December 25, 1977

To My Sweetheart
With All My Love
Doc

# MAXWELL STREET

# MAXWELL STREET

## SURVIVAL IN A BAZAAR

### IRA BERKOW

Special photographs by Walter Iooss, Jr.

DOUBLEDAY & COMPANY, INC., GARDEN CITY, NEW YORK

1977

*Photos courtesy:*

Acme, Leonard Balaban, Ira Berkow, CBS, Mike Chiappetta, Chicago *Daily News,* Chicago *Herald American,* Chicago Historical Society, Chicago Maternity Center, Chicago *Sunday Times,* Chicago *Tribune,* City of Chicago, Department of Urban Renewal, Albert Fenn Collection, Arthur Goldberg, Bruce Iglauer, Walter Iooss, Jr., Irving Jacobson, Michael Mauney, Jim O'Neal, John L. Keeshin, Schocken Books, Theater Historical Society, Dr. B. E. Tucker, United Press International, Inc., John Vidovic, Wide World.

Library of Congress Cataloging in Publication Data

Berkow, Ira.
Maxwell Street.

1. Jews in Chicago—Biography.  2. Chicago—Biography.
3. Chicago—Streets—Maxwell Street.  I. Title.
F548.9.J5B47      977.3′11′04924 [B]
ISBN: 0-385-06723-2
Library of Congress Catalog Card Number 76–42060

*To my mother, father, and brother*

# ACKNOWLEDGMENTS

In the preparation of this book, I had a great deal of help. Most obviously are the interviews included in the book and the selections from books and periodicals that I made such liberal use of. But there was much more that does not meet the reader's eye. There were people who loved the concept of the book, who encouraged me, provided me with ideas and leads and sometimes entrées:

Mel Wolff, my cousin, provided sources, transportation, and friendship. For me, he is beyond praise and always has been.

Mike Chiappetta opened doors, particularly in the chapter entitled "Potpourri," that otherwise would have remained closed to me.

Janice Diehl gave me tender and painstaking assistance with her transcriptions of my tapes. In this respect, I am also grateful to Jennie Lightner and Ann Sanger.

Walter Iooss, Jr., an artist and a joy. Larry Jordan, an editor of remarkable insight and skill; he gave the project wings. Toni Mendez, my literary agent and friend.

Nancy Berkow and Timmy Pratt, who mean so much to me.

For their important contributions, I want to also thank: Jerry Feig, Ian Levin, Howard Noel, Bernadette Birkett, Curt Cole Burkhart, Stacy Noel, Mike Cohen, Mrs. Frances Cohen, Leonore Glazer, John Corcoran, Al and Betty Halperin, Jerry and Lillian Halperin, Howard "Hershey" Carl, Hope Wolff, Leo Robinson, Arnold Gilmore, Bob Herb Gilmore, Harry Breslaw, Art Shaw, Kenny Moss, Willie Hale, Dolly Case, Wilda Lewis, Rich Huttner, Rae Schleicher, Fritzie Menaker, Judy Berkow, Daryle Feldmeir, Herman Kogan, Sol Rosenshine, Gary Stutland, Minette Saxner, Jean Palmer, Lew and Joanne Koch, Irv Kupcinet, Steven Ford,

Ike Eppenstein, Decatur Miller, Harry Hartman, Tyner White, John Henry Davis, Dave Lunde, Ira Colitz, William Zaret, Leone Rimmerman, Irv Seifer, Sam Hessing, Martin "Colonel Gimp" Snyder, Al Reisin, William Cozzi, Goldie and Bob Bluestein, Paul Goldstein, Mrs. Louis Leavitt, Louis Steinberg, Mike Novotnak, Jerry Snower, Ross Gelbspan, David Hendin, Hana Umlauf, Sarah Juon, George DeLury, Janet Tara, Paul Dugan, and Bill Grisham.

A special thank you to Federal Court Judge Abraham Lincoln Marovitz, born and raised in the Maxwell Street area. He told me, "I don't know of any self-made men or women. You go through life—somebody has given you a friendly pat on the back or a little word of encouragement. And that's what I got. That was important in my life. You know, I think the only thing a guy can do by himself is fail."

# CONTENTS

## III
## THE SMOKESTACK EXPRESS

## IV
## POTPOURRI

## FISH CRIER

I know a Jew fish crier down on Maxwell Street with a voice like a
    north wind blowing over corn stubble in January
He dangles herring before prospective customers evincing a joy
    identical with that of Pavlova dancing.
His face is that of a man terribly glad to be selling fish, terribly
    glad that God made fish, and customers to whom he may call
    his wares from a pushcart.

*—Carl Sandburg*
*CHICAGO POEMS*
*1916*

———————◆———————

—Little Louie Epstine, age nine years . . .
lived on Maxwell Street. His mother had five
more like him, and they all lived together in
two large rooms back of a bakery. . . . They
almost always had something to eat. . . . [In
winter] Louis' mother bundled him up the
best she could. His shoes were not very good.
He had bought them "second hand," or
whatever it is with shoes. . . . Both of them
were pretty large, but his mother had always
told him that large shoes were the best and
would wear the longest and would not make
corns.

*—Clarence Darrow*
*from his short story,*
"Little Louie Epstine"
*THE PILGRIM MAGAZINE*
*1903*

---

My baby don't wear no drawers, my babe,
 my baby don't wear no drawers,
She wash her clothes in alcohol
 and hang 'em on a hook in the hall.

*—by street musician "Maxwell Street" Jimmie Davis,*
*from his original composition,*
"My Maxwell Street Babe,"
*1971*

# MAXWELL STREET

# I

# DAYBREAK

There is a sense of abandonment about Maxwell Street. A number of stores are boarded up; other stores still in business have awnings that sag desolately. There is no foliage on the street, and there hasn't been any for more than seventy-five years, or before the street developed into the center of the tumultuous bazaar, thieves' market, and immigrant ghetto that it became. But the street now bears little resemblance to the marketplace that once was, except on Sunday.

No area in Chicago is frowzier than Maxwell Street or more neglected. It is virtually in the shadow of towering downtown Chicago, and the contrast between old and new is striking.

Urban renewal and the inexorability of time have taken their toll on the old street. Maxwell Street once extended east to west for a city mile. In the 1950s and '60s it was cut to half that length. Of the four remaining blocks, only one—the block from Union Street to Halsted Street—mirrors former times.

Nearly twenty-five stores or empty stores occupy the one-, two-, and three-story wood and brick buildings that dip and rise on either side of that block on Maxwell Street. Clothing and home-furnishing stores dominate. A medley of signs swings on chains in the wind—particularly in wintertime, when the infamous chilling "Hawk" (local name for that wind) whips in from Lake Michigan about a mile west. Summers are hot; the air is stagnant and the street simmers with a white glare.

The coolest place in summer is under the awnings that stretch from the stores to the permanent wooden stands at the curb; a kind of tunnel is created on the sidewalk, distinct from the openness of the sixty-foot-wide street. The sidewalks are so dark, in fact, that even in midday bare lights are strung up to enable passersby to view clothes and shoes and rugs displayed in front of the stores.

The wooden stands are spaced here and there along the curbs of Maxwell Street. These stands are about seven feet high and three feet wide and built with slats so weathered now that they look as pickled as driftwood.

Once, the stands made a continuous line along the curb for eight blocks. Many stands were torn down while others collapsed from sheer disregard, as Maxwell Street's business declined. Even the Sunday market—always bustling—gave way to the emerging Sunday commerce in neat and safer suburban shopping centers.

One can get a good perspective of Maxwell Street from the walk of the low-arching Dan Ryan Expressway, the structure that lopped off the eastern end of the marketplace. From the expressway, Maxwell Street, with its hollow spaces between wooden stands, has the peculiar gaping smile of a Halloween pumpkin.

To the west, much of Maxwell Street and the surrounding area has been razed, though a few three-story, pitched-roof buildings from the turn of the century remain among the rubble and are still lived in. The most dramatic change in that far part of the street is the deep green athletic field of the new University of Illinois-Chicago Circle campus.

Although truncated and waning, some of the old-time mood of Maxwell Street remains, recalling its heritage in the ancient labyrinths of Baghdad and Jerusalem.

On a good, sunny Sunday, the street again shimmers with vitality, evidenced by the gaily dressed crowds, the hustlers, the smells.

A different smell greets the walker every few feet. The aromas of the foods are particularly enveloping. The steam from boiling hot dogs billows out like clouds and is bracing to the nostrils. Walking farther, one is confronted by lamb chops sizzling on charcoal and pork sausages frying in a pot of grease thick as slush.

The unmistakable smell of frying onions is sharp and pervasive; the scent is as great a part of this open-air marketplace as the broad Midwestern sky above.

There are stands devoted exclusively to spices. Even more specialized is a stand stacked solely with garlic. Present, too, is the fragrance from stands of fresh fruit. Beside a truck, big ripe watermelons are heaped in several mounds, and at the top of each is a watermelon cut in half and looking luscious in its redness.

Not all the smells are embracing. Maxwell Street is one of the filthiest streets in the world: the sour odor of garbage scattered in alleyways and along the curbs holds its own on the street. There are greasy rags, fruit rinds. Urine. Tufts of yellow smoke carry the stink of garbage burning in big dark trash drums.

The smoke and smells curl and drift through Maxwell Street and down the streets feeding into it—Union and Halsted and, at half blocks, Newberry and Peoria and Morgan and Sangamon and Miller and the nearby parallel streets of O'Brien, Liberty, Barber, Thirteenth, Fourteenth, and Fifteenth.

On Sunday, a spectrum of merchandise is displayed in stalls and stores; sundry stuff is spread out on card-table stands and piled on blankets on the pavement. Crowds flow over the sidewalk and out into the streets and over the empty lots.

One may buy a used toothbrush, bundled-up socks with no toes (let the buyer beware), an outboard motor, a raucous rooster, an authentic mink coat, a purported money-making machine that seems to resemble nothing but a cigar box with a crank attached.

Thousands of people talk at once, though some louder than others. Some are momentarily silent, like the woman burrowing into a heap of colorful dresses.

There is a torrent of haggling and hawking in languages from Yiddish to Spanish to Polish and curious versions of English.

"How much is the radio?"

"For you, two dollars."

"But it doesn't work."

"So from where else can you buy a radio for two dollars?"

A man in an Indian war bonnet wearing penny loafers pitches snake oil with a megaphone. There is a hurdy-gurdy man, a balloon hustler, a concatenation of black street musicians.

A stocking salesman shouts, "Hey, lady, only one hole in these socks—where you put your foot in." The woman walks on, undaunted.

The salesmen or "pullers" in front of the stores are generally voluble, though lacking the fervor and boldness of days gone by.

"In the old days," wrote Mike Royko, the Chicago *Daily News* columnist, "they didn't stand outside and coax you into the store. They hauled you in, if you weren't big enough to resist. The only reasons they stopped was because an ordinance was passed prohibiting the kidnapping of customers."

The quietest hustler is one who whispers, "Watch, mister?" You turn around. He reveals a watch on his wrist. You shake your head no and take a step forward. He takes a step forward.

"No."

"No?" he repeats furtively.

You step forward. He steps forward. His sleeve goes up another notch. The man has watches all the way up his arm! *Both* arms. He eventually accepts that you are truly not interested in his merchandise, though curiosity lingers whether he was about to raise his pants leg, too.

Maxwell Street is the center of a ghetto about a mile square which served as a blighted garden of promise. From 1880 to 1924, two million Jewish immigrants—despised and repressed and the object of murderous pogroms in Europe—sailed in teeming steerage to port cities such as New York, Boston, Philadelphia, and Baltimore. Many stayed. Others would sooner or later go on to Chicago, called by them "the city on the lake" or "the Klondike of America." Chicago was located in the American heartland and seemed far away from the overwhelming congestion of the cities in which those immigrants had first landed. There is a record of Jewish peddlers in Chicago dating back to the days of Fort Dearborn in the early 1800s. And in 1834, Peter Cohen advertised in the Chicago *Weekly Democrat,* "a large and splendid assortment of winter clothing . . . a fresh supply of provisions, groceries and liquors."

The Maxwell Street area is about a mile southwest of downtown Chicago. It was little developed until the 1850s. Then railroads began to lay their ties through the South Side. Before this, it was just a sandy wasteland crossed by wagon trails and Indian paths.

Chicago became "a town among the routes of trade," wrote Oscar Handlin; "concentrations appeared at the inland termini, the points of exchange between rail and river or lake traffic. In all such places the newcomers pitched themselves in the midst of communities that were already growing rapidly and were therefore already crowded."

Chicago's population grew from four thousand in 1840 to 1.7 million in 1900. By 1900, Chicago had become the world's greatest railroad center; four hundred trains a day puffed into Chicago.

Establishment of factories around the railroad yards and shops created a demand for workers who, in turn, sought inexpensive lots and homes near their work. Workingmen's frame houses and boardinghouses rose on the once unsettled prairie and wasteland south of Roosevelt Road. The horse-drawn trolley-car system was begun on the South Side in 1859 and was extended in the early 1860s; this meant greater residential growth for the Maxwell Street area.

The Civil War and postwar boom in trade and manufacture brought wealth and an increased population to the city. The Great Fire of 1871 halted progress but only briefly. The fire began in the barn beside the house of Mrs. O'Leary when, legend has it, her cow kicked over a lantern. Whatever, the blaze was carried north and west by the wind. The fire leaped across the Chicago River, raged for two days, and could be seen as far as Peoria one hundred miles south. The aftermath left much of the city in charred ruins, but Maxwell Street was untouched since it was just south of that infamous cow on DeKoven Street.

As Chicago rebuilt after the fire, the neighborhood around Maxwell Street received a surplus of population from the burned-out areas. Soon, recognizing that this area was becoming one of Chicago's most densely populated sections and that its population would require consumer goods and services, Jewish peddlers with two-wheeled pushcarts appeared on Jefferson Street, selling small household items, shoes, and notions. Jefferson Street was a major thoroughfare with horse-drawn trolley cars clanging and clopping down the middle of it. Maxwell Street, perpendicular to Jefferson, was still completely residential.

By 1912 Jefferson Street had become so crowded that pushcarts were forced to move westward along Maxwell Street. With a large local market, small operating expenses, and the opportunity to move freely in search of trade, the pushcart trade prospered. The area became unique and so significant that the Chicago City Council passed an ordinance in 1912, recognizing it as the Maxwell Street Market.

Irish and German immigrants who had fled famine and depression in Europe were the earliest inhabitants of the area. With the Jewish influx, the Germans and Irish moved out, just as several decades later the Jews would move when blacks and Mexicans moved in. Gypsies have long lived there. Italians and Poles and Lithuanians and Greeks and Scandinavians lived on the outskirts of the area.

During the last two decades of the nineteenth century an estimated fifty thousand Jewish immigrants arrived in Chicago, most from Eastern Europe. Some went to the South Side, some to the West Side, and some to the Near North Side, but most went to Maxwell Street, closest to the railroad stations where they had arrived and where the greatest number of synagogues and kosher food stores were.

The Jewish immigrants of those times landed in Chicago with little more than their small bundles of belongings. They were forced to live in the least expensive area—a place where they could practically begin to pull themselves up. That was usually the Maxwell Street area.

In 1891 a survey showed nearly sixteen thousand immigrant Jews living around Maxwell Street. Streets were mud; sidewalks were wooden slats with nails protruding. Garbage was rarely picked up. When the lungs of an overworked peddler's horse burst in the heat of summer, the beast might lie in the street for days, a feast for flies and maggots, before the fire department got around to dragging the carcass off.

For every ten people, only one toilet was available. Three and four people slept in the same bed. One small, dank, dark flat might house several families. Ventilation in bedrooms was considered a luxury, or a curse, depending on how one withstood the stink from the stables and outhouses in the alleys.

Sweatshops sprang up here. The sweatshops were, without exception in this area, located in the tenement houses. The noxious odors from the alleys, the close and unsanitary conditions, the lack of light and air insured the maximum probability of disease.

Diphtheria, scarlet fever, smallpox, typhoid, scabies, and various forms of skin diseases were found in alarming proximity to garments of excellent quality, in process of manufacture for leading firms. If a sweat-shop owner had a social conscience, it was generally a well-kept secret.

A report by inspectors from Hull House, the famous settlement house near Halsted Street, found that "Every tenement-house shop is ruinous to the health of employees." Basements were damp; attics dark and foul. One cloakmaker was given as a typical example. Like most workers in Chicago sweatshops at the turn of the century, he had begun to work at his machine at the age of fourteen and was found, after twenty years "of temperate life and faithful work, living in a rear basement, with four of his children apparently dying of pneumonia, at the close of winter during which they had had, for weeks together, no food but bread and water, and had been four days without bread." The father had difficulty keeping a job because he was so plagued by rheumatism, among other ailments. Physicians found that he was indeed suffering from "old age." Twenty years at the machine had made him in fact an old man at age thirty-four. During those twenty years, his meager earnings had ranged from $260 to $300 per annum.

Child labor was also rampant before the advent of unions. The Hull House inspectors' findings were gruesome in this area: "Among the occupations in which children are most employed in Chicago, and which most endanger the health, are: The tobacco trade, nicotine poisoning finding as many victims among factory children as among the boys who are voluntary devotees of the weed, consumers of the deadly cigarette included; frame gilding, in which work a child's fingers are stiffened and throat disease is contracted; button-holing, machine-stitching, and hand-work in tailor or sweat shops, the machine-work producing spinal curvature, and for girls pelvic disorders also, while the unsanitary condition of the shops makes even hand-sewing dangerous; bakeries, where children slowly roast before the ovens; binderies, rotting paste, and the poison of the paints are injurious; boiler-plate works, cutlery works, and metal-stamping works, where the dust produces lung disease; the handling of hot metal, accidents; the hammering of plate, deafness. In addition to disease incidental to trades, there are the conditions of bad sanitation and long hours, almost universal in the factories where children are employed."

A CASE HISTORY: "Bennie Kelman, Russian Jew, four years in Chicago, was found running a heavy sewing-machine by foot-power in a sweatshop where knee-pants are made. A health certificate was required, and the medical examination revealed a severe rupture. [It was learned] that the boy had been put to work in a boiler factory two years before, when just thirteen years old, and had injured himself lifting heavy masses of iron. Nothing had been done for the case; no one in the family spoke any English, or knew how to obtain help. . . ."*

The owners of most of these sweatshops in the area were Jews themselves who, perhaps literally, had been in the same boat as their employees. How did they reconcile their Jewish heritage with the sordid working conditions and the brutality sometimes used in quelling the periodic strikes? Competition was stiff, and the future of their business uncertain. "Had the immigrant workers not forced recognition of their unions and improvements in conditions, most Jewish employers would not, and probably could not, have allowed traditional sentiments of justice to overcome economic urgencies," wrote Irving Howe.†

In 1910 a major strike by Chicago garment workers lasted four months, involved forty thousand workers, and expended $200,000 in relief; 874 were arrested and seven killed. The focal point of the strike was the huge Hart, Schaffner and Marx factory. The organization of garment workers selected Clarence Darrow for their representative in arbitration. A young man named Sidney Hillman emerged as an important union leader. But "what broke the unity of employer resistance was, to some extent, the moral qualms of Joseph Schaffner, who so took to heart the criticism of rabbis, ministers, and social workers that he began to wonder whether he was 'a moral failure.' "‡

The strike was successful in that it forced limited recognition of

* *Hull House Maps and Papers: A Presentation of Nationalities and Wages in a Congested District of Chicago* (Boston: T. Y. Crowell, 1895), p. 63.
† Irving Howe, *World of Our Fathers* (New York: Harcourt Brace Jovanovich, 1976), p. 303.
‡ Ibid, p. 304.

the needle-trade unions by the owners, gained improved sanitary conditions and a uniform wage increase of 10 per cent; also, a fifty-four-hour work week with time and a half for overtime was granted. "This marked the beginning of the most highly elaborated industrial government in America based on the equal participation of employer and union."*

In 1900 a social scientist determined that if all of Chicago were as densely populated as its average slums, the city would have 32 million people instead of 2 million, and if it were as densely populated as its worse slum, such as Maxwell Street, then the whole of the Western Hemisphere could have been housed in Chicago.

Housing in the area has undergone immense change in the one-hundred-twenty-year history of the street, going from small cottages of wood and brick, at about the time of the Chicago Fire, to two- and three-story clapboard buildings, so narrow that the staircases had to be put on the outside of the structure. The roofs were pitched, or inverted "V-shaped." They became abundant at the turn of the century to accommodate the swelling hordes of impoverished settlers. In the early 1900s many of these buildings were replaced with the "tenement" or "double-decker." They were usually three stories high, built with brick, and were a response to the even greater demands for low-cost housing. "Yet to those who knew, these new structures concealed a new level of congestion and degradation," as noted in *Chicago: Growth of a Metropolis.*† A 1901 survey found 127 people living in a single six-flat building. In one three-room apartment, occupied by at least a dozen people, there were no windows at all.

Chicken stores and butcher shops and the kinds of stands that still exist on Maxwell Street began to flourish. Bewhiskered patriarchs in faded black derbies and long caftans peddled their simple wares on the street. So did their spouses and their children.

"There is something of the pitiful in this . . . traffic of the curbstone," said a Chicago *Tribune* article in 1896. "No pride embarrasses the purchaser who stands haggling. There is no senti-

* Selig Perlman and Philip Taft, *History of Labor in the United States, 1896–1932* (New York: The Macmillan Company, 1955), p. 464.
† Harold M. Mayer and Richard C. Wade, *Chicago: Growth of a Metropolis* (Chicago: University of Chicago Press, 1969), p. 256.

ment regarding the material things which he needs; utility is the one thing dominant in his mind as he seeks to buy for the least money which his small Shylock will accept. . . .

"In all the wildernesses of narrow by-streets garbage [is] everywhere. . . . The average merchant moves his family into the backrooms of a tumble-down building, puts wooden shutters on the front windows, and spreads his stock-in-trade on the pavement. There is more room for haggling out-of-doors.

"La Salle Street and Dearborn Street [Chicago's financial center] may busy themselves with a business which involves millions every week. But both of them combined will not expand more nerve tissue, action and volubility than does commercial Maxwell Street in this very center of hard times."

America, however, as wretched as it was around Maxwell Street, still held out hope for a life better than anything the immigrants had ever known. Maxwell Street appeared, then, a welcome step for them, a chance to climb up in the New World, or "Columbus's land," as they called it. And if they themselves couldn't make it, they dreamed that opportunities would be created for their children.

Joseph Goldberg was one of these immigrants. He came to America from Russia and eventually landed on Maxwell Street. He bought a blind horse, the only horse he could afford. He became a fruit-and-vegetable peddler; his son, Arthur, would serve in President Kennedy's cabinet and become a Supreme Court Justice of the United States.

Samuel Paley became a cigar maker in America, as did Max Guzik. Samuel's son William, born in the back room of the modest family cigar store near Maxwell Street, is founder, president and chairman of the board of the Columbia Broadcasting System. Mr. Guzik's son Jake, known as "Greasy Thumb," became the brains behind the Capone gang and, when he died in 1956, was among the top three on the FBI's list of public enemies.

Eastern European immigrants David Goodman and Abraham Rickover took jobs in Chicago as tailors. Their sons are Benny Goodman and Admiral Hyman G. Rickover.

The father of Barney Ross, onetime world lightweight boxing

champion, and the father of Barney Balaban, the late president of Paramount Pictures, each owned a tiny grocery store in the Maxwell Street area.

Paul Muni's father owned a Yiddish theater near Maxwell Street. Jack Ruby's father was a carpenter there.

John Keeshin, once the greatest trucking magnate in America, is the son of a man who owned a chicken store on Maxwell Street, as did the father of Jackie Fields, former welterweight champion of the world. The father of Federal Court Judge Abraham Lincoln Markovitz owned a candy store near Maxwell Street.

Colonel Jacob Arvey, once a nationally prominent political power broker, is the son of a Maxwell Street area peddler.

And it was around Maxwell Street at the turn of the century that the phenomenal con man Joseph "Yellow Kid" Weil, son of immigrant parents, learned to inveigle people to gladly hand him their money for nothing but a sweet song.

Countless others, though, lived, sweated, and dreamed on Maxwell Street and never got a mention in the newspapers at all until their scant and obligatory obituary.

One of those whose dream evaporated on Maxwell Street was a young Jewish immigrant apparently dying of tuberculosis in a crowded tenement flat on Liberty Street, just off Maxwell. He was described in a book, *The Tenements of Chicago,* at the turn of the century:

"The name Liberty Street, where a friend from his village lived, had fired the imagination of the Russian youth. He thought Liberty Street would be a wide and beautiful avenue. He dreamed of a parkway with a great statue like the Liberty he had seen pictured, enlightening the world, welcoming poor immigrants to the land of promise. He then told of his bitter disappointment—the small, mean streets, the miserable houses, the vermin, the dirt, the sky dark with smoke, no parks, nothing but defeat and despair."‡

Hamlin Garland, a widely known writer of the time, when first arriving in Chicago from his small northern Illinois hometown, wrote, "I took the train for Chicago, and I shall never forget the

‡ Edith Abbott, *The Tenements of Chicago: 1900–1935* (Chicago: University of Chicago Press, 1936), p. 36.

feeling of dismay with which an hour later I perceived from the car window the huge smoke cloud which embraced the whole Eastern horizon. This was the soaring banner of the great and gloomy inland Metropolis whose dens of vice and houses of greed had been so often reported to me by wandering hired men. It was in truth only a huge flimsy country town in those days, but to me it was august as well as terrible."*

And Rudyard Kipling, after a visit, said, "Having seen [Chicago], I urgently desire never to see it again. It is inhabited by savages."†

The most vicious area, according to *Gem of the Prairie,* a book published in 1940, was "the Maxwell Street district, but was more commonly known as Bloody Maxwell. Bloody Maxwell was bounded on the north by Harrison Street, on the west by Wood Street, on the south by Sixteenth Street and on the east by the south branch of the Chicago River."‡

The precinct police station was on Maxwell Street three blocks west of Halsted and "on all sides of the station," wrote the Chicago *Tribune,* "are corners, saloons and houses that have seen the rise, the operations, and often the death of some of the worst criminals the land has ever known." Two blocks from the station was the corner of Sangamon and Fourteenth Place, notorious for more than twenty-five years as "dead man's corner." More criminals were shot by policemen and more policemen by criminals than at any other location in Chicago.

On February 11, 1906, the *Tribune* added that the Maxwell Street area "is the crime center of the country . . . murders, shootings, stabbings, assaults, burglaries, robberies by the thousands . . . by people living in these areas in many instances more like beasts than human beings."

One of the most famous gangs of the period following the Fire was the Johnson Street gang, captained by Buff Higgins. Higgins was hanged on a scaffold for shooting a man who had the indecency to wake up while Higgins was burglarizing his bedroom.

There was Chris Merry, who was hanged for kicking his invalid

---

* Mayer and Wade, op. cit., p. 192.
† Ibid, p. 192.
‡ Herbert Asbury (New York: Knopf, 1940), p. 211.

wife to death; his other claim to fame was that he once fought a two-hour pistol battle with a posse of policemen. Ostensibly, Merry was a peddler, but he and his men would frequently drive along Maxwell and Halsted in their horse and wagon and take whatever they wanted from stores and outside stands in broad daylight.

When the Jews moved in en masse, they organized gangs of their own, since they found themselves enclosed on all four sides: To the north were the Italians, particularly the 42-gang, with a young leader named Sam "Mo" Giancana; to the south were the Irish, the Valley gang; to the southwest and west were the Poles and Lithuanians.

Maxwell Street bears the name of Dr. Philip Maxwell. No evidence exists today as to *why* the street was named for him, other than that he was a surgeon at Fort Dearborn in Chicago. But the naming was fortuitous, nonetheless, since Dr. Maxwell seemed as singular as the street would become.

A newspaper of the day described Dr. Maxwell as "Falstaffian in his abdominal rotundity." He weighed two hundred eighty pounds, yet dashed through the streets of Chicago on his favorite gray horse "with all the chic and erectness of a soldier and with the abandon of an Indian." The grace with which he mounted and dismounted the steed "was the subject of comment among bystanders," according to the Chicago *Republican*. The bystanders may also have been surprised that the horse didn't buckle when the good doctor mounted and dismounted his steed.

In the one hundred and twenty years since Maxwell Street was first officially recognized with a name and was no longer just a trail, unimaginable transitions took place. People and houses replaced grass and trees. Smoke from chimneys replaced smoke from Indian campfires. And the call of street hawkers replaced the cry of hawks.

The world came to Maxwell Street, and Maxwell Street went out to the world. Each in degrees mutually influenced the other. How did it happen? Why did it happen? What was it that produced such people as the Paleys and Goldbergs and Guziks and Rubys and Munis and Balabans and Arveys? Is there a common thread? What motivated and sustained all the other immigrants and their children—including my parents and grandparents—who also struggled to survive in America and, particularly, in that loud, smelly, crowded kaleidoscopic place named Maxwell Street? I attempted to learn.

Today, from the walk on the expressway beside Maxwell Street, one may turn and see the one-hundred-story John Hancock Building and the Sears Tower and the lights and beacons of imposing buildings that comprise the soaring sweeping skyline of Chicago. For some of the people inside offices in those buildings, journeying that mile from Maxwell Street was longer by far than going several times around the world.

2

Starting from age eleven until I began college, I regularly hawked women's nylon stockings on Maxwell Street. They sold for three pairs for a dollar and they were not firsts. I sold them on a stand made up of four card tables. I had a small wooden sign which I tied with shoestring to a table leg. The stockings were displayed in cellophane bags. The hot items when I started in 1951 were the "Red Fox" and "Sunburst" colors, with black butterfly heels and black seams. Sometimes, though, a single stocking might have more than one seam sewed in it.

I traveled to Maxwell Street on Sundays from my home several miles away. Maxwell Street, dark and seemingly moribund, would shortly after dawn come brightly and boisterously to life.

I sold the stockings for a glum man who wore a cap so low you could not fully see his eyes. He ran numerous men's socks and nylon-stocking stands on Maxwell and the adjoining streets of the market. In a dark, long, musty basement, the stockings were taken from shelves and placed in cartons and put on red wagons. In the rotting rear shed of the two-story building, I rummaged among the piles of folded-up cardboard-top tables. I looked for tables without breaks in the middle. This process sometimes demanded that I perform a jerky dance, since from behind a disturbed pile rats would jump out.

Before going to work I stopped in a coffee shop. It was an odd and exotic place, being half coffee shop for awakening Sunday-morning workers and half night dive for the drowsy Saturday-night revelers.

The workers sat in the front on tilty stools. We ate plump jelly sweet rolls and hot bagels thick with cream cheese. The men drank coffee, and so did I; it was a daring thing to do at age eleven, but the place lent itself to such a carefree spirit.

In a back room a jukebox played. A purple curtain divided the two rooms. There were a few people left in the back, all of them black—hazy survivors of the night who still floated through woozy dance steps with now and then a flamboyant twirl in slow motion. It was a ballet of the sensuous and sodden. Powerful smells emanated from that darkling room, mixing booze and smoke and sweat. The women were not young and looked lumpy. The men were not much sleeker. Yet their movements were very silky, very sexy. I remember the first time, standing and watching in the doorway and feeling a flush creep over me.

Recalling the smells of Maxwell Street, particularly the oniony odors wafting from the several hot-dog stands, brings to mind the kind of excitement—the casual and regular but always unexpected encounters with the bizarre, the queer, the extraordinary, the wondrous—that gave me a notion of adultness and distinctiveness. It was similar to Sam Clemens' feelings when he became a Mississippi River steamboatman. "I had an exultant sense of being bound for mysterious lands and distant climes," wrote Mark Twain. Maxwell Street was like that for me.

My friends were envious that I could be privy to the supposed secrets of the street. I basked in my little celebrity, much like young Twain who relished being "stared at and wondered over" by less fortunate landlocked chums.

I remember once talking with a man bedecked with placards who claimed to be king of the hoboes. I later learned that there is a king of the hoboes found all over the country, and each claims that only his is the true bloodline of royalty. I remember a legless man who sold snake oil for treatment of everything from hiccups to social disease. He had a horse as a come-on, a horse he could speak to. The man placed a stump of chalk between the horse's teeth and then snapped out a count from one to four with a whip. As he did so, the horse shakily but nonetheless incredibly wrote the number on a blackboard.

I remember a one-man band, complete with harmonica, drums, and a pot. The virtuoso played the pot with the tablespoons he tied to his foot. There was a man with a dancing chicken on his head who sold one egg for a dime, two eggs for a quarter. A woman peddled for one dollar mangy curs she had found on the street during the week.

I remember the pretty Gypsy girl, about my age. She had long, pleasingly careless blue-black hair, half-hidden golden earrings, knowing eyes, swaying patterned skirt, and low-cut blouse that showed her already compelling, smooth cleavage. She also wore gold-flecked high-heeled shoes without straps that made a slapping sound against her very naked heels when she walked. The sight made me swallow. Her charms had a considerable effect on me.

From some of the black minstrels on the street and from the music on the jukebox in the coffee shop, I learned blues and rock-and-roll songs, funny-seeming songs, sung by funny-seeming names like "Howlin' Wolf" and "Hound Dog" Taylor and "Muddy Waters" and "Daddy Stovepipe." I remember singing—clowning —one of their songs, "You ain't nothin' but a hound dog," to the laughs and, I imagined, respectful fascination of my friends. The song was popular on Maxwell Street several years before Elvis Presley made it nationally famous, and, when he did, it fortified, to my mind, the esoteric place I held in my other, more conventional society.

I learned the hambone from Alexander, a black fellow my age. He was long and bony and his thick glasses streaked with perspiration as he did this hambone, or hand jive. He sat on a stoop and with limber wrists slapped and thumped chest and thigh. His hands flew in a blur, like the wings of a frightened chicken. *Plus,* he would sing in his hoarse voice a rendition of "Mockin' Bird":

> "Hambone, Hambone, have you heard
> Mama gonna buy me a mockin' bird
> And if that mockin' bird don' sing
> Daddy gonna buy me a diamon' ring. . . ."

I can still hambone, and sing "Hambone," and it is always a conversation piece, especially when people try to and, invariably, cannot perform it correctly, according to my lofty standards—which are Alexander's standards. The hambone is one of the most satisfying and worthwhile things I have ever picked up.

I can also remember the slippery, three-card monte man—a black man with veiny, velvety hands. He showed you the cards, two black and one red. Then, with cards face down, he shuffled them in a tantalizingly slow fashion and placed them on the street. Which one is the red? I remember with terror the time a heavy, red-haired young guy got involved. He sold socks on a stand near mine. With socks and tables loaded on his wagon at day's end, he stopped to try his luck. A crowd watched the three-card monte man take his entire day's wad, something like two hundred dollars. He worked a couple of months to pay our boss back.

One of my first personal lessons in the wiles of mankind came on the first day I worked Maxwell Street. I was taken there by my friend Bobby Popowcer, along with his father. Bobby was several years older than I and, like his father, sold stockings on the street. I admired Bobby. He made me laugh, played the trumpet and second base with an equally high degree of skill, as I perceived it. I looked forward to the work adventure, having been to Maxwell Street on shopping excursions with my parents and thrilled to its arcane, carnival aura. My parents, who owned a dry-cleaning store, approved of my earning whatever money I could, wherever I could.

I got my assignment in the basement office. I was told that I would probably need a helper around outside the basement storage room. It was suggested I pay him a dollar at day's end. I hired David, a pudgy kid with a beatific smile. After David helped me set up the stand, he requested the buck because it was his mother's birthday, he explained, and he wanted to buy her a present. I said sure. David left. I didn't see hair nor hide of him again.

My mother and my father were born and raised around Maxwell Street. My maternal grandmother, Molly Halperin, owned a chicken store on the street. It was located across from the police station. The chicken store has since been leveled to make way for the university athletic field. My grandmother sold the store before I was born. According to my mother and her three brothers, there was a flurry of activity there. Chickens squawked and fluttered in coops as they were pinched and jabbed to test for meatiness by customers, and then plucked out for slaughter.

The wooden chicken coops served another purpose as well. One of my uncles explained to me that young lovers in the congested ghetto had difficulty finding privacy. So at night he would sneak into his mother's dark chicken store. He and his sweetheart would tryst atop a coop as the frightened hens hopping in their box pecked at the couple.

In the fall, my grandmother placed turkeys on the sidewalk to advertise her Thanksgiving wares. She tied the turkeys to the steel railing beside the building. This precaution did not always keep the turkeys where they belonged. Theft was a constant problem, even with the police station across the street. One morning my grandmother left home from her flat around the corner and came to the store and was shocked to find it had been emptied. During the night everything had been stolen. She stood amid the desolation of sawdust and feathers, and she cried. Then, still in "turby," or cobbler's apron, and babushka, she went to the bank, waited for it to open, called on her friend at the bank, a vice-president with whom she had established her business respectability, borrowed money, hurried to the nearby South Water Market, bought new coops of chickens, and was back in business by midmorning.

She had no choice. She had to feed a family of three sons, a daughter, and a husband, my grandfather, Max. He was as spare as she was thickset. In America, he was a broommaker, when a hangover did not prevent him from going to work. He had been studying in Russia to be a religious scholar, according to family legend, until he was drafted into the anti-Semitic Russian Army. Hating the army, he stole away to America, determined to send for his wife and young son as soon as he could earn enough money. He found New York unbearable and a great culture shock, after coming from a tiny town in Eastern Europe. He returned to Russia, quickly grew disenchanted again, and came back to America, this time to Chicago, where relatives lived; he earned enough to send for his family. But he never seemed to adjust to being a laborer when he prided himself a scholar. He attended synagogue faithfully, but at home he might be careless about wearing his yarmulke unless a visitor called, and then he made a furtive dash for the headpiece.

Yiddish scholars, however, starved in America, unless their wives helped feed them. My grandfather's wife was just such a *shtarker,* a rugged and efficient and responsible woman. Her problems did not rest with helping her husband financially. In America now, she could not be the ever-watchful mother. Her children, like many of the children of the swarming neighborhood, took to the streets and learned of the raw city life among the melange of people and pushcarts and horses and wagons. My grandmother's problems were compounded by her eldest son, a graduate of this tough street existence. Once, in 1921, at age sixteen, he held up a man in front of the Maxwell Street police station, of all places, and was pursued by cops through the backyards and alleyways of the area. He flung the loot away and, when finally caught, would not tell where it was. In accordance with the custom of handling ghetto troublemakers, the policemen beat hell out of him. My uncle died in 1953, an epileptic, a sickness he suffered only after that brutal encounter.

My grandparents were married by a *schatchen,* or matchmaker, in Russia. They lived in neighboring *shtetls* fifteen miles apart in the Ukraine. (A shtetl has been described as being no bigger than a yawn.) "Neighboring" may be a proper adjective when viewed on a present-day map of Russia, but not necessarily when considered in light of travel for Jews in nineteenth-century czarist Russia.

Jews were given little opportunity to earn a good living, so most were poor farmers or poor peddlers or, like my grandfather, poor religious scholars. Fifteen miles by creaky horse-drawn wagon was an all-day and part-of-the-evening affair. The courtier would visit his intended and then leave for home. About midway back he would usually flap the reins and pull his meager horse off to the side of the snowy road amid vast, white farm fields. Breathing white puffs in the cold air, I picture how man and horse spent the rest of the night there. My grandfather, in thick winter's coat and still wearing his heavy furry hat, would slip under the hay in his

wagon. Before curling up he sought a last palliative for warmth.
He drew from his coat a flask, and he drank deeply, making a
silhouette in the big, round, pale Russian moon.


When she retired from business, my grandmother came to live
with us. I was nine years old. Her husband had died. She was
quiet, a woman of unobtrusive dignity. She sat alone in a corner a
great deal, hands in lap, trying not to be a burden, as I imagined.
She would stare at the new invention, the television, when others
turned it on. I never got the impression she took joy from it. We
spoke very little because she spoke Yiddish and only a sparse
few words of English. Once, upon leaving the house, I cautioned
her that if my friends called—I was sure they would—and asked
to borrow my new baseball bat that I placed in the closet, please
not to give it to them. The next day I went for my bat. It was in
the same place I had left it, but it had a fresh crack in it. I was
unhappy, but I could not get very angry with her.

In the middle of a night when I was ten, my mother woke me.
"Ira, I want you to see *Bubbie*," she said. "It may be the last
time." I rose, padded into the living room where ambulance men
carried Bubbie on a stretcher. Her face was in repose, and a blanket had been tossed over the yellow nightgown she wore. Her
white and purplish leg was slightly exposed. They went out the
door and down the stairs. I heard a motor start up and, abruptly,
a siren. I went back to sleep as the siren receded in the distance.
My grandmother died about an hour later.

My mother's family had once lived in an apartment house on
Morgan Street, around the corner from Maxwell, where next door
lived their friends the Rubensteins; several of the Rubenstein
children would eventually "Americanize" their last name to Ruby,
including Jack, when he moved to Dallas.

A few blocks south and east from there is the apartment building on Fourteenth Street and Newberry in which my father was
born in 1914. It is a large building, three stories high and with
columned entrances. It contained a minimum of eighteen apartments, which over the years were split into many more flats. The
address is 814 West Fourteenth Street. (A matter of interest to me
is that it is the same address in which Samuel Paley—father of

William Paley of CBS—lived with his father, mother, brothers and sisters sometime after arriving in Chicago from Russia, in the latter part of the nineteenth century.)

My father's family then consisted of his parents and some ten to fifteen children, depending on who was living at home, who was living at a friend's house, and who had left to strike out on his own. They left home, often, to escape the bickering and over-crowding commonly integral to the households on Maxwell Street.

My father's brothers and sisters were the sons and daughters of a Rumanian-Jewish sheetmetal worker, poor and never comfort-able with his adopted country's language. Like most of the bread-winners in the area, my grandfather, Israel Hersh Berkovitz, moved his family from flat to flat, seeking little by little to better their lot.

The building my father was born in is now heavily damaged. A fire several years ago reduced it to a shell. Boarded-up windows and charred doors now beckon the neighborhood's derelicts. They sleep in the blackened hallways while the building awaits the wrecker.

One of my father's early boyhood memories is of cracking his glasses and being unable to afford new ones. His nickname was "Blinky" because of the effort it took to peer out at the world through shattered spectacles.

On Saturday nights my father recalls accompanying his parents to Rumanian restaurants which were everywhere in the neigh-borhood. There was fiddle music and singing. My father's uncle, Baruch, owned such a restaurant for a time, on Newberry just off Maxwell. Uncle Baruch was a great sport and made his own wine, which he also drank in abundance. My father remembers that, as a Saturday night would grow later and later, Uncle Baruch drank more and more. With an expansive wave of his hand, Uncle Baruch would tell customers who were about to pay, "Forget it . . . on the house." This after they had eaten huge steaks and the pickles and tomatoes and big brown breads that weighted down the tables. It was no surprise when Uncle Baruch lost not only his business but his wife as well.

My father's mother died when he was thirteen. My father, youngest in the family, went to live in a boardinghouse with his father. The rest of the children had by now gone on their own. There was a wide gulf between father and son. It was the time of the Great Depression. The old man was rapidly losing energy, had little work, and even less money. My father was forced to go to his married sister, Rose Wolff, to receive three dollars for the week for food. My father told me he spent fifty cents a day for food. I said, "That's only six days." He replied evenly, "Never on Sunday."

The Wolffs were special people to me, as well as to my father. My Aunt Rose was supposed to be able to tell fortunes from tea leaves at the bottom of a cup. Her husband, Leo Wolff, was a husky, deep-voiced, highly respected Chicago detective, who had the ominous nickname "Jim Boston." When, for example, a death threat was made on the daughter of Colonel Jacob Arvey, the two best detectives in town were called on the case. One of them was Jim Boston. In 1919, Leo Wolff and Rose Berkovitz were dating. One day he was in a barber's chair and being shaved. He saw in the mirror my Aunt Rose walking down the street. She was a striking redhead. An idea hit. Uncle Leo jumped out of the chair and in flowing white sheet and shaving cream ran after her and proposed.

The couple had one son, Mel. One Saturday when Mel was five, he attended a local Chicago theater. Some theaters had talent contests in those days. This one had a Charleston dance contest. Mel, seeing other kids in the family competing, rushed on stage and began jumping up and down in imitation. A long hook reached out from the side and dragged him off.

Near the end of my Uncle Leo's life, he lost the use of his deep, awesome voice. My Aunt Rose and he would communicate on the telephone this way: She would ask a question and he would rap on the table. One rap no, two raps yes.

In the night and gray dawn, the stores on Maxwell Street today are locked and padlocked and gated and grated and bolted and barred and alarmed and boarded and shuttered and chained. Those heavy precautions mean in the end just one thing on Maxwell Street: the building will probably not be stolen from its moorings overnight. Thieves break into buildings by drilling or hacking in from the top, the bottom, the sides. At one liquor store, a thief spent all night with chisel and hammer carving a hole in the side of a brick wall. He was caught the following morning beside the wall. He had got drunk and fallen asleep before he could make his getaway.

## 3

From morning to night, and from night to morning, the street today is never without people; but in the smallest hours are the fewest people. Disparate noises break the eloquence of night silence. Jimmy's hot-dog stand is on the main corner of Maxwell and Halsted. With stark lights in the otherwise dark night, it resembles the lonely oasis of Edward Hopper's red-and-saffron painting, "Night Cafe." There is a little crash of the cash register, and then silence. The groan of a car pulling away, and then silence. A cackle of laughter, and then silence. Glass is broken. The sound of someone running down the street. Someone else running. And the sound dissolves into the night.

In the Sunday morning darkness cars bearing merchandise begin to appear. Doors open. Tables for the stands are put up, as are wooden horses with wooden boards and blankets on the street for display of merchandise. Clothes that fill some cars are removed and placed on the car's roof, hood, fenders, trunk, and hung from its doors and windows. No longer is the car choked; it is smothered. A vendor turns up his collars; his blood is thin in the waking morning; a chill ripples through his body, along with a thrill of expectation of good crowds, good sales, little theft. Another man glances over his eyeglasses and scans the sky for hints of rain that would keep shoppers home.

The street grows lighter as the soot-colored sky draws open. Pigeons come out early onto the building ledges and lopsided frontal fire escapes and looping wires of the telephone poles; they sit as mutely as members in a British clubroom.

The sun is rising. Buildings on one side of the street take on a pinkish tint, are in shadow on the other. Store gates rattle open. Locks unclick. Adam Cussberg, who always rises early on Sundays, did not wait for the tardy alarm clock to jangle and was up walking about his house, in anticipation of, now, pacing on the sidewalk in front of his basement shoe store and, soon, mumbling enticements to prospective customers.

Sidney Goldstein, wearing a square cap made of newspaper, a torn fleece-lined vest, and baggy pants, unbolts the front of his long, wooden-and-tin stand from the sidewalk and climbs up and in. He turns on the naked light bulb overhead. He crawls onto the pile of boxes on which he will sit all day. He has a potty, a heater, and during the day neighboring businessmen get him coffee and food. Sidney Goldstein puts out his display cases of watches and rings. He hangs necklaces and earrings of gold, crimson, turquoise, chartreuse. One views him from behind those necklaces and the light from the bulb casts an eerie, purplish glow. He can quote Milton and Shakespeare and Oliver Wendell Holmes. He has crawled in and sat for hours and hours like this nearly every day for the last forty years.

A big, colorful sun umbrella pops up on the street. And another. A third. Springtime in a concrete mushroom field. The socks stand opens. The panties stand opens. The Spanish tapes and records stand opens. The wig stand sprouts.

A black man with a small truck unloads buckets filled with ice and dead fish. Only the heads of the fish—carp and buffalo—are seen; fish with big cold white eyes. At another stand, actual heads of pigs with great snouts glare from inside bloody plastic bags.

There is a plastic-flowers stand. A garlic stand. Old shirts, one with one sleeve; and old pants; and old steam irons, one without a handle, and old shoes without laces. There is a fringed lamp shade which looks half-eaten. Crystal chandeliers are strung between two poles on coat-hanger wire. Tires lay flumped in heaps on a curb. A screech of live chickens. A quack of ducks. A roach-killer stand. Used toothbrushes. An assortment of old toilet bowls, some cleaned, and hubcaps, some not dented. Rusty saws. Dogs barking. Good antique clocks. Oranges and lemons and apples and grapes and cabbages and grapefruits piled up. There are hundreds of stands.

One day one of the regular stands did not open. It was a big appliance stand where television sets and radios and hi-fis were sold at very low prices. The proprietor, Ron Magliano, did not show up because he was in the morgue. He had been murdered in his home, a towel wrapped around his head so he wouldn't bleed on his nice carpet. Magliano had recently been convicted of transporting stolen merchandise across state lines, from Indiana to Illinois. He was awaiting sentencing. The police chief of the district in which he was murdered offered that friends and business associates of Magliano may have feared that, in return for a reduced sentence, he might have given evidence against them.

There are also some stores that no longer open. But that is because business, particularly during the week, has so diminished that those stores had to completely close down.

The market master, Irv Gordon, in white raincoat and white sporting shoes, comes up the stairs from Nate's Delicatessen, popping into his mouth nitroglycerine tablets that have kept him alive after two heart attacks. He has an "office" in Nate's, the third table from the door, the last table. Nate only has three tables. The tables are tiny, with three chairs and the wall on each side of them. But the market master doesn't need much of an office, anyway. He has his few policemen who walk with him to collect his "official" seventeen cents for the City Clerk's office. "Do you ever see him collect change?" a vendor once asked. "If he did, he'd need a wheelbarrow. But you don't need a wheelbarrow for bills."

There are shoppers on the street now, poking and sniffing and plucking something up and asking the price and shaking a head and walking on, being called back, stopping, haggling—buying grumblingly, or walking off. Perhaps returning. More people. The cars that bore merchandise are driven off to be parked. As more people come, cars now have tougher times getting through. Curses.

Serious shoppers like to come early. The tradition is that the best bargains are obtained on the first sale of the day, when the merchant wants to "break the ice." No one knows how many "first" sales the merchants, perpetrators of that myth, make in a day.

The street is crowded now. People jostle, bump into each other; the sun is out and warming.

There once were as many as seventy thousand shoppers and thieves among the tumultuary; on the best day in the 1970s, there were fewer than half that number. The Maxwell Street artery, which always has had branching and tributary streets for several blocks around, has grown at one end while being stunted at others. When the street had been chopped off to the east, north, and west, the vendors moved their stands to the south. Maxwell Street survives. Some of Maxwell Street has always survived. For much of the last one hundred years, there have been recurring civic movements to destroy it, thwart it, delouse it, ignore it, revamp it, rename it, remove it, and renovate it. All of these well-meaning, or politically motivated attempts have, in varying degrees, been successfully resisted by the street. But the effects of the battering attacks have taken their toll, to be sure.

Black bluesmen stomp and wail in a cacophony of amplified grunts and plucks to a desultory crowd. They are in a rubble-filled empty lot beside an apartment building on the corner of Newberry and Maxwell. Their wires and cords are plugged into outlets in nearby apartments and run umbilically through adjoining second-floor windows to their instruments.

Porkchop, a wiry, elderly man in dapper cap and stump cigar, beats and brushes a good drum. In due time, he may rise and join one of the heavy women in threadbare spring coat in the crowd and dance, kicking up stones in the empty lot.

There are antagonisms. John Henry Davis, group leader, sometimes will not permit "Maxwell Street" Jimmy Davis (no relation) to "play in" because Jimmy may be too "sauced up" and disruptive for John Henry's tastes. Maxwell Street Jimmy, however, has been playing there for years, has cut an album, but hasn't hit it big yet, not like Muddy Waters or Howlin' Wolf or Hound Dog Taylor. And so, Jimmy, unlike those stars, must return to Maxwell to gain an audience. He also has sentimental reasons for returning. It was here that his father would come and listen to him. His father was murdered a few doors down a few years ago by a girl friend, who stabbed him repeatedly as he ran into the street from Don's Liquor Store. To this day, when Jimmy plays his blues, he will see his daddy in his mind's eye standing there in the crowd, giving a little bob to the beat, and saying, "Sing it, son."

Down the street, Spanish tape decks whine from an old phonograph; Homero Prado croons "Humilde Corazon."

The most powerful smell, without question, issues from Jimmy's hot-dog stand on the main corner of Halsted and Maxwell. The enclosed stand with six open windows props against a two-story brick building. A "Vienna Red Hots" sign tops the stand. Above it rises into the sky a great cardboard 7-Up bottle and a green, white, gray, and red sign which reads, "Leavitt's, Famous for Sandwiches." Leavitt's has been out of business for a decade. Eight workers in Jimmy's fork out hot dogs from steamy tin bins, tuck the dogs into buns, slap on mustard, pinch in peppers, stuff in pickles, flap pork chops on the open grill, scrape the frying onions in pork fat and gristle for the Polish sausages and hamburgers. On a Sunday there a ton of onions, literally, are used. Thousands and thousands of soft drinks are consumed. The grease from the cooking is so great it seeps onto the sidewalk as customers, three and four deep, waiting to eat or eating, stand with shoes sticking to the grease. They walk away with shoes making sucking sounds. Special details are periodically sent by Jimmy to sop up the grease. Customers cough from the steam and the smell. The odor is cloying. Mike Chiappetta, a cop on the beat, spends much of a Sunday across the street from the stand. When he returns home his wife, Josie, complains that he reeks of onions. She stops him at the front door and sends him to the basement to change clothes and wash down.

Shoppers here are now primarily people from the area, and this is the way it was when the street first began to develop as a thriving marketplace, in the time following the Chicago Fire of 1871, going through the great immigration period from 1880 to 1924. As newcomers to America began pulling themselves up the economic ladder, they pulled away from Maxwell Street. But many returned to shop there. This lasted until the late 1960s, when whites became reluctant and fearful to come to the street, now inhabited primarily by blacks (though the businesses are owned mainly by Jews).

The buildings on Maxwell from Union to just past Halsted have stores on the ground level and sometimes the second floor. The

second and third floors are also often used for storage of merchandise or storage of impoverished tenants.

At the time of World War I there was a construction boom,
which lasted intermittently until shortly after World War II. That
boom is reflected sparingly in the buildings on this stretch of
street. The architects here were more builders than creators,
though there are indications of a little fancy stuff. The three-story
building housing Jack's Textiles on the southeast corner of Union
and Maxwell, for example, sports a mansard roof, rather, what architects call a "bastardized" or halfhearted mansard roof—as if the
builders hadn't had enough time to fool with the full slope. Some
of the buildings here have capitals atop pilasters; these are columns built into the brick, and they are fairly thin and forlorn columns. It seems as if the builders had seen these columns in a book
or in a newspaper picture, committed them to faulty memory, and
then endeavored to reconstruct them here. One building, made of
the popular Indiana limestone, is topped by a dome that resembles
the Kaiser's pointy helmet.

The tradition of famous architects coming to Chicago began
after the fire of 1871. The architects had seen Chicago as the
land of opportunity for their ideas—men such as Root and
Sullivan and Adler and Burnham and Richardson and Frank
Lloyd Wright and van der Rohe. They concentrated primarily on
commercial buildings in the downtown area. There, the beginnings
of skyscrapers appeared, such as the then soaring ten-story steel
structure, the Monadnak Building, which into the 1960s was still
considered a marvel. "The airy and vigorous articulation of elevation" of the Rookery Building, the spectacular and innovative
caisson foundations of the Chicago Stock Exchange Building.

However, there is not a brick on Maxwell Street that in any way
reflects the work of those monumental and original architects of
Chicago.

The first great movement of population, from the Maxwell Street
area to the West Side of Chicago, began in 1916. Jews began more
and more to assimilate. Beards were shorn. Women allowed the
hair on their heads to grow. Hot water and bathtubs and indoor
plumbing and room space and air were the lures.

But cable cars along nearby Roosevelt Road—the highway of the hegira—made it possible for the families to still return to Maxwell Street and its kosher meat markets and synagogues and fish stores and bakeries and clothing bargains. Besides that, Jews were not yet permitted to work in many of the grander stores and banks and office buildings in the Loop, so thousands of Jews still worked in the Maxwell Street area. However, by the 1950s, no Jewish families remained living there.

The number of residents around Maxwell Street had diminished by the 1970s to fewer than a thousand. And those remaining live in some of the same buildings and surroundings considered intolerable nearly a century before. One pooped two-story pitched-roof structure leans so far to the left it appears held up by the building beside it. And that building tilts slightly right. The impression is of two fatigued fighters propped up by each other and who can neither fight any longer nor fall. People still live in both buildings. In the second-floor window of one, in the spring, was a shedding Christmas wreath.

There are still cold-water flats in buildings here. Chimneys sag. Sides are cracked. Wooden porches are frail, and people have taken a step onto them and fallen right through. Railings are busted.

Except for the few vigorous hours on Sunday, it is not much of a place for a young man and his visions. At night, the windy flap of a store's torn awning has the sound of death. The people who live on Maxwell Street live there for the most part with no thought of a stepping stone any more, other than through robbery or narcotics. Few are white. Most are poor blacks or Latins. Some are elderly, like Bennie Maurice, called "Cuz" because he calls everyone "Cuz." Cuz is a spare, gray-haired black man with blue eyes, an ex-convict, who now walks with an aluminum walker and must clump slowly and painfully down the loose wooden stairs from his dreary second-floor flat on Maxwell Street. He clumps down the street to the main corner of Halsted and Maxwell where he spends most of the day in the tavern located across from the hot-dog stand; in the tavern the jukebox is loud and now and then gunshots whistle through the air.

Cuz had moved to Maxwell Street with his mother, a lady of

the streets, from New Orleans, in the transition that brought in black families to the neighborhood and drove out the Jews, just as the Jews had driven out the Irish and Bohemians and Germans before them. The blacks, who began to move to the Maxwell Street area—coming up from the South and bringing their cotton-field blues which they now sang on the streets for coins—were the new immigrants. Congress, in 1924, had decided that tighter immigration laws would keep America purer and that enough of this melting-pot business was enough already. Thus, there were few European Jews to take the place abandoned by the newly "Americanized" Jews. So the street at night was left to blacks, and later Mexican and Gypsy families.

There is at once a curious intermingling and separateness among the groups. The Jewish merchants who devour what they can of Maxwell Street by day, spit it out at night, and drive off to leafy suburbs. The blacks are themselves splintered into several groups. There are the tired old ones like Cuz, some youngish business people like Nate Duncan. There are the neighborhood people who wait for nightfall to turn tricks, peddle junk and needles, boost merchandise. There is an odd kind of fraternity between them and the local cops. Once walking the beat at night, patrolman Mike Chiappetta heard tapping noises coming from a rooftop of a clothing store at 729 Maxwell. Mike's headquarters is Jimmy's hot-dog stand on the corner. It is common knowledge among the crooks that Mike is usually there. It is also from the hot-dog stand that Mike's antennae for the smell and sounds of neighborhood iniquity is most acute. He now investigated the noise, climbing quietly up the back stairs. He saw two young men hammering a hole into the roof. One of them looked up in the dark and exclaimed, "Mike, what are you doing here?"

"Sylvester," Mike replied, "what are *you* doing here?"

There are two groups of Mexicans on Maxwell Street. Cisco Rodriguez, twenty-one-year-old owner of a shoe store on Maxwell Street, represents one. His is, perhaps, the cleanest, brightest, neatest, and pluckiest store on the street. And prospering. Cisco began his store career as an assistant to one of the other shoe merchants on the street. When Cisco broke away to seek his fortune a few doors down, the merchant tried to have the shoe jobbers boycott Cisco. The merchant liked and respected Cisco, and the feelings were mutual, but business is business, the merchant explained to Cisco. But Cisco persevered, a trait he inherited from his father, who entered the United States from Mexico twenty-four times, by illegally swimming across the Rio Grande, and was deported twenty-three times until he and his wife, while employed as fruit pickers in Texas orchards, gave birth to Cisco, their firstborn. The parents of a citizen may by law live in the United States with their offspring.

Other Mexicans in the Maxwell Street area are, as Cisco's father once was, American by stealth. They live huddled in dingy and damp and sparse rooms, shades drawn all day, and work at menial, clattery jobs by night—dreaming of making the fortunes they have heard exist in America, and then planning to return with their lode to the soporific Mexico of fond memory.

Gypsy families live above a hot-dog store on Halsted Street just south of Maxwell. Gypsies have been around Maxwell Street as long as anyone can remember, leaving each winter to see the world and returning each spring to see the world. The old heavy seeress, Mary Montes, sits regally on a groaning folding chair on the sidewalk in front of her hallway. She wears a black dress because of the recent death of her husband; her face is kindly, puffy, and bewhiskered. Her daughters and nieces and grandchildren who call her "Madonna" sit and stand beside her. The women in turn openly express willingness to share with a passerby the arcane wisdom of the ages and the contents of his wallet. The Madonna has lived here on Maxwell Street since the 1920s, when her uncle Tene Bimbo, the self-styled "king of the Gypsies," terrorized the other gypsy families and fancied himself the Capone of the Gypsies, and, said the Madonna, "was known to cut off the ear of anyone who acted cross-eyed to him." She has lived here through the great shifts of population and generations. At night, the Gypsies rarely come out. "Because we are private people," says the Madonna. "No, we are not scared of the neighborhood. The people are more afraid of *us*. They worry we will make a hoodoo on them."

A Korean man, quiet and with a cowlick, owns the wig store, that odd little dreamworld of glass cases with shelf upon shelf of bodiless heads containing unblinking eyes and flowing hair—curly hair, straight hair, brown, black, blond, orange, banged, speckled, swirled, pyramided, bunned, braided, and beribboned hair.

Another Korean across the street owns an unpretentious restaurant serving oriental food, with "fire beef" the specialty.

Signs on the street proliferate: "The Mexican Gift Shop," with a hand-drawn purse floating on the hanging sign; "The Beef Stand," with a snorty, cartoony cow; "Makevich's," a devastated neon sign. Makevich's was once the most spectacular department store on the street. It sold everything from caviar to bicycles and catered to shoppers from as far away as Iowa and Michigan and southern Indiana and Minnesota. When it shut down in 1974, a blow was struck to Maxwell Street; but the great sign, now without lights, still proclaims, "Your Credit Is Good."

"Esquire Joe's 719 Maxwell." Owned by Joe and Ruth Glassman since the 1930s, when they had empty boxes lining the shelves and only a handful of merchandise, but told customers that they must sell what was out because they hadn't yet taken inventory on "all those boxes on the shelf." They also slept in the window then, to guard against thievery. They still hold hands. Ruth tells how she had wanted to break the wedding engagement to Joe when she learned she had a spinal infection (a childhood injury incurred when she tripped in a hole in the Polish forest as she and her family ran away to America one night just before a pogrom broke out in their town). She wanted to break the engagement because she feared she would have to wear a back brace the rest of her life, and no husband would want a cripple for a wife. Joe sneaked up eleven flights of stairs to her hospital room and proposed again. She accepted. When a couple of years later she found she was pregnant, she said it was the saddest moment of her life. She cried and said to the doctor, "I'll never be able to have a baby because of the brace." The doctor said, "Wipe your tears. We will have your baby." And *they* did.

More signs: "High styles in Men's and Boy's Wear." "Superior Clothing." "Kelly's Sporting Goods." "Jay's Shoes." "Dunne's Hats." "Jack's Textiles." "Tannenbaum's Hardware." "Schauer's Luggage." "Hy's General Merchandise." "Toys." "The Earring King."

There are two hot-dog stands on opposite sides of the Halsted and Maxwell corner. One is owned by a Yugoslavian immigrant, the other by Italians.

There is a liquor store, "Rush Liquors," on Maxwell and Sangamon. The owner is Louis Briatta. On Maxwell Street, he is called "Uncle Louie" and is notorious for having alleged underworld connections. He had recently been in the headlines again. This time, it had nothing to do with income-tax evasion or alleged mob activities or any of those odd people he has been linked to in the press in the past, such as Rocco "Parrot" Potenza, Frank "One Ear" Fratto, John "Mule Ears" Wolek, Anthony "Peaches" DeLordo, Jack "Pippy" Green, Anthony "Pineapples" Eldorado, Edward "Big Head" Vogel, Mitchell "Firebug" Glitta, James "Bomber" Catura, Murray "The Camel" Humphreys, or Willie "Potatoes" Daddano. This time, the newspapers announced that Briatta's daughter was marrying the son of the mayor of Chicago, Richard "The Great Dumpling" Daley. And so the mayor's son married into Maxwell Street money.

Politics and hanky-panky and Maxwell Street have been inextricable. Through the years, the market masters, who decide whose stand may be placed at what advantageous spot, have been political appointees, some becoming tolerably wealthy on a surprisingly paltry City Hall salary.

There are those who believe that Maxwell Street, even the little that is left of it, has survived—while much of the area around it was being razed and "renewed"—because of political "clout." An example of the benign attitude of City Hall for this disadvantaged area is the fireplug on the corner of Halsted and O'Brien where, some seventy years ago, Arthur Goldberg was raised. Today there is a permanent wooden fruit stand located *on* the street, beside the curb. It is a fine location and business is good. Unhappily, a straitlaced policeman discovered that the stand was situated too close to the fireplug and violated a municipal ordinance. The stand was ordered removed. The owner, a reputed onetime bookmaker and currently a Democratic precinct captain in the area, protested. His protests proved convincing to city officials. The stand stayed. But the *fireplug* was dug up and set down across the street.

In the old days, before election machines, political enthusiasts would bring into a polling place from the rear door a stuffed ballot box with ballots already marked for the favored candidate. The original ballot box was then picked up and carried out the back door while the policeman on duty gazed with consuming interest out the front window. It was in this atmosphere, however, that the Jewish immigrants, accustomed to powerlessness before subjugating Eastern European authorities, quickly learned in America how votes could equal muscle in order to attain rights and privileges in a democracy.

From these beginnings came Jacob Arvey, one of America's most influential politicians of the 1940s and '50s and at one time an alderman of the most powerful ward in the United States. (During the 1936 presidential election, for example, his ward, the twenty-fourth, a few miles down Roosevelt Road from Maxwell Street, gave Franklin D. Roosevelt 29,000 votes to 700 for Alfred Landon.) Later, as Illinois Democratic National Committeeman, Arvey helped Richard Daley gain office. Arvey was also credited with delivering Illinois to Truman in 1948, thus spearheading a tremendous upset over Dewey. It was, in part, Arvey's influence in these matters, and the dues owed him, that persuaded Truman, in 1948, to have the United States recognize the State of Israel.

Today, at the opposite end of the street from Uncle Louie's tavern is "Jack's Textiles." It is a tidy store run by a quiet elderly couple named Jack (or Jakov) and Sonja Karchmar. They represent a wholly different background from the one that has been attributed to Uncle Louie. The Karchmars came to America in 1949, after having spent most of World War II in Nazi concentration camps. They are retiring people. Mrs. Karchmar, a small-boned woman in a deep-pocketed smock, hauls down a great long roll of material from a shelf and thumps it on the long wooden counter to show a customer; she is especially circumspect in her selling technique. Mr. Karchmar, a little taller, with ready smile and doelike eyes, is spiritedly showing a red rug with a bear emblazoned on it to another customer. He is less reluctant to talk about their experiences in Europe in the 1940s than is his wife. The Karchmars and their three children were awakened in the dead of night in their house in Warsaw, Poland, and dragged off to separate German camps. The three children did not survive, apparently, since after the war the Karchmars searched unsuccessfully from city to city, stumbling over the rubble of Europe as they did. They eventually gave up and came to America and to Maxwell Street, which they heard was a place where they could start with little and build a future. They did. They also began a whole new family, of which their three American-born children have, they say with undisguised pride, graduated from college.

How was it that the two of them, having been separated by the Nazis, found each other in the confusion after the war? Mrs. Karchmar said quietly, as if some unfriendly authorities might be listening, that when she was released from Auschwitz and was in the crowded processing center in Poland, she noticed a man who was "a bag of bones" and had a shaved head but who looked familiar. She peered closer. "Jakov!" she cried.

"My husband had changed so much," she says now, "but I knew it was him. I could tell by his eyes."

Schauer's Luggage is one of the oldest established continuous stores on the street. The store is run by the son and daughter of Max Schauer. When Max Schauer came to America from Poland at the turn of the century, he decided that the first job he wanted to get was in a restaurant. In that way, he figured, he would be sure of eating. He found what he was looking for and was required to wear a tuxedo in this restaurant. As he walked down the street going to work, one day that first week, he met a man from his small hometown in Europe. The man was amazed.

"Max," he said, "how long have you been in America?"

"Two days," said Max Schauer.

"And already you can afford a tuxedo? Such an America!"

Max Schauer saw greater possibilities in America than wearing a tuxedo for an employee. He would become an entrepreneur. He began to sell small items on a stand on Maxwell Street. One day he heard of an auction. There he saw silk shirts that buttoned up the back; they were being sold at a great bargain since up-the-back buttons were no longer in style on shirts. Max and his wife spent all night taking the buttons off. The next day they sold all of their silk shirts, and gave buttons free so that people could sew them on and wear them in front, as was now the fashion. Schauer and his wife and their children spent all that night joyously counting the money.

The sign "Sherman Pants, sizes 6 to 60" leads to a basement store where they have a sixty-inch-waist pair of pants, looking like an elephant's drawers, hanging up over the sidewalk in front of the store.

"Max's Adult Book Store—Peep Shows, Novelties," the newest store on the street and the most controversial.

"Paul and Bill the Tailor," with a big arrow pointing to their second-floor shop; the sign is sometimes lost in the steam which billows out the windows from the pressing machines.

"Continental Bargain Store." "Wigs." "Hass Brothers Clothing." "Kelly's Sporting Goods." "Mother's Threads." "Ethel Brodie's Corsets." "Hy's General Merchandise."

At the corner of Halsted and Maxwell, tattered green and red plastic strips cross from the top of two telephone poles on opposite sides of Halsted. The strips are there to add pizzazz, but are remindful of a bum wearing a wilted boutonniere.

Halsted Street has changed over the years. The stores on Halsted Street have similar merchandise to those on Maxwell, and many of the stores there have, over the years, moved from Maxwell. One difference, however, is that most of Halsted Street is "one price," as opposed to the haggling of Maxwell. And Halsted Street owners are not delighted to be considered Maxwell Street owners. Sheldon Pinsker, who in his twenties in the 1970s opened "Mother's Threads," alongside his father's clothing store on Maxwell Street, said that when he was in school he was ashamed to tell people that his father worked on Maxwell Street. "I would say 'Halsted Street.' It had more prestige, I thought, until I got older and realized the difference was minimal." There are signs for bargains on Halsted just as on Maxwell. Sid Wexler, owner of a shoe store on Halsted, has Christmas tinsel hanging all year round in front of his store. "I keep it because when the tinsel blows in the wind, it's like it sings a little song out there," he said. "It's good for business."

Back on Maxwell, on the west side of Halsted, are signs: "Nate's Kosher Delicatessen," owned by Nate Duncan, a black man, and "Harry's Paints."

"Maxwell 831—Records. TV." Boarded up instead of locked up for the night, until Bernard Abrams, hefty, one-eyed, wearing a hunter's cap with earflaps up, and his wife, a babushka over her red hair, take down the slats and reveal inside a jungle of wires and cords and knobs and stacks of old radios and record players and TV sets and sundry parts from musical instruments. Bernard and "Mrs. Bernard," as the customers call her, were the first to sell the blues records of Muddy Waters and Little Walter and Howlin' Wolf. They did this after World War II, when no one else would sell their stuff. Bernard, though, admits he did it only for money and not for love.

"I never could understand what those blues singers were about," he said. "I like talented singers, like Perry Como."

In the dilapidated toilet in back of the store is written on the wall, in black crayon: "Directions on Use of This Washroom: 1. Pick up Board. 2. Direct Stream *in* Bowl. 3. Don't Steal the Toilet Paper, Please. Your continued use depends on your obedience to these rules."

The last building left standing on the following block is the police station, the oldest building on the street, having been built in 1891. It looks like a fortress, with foot-thick russet brick walls. The station house is expected to be torn down in a few years. Much of the work that goes on now has been moved to another precinct. The lockup in the basement, for example, is no longer in use. Lying dormant is the open drainage pipe that protrudes from the wall and once carried prisoner's excrement and urine past the other prisoners.

Gone too are the fat rats who would sit and watch from wooden beams above the cells, their long tails hanging down. Long gone, too, is the lockup keeper who, knowing the drug addict's craving for sweets, would buy a box of five-cent candy bars and sell them to the prisoners for a buck apiece.

Beyond the police station is a parking lot for squad cars, and that's where Maxwell Street physically ends now. In the distance is a new school, relatively new housing projects, and the spires of two churches.

One other building still standing on the street is of historical and until 1975 practical importance. That is the Maxwell Street

Maternity Center. It was the last home-delivery service for births in America. It closed down for lack of funds and lack of inspiration, when Dr. Beatrice Tucker, its director for forty-one years, retired.

There are more empty lots on the west side of Halsted Street than on the block east. One empty lot, directly across from the maternity center, is where on Sundays the surreptitious and whispery watch sellers congregate with hats lowered and sleeves rolled down.

Newberry and Maxwell is also the main corner for prostitutes and was once the hotbed of the whorehouses. But now most of those buildings have been torn down. One was on the empty lot where the bluesmen play, and once the gold-toothed pimps under wide-brim hats lounged beside the cyclone fence. They watched and counted the tricks come and go from the houses so that their women couldn't keep any sly change for themselves. The pimps never wrote down this information with pencil and paper but kept it all with a mental abacus. Leisurely, they watched the events of the market day pass before them. And none will ever forget the day when a dispute between two adjoining and competing whorehouses culminated with the ladies streaming into the street, with their mini-skirts and wigs and double false eyelashes and negligees and tall, tall heels and switchblades and tire irons, and engaged in a furious battle.

The scene, despite its comical and prurient aspects, combined the historic elements of Maxwell Street: entrepreneurs and residents battling, sometimes literally, to survive.

# THE STREET, 1895

## LITERALLY, MAXWELL STREET
## NO LONGER EXISTS

—You might look for a whole week by consulting lampposts on the West Side and you wouldn't find "Maxwell Street." The hand of the iconoclast has been busy with West Side tradition and the street to which the famous police station gave dignity is simply and flatly West Thirteenth Place.

But the Maxwell Street Station is still there, and the street is still called Maxwell Street by everybody except the postman.

CHICAGO *TRIBUNE*
*September 20, 1895*

Earlier that year, in 1895, a committee of city councilmen had begun a program to rename city streets, thereby trying to avoid the confusion that existed by having such things as two Avenue A's, two Avenue B's, and five Center avenues. Even though there was only one Maxwell Street, the street still found itself in the middle of this civic crusade for order. Thus did it become West Thirteenth Place.

But one year later, Maxwell Street's marked recalcitrance to suffer change of any sort resulted in the following minutes of the Council meeting of March 30, 1896:

The committee on streets and alleys to whom was referred an ordinance changing the name of 13th Place [back] to Maxwell Street, submitted a report recommending that the same be passed.

Yeas 62. Nays 0.

Be it ordained by the City Council of the City of Chicago.

# II

# FLIGHT TO COLUMBUS'S LAND

"The year 1881 marks a turning point in the history of the Jews as decisive as that of 70 A.D. when Titus's legions burned the Temple at Jerusalem, or 1492, when Ferdinand and Isabella decreed their expulsion from Spain," wrote Irving Howe. "On March 1, 1881, Alexander II, Czar of Russia, was assassinated by revolutionary terrorists; the modest liberalism of his regime came to an end; and within several weeks a wave of pogroms, inspired by agents of the new government, spread across Russia."*

Hordes of soldiers stormed in and burned and looted the homes of Jews living in the Pale. The Pale of Settlement composed the area of czarist Russia in which Jews were legally authorized to settle. The Pale covered an area of 386,000 square miles, from the Baltic Sea to the Black Sea. By 1897, slightly less than 4.9 million Jews lived there, forming 94 per cent of the total Jewish population of Russia and about 12 per cent of the population of the area.

The overwhelming number of Jews living in Europe resided in Russia and in the Pale; there were substantial numbers of Jews living in nearby Rumania and Poland, as well. Persecution and second-class citizenship existed for Jews throughout Europe.

The Jews had been severely limited in Russia. They were not allowed, generally, to own land, join the guilds, or hold jobs in government. They were often not permitted to attend the Russian schools. They had been forced into money-lending and peddling, both occupations scorned by the gentile populace, and into small trades such as tailoring. Yet they were forced to serve in the army of the despised czar.

They were forced to live in poverty and in seclusion from the

* Irving Howe, *World of Our Fathers* (New York: Harcourt Brace Jovanovich, 1976), p. 5.

rest of society. Because they were so adamant about not converting to Christianity, the Jews in Russia—as in most places they lived in after the Diaspora in A.D. 70—were often considered strange, sometimes accused of "ritual murders" and, in times of upheaval (such as the assassination of Alexander II) were rendered scapegoats.

As the industrial revolution developed in Russia, Jews after 1881 gradually began leaving their tiny shtetls for cities where they often worked as cheap laborers.

Until the murder of Alexander II, there was only a relatively small amount of immigration to America by Jews; seventy-five hundred between 1820 and 1870, forty thousand in the 1870s, but from 1881 to 1924, the figure swelled to two million.

# JACK GREENBERG

Jack Greenberg, aged seventy (in 1975), came to Chicago from Russia when a youth. He has worked in America mainly as an appliance-maintenance man, though he briefly owned a textile shop and a dry cleaning store. He now lives with his wife in a one-bedroom, first-floor flat on the North Side of Chicago.

"My family lived in a town by the name of Proskurov in the Ukraine, a town of twenty thousand people. The town was mostly Jewish and especially the district where we lived, which was, I would say, 90 per cent Jewish and maybe 10 per cent Gentile. During some pogroms sometimes friendly *goyim,* these Gentiles, would hide us. They would protect us. They would help us along. I can tell you about a pogrom that happened. This was in 1918. It happened in our town. Five thousand people they killed on a summer afternoon, Saturday afternoon. It was a nice warm day, a sunny day. I remember it just like I'm sitting right here. I saw it. Since I was a little guy, I was on the street. I was eight years old. While they were killing people, I was on the street.

"The soldiers came up more or less on the main street and then there were side streets. We lived on a side street. We lived on Naberaznia Boulitsa, *boulitsa* is Russian for street. Actually, we lived near the river at the end of town, so there weren't many businesses, mostly homes. The soldiers would come and shout *'Podamom, podamom.'* That means, 'In the house, everybody in the house.' They were chasing everybody in the house with their swords swinging. Some were on horseback; some were on foot. Most naturally, when something like that happens, everybody gets in the house. We don't know what will happen, especially in that town. I can't believe it today. It's hard for me to believe. Everybody went in their house, and before you know it, I was on the

street. I was running around the street. A kid! What the hell am I
going to go in the house? I was four blocks away from the house,
running around with kids. I was a little punk. But I wasn't out
there very long. I saw what was going on. They were starting to
kill people. I saw them shooting and chopping people's heads off,
killing people. The screaming was murder. Everybody was being
killed. And there was a lot of screaming going on, so I finally ran
home. When I ran home, my father wasn't home. My father was
in *shul*. Saturday that was the place for him to be, in shul. He was
praying all day long, and this happened to be in the afternoon already. My grandmother, my uncle, my aunt all lived together in
two houses adjoining each other, and here the soldiers were killing
people all around, and I came into the house. My mother grabs
a hold of me and we went and hid ourselves. We had my uncle
next door. He was in the rag business, and we had a storage area,
a garage you might say, right next to the house, adjoining our
house and his house—full of sacks with shoes, rubbers, rags,
pieces of material, sacks full. So my mother, the whole family, we
all went into the garage where that stuff was, and there was a
basement there under the stuff. There was a big hole. You would
crawl in there, and then you would put a sack over and nobody
would know, and this is how we were saved. But at the time my
older brother Sam hollered 'Where's Pa? Where's Pa?' and Sam
ran out. He was very lucky. He ran out to the shul where my father was, a block and a half away. He ran right across the street,
mind you, while they were killing people. He ran to save my father. He came in there, and everybody in that shul ran up to the
roof to hide themselves. My father says, 'Nothing doing.' He
believed God would save him. He just put his *tallis* on and stood
there praying. And the soldiers skipped that shul! There were four
other shuls in that vicinity. Every other shul they went into, but
that shul they did not come into.

"That was Pa's theory. God will save him. He believed so much
in God that he would go to any length to prove his faith. It's hard
for me to believe today why people would let themselves be killed
like that, why they didn't prepare themselves, why they didn't put
up a fight, fight back. But nobody did, and there were quite a few
able-bodied people. But they had such a belief in God, that God

would look after them, in life or in death. That it was God's decision. They were in his hands.

"Half the town's Jewish population was killed, about five thousand Jews. But my whole family was all saved by some miracle. The day after, there were bodies all over the street. The survivors collected them and buried them. According to the Jewish Law, you've got to bury them separately, not just throw them in a mass grave. They were all crying. Whoever was left was crying and crying.

"They piled the bodies into wagons. Whole families were piled in. They carried them in black stretchers. Four people would carry a dead person all the way through town, and other Jews would follow to the cemetery, which wasn't very far. Everybody was crying, most naturally.

"Everybody who had fathers and mothers dead ran to the cemetery to pray. You know how Jews are. Jews always believe that the dead people pray for them. That's the Jewish religion, that they can do a lot for you down there. That they should pray for us and keep us alive and all this and that. This is the Jewish belief, anyway.

"We had other pogroms, from time to time, but none as bad as this one. Maybe you wouldn't call them pogroms. Just robberies and stuff like that.

"They were all done by soldiers, never the local police. The soldiers would come in and they would confiscate our house. They would take over our house. There were five people in our house—my mother and father and three of us guys, three boys. We had, let's say, an apartment like this here for five people. They would come in, take away the living room. They would take this room and this room, and they would give us the bedroom, that's all, all five of us. So most naturally, my father and mother, they would not allow us to sleep in there, so they pleaded with them, so we slept over here on the floor.

"Once the soldiers had a couple of broads. They pulled a couple of broads through the window. They wouldn't take them through the door. My father locked the door at night, so they pulled them through the window, and here I was sleeping! But I was also watching. Why not? Sure. What the hell? This wasn't the first time I had seen anything like that. It happened at the time I was already thirteen years old. I was already screwing my boyfriend's sister.

"Life wasn't good there, when you look back on it from America today, but it wasn't bad, as far as I was concerned. I was a kid. I was growing up without the luxuries they have here, but nobody over there had them.

"At certain times we were starving, sure. We didn't have nothing to eat. Not only because we didn't have much money to buy it. But there was many a time in which there was nothing to be bought. At one time I remember my father went out to get bread, to get food in the house. So he went out—with money, mind you —and the only way he could get bread was from beggars. He bought bread from beggars. Beggars over there used to go around with big bags, to houses, and instead of giving them money, everybody used to give them a piece of bread. A piece of bread would be like a loaf of bread, that big—a quarter of a loaf. Here, that's for the beggar. Nobody ever refused a beggar a piece. At that time there was such a famine in our city—there was nothing ever like it! My father had to buy it from the beggar, of all things. There was nothing to be gotten anywhere else in the whole town.

"We were very, very poor, like most of the other Jews. The government didn't encourage me to go to the Gymnasia, the Russian school. I went to *cheder,* the Jewish school. Few of us ever learned how to speak Russian. We spoke Yiddish. My parents never learned to speak Russian, the language of the land they lived in. My father's job was primarily a chicken killer. But he was a religious man and he mostly studied and prayed. He was a follower of the great Barditschiver rabbi. He lived in Barditschev, which was another town fourteen or fifteen miles away. We had to go by horse and wagon and it was a plenty long way. It took a good part of the day to get there.

"We lived in a wooden house with a wooden floor. Prior to that we had a dirt floor, when we lived with my grandmother over on another street. In the kitchen of our house was a simple wooden table with four wooden chairs. In the bedroom were two broken-down beds. In the front room was what you might call a commode and a couple of cots for us to sleep on. That was it. There were only four chairs.

"In 1918—right after that pogrom in 1918, we knew we wanted to get out of Russia. But it was hard. We wanted to go to America. That's all we envisioned was America. Everything was supposed to be rosy there. But you had to have somebody there send for you, and send you money for passage. We had nothing.

"I had two older brothers who were of age to be conscripted into the army, they were seventeen and nineteen. Everybody tried to get out of it, if you possibly could. My brother Sam's boyfriend went and it wasn't very long before he came back without a leg. That was during the Russian Revolution. It wasn't good to be a Jew in the Russian Army. They would put you immediately in the front line. And they drafted you for twenty-five years.

"Everybody tried to get out. They might poke their own eardrum out or mangle a finger to stay out. My brothers ran away early one morning. There used to be a time when they would conscript guys, and they would go and you'd never hear from them again. They would kill them. They were killing Jewish boys like flies. They'd just disappear. Neighbors of ours. Anyway, one nice morning my father told my brothers, 'Make your way the best way you can.' So we had an uncle here, in this country, in Chicago. My uncle Dave. He was the only one. This one uncle was a brother of my father's. And we wrote letters and he sent money. Now, my brothers snuck out of Russia and went to Rumania. They stole across the border. It wasn't easy. So this uncle brought over my two brothers. This was 1918. And most naturally, once they got here, they used to correspond with my folks. They used to write letters, send money. . . . We used to get pictures of them. My brother would send a picture, and in the picture—we knew already—was a five-dollar piece. And they always said, 'We'll get you over here, too. We'll work hard.' They did work very hard over here, and they brought us over with the help of my uncle.

"I was fourteen years old at the time we left Russia. It was 1924. I left my girl friend over there who was crying—girls galore! I hate to brag about it, but God! That's all I had was lots of girls. She was crying. Oh, did she cry when I was leaving! But to me it didn't make no difference. Love 'em and leave 'em. That was me. I had plenty.

"So we packed up. There wasn't much to pack up. We packed up Proskurov. We left. We took nothing from the house except my father had maybe ten gold pieces. Naturally he took his religious books.

"We were excited. America meant an awful lot. The biggest thing was my brothers—to see my brothers—and freedom. The way my brothers were giving us to understand—they sent us money for coming here, three hundred dollars for the ship, tickets, and all that, and they were only here four years, so we thought you come over here, you get to be a millionaire overnight. My older brother was in business for himself. He was a peddler. So you get a feeling about over here; my feeling was that over here money grows on trees.

"So I packed up my *klimical*. That's a little package that you take like in a pillowcase, and you put things in. And my suit was in there. My suit which my boss at the feed store gave me when I was Bar Mitzvahed. It was a long-pants suit. It was my first long-pants suit. Mostly you wore knickers as a little boy. Now I was a man. At thirteen you were considered a man. And this boss gave me a suit with long pants and, boy, was I in seventh heaven at that time! That's the suit I carried with me—that suit and maybe underwear, a couple of pairs of underwear, and that's it. Shoes? What I was wearing, no extra. I had a cap, one of those little caps. We left nothing behind. We took nothing and we left nothing."

# MORRIS KURYOL CARL

Among the fears Zvi Kuryol had in 1918 was that of his sixteen-year-old son Morris being conscripted into the Russian Army. The Russian military took Jewish boys as young as eight into service, and not without disdain. (A Russian officer was quoted, "A Jew boy, you know, is such a frail, weakly creature. . . . He is not used to tramping in the mud for ten hours a day and eating a biscuit . . . being among strangers, no father or mother nor petting; well, they cough and cough until they cough themselves into their graves.") One of Zvi Kuryol's older sons had run off to America to avoid the army; and began sending back small amounts of money in hopes that the rest of the family, his mother and father and seven brothers and sisters, would follow.

One night in 1918, in the Kuryols' little town of Miaskovka in the Ukraine, the Jewish section of about two thousand dwellers experienced a pogrom.

The soldiers came, recalls Morris Kuryol Carl today, and then they ravaged the town. "There was a saying by the Russians, 'Kill the Jews and save Russia,'" he said. "They came tramping into our house. My father begged them, 'Take what you want, but don't kill anybody.' They didn't. We were lucky. When I got married, I learned that my wife's father was murdered in a pogrom. He was hit on the back of the head with a club and died a couple of months later. But I can never forget that day in 1918. I was cowering in a corner so scared I could not move. I wished I had wings so I could fly away."

A few days later Zvi Kuryol urged his son Morris to leave Miaskovka and go anywhere. Zvi, a poor peddler, gave young Morris all the money he could, fifty dollars. It was enough to send Morris thirty-five miles away to Rumania. Morris crossed the border at the river by night in a rowboat. He was on his own and frightened. As soon as he landed, he was pounced upon by a Rumanian who ran off with his one bundle of clothes. Morris found his way to a synagogue in Bucharest and was helped to find two jobs.

Morris worked in a factory and also taught Hebrew to youngsters. He saved all he earned in order to get his parents out of Russia. It took him two years to do it. He arrived in Rumania with one shirt, and two years later it was still the only shirt he owned.

He had also saved enough to get to America. He went by train to Le Havre, France, and from there boarded a ship to America, where he would eventually raise the money, with his brother, to send for the rest of the family who had remained behind in Bucharest.

"I cried when I boarded the boat because I was so happy. It was like going from a prison to an open society. I cried not once but a dozen times. I cried on the boat, I cried when I saw the Statue of Liberty, I cried when I landed. . . .

"I was so anxious, I can't tell you, to see the Statue of Liberty. We had heard about it so much. It was the symbol of freedom for all the oppressed people of the world. I wanted to get close to it, to kiss it. But once we landed we had so much to worry about. There was concern about being sent back. We talked about that on the ship. People who weren't healthy were sent back. Not many, but some. The officials looked especially for bad eyes, we heard. My eyes were good. I didn't worry so much about that. The building in Ellis Island was very, very big. It made you feel so small. So much confusion. So much noise. People from all over the world, talking in all different languages. Lots of tables and doctors, and we were sent here and there. I was lucky, too, that I had met a lady on the boat. I told her I didn't have twenty dollars left. That's what you needed to enter the country. All I had was Rumanian money, and you'd need a bushel of it to make twenty American dollars. This lady, so she gives me twenty dollars. Can you believe this?"

The immigration official, as was the wont of many of those men in those days, did not listen very carefully to these strange-speaking foreigners. One in particular took the easy way out with "Kuryol" and wrote "Carl" on the young man's documents. Morris accepted humbly, and it was Morris Carl from then on.

Morris Carl as a young man opened a dry goods store at 704 Maxwell Street. He labored there from twelve to fifteen hours a day nearly every day for twenty years. He never took a vacation. He left Maxwell Street when he felt a sense of entrapment, a feeling reminiscent for him of Russia. He had worked so hard he had begun to neglect observing his orthodox Jewry. When his father died, Morris Carl experienced a sense of guilt and returned fervently to religious rites. Every day since then, he says, he has praised God—praised God for the freedom to practice his religion, to be an American, to earn a good living for his family.

One of his sons, Howard Carl, became a determined and spectacular basketball player. He eventually played for the Chicago team in the National Basketball Association. But before that, Howard broke scoring records at his college, DePaul, that had been set by the widely acclaimed George Mikan. Mikan stands six feet ten. Howard Carl is five nine. Howard received a scroll as a member of the "Catholic Digest College Basketball All-American Team." The scroll had a crucifix on it. Howard hung it on his bedroom wall. Morris Carl was proud of his son's achievements (though he never understood the tumult about games in America) but believed the "crucifix" a sacrilege in his home. He discreetly stuck a piece of tape over the crucifix.

# MORRIS MILLER

"On the boat we had a whole sackful of black Russian bread that my mother had made. There were about twelve loaves. It was for the six of us. That was our food for three weeks, the time it took to cross the ocean. Black Russian bread, if you ever saw it, is, oh, about twelve inches in diameter. You take that bread and you soak it in honey and you dry it in the oven. My father had been in America and worked for five years as a blacksmith to save five hundred dollars to bring us across, and we had no money left to buy food on the ship. My mother and five kids. All we had to eat was those twelve loaves from her burlap sack, plus some herring the ship provided free. We didn't have one slice of bread left when we got here."

Morris Miller recalled that trip from Poland made in 1912, when he was eleven years old. He sat now, at age seventy-seven, hunched on a ladder that leaned against the stacks of baseball gloves in his brother's sporting goods store at 729 Maxwell Street. His brother is Irving Miller, though known as "Kelly" most of his life. The store is called "Kelly's." Kelly is two years younger than Morris. Morris, a retired carpenter, works in his brother's store from spring to fall, then spends winter in Miami Beach. He has cheery blue eyes that are emphasized by glittering glasses. He wears a golf cap cocked on his gray hair, a red windbreaker, neatly creased black pants, and shiny shoes.

The crossing by the Millers was reminiscent of the crossings of many of the immigrants. They came in steerage, the underdeck compartments near the rudder—a part of the ship without light or ventilation. Steerage was packed with thousands of impoverished immigrants. The din was great. They packed on deck in motley shawls and fur caps to gather air in the afternoon. At night in steerage, three and four people huddled in bunks. When one turned in his sleep, they all turned. Smells grew strong, especially when storms raged and masses vomited.

The Millers landed in Baltimore. A majority of immigrants landed at Ellis Island, where as many as fifteen thousand immigrants would land in one day. Others landed in Philadelphia, Boston, New Orleans, and Galveston. They were herded behind screens and into penlike areas by officious, uniformed, and booted bureaucrats. They were poked, prodded, inspected, questioned.

"The customs," said Morris Miller. "I thought I'm back in Poland. You can't go here, you can't go there, you had to stay in your place. Like the little town I came from in Poland. Maybe twenty Jewish families there. The Polish people didn't like the Jews too well. They'd look at you in the streets and like to spit on you, right in the street. Actually, there was no street. It was a mud road. Just stones on it. The Gentiles, the butchers, they'd take a hog and butcher him right out in the street. The blood poured in a bucket and sloshed over into the street. It wasn't too pleasant. And the pigs would run around the street. I felt like one of those pigs in the customs building.

"But it was all right once we got out of there. We got on the train and we knew we were on our way to Chicago, to see Pa. It was exciting.

"I looked out the window and I saw nothing but fields passing us by, nothing but fields. I knew I was in America, but this looked like Europe. And the train car was filled with others from Europe, some of us with tags tied to our lapels, telling our name and destination because we couldn't talk English."

The train huffed into Chicago's Grand Central Station, with its Norman tower rising 247 feet at the corner of Harrison and Wells. The railroad tracks and the crush of trains amid the smoke from engines made the scene gauzy and unreal to Morris Miller, as it did to many more like him.

"And Pa was there to meet us. It's hard to describe how I felt. Happy, happy. It felt like in a new world. You know, in a new world, which it was. The buildings looked so tall. But now, of course, they're just babies. But then, oh my God! And the cars driving around, the old Fords. Coming from a depressed village like mine, and America looked bright and big and lively.

"My father had a couple little wagons, and we pulled them to my father's apartment on Fourteenth and Jefferson, that's a half a block from Maxwell Street. Pa lived on the third floor. I was hungry. So I poked around. He had an icebox. I opened the door. And what I saw amazed me. Grapes, pears, apples, oranges. When I saw that—you can imagine, a youngster—I never saw fruit where I came from. Maybe a banana I once saw. But I didn't eat it. We had only black bread and milk, lots of milk because we owned a cow. And eggs. And chicken on Friday night. And candy, halvah, once a year at Purim. We were always hungry. We never had to clean the plates after dinner. We licked them clean. When I saw all the colorful fruit, that's when I was sure I was in heaven!

"Now this was Yom Kippur, it happened. So you're not supposed to eat. But I couldn't resist. I sneaked it. It was so good. I couldn't get my fill with all that stuff. I ate so much I got a bellyache.

"I was entered in school right away. And I remember the first day when they hoisted up the flag. That was a thrill. You have no idea. To be in America. To be an American. That was really a thrill that I can feel the goose pimples on me yet. I thought I was in heaven. But you want to know when I realized that I wasn't in heaven? When the Gentiles came over from the other side of the tracks and burned my father's beard."

# SAM TAXMAN

"When I first saw Maxwell Street, I was very enthused. I saw my country over here. I felt like I'm in Europe. How did I first hear of Maxwell Street? When a man comes from Europe in them days, that's all you hear. You go in a city—in Chicago you had Maxwell Street. In every city they had a thing like that years ago. So where does a greener go? He goes to his own class. That is where you get started. Over there he can talk Polish, Russian, Yiddish, Crimean.

"In my hometown there was every Sunday like a bazaar, like Maxwell Street. I was from a small town, Byelorutkey, in the Crimea. People from in the town and around in the farms would bring all kinds of fruits, vegetables, live poultry, eggs, stuff like that. They'd buy shoes and clothing from the Jews and bring them back to the farms.

"I liked it better than Maxwell Street. I don't know why. Maybe because I didn't know any better. It was nice until the end of peacetime and the Russian Revolution began and they started pogroming.

"And there was typhus very bad there. People died like flies. We didn't have no sanitation. Like we never had a toilet in the house. We went outside. Twenty below zero—we went outside all the time, when I was a kid. I tell it to my kids. They don't believe it. It's unbelievable. But you get used to it.

"I was nineteen in 1922 when my uncle sent me three hundred and fifty dollars to come to America. It took me about six months to come here. I had to wait to get a number. In them days, in order to come to this country you had to have a number. There was too many people coming. I was in Poland six months waiting. When I came here, I had fifty cents left. You had to have fifty dollars in your pocket at that time. They wouldn't let me in. My uncle sent me fifty dollars after I waited three days, and they let me off.

"I went first to my uncle in Iowa, in a little small town. My uncle had a grocery store. I could get enough to eat and drink and have a pair of pants to wear, but I didn't see no future, so I came to Chicago. I had cousins here.

"The first job I got was at Goldblatt's, a little department store, for eight dollars a week. And on Saturday and Sunday I sold caps on Maxwell Street. I had a pushcart. I bought, from a friend of mine, six dozen caps. My investment was forty or fifty dollars, that's all. I didn't even have the money. But he gave me credit. After Sunday, whatever I took in, I gave him the money. He gave me the caps for no money down. He liked me. We didn't sign no paper. We shook hands. Years ago, they used to do business on a handshake. On a man's word. Today is different. Years ago, most of the people didn't know how to sign their names.

"Then when I made a few dollars, I opened up a second floor. Then I went in partners with Dlugach and we opened up a big store at 711 Maxwell.

"It became a very respectable store with a high reputation. I am proud of my customer list. People would come from miles and miles away to shop at our store.

"Well, getting back. When I made money I immediately paid back my uncle. And I started bringing the rest of my family to America. I brought my brother here, and I brought my father here. Then U.S. immigration got stricter. The rest of the family remained in Europe, and when Hitler got in there, he ruined the town. He killed everybody there. I left two brothers and a sister. The Germans put them in a wooden barn. The roof was tarpaper. They poured kerosene on it and burned them up alive."

# MEYER LASER

Meyer Laser sat in a room of the mammoth Globe Feather and Down Company, one of the largest businesses of its kind in America. The three-story-brick factory and office building is located on North Avenue, a few miles from Newberry and Maxwell where Globe maintained headquarters for decades. Laser wears glasses, a hearing aid, a conservative suit, the traditional orthodox Jewish fringed undergarment (which he showed, smiling, by unbuttoning his shirt), and walks with a slightly stooped yet dignified carriage. He was born in Chicago in 1893.

"There was a philanthropist by the name of Phillipson, who had a department store on O'Brien and Jefferson. Whenever immigrants came in who couldn't make a living, he'd fit 'em out with a basket, needle, thread, and accessories, and they'd go from door to door and sell that. My father was one of those peddlers. He came here in 1885 from Russia. Now, in walking down Maxwell Street, there were a lot of kosher poultry shops. My father noticed all the garbage cans filled with feathers waiting to be taken away as rubbish. My father knew that dry feathers are used for bedding. So we used to go around to the different shops and make 'em a deal. 'Put the feathers in the barrel instead of throwing them in with the other garbage, and I'll pay you so much a pound for 'em, and I'll pick 'em up every week.' Or whatever the interval he wanted them to be picked up. Maybe he paid two cents a pound. I don't remember. But the shopkeepers realized something. They wouldn't care even if they only took in a dollar a week. It meant a dollar profit. See, otherwise it was just rubbish and they had to pay to have the garbage taken away. So here comes along a man who pays to take the rubbish away. And this is how my father started the feather business. And from that grew up this. Eventually. But it is a long time. Over eighty years.

"We lived a block away from Maxwell Street, on Liberty and Jefferson. We lived up on the second floor, and the first floor is where we had the feathers brought in. My father hired a workman who had a horse and wagon. They used to make the rounds and then they'd separate the feathers. The goose feathers and duck feathers are worth ten times as much as chicken feathers. Goose feathers and duck feathers are more flexible, and the pillows that you make from them are more buoyant.

"This business developed. And pretty soon, he had to have two wagons. We bought machinery that would even dry feathers and machinery that would fluff 'em.

"Then along came turkey feathers. My father made a big deal when the feather boas came into existence. It was in the 1890s, and the early part of this century, 1901, '02, '05. They had feather boas. They came from turkey feathers, which were big and fluffy.

"Pretty soon, our place was too small, on 90 Liberty Street. We lived upstairs, and downstairs in the basement we had all these feathers. So we moved to a little factory on Newberry."

Meyer Laser has bittersweet memories of the area. "It was a unique place. You couldn't walk down the street because you were pulled in. And they had shills at different stands. On Sundays, for blocks and blocks, it was thick with people, shoulder to shoulder.

"Some of the shopkeepers, I remember, took advantage of the unfortunate immigrants. They would cheat them mercilessly. Not all, but some. And not long before, these shopkeepers were immigrants themselves. For instance, in the butcher shops. I used to pick up these feathers. And I'd wait while the boys packed these feathers in the bags. We'd weigh them and I'd pay them. In the meantime, I watched the transaction. Now, they never sold chickens for 20, 30, or 40 cents a pound. It was always 27½ or 39½ or 32½. You take an ordinary Pole, or a Negro, or a Jew who hadn't had much education. You tell 'em, 'This chicken weighs 7¼ pounds times 39½—$4.85.' He'd go down the street and scratch his head and try to figure out. He don't know. He don't know he's being cheated. By a couple of dollars. Once you throw in half a cent a pound, now they're lost.

"It was pitiful. I'm sorry now that I didn't take it up with some association. You talk about the thumb on the scale. I saw that so often. If the chicken weighs 4½ pounds, it weighed six pounds when he got through with it. And if that wasn't enough, he'd miscalculate.

"Well, it was the beginning of the century. The largest influx was the first two decades. The 1910s and '20s. And there was hardly a week or a month went by that some new greenhorn came into our neighborhood and we had to introduce.

"We had the first telephone on our street. I remember our number. Loomis 2. And not only that, we had the first bathtub. In the house. And toilet. In the house.

"My father was a little more affluent than a lot of other people around there. I'm talking about this little neighborhood that we were in. Doesn't mean on the outskirts, too. Those people on Ashland Avenue, less than a mile away, they lived in castles. But in our neighborhood what we had was unusual. Everyone had outhouses. The phone was on the wall. And people, we called 'em greenies, to hear the phone ring and hear somebody talk! To somebody else! Coming out of the wall! Why, it was the most miraculous thing they ever heard of. Couldn't believe it. But that's neither here nor there. Maxwell Street itself was a poor man's paradise. They really bought bargains down there. But later on, there came the fence. They had a lot of stuff that was stolen. The State Street of the ghetto, it was known as. Most of the material was shoddy. In the first place, they wouldn't have the call for anything else. Who would pay thirty dollars in those days or thirty-five dollars for a suit when you can get 'em for ten or twelve?

"The more people came streaming from Europe, the bigger the neighborhood got. At first the market was Jefferson Street—even before that it was Canal, but the railroad—the Soo Line—was built, knocked out Canal, and the market moved to Jefferson. But Jefferson began to overflow. There weren't enough stores or space for stands. In about 1912, people began renting space on Maxwell Street from the landlord of the building. And soon you could not go through the street, it was so crowded. Horses and wagons couldn't get through. Cars couldn't get through.

"I saw it all grow so fast. Just before the turn of the century, I can remember playing ball in the middle of the street. And very,

very seldom were we disturbed because an automobile went by. Horses, yes. Automobiles really didn't start coming in until the 1920s. But there were horses and stables all over. I remember that on my way to cheder, Hebrew School, I would pass the blacksmith shop. I used to pause there. Both going and coming back. It always intrigued me. I loved horses, anyway. We had horses. Everyone had a horse in those days.

"And I would bring our horse over there to be shod. Then I used to stand around and maybe kibitz with him or talk to him. But he didn't have much time to talk. And we had to talk Yiddish to him, incidentally. He didn't speak any English.

"It was on Jefferson and O'Brien. I was intrigued by the smell. It was a lousy smell, but I loved it. The smell of the horseshoe on the hoof. The minute they put that hot horseshoe on the horse's hoof, there was the smell.

"It was a dank, dark place. I mean, there was no electric lights in those days. He had lamps there. And they, too, smelled. He had the lamps that burned oil. It smoked all the time. Later on, he had lanterns. It wasn't a very big place. He might be able to fit two, three horses at the most. A wooden structure. A low wooden structure that looked like that you build in the back of the house sometimes to put storage. It was one story. It had the brick walls on both sides, but it was a tar roof, as I remember it. Wooden roof with tar paper on it.

"This blacksmith had a great big black beard. In the summertime all he wore was his pants and a Jewish undergarment. He would stand there with his bare chest, bare shoulders. He had a pair of shoulders like you see on wrestlers today. And it was really a pleasure to look at him. A short fellow. Not big. But powerful. And when he grabbed the horse's foot, he would practically pick the horse up at the same time. And he knew his business. And the way he used to shape those horseshoes to fit the horse's hoof. It was really intriguing. I remember—what was it? Longfellow's poem of the blacksmith? 'Under the shade of a tree the mighty smithy stands?' Well, he reminds me of that mighty smithy, excepting there was no tree over there. The tree was in Brooklyn. Not on Maxwell Street.

"I remember it was hot in there. Especially summertime. And wintertime, he wore a sweater and a leather vest. The sweat running off of him. All the time. And it was a wonder to me that the shop didn't burn down. Because he had that fire going there all the time. And he would pump the bellows so the flame would get larger, stronger.

"He also wore a skullcap—a yarmulke. He was a pious man. He worked on Friday until he thought that the sun had set. That was the beginning of *Shabbes,* the Sabbath, you know. And if you would come in an hour before sunset and offer him a thousand dollars to put a shoe on a horse, he wouldn't do it. And closed Saturday. In fact, all of Maxwell Street was closed Saturday then."

Eventually, young Meyer Laser would pull himself away from the blacksmith shop and go to cheder. Cheder was rarely a pleasant experience for Jewish boys.

"We lost two generations of Jews because of the inadequate teaching that we had. The teachers that we had in my days were usually frustrated. We called them *rebbe.* Not rabbi, but rebbe. A teacher. They were frustrated old men who couldn't make a living in any other line of endeavor. And they took up this, and they knew very little themselves. And they took it out on their kids. They believed in the bibilical saying, 'Spare the rod and spoil the child.' Many boys I knew, dozens of them, quit cheder because they were being beaten up by the rebbes. And so we lost two generations of Jews. But it so happens, not in my case. My father after a while got me to a private tutor. And later I went to the Yeshiva, the theological seminary.

"But before that, I lost a brother from a beating by a rebbe. My brother died of a hemorrhage of the head, and we didn't know about it until several months later. One of the boys in the class said to one of my other older brothers, and I'm going back now sixty, seventy years, maybe, 'You know why your brother Hermie died? The rebbe hit him on the head with a stick.' This is exactly what happened. Now this will give you an idea of the brutality. They all had straps, machine straps. And a ruler. They'd hit you over the knuckles. I know of a man that after fifty years still bears the fingerprints on the cheek of when a rebbe slapped him. They were just brutal. You couldn't concentrate on your studies. Sometimes the cheders would be in dark, musty basements, and you sat on like picnic benches. Boys would get so frightened they'd crawl out the windows to escape the rebbe.

"I remember when I went to cheder at first, before I got a private tutor, we went to a private home of a rebbe, and he had about five, six children. We studied in his kitchen, and there was always the smell of cooking or the smell of washing. His wife was washing clothes, and this is what the environment was for studying. You smelled the dirt from the clothes boiling in water and then she hung it up there to dry, and you smelled the chicken fat frying. And you don't ask questions.

"If you ask a question, you don't get an answer. You get a rebuff because he doesn't know the answer. No, they'd usually say, 'Ask your father.'

"Maybe you couldn't blame the rebbes if some were phonies. Especially these poor people who look for an extra dollar, to whom it means bread and butter. And most of the people there were poor, on the West Side. There were a few rich people.

"My father, as I say, had become pretty well off. And at fifty years old, retired. He'd spend his time now working for the synagogue and for the seminary. Well, there was a rich Jew on the West Side, richest Jew on the West Side, a fellow by the name of Morris. We called him Monkey Morris. Any time there was a drive for anything they went to him for money.

"My father went to him one time. They were building a new school and he came over and asked for a donation. This Mr. Morris, he wasn't in a good mood. He said to my father—he spoke Yiddish—he said, 'You beggar, you *shlepper*. You beggar, you. Why do you come begging all the time from me?' Morris said, 'I have made a will, and in this will I have taken care of everybody. I don't want you to ever come around and bother me anymore. Keep away from me.'

"My father said, 'In the first place, I want you to know I am richer than you are.' This man, Mr. Morris, was a millionaire. My father wasn't. Far from it. But Morris said, 'How's that?' My father said, 'Because I've got enough, and you *still* haven't got enough. You're still working in your junkyard. So I am richer than you. And there's a Hebrew expression, one of Solomon's quotations, "Who is considered a rich man who is satisfied with his lot."' My father said, 'But leave that aside. You know, you remind me of a story, Mr. Morris. The pig came to the king of the animals—the lion—and said, "I want to ask you a question. Why is my lot worse than any other animal on the farm? Comes the nighttime, the farmer takes the cows in the shed, he takes the horse in the shed, lays out hay, straw for them, gives them food. Even the dog he takes in the house. But me, poor pig, nobody bothers about me. I must wallow in the mud."

" 'So the lion said to him, "Well, let's consider this. You're comparing yourself to the horse. Where could the farmer plow his field if he didn't have a horse? You're comparing yourself to the cow. The cow gives milk, butter, cheese. Even a dog, there isn't a better friend to man than a dog. But you, the only time we can get any use out of you is when you die.' "

"This is what my father told Mr. Morris."

On the West Side of Chicago at about this time, 1916, also lived the Abraham Rickover family. They had a teen-aged son named Hyman George Rickover, who would soon graduate from Marshall High School and leave for the U. S. Naval Academy on scholarship. His father, a Russian immigrant tailor, could not otherwise have afforded to send his son to college.

"Our family did not know the Rickovers then," said Mr. Laser, "but I have a great warmth for this Rickover. I have a son, Alan, who is an atomic engineer. When Admiral Rickover was building that first atomic submarine, he chose twenty of the leading engineers in the United States to build it. And my son was one of the twenty.

"Alan worked out in Arco, Idaho, on this project, the nuclear submarine. It was in the late 1940s. Admiral Rickover used to call up every once in a while. Now he called from Washington. There's a difference of three hours. And so once in the middle of the night in Idaho the admiral called. And my son was always clowning around. So the phone rings and Alan says 'Schultz Meat Market.' And the admiral says, 'Cut out that shit, Alan. How are you coming along?' " Mr. Laser laughed.

"Admiral Rickover perhaps did not think it was so funny, this Mr. Schultzing. It reminds me of when I was a young fellow and used to stand on a truck, when me and some workers would pick up feathers. I would be handed burlap and cotton bags full of feathers. I used to pile 'em up in the truck. I was by now full of

# IRVING JACOBSON
# and PAUL MUNI

On the walls of Irving Jacobson's study are, among other items, an autographed picture of Bobby Kennedy and a color drawing of Jacobson when he played Sancho Panza in the Broadway production of *Man of La Mancha*. He is a man of great vitality. He spoke animatedly at his desk. He lives in an apartment in the sprawling Peter Cooper housing complex on East Twenty-third Street in New York City. He was born in 1904 in Cincinnati, while his actor-parents were on tour. His father died shortly after his birth. Mr. Jacobson grew up in Chicago and in its Yiddish theater.

"In those days, don't forget, the Jews that came over from Europe, they didn't know English. It took 'em quite a while before they learned it, and they used to speak with the broken English. So the only entertainment they had was in a Jewish theater. At one time Greater New York had thirteen Jewish theaters. In Chicago, in the Maxwell Street area, there were three.

"I was onstage ever since I can remember. I had a terrific voice. I had an outstanding register. I had at least two and a half octaves. A snot-nosed kid, seven, eight, nine years old. I sang with a lisp. And some people laughed. But they called me 'the Little Caruso.' They also called me Pesick. Pesick is a dwarf. When I was two years old, three years old, four, I didn't grow. I'm still five six and a half. That's all. And the only one that still called me Pesick was Paul Muni until he passed away. He was nine years older than me. I went to see him backstage when he was doing *Inherit the Wind*. I hadn't seen him in years. 'Pesick!' he cried. 'Come over here. On my lap.' And he bounced me like he used to as a kid. And he said, 'Pesick, where's the roller skates?' And he got hysterical. Why? He used to have roller skates. I would tighten them for him and he'd roller-skate on the cobblestone in back of the theater, the Weisenfreund Theater, the one his parents owned on Twelfth Street not far from Halsted.

"The stagehand there at the old theater, when I was going to sing, would pull the curtain, move the props, and right away they brought out a big box, like a fruit box. I would get up on it to sing. So the audience should see me. Otherwise they would hear a voice and they'd ask, 'Where's it coming from?'

"So I would sing. I can still remember the songs. It's funny. I forget so many things that happened yesterday, but I can remember 1912 vividly. I sang one song called 'The *Titantic*.' They called it 'The *Tetonic*.' A terrible thing happened. The *Titanic* sunk and people were dying. There were rescue rowboats. There is a mother with a child. She was begging the people to save the child, at least. She'll sacrifice herself. She said, 'But save the child.' And I had to sing that song every day. On Saturdays and Sundays, eighteen times a day. We had eighteen performances. I had to sing that song until I was blue in the face. And I used to cry every time. Everybody cried.

"I remember singing a song about remaining a Jew. Some Jews would change their religion. This song said, 'The Jew in his heart is a Jew. Remain true to your heart. Come home to Israel, your homeland.'

"In the summertime, the people had nowhere to go to escape the terrible heat, so they'd spend many nights on rooftops. Playing casino, sleeping, having picnics and parties. I sang about how they ran from their rooms to escape the heat and the flies. They ran to the roof to get free. There's no police come up on the roof. You can do everything there. You never saw anything like it if you were never on a roof on a summer night.

"Do you know who used to write most of those contemporary Yiddish songs there? Elaine May's late father. He was called 'Connoso' Cohen. The pug-nosed Cohen. His name was Cohen. I knew him and Elaine May's mother, before her marriage. When Elaine and her partner, Mike Nichols, came to visit me at *Man of La Mancha,* she said, 'I must meet the man my mother was in Yiddish theater with and told me so many stories about.' Yes, there was something there. But I said, 'Your mother was an honorable woman, an honorable woman.' She said to me, 'Maybe if you would have married my mother, I would look different.' I said, 'You should thank heaven, because then you might not be so pretty, so all right.'

"You know, performers more or less had a reputation for loose morals. That irks me to this day. I'm very, very thankful to my late parents, a memory that they were performers. They were honorable. When people ask me about the reputation of theater people, I tell 'em, 'I know a couple of lawyers, I know a couple of doctors, they're fooling around with their nurses and everything. It's none of my business. Okay.' You know about Paul Muni's mother? About that story?* I knew the prompter, her boyfriend. You know the Yiddish theater had prompters. This prompter's name was Nesiter. A little guy. I knew there was something between them. But I never wanted to know. But so what? The only angels I know of are in heaven. I've never seen an angel on this earth. Not one.

"At that time, Paul Muni was Muni Weisenfreund. He played the widest range of parts. He used to put make-up on and he'd play his mother's father. He was seventeen, eighteen, he used to play his mother's *grandfather!* He used to make beards, you know. He used to come at 6 P.M. in the dressing room. The show starts at eight, eight-fifteen, eight-thirty. He used to work for an hour, an hour and a half, putting on different make-ups all the time. I used to watch.

"Everyone said about him, 'This is going to grow up a genius.' It was my older brother Hymie who was the matchmaker for Muni and Bella Finkel, his late wife. She was a niece of the late Boris Tomachefsky, a Jewish star years ago. Hymie introduced them—Muni and Bella.

* "Muni saw tears in his father's eyes. . . .

" 'Papa, are you all right?'

" 'No, Munya, I am not all right. . . .' And then (his father) began to sob. It was the first time Muni had ever seen his father cry. . . . Muni was sure it was a scene from a very bad play which never should have been written.

" 'Your mother—your mother,' he said in Yiddish, 'she is a *curva,* a *nafka,* a whore. She is sleeping with other men. . . .' "

"Muni ran out of the theater. . . . He didn't speak to his mother again for twenty years." From *Actor: The Life and Times of Paul Muni,* by Jerome Lawrence (New York: G. P. Putnam's Sons, 1974), p. 61.

"Now Muni is keeping company with her. He asks my late brother, 'Hymie, do you think she's a virgin?' He says, 'Sure.' He wasn't going to say he didn't know because he had introduced them. He was the schatchen—the matchmaker. So Muni says, 'Hymie, we're getting married. Bella and I are getting married. And if she's a virgin, you get a suit of clothes.' They got married. And soon he sees Muni. Muni says, 'Come on, Hymie, I'm getting you a suit of clothes.' So my brother said to Muni, 'All right.' And to himself he said, 'Thank God!'

"The Weisenfreunds had their own theater, on Twelfth Street near Waller, which is now Morgan Street. The father and mother were both performers. There were three brothers—Joe and Al and the youngest was Muni. Alex was the fiddler. Joe played piano. My late brother used to play drums and then run and pull the curtain when the show started. The curtains would roll up, not like the travelers they have today that pull to the side. And when they'd drop the curtain in those days, you had to be careful or you'd be hammered into the stage. Especially a pesick like me.

"Muni's oldest brother, Joe, had the widest shoulders you ever saw. If someone had sneaked in to see an extra show, he'd pick 'em up as though they were a herring and throw 'em in the alley.

"They had movies and legitimate theater. The picture would last half an hour and the show, the act, about three-quarters of an hour. Always it was packed. The theater held about four hundred people. We did so many shows. And benefits. This organization bought a benefit, they wanted a musical. This one, they wanted a Russian show, a Tolstoy or Dostoevski. This one wanted a Sholom Aleichem comedy. Who could memorize all those in one day?

"That's why they had prompters. We studied, but we needed a prompter. He used to have a little box in center stage. And the man used to prompt, whisper. He used to come from underneath the stage. Just his face would be above stage. And a little piece of wood hid him from the audience.

"We had one incident. There was a great actor by the name of David Kessler. I had the pleasure of playing with him when I was a kid. Everyone said, 'Oh my!' when you mentioned David Kessler. And he was playing a show. *The God of Vengeance.*

Something like that. It was by Jacob Gordon. Yankel Gordon. He was like our Jewish Shakespeare. It was a classical show. And he's playing and he's got a certain scene there where he's got a safe and money was taken out and he wants to commit suicide, and he puts a cord around the safe, puts the other loop around his neck, and hangs himself by the safe. While he's doing this, the people are laughing! It's a dramatic scene. So, sotto voce, he says, 'What is that?' The prompter says, 'A cat has come on stage.' The cat walks toward the prompter's box. He turns his backside to the audience and he's watching the act. So David Kessler yells in this sotto voce to the prompter, 'Chase him off!' So a stagehand takes a brace with a hook—they used to have that to change a piece of scenery in those days—and tries to move the cat. The cat won't budge.

"And Kessler says, 'Throw him out!' The prompter threw a book at the cat. Now there's a hook on the floor of the stage and a book on the stage. The cat keeps watching the show.

"Finally Kessler got so mad he leaves the safe upstage and goes right down there and bends over to the cat and says in English—when he was mad he'd talk in English—he says, 'Will you get the hell out of here!' The whole audience fell apart.

"They used to have two-reeler movies and then vaudeville. The two reelers often had Indians and cowboy stories. So naturally when the cowboy rode off in the sunset in the dust, they showed the dust flying and that. When it was over I remember a comedian, Moe Schenkman, used to come on stage, coughing from the dust. 'Such a dust!' and he told them they should please excuse him until he gets the coughing out. Everybody was laughing.

"He was terrific. And then he says, 'How would you like to hear this song?' And then he'd mention the name of some famous number. Oh, they'd applaud. He says, 'I wouldn't know it.'

"My late brother Hymie and I were a hell of a dance team. We could do any kind of dances, the Highland fling, the Russian crane. . . . We used to fly across the stage, climb up the sides. And then we'd sing a duet. Then we'd bring out two cups. And we always had a shill in the audience. Somebody would throw a nickel on. So the others would throw a nickel, a dime. One thing I'll never forget. Some rich guy threw a quarter. In those days!

"When my brother saw the quarter, he put it in his shoe. I said,

'I'll tell Mama.' He said, 'Well, I'll get you after the act.' He called me in Yiddish, *'Moosa.'* Squealer. 'Moosa. I'll get you later!' He wanted to cheat Mama out of a quarter. Mama needed it for gas. They had quarter meters then. Put in a quarter and you'd get gas for four, six hours.

"We were poor. Sometimes I'd ask Mama, 'Should I come home for lunch from school today? Do we have any lox and herring? Or should I stay there?'

"We moved to New York when I was nine years old. My mother thought we could make a better life there. More of a theater there. And I was there in the Yiddish theater, playing in it and owning theaters until 1962.

"I was sorry to see the Yiddish theater in America collapse. It had held a lot of joy for the many immigrants who lived in despair and poverty. They spoke almost all Yiddish. Then their children spoke less Yiddish. And their children's children speak and understand almost no Yiddish now. So most Yiddish theaters here have disappeared. Much to my deep sorrow. I thought it provided an important link between the past and the present.

"My first play in the American theater, on Broadway, was in 1963. I got the part of a Jewish refugee in *Enter Laughing.* It was a comedy. And it was Alan Arkin's first play on Broadway. In rehearsal one day, he said, 'That Irving Jacobson, he's going to steal the show.' I said, 'Come here. There's seventeen scenes in this play. How many are you in?' He says, 'All of them.' 'I'm in four scenes. How am I going to steal the show? And God forbid, if I steal the show, we got no show. And I want to make a living.' The play ran for a year and a half.

"I got a call to be in *Man of La Mancha.* The director, Albert Marre, says, 'You're in the play, but can you sing?' He asks me to come up on a Saturday morning to hear me sing. Richard Kiley, who will play Don Quixote, was there. I told them, 'I'll sing a parody, an old parody, of "In the Shade of an Old Apple Tree." It goes:

> An Irishman, a Frenchman, and a Hebrew
> Were going to be hung one by one.
> The judge said, 'Choose a tree that will please you.'

The Irishman said, 'I choose a pear tree.'
And on that pear tree he did die.
The Frenchman said, the peach tree would please him.
'Please hang me on mine favorite tree.'
Then the judge said to the Hebrew, 'What shall it be?'
'Oh, the one I love best, it's my dying request,
Please hang me on a gooseberry tree.'
Then the judge said, 'Why, fool, don't you know
That a gooseberry tree is so low?'
'I'm in no hurry,' said the Jew.
'I'll wait till it grows.
But please hang me on a gooseberry tree-e-e-e-e.'

"Richard Kiley ran down and said, 'God love you. God love you. He's gonna steal the show.' I said, 'I'm not singing *that* in the show.' And the rest was history. I played Sancho Panza for five years on Broadway.

"I'm very grateful that I had the great pleasure of playing that role. Of being in something that was written by Miguel de Cervantes. He was one of the great writers of all time and had the qualities of a Mark Twain and a Sholom Aleichem. He must have meant something because he has lasted for four hundred years. They're still playing it. *Don Quixote!* And Sancho, he did a lot for me. What was Sancho? He was an illiterate. He couldn't read. He couldn't write. But he loved life. He had two passions in his life. His fear of God and the love for Don Quixote, his boss. When he was told to deliver a missive to Dulcinea, he takes the paper and tries to memorize. And fouls it up. But he studied it and studied it.

"One night Lynda Bird Johnson came backstage. Now I'm talking to the President's daughter! She said, 'You know, Mr. Jacobson, you as Sancho Panza show so much love for Don Quixote, so much loyalty, I wish my father had a Sancho like you in Washington.'

"And there was one night, one night I will never forget. There was a knock on my door after the show. My production manager said, 'Jacobson, are you decent?' I said, 'I always try to be. Why?' He said, 'Senator Robert Kennedy and Mrs. Kennedy would like to come in.' And I got all excited and I put my robe on. And a towel around here, and there he was. He had tears in his eyes. It was from the last scene. I got tears, too, when I did that scene, the Requiem. I would stand over the dead Don Quixote. I'd cry. I said I felt like an orphan. I can't read. Who's going to take care of me? He's dead. Who'll take care of me now? When Robert Goulet played Don Quixote, he once whispered to me as I'm crying over him. 'Irving, for God's sake, move away. You're giving me a shower.'

"Bobby Kennedy had been sitting in the second or third row of the audience. This was 1967. He was once loyal to his brother John the same way Sancho was to Don Quixote. Bobby came into my dressing room and I saw the tears in the corner of his eyes and he took my face and he kissed me on both cheeks and I melted."

# NEWSPAPERS AND THE JEWISH GHETTO

The Yiddish-language newspaper, the *Courier,* was a paper serving primarily the religious people, and, to some extent, reactionaries. The *Forward* is a Jewish socialist labor paper. Consequently, when one took a stand on some issue in Chicago, the other had to retaliate. The papers split the Jewish community, and one or both were read by most Chicago Jews. The *Courier* was at first published in the Maxwell Street area. The *Forward* was delivered from New York, but had offices on the West Side of Chicago and carried special Chicago pages. The rivalry of the two papers was reminiscent of the two newspapers in the somewhat fictional town of Kasrilevke that Sholom Aleichem wrote about. The two Yiddish papers were called the Skullcap (naturally the traditional daily for the orthodox) and the Bowler Hat (the modern, radical gazette):

"[Sometimes] the Skullcap would call its rival 'the battered Bowler Hat,' and the Bowler Hat would call its opponent 'the moldy numbskullcap.' For the most part, though, they approached the problem under cover. . . .

"For example . . . the Bowler Hat, instead of saying Skullcap, would think up an alphabetic acrostic like this:

"'That asinine, beggarly, crooked, drunken, envious, feeble, galling, hair-splitting, idiotic, jagged, knee-bending, leprous, mangy, nefarious, ossified, provocating, querulous, rabble-rousing, skimpy, tottering, ugly, venomous, wayward, xenophobic, yellowing and zig-zagging rag whose name we don't ever want to mention.'

"That was a great success in Kasrilevke and the copies sold like hotcakes. . . . Naturally, this stung the Skullcap to the quick and it came out with its alphabetic answer the next morning.

" 'We have read the "a-b-c" of that ass, bastard, coward, dunce, eel, fool, gyp, hound-dog, inquisitor, jellyfish, knave, liar, miser, nihilist, ox, patan, quack, reptile, scandalmonger, terrorist, unmentionable, villain, wastrel, Xerxes, yokel, and zoo of a paper, but we're not answering for we have no desire to defile our pens.' "*

Although the *Courier* and the *Forward* usually did not go to such castigating extremes, they did grapple. More important, though, they served the Jews of Chicago in a powerful way.

First, they did in fact bring a sense of community and togetherness to this transplanted people. And spoke in their own familiar language. They raised the peoples' spirits, talked to them of their problems, gave answers, tried, in general, to ease their adjustment; they even served as a place where "schatchens" or marriage matchmakers placed huge ads.

The Bintel Briefs, or "A Bundle of Letters," was a crucial aspect of the *Jewish Daily Forward*. People would write in about personal problems, and the editor of the *Forward* would print the letter with an accompanying home-remedy answer. He was the precursor of Ann Landers. Following is an example from 1910:

Worthy Editor,

My husband,———[here the name was given], deserted me and our three children, leaving us in desperate need. I was left without a bit of bread for the children, with debts in the grocery store and the butcher's, and last month's rent unpaid. . . .

It breaks my heart but I have come to the conclusion that in order to save my innocent children from hunger and cold I have to give them away.

I will sell my beautiful children to people who will give them a home. . . . I, the unhappy young mother, am willing to sign a contract, with my heart's blood, stating

* Sholom Aleichem, *Stories and Satires* (London: Collier Books, 1959), p. 19.

that the children belong to the good people who will
treat them tenderly. . . .

> Respectfully,
> Mrs. P. (Full name and address given here)
> Chicago.

Answer:

What kind of society are we living in that forces a
mother to such desperate straits that there is no other
way out than to sell her three children for a piece of
bread? Isn't this enough to kindle a hellish fire of hatred
in every human heart for such a system?

The first to be damned is the heartless father, but who
knows what's wrong with him? Perhaps he, too, is
unhappy. We hope, though, that this letter will reach him
and he will return to aid them.

We also ask our friends and readers to take an interest
in this unfortunate woman and to help her so that she
herself can be a mother to her children.†

Sometimes there was a letter that needed no reply. Such as this
one in 1906:

Dear Editor:

In the name of all the workers of our shop, I write these
words to you:

We work in a shop where we make raincoats. With us
is a 13-year-old boy who works hard for the two and a
half dollars a week he earns.

Just lately it happened that the boy came to work ten
minutes late. This was a "crime" the bosses couldn't
overlook, and for the lost ten minutes they docked him
two cents. Isn't that a bitter joke?

> Sincerely,
> V.‡

† *A Bintel Brief*, edited and with an introduction by Isaac Metzker (New
York: Ballantine Books, 1971), pp. 104–5.
‡ Ibid., pp. 53–54.

In its editorials, the *Courier* tried to instill pride in Jewishness and the history of the Hebrews. Such as, "Throughout all the happenings of our 5,000-year-old history the connecting link is very prominent. This spirit that is reflected in all national events may be styled a revolutionary attitude, ever to react to reactionary tendencies, always to look forward and not backward. . . . Abraham, the son of the idolatress Terah, quickly rises from out of the morbid atmosphere of his time and proclaims monotheism to the world. Abraham was a revolutionary par excellence, a rebellious mind of the highest caliber."

The Jews were living in the most squalid circumstances possible, and pointing out sources of pride was, most agreed, essential to the pursuit of survival. For example:

"Our share in the development of the modern stage is too well known to need special mention. Max Reinhardt, who revolutionized the modern stage. The four great actresses of modern times, including Rachel, Sarah Bernhardt, Irene Trish and our own Bertha Kalich, belonged to our race. In America at least all the great producers, Balasco, Schubert, Wood and Hammerstein, etc., are Jews. There is only one great man among the producers who is not a Jew and his name is Cohan."

The papers told about anti-Semitism, particularly that of Henry Ford, and about who Ford's antagonists were, especially Arthur Brisbane, famous writer for the Hearst newspapers.

What was happening to Jews in Europe also was news of the essence. HEADLINE: "ANTI-SEMITIC EXCESSES CONTINUE IN RUMANIA."

"In Bucharest a band of two hundred students surrounded the northern depot conducting an attack for many hours on all Jewish passengers who left the train. The minister of the interior is reported to have staged the anti-Semitic excesses."

A note was printed lower on the page. "King Ferdinand of Rumania is reported to be dying but radiograms from Queen Marie on the Berengaria are said to be less optimistic."

And they were also filled with jokes:

ITEM: The bones of a woman, presumably a million years old,

have been found in Asia. But you'll never get her to admit she is a day over a hundred thousand.

HEADLINE: "Thirty-eight caliber."
HOTEL CLERK: "Just got in from Chicago I see, Mr. Smith."
MR. SMITH: "No, that's a moth hole in my lapel."

And "The sweet young thing was saying her prayers. 'Dear Lord,' she cooed, 'I don't ask for anything for myself, only give mother a son-in-law.'"

The local big daily newspapers did not believe it necessary to spend much time reporting on the affairs of the ghetto people (in the same way that for years the local papers saw no urgency in writing of the black community except to report an occasional murder, and then only when the victim was white and the assailant black).

There was one instance, though, when the Chicago *Tribune* broke that routine. On April 25, 1914, it reported:

"Chicago is taking proper pride in the Jewish lad, Samuel Meisenberg, who was one of the first to give his life at Vera Cruz for the honor of the American Flag. Samuel Meisenberg was not born in this country. He came here as an immigrant. In the brief span of time he had been in the New World he acquired not only the language and outward characteristics of an American but also the high American ideals, as all who knew him testify.

"He is a credit to the city and more especially is he a credit to the Ghetto of the city, for he is a product of that Ghetto. The struggle for bread is nowhere so keen as in the congested immigrant district on the West Side. The drab, colorless existence there, when viewed merely from the surface seems extraordinarily foreign. Sammy Meisenberg shows that beneath the foreign exterior of the Ghetto is a heart that beats with loyalty to the United States. . . ."

The body of Samuel Meisenberg was brought to Chicago and buried with military honors.

# DORA BERKOVITZ

Dora Greenberg was born on December 22, 1897, on Des Plaines Street near the corner of Twelfth Street, close to Maxwell. She had two older brothers and a sister, who was lame. Her uncle was Morris Eller, the powerful committeeman of the Twentieth Ward, the Maxwell Street ward. In 1921 Dora married Max Berkovitz, my father's brother. Although her husband has been dead for twelve years, she still lists her phone number under his name. She lives in a simple one-bedroom apartment on the North Side.

"My father came to America from Poland at the age of thirteen and never became Americanized. He worked in shops where they talked nothing but Yiddish. My mother was born here and spoke English. They seemed to come from two different worlds. But I'll tell you what it was. My father had at that time a thousand dollars. That was like a million dollars today. And they thought he was wealthy. They got married from a schatchen, a matchmaker. It was common in those days. Today we marry for love. I married for love. Love at first sight it was. But in those days, it was the match-maker.

"My father was the lord. Right. In every family in those days it was that way. The man was regarded as the lord and master of his home. At nights we'd play cards or checkers and then be in bed by nine because my father used to get up at six for work. And it had to be quiet in the house. So everyone would go to sleep when he went to sleep.

"I used to have to go shopping for my mother before I went to school. I used to go every day to the butcher shop a block away, no matter how bitter cold it was. We didn't have no refrigerators then. I got the meats, and a lot of times I'd help bring the ashes down and bring coal up if my brothers would get into a fight and

wouldn't do it. My father wouldn't do it. My father was a good man, but he still never brought up coal or took down the ashes. The role of the man of the house was different than it is today. He was respected more. Life was different.

"My mother did all the disciplining. When my father came home from work, he rested. My mother was worldly. She read the English language newspapers. That's how I came to see the Wright brothers demonstrate their plane. They came to town, to Grant Park. The only way you knew about those things was the newspapers. There was no radio at that time. This is 1906, '07. There were thousands of people there to see the plane. Everybody was amazed. 'Lookit, flying in the air.' I mean, it was such a great thing, people never believed it. My mother used to say to me, 'There'll be a time when people will be flying in the air.' But when we were little children who ever believed anything like that? Like, fifty years ago, who would believe about the atomic bomb or flying to the moon? And like when my husband, Max, used to say to me, when the planes were going a couple hundred miles an hour, 'Gee, there'll be planes that'll be going a thousand miles an hour someday. You wait and see.' But he never lived to see it, though I did.

"But by the time they landed on the moon, I was amazed, yes, but, well, it wasn't like seeing the Wright Brothers that time. Because there was so much that had happened in between. Like Lindbergh flying to Paris in 1927. Flying across the Atlantic!

"It was in 1909 when I rode in my first automobile. Nobody had ever seen cars at that time. All we saw was horses and wagons around there—teams, they called them—or horses and buggies.

"I went to my cousin's wedding in 1909. The daughter of my uncle Morris, Morris Eller. He was ward committeeman and the City Sealer. He sent a limousine to pick us up. The neighbors all gathered around and 'Oooooo.'

"It's funny about rich people in those days. They had more to eat then we did, but they didn't live much better than we did because they all had stove-heated apartments. Steam heat didn't exist then. And they had to carry coal or somebody had to bring it up for them. And take their ashes down. And there were no bathtubs. They had to use kettles and pots to boil water for the bath, like the rest of us.

"But the rich did have private toilets. We shared a toilet with our next-door neighbor. We had five kids. They had five kids. Used to have to knock on the door and 'hurry up.'

"Some rich people shopped downtown, but some shopped on Maxwell and on Halsted. They shopped there if they knew value. There was a dress shop on Maxwell that had a lot of cheap stuff in the front and in the back they had original dresses that sold for hundreds of dollars. And women with limousines would pull up and go into the store. They had a red velvet drape separating the back from the front of the store. The owner's name was Davis. He'd pull the drape back and then you'd see the most gorgeous dresses that you've ever seen in your life.

"And there was a jeweler there selling rings for thousands of dollars, that were worth every bit of what he was asking. You might also find on Maxwell Street a beautiful rug, but it might be damaged in one corner. From a fire. They'd have a way of hiding the damage. You had to know, had to be watchful.

"You learned. You got an education that way. It wasn't such a thing as educating the children formally like it is today. As soon as they were fourteen years old, and they were out of grammar school—very few children went to high school—they went to work. I went to work in a department store, a salesgirl. And then I went to high school at nights. I didn't know anybody that went to college. Even my relatives that were so well off. Except one son, he went to college. He became a lawyer. Later he became a judge in Chicago. That's my uncle's son.

"People started getting more education as years went on. All three of my children went to college. One of my sons is a psychologist. My son-in-law is a judge.

"Times change, but then I hear on the radio now that the stock market is dropping and the World Bank says we're going to go into another Depression. It doesn't scare me anymore. We went through a recession when I was a kid, in 1914. And again when I got married, in 1921. And in 1929 the stock market crashed. We lived through all those years. For myself now, I don't care. I worry about my kids. I hope they never have to suffer and struggle like we did. I would walk in the bitter cold and the wind and rain selling door to door during the Depression. I sold women's hose and I sold salamis. I had holes in my shoes. I had to put

Maxwell Street during its heyday. (Chicago *Tribune* Photo)

Maxwell Street now . . .
(Photos by Walter Iooss, Jr.)

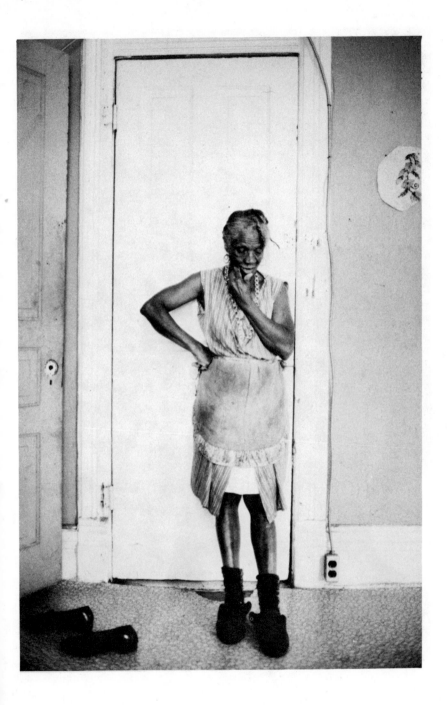

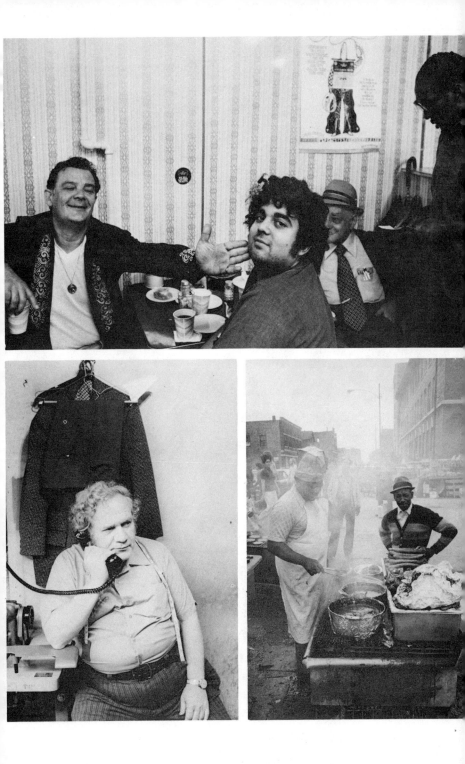

cardboard in my shoes. That's how I walked around. And the tears I shed, so many dollars you should have in your life. Walking and crying. Not selling very much, but glad to sell whatever I did.

"The future looked very black, very dim, you know what I mean? People were jumping out of windows. At that time, landlords were losing their buildings 'cause people couldn't pay their rents. Even people that had money. We lived in a six-flat building where the landlord just walked away from the building because nobody could afford to pay the rent. At first they used to put the tenants out on the street. Put the furniture right on the curb. But then how could you take and put everybody out on the street? So they stopped that.

"Max was driving a cab. But people weren't taking many cabs. The only ones that would ride cabs would be salesmen. He was bringing home five, six dollars a week. There were cab wars in those days. Yellow and Checker cabs. They would fight amongst themselves for a load. In fact, we had a neighbor, guy by the name of Fox, that went to prison for life for killing. He was a Checker cabby and he killed a Yellow Cab driver. Max also sold stockings on Maxwell Street in those days. My uncle got him a good stand. Then Max got a good job with the cab company as the employment officer. It was in the late '30s, when the country began coming out of the Depression.

"But, well, overall, God has been good to me. My life was very happy because I always did what I wanted to do. And I never was the type of person that wanted a lot of material things in life. Never did. That's why I was usually contented. If there wasn't enough, I went out and made it enough. Even now, I'm independent. I don't take anything from my kids. I have Social Security from my work in private industry, working in the cab company. And I have a little income from bonds.

"And thank God for my health and for my mind. That is God's gift to me. I know a lot of people younger than I am who are senile.

"But I've got a neighbor down the hall from my apartment here. She's eighty-seven years old and has a terrific mind. She says, 'You're a kid compared to me.' I'm ten years younger. I hope I live to be her age and have her mind."

# BERTHA EPSTEIN

She is eighty years old (in 1975), lived on Maxwell Street for many years, lives now with her husband, Joseph, in a middle-class apartment in Miami. Joe is retired, a onetime milkman.

"The women were in the background. Just like in the old country. It was taken for granted that the man is the man. He's head of the house, and you do as your husband wishes. There was no women's lib then. I raised the four children. He was the provider.

"I used to smoke cigarettes in those days. But I would never let anyone see me smoke. I'd smoke, and then I'd burn incense so my neighbors don't smell that I'm smoking. Otherwise I would be considered a woman of the streets. In those days, a bum.

"It's funny. My mother used to smoke. The old women in Russia used to smoke pipes. They sit around at home and smoke pipes. That was all right, but us, we'd sneak it. Today a woman has no shame. She smokes on the street. She considers if a man can do it, I can do it.

"What shame do they have? You see over the television the shame they've got. 'I'm living with him.' And that's all. If people ever lived together in the old days, and we knew, we didn't say anything. We'd just raise an eyebrow.

"The intermarriages of today, they're so common it doesn't mean anything anymore. I remember when a girl in the neighborhood married a colored man. Her people sat *shivah* right away. They sat for a week, mourning her death, as they called it.

"The moral code was very strict. For example, some friends and I would go to Thompson's Restaurant on Halsted Street for a piece of cheesecake. Mostly men went to Thompson's. So we would say, 'All right, whose turn is it to go in and buy?' Then we'd come home and divide it. We'd have a ball. That was our entertainment. That and playing pinochle for toothpicks.

"There wasn't much else to do. We didn't have the luxuries of today. Like we used to live on the third floor. We'd have a rope to pull up the coal when it was delivered. Or take New York, we lived there for a while. If you lived in a six-floor walk-up—you call it a walk-up because there was no elevators—six floors high, you had to bring up your coal or your ice for your icebox. You'd order a fifty-cent piece of ice. By the time it was brought up to the sixth floor, it was a twenty-five-cent piece of ice.

"When I was a girl I worked in a clothing factory—a sweatshop —at a sewing machine. I used to work for ten cents an hour. Eighty cents a day. Until these clothing unions began to organize. According to my thinking, without unions we might still be working for ten cents an hour.

"There was a lot of sickness, too. I remember a big influenza epidemic. The people died by the hundreds. We used to have funerals, five, six a day, one on top of the other. They were dying like rats in Chicago. They didn't have enough cars to take everybody.

"I remember visiting a friend who had gone to a funeral. Her baby was crying. I asked the older daughter, 'What's wrong with the baby?' 'Well,' she said, 'the baby's hungry.' I had a baby of my own then. So I took the baby and I breast-fed her. We breast-fed all our babies. We didn't give them bottles like they do now. It was cheaper that way.

"But if I didn't feel that I was a friend, I wouldn't do it. My daughter not long ago said, 'Ma, would you want to go back to those days?' Well, I'm not physically fit to go back to those days. But we did have some kind of security. We had some kind of social life. More congeniality. Your friends were friends. They weren't good-weather friends. You lived on one street. You knew everybody on the street. If you had sorrow, they had sorrow with you. They mourned with you. Or we'd laugh. There were stories told that tried to break up the sorrow. You'll find that very, very much among the Jewish people. When they see that people are getting too depressed or too uptight, somebody will come in with something funny—say something or do something funny—and no matter how the tears are running, you'll have to laugh.

"Today, you very rarely can say you have a true friend, very rarely. Today, friends are 'What can you do for me?' It came in when people got richer. The men shaved off their beards. A lot of people prospered after the First World War and the Second World War. The standard of living went up, and if you weren't equally equipped financially as they were, they would sort of not include you in their social functions. They divided themselves by their apparel, their way of living, their apartments, their furnishings.

"For me, I didn't care about standards. My husband usually made a decent living. And I always had my dreams. I'm a dreamer. I'm a big dreamer. I always visualize someday this, someday that. I used to sketch with crayons when I was younger. But I didn't study it in school. I left school for work in the seventh grade. But I always thought one day I'll do art work. My art came in when I was seventy-four years old, six years ago. One of my granddaughters used to take art lessons. She did watercolors and acrylics. And she went to register in an evening class at a public school in Miami. She says, 'Grandma, come along with me.' I went along and she went to sign up. I was saying to the man that was taking her registration, 'You know, if I wouldn't be ashamed at my age, I would love to do it because I always had an ambition.' He said, 'Why don't you?' So I gave him five dollars and started to go.

"And then I got involved with a choral group. I direct and help set up the programs. I always dreamed about being in music. Yeah, and I myself am what you call a humorist, a monologist. That's what I do. I give monologues and I pantomime.

"But maybe that's why, even though I had dreams and ambitions all my life, I never felt depressed when I didn't try to carry them out. I always tried to—how can I say?—I like people. I love people. And when I'm among people, I just explode."

# THE STREET, 1921

## MAXWELL MARKET NEAR DOOM

—Reformation hit the Maxwell Street Market today as dealers are contemplating forty-eight-hour notices for the removal of the permanent stands they have occupied for years. . . .

Charging the existence of graft, bribery and political favoritism in the Maxwell Street market, Alderman Henry L. Fick . . . filed a writ of mandamus in the Circuit court today to compel the city to remove the permanent stands. . . . The street was called "the greatest fence for thieves in the world."

Also, the existence of the stands is described as one of the worst fire hazards in the city, all of them "being of wooden construction and therefore highly inflammable."

Fick, a political opponent of Mayor William Thompson, is alderman of the 20th Ward, known as "the bloody 20th," the ward in which the Maxwell Street market is located.

CHICAGO *DAILY NEWS*
*November 29, 1921*

# BEN AND CELE LYON

They owned a landmark delicatessen at 807 Maxwell Street. His father and mother owned it before him. Lyon's Delicatessen, three steps down from the street, had been at that location for fifty years. In 1974, at age sixty-five, Ben Lyon retired and sold the kosher delicatessen to his trusted employee of twenty-five years, Nate Duncan, a black man, who has kept the restaurant kosher. The Lyons live in an unpretentious ranch-house-style home on a tree-shaded street. It is in West Rogers Park on Chicago's North Side.

"My name when I was a youngster was Benny Wurstel. Wurstel. That means salami. That was our business. So that was my nickname. People still remember it. And you know, like when Barney Ross, who was a neighbor, became the world boxing champion, he'd always come back and visit the old street and he'd see me and hug me and kiss me and he called me by my name. He never, never forgot it.

"My wife and I met on Maxwell Street. We could hardly avoid it. We lived in the same building. Her mother owned it. We had our delicatessen in the basement. She had a restaurant on the first floor and lived on the third floor.

"We met when we were sixteen. We'd go to Stanford Park on Fourteenth Street. They had a social and dance every Friday night. We'd sit around and chew the fat. There wasn't very much to do in those days."

CELE: "He had a fight with his girlfriend and I went down to make them up." She laughs. "And I ended up with him."

BEN: "Her mother never approved of our marriage. She wanted her daughter to marry a lawyer, or a doctor, high class, not a Benny Salami, but I think in later years, I think she learned to like me. She saw I was good for her daughter. But when we were going out, we'd come home a little late at night. She used to sit up and wait for Cele and throw a milk bottle out the window at me. She was really a character. She had a lot of money accumulated from her restaurant and from gold bonds. So she took Cele to Europe to meet a man to marry. Better-class man."

CELE: "And I did meet someone. A lawyer. Couldn't stand him. My mother was all for it. So I told *her* to marry him. She was marvelous. She could spot the phonies. She'd stand outside and I'd introduce her to my dates. At that time we wore raccoon coats. I remember a date with a North Side boy. The North Side then was supposed to be exclusive. He came to pick me up in a roadster. My mother looks him over. She says, 'Turn him upside down, a dime won't fall out.'

"When she was going downtown I used to say to her, 'Don't wear a babushka. Put a hat on. It's the American style.'

"She'd say, 'We'll go to a bank. You'll be dressed up in a fur coat, I'll go in a babushka. We'll see who they give the money to.' And she had another saying: 'I could dress you in hundred-dollar bills.'

"My brother used to be a playboy. He used to run around with a lot of girls. Once a girl friend called up. My mother answered. She said, 'He's not here. He's a sick boy. I took him to the doctor and the doctor looked and looked and looked and found out he's only got one ball.' When my brother came home and was told what happened, he said, 'Ma, why'd you have to tell her that? She knows I got two.'

"I had a stepfather, Joe. He wasn't an aggressive guy. She was really the boss in the family. He actually worked for her in the restaurant. It was a small place. Had no name. Chicken, gefilte fish, soup. An eight-course meal was forty cents. Customers used to eat part of the meal in the morning, part in the afternoon, and the balance for dinner. They'd come in three times in the day. Stretch it out. My mother would have signals with my stepfather. She'd make homemade wine and if a customer came in and said he wants a gallon, she'd holler for Joe to fill the order, but sometimes she'd signal to him, by crossing two fingers. Half and half. Half wine, half water.

"She used to get these construction workers in. They'd come in just for one meal. They used to drink. She used to specialize in roast duck. So the guy would order a duck dinner. Joe would put the duck down in front of the man, and the guy was so drunk he'd fall asleep. While he's sleeping, my mother took the plate away and replaced it with a plate of bones. When the guy woke up he didn't remember if he ate it or not. He had a plate of bones, but he was still hungry. He'd order another duck dinner.

"Joe worked hard there. After a while it got to the point he demanded a salary from her. You see, she held all the purse strings in the family. So she gave him ten dollars a week. He hid it under the rug in the living room. She spied on him. Saw him just pick up the rug a little, shove the bill under it. When he left, she came in and took the money. The following week she'd give him ten dollars. Same ten. Well, after a couple of months he figured he'd put it in the bank. Figured he had seventy, eighty dollars. He was upset when he found he only had ten. But she talked him out of being mad.

"Another time he was going to a movie. She decided to play a trick on him. He liked the hard candy, little licorice drops. Instead of licorice, she took a few pieces of coal and put it in the bag. He goes in the show and bites on a piece of coal and breaks his bridge. Her joke cost her a lot of money because she paid for a new bridge."

Ben Lyon's mother was, similarly, the "boss" in their store, but she did not wear the pants in the family.

BEN: "My father was never a worker and he was never a worrier. He was an executive, my father. He was a wonderful man. He was always good to us. But he was never a worker. My mother ran the store. He would order ten cases of something. He liked to order in big quantities, even when he didn't have the money. I took care of the books, even when I was a kid, and I knew we didn't have enough money to pay for it. He'd tell the salesman 'ten,' but behind his back I was motioning to them, 'two.'"

CELE: "When we got married he bought me a trousseau for $750. I took it back. We didn't have the money to pay for it."

BEN: "He never had any money. Always spent everything he

made. He liked to dress in the very finest clothes. Silk underwear, silk shirts, silk socks. He had his clothes custom made. Had a beaver hat, a Borsalino hat in those days. These were expensive things. Even had a Montagnac overcoat from France. That's a very fine woolen.

"He liked to drink. He had a lot of friends from the old country, and they'd sit in the saloon most of the day. Or he spent a day in the Turkish bathhouse. And he was always picking up the check for everybody. He died from drinking too much, cirrhosis of the liver."

# BUDDY DAVIS

Bernard "Buddy" Davis, a baldish man in his late forties, points with pride to a framed impressionistic oil painting of Maxwell Street by an obscure Chicago artist. The painting hangs on the wall of Mr. Davis's dress shop on Howard Street on the Far North Side of Chicago. Mr. Davis's father owned an extraordinary dress store on Maxwell Street for nearly forty years.

"I told my wife that this is going to be a store like Dad's store. But he had a wider front because the store narrowed off into a V, and then the L-shaped room started. His was all fuel oil. It had potbelly stoves that we'd heat up every morning. The floor had pieces of carpeting nailed together. Seventeen different carpetings. As one wore out, we'd put another piece on top and nail it down with tacks. The walls were raw brick until I painted them gray. There were upholstered chairs. The store was bright. It had about fifteen 200-watt bulbs, those old pear-shaped bulbs.

"It had all kinds of fabrics in the front. Hanging all over. On the walls, from the shelves. Hanging as high as the ceiling. Fabrics lay on tables, all strewn around. Silks. Pure silk. Gold lace. Velvets. Velveteen. Sateens. All these exclusive fabrics of the day. Every kind of color. Gorgeous, just beautiful. We also had custom jewelry. And at one time my father carried millinery. A factory went bankrupt. We bought boxes of millinery. The feathers and the fruit on the hats. And women came from all over to buy 'em. We were selling it for one third the price. Just like our dresses. The best and most expensive fabrics would be sold for one third the price. That's why we had such a tremendous clientele. And varied. We had gigantic Cadillacs with the drivers pulling up and waiting outside on Maxwell Street.

"We had hundreds of people in the store on Saturday and Sunday. Maxwell Street was open on Sunday before the whole world opened on Sunday. We used to have swarming crowds of women waiting when we brought in a new shipment of merchandise in the morning.

"In the middle of the back room was a large table where we'd throw the new dresses to mark them and put them in stock on the racks. But as we were unpacking, the women with frenzy would scramble and grab at them. It was getting dangerous. So I got a big heavy rope and wound up a hook on it and pulled it across the door of the back room to keep the women out until we got the merchandise in order.

"The women would all be trying on dresses together in the back room. Were they embarrassed? Hardly. My father would walk through. He was a short man, robust, with a mustache. They might give him a glance. He said, 'Ladies, make like I'm the doctor.' He was watching they shouldn't steal. We used to have signs in the store. I remember one sign he had up there, 'Please select carefully. Save time and save money. Also, please do not put anything in your shopping bags or umbrellas.' Today it's all modern. Today I take a photograph, with an electronic eye that I installed myself, of everybody that walks in and out of the store.

"I remember we always had to watch the Gypsies. Fat Mary, I remember, that was Eli's wife. Eli was considered king of the Gypsies. Fat Mary would grab a piece of fabric and slyly make a little ball as she's talking to you to distract your attention. And the whole piece of fabric would quickly disappear in her hand, inch by inch, like a snake swallowing a rat.

"When my father walked around in the back room with the women trying on dresses, he also watched they shouldn't get lipstick on the dresses. In those years lipstick was a problem. After college I took up a year's work at textiles at the Illinois Institute of Technology, mainly to take out lipstick and other spots. But today lipstick is not a problem because so many of these dresses have polyester which washes the lipstick right out. But in those days, the dresses all went over the head with the zippers on the side. My father would say, 'Ladies, vatch the lipstick.' He asked them to wipe their lipstick off. He had boxes of Kleenex all over the store.

"My father was born in Russia. He then emigrated to Paris. In Paris he spent ten years in the women's trousseau business. He used to tell me that Captain Dreyfus was his customer. After he had returned from Devil's Island. If you remember Dreyfus had been convicted of high treason in the French Army. He was later exonerated. He used to say, '*Bon soir, Monsieur* Davis.' He would come in and always buy a lace handkerchief. Either for himself or for a gift. He was an old man then.

"My father said that he had never heard of anti-Semitism until he got to France. I remember him emphasizing that. My father was never fond of the French. On no. He finally left France. Just picked up, took his money, and came here. It was about 1914 or 1915.

"He came here and at first opened a shoe store in a basement on Maxwell Street. He struggled there for ten years. One day he bought a few dresses. And sold 'em. Went back and bought more. And from that, he became quite a dress tycoon, owned one of the biggest dress outlets in Chicago, at that time.

"I remember on Maxwell Street the hoochy-koochy girl. A man with a turban threw a couple dozen knives at her. She was in a box. Later for a nickel we'd look in the box to see how the knives missed her. She was all contorted. It was a terrific trick.

"Then there was a guy that washed hair. He had a special soap. He gave a nickel to any of the kids who'd have their hair washed. So I had my hair washed. He gave me a nickel. But I had to hide the fact that I got a nickel because my old man would have killed me. Because I made a spectacle of myself. But a nickel was a lot of money in those days. And my father didn't dole out the money that quick to me.

"I went to college at the University of Miami. Majored in marketing. I had dreams of studying mechanical subjects. That's my hobby. But I wasn't guided right. I've always regretted not having done that. But I was in a sort of European atmosphere at home. That you take over your father's business. He didn't comprehend my electronics interest. He wasn't from that world. Oh, my wife had made the point more than once that my parents didn't realize my potential as a young man. I wired up a whole sound system so that there was music from the radio throughout the store on Maxwell Street. And I finally convinced my father to let me install fluorescent lighting. You know, the first toy I ever gave my son was a piece of wire. Yes. My wife says I should have been in anything but this business because—although I like the business—I mean, my heart was always, well, frustrated.

"So I'd do things like install alarms in the old store. I wired up a jewelry case so that if you just touched it, bells would ring. I took pride in that."

# MAVIS GOLDSTEIN

Mavis Spetner Goldstein, blondish, steadfast, in her early sixties, sat in the back of her corset shop on the North Side. She owns the store with her husband, Bob. Her father and mother owned a similar kind of store on Maxwell Street.

"My parents started on the street by building a wooden stand with a long dark-green window shade. Right at the center was an opening where a customer could walk in. Then they'd pull the shade down behind you so you could try on the girdle or corset in private.

"My mother used to stand there in the cold and pull in all these people and fit them—not fit them—they didn't take off their clothes. She used to put it around them. It was sometimes hard, what with the overcoat and all that heavy underwear. And some of these women, you know, were pretty fat. My father would stand outside and wait until they were finished. Then they'd both stand inside. The stand had a stove.

"We had a special thing. 'Scampies.' Very fancy. They used to be a corselet with lace all around. And we had corsets with laces up the front. You'd take them three inches smaller than you measured, and you'd put it on. You'd tighten the laces and pull yourself in. Lots of bones and steel, you know. Word got around about us. And pretty soon we had a clientele. When we moved into the store, we'd have chauffeur-driven limousines pull up with customers.

"My father worked seven days a week. He and my mother both. They used to come home seven, eight o'clock at night until the thing got going.

"Now my father began to make a little money. He rented the second floor, and he put sewing machines upstairs. He made an opening from the store to the second floor, like a laundry chute. He had a bucket on a string and we'd sell something, we'd send it upstairs to be fixed. On Sunday you could not get in that store, it was so packed. During the week not so much, but on Saturday and Sunday, it was absolutely mobbed. Sometimes on Sunday we had to lock up the store at five o'clock and not let anybody in.

"I have children now whose mothers were fitted on Maxwell Street as children. When a girl had a Sweet Sixteen birthday, her mother, instead of making a party that's like a wedding, they took them to us on Maxwell Street and got fitted for a corset or girdle or brassiere or whatever she needed. Otherwise, they used to buy things in a dime store. This was the coming of age where you went into a shop and you were fitted.

"You know, my father had a chance to become a millionaire during the Second World War. He could have bought two-way stretches, that's girdles, on the black market. They needed the rubber for the war. So they started making synthetics. But synthetics had an odor to them. Now you couldn't buy rubber on the open market. My father refused to buy it black market because he was a very patriotic American.

"He loved America. He came from Russia, and evidently when he was a little kid they broke his finger, you know, so he shouldn't have to go in the Russian army, and for all his life he could never bend his finger straight.

"He came here when he was fifteen or sixteen years old. He got his citizenship papers in 1896. He was seventy-nine when he died in 1954. He always kept his citizenship papers with all his important stuff.

"First he went to St. Louis, where he had relatives. He eventually owned a dress factory in St. Louis and was rich. I remember in 1924 he decided to take a trip with the family to Chicago. He bought a Chevrolet touring car. And he didn't know how to drive! He put five American flags on it, with a big flag on the radiator. He didn't even know how to drive. The car broke down in Joliet. He had broken the axle from the way he was driving.

"Then he lost everything in the crash of '29. We came to Chicago. We came to Maxwell Street. It was the only place you could start with ten dollars and start a business. He couldn't get a job. At first he was selling ties on the street. And the store owners kept chasing him from one place to another. They'd say move, so he'd move. I used to come down to visit, to see how Papa was. It was very sad. It hurt me terribly. I remember seeing him shuffle from one store to another, a small man and very thin. I was about fourteen years old. I recall it vividly, how he'd be standing there in a doorway, and they'd shoo him away like a dog.

"And when I didn't see it, I used to hear the stories at home because he'd come home and tell Momma what happened. And Momma used to cry because Papa had been so dignified and had been a businessman. My father was fifty years old when the Depression hit.

"So he started all over and made another success. He loved this country with such a passion. He hated Russia with an equal passion. I remember how he would say, 'the Communists,' with such scorn in his voice. He couldn't understand how any of these people in the 1930s could feel any sympathy for Russia because he really knew what Russia was about with the pogroms and the rest. But, oh, did he love this country! From my earliest childhood I remember Papa was a flag-waver."

# DONJO MEDLEVINE

Daniel "Donjo" Medlevine is owner or part owner of several theater-in-the-rounds, including the Mill Run in Chicago, one in Cleveland, and one in San Francisco. He was once part owner of the widely known and now defunct Chez Paree nightclub in Chicago. In later years he was for a while the business manager of Sammy Davis, Jr. He continues to book acts for Don Rickles, Steve Lawrence and Eydie Gormé, and Marvin Gaye, among others. He lives in San Francisco, but his Marquee Productions has offices in both San Francisco and Los Angeles. He was born in Paris in 1915.

His brother, Maurice or "Frenchy," was recently released from a California state penitentiary where he had been sent up on conviction of a bonds fraud. He is four years older than Donjo and also was born in Paris. The Medlevine family moved to Maxwell Street in 1922.

The brothers bear a close physical resemblance. Each is stout, though Frenchy is somewhat stouter. They are about five eight or five nine. They wear glasses, have roundish faces, broad shoulders, and firm handshakes. Donjo sat now behind his large desk in the L.A. office. Frenchy arrived early into the conversation and sat to the side of the desk. Each wore shirts open at the collar of their thick necks.

DONJO: "It was a ghetto, Maxwell Street. At nine, ten, you had to go out and scuffle for yourself. My parents had a dry goods store on Maxwell, and we lived above the store, at 912 Maxwell. My folks worked all day and a lot of the night. It was a rough street. Every corner had their own thieves. They went out either boostin' or hijackin' or bootleggin' or something.

"When I was a kid, the guys we idolized were big-time bootleggers. They had the big touring cars and Homburgs and spats. Like today in the black ghettos. The top pimps have the big cars, the one hundred dollar shoes.

"Street fights, we had enough of them. We were surrounded, you know. Across Roosevelt Road, there was the Italians. Another side from Maxwell was the Polish. Another the Irish. And the Bohemians.

"I remember once I crossed Roosevelt Road. I run up against a couple guys. One guy said, 'What nationality are you?' I says, 'French.' He says, 'Take your penis out.' Well, they didn't hurt me. One guy hit me with a pie. But you had to learn to run. Anytime you went into their area, you were usually outnumbered.

"I've seen street-gang fights where there were twenty, thirty on a side. I remember one on Newberry and Roosevelt, right in front of St. Francis Church. We'd fight with anything. Blackjack, club, a baseball bat. I've had my nose busted. I've had my head busted. But we learned young to protect ourselves. And we healed real good. And quick.

"It happened that in our neighborhood we had a bunch of fighters. Some states never had a world champion. This one little street coulda had maybe ten. We had two world champions, Barney Ross and Jackie Fields. And we had half a dozen contenders. King Levinsky fought five world champions, including Jack Dempsey and Joe Louis and Max Baer. Davey Day fought Henry Armstrong. Joey Medill once won forty-eight straight fights. Sollie Schuman, Heckie Schuman. Heckie could have been great. I saw him fighting Johnny Battaglia, who was number-one middleweight contender. Heckie was kicking the shit out of him. Then Heckie took a shot and he was finished. Heckie had a saying, 'Hit me in the pocket and I drop.'

"You see, in those days, Jewish kids went into fighting to make a buck. There was no money in entertainment then in Chicago like there was in New York, say. In them days, jobs were tough to get. So you knew if you knew how to fight, you could make some dough. We'd go down to Marcy Center on Maxwell. 'Machine Gun' McGurn used to go down there, too, and hit the bag. He was the one accused of pulling the trigger in the St. Valentine's Day Massacre on Clark Street.

"It was some street. I'm not ashamed of that street. I think I'm very proud to have been associated with the element of people that were there. Like we'd have a crap game. Well, nobody would get all the money out of that crap. If the game did fifty dollars a week, well, everybody ate on it. And nobody went off to eat by himself. If he had a dollar, then he'd cut it with two or three guys. Something you don't see in this generation.

"There were no stool pigeons, and they all had a little balls."

FRENCHY: "But today you get a kid and right away, he's like a canary. And in them years, the police department used to hang you on doors and everything."

DONJO: "Like English, a guy in the neighborhood named English. His family came from England. I don't know what he did, but whatever it was, the cops thought he was the guy. And they had him hanging on the door. I got called down to finally get him. He was stretched out and he was black. Every inch of him was black. Everything but his face. They had put his hands behind his back and put a pair of cuffs on him. They opened a door and lifted him up and hung him on the edge of the door. And he wouldn't talk. It took three months before his arms went back in place. They finally gave him fifty dollars so he don't say anything about it. And he stood up—never said anything."

FRENCHY: "Talk about sadists down there. The cops killed guys. You know what it took to be a cop in them days? Five hundred dollars. You bribe yourself onto the force. Sometimes they'd give you a bum finger, just because they had to have an arrest for their quotas."

DONJO: "Sometimes they'd give you a pass. I was thirteen years old and they raided my moonshine joint. It was on Peoria, between Maxwell and Roosevelt. There was a barbershop downstairs. We had the second floor. I used grain alcohol and mixed it in the bathtub—180 proof.

"And so the liquor-control guys—like the guys with Ness—they chased me out. One of 'em said, 'What's a nice, clean-cut kid like you doin' here? Get the hell outta here!'

"Thirteen years old. Young to be in that business. But you start young on Maxwell Street. When I was a little kid, eight years old, I'd sell shopping bags. Three cents a bag. When you grow up, twelve, thirteen, you got the rubbers concession. French ticklers, and those dirty books—you know, we used to call them the Tillie Toiler books. You'd flip the pages and you'd see sex acts.

"But by then—before then—nine, ten years old, I was already doing six months. They had already took me away. What the hell.

"Took me to parental school. And I passed Frenchy in the hallway. He was comin' out. I look back now, I think it was a good experience. It really taught you to shuffle for yourself in there. You know you had to make some moves. As soon as a Jewish kid went into a school like that, everybody challenged him."

FRENCHY: "Donjo was the champ."

DONJO: "French was too. That fuckin' Burns used to make me fight every day. He was an officer that ran a cottage. As soon as a new big kid came in, he'd bring him down to fight me.

"We used to have what we called a 'battle royal.' They'd put six guys in a ring. And only one guy would come out. We'd fight each other till there'd be only one left. The toughest guy always became captain of the cottage. Frenchy and me usually done pretty good in it."

FRENCHY: "Before you, Donjo, when I first come there they used to have rooms upstairs for the bad boys."

DONJO: "Yeah, but do you remember that cage they had outside? Till a few guys died of pneumonia? That the cage you're talkin' about?"

FRENCHY: "Yeah, upstairs, even the little kids, they were put in an outside cage. After too many guys died, they finally done away with it."

DONJO: "Remember Popeye? This officer who looked like Popeye and had a long chin? He was in B cottage. That was my first cottage. Remember how you'd get up in the mornings and there was no toilets? And sometimes a guy would take a shit in a bucket in his cell in the middle of the night. In the morning they had the bucket brigade. You'd toss the shit in a big trough.

"I read a lot now. I read probably somethin' like three books a week. What I missed when I was a kid. I caught up, you know, in the years. And they say that our penal institutions are obsolete. They're fifty years behind. They breed crime. They don't stop it. You take a kid and throw him in that jungle and he's gotta come out mad at the world. If a guy straightens out, he's gotta be very lucky. Or scared to death.

"In later years I saw how much luck played in people's lives. When I owned the Chez Paree, I got to know the top. All the best acts worked for me there. Durante, Sammy Davis, Nat Cole. Henry Ford once said to me 'Can I meet Nat "King" Cole?' He wanted to hire Nat for his daughter's coming-out party. And he did hire Nat, and from that day on, he used to send Nat a Lincoln and a Thunderbird every year.

"And the politicians—I remember entertaining John Kennedy all night. The time he almost made Vice President. That night in 1956, after the Democratic National Convention in Chicago. JFK didn't drink. But he sat there all night sort of glum. He came there with Peter Lawford, who worked for me.

"I'm still friendly with the retired president of Standard Oil of Indiana. Governors, senators, judges, hoodlums, they all came to the Chez Paree. I got along with everybody in all walks of life.

"They're no different from the kids from Maxwell Street. They're all hustlers."

FRENCHY: "You know, Huey Long once said, 'Show me a politician that's up there, and I can send him to jail.'"

DONJO: "That's true. I could talk to you for three weeks on individual guys that I've been connected with. They're not any better than that kid I knew on Maxwell Street that went to jail or got his head shot off. There are judges I wouldn't trust. I zipper my pockets when they come around me. Same with some businessmen and some politicians. Who's in jail and who's out of jail. What's the difference? Luck.

"I think I've had a lot of help in my life. I've been very lucky. To be here, sitting here after some of the things you went through, you'd have to be lucky. For him, Frenchy, to still be here, he'd have to have been very lucky. After what he went through. Most of 'em never made it. He's been shot three or four times. He's been cut. He's had everything happen to him."

FRENCHY: "Shot here, one here, one here."

DONJO: "He looked like a yo-yo."

FRENCHY: "I got one still in here. Right here. Right shoulder."

DONJO: "Once he got shot in a crap game. He tried to stop a guy from getting killed. Tried to grab a guy's arm. He killed the guy. What happened, Frenchy?"

FRENCHY: "I wound up in Bridewell jail hospital."

DONJO: "Then he copped one to life."

FRENCHY: "Well, one of them things, like they say."

DONJO: "It's funny. Some of the most respected people in the country are here in Los Angeles. In fact, I know a couple right here. I'm lookin' out the window. I could almost touch 'em. They were ex-bootleggers. You see, if you were ever going to make any money, it had to be illegal in those days. The cops would let you do practically anything as long as you paid off. The only guy who suffered is the guy that couldn't afford to drop it.

"The whole world should be Maxwell Street. It's not. I think we'd have a better world. We used to say, 'If you can't make no money on Maxwell Street, you ain't gonna make no money nowhere.' It was a good street, and we all looked out for each other. The problem with our country is we don't look out for each other, don't trust each other enough.

"I have half a dozen of the biggest acts in the country. And I don't even need contracts with 'em. We shake hands. Like, here's a kid, Marvin Gaye. He's probably the best in his field. Now I had a contract with him for a quarter of a million dollars. Not a contract. I had a verbal with him. He's off a Detroit ghetto. He did everything. Slung hamburgers. He'd get on a boxcar and ride the rails. Finally he found out he could sing. And write music. We understand each other because we got the same upbringing. Only trouble is, the blacks been there a lot longer than us. The Jews managed to squeeze outta there. They didn't. Sammy's had a lot of experiences, too. There's many a day he told me he lived on a candy bar.

"Now he's got the biggest wardrobe in the world. By far. I'd say he's got five hundred suits. And he doesn't throw anything away. Every little gimmick that's been given to him, you'll find it in that house. He reminisces with everything.

"But the clothes, when you're a kid and don't have nothin', as soon as you get old enough, you buy clothes. I had two older brothers. When I was a kid everything I ever got to wear had two or three patches."

FRENCHY: "I remember when you had about a hundred suits hangin' a few years ago. Then they made the lapels to a smaller style and you never put them suits back on."

DONJO: "I can have six, seven suits being made up in shops at the same time. Once you didn't have it, you spend the rest of your life trying to get it. What is life? You scuffle to get what you don't want.

"I got a friend of mine that died about two years ago. At one time he was worth $250 million. He was a poor kid, made it all by himself. His name was Ralph Stoken. He had like ten washrooms in his house. I said, 'Ralph, what the hell you need ten washrooms for? You only got one asshole.'

"But it's the same with me. I understand. And I think that's helped me in my business. People say, how do you get all the top acts? I've got one thing in my life. I always treat people the way I want to be treated. I got one policy. Once a year I sit down with all my help and I say to 'em, 'Look, fellas, 99 per cent of our business is the act. We are only 1 per cent. We can all be replaced. Never use the word "no" to an act. If he asks you for the most ridiculous thing, do it.' We give 'em limousines, the suites, catered dinner every night. And when they walk outta our theater, they wanta come back. Sometimes it's tough to do.

"I had one act, Betty Hutton, it was below zero and she wouldn't allow the heat on. I had another one, Tony Martin, it was a hundred outside and he wouldn't allow the air conditioner on. Tony couldn't work with the air conditioner on. Betty couldn't stand heat. The room had to be freezing or else she'd walk off the floor. See, but I know the need to be comfortable. A man once asked me, 'What's the biggest thrill in your life?' I told him that I slept in a little bedroom on Maxwell Street that was so hot. A hot, hot room. No window. Too small even for a dresser. Just a bed. I scored enough money to buy an oscillating fan. I pulled up a chair and put the oscillator on the chair. And that fan would hit me in the ass up and back when I was sleepin'. *That* was the biggest thrill of my life.

"The way I would treat Betty Hutton or Tony Martin or Sammy or Henry Ford or Kennedy, I would treat others. When I was in parental school, I tried to take care of my bed partner or my room partner or any kid that came there and started to cry at night. I tried to make him feel at home. The way I wanted to be treated. I remember a lotta kids when they'd come. They weren't criminals. They were kids who didn't want to go to school. You sit down; you talk to him. Like I remember the rabbi would come once a week. The rabbi'd bring the matzos for the holidays and that. A couple kids would come to me from other cottages. 'Hey, they're pickin' on me because I'm Jewish.' And I'd grab the guys that were pickin' on 'em. Well, the guy who came to me was probably doin' the same thing. So what. I felt for 'em.

"My wife thinks I'm taken advantage of a lot. So what if you do a hundred nice things, and you only salvage two outta the hundred? Two people that appreciate it. You're a big winner! I remember givin' a guy my last money, two hundred or so, and he walked around the corner, he says, 'I beat that schmuck outta two hundred.' I woulda felt worse if I thought he really had needed it and I didn't give it to him.

"Tell you a funny story that happened just lately. Watergate is all over the papers. I was being questioned by an FBI man about who I socialize with. It happened right here. He's askin' me about certain people I run into. Well, I've met people in all walks of life where people that I was raised with became hoodlums or whatever you may call 'em. So he kept askin' questions. When he was ready to leave, I says, 'Wait a while. Sit down now. I want to ask you something. You know, my grandchildren are gettin' to an age where you gotta talk to 'em. And a couple years ago, I told my grandson to pick up everything he can read about Nixon, Mitchell, Erlichman, Haldeman, all of 'em—our *leaders*—because these are the people I want him to follow in their footsteps.' I says to the *FBI* man, 'Now, did I do the wrong thing?' The poor son of a bitch couldn't even answer me. That's the truth. Here's a guy questioning me about my associations. I says to him, 'I want to tell you something. You, your boss, your boss's boss should just have the character I got. You're up here questioning me. You should just have the same character in life and feel in your heart that you been a good man all your life.'

"A lot of the wrong people are in jail. It's always been that way. There were such injustices. I remember Nicky. You remember Nicky, Frenchy. He got pinched holdin' up cabs and takin' the driver's pants. He got pinched and he done seven years. And he got out and the first winter he was so cold—Chicago is so cold in the winter—that he seen a coat in an automobile and he went and took the coat and got pinched again. Just to keep warm."

FRENCHY: "He done another ten."

DONJO: "Nobody ever wrote about the injustices of them kind of streets. Of what made the difference. That's like *Les Miserables,* where he did all that time over a loaf of bread. Here's a man freezin' to death and he sees an old coat in a car. And some hero cop wants a feather in his cap.

"There's some nice cops, too. Just like there are some bad crooks. I remember one guy, they made a heist and one guy who was countin' up the money kept the thousand-dollar bills and gave the others the hundreds. They never saw a thousand-dollar bill."

FRENCHY: "Yeah. And who's that got killed in a barber's chair on Fourteenth Street for a bootleggin' double-cross? And they found Yager in an ashcan on Western Avenue."

DONJO: "There was one year, we lost seven in one year. They got killed. It was a bad year."

FRENCHY: "It's who you hang with. You're with legit kids, you're legit, you know?"

DONJO: "Right. We got kids that never mingled with us. There's about thirty, forty families on the street. Lawyers, judges, doctors. We were talkin' about Ben Schwartz. Shorty Schwartz. Highly respected circuit court judge in Chicago. Schiller's a judge there. And he'd never come near us. He'd go home and study.

"And I'd go to Finaman's candy store and throw my lunch money into the slot machine. And later I had my own book joint in Chicago. It wasn't legal, but I run wide open. I learned that business from Maxwell Street. I remember the grocery store on Maxwell, and they had a buzzer for the back door and they'd let you in and there was a crap table and they was bookin' horses with a blackboard and sheets on the wall."

FRENCHY: "They had all the phones around. Remember the phones ringin' off the hook?"

DONJO: "Then I got married and I straightened out. I was married at nineteen. And we moved out of Maxwell Street. 1935. Everybody had been movin' out by now. We didn't have no steam heat. As soon as a Jew could make a little money, he moved into a steam-heat building, and he hadda go west. I was in the jobbing business now. Getting merchandise for the family store. And we made a living from then on.

"Then I got into the liquor business. I bought a bar. I was havin' some trouble with my old lady and I figured, if I have a bar I can always say at any time, 'I gotta go to my joint.' I was in partners. We bought another place. Then the Chez Paree. We closed it when we saw it was the end line for nightclubs.

"But I'm lucky. I handle now about ten million dollars worth of talent a year. My parents were lucky to escape the czar. And then they went to Paris. They were called dirty *Juif*. Juif means Jew in French. Then my parents left France. That was lucky. Otherwise we'd have got caught in the Hitler thing over there.

"My father never talked about it. He wanted to forget. I like to remember. I even talk the same way I always talked. I say t'ink instead of think I say gettin' instead of getting. It's like a combination Brooklyn and Maxwell Street accent. Sometimes it helps when I do business. Maybe they think they're dealin' with a sucker. But after all these years, why should I change? I'm the same guy.

"I've had a very enjoyable life. Nobody appreciated life more than I did. Everytime I woke up—every morning I woke up, I thanked God I got up, and let's have some fun. And when I look back, I realize what made the difference in my life. It's not what I did. It's what I didn't do."

# JUDGE ROBERT CHERRY and JUDGE BENJAMIN SCHWARTZ

Judge Cherry, a somewhat florid-faced man wearing black judicial robes, has stopped by Judge Schwartz's office for a brief lunchtime visit. Both are circuit court judges in Cook County and have adjoining offices. Judge Cherry, born in 1911, is three years older than his colleague. Judge Schwartz, a trim man, sits now in suit and tie. Behind him is a glass case full of law books and transcripts. Although they had been discussing a case in which Judge Cherry is about to return to the bench to make a decision, Judge Schwartz takes a playful bent. Judge Schwartz had just begun talking about his Maxwell Street days when Judge Cherry entered.

JUDGE SCHWARTZ: Let me start all over again. Judge Cherry, were you born in Chicago?

JUDGE CHERRY: No. I was born in Philadelphia and came to Chicago at age three. We then resided on Maxwell near Union. 657 Maxwell.

JUDGE SCHWARTZ: That's quite a coincidence. You know the address of where I was born? 648 Roosevelt Road. Do you know the Gertner Yiddish Playhouse? We resided right by it.

CHERRY: My father and mother went there often.

SCHWARTZ: Well, then perhaps they saw me on the stage. Whenever they needed a baby, I—

CHERRY: Were you an actor?

SCHWARTZ: No . . . but whenever they needed a child performer—and this is the way my mother and father, may their souls rest in peace, got passes to the theater—I was the baby in the play.

CHERRY: Hmmmmm, well, that explains it. That explains some of your activities, Judge Schwartz.

(Judge Schwartz tosses back his head and laughs.)

CHERRY: My father started in business with one or two barrels of herring on the sidewalk on Maxwell Street. And from there he apparently accumulated sufficient money to open up a grocery store on Maxwell Street. My father was an excellent businessman.

SCHWARTZ (referring to Judge Cherry's former position as Illinois state senator): Then he should have been the politician in the family.

CHERRY: My father never engaged in politics. Things were very, very tough then, and he had a wife and two children to support. A third child was soon born to them on Maxwell Street. So he didn't have any time for any outside activities. And he concentrated mostly on being able to earn sufficient money to support his family.

After working very hard—I remember specifically that we lived in the back of the store and the store was in the front and my mother worked together with my father and they worked from early morning, possibly seven in the morning, until maybe ten, eleven at night. I remember it was messy back there. We had three or four rooms. Our living room was separated from the dining room by tassel drapes. We had two bedrooms. My brothers and I all occupied the same bedroom. We continued to occupy the same bedroom for years. We all slept in one bed. That's right. One bed. We moved west in 1918.

SCHWARTZ: Did you learn any values as a boy from 1911 to 1918, when you moved away?

CHERRY: You learned that you came from people who don't have the luxuries of life, that you had to work hard from early morning to late at night. I used to help in the store when I was eight, nine, ten years old. I was the cashier, and I had to learn to make change. I also worked as a clerk there and stockboy.

Neither my father nor mother had a formal education. But the children addressed themselves to becoming educated.

SCHWARTZ: Were there books in your house?

CHERRY: Not too many.

SCHWARTZ: The only books in my house were religious books. My father was not a religious man, but my mother was very religious. She would be constantly reading. Reading came naturally to me. But I was a typical boy in those days. My life was on the street there. And instead of devoting most of our time to education, it would be devoted to play. I remember we organized baseball teams at Stanford Park.

CHERRY: And we played street hockey. Do you remember those games?

SCHWARTZ: Oh, sure.

CHERRY: On Maxwell Street. Not on Saturday or Sunday, of course, but during the rest of the week. There were not too many automobiles at the time, and the only traffic was really horse and buggy. My father owned a horse and buggy, after he became a little affluent and was able to engage in business in a store, as distinguished from the sidewalk. I remember on nights in the summertime, my father would hitch up the horse and wagon and take the family for a ride. I remember that very vividly because we enjoyed it so much.

I used to love to go into the stables. My father's stable where he kept the horse—or horses. At one time we had *two* horses. The smell of the stable was just beautiful. I loved it. As a matter of fact, I got a beating once from my father because Jack Keeshin's father bought Jack Keeshin a pony, and he used to race down the streets—the cobblestone streets. Others on the street had ponies, too. One of them was Yonkel Finkelstein, who was later known as Jackie Fields. And there was a competitiveness that existed between them, and I remember, in fact, when Jackie Fields's father bought him a pony. He used to race it down the street. And I became so much interested in that, and I wanted to get involved, so I started harassing my father to buy a pony. Well, I didn't get a pony. But I did get whacked pretty good.

SCHWARTZ: Our family had a pony, too. It wasn't our pony, though. It was the pony of the then market master of Maxwell Street, name of Krakow. And there was a stable in the garage back of our house. At that time we lived on Peoria near Maxwell. Now, I used to take the market master's pony, which was purchased for his son, for his children, and I would race him with the street cars on Roosevelt Road. Because I, too, used to love to ride the horses.

CHERRY: Going back to Jackie Fields, we had fights like kids do, you know. Over disagreements about nothing. And as a matter of fact, when I recall to him the time that I whacked him around during a fight we had—long before he became a professional fighter—

SCHWARTZ: Who witnessed this altercation?

CHERRY: Well, not you. You were a little too young.

SCHWARTZ: What evidence do you have? Jackie Fields denies it, though.

CHERRY: He doesn't deny it. No, no. He doesn't deny it at all. We put our arms around each other every time we meet. (Judge Cherry now excuses himself to return to the bench.)

SCHWARTZ: "Before speaking about Maxwell Street, I had kidded Judge Cherry about a sentence he had just imposed. You see, our philosophies are entirely different. My philosophy is, I always believe in giving a man, a first offender, a second chance. Always. It would be a most unusual case where I wouldn't give a first offender a second chance.

"Although Judge Cherry and I grew up in the same general neighborhood and shared some of the experience of that neighborhood, we also had personal experiences that shaped each of us differently.

"First of all, I committed two crimes as a boy. The first one was when I must have been all of about seven years of age, just a kid in cap and knickers. There was a livery stable on Fourteenth Place. I can't remember the exact address. But we went there at night and stole some salamis and some cigarettes. Merchants had left the merchandise there overnight. I remember sneaking into the stable in the dark of night and looking around to see if anyone was around. Then I climbed into a wagon to steal the salami. Then we ran. Oh, sure, we ran. Even at the age of seven, I knew I was doing the wrong thing. I smoked one of the cigarettes and ate part of the salami. I had never smoked before. It was very distasteful. So I never smoked after that until I went to high school.

"The second crime, this was a tremendous experience. I was all of ten years of age. I was already in my last year of grammar school. I was under eleven when I graduated grammar school, and I graduated Crane Technical High School when I was a little over fourteen. Everyone I traveled with was always three to five years my senior. At this time that I'm describing, three of my companions were going to graduate Foster grammar school with me. They were fourteen years old. It was a hot day. We wanted to do something with ourselves. This was in the summertime. We decided to rent a horse and buggy to take a ride out into the country. Well, we didn't have the moola, and so . . . I'll never forget this . . . how we conceived of getting the necessary funds. We devised a plot.

"There was a grocery store, Peskin's, and that was two doors south of where one of the other boys lived. Saul. I forget his last name now. He lived at 1301 Peoria. We lived at 1303. Peskin's was 1305. The Peskins were an elderly couple. Very elderly. And they had a very limited grocery store. This was a three-story building, and there was a basement with a large picture window, so that you can see what's going on inside the store from the outside, from the street. And so my two friends—one was going to stand outside looking guard, watching if anyone would come into the grocery store, and the other would engage the old gent in making a purchase of a bottle of pop. The pop was in like an icebox, away from the counter itself. So in order for Peskin to get your bottle of pop, he had to leave the counter and go to this icebox. And I—youngest and smallest—while Mr. Peskin was being engaged in making this purchase, I would sneak around the counter. They didn't have a cash register. They had a drawer where they kept the money. I would then go to the drawer there and get his money and then leave with my friend.

"As luck would have it, Saul's mother was coming up the stairs and could observe from the outside what was going on inside the store. I was caught red-handed with my hand in the drawer. When they counted the money out, it was a dollar nineteen cents I had stolen. This was reported to my parents. My father, may his soul rest in peace, said, 'From now on, you don't even go on that side of the street where those boys are. No longer do I ever want to see you in company of those two boys.' He figured they were the bad influence on me. For several weeks I kept my promise, didn't see my two companions, nor did I venture on the other side of the street. But one particular day, several weeks later, I ventured across the street, saw my two friends, and just sat on the stoop and merely engaged in conversation.

"This was about five in the evening. And who should be coming along but my father on the horse and wagon, after having closed up for the day his vegetable stand on Maxwell Street. He observed me sitting with my two friends. He reined up the horse, got off the wagon, and with a clenched fist—not an open hand—grabbed me by the collar and hit me right on the jaw. Knocked me flat on my— He didn't knock me out. He knocked me down. And from that day forward I never stole, never did anything bad like that again.

"In that neighborhood, there were a lot of success stories, but a lot of people went wrong, too. I remember Moishe the Goniff. He went to the penitentiary for being a participant in a hold-up of the Rumanian synagogue. And there was Barney the Bum, the notorious tire thief. But that punch in the jaw helped me a great deal. Because to this day, as I relate the story to you, I can still feel it.

"My father was some teacher, even though he was not at all an educated man. When he came from Russia he landed in New York and worked there for a short time before coming to Chicago. He worked in New York as a dockman, although he was a smelter by trade. He worked with a man by the name of Schwartz. And Schwartz taught my dad how to write the name 'Schwartz.' So he adopted the name Schwartz. I later found out my father's last name was Smilovitz.

"After he'd moved to Chicago, his brother who had been residing in New York came to visit us. I was about nine and when his brother was introduced as Smilovitz, I said, 'Hey, Pop, how come your brother is Smilovitz and we're Schwartz?' And that's how I learned the story for the first time.

"My father, every morning at about four, would go to the Randolph Street market where he would purchase from the farmers the vegetables that they brought in from their farms. I would quite frequently go with him. To me, it was a thrill. Just being with my father and watching him and with my older brother, incidentally, who, being the oldest in the family, didn't go beyond grammar school. He stayed behind to help my mom and dad work the stand. And he, too, became skilled at buying. So I would even go with my older brother, Harry.

"Well, the thing that impressed me was the skill developed in bargaining. You'd go from one farmer to another because there was no stability in prices. Each farmer had different prices for his commodity. And so when you pick up a bushel of tomatoes, if it's not cheap at one place, you can get it at another. Or even a box of peppers or a crate of lettuce. The experience that I would carry is that everything had a price. And that you never accept the first price offered. You're always bargaining. Except of course if you went to a department store like Marshall Field. It's a one-price store. No matter where you went on Maxwell Street, you could always bargain. As a matter of fact, it's like in many foreign countries in the flea markets that if you didn't bargain, they'd think there was something wrong with you.

"You learn then, if you can bargain well and know value, that the one who had the article to sell wasn't quite truthful as to the real value of the article. So you always look upon someone who has something to sell with suspicion. It does lead to cynicism. No question about it. There's a tendency to lose faith in your fellow man. And you doubt his integrity and veracity. So how do you live with that? Well, take, for example, if you are presiding over a trial, where there are no independent witnesses. Just the plaintiff and the defendant. So that it's the plaintiff's word against the defendant's word. And then the judge becomes a human lie detector.

"He has his antenna up because he's got to determine who's telling the falsehood. Unless it's simply a matter of opinion. The telltale sign is observing the witnesses very closely. There are certain nuances, and if you use a word that's quite familiar in the vernacular of my people, a certain *shtikeleh* that gives a person away. Certain inflections in his voice, the manner in which he would look at you as a judge, and the manner in which he is testifying. Some of it is really very simple, but you have to be watching for it. One witness would turn to you while on the witness stand and relate the story, looking you straight in the eye. Whereas the other witness wouldn't even attempt to look at the judge, nor even at the lawyer if the lawyer is asking the questions.

"Of course, there are some pathological liars, who never even know when they are lying. So these are the trials and tribulations of a trial judge. This is why, for example, when in an appellate court they review a record, and all they have to review is a cold, naked record, and so it is a hard-and-fast rule seldom breached that when it comes to the credibility of a witness, they will leave that up to the trier of the fact, and if there's any evidence in the record to support the trier of the fact, they will affirm the trier of the fact because he is the one who has had the opportunity to observe the witness. They didn't.

"And I think the kind of life I led on Maxwell Street has made a better judge out of me, having observed life now at every level and on every plateau, or to put it another way, having now lived on both sides of the tracks, I think it's made a whole man out of me. As a result of this, I think it's made a whole judge out of me. It's made a more competent judge out of me. More sympathetic. Now, I'm quite aware of the criticism of the courts in being too lenient. But that would not in any way affect my judgment if I thought that the defendant before me, after a finding of guilty if he pleaded guilty, is deserving of probation. I wouldn't hesitate to put him on probation. Let me give you an example.

"Approximately eleven years ago, I sat in Boy's Court. The case load was very heavy. They probably would have seven, eight sheets a day, a hundred to a hundred and fifty cases a day. Tremendous case load. Totally unfair to the sitting judge because if you wanted to do substantial justice, well, you could become a machine instead of remaining a human being. One case. A boy of eighteen charged with three felonies, one burglary, and two larcenies. He looked like any ordinary boy. White. Blond. His eyes told me nothing. Looked like a fine young man. Did not look like the criminal type at all. But he had two prior records. So the record alone told me he had criminal tendencies. He had been placed on probation on two previous occasions by two other judges. I was going to impose a sentence of three years. At that time, his attorney had pleaded for probation and asked the court to hear five citizens whom he'd brought to court. One was a priest, one a social worker, one was a Boy's Club executive, and two independent citizens. They were confident they could rehabilitate him.

"I said, 'Notwithstanding his prior record, he was placed on probation on two prior occasions, and you're still willing to recommend to this court leniency for this boy?' And each in turn said, 'Yes.' Well, I yielded.

"The Assistant State's Attorney said, 'Judge, how can you do this? Here you were ready to sentence him to three years, and now you're going to let him walk the streets again on probation.'

"I said, 'Remember, we've observed him for only thirty minutes. These five respectable and responsible citizens have had him under roles of supervision far longer and see some redemptive qualities in this boy which we can't observe in such a short period. And if they are willing to risk him on the streets, why shouldn't this court? They are the citizens whom we're concerned about. If he should go back to committing a crime, the fault is not yours. The responsibility is mine and mine alone.' So I placed him on probation.

"Twenty-eight days later I get a call from Frank Sullivan, a reporter on the Chicago *Sun-Times*. 'Judge, remember this case?' I said 'I certainly do.' He said, 'Well, this man that you placed on probation is now in the criminal court before the chief judge and was indicted on other charges. What do you intend to do about him?' I said, 'Apparently, Mr. Sullivan, you have the transcript of the proceedings. And you have read it. Now, you as a reporter, you do what you think is best for you and society. If you feel I'm deserving of criticism, be my guest.' He laughed and said, 'I could never do that after reading the transcript.' I said, 'When the case is formally called to my attention, I will issue a warrant for revocation of probation. And then when the warrant is served he will appear before me. A hearing will be held, and I want you to know that a full-scale hearing will be held with all these five witnesses who will be called back before me, and I want to say, "Now, where did *we* go wrong?"'

"And just like the rest of society, a judge is not always right. No matter how skilled, no matter the depth and range of his experiences and background.

"But I love the work, love it intensely. However, I suffer from angina and it is debilitating so that I can't work for the long stretches that I must. I may be forced to retire. It's going to be a great sorrow if I do. I always wanted to become a judge.

"Even as a youngster I was always engaging in arguments and loved to debate. A lot of my friends said, 'Why don't you become a lawyer?' As long as I can remember. But I always wanted to be a judge because of my mother's urging about—you see, I'd listen to her reading the Talmud on the Sabbath and then reading the laws. This literature made a great impression upon my mother. We had discussions on religion and law. More than my father and I because he was too busy working day and night. She constantly helped him out at the stand until my brother came of age, when he finished grammar school. Then he helped my father. That's why he didn't continue on with his education. Same for my sister, who went to work to help support the family, and the others, seven children in all. I was the most fortunate one. I was the one who was blessed. I could go to college.

"My mother always talked about Mishnah and doing substantial justice and walking humbly with your God. I used to always question Ma about religion. And I'd get only one response. She'd say, in Yiddish, of course, 'You musn't ask questions.' In other words, just take it on blind faith. Well, this I never did. Even though I attend synagogue on the High Holy Days, and do a *Yizkor,* you know, prayer in memory of my late parents, I am now somewhat of an agnostic.

"Well, we had a large family and so when I wanted to do homework and have some quiet, I went to my friend Shmopy's apartment. He had a bachelor apartment above a tavern on Maxwell Street. I would go there to study. I was attending DePaul University College of Law, from 1928 to 1931. I graduated at twenty. But I had to wait until twenty-one, the legal age to obtain a law license, before I could take the bar exam. After I took the bar we waited anxiously for the results. Every day we'd look in the mailbox or await the arrival of the mailman. I'll never forget the day the results of the bar came in the mail. It was a Saturday. *Shabbes.* The Holy Day for my mother. My mother was home. It was just the two of us. I knew from the big envelope that I had passed, just the size of the envelope, because along with the results you had to fill out documents relating to character and fitness. If you failed, you just got a postcard. Ma was in the kitchen. 'Ma,' I said, 'I passed.' And this I'll never forget. In the kitchen we had a round table. We embraced. We danced around the table. And she says in Yiddish, 'Maybe someday you'll be . . .'" Judge Schwartz's words thickened. He paused. "And she says, 'Maybe someday you'll be a judge.' She was sitting in the jury box on the day of my induction and I related the story, and there she was proud as a peacock. And then she began to cry. And I began to cry. Everyone in the courtroom began to cry."

Judge Schwartz, smiling, took out a handkerchief. He wiped his eyes and blew his nose.

"I didn't go into private practice for two reasons. One was economic. We were in the throes of a depression, and I wanted to be certain to earn a living. But two, and this is really foremost, I wanted to be a judge. It was more than just becoming a judge. It was the recognition of what kind of judge I would make. To be recognized by my professional peers as being an outstanding judge. And I think it has happened. The last two times I ran for retention, in 1966 and 1972, I received the highest number of votes by the Chicago Bar Association each time. The Chicago Council of Lawyers, a newly created organization, recognized by the American Bar Association, also voted me one of the six outstanding judges. That's the recognition I wanted. Not merely the title of judge.

"Coming from humble surroundings, I believed that the only way to achieve my goal would be to enter politics, and perhaps through this attain the bench. As one former president of the Chicago Bar Association said, you earn brownie points so that the party would recognize you not only for your legal ability, but also for your political efforts. In other words, I saw it as the means to an end. I eventually served for twenty-four years and three months as an assistant attorney general, serving under seven attorneys general of the State of Illinois. And in 1959 I was elected to the bench.

"Politics, when I began, did have a bad name. You heard about the ballot stuffing and various shenanigans. But once again, to achieve my goal in life, it was the only way I could conceive of at that time to accomplish it. It's as simple as that."

# RALPH BERKOWITZ

"Battling Berkowitz" was the name the Chicago *Daily News* used in the headline of the April 10, 1975, feature story on Ralph Berkowitz. "The feisty [seventy-two-year old] gentleman with a bit of a brawler in him is the first assistant to Cook County State's Atty. Bernard Carey." It added that "this son of a Maxwell Street rabbi" is a hustler, a behind-the-scenes manipulator, a "straight-shooter," and "a generally compulsive guy."

On the day that the interview with Berkowitz was taped, he was in rapid transit. We talked in his office in the County Building in Chicago, in his car as he drove carefully but quickly to the court-house, up and down the elevators in both buildings, and as we strode briskly. He speaks as swiftly as he moves. Gray-haired, five feet five, a hundred forty pounds, natty dresser, serious eyes. He has nine grandchildren.

"My father wanted me to be a rabbi like him. Hell, yes. And he wanted my brothers to be rabbis. None of us wanted it. We had known the poverty that goes with it—hand-me-downs and stuff like that. And the indignities a rabbi suffered in America. He felt that he had to bow and scrape to the guys that were supporting the shul. And as he said, any *grauber yung*—any peasant—can tell him what to do. Not for us. We liked independence.

"It wasn't that way for a rabbi in the old country. In our small town in Poland, my father, as the rabbi, was by social tradition the respected leader of the community. And his training was in the Lebovich *yeshiva,* the oldest yeshiva of Poland. So when we came to America, in 1907, and came to live in McKeesport, Pennsylvania, where we had relatives, my father discovered that the rabbi in America has to pamper and pander to the tastes of the local rich man. He usually had a small factory or a department store in that town. They had a small synagogue and a small Jewish community. So here he had to please the grauber yung to get along and he hated it. As a result he just about made up his mind to abandon it the first chance he had, and he was given a chance quite early. The local department-store owner had a son and the man wanted his son to learn to say *Kaddish*. The kid was very dumb from my father's point of view; he was very, very dumb. And my father in those days was not a very patient man. He couldn't stand ignorance. The man asked him, 'Well, Rabbi, how long do you think it will take my son to learn to say Kaddish?' And my father said, very complimentarily, 'You should live so long!' The guy took it wrong. So my father quit. He came to Chicago with absolutely no intention of being a rabbi.

"We moved to Sangamon Street, just off Maxwell. My father thought he'd give it another try, being a rabbi in America. He opened a storefront shul on Maxwell. Most shuls in those days around there were in storefronts. My father had an altar up in front. In the back he had the cabinet in which the Torah was deposited, and he had benches. There was a curtain to separate the men from the women, and women, as was the tradition in orthodox shuls, sat behind the curtain in the rear. It wasn't much of a shul. The important thing that happened was the holidays. You made a few bucks on the holidays. You sold tickets. You had to be your own promoter and sell your own tickets. But my father was not much of a money-maker. He felt he should be above that. He was a very proud man. It was so difficult for him to ask for money from anyone. You know, in later years, when my father was very old—he lived to be ninety—you couldn't give him a handout. So my brother and I used to deposit money in the bank in his account. We never handed it to him. He would go to the bank and take the money out. It was sort of a charade. If I handed it to him, he'd get very angry.

"Well, I think my father lasted altogether about two years as a rabbi. He wanted no part of it. He soon became very bitter and finally went into the business that was operated by my mother. That's in the tradition. The man, the religious man, he shouldn't dirty his hands. He should spend his time learning. That wasn't unusual.

"We had a grocery, with my older brother and I helping. My

mother was a charitable institution for all the Maxwell Street area. You see, people bought on credit, and if you couldn't pay your bill, my mother would let it go. 'Later, they'll pay,' she'd say. 'Are you going to let them starve?' So she wasn't much of a business person herself. I remember during World War I we had a store at 800 something Maxwell, and we lived in the flat above the store. There was a flat behind the store that we were no longer living in, and we had every room filled with sugar and flour, hundred-pound bags of sugar and flour, piled to the ceiling. During World War I sugar and flour rose in value 500 per cent. In other words, sugar that used to be four cents a pound was being sold for twenty-five cents a pound. Flour the same. Now, what my mother had represented substantial wealth, and yet we went broke.

"It's simply that my mother—she was just bighearted. She couldn't let anybody starve, and everybody owed her. I see men sitting on the Judicial bench today whose mother and father owed us money and never paid us. I don't say anything about it. I'm aware of it. I won't tell you who they are. I will tell you that Judge Schwartz is not one of them. He is not in that category. Schwartz is a *landsman* of ours. Our families were from the State of Gabernya. I don't even know the name of the town—the town I was born in. Schwartz may not know this, but his mother was a maid in my maternal grandfather's home. My maternal grandfather, for his time and place, was one of the few Jews that owned his own land. He had a factory, and he was the *poritz* of the town, the Jewish big shot. How I know about Schwartz's mother is because one day my mother said to me that she met a woman by the name of Schwartz. This woman told her that her son was a lawyer and is a good friend of mine and she wanted to know if I knew him. I said, 'Yes, Mom, I know him very well. He's a very bright person, really a lovely person and a very bright lawyer.' And my mother said, '*Aclog ov Columbus' medina.*' That is, 'A plague on Columbus's nation.' And she said, 'My God! The son of a servant of ours is my son's friend.' She said, 'This couldn't happen in Europe.'

"They were snobs. You have no idea of the snobbery that must have existed because she was married to a rabbi, and her father was the rich man in the town. That gave my mother social standing, and she was the best-hearted person in the world. You have no idea of the snobbishness because there were three social classes in the old country. The grauber yung, the peasant; the rich man—what they would call rich, it wouldn't be very much; and, of course, the learned. The learned ranked highest in the social scale. There was no middle class.

"The respect for the rabbi was tremendous. Some rabbis would represent the Russian government in the shtetls and preside as arbiters. It was a civil position, and they would decide civil cases. Rabbis would decide a religious issue, primarily, such as which dishes could be used at Passover. I remember my father had a problem over ownership of a cow. The details are vague to me now. But it was something about a cow having strayed from its owner and someone else claimed it. The question: Should a cow be on a leash like a dog? I don't remember how my father resolved it.

"So my mother found it a culture shock to come to a world turned upside down from the one she grew up in. And I remember once, someone was criticizing the rabbi of a shul they were attending. They were now just members of the congregation. And somebody got up and criticized the rabbi. My mother got up and said, 'Sit down, you peasant. You can't talk that way to a rabbi.' She wouldn't stand for it. She cursed the person. Something like, 'You'll go to hell and you'll bake bagels.' or 'You should itch in places impossible to scratch.' Yiddish curses never *quite* wished you harm. Even if someone wished you to break your neck, they used to soften it, so it comes out, 'but it shouldn't be painful.' That kind of business. The curses are basically epigrammatic in their expression.

"My mother, who was very blunt, could tell you off in the most beautiful language. You can say so many things in Yiddish with its limited vocabulary that you can't say in any other language. I remember when my mother wanted my brother to marry a certain girl. A cousin of mine met the girl, and he made better time with her than my brother did. So one Saturday night, this cousin and his mother, my aunt, called at our house. They came to announce the engagement. They wanted my mother to be the first to know. Well, that aunt of mine was never exactly my mother's cup of tea, anyway. So the aunt walks into our house and says, 'Why so dark?'

"And my mother says, 'For bad guests we don't turn on lights.'

"My parents maintained certain moral standards that were inflexible. I had never seen my father when he wasn't completely dressed, for example. I never saw my father in underwear. I remember one time I came home at about two in the morning. I didn't have a key so I had to wake my father. My father asked who it was, and I told him, and he says, 'Wait a minute.' He didn't see that there was anybody else. He knew it was me. He went into the bedroom, stuck his head out and said, 'Okay,' so I wouldn't see him not completely dressed.

"Honesty was almost a fetish with him. It was common in the neighborhood for kids to steal—off a fruit stand, or something. I never would even think of it. Never. I recall a time there was a crap game in an alley near the grocery store. I became interested. And I won about twenty-five dollars. I was a kid, and now, what to do with the money? So I hid the money under the mattress. But in our house you had to clean up the house for Shabbes. The house had to be scrubbed clean for Saturday. That meant airing everything, turning the mattresses over, so I had to find a place to hide it for the Sabbath. I used to do most of the cleaning because there were no girls until my younger sister was born. My mother was busy in the store. And my father didn't do it, of course. I finally decided to hell with it! I'd lie! 'I found this money, Pa.' My father wouldn't believe it. Where did I steal it? My God, I had one hell of a time to convince him that I found it. I turned it over to him. I practically had to swear myself on everything that was holy to convince him that I was walking in an alley and I saw that money in a bag. I came up with a fanciful story. I never shot dice again after that. Ill-gotten gains. Believe me, it was ill-gotten.

"All this fortified my father's opinion that this country was a *goyisha* land, the Gentile's land. Like most of these people, he would always have a yearning, a nostalgia for the homeland. He used to tell how the winters were more terrifying there, and everything that grew was bigger there. And even though the czar was *fonya*—one to be damned—you still had to pay deference to him. As far as he was concerned, lip service he would give the fonya, but at heart he wouldn't so that he was never kindly toward the czar.

"Now, another thing that was interesting. Radicalism. There was no radicalism in him. There was a member of the family who was a radical and was sent to Siberia. And that was terrible, he thought. It was a shame. You didn't talk about it. It was wrong to oppose the system, no matter how bad the system was. It was wrong under any circumstance to engage in violence.

"He never quite adjusted to Maxwell Street. It was too crowded, too noisy, too dirty. He came from a small community where you had land, and you had room.

"I liked Maxwell Street. The street was an exciting place for a boy. There was something about it. On summer nights, going to bed before one or two in the morning was unheard of in those days. Something was always doing on the street. Just between you and me, we didn't think of ourselves as living in the ghetto. We didn't think of ourselves as poor, and, when thinking back, I don't remember ever thinking of myself being hungry or in need. Even when we were broke, we weren't poor. We always had enough to eat. One or the other of us made enough money to pay the rent.

"And it seemed we always had enough to go to the Yiddish theater. You either laughed yourself sick or cried yourself sick at the theater. The humor was broad and the pathos was deep. I loved it. I don't remember ever enjoying the theater as much since. I remember one Yiddish theater had a chorus girl there whose name was Rosie Margolis—I still remember her name. She used to sing a song in Yiddish. Translated it goes something like 'Pretty girl, lift your dress just a little, and a little more.' I don't remember much more, but that was Rosie Margolis. She would sing the song and lift her dress a little bit up to about her knees, not even that much. Oh, that was real risqué. And we'd say, 'Nok, nok, nok.' More, more, more. And even the women liked it. That was Rosie Margolis. I'll never forget her.

"In later years we went to Dreamland, a dance hall. A lot of the great bands of the day played there. Like Duke Ellington, Louie Armstrong, when they were first coming up. The dance hall had those reflecting lights. It was set up like an old skating rink, and you danced around the band. We did the fox trot, one-step, waltz, two-step, that kind of dancing. One of the things that you found a lot of is what we used to call floozies. You know, the guys would stand there and rub against the girls. When you think back, it was quite a place. The girls were dressed in party dresses. Nice girls wouldn't go there. And you would very seldom see a Jewish girl there. But a lot of Jewish guys would go, of course. As a matter of fact, a Jewish boy would hardly make a pass at a Jewish girl because you were supposed to marry a Jewish girl. That was the rule of life.

"I started working for a living rather early in life, at twelve or thirteen, which meant I was on my own. I worked downtown. By the time I was seventeen or eighteen, I was really pretty sophisticated. To me, it didn't make much difference about girls, Jew or Gentile. If I thought she was willing, I'd find out.

"I was going to high school about this time. I went to a hell of a good high school, McKinley High. Two teachers there made a lasting impression on my life, one particularly. One teacher, named Fred Turner, taught me to love reading. He taught me the beauty of Shakespeare and the classics. Part of his life he had spent on the stage, and so he had a class where he'd do nothing but read, and word would get out—'Oh my, come and listen to Fred Turner read.' You'd come and sit there fascinated. Pretty soon, as tough as we were, we'd come over and listen to Fred Turner read.

"I was fortunate in that I was able to go to college. I worked as an auditor. My father still wanted me to be a rabbi despite his own experiences. He felt I would be a modern rabbi, and a modern rabbi had greater advantages.

"He had wanted me to be a rabbi since the time I was three or four years old. Oh, I remember, he would kick the hell out of me. I had to be the example for the other kids, the model for everybody else. He would brag, 'He does it by heart. He can read and translate a page of the Gemara.' That made me brilliant. That was the most important thing in my father's life. The minute I could be taught to remember my name, I was taught to read. And when we came to Chicago, my father still showed me off. I'd read part of the service.

"I became a lawyer. And I became a Republican soon after I started my practice. Before that, like most Jews, I had been a Democrat. But I went to a speech and heard a Jewish judge say that we Jews owe it to ourselves and to our families to be Democrats. It was our salvation. Well, I resented this approach. Especially since in high school I had been impressed by a teacher, William Morton Paine, who preached against hyphenated Americanism. He resented people being Irish-American, German-American, Jewish-American. He argued that this was a melting pot. This is America. You are either American or you are not. So that judge's approach got me mad enough to want to go into politics actively, against the Democrats. And then I was very much interested in what Roosevelt really meant to the Jew. I found that he was phony as hell. In retrospect, I'm right because he ignored every bit of information he got, every sounding of warning he got about what was happening to the Jews in Hitler Europe.

"In the 1948 presidential campaigns I was for Dewey, the Republican, and Dewey was very pro-Israel in that campaign. The State Department was all for ducking the issue until certain political considerations made President Truman see the light. Jack Arvey had taken credit, covertly taken credit, for persuading Truman to take Israel's side. I'm inclined to believe that Arvey did it; he was supposed to have told Truman that he couldn't even carry the Twenty-fourth Ward—he couldn't even promise him the Twenty-fourth Ward—unless he changed his stance on Israel. Then came the de facto recognition of Israel. When that happened, I had a problem with my mother and father. I had a hell of a time, and to this day I never did know how they voted. Then, you see, they were emotional about it—'Well, in the end, Truman did recognize Israel,' they said. I said, 'But he didn't do it from the heart.'"

# THE BATHHOUSE

The bathhouse on Sunday was to many Jewish immigrant men what the country club would become to their grandsons. The bathhouse was a place to take a deep breather—literally and figuratively, for the brick-burning ovens would heat the steam room at temperatures of up to 250°. The men in the neighborhood would come and often spend full days on the weekends sweating, eating steaks, lox, schmaltz herring, and black bread and drinking homemade wine with seltzer water in jugs. They wore sheets and sandals, played cards, talked endlessly about the New World and the Old. This was the social highlight of the week.

The primary Russian bathhouse in the neighborhood was on Fourteenth Street, one door west of Peoria Street. It was located in a two-story building. The bathhouse was on the first floor, and families lived on the second floor. A turnstile was at the entrance to a long hallway of the bathhouse. Off the hallway was the enclosed steam room, with its three wooden tiers, its oven, and its buckets of cold water and soapy warm water, and in the soapy water, thick brushes made of dried oak leaves so that the bather might paint himself soapy white. The men would also soap up each other. They wore funny wide-brim felt hats in the style Americans think of as the Hatfields and the McCoys. Every few minutes, a man would dip his felt hat into a bucket of cold water and then splash the hat on his head to cool off, the heat being so intense.

Another room off the hallway was partitioned with wire cages and in each was found double-decker cots for sleeping.

There were no Turkish towels in those days, and the men used sugar sacks with linings sewn in which had been bleached and cut to look like towels. The sheets were worn like togas.

A third room contained a small dining area with card tables and folding chairs. Coming in after the steam, the abundance of salt from the men's pores would be used to advantage in that they'd eat the schmaltz herring with their hands, the herring tasting all the better with the added salt.

Almost every masseur was known to be an alcoholic. They lost so much salt in the steam room that, they decided, only great belts of liquor could restore their energy.

The clientele was mostly neighborhood Jews. But in many cases Irish and Italian and Lithuanian customers came for a steam. Politicians and gangsters and potato peddlers sat side by side, soapy and gasping and sweating, in the billowy steam room. A man like the Kansas City gangster Spike Kelly, when he came to town, would interrupt his business affairs to travel down to the bathhouse, bowlered and bespatted, with bodyguards. When he went into the steam room, he removed his hat and spats; he did not remove his bodyguards.

Legend has it that one local hoodlum, who had turned stool pigeon, went into the steam room to explain his unseemly action to a few of his colleagues and came out as smoke from the oven's chimney.

Once, a big black sedan pulled up in front of the bathhouse. Four men in black suits walked in carrying violin cases. Soon after, another man burst out of a room and fled naked down the hallway and disappeared onto snowy Fourteenth Street, followed by four men chasing him with violin cases.

The bathhouse also served a religious purpose. Women attended for *mikvahs*. It was an observance of ritual purity. On the first day of her menstrual flow each month, a wife was rendered "unclean" by Orthodox Jewish law and sexual relations were forbidden for a minimum of twelve days—at least five days for the menses to end, and then seven consecutive "clean" days. At the end of this time she must go to the mikvah to be bathed.

Customarily, a husband anxiously remained outside the bathhouse and paced back and forth after having relinquished for nearly two weeks, in the name of God, his conjugal rights.

# THE STREET, 1926

## MAXWELL STREET
## MAY BE ABOLISHED

—Action by the city council to abolish the Maxwell Street market loomed as a possibility today as a result of renewed squabbling between Ald. Henry J. Fick and the curbstone venders.

. . . [Mayor Dever had] ousted Harry Lapping, for four years market master, and transferred several policemen after which, as a move toward peace following a rebellion among venders, he appointed Max Janowski to be director of the market.

In dismissing Lapping, the mayor warned Ald. Fick he would tolerate no further trouble at the market that might reflect on his administration, and during a discussion on the floor of the council of charges that upward of $250,000 a year was being collected in graft from the peddlers and hucksters on the street, several aldermen urged the abolishment of the market.

The latest feud developed ten days ago, when the banana cart of Edward Schatz and his son, Benjamin, was literally "kicked off the street." Among the venders it was whispered that Ald. Fick was squaring accounts with the Schatzes for carrying a "shakedown" complaint to the mayor, which ended in the firing of Lapping. In sworn affidavits the Schatzes charged that, for several years, they had been compelled to contribute $300 annually, in addition to the dime a day collected by the city, in order to remain undisturbed in business on the street.

The money, it was charged, was paid to Victor Cohen, who masqueraded with Fick's consent as assistant market master. . . .

"No one can come into my ward and defy me," the alderman is quoted as saying. "The Schatzes have made their bowl, now they're through peddling bananas on the West Side."

CHICAGO *DAILY NEWS*
*July 15, 1926*

# JAKE "GREASY THUMB" GUZIK

When French *littérateur* Marcel Proust said that "Each of us has a thousand selves," he wasn't thinking of Jake Guzik, though Jake Guzik fits the description more than most. These are some of the *noms de guerre* Guzik was known by: Dean Jake of Old Scarface U., Mr. Five by Five, the Little Fellow, The Jew Kid, Top Noodle, the Mayor of Cicero (when Cicero was the place where, it was said, if you smell gunpowder you know you're in Cicero), Mr. Fix, Old Baggy Eyes, Chief Panderer, Potbelly Toughie, Gangland's Fearless Fosdick, and, of course, Greasy Thumb.

He also had a passal of aliases, including Anthony Guisak, George Cusik, John Cuzik, Jose Garber, Joe Graber, Mike Brown (Al Capone's famous alias was Al Brown), Julie Gordon, and, when he expired at age sixty-nine, he was going under the name of Jack Arnold.

What he looked like was a matter of considerably less conjecture. He was short and he was fat. He stood sixty inches high and not quite sixty inches round. "A short, penguin-shaped man, wattled, dewlipped and pouchy-eyed, he wore a perpetually plaintive air," wrote John Kobler, author of *Capone*.* Len O'Connor, author of *Clout*, described Guzik as "a sad-looking little guy with one kidney and a calculator in his head."† John H. Lyle, the late Chicago judge, saw him as "a pint-sized bookkeeper."‡

In the end, though, the name posterity will remember him by,

* John Kobler, *Capone: The Life and World of Al Capone* (New York: G. P. Putnam's Sons, 1971), p. 118.
† Len O'Connor, *Clout: Mayor Daley and his City* (Chicago: Regnery, 1975), p. 63.
‡ Judge John H. Lyle, *The Dry and Lawless Years* (New York: Dell, 1971), p. 80.

and the name in his own lifetime he could have signed checks with, was, lugubriously, "Greasy Thumb."

How he got the name remains mere speculation. Perhaps, by dint of his duplicitous intellect, he stood out among his slimy peers like a greasy thumb. Or the thumb had to be highly lubricated to count the mob's millions. Another version is that the name was nothing more than an allusion to Guzik's beginnings as a waiter whose clumsy thumb constantly plopped into the soup.

Kobler described the most widely accepted theory: "Probably nobody ever walked up to Guzik and said, 'Hi, Greasy Thumb.' Nor did gangsters address each other as 'Schemer,' 'Enforcer,' 'Potatoes,' etc., except in movies and fiction. Such nomenclature was chiefly played by newspapermen. Legend ascribes many of the more picturesque sobriquets to James Doherty, a Chicago *Tribune* crime reporter, and Clem Lane, a Chicago *Daily News* rewrite man, who supposedly amused themselves on slow nights by coining them."

The writers on the local papers took great joy in caricaturing the infamous. When, for example, "Machine Gun" Jack McGurn, a golfing enthusiast, was slain near Eightieth Street on Chicago's South Side, Ed Lahey of the *Tribune* began his story, "Machine Gun Jack holed out last night. He died in the low Eighties."

And after Richard Loeb was stabbed to death in Statesville Prison in what was reportedly a homosexual quarrel, Robert Casey of the *Daily News* wrote: "Richard Loeb, who graduated from college with honors at the age of 15 and who was a master of the English language, today ended his sentence with a proposition."*

What Guzik was about is, to some extent, public record. His FBI dossier is number 561475 and it includes this information (from a 1950 updating): "Occupation: gambler. Evasion of income tax, sentenced to five years at Leavenworth, April 8, 1932. Alleged income in 1927 was $970,302. Income tax in 1928 was $642,000, but filed a return and paid tax on income of $18,000. Convicted of evading $800,000 in income tax from 1924 to 1928. Alleged bootlegging, pandering. By 1949 owed $892,233 to the Govern-

* Irv Kupcinet, *Kup's Chicago* (New York: World Publishing Co., 1962), p. 97.

ment. Settlement was for $100,000. Admitted he was business manager for Capone's organization, had mastery of figures and details that may never be equalled. . . ."

Guzik once said, "I don't know why they call me a hoodlum. I never carried a gun in my life." That was supposed to be true. Violence was not his game. Accountancy was. And so for protection he always carried $10,000 or more in currency. Once, when arrested, he had a roll of $21,000 in his pocket. He explained, "I never fear kidnaping because I'd just give the roll to the guys who snatched me. They'd be more than satisfied." He returned safely from three kidnapings.

Guzik is credited with having invented the "Crime Syndicate." After prohibition, organized crime needed another big money-getter. And so in the '30s, "largely through the wizardry of Guzik," wrote O'Connor, "[the Outfit] brought to its finest flowering the nationwide racing wire.

"This was the system over which, on wires leased from American Telephone and Telegraph, running descriptions of all races at all tracks were transmitted almost instantly to betting parlors in all sections of the United States.

"If there is any single thing that can be held responsible for the development of the unique American phenomenon that is called a national crime syndicate, it was not booze but the ingenious method employed by the Capone gang to ensure their control of the information that was the lifeblood of bookmakers throughout the nation. The profits generated by the Chicago wire proved to be the catalyst of syndicate crime. The basic conclusion of the U. S. Senate Crime Investigating Committee headed by Senator Estes Kefauver was that the interstate transmission of race track results was the heart of the national crime problem; the evidence turned up in committee hearings clearly showed that instantaneous transmission of information vital to illicit bookmaking was the nerve system of organized gambling, the foundation stone of syndicate crime.

"The Chicago race wire was the nation's bookmakers' only available source of instantaneous information concerning *all* the betting opportunities currently existing at *all* the tracks, and, indeed, the cash flow of the bookie joints was significantly greater than that of the tracks. The total pari-mutuel betting at the tracks runs into the hundreds of millions, and it is beyond question that the take in the nationwide network of bookie joints ran into the billions.

"The Capone gang fed its wire into its own horse parlors and those of its politically connected friends in the Chicago area and wholesaled its information to bookmakers everywhere, with trusted crime syndicate people in various parts of the nation serving as middlemen. The profits everywhere were far in excess of the sum needed to cover the necessary operating expense of corrupting the politicians, the courts and the police departments.

"In Ed Kelly's day as mayor of Chicago, 1933–1947, an educated guess is that the mob was laying out locally something like $20 million a year for 'protection.' "

Guzik was a cocky, stocky peacock because of his accomplishments and connections. He wore $300 suits, flashy rings, broad straw skimmers, puffy silk handkerchief in his suit-coat pocket. When in 1945 he was arrested on suspicion of murder of James M. Ragen, a rival race-track wire-service operator, Guzik said to the cops who made the pinch, "I've got more cash than Rockefeller and there's twenty of us with more than I have. No one's going to push us around." A Treasury Department official, investigating Chicago organized crime at that time, said that although Guzik was inclined to boast, he was certain "Greasy Thumb" had as much as $150 million in cash in Chicago safe deposit vaults.

There is at once a frustrating lucidity and opaqueness to the life and times of Guzik. It is as though we are watching through glasses that every so often get befogged, and we must take them off, wipe them, and put them on, and in the process miss some stuff.

He was born in Russia on March 25, 1886. The family moved to America in 1891 or 1892. At one point, it is known that they lived near the corner of Lytle and Taylor, a few blocks northwest of Maxwell Street, in the area in which author Meyer Levin and federal court judge Abraham Lincoln Marovitz, grew up. The family later moved to Ogden Avenue, where the father had a small cigar store. It was about the same time and on the same

street that Samuel Paley had a cigar store in the back of which in
1901 his son William was born. Ogden Avenue was also the street
to which, in the early 1900s, the families of Barney Balaban and
Benny Goodman moved—moving *west* from Maxwell, the equiva-
lent in those days of moving *up*.

Guzik's father, Max, was naturalized as a citizen on November
5, 1898, and that made his children citizens as well.

Jake spent two years in high school and, in adulthood, would
brag that he had been a classmate of "some people who achieved
distinction on the right side of the law." His parole record lists
employment as: 1901–2, sold newspapers during vacation; 1902,
with Sears Roebuck; 1902–14, with father in Chicago, delivering
cigars from his father's cigar store; 1914 to present, in business
for himself.

Authorities believe he may have spent several months in Bridewell Penitentiary in 1917, but if he did it was under one of his
aliases, one authorities can't precisely pin down. Guzik himself always denied it.

Guzik left home at age twenty-one to marry Rose NeuLe-
poschultz, age sixteen. They eloped and were married immediately
in Crown Point, Indiana.

He had three brothers—Harry, Sam, Joe—each of whom was
in the rackets. Harry was a notorious panderer and collection man
for Capone in the '20s; Sam was a burglar and served a sentence
for income-tax evasion in Leavenworth (his wife was also charged
with soliciting); Joe was a saloonkeeper and handbook operator.

It is known that he became interested in affairs of corruption
since his father was a precinct captain for Michael "Hinky Dink"
Kenna and "Bathhouse John" Coughlin, political bosses of the
Loop area.

He came in contact with hoodlums, apparently, through his
brother, Harry, who ran brothels. Harry, it seems, decided to join
the Capone mob instead of battling it. He ran one such house of
prostitution in the old Levee area, where the Johnny Torrio-Al
Capone gang had its headquarters. Harry, according to legend,
was the direct cause of the passage of the Mann Act. In *Chicago
Confidential,* Jack Lait and Lee Mortimer, wrote: "[Harry] was
chosen to be the first man to be arrested under the new law.

"The historic anecdote that came out of Harry's whorehouse gave a fantastic origin to the term 'white slave' as it became and is now applied.

"A girl named Mona Marshall, one of Harry's inmates, who roomed upstairs, got doped up one night, and, morose and melo-dramatic, wrote a note on which she stated: 'I am a white slave.'

"She signed her name. She attached the paper to her room key and threw it out the window, to the street, one floor below.

"She was no slave in truth. She spent half her days and nights on the street level with open doors. She strolled and solicited on the sidewalk in hot weather, though that was forbidden even then. She had a night off every week and went out.

"But an honest milkman came along in the gray dusk just before sunrise. He saw the note, picked up the note and the key, and read the lurid lament. He galloped to the 22nd Street police station with it. . . . Mona, to her immense surprise, and Harry, to his intense indignation, were hauled into custody. . . . Mona mumbled she didn't remember writing the note." But the prosecu-tor declaimed against the "empire of vice" and railed about "enslaved weaklings like her."† His purple oratory was published. A great commotion ensued among ministers and women's clubs. Then it died down. Mona and Harry returned amicably to work.

Jake was a waiter in Harry's place. That's where Jake first met Al Capone. It seems that Capone took a liking to the pudgy, mel-ancholy waiter. Capone listened with deep sympathy one night when Guzik told of being slapped and kicked by a speakeasy pro-prietor named Joe Howard, during a barroom argument. The ro-tund Guzik was hardly a physical match for the larger Howard. Capone was outraged at Howard to begin with, since Howard boasted how easy it was to waylay beer runners—Capone's beer runners.

Capone located Howard in Heinie Jacobs' saloon on South Wabash Avenue. When Howard saw Capone, he went forward with outstretched hand. "Hiya, Al." Capone grabbed him by the shoulders and demanded to know why he had picked on Guzik. Howard is supposed to have said, "You Dago pimp, why don't

† Jack Lait and Lee Mortimer, *Chicago Confidential* (New York: Crown, 1950).

you run along and take care of your broads?" In a rage, Capone pulled out a gun and shot Howard five times. There were two witnesses to the murder. Both told substantially the same story, and police went after Capone. But Capone had disappeared. About a month later he walked into police headquarters and said, "I heard you're looking for me." In short order, however, both witnesses underwent losses of memory. And Capone, questioned for hours by the young, energetic prosecutor, William H. McSwiggin, admitted only that he was a reputable businessman, a dealer in antiques. The case went to court. Jury's verdict: Joe Howard was killed by white, male, party or parties unknown. The prosecutor, McSwiggin, was eventually murdered. No killer was ever apprehended.

Capone and Guzik became so close that Capone used to say, "Jake's the only friend I can really trust." Capone quickly came to appreciate Guzik's acumen. He soon made him financial overseer of his organization. Guzik's business establishment was at 2146 South Michigan Avenue. It was made to resemble a doctor's office (with a shingle reading "A. Brown, M.D."). Guzik had his clerical staff and records of all the syndicate's transactions in six different ledgers. John Kobler described it: "One group of ledgers listed wealthy individuals, hundreds of them, as well as the hotels and restaurants buying wholesale quantities of the syndicate's liquor; a second group of ledgers gave all the speakeasies in Chicago and vicinity that it supplied; a third, the channels through which it obtained liquor smuggled into the country by truck from Canada and by boat from the Caribbean; a fourth, the corporate structure of the breweries it owned or controlled; a fifth, the assets and income of its bordellos; a sixth, the police and Prohibition agents receiving regular payoffs."‡

When Capone was sent to prison in 1930 for income-tax evasion, he left the running of the organization to his brother Ralph and to Jake Guzik. Guzik was regularly one of the headliners on Public Enemies lists.

Some people, however, did not consider him an enemy at all. Quite the reverse. Guzik and other hoodlums frequented Meyer Gold's restaurant on Roosevelt and Halsted, just north of Max-

‡ Kobler, op. cit., p. 119.

well Street. It was a fine, respectable restaurant run by a respectable owner. The restaurant included dinner music with a piano player and a violin player and had some of the best corned beef in town. It seated 250 people on the main floor and had a banquet hall upstairs, where Benny Goodman in his early days would practice with a small band.

In that banquet hall, Guzik threw the golden wedding anniversary for his parents. The place had been lined with gold trimmings. Meyer Gold remembers that there was a huge loving cup on a table at the hall's entrance. And all the elegantly attired hoodlums dropped gold coins into the cup. Meyer Gold estimates that there was between $20,000 and $30,000 in that loving cup.

Gold remembers that Guzik and his friends were well liked by the employees of the restaurant. "They were quiet, no trouble and, best of all, big tippers," said Gold. "They'd leave a dollar tip when in those days a nickel tip was a big deal. Things like that helped me keep good help."

Guzik helped Gold in another way. Recalls Gold:

"Morris Eller, the alderman for the ward, tried to intimidate me. Once he came in with two henchmen. Now I had about sixty people working for me. Eller wanted all these people to register so they could vote for him. I told him that these people just work here, they don't live in the neighborhood. I said I couldn't tell them what to do. So Eller got mad at that and began to harass me. While the restaurant was full, he would have the police come in and start searching my customers. It was embarrassing. So one time I decided to go to my friend Guzik and told him what was happening.

"Guzik went to Eller and said, 'Gold's a good man. He doesn't cause anybody any trouble. He's a credit to the community. Let's just leave him alone.' Eller listened.

"Another time there was some union organizing. A couple of Italians came in to the restaurant. They wanted a hundred-dollar initiation fee and some weekly payments. As they left they just sort of rapped on the window as if to say 'You better do what we say.' So I went to the Congress Hotel where Guzik hung out. Guzik was in the lounge. Jake said, 'Hello, how're you doing?' I said, 'Not too good.' He asked what the trouble was. I told him the story. He said, 'Forget it.' I went back and never heard from those guys again.

"One thing more. My wife was always active in the B'nai B'rith, and other Jewish organizations, trying to raise money. She might be in Fritzel's Restaurant where he used to eat. He'd say hello. She'd tell him what she was doing, and he'd always give a donation, maybe two hundred fifty dollars or so."

In 1951, the Kefauver committee called Guzik to testify. He refused on the grounds that his answers might tend to "criminate" him (not "incriminate"). When asked his occupation, he said, "I'm retired." Asked from what? He replied, "I won't answer that."

He lived in a house in one of the finest residential neighborhoods in Chicago, had nine rooms on three city lots, and two maids. He spent a lot of time strolling around hotel lobbies in the Loop and sauntering through the corridors of City Hall and the County Building.

He was embarrassed by his son Charles, a notorious homosexual, who was imprisoned in an Arizona jail in Florence Junction.

Charles was a prison photographer. It was discovered that in prison he lived in an air-conditioned private apartment, equipped with photo lab, refrigerator, stove, and television set. His door was locked from the inside so that prison officials had to knock and wait for him to open the door. Greasy Thumb's son had his own provisions brought to him and did not eat with the other prisoners.

In his last years, Guzik took delight in suing newspapers and the police for harassment. He had a $50,000 damage suit brought against the police at the old Canalport Station. He said he was forced to climb several flights of stairs even though he had a heart condition. This is when he was arrested in an investigation. He went to the American Civil Liberties Union and asked that group to defend him. It did.

He also brought suit against the Chicago *American,* which had called him, "Dean Jake of Old Scarface U.," and "Gangland's Fearless Fosdick," and "Chief Panderer," etc. When brought to court, Judge Salmon said, "Failure of the plaintiff to allege that said statements were false must be considered as a tacit admission that they were true. The truth is a complete and sufficient defense to a civil action for libel."

Another time he was called to court to answer some questions. He was given a list of names and asked if they were associates; about halfway through the long list he turned to his lawyer and asked loudly, "When are they going to come to Jesse James?"

The lawyer said, "They haven't got to the J's yet."

Guzik died on February 21, 1956, of a heart attack. The Chicago *American* described the end of Guzik:

"Four hundred mourners including Alderman John D'Arco of the First Ward paid their final respects to Jake Guzik. He lay wearing a skullcap and clad in a brown, single-breasted business suit, in a $5,000 bronze coffin."

Manny Capone, younger brother of Al, was there. So was Mae Capone, Al's widow. (Al Capone had died in 1948.) There was a public relations agent to meet the press at Tancel's Chapel. Rabbi Noah Ganze of the Chicago Loop Synagogue gave a twenty-minute eulogy. Around him were three floral pieces, one of which was sent by Mae Capone. Guzik was described as loyal to his parents and the *Yortzeit,* which is the anniversary of the death of his parents. And he was said to be loyal to his wife, Rose, who wept softly during the orthodox services. The rabbi said, "Jacob Guzik never lost faith in God. Hundreds benefited from his kindness and generosity. His charities were performed quietly. And he made frequent and vast contributions to my congregation." The Twenty-third Psalm was read.

The service had to be held outside Chicago, in Berwyn, so that Tony Accardo, known as 'Big Tuna' and now syndicate head, and other hoodlums could attend. They were subject to arrest on sight in the city.

Accardo, well-tanned, wearing cashmere overcoat, sunglasses, sat in an alcove where he could hear the services but not be seen by the other mourners. He had ten bodyguards around him. Two at a rear door, two at a side door, one sat on either side of him, and four others milled around.

After the services, Accardo stood up to go but was stopped by one of his men. "The G are outside. Wait a few minutes. No sense taking chances," the *American* quoted the man as saying.

Accardo was the last of the mourners to leave. He did not accompany the thirty-five-car entourage to Oakwood Cemetery at Sixty-ninth Street and Cottage Grove, but drove off in his red-and-cream Studebaker by himself. The G, or federal agents, took down the license number: Illinois 1-677-811.

Guzik, apparently, thought himself not a hoodlum but an American businessman. He was certainly no gunslinger. And as a contemporary "businessman" in pursuit of wealth and position, he considered himself a great success story—a rags-to-riches story in the glamorous fulfillment of the American immigrant's dream. But in the tradition of the Judaeo-Christian ethic of morality, Greasy Thumb left much to be desired.

# JACKIE FIELDS

Inside the Sands Hotel in Las Vegas, there is a congestion, a clamor, a glitter of people and money and calls that are not unlike a marketplace. Jackie Fields is at home here, having been born on Maxwell Street. He is a "casino host" or "greeter," which is a kind of public relations position. Jackie wears a tuxedo and wears it well on his trim frame. At sixty-seven (in 1975) he has thinning hair, wears horn-rim glasses, and his overall aspect is quite unlike that of a tough fighter. However, his mushy nose, cobbly speech, and puffy knuckles indicate otherwise.

In the Olympic Games in Paris in 1924, Jackie Fields won the gold medal in the featherweight division. On March 25, 1929, in Chicago, Fields beat Young Jack Thompson to win the National Boxing Association welterweight title. Four months later he beat Joe Dundee, the "other" titleholder to win the undisputed world title. He later lost the title, and then won it back in 1932.

In 1933 he lost the title for a second time and retired shortly afterward. He had lost the sight of his right eye.

He lives today in a house on a quiet street in Las Vegas several miles from the strip of casinos. He lives with his second wife and her two young children. We spoke in his den, which has medals and his boxing photos on the walls.

"My father had a butcher shop on Maxwell Street," said Fields. "Half butcher shop and half poultry store. He musta been a butcher in Russia and then opened up on Maxwell Street. I was born Jacob Finkelstein. But nobody ever called me Jacob. They called me Yonkel then. That's Hebrew for Jacob. 'Yonk.' When I hear a guy say 'Hey, Yonk,' I know he was from Chicago from way back. I look around. Oh, here's a guy I haven't seen for thirty, forty years. I love to hear that name.

"How did I get the name 'Fields'? Well, in the amateurs they said, 'How can you fight with a name Finkelstein?' A Jew wasn't supposed to be a tough fighter. A Jew is supposed to be a guy for books. So they said pick another name. The first one I could think of, the first high-class name was Marshall Field's, from the department store in Chicago. And Jackie, Jackie is just American for Jacob.

"I musta been about six or seven when my older brother, Max, got the idea to sell our meat to Jewish restaurants. And at one time my dad had over one hundred restaurants he was selling to in Chicago. I remember being the helper, delivering. In fact, when they say, 'God has his arms around you,' it's true. One night I was driving a horse and wagon delivering the stops—I musta been ten years old now—and the horse started to run away from me. I was running up west on Roosevelt Road toward Ashland Avenue. I'm trying to stop the horse. A streetcar is coming from the opposite way. The shaft of the wagon hit the streetcar, knocked the wagon over, and I wound up in the mud, in the snow with the meat all sprawled out.

"I was afraid my dad would punish me, so instead of going home I went to the Turkish Bath which was about three or four blocks from our house and slept there all night. They knew my dad. We used to always go. So they let me in.

"I was a kid. What the hell. What did I know? Just like the neighborhood itself. We didn't know the difference of a good neighborhood or a bad neighborhood. Pushcarts on one side, pushcarts on the other. We'd play in the streets, play in the alleys. We had Stanford Park three blocks away where you had to fight your way to the swimming pool because the Italians, the Polish, the Irish, the Lithuanians, were there. The Jews were surrounded by all of 'em. So in order to go to the pool you had to fight. 'What are you doin' here, you Jew bastard?' 'Hey, Kike.' You know. We'd start fighting right away.

"Now, they had benches, maybe thirty benches, before you go into the pool. The waiting room like. It was about an hour of swimming. The first, second, third benches were the first ones in, and you'd be able to swim ten, fifteen minutes longer. So they'd fight to get up front. 'Get out of here.' And you start a fight again. So we were always fighting for position.

"In that neighborhood you had to be tough. A kid that couldn't take it—you'd call him a sissy. We wouldn't let him with us. And there musta been twenty or thirty kids on the street. And out of them, the two toughest I had to fight—one by one. Charlie Schwartz and Joe Wilmer. Joe Wilmer was number two and Charlie Schwartz was number one in our group. And they were bigger. One or two years older than me. One year is a big age limit when you're a kid. I was ten, eleven years old, and I finally got to 'em. They used to bulldoze me, you know, being boss. And I just wouldn't stand for it. We fought it out. Maybe half an hour in an alley off Maxwell. Joe Wilmer and I fought behind our store, by the barn where we kept the horse.

"Sometimes on a market day guys would wrap towels around their fists and box for coins from the shoppers. We'd also go to the gyms around the neighborhood. Then I used to ditch school to go downtown to Howard's Arcade where the professional boxers used to work out. When I became about eleven, I joined there.

"Sam Langford, the tar baby, the heavyweight, a great fighter, taught me how to punch a bag. Yeah. One-two-three-four-, one-two-three-four. Little by little. I was this high. He was a short one, too, but he took a liking to me. And Jack Blackburn, who became Joe Louis's teacher, he taught me how to box. But Benny Leonard was my real idol.

"I saw Benny Leonard fight when my dad took me and my brother, Max, to Benton Harbor, Michigan, and he fought Charlie White. And Charlie White almost knocked him out in the seventh round. He knocked him down, and Joe Leonard, Bennie's brother, threw a bucket of water in his face to revive him. But Benny was so smooth. Oh God, he was."

In 1921, when Jackie Finkelstein was thirteen years old, his family moved to Los Angeles. His father suffered from consumption, a disease presumably derived from his having, as a butcher, to go in and out of cold storage. "And in those days," said Jackie, "all the consumptives went to California for the warmth.

"We bought a nice home in a nice section, the Wilshire District. Then someone sold my father an idea of opening a restaurant in Ocean Park. One of his friends unloaded his restaurant, and my dad lost a lot of money there. My big brother, Max, he left us. He went to Chicago. He was sort of a hoodlum. And things went bad because the money my folks had was tied up in this property, and the restaurant was losing money.

"I started to go to Lincoln High School, but I didn't like it. I wanted to be a fighter. I went up to the Manhattan Gym. I skipped the rope and boxed. Couldn't box. I mean, there was nobody that small enough for me to box with. I weighed ninety-two pounds, with my sweater on. Then I met Irving Glazer. He was a flyweight and fighting professional to make money to take up law at Stanford College. We're in the dressing room and he said, 'What are you doin' here?'

"I said I want to be a fighter.

"He said, 'Why don't you go to school?'

"I said, 'Why don't you mind your own business?'

"He sent me to see George Blake at the Los Angeles Athletic Club. Blake looked at me. 'Where did you box before?'

"I said, 'The Illinois Athletic Club.' 'Cause I remembered the Illinois Athletic Club having fights. Well, Blake was the boxing instructor once at the Illinois Athletic Club, and so he knew I was lying. But he got a kick out of it, he told me in later years. He saw I was enthusiastic. He told me to take my coat off and put the gloves on. He called over Billy Zukal, who was amateur featherweight champion of the Pacific Coast. Blake must have thought I looked good. He said, 'You sure like to fight, don't you?'

"I said, 'Yes, I do. I want to be a fighter.' And from that day he began teaching me how to box.

"But it was inborn with me, fighting. It's just like any other profession. A doctor, a lawyer, it must be instinct. My first fight, my father was my second. Without my mother knowing it. 'Don't tell Mom,' he said. We snuck out of there. My first fight was against Fidel LaBarba, the flyweight champ of the Pacific Coast. He kicked the shit out of me. But he didn't knock me out or knock me down. Now Blake saw for sure I was a tough kid, and I loved to fight. He gave me twenty dollars. I bought myself a cap for five dollars and the rest, fifteen dollars, groceries. And we had groceries for six, seven months.

"But when I came home, my face was this big. My mother, she slugged me. 'Bandito.' You know, she spoke Jewish. 'Meshugge!' She hollered at my dad for taking me there.

"But I felt I was part of the game. I felt I was a fighter, so I kept at it. And it's hard. Hard to train. Hard to keep your hands up at first, especially when you're getting hit. I was getting better all the time. Advancing. The inducement was to get somewhere, to become champion. That's the instinct I had. I wanted to become the best. As a punk, I had, you know, the conceit. Or whatever you call it. The desire. And what else could I do? I wasn't a studious kid. I quit school.

"My mother was so nervous about my fights. First thing I'd do after the fight, I'd go to a telephone and call her. 'Ma, I won. I'm all right. I'll be home. Don't worry.'

"My father died in 1925. I turned professional then and little by little, you know, I'd bring home money. I bought a home for my mother. A little house. And she was like my sweetheart. Every Saturday night, I'd take her to a cabaret. Show her how life is.

"And she was proud now. Her friends that were Jewish, they'd say, 'There goes Yonkel.' 'Yeah, your mommy told us about you.' 'We all know about you.' 'A champeen, huh?' Champeen. They knew what champeen was. And they'd say, 'the *gonster macher*.' The big man.

"Oh, I got a big kick out of it. I used to get a bigger kick when I'd do down to the ghetto. First thing I'd do is check into the hotel in Chicago, take a cab, and go down to Maxwell Street. Never failed. First trip into Chicago was Maxwell Street. Couldn't wait to get there. I dressed like I always dressed. Suit and tie and hat. I wouldn't outdo myself. I'd walk up and down the street with the people that were still there with their pushcarts, with their stores. 'How are you?' Shaking hands. I'd go down to Lyon's Delicatessen for a corned beef sandwich.

"I never forgot where I came from. Can we help what we were born? Some people try to hide it. Who're you cheatin'? I'm proud of what I am and how I started. If somebody don't like it, they can go fuck themselves. I don't give a shit what they like. Some people deny being a Jew. I'm a Jew. I'll be a Jew. I'll always admit it.

"I remember in some fights, I'd be in the ring with a guy and he called me a name. 'Kike.' 'Jew.' You son of a bitch. I'd go after him. Pow! I'd just try to tear his fucking brains out. But sometimes you just couldn't do it. They were tough, too.

"But the people in the old neighborhood. They were behind me. And you know who else was? Al Capone. I knew Al Capone very well. Through boxing. He was from over on Twenty-second Street, about a mile or so from Maxwell Street. Him and his friends liked the kids that they saw comin' up from the neighborhood. Me and Barney Ross and King Levinsky. They were from Maxwell Street. One of his closest associates, Guzik, was from our neighborhood.

"When I fought for the second championship, against Lou Brouillard in Chicago, Capone was in County Jail and I went up to see him. It was the day before the fights and I brought him twenty tickets so he could give them to his friends. And he was walkin' around. He wasn't in the can. He was in the office, you know. And he said, 'Champ, don't come back unless you're a champion again.' And I said, 'I'll see you tomorrow.' He hit me on the back and says, 'OK, champ.'

"After the fight, I called to come over but they wouldn't let me in. Because that's the day, if you remember hearing about it, he was supposed to escape. So they wouldn't let me see him. No visitors. So I sent him a wire. 'Will see you tomorrow. I'm champion as you did wish.' He was a great guy. I remember he would give free lunches in the winter to poor people. But what else he did, that wasn't my business. He helped a lot of people. Many a person and many a family he helped. He was maybe mean or destructive in his business, or he was just protecting his own.

"I was never in any business with him, and he never did nothin' for me. I just would talk to him. All those guys loved athletes, especially fighters. In those days, boxing was the number-one sport. Basketball was nothin', football was nothin'. Baseball was good, but you know there's 86,000 players. Boxing, there's only ten champions. And they all liked to meet the champs.

"I met a lot of people through boxing, from the lowest—what's that, a pimp?—to the highest, including two Presidents. I met Calvin Coolidge when I was on the Olympic team in 1924. Just before we went over to Paris we were invited to the White House. That was a thrill to me. He wished us luck. He looked at me and he says, 'How old are you?' I said, 'Sixteen.' I was the only one on the team still wearing short pants. And he said, 'You're going to fight in the *Olympics?*' 'Yes, sir.' He said, 'Good luck.'

"I met Franklin Roosevelt through my friend Jim Farley, who was the Postmaster General. I met Farley because he was boxing commissioner of New York when I first fought in New York, in 1927. And to this day, Jim Farley sees me and calls me 'Champ.' 'My little champ.' And when my mother's house was going to be lost because I couldn't make the payments after I lost all my money from boxing, in 1934, he helped get me financed through the Federal Government Housing Authority."

Fields said that he grossed over half a million dollars in his seven and a half years as a professional boxer. When he retired, in 1933, he had about $300,000. Within two years he was nearly broke. The Depression, investments in real estate and stocks, and general mismanagement blew the money away.

"I've had one nickname in my life," said Fields. "It's *'Shmuck.'* You gotta be a shmuck to have a lot of money and then go broke. To tell you the honest-to-God truth, I don't even remember feeling that low about life. I was a fatalist. I believe that that's the way it should happen, and that things happen for the best. And I thank God when I went busted that I was young enough to feel that I could get another chance to get ahead. I mean, I was only twenty-five years old. Just beginning life.

"I've been lucky all my life. Like I could have been killed by that streetcar when I was ten. And when I won the title back people had been saying I was washed up. And I was twenty-three years old! Then I lost my right eye. I was hit by a car and my retina slowly got detached. Then boxing didn't help it either. But I was lucky again. It was my right eye. And I'm a right-handed fighter. So in your stance, you peek over your shoulder with your left eye. I didn't tell anybody about it. And before fights I memorized the eye chart. E. E-f-f-a-g-r. They'd only give me three or four lines and then they'd say, OK. I was taking a chance. I lost the crown for the second time, to Young Corbett III, in San Francisco, in February, 1933. I beat Peter Jackson in May and was supposed to get a match for the middleweight title. But my mother died, and I had lost the title. I felt hard luck was changing me. So then I remember the one eye and if I lost it I'd be totally blind. I said, 'Fuck it. I'm through. I don't want to fight no more.'

"I remember after I won the title for the first time there were all these people around me as we walked out of the dressing room. 'Champ, hello.' And I said to myself, 'I hope these guys are around here when I lose. But I don't think nobody'll be around.' A year and a half later, I lost. I was with two friends. That's all. 'These son of a bitches—the crowds—where are they now? The king is dead. Long live the king.' And one of my friends said, 'Yeah, you're right, Jackie.'

"And one guy, he always gave me suits as champ. 'Anything you need champ.' Blah, blah, blah. One day I went to him to ask for money for an eye operation. He said come back tomorrow. I came back and they said he was out. I knew he was duckin' me. I was disappointed. But I came to expect it, part of life. You have to learn to take these things.

"But a lot of others stayed with me."

He got jobs as a bookie and as a film editor for MGM. He later was distributor for Wurlitzer Juke Boxes and represented J&B Scotch Whiskey in Chicago.

"Friends helped me get those jobs," he said. "And I was proud of my name. I'd say, 'Jackie Fields calling.' And I think it opened doors, made a difference. So I was lucky in that respect, too. Lot of guys don't get a chance to prove themselves. Make a name for themselves. Become a champ. That I rose out of the ghetto and earned a good living. And I was happy to help others. Like Barney Ross. He was a doll. He was three years younger than me. I always knew he'd be a good fighter. I take pride in saying that I was a good teacher to him.

"I told him to stay in shape because half the guys can't go ten rounds at top speed. And if you can, you're the boss. I'd say, 'Get your hands up a little higher,' or, 'Jab it out a little stronger. Instead of tappin'. Jab in. Hook 'em. Jab 'em.' But I taught him the first thing, 'Be careful of the stooges around you. They hang with you because you're Barney Ross. They'll suck your blood.' And sorry to say they did. Barney was in my stable, fought in all the preliminaries when I fought. He was my sparring partner.

"He became a great champ. A great champ. But it was sad for him when he got on the dope stuff. And the hangers-on sucked him, then they left him dry.

"And I see someone like Mickey Walker. The toy bulldog. A wonderful fighter. Found on the street recently. I was shocked. I almost cried when I heard that. I called him but they wouldn't let me talk to him when he was put in the hospital. Drinking problem. Broke.

"And I know how lucky I am. I'm not punchy. I got a wonderful wife and two children. My daughter's married, happy, lives nice. I bought her a condominium over on Valley Drive. My health has always been good. But once about a year ago I keeled over in the casino. How do you like that? First time in my life I ever fainted. It was high cholesterol. And I was up to about a hundred ninety. I've lost twenty-two pounds. I'm back in shape. A blessing from upstairs. I take it easy now. No more rough stuff."

He smiled and lit up a cigar. "The kid from the ghetto. He's a gentleman now."

# ESTHER LEVINE

Esther Levine, with one long fingernail tapping the ashes from her cigarette, sat in the kitchen of her comfortable two-bedroom home in a conventional Chicago suburb. She lives here with her husband. Her two children are married. A part-time manicurist, her hair is bleached blond and she wears glasses with rhinestones on the rims. She speaks with pleasing animation. She was born in 1916 near the corner of Fourteenth Street and Racine and lived there for eighteen years.

"All my friends used to congregate at Flukey's hot-dog stand, on the corner of Maxwell and Halsted," she said. "It was only a few blocks from where I lived. Well, that area was all considered one, you know. I lived with my family in the back of my father's store.

"My father was a bootlegger. At that time bootlegging was forbidden. Selling whiskey was against the law. He did it from the time I was a little girl until the end of Prohibition.

"Of course I knew. Was I a stupe? We all knew what was going on. I remember when I was a little bitty of a girl, he made his own. I don't remember whether he got caught or what, but he stopped making his own. He felt it wasn't worth it. So there were other people that made it, and he went and bought it from them. I went with him a few times. You bought cans, great big five-gallon cans with alcohol in them. We went to houses to buy the stuff, very clean immaculate houses. And if you looked at the house you wouldn't dream that anything is being done there.

"Then he'd pack up the back of his car, a Maxwell or a Peerless, whatever he was driving. And you prayed you didn't get caught, that's all. Then we drove home.

"We had a store, a clean, plain place with maybe three tables. It was supposed to be a restaurant. But it didn't look like a restaurant. I don't know what it looked like. If a policeman walked in, he got coffee and sandwich. But anybody else came in, they got my father's whiskey.

"We lived in the back. A couple steps up from the store. It was two bedrooms, a living room and a kitchen. A curtain separated the store from our home. We had bottles all set up in back, and sometimes I sold them. There were glasses. Some liked to slug it from the bottle, and some would be refined. They drank from a glass. Very few refined ones.

"My mother used to wait on a customer and hold my baby sister in her arms. My sister would be drinking milk from a pint bottle with a nipple on it. My mother would wash the bottle out and use it for the baby's milk. Sometimes my sister would stick her finger in the alcohol, the hundred-proof alcohol, before it was diluted with water. Stick her finger in and suck it off.

"There were a lot of people there in the alcohol business. You better believe it. A lot of the respectable families today, they started out making money by bootlegging. They'll deny it. But I know it. I practically lived in their houses. Their kids were my friends.

"We were ashamed a little that Pa was bootleggin'. We knew he was doing something illegal. And when you're young, you're ashamed of it. I remember when a teacher of mine would walk by the store I used to hide. So I knew I was ashamed.

"My folks never discussed it with the children. Children at that time were raised to be seen and not to be heard. You couldn't talk back to your parents in that day. If you did . . . In the first place, my father was very, very good, but, oh, we dared not talk back. All he had to do was look at us and we read him. But we weren't lacking in anything. I mean, as far as money was concerned, money was plentiful. Bootleggers did very good. That's if they hung on to their money and if they weren't pulled in where you had to pay off the police.

"I remember when they raided our house. At the time, we didn't live in the store. We lived across the street in a two-flat on the second floor. The police crashed into our home. My father jumped out the window. And they pulled my mother into the station. She was sitting in the hoosegow. At this time, we couldn't pay them off. When they really want you, forget it. So they decided at the time that I'm a very good speaker. My mother was a foreign-born person. She spoke with a foreign tongue. They decided I should go before the judge. I pleaded for my mother. So they let her go.

"Meanwhile, my father had to hide. A man they put in for worse. A woman, they have a little more sympathy. Pa went by his friend's house. And the house got held up and a colored guy cut Pa from one ear to the other. Pa survived. It was a very dangerous area. Very. Very.

"There were a lot of gangsters in those days. I remember Bummy Goldstein. He was a big hood at the time. He'd sooner kill you than look at you. He was a very mean person. But very good-looking. As handsome as could be. I remember me and my sister were standing on the corner of Fourteenth and Racine, in front of a drugstore. All of a sudden, a black sedan pulls up. The druggist disappears. Some hoods walk in with masks on. Bummy was behind the counter. They shot bullets in him like you wouldn't believe. And they took him out dead. My sister and I, we didn't know where to hide. Walked out of there, I was shaking. And they were busy shlepping me to the Maxwell Street Police Station for a witness. They wanted to take our pictures, and my father said he'd break the camera if they took our pictures.

"Oh sure. Well, listen, you're dealing with gangsters. And if I said I could identify them, before I'd know it, I'd be laying right along Bummy. Did I know what he did? All I know is when he walked in, everybody shut up because he was mean. I saw him beat up a man. It was unbelievable. Unbelievable. His father used to tell him, 'God should be good to me, and they should bring you home dead.' He was only in his twenties, I think, when they killed him.

"By the early '30s, the colored had moved in and we were the only white on the street where we lived. Matter of fact, there were streetcars at the time and we lived at the center of the block. All the conductors knew us. When we'd come home from a show or something, at night, they'd stop in the middle of the block and leave us off, and wait till we got into the house. Then they'd pull away. It was dangerous. I used to walk down the street at night if I'd go to the show. I was one of these little smart punks. I'd go and I'd have a knife, an open knife in my sleeve. And I'd walk in the middle of the street.

"And there were plenty of whorehouses on Fourteenth Street, but I was too naïve to know about it. I was going around with a girl—I'll never forget it—and we slept at another friend's house. And I didn't know that that was a whorehouse. And we slept there! We didn't sleep all night. We found out what it was. I mean, this girl, she was Polish, and her vocabulary was unbelievable. I don't think a man could repeat the words she spoke.

"We didn't know her mother was running a whorehouse there. We were up all night because there's so much tummeling.

"We were hearing things. What seeing? I'm gonna get out of bed and go look? I was scared. I didn't know about such things. I mean, I wasn't brought up with a whorehouse and all that. I knew I was a bootlegger's daughter, but that's as far as it went. In the first place, if we'd go to a place for chili or chop suey, say, and my father didn't like the way the place looked, he wouldn't let us go in there. 'Cause it wasn't nice for his daughters. He was only concerned that we should be raised right as far as that goes. We were taught right from wrong. He only wanted the best.

"You know, my father originally was a peddler. Junk peddler. Came over from Russia when he was young. He was from Minsk. My mother was from Pinsk. Or was it the other way around? He went to night school. He was the type of man that wanted to know everything, so he went to school and learned to read and write. He spoke with a slight accent, but he could read English, write English, and speak. And he became a Yankee Doodle Dandy. Whatever new cars came out, he had. He was always dressed good, and so was his wife and kids. My mother would go to the beauty shop and have her hair bleached blond. Had her eyebrows arched. She never learned much English. But she was good with the Yiddish curses. I remember she once said to somebody who had made a dumb remark, 'I wish I had in health what you don't have in brains.' My father always dressed the kids good. He bought my sister and me diamond rings. Then he died. He died at forty-four, in 1932. That's when hardship started.

"He didn't believe in insurance. It was the middle of the Depression. End of Prohibition had come and bootleggers didn't make such big money anymore like they once did. So by 1934 we had very little. My mother went on relief. The relief people, they should choke. Because they're rotten. They made us sweat to get whatever we got. My mother became a cook and took care of other people's children when they went to work. The relief got me a job. I did office work in the Field Museum. We were sad. Sad about being in a home where, when my father was there, it was a very lively house.

"You ask me what my father was. He was a bootlegger. Big deal. What have I got to be ashamed of? He didn't kill anybody. He didn't commit crimes. Look at the politicians. Look at the union leaders. When you want to make a living, you have to pay off. My father sold something. What'd they sell? I'd be more ashamed to say I'm a politician's daughter because they're doing more than my father did. At least my father wasn't a crook."

# THE STREET, 1926

## EXPLOSION ROCKS
## MAXWELL STREET AREA

—Midnight in Maxwell Street. All was quiet save for crashing echoes and the jingling of phone calls in the police station.

"An explosion?" shouted the lieutenant as he shook the glass of the broken windows out of his wavy hair. "Call out the reserves."

"Somebody just shot off a carload of TNT at Taylor and Halsted streets," came an agonized voice over the shivering phone.

So the white-faced squads were loaded into cars and hurried to the scene. Taylor Street lay calm and dead before them. They rang a doorbell. They rang other doorbells. Sleepy householders told them to go away.

They found no wreckage or evidence of a blast.

In Maxwell Street, when a still blows up they bury their dead without the help of the police.

CHICAGO *DAILY NEWS*
*November 12, 1926*

Perhaps the best known still in the Maxwell Street area during Prohibition existed in a hollowed-out movie house, the Model Theater, on Halsted Street just south of Maxwell.

Outside, the theater was boarded up. But inside where the seats had been removed was a large sophisticated distillery. It was described as looking like a little factory. A tunnel led from the theater to a house on the adjoining street, Newberry, where electricity was provided.

One night in the late 1920s the neighborhood was again awakened by a great hullabaloo of sirens, followed by the whacks of axes from Federal agents busting into the still.

# JOHN L. KEESHIN

From at least the time he was twelve, in 1914, Jack Keeshin understood the need for cross-country transportation. He had been a mischievous kid at Foster School, on Union and O'Brien streets. A teacher threatened to flunk him when he put glue on her chair and, upon rising, half her dress ripped off. Jack Keeshin then hopped a rail freight car, hid in the blind, and hoboed west for a year.

It was the third time he had run away from home and from school. When he returned from his wandering, his father shortly bought him a horse and wagon to start him in business and induce him to stay in Chicago. It was a mutual agreement to forget about school. Jack and his brother, Charles, began a delivery service. One of their first customers was, not surprisingly, their father, Abraham, a German-Jewish immigrant, who had come to own several poultry stores on Maxwell Street. It was near their home on Clinton and Bunker, the area in which Keeshin was born.

It wasn't long before Jack bought another horse and wagon, then a truck, another truck. He had twenty-six vehicles by 1920, thirty-six in 1923, eighty in 1929, two hundred fifty in 1933, three hundred seven in 1934, eight hundred in 1936. By then, he had become the largest individual trucking magnate in the United States. A millionaire operator. And soon, an international power broker with a line to the White House. In a lengthy, flattering article on Keeshin, *Fortune* magazine said that "besides muscle and guts he has brains and persistence and ambition and prodigious energy. For these reasons he also has money, and he flaunts the title of Keeshin Transcontinental Freight Lines."*

The trucking industry was always a rough and bruising bare-knuckles business, never more so than in its earliest years. There

* *Fortune,* "Freight by Highway," February 1936.

were fistfights. As tough a place as any was the notorious South Water Market—adjacent to Maxwell Street—where the driver with the hardest punch got the best loading space.

The breadth of the violence was demonstrated in Keeshin's dank office in his one-floor garage on nearby dreary Washburne Avenue. Keeshin, according to *Fortune,* had once found it advisable to install above his door two guns that protruded about five inches through the wall, their muzzles fixed at each of the two visitors' chairs flanking Keeshin's big desk.

Keeshin had immense physical power. He could, for example, tear in half a Chicago telephone directory with his bare hands. He had always, apparently, been rugged. His numerous fistfights in school attested to that. But regularly lifting huge crates onto trucks enhanced his physical strength; Keeshin, at five-eight, developed into a brawny two hundred-pounder.

The better to defend himself: A story in the Chicago *Tribune* of May 13, 1934, read: "An apparent plot to kidnap John L. Keeshin, head of Keeshin Motor Express Company, was thwarted by the intended victim's struggles at a busy West Side street intersection shortly before noon yesterday.

"The would-be kidnappers fled after slugging their victim to unconsciousness in the front of his car." He had left his offices on Washburne Avenue and started toward the South Side. He was driving along in his car. He had discharged the Negro chauffeur the night before.

"At 18th Street and Blue Island Avenue, he stopped for a traffic light. As he did so, he said a gunman opened the right-hand door, slipped beside him and pressed a revolver against his side. Keeshin grabbed the weapon, but another man boarded the car and threatened him with a gun. Both men aimed the revolvers at him. 'Just keep driving,' they said.

" 'What do you want? Money?'

"He reached in his pocket and pulled out $150. He was wearing jewelry valued at three thousand dollars. He had an additional $300 in cash in the other pocket.

" 'We want you,' one of the men replied. 'You're going for a ride. Keep on driving.'

"At this Keeshin renewed his struggles and the man on his right struck him on the head with the butt of a revolver. Apparently frightened by the attention they had attracted, the two men leaped from the car, leaving Keeshin unconscious, and entered another car which they had parked nearby."

Another time a masked gunman broke into his home intent on killing him, Keeshin believed. Keeshin jumped out of bed, threw a blanket at the intruder, and followed through with a punch that sent the man reeling against the wall so hard that the plaster cracked. While Keeshin hurried back ino his room for his revolver, the man fled.

Other problems over the years: He had been indicted for a conspiracy to slug employees of the Keeshin Company presumably because they were labor agitators. But the case was dropped when Bruce "Bud" Borrelli, a guard at Sportsman's Park and believed to be the only witness who could connect Keeshin to the conspiracy, surprisingly refused to testify. Borrelli had earlier implicated Keeshin in grand jury testimony. This case followed that in which Keeshin had punched a burglar, identified in the *Tribune* as "Nathan Metcalf, colored." Metcalf had allegedly told Keeshin, "I'll cut your heart out." Whereupon, Keeshin punched him, knocking him down. Metcalf died of a skull fracture. The coroner's jury found that Keeshin acted in self-defense and was justified in striking Metcalf.

*Fortune* described the people in trucking in the early years as "a brawling, noisy mob of individual operators, each answerable only to himself and to a state administration which takes scant notice of the trucker's methods so long as he keeps his licenses up to date and pays his multiple taxes. . . . It was no business for sissies."

Keeshin recalls his first "long distance" haul with a load of wine grapes to Joliet, thirty-six miles away from his one-floor garage on Washburne Street near Maxwell. He drove a two-cylinder truck with hard tires, no windshield, carriage lamps with candles for lights, and a chain drive in which the chain fell off every few miles. That journey took two and a half days.

One winter night, Keeshin lay under his truck repairing a broken bearing by the light of a bonfire. When he tried to rise, his back was frozen to the ground. To start the engine he built another fire under the crankcase, poured ether into the engine pet-cocks, turned the crank, them jumped for the seat to get off the fire before the whole thing could blow up.

He boiled eggs four at a time on the radiator. He sucked on clogged gas lines and changed four one-hundred-pound wheels. He ripped up fence posts to get out of the sand. Once, stuck in mud, he had to borrow a few tombstones from a nearby cemetery to give the spinning tires some traction.

He hauled brick, tile, cement by night and continued to deliver produce by day. Every penny made went into new equipment—"baking my cookies." All the while, he made it apparent that the boss could whip any of his employees, a band of rugged fellows.

Keeshin landed the A&P trucking contract to Sterling, Illinois, opened up the big shippers—Montgomery Ward, Sears Roebuck, General Foods, Walgreen's—battling competitors, and brokers, and state utility commissioners, and railroads.

Railroads applied pressure to state agencies not to allow out-of-state truckers to stop overnight. So Keeshin devised a pony-express-type system, where a truck ran for eight or ten hours and then a new driver picked it up and took it highballing down the road. In December of 1936, he sent a fleet of loaded trucks and trailers across the United States—from Chicago to Los Angeles—for the first time. It took five days, three to four days swifter than it normally took railroads to deliver freight. Then Keeshin's trucks turned around and roared to New York, in six days, twenty-three hours, and forty-eight minutes. "We beat the hell out of the damn railroads," he said.

He was also developing a sophistication. He was the leading spokesman for federal control of trucking. "And I was learning my way around Washington," he said. His efforts helped bring about the Motor Carrier Act of 1935, which stimulated the big, well-financed operations of which Keeshin's was the first in the nation.

While in Washington he met many people, including the President of the United States, Franklin D. Roosevelt. He remembers that in the mid-1930s, Cardinal Pacelli, later Pope John, made a visit to the United States; Roosevelt asked leaders of industry to escort the cardinal on a tour of America. Keeshin drew the assignment for Chicago. He remembers handing Pacelli an envelope. "You'll need cash to get around the United States," said Keeshin. Pacelli accepted with gratitude.

From that sprang a friendship with Rome that continued with three popes. They have traded gifts. Keeshin says with pride that he gave the first television sets to the Vatican, sent Pope John a stereophonic hi-fi set when he learned John was an ardent music lover, sent him the first watch a pope ever wore (sent along a black band but had to change it to white when he learned popes do not wear black). He also air-conditioned the Vatican.

"One hot afternoon I was sitting with Pope John in his study. It's a small room and it was hot as—it was hot! I was in suit and tie. He was in his robes. We were soaked with sweat. I said, 'Your Holiness, if I may be blunt, I'm a heavy-set man, and you're a heavy-set man, and I think we could use an air-conditioner in here.' When I got back to the states, I sent air-conditioning units to Rome and with men to install them."

In the drawers in his office desk, Keeshin keeps gifts such as Pope John's rosary beads, given to John by his father when he entered the Italian Army as a corporal in World War I. He also has a small gold clock from Pope Pius and a lock of Pius's hair that Keeshin carries with him for luck.

In November, 1945, Keeshin, who was still the largest individual truck operator in the nation, resigned as president of Keeshin Transcontinental Motor System, after a long power struggle with John Hertz, the Chicago taxicab and rent-a-car magnate. Hertz had become a partner of Keeshin's, in 1936, and helped finance the tremendous expansion. Hertz became Chairman of the Board. Various labor problems also contributed to the breakup. Keeshin said labor costs had gone up more than 56 per cent. Maintenance costs had also risen from three and a quarter to nine cents a mile. He said his action would draw attention to "the critical situation of the trucking industry."

He did not leave the business entirely, however. He was still president of Keeshin Transport System, a division of Keeshin Transcontinental Freight Lines, with a stronghold in the Midwest. But in 1967 he sold out to Murphy Motor Freight Lines of St.

Paul, Minnesota, while the company was grossing $9 million a year. "Doctor's orders to cut down," he said.

The Keeshin Company retains a limousine and bus service from O'Hare airport to various parts of Chicago and suburbs. The company is run now by Keeshin's son, Paul, who was born in 1937.

John Keeshin (in 1975) maintains a three-room office on the forty-seventh floor of the First National Bank Building in downtown Chicago.

He employs one secretary, Leone Rimmerman, who has never married and has been a devoted employee of his for forty years. On the wall of one room, a kind of conference room, are photographs of popes and rabbis and ministers with whom he has been friendly. His office is distinguished by an antique grandfather clock and, on his desk, a telephone which has no receiver. He presses a button and leans back in his chair or walks around the room, talking on the receiverless phone. He speaks with a deep, rough-hewn, yet studied, tone. Even at seventy-five, he seems rugged. Sometimes his teeth clench, and he smacks his palm emphatically. He wears steel-rim glasses. His eyes are piercing and vigilant. His gray-black hair is slicked back. His chin is good. He wears a blue suit and a gray silk handkerchief in his breast pocket. His chest is big, his hands are flecked with liver spots, but are sturdy. Out on the street he walks swiftly and with his chest thrust out. "The doctors tell me I shouldn't walk so fast," he said, "but I walk the way I've always walked." He has had two heart attacks and two serious operations in recent years. One operation was a mastectomy; he had a cancer on his breast, developed, he believes, from years of loading boxes of apples and produce and poultry onto trucks. He also underwent an artery operation behind his ear. He continues to suffer headaches from the effects of it.

He still receives numerous phone calls. A fire department chief, the chancellor of a local university, a banker, a business friend. Lunch dates, dinner dates. Various philanthropic and financial dealings are weighed. He is closer to his family now than ever before. "I had always been too busy building an empire to spend enough time at home," he said. His son, Paul, calls to ask advice on a business matter. John Keeshin discourages it—it would mean unnecessary mortgaging—and then listens to a retort. "You'd better listen to me," said Keeshin, joking, "because I can always change my will."

Keeshin has another son, who had begun a career in trucking. "But I lost him to real estate," said Keeshin. That son did not take to the urgings of his strong-willed father, just as Keeshin himself had veered from his father before him.

"My father never liked me to be in trucking," said Keeshin. "He had a low opinion of truckers, called 'em teamsters. He always wanted me to stay in poultry like him. He eventually expanded to where he owned a couple poultry factories in the Dakotas and Indiana. And he owned a great wonderful house on the West Side of Chicago, at 1822 Miller. He lost about a million and a half dollars in the Mercantile Exchange in the Depression. The bank took away his home. Seven months later he died, in 1930, of a broken heart, I'd guess.

"I learned from that, that you stay liquid. You don't have mortgages. I like it that I can go into a bank and see the president and not have to take my hat off. I can tell the president that I don't have any of his money, he's got my money.

"I did learn from my father that no matter what, always have a buck in your pocket. My father gave me a silver dollar when I was a year old. I still have it. Still shine it for luck." He pulls a silver dollar from his pocket. He says it was minted in 1890. The coin is rubbed smooth. All that remains visible are the letters PLUR and parts of points of a few stars.

"I still have a bump in the middle of my forehead from when I was hoboin' and someone tried to take away my silver dollar," he said, "and I protected it."

Keeshin's childhood has emerged in his adulthood at the oddest moments.

When he owned Sportsman's Park, for example, he was told that the Outfit—the Chicago crime syndicate—wanted a piece of the action, some patronage at the race track. They wanted Keeshin to meet the boss. Keeshin said, "Well, they have to come to my office. Anybody who wants to talk to me has to come to me."

Keeshin recalls: "So one day I'm sitting in my office in the penthouse at the Park and in comes the man I'm supposed to meet with. It's Tony Campagna, of all people! Tony from Foster grammar school. And he's with a couple of plug-uglies. Neither of us knew what the other had been doing all these years. And we busted out laughing. He was called 'Little New York Tony,' and I don't know why, because he's from Chicago. He's supposed to be a rough, tough, mean guy and he tells me he has thought about me through the years because of his hearing aid. We were about eleven years old and he hit me in the hallway of school when I wasn't looking. This was when the Italians and Jews didn't get along so good. I chased him down the hall and punched him so hard, banged him against a steel bannister. And Tony broke his eardrum and lost his hearing in one ear. He says he's wanted to thank me because when he doesn't want to hear something, he just turns his hearing aid down.

"He said, 'We got to talk.' I said, 'Okay, but we'll do it in private. I'll send my men out and you send yours out.' Then we sat down. I said, 'What do you want?' He said, 'Jack, we're going to have to have some help over here. We're going to have to have some people. You're going to have to help us out.' And I said, 'I'm not giving you any of that stuff. Look, you know, you don't watch your step I'm going to break the other eardrum.' And he said, 'I bet you would.' We didn't have a hell of a lot more to discuss after that."

One of the most important discussions—one that shaped his business philosophy—came a few years after he had been in the horse-and-wagon delivery business. "I got myself a truck," said Keeshin, "and I went to the National Biscuit Company and talked to the manager there.

"I said, 'I'd like to know if you'd like to truck with me. I'd like to expand my operation.' The man said, 'Well, come back here. I want to show you my plant.' He showed me rows and rows, stacks and stacks, boxes and boxes of cookies. He said, 'Now, if I called you up at your stable, or your garage, and said 'Okay, we want you to transport some of our cookies, would you be able to handle this?' I said, 'No, I'd have to buy more trucks.' He said, 'That's the thing. You get *your* cookies in order and then come back. You have to prepare your cookies first, and you have to get your trucks first. You've got to be ready and move fast.' So I learned from that. When my business grew bigger and bigger in the '30s, I'd buy a hundred more trucks and fifty more tractors, and people around me would say, 'But we don't have the business yet.' And I'd say, 'I'm baking my cookies.'"

Keeshin learned so well, became so powerful, that in 1939 the White House called Keeshin for assistance. The U. S. Government wished to help the Chinese build roads across China and Burma. Keeshin was asked to send trucks for the enormous project. One reason for building the now famous "Burma Road" was to speed the transportation of goods and munitions from the British and French ports of Rangoon and Haiphong into the interior of China. At the time, the Chinese were at war with Japan. The Chinese railways had been wrecked by bombings. The Pacific sea routes were considered too risky for shipping. A second reason for the road: the U. S. Government was greatly concerned about continuing to get the valuable tung oil found only in China. Tung oil was instrumental in the assembly-line painting of American automobiles. Tung oil has properties that allow paint to dry within hours. Before the use of tung oil, it took Detroit twenty-one days to paint a car. The White House now reasoned that if the U.S. couldn't get this oil out of China, then automobile production in America would dramatically drop, unemployment on a mass scale would result, and the country would fall back into the depression that it had been climbing out of. Finally, China had made a $25 million loan from America, and it would be with tung oil that they could pay back.

So America's leading trucker was called to help. Keeshin still has the diagrams of that enterprise. He has also saved a letter from Secretary of the Treasury Henry Morgenthau. Keeshin insisted on the letter, which would acknowledge his activities. "Otherwise," said Keeshin, "if caught I could have been tried as an international spy. I mean, we were helping China in a war effort."

What he did was so top secret, he says, that when he went to the East he told his family he was going off somewhere in the continental United States.

He remembers going days without sleep, working in torrential rains, directing some sixty-five hundred yellow Keeshin trucks and tractors and trailers over eight hundred miles of mountains. Some 150,000 coolies labored. The roads were built along with detours in case the original roads were bombed. Body shops were established in caves all along the way. Rickety bridges were fortified. Within eight months the job was done.

Not long after this development, Keeshin learned that five freighters of—he has never forgotten the precise figure—12,663 Jews fleeing Hitler Europe "were floating around the high seas." (A sixth freighter came later.) "They were on the high seas for three months."

"To this day," said Keeshin, "people ask, 'What happened to these Jews? Did they sink?' No one knew. England wouldn't take them. They went to Cuba. Batista wouldn't let them in. They went to Palestine, but the British, who hated Jews, again said no. The U.S. wouldn't let them in. They were illegal immigrants. They had no passports. I got an appointment to see Roosevelt. I said, 'Mr. President, I have a place for these Jews to land. I want to get them into China.' He thought about it, then said, 'Well, okay, as long as I don't know anything about it. You have my blessings, but, remember, if you're caught, it's your fault. Yours alone.' Again, if I was caught I could be shot as an international smuggler. The freighters landed at night in Rangoon. We got the people onto trucks, some huddled in the trucks, some lying flat on the top of trucks, and they spread out all over China. They were safe."

# DR. BEATRICE TUCKER

—Dr. Beatrice E. Tucker is the medical director of the Chicago Maternity Center (opened in 1932), on the corner of Newberry and Maxwell. In the first year there, she lived in a small dark room in the basement of the building. This made room for the swarm of young interns, medical students, nurses, who crowd this ancient barracks—to watch obstetric demonstrations, to examine rows of expectant mothers, to boil urines in the miserable little laboratory, to catnap while they keep one ear cocked for the telephone that jangles to bring news from expectant poor women all over Chicago. . . .

In her basement boudoir Tucker was blown upon by grime from what's as filthy a street corner as you'll find in our so-called civilized world. Sleeping a couple of hours in the gray of morning after a night of birth-helping, she'd be roused by bawling hawkers and a terrific quacking of doomed ducks of the Maxwell Street Market.

She was called to frightened households where bungling midwives had delivered babies' heads but could not bring their shoulders. Where a baby's head had actually been torn off by an incompetent attendant. Where an agonized mother had been found on the floor by neighbors, with her baby half-born and on the verge of a deadly rupture of her womb. . . .

This tall woman, always carrying her black obstetrician's satchel, might come back tired from a vigil against a mother's threatened disaster. In front of the building of the Center, she'd notice a crowd of people peering at the just discovered body of a gangster done to death. She'd forget her tiredness. This was life.

*Paul de Kruif,*
*THE FIGHT FOR LIFE,*
(New York: Harcourt, Brace, *1938*),
pp. 89–90.

———◆———

Shortly after her seventy-fifth birthday, on October 9, 1975, Dr. Beatrice Tucker came out of quasi-retirement to deliver a baby at the mother's home. It was a relatively easy affair, in clean, efficient surroundings and was reminiscent of her delivery of her first grandchild on a kitchen table a few years back. (She never married but became one of the first women in Illinois to adopt children.)

The delivery wasn't like that of the old days as described by de Kruif. All that and more occurred in Dr. Tucker's forty years as director of the Center, from 1932 to 1973. In that time, the staff delivered over 100,000 babies in private homes. And the Center was where obstetrics was taught to hundreds and hundreds of students, doctors, and nurses. It was the only home-delivery service in the United States staffed by physicians. Shortly after Dr. Tucker retired, the Center itself closed its home-delivery service for lack of staff and, conceivably, lack of inspirational leadership.

De Kruif called Dr. Tucker "the woman of the future." She calls herself, today, "the last rose on the bush."

She became the first woman resident at the University of Chicago Lying-In Hospital, in 1929, and worked under Dr. Joseph

Bolivar De Lee, a gruff but internationally-respected obstetrician. He was the founder of the Chicago Maternity Center.

Today, Dr. Tucker remains active in medicine. She is a family-planning consultant in prenatal care and adult medicine in a clinic in a Chicago South Side ghetto.

She is nearly six feet tall, trim, with short fluffy gray hair, owl-rim glasses, a quick, high, delighted-sounding voice. On the evening of one of our talks, she wore a black turtleneck dress with a silver-and-turquoise Apache-made necklace, and black low-heeled shoes with gold Gucci-like buckle and trim. She drives a canary-yellow Volkswagen. Her house is uncluttered, simple. We sat in a small room, and behind her was a painting of a little black girl with a red rose in her hair.

"Dr. De Lee began the dispensary, which was later called the Chicago Maternity Center, on February 14, 1895, Valentine's Day, don't you know," said Dr. Tucker. "Obstetrics was barely a specialty at that time. Doctors knew very, very little about it. The mortality rate was high for mothers; the mortality rate was high for babies. He became expert in prenatal care, learned how to use the forceps, knew how to prevent childbed fever. Dr. De Lee decided that the only way you can teach doctors and medical students and nurses how to take care of, or deliver, a baby is to do it. And the only way to do it, you have to have cases. There wasn't a hospital for indigents outside of Cook County Hospital, and that one was overcrowded. So he started the dispensary. He had a cold-water flat, which was torn down just this year, kitty-corner from the Center.

"Oh, first he didn't have any patients. And he couldn't get any. He was on the fourth floor and pregnant women didn't want to climb four flights of stairs. So he took a first-floor cold-water flat. He put up signs, 'Free Delivery Care,' 'Free Prenatal Care,' and nobody'd come. You see, they were used to midwives. Then he began house-to-house canvassing until he got a handful of mothers. He told them it was safer to have a physician deliver their baby, that the prenatal care was free and that the mortality rate for them and their babies would be less. He was a convincing man. He was able to identify with the needs of the patient he talked with.

"He was Jewish, and this was primarily a Jewish neighborhood then. His father was an immigrant from Russia. I think De Lee changed his name because he had a Russian Jewish name which was, I guess, very definitely Jewish. He said he never denied being Jewish, but he never advertised it, either. He said he never would have got where he did if he had. I think there was a strong anti-Jewish element, especially amongst people who had money, and he had to have money to build a hospital. Sometimes he was treated terribly when he went for a donation. He was once even kicked down a flight of stairs.

"He worked for ten years *'schnoring,'* as he called it. That's Yiddish for begging. His father sold horsewhips. He'd send De Lee out to sell his merchandise, but De Lee couldn't sell it. He'd get his friends to sell it. But he could sell the idea of good obstetrical care because, well, he believed in it. See, I guess he didn't give a damn about a horsewhip.

"He made a good appearance. He was a very handsome man, six feet tall, thin. When I met him, in 1929, he was about fifty years old and had white hair—pretty hair—a white mustache and white goatee. He wore nothing but white in the hospital. White morning coat, white starched collars, white-wash ties, white shirt, and stiff white cuffs. Meticulously groomed. And aesthetic. He wouldn't go to a football game if he could help it. He said, 'I'm not going down there and spend two hours looking at eleven backsides. I think it's downright vulgar.' He was a great teacher and a great obstetrician and was internationally famous in his field. But still, I wasn't 100 per cent sold on him as a man.

"For example. I got my residency when De Lee was out of town. When De Lee came back and found a woman resident, the very first one at Chicago Lying-In, he was not happy. And not long after, De Lee introduced me to another doctor in a meeting. He said, 'This is the new resident, Dr. Tucker.' And then in front of everybody, said, 'Of course, she'll never be able to do what you've done Dr. So-and-So.' I was just furious. After this meeting ended I went trouncing into his office and I said, 'Dr. De Lee, I would like to have a word with you.' You'd think *I* was the professor. I said, 'You know, I don't think you are a very nice man. I do not think you have treated me properly. You shouldn't have talked like that. You don't know what I can do. You haven't got the slightest idea of my capabilities. And until you do, I think you should not make any remarks in front of anybody. That staff is my staff as well as your staff.'

"Well, he was quite taken aback and he never did it again. I never did it again. I never had any trouble with him again. I worked like a dog to gain his respect. I'd work forty-eight straight hours. I'd work six, seven days a week. I played up to him like mad. I'd call him in on every case I had. He used twice as much catgut as anybody else. So I did. He used interrupted sutures. I used interrupted sutures. I also did a lot of things that, well, that I'm not too proud of. There was a German book that came out that he said was by the greatest obstetrician in the world. I got the book out of the library. I got a tutor who read German. And I learned to read one little passage. Now, I had an office across from De Lee's. I planned it that way because I wanted to keep an eye on him. So when De Lee's office door was open one day, I opened my door and I sat down at my desk and put this book in front of me. I didn't know how long I'd have to sit there before he came in. Pretty soon he wanders over. He said, 'What are you reading?' I said, 'Oh, I'm reading this book that you recommended.' He said, 'Oh, I didn't know you could read German.' I said, 'Well, maybe not very well'—but I had my little paragraph to read, so I started. 'Why,' he said, 'that's wonderful!' And I said, 'Yes, this passage, very interesting, isn't it?'

"I remember once I gave a speech to a medical society and De Lee was sitting in the first row. He was beaming. It was obvious he was quite proud of me. But he couldn't come right out and say it. The closest he got was one day shortly after in his office. He said, 'Tucker, you did fine with your speech. But you know, you would be top-notch if only you were a man.' Then he began to tell me about experiments in which hens were injected with male hormones and became roosters.

"He said to me—and I really wasn't sure if he was joking or not, I suspect he wasn't—he said, 'Would you ever consider being injected with those hormones?'

"I replied, 'No, Dr. De Lee, I have no wish to become a rooster.'

"Since the maternity center was built in 1908, the board of Directors of Lying-In Hospital had been financing the dispensary on Maxwell Street. By 1930, they didn't have the funds for it anymore. It was the Depression, of course, and they were going to close it down. De Lee felt it was too important a teaching institution to close down, so he convinced them to turn it over to him. All this time, he had been trying to raise money for the Center. You know, he wrote *De Lee's Obstetrics* while possible donors kept him waiting in their offices three and four hours before they'd see him.

"When the university turned the dispensary over to him, he called me in his office at Lying-In. He said would I go down there and take charge of the professional work at the Center? I said, 'Oh, I was going out to make some money in private practice.' He said, 'You don't know enough.' I said, 'Well, I've had three years residency in this hospital.' He said, 'That doesn't mean much.' I said, 'Dr. De Lee, that's terrible.' He said, 'Well, if you go down there on Maxwell Street and work in those homes, you'll see more than you've ever seen in the hospital, and you'll be a much better obstetrician when you get out.' I thought, well, if I was going to starve to death, I might as well do what he wanted me to do.

"The first thing, he changed the name from Maxwell Street Dispensary to Chicago Maternity Center. Give it dignity, you know. The building was horrible. It was an old three-story brick building. Most of the window panes had been knocked out by gunshots from the street. The walls hadn't been washed in three years. It had battleship-gray linoleum on all the floors. Clear up and down the stairs. There were no curtains on the windows, except some dirty old torn shades. There were old electric-light fixtures. The pipes were full of sediment. It was old; they were going to shut it down. It was a very dismal-looking place. One night, I had a medical student working in the kitchen when a stray bullet came through the back window and richocheted around. He dropped down like he'd been shot. It was funny, though it wouldn't have been funny if he had been shot.

"The first thing I did was clean the place up. This was how: We didn't have any money for it, so when we'd deliver a baby, I'd say to the father, 'Well, will you work for ten days? We'll pay you a dollar-and-a-half a day, which will pay for your expenses, and we'll give you your food while you're there.' So they'd come and paint and clean. You see, most of these people were unemployed at this time. We'd go through files looking to see if painters' wives or plumbers' wives or electricians' wives were pregnant.

"We got paint from a woman De Lee delivered who owned a paint store. We ripped out all the linoleum. We got red paint and yellow paint and black runners for the staircase. I had a house-keeper sew little curtains, and I told another doctor, my partner, Harry Benaron, 'We'd better hurry because if De Lee ever sees it, he'll think we're running a whorehouse over here.' In a week it was done. And De Lee came over. I was scared. He thought it was great! I was never so surprised in my life.

"But you could never trust him. He used to come snooping around. He wouldn't let me know when he was coming. I had that basement room. I had taken so many doctors and medical students and nurses, there was no place else, and I wasn't going to ask anybody else to live down there. I didn't care—I was in and out and all over. Anyway, a lady friend of mine and I were sitting and laughing and joking in the room, and you can hear me for a mile. I was roaring with laughter. And I'd had a bath and I didn't have a stitch of clothes on. I was brushing my hair, I had long hair, and I was standing in front of the mirror and De Lee opens the door without knocking. I was just furious at him.

" 'Is there anything I can do for you, Doctor?'

"He turned red as a beet and left. But, you know, I don't know what he thought I was doing there. And he also had his snoopers. This I don't like. 'Cause he's too great a man to act like that.

"One day he comes to me and says, 'You want to join a cabal?'

"I said, 'Well, I don't know what a cabal is.'

" 'Well, that is a group for intrigue and plotting to raise money for the Center.' He said, 'You can raise money.'

"I said, 'I can?' He said, 'Sure.'

"He said, 'Think how fortunate you are. When I started out, I didn't have a single case. You've got thirty-six hundred babies a year to deliver, to take care of.'

"I said, 'I think that's a dubious advantage, Doctor, when you've got no money.'

"And he said, 'Well, if you go out in the Sahara Desert and shout long enough and loud enough, you'll get money.'

"He taught me his tricks. He started the Center by first organizing a Board of Directors for the Center. He said, 'If you're going to get money from people who've got it, you've got to be a success. You can't let them think that you don't have anything.' So he used to meet in the First National Bank, downtown where the vaults are. You know, that's pretty swank-looking down there. And the only person who came was Mrs. Mandel of Mandel's Store. And at every board meeting, every month, it was he and Mrs. Mandel. He also said, 'Never name a hospital after yourself because anyone has so many enemies you'll turn off money.' He eventually got a lot of wealthy people on the Board. Most of them there were Gentiles. I don't know how that happened. But De Lee said, 'You know everybody says the Jews have all the money. But all the big money in this town is in the hands of the Gentiles. That's where you go.'

"Did you ever hear of Lady Esther? One day, De Lee calls me up and says, 'Tucker, Lady Esther has invited us to dinner, and I would like to have you show the movie about the Center.' We had made such a movie. Now, Lady Esther was this wealthy and good-looking woman who owned a cosmetics-supply line. 'Lady Esther' I called her, I don't know what her real name was. I said I'd go. But first he looks at my nail polish, and says it would look better if I'd take it off. I said, 'It's more sanitary on because bugs can't live in nail polish.' 'Another thing,' I said, 'if she serves liquor, I am going to drink it.' He didn't approve of drinking.

"Lady Esther lived in a mansion in Lake Forest. A great big place along Lake Michigan. She had a theater in the house. A butler meets us at the door. Now I think she had designs on De Lee. De Lee wasn't married. Nooooo. Women adored him, but nobody'd marry De Lee. They couldn't live with him. And I think women made him uncomfortable, outside of the profession. But I guess Lady Esther didn't know this at the time. We waited for her in this living room, with all kinds of Dresden things. And De Lee was jumping around like a cat on a hot tin roof. I said, 'Will you

please sit still?' De Lee said, 'I've got to get ten thousand dollars.'
I said, 'Well, you will.'

"Lady Esther now made her entrance. You could see the winding marble staircase from where we were sitting. She wore a
flowing gown, and she came swooping down the staircase. She
looked just lovely. Just beautiful. This made him more nervous
than ever. She had a nice dinner. Then I showed the movie. I
didn't know why he wanted to show it to her. It should be attractive. It showed a slum, a slum room with a woman having a baby.
Showed how we set it all up. Then he gave his little talk on the
teaching of doctors that we were doing, and so on. On the way
home, he said,

" 'You know what she wanted me to do?'

" 'I have an idea.'

" 'You do?'

"He said, 'She told me there was a beautiful view of the lake
from her bedroom.'

" 'Well, didn't you find that interesting?'

" 'Tucker!'

"And I said, 'I think you should have definitely gone up there.'

" 'I'm shocked at you.'

" 'Oh no, you're not, Dr. De Lee. I know what the score is and
you know what the score is.'

"And so I think in the next day or two he got a check for ten
thousand dollars from Lady Esther. Soon after, De Lee calls me
in. 'Tucker, Lady Esther's got feet that itch.'

" 'Well, so what?'

" 'I want you to go see her and do something about it.'

" 'What do you want me to do?'

" 'Anything, Tucker, anything. Let's get another ten thousand
dollars.'

"I said, 'Do you really think this is a nice way to treat her?'

" 'Will you do as I ask you to do?'

"Well, that poor woman—she didn't want to see me. She wanted
to see De Lee. And he didn't want to go. I went up to see her. And
there was nothing wrong with her feet. So I put a towel down on
the bedroom floor, and I put an apron on and I got out the gen-
tian violet. That won't hurt anybody. I took out the applicator

and I painted both of her feet purple, clear up to her—not her knees—but past her ankles. I'd gotten tired by that time of being a party to this thing between her and De Lee. But you know, she talked to me a lot while I was doing it, and I really think she was a very lonely woman, as rich and smart and beautiful and decent as she was.

"He wanted me to go to the opera with them one night. She had called and said she had tickets. But that's where I drew the line. 'I cannot do it,' I said. 'She won't hurt you at the opera.' He looked at me, and he's like a caged animal. I said, 'I think it would be nice. She's given you ten thousand dollars.' He went, but I never did ask him how he made it through.

"I was too busy. Oh, I saw everything under the sun down there on Maxwell Street. I delivered babies in alleys, on dirt floors, by candlelight, with a heated iron stove, crawled into attics. I remember one, she was all bled out by the time I arrived. I thought she was going to die. I got the hemorrhage stopped. I got her uterus packed. And I said to the medical student with me, 'I've got to get her in an ambulance and over to Lying-In.' I didn't yet have a setup at the Center. 'She's going to have to have blood if she doesn't die on the way.' We called an ambulance. The ambulance couldn't get their carriage up because the stairs were so narrow. She lived in the rear on the second floor. So I said, 'We'll have to go through the front.' And I banged and banged on the door, and nobody came. So I found an ax and gave it one good crack. And there are these two men in long underwear. They had big beards. They looked like the Smith Brothers. They couldn't speak a word of English. They looked at me, they looked at her, and I tried to make them understand. Ambulance. They finally did, and let the ambulance people out and we got her down. It was in late February, icy night. It was snowing and blowing. You couldn't see anything. They had the siren going and you know the ambulance—hell-bent to get there. Well, there was a broadside collision of a car coming this other way. And this ambulance swung up on the sidewalk, turned around, and it turned the woman over. It knocked the thing that carried her over. It knocked me under that carriage so I broke my little finger. Didn't hurt much. The medical student and the baby were thrown a couple of feet. It

Market day in Kazimierz-on-the-Vistola River, Kuzmir (Yiddish name), 1920.
(Photo by Alte Kacyzne, courtesy of Schocken Books)

Information desk of the Hebrew Immigrant Association in Warsaw office,
1921. (Photo by Alte Kacyzne, courtesy of Schocken Books)

Author's maternal great-grandparents taken in Bialystok, Russia.

Below: Molly Halperin and son Julius, author's grandmother and uncle, taken around 1902 in Russia, perhaps in the town of Grodno.

At right, Author's grandfather, Max Halperin, and brother, in Chicago, around 1915.

*Below left:* Mr. and Mrs. Israel Hersh Berkovitz, author's paternal grandparents.

*Below right:* Author's mother, Shirley Halperin Berkow, at age six, in 1922. Photo taken in front of her home at 1302 Morgan Street, just off Maxwell Street. At left is her brother Al. At right, her brother Jerry.

Storefront tobacco factory in Maxwell Street area, about 1905–6. (Chicago Historical Society)

Area around Twelfth Street and Jefferson Street, about 1906. (Chicago Historical Society)

Maxwell Street market scenes, about 1906. (Chicago Historical Society)

Sunday market, Maxwell Street, 1917. (Chicago Historical Society)

Glickman Building, 936–40 West Fourteenth Street (the northwest corner),
1965.

didn't hurt the baby any. And the patient improved under this treatment. She hadn't been speaking or anything. Then she wanted to know where she was and what was going on. And I had the hemorrhage controlled by then. All the pinnings of the ambulance were hanging down, dragging on the street. I said to the driver, 'We've got to get her to the hospital. Will the thing run?' He said it would. So we went to the Lying-In with all those things scraping along, and I felt more comfortable because I thought the ambulance couldn't possibly skid with all those things on the ice. We got her to the hospital. Fortunately, the student's blood matched hers, and he was willing to give it to her. We got her transfused and she got along fine.

"And then once I had a breech baby. Feet first. These people lived under eaves, where the whole roof slanted down, and if you stood up any place other than in the middle, you'd knock your head off. The woman was all ready to deliver. One of the baby's legs was already sticking out. The woman had a very bad pelvis; she was forty-one years old, and I knew I couldn't get that baby's head out. I wanted a live baby, of course, and a live mother. So I thought, well, you know, De Lee always said, 'If you don't know what to do, Tucker, you go off by yourself and don't listen to anything anybody says, and make up a plan.' He said the best place to go is the bathroom because nobody can get at you. So I thought of De Lee and I went to the bathroom, and I sat down on the toilet and I thought. All right, I had to stop labor and get her to the hospital. If I let her labor, she'd push the baby out, and it'd get strung up with the head. I had to get the leg back in. I didn't want it dangling all outside and getting contaminated. So I cleaned it up, put the woman to sleep with ether, and then I sewed the baby back into her womb. I had to get her to the hospital. And at this time, I couldn't afford an ambulance. It cost thirty-five dollars or forty-five dollars. I called a paddy wagon. We drove down Michigan Boulevard and I was pouring ether like mad at one end. Because if I didn't keep her labor pains relieved, she'd rupture her uterus and die. When I got her over there, the doctor believed that the baby couldn't be saved and wasn't going to try to do the operation. I said, 'You can't do that to me. I've been working this case for hours now.' I argued and argued. So I finally got discouraged and just sat down and wept. Once in a while that works. And it worked with him. He said, 'All right.' You had to take the woman's uterus out because of danger of infection. But she lived, she got along fine, the baby lived. That case gave me great satisfaction.

"When you deliver in homes, you develop your ingenuity. You don't show your needles. It scares people. And you can make a delivery room in the most shabby surroundings. You can use an ironing board with all your instruments on it, and you use a lot of newspapers. You just don't touch anything. You use sterile gloves. But even with the dogs and the cats and the animals swishing about and the flies all around, very rarely were you in trouble with an infection. It just seems as if people in their own homes are probably immune to the kind of bacteria that they're living in, and they don't have pathological bacteria like you have in the hospital, like Staphylococcus and Strep and this kind of thing.

"I liked living down there. You know how the street is on Sunday now, well it used to be that way every day and all night long. I'd walk along the street and talk with the people and shop. My silver *menorah* came off Maxwell Street and so did my Russian samovar. The only thing, I get a little insulted when these prostitutes would come out and proposition whoever I was with. I got slightly jarred up. I mean, who does she think she is? I identified with Maxwell Street, certainly. I think it's because of my background probably that I fitted in so well.

"My father made his money practicing medicine without a license. He was an illegal doctor. The first nine years of my life, the sheriff was about one step behind us."

Dr. Tucker's father had come to America from a Welsh mining town. The men in his family were coal miners. He refused to go into the mines. He worked in the mines one day and quit. He apprenticed himself to a Jewish grocer in nearby Cardin. Then an aunt in America sent $350 for the boy to come to America. But his father, a heavy drinker, consumed the money on alcohol. In four years, working and stealing what he could, Dr. Tucker's father finally saved enough to come to America. He came over at seventeen, worked in a grocery store in Carbondale, Pennsylvania, and at twenty-three owned the store. He had bad eyes, but nobody there could fit him for the glasses he needed. He enrolled in a correspondence course in optometry, graduated, made himself glasses, then found a book called *Medical Specialties,* and he "settled" on the removal of cancer spots with a "cancer paste" as his area of medical—and, he hoped—financial expertise.

"You put the paste on the cancer," said Dr. Tucker, "and it ate it out. It truly did if you made the correct diagnosis and got it before the cancer was too big. My father was shrewd. He never got in trouble with a patient. But he got in a lot of trouble with the medical profession. His knowledge of medicine was strictly limited, and he wouldn't have been able to pass any of those tests. We went prowling up around Maine, along the Canadian border, so he could get out of the States fast if he got into trouble. And there was a lawsuit against him for going into bankruptcy. I don't know what happened with that. I'm sure he didn't abscond with funds. At least my mother said he didn't. But he did steal that money to get over here from Wales. When I got to be about six, old enough to remember, he changed our name, and told me if I forgot I was Beatrice Harris, he'd end up in jail. I didn't want that to happen. I adored my father. And he loved me, thought I was perfect. I always thought, Isn't he sorry I wasn't a boy? But no, he thought I'd make just as good a doctor as anybody. A damn sight better than the ones he knew. I always thought I'd be a doctor. My father kept talking about it all the time. We had a team of horses and a sleigh up here in the north and I'd go with him all over. Never got caught. He made a lot of money. I went to school. He gave me a very fine medical education, a big allowance, everything I wanted. I did quit working at my studies a couple of times when I got mad at him about what he was doing. But then he settled down, and he had the biggest optometry practice in Southern Illinois. That was legal.

"I liked him. I admired him. He wasn't good for my mother because he had an illegitimate child. He'd be gone on the road for months. And he gambled like a fish. My mother was really a born lady, although she came off a truck farm. She was fastidious and intelligent and I'm sure she wasn't happy about the way he made his living; although when I got old enough to be embarrassed about it, she told me she didn't think it was any of my affair. I was very unhappy. We didn't have a telephone because he was afraid somebody'd trace him. I had to work at being normal. I felt degraded by this then.

"Once I remember my mother getting mad at him too. My father sent my mother two beautiful hats with birds of paradise and egret feathers on them. He sent me three diamond rings. He'd been up in Canada, he wrote, and he'd gotten a farm in trade for taking a cancer off of a woman's breast, and all this stuff came down. I don't know whether my mother thought he was having an affair with a milliner, but she sent those hats back so fast that it made my head swim. And I thought, I hope she doesn't take my diamond rings. She didn't. I was sixteen or seventeen at the time.

"I was never married. I was dedicated to my work. And I never found anybody I loved; but I also wonder if I didn't want to subject myself to the suffering that I know my mother went through. And after my father, I was hungry for respectability, for status.

"And yet I think I identified with my father, with some of his vices, and with a lot of his personality. I wasn't at all like my mother. But I thought if I ever wrote a book I'd dedicate it to my mother, one of God's chosen people. She probably did more for me through discipline and keeping me on a level key than my father did. But my father was, you know, stimulating and of course girls do like this. I think this is pretty normal. But my father was a lovable, vital, wicked man."

At age seventy-five, Dr. Tucker had retired from making home deliveries. "I'm no longer adequate physically, and I think my skills are slipping," she said. An operation is often two hours long, and she says she can't muster the strength for it anymore.

She retired from the Maternity Center in 1973 because the influx of students diminished. More and more universities began broader obstetrical programs. Without residents, the Maternity Center could not continue its program. Today there is only a little prenatal care done there along with some administrative work. It is an old, dark, and gloomy place. It is remindful of the hotel room where Dr. De Lee lived his last days. In 1941, at age seventy-one, he had had a gall bladder operation. Dr. Tucker remembers visiting him. The shades were drawn.

"I would come down and visit him, but he would say, 'I don't know if I'll have time to see you.' Then when I got there he'd talk for hours. They weren't some of the nicest talks we'd ever had. He had got his stocks in order and made out his will and the Center was going nicely and he really had his life all straightened out. And it looked like he was going to die. And then the operation was successful and he recovered. He said, 'I was very disappointed. I was all set to die and now I've got to live a little longer.' I thought he was only half joking. Anyway, he died a year later."

# KING LEVINSKY

Shortly before the remarkable bout on August 8, 1935, between the great heavyweight boxer Joe Louis and Maxwell Street's King Levinsky, an unusual kind of tension was building in the King's dressing room. According to Barney Nagler, author of the Louis biography, *The Brown Bomber,* the fight promoter feared that the trembling Levinsky might bolt the dressing room at Comiskey Park and run home to Maxwell Street (about three miles north), where his family had been long-time fish peddlers.

The promoter hurried to the boxing officials and said, "We'd better start the fight now."

An official said, "But we have a half hour to go."

"Well, but it might start raining," replied the promoter, looking up into the balmy sky.

The King went down and out in the first round. Some ringsiders say that the King wasn't really knocked out; what happened was he fainted. Still others, thinking back, wonder if he hadn't been weakened by pain in his feet. Legend has it that the King once complained to his trainer that his feet were killing him. The trainer duly checked and found that the King had put the right shoe on the left foot and the left shoe on the right foot. Old-timers are in conflict as to whether that took place at the Louis bout, a Max Baer bout, or the Jack Dempsey exhibition bout. Others say the King would complain about his tootsies while sitting in a restaurant, as well. For the record, this is the full, unexpurgated, objective, definitive and running account of the Louis encounter as reported in the Chicago *Tribune* the following day:

First round (the writer took the liberty of assuming there would be others): The boy (referring to the black man, Louis) shuffled forward carefully. Levinsky crouched protecting his jaw. Louis jabbed lightly to the body. Levinsky slowly retreated. Louis hammered home lefts and rights to the chin, and Levinsky went down for the count of 2. King backed up. Levinsky missed with a wild right, and Louis followed in and hammered a right . . . a hard right to the body. In a half-clinch, Louis pumped both hands to the King's stomach. The King still retreated.

The King took a hard right to the side of the head and went down for the 5 count. Louis came in with a left and a right and Levinsky went to the floor again for a 5 count. Again, Louis sent home a right, a hard right to Levinsky's stomach, knocking him down for a 4 count. The King sat on the ropes during that period. Referee McGarrity stepped between the men, and Louis was declared the winner. Time elapsed: 2 minutes, 21 seconds.

Forty years later, the Louis match remains pretty much the King's major claim to fame.* He is an independent, traveling tie salesman living in Miami Beach, Florida, and is as devoid of malice and a violent nature as when he was a pugilist. His sales technique is as unconventional as was his looping-right fighting style; he rarely used his left at all. He may with great good-nature wrap a tie around a prospective customer's neck and, pulling cross-handed, tell him "It fits good."

The King hustles his ties in the coffee shops and lobbies of selected hotels along the Beach. The Fountainbleau and the Diplomat are particularly fertile haunts for the King. Everybody knows the King. His name invariably draws a smile. And cigarettes are hidden when he comes around—"He'd smoke your whole pack while standing and talking to you," one hotel clerk said. Sometimes, a starchy assistant manager will shoo the King off the premises. But the King is indomitable and shall prevail. He simply hoofs it to another hotel. When the heat cools, he may return to the scene of his eviction.

You cannot miss the King. He is a six-footer and still husky, at age sixty-nine (in 1976), but now walks in a hulking manner: he drags his left leg because of a painful, pinched nerve. His hair is

---

* Red Smith, in his sports column for the May 21, 1976, New York *Times*, also recalled this: "The Kingfish was a fairly vincible heavyweight, but when he wound up and pitched his right hand from deep center field he could make the arena sway. . . ."

gray and sparse. He wears glasses that he continually props up because they frequently slip down his flattened nose.

On a particular spring day, he wore a baby-blue Banlon shirt that clung to and accentuated his ample belly, a jazzy white belt, nondescript gray-checked pants with cuffs that drooped around his black buckled shoes. He carried under his arm a battered gray tie box. He set it down on a small table in the coffee shop, right near the cash register. He greeted the regulars on the stools. "How's the action?" he asked. His voice sounded as creased as his rough, kindly face looked.

He opened his tie box, where colorful ties are held together in clumps by rubber bands. The most distinguishing aspects of the ties are the two labels on the back. One says "King Levinsky" and has a drawing of two boxing gloves to prove it; the other label reads "5th Ave cravat" and, the *pièce de résistance*, "WRINKLE-FREE." In the box are also old photographs preserved in a moldy plastic. The pictures show the King with Bobby Kennedy and with Frank Sinatra, and with Joe Louis. There is another, nearly a half-century old, which shows a posed, serious-visaged, gloved fistfighter with lustrous, wavy hair falling over his forehead. He has a thick hirsute chest.

"That's me," croaks the King. He pulled a cigarette from a friend's pack, stuck it between his teeth. He has partially broken off the filter and commences to puff with some frustration upon the cigarette.

He sells the ties—"For you, a deuce," he says. "For others, four bucks, or even a fin." He grabs you close and inflicts a hug, adds a loving little punch, and then wraps a tie around your neck. "Nice ties," he says. You buy. He says the most anyone ever paid for a tie was Sinatra, "a C note." Al Capone was second, at half the price, fifty dollars.

He earns enough to drive a big car, live in a comfortable though not lavish home with his third wife, a rather dour, rough-and-tumble lady who is a masseuse in a local hotel. ("No, I don't know where the King is and don't bother me," she said to one visitor.)

A question concerning the King is, What happened to the nearly half-million dollars he made in the ring as one of the top-flight heavyweight and lightheavyweight challengers in the early and mid-30s? "Bad managers," he whispers coarsely in your ear.

One of his managers was his sister Mrs. Lena Levy known as "Leapin' Lena," who was quite comfortable with the language of the docks. She was also strong and would carry by herself the barrels of herring that she and King and the rest of the Krakow family sold on the sidewalk and in their store on Maxwell Street just west of Halsted.

In the King's corner, Lena acidly and vociferously urged him on. One stratagem of hers has filtered down through history: The King signed to box a four-round exhibition with Jack Dempsey, on February 18, 1932. There were over twenty thousand people there to see if Dempsey, attempting a comeback, had anything left, and to see what the upstart Levinsky had. Yet it was an exhibition, and people don't usually take these things too seriously. Lena, though, figured that if her charge could wallop the ex-champ, it would be a great hot-foot to his young career.

The *Tribune* reported: "Dempsey's black whiskers covered his face. He scowled out at Levinsky as he had scowled out at Jess Willard and others. He came in low, his head weaving and bobbing, aiming at the left side of Levinsky's body. . . . But the old power was gone in his blows. . . . Dempsey took so many of the Kingfish's wallops in the first round that he came back to the corner wobbling on his ancient legs. He fought back in the second round and won that session. He took it on the chin, in the mid-section and other parts in the last two rounds. . . . The 14 newspapermen at ringside were asked to cast their votes. Eight gave the decision to Levinsky. Two for Dempsey, four called it a draw.

"Dempsey said afterward: 'Levinsky's a dangerous boy, but not one of his punches hurt me.'" It was enough for Dempsey, though. He figured if he could lose so decisively to King Levinsky, then the sun had surely set on his career. Dempsey never boxed professionally again.

Such untoward strategy was effective in getting Levinsky big bouts with Jack Sharkey and Primo Carnera, other top contenders and former champions—whom the King beat—as well as two bouts with Max Baer, who beat the King in two hard-fought decisions of ten rounds and twenty rounds. That was before Baer became heavyweight champion in June of 1934. At the end of the year, Lena arranged another "four-round exhibition" at Chicago Stadium, this one with Baer. She thought the King might ambush Baer, who ought to be taking the exhibition as just that—a light workout. Meanwhile, she plotted to instill murder in the gentle King's heart.

The King rushed Baer in the first round. Bair recoiled, with this result: "Max Baer last night plum forgot that he was appearing here in an exhibition with King Levinsky, and proceeded to knock out the Kingfish in 23 seconds of the second round," reported the *Tribune*. "It was the first time in the King's career that he was knocked out stiff. The King, upon awaking, danced over to Baer's corner and began to joke and tossed his arm around Baer's shoulders. Baer knotted his brow at this mad scene and proceeded to ignore the lug."

The King's boxing career began to decline. His fight with Louis nine months later resulted in the Illinois Boxing Commission turning down his next application for a fight. "The Commission's refusal," said the *Tribune,* "was due to a sorry display against Joe Louis, in which Levinsky received $30,000 from the $215,000 gross receipts." On January 19, 1938, the *Tribune* reported: " 'Kingfish Levinsky doesn't know how to wrestle,' referee Curly Fowler said tonight in disqualifying the Chicago ex-pugilist in Louisville. Fowler stopped the match between the Kingfish and Alonzo Wood of Pittsburgh after three minutes. The referee explained to matchmaker Haywood Allen, Sr., 'This man doesn't know how to defend himself. I can't let the match go on.' At that time, the Kingfish was sprawled on his back."

The King was caught in a crap game on June 29, 1941. He was one of eight men who were chased, but the lumbering 225-pound Kingfish was the only participant pinched. The judge asked if he was in the crap game. The King said no, that he was only a kibitzer. The judge believed.

(Crap games and various forms of games of chance were popular with Levinsky when growing up on Maxwell Street. He was often in crap games and, when a heavyweight contender, would

stop by even a marbles game to try his luck, always backing it up
with a generous cash wager.)

The King was inducted into the Army on July 7, 1942. Although he had bad teeth, flat feet, was overweight (now he was at
240) and illiterate, the Army said he was a fine specimen for
them.

The King's personal life was always a bit rocky, apparently. On
October 14, 1934, Chicagoans read in the morning paper that the
King was being sued for divorce from his estranged wife, "Rox-
anne the Fan Dancer," who called her husband, "an alleged
fighter" in her charges. The King was miffed only that when she
left "their abode" she took his prized Scotch terrier. "That dog
has personality just like me," the King was quoted. "I don't mind
losing my wife, but when she takes my dog, that's too much." The
King said he would not contest the suit.

The *Tribune* said: "Those who do not agree with King Levinsky that King Levinsky is a prizefighter were joined yesterday
by his wife. . . . Last week she sued her husband on charges that
he punched her and was unfaithful to her. In the new bill, the former fan dancer alleged that his sister and manager, Mrs. Lena
Levy, hated her because of an intense jealousy of Levinsky and
often twitted her on her ability as a dancer.

"On the third night after the couple's marriage in Crown Point,
Indiana, the bill alleges Mrs. Levy climbed in bed with her sister-
in-law, the plaintiff, and announced that 'From now on, you'll
sleep with me.' Thereafter, Mrs. Levy encouraged her brother to
go out with other women, the bill charges."

On September 7, 1944, the King was in the news with his second wife, Freda "Fritzie" Bay, twenty-seven, also a former
dancer. He filed a suit for divorce, saying that he was, in effect,
overmatched and beaten up. He charged that his new wife threw a
cup of coffee at him, struck him and pushed him out of their
apartment. When the case came before the judge, Fritzie complained now that the King had in fact also struck her. The judge
showed no mercy. "Were you the only person he ever licked?" he
asked.

"Levinsky waited anxiously in the corridor during the hearing,"
the *Tribune* reported, "and when his freshly divorced wife

emerged, he planted a resounding kiss on her lips. 'Come on, take me home,' she told him. And they walked away together."

Levinsky was born Harris Krakow in New York in 1907. His family (which would include four sisters and two brothers) moved to Chicago and Maxwell Street when he was two. Levinsky worked in the family fish store as a herringmonger, and performed such chores as lugging the barrels to filleting the fish. He attended the Garfield Public School but retired from formal education in the fourth grade. He had his share of street fights, and, being so big and strong, he gravitated to the ring, though it seemed the most incompatible occupation for his clownish nature.

His family, however, was known for its roughhousing. In the mid-30s, the King used some of his money to open a restaurant and bar on the corner of Halsted and Maxwell. It was a lovely place and for the opening Jack Dempsey showed up and gave the King a watch which he carries to this day. But that night, the family got into a squabble over some long-forgotten matter, and they tore the place apart.

In 1939, after his boxing, wrestling, and restaurant careers had collapsed, he went into the tie business. "I saw Swifty Morgan—a sharpie—selling ties. So I tried it, too," said the King.

Swifty Morgan was immortalized as the Lemon Drop Kid in a short story by Damon Runyon and in a movie of that name starring Bob Hope as "the Kid" in the early 1950s.

Levinsky observed with awe Swifty Morgan peddle his ties in Chicago, around the Loop area as well as around Maxwell Street. Swifty would put a tie around the neck of a well-heeled gent and then take off. A few days later he'd catch the man in a group and ask loudly where his money for the tie was. The man, to avoid embarrassment, would fork over several bills.

Swifty was a hustler of the most flagrant order, and with great dollops of courage. Once, legend has it, he took Al Capone for two grand.

Capone, while in a steambath, struck up a casual conversation with a man seated beside him. The man—the Lemon Drop Kid— talked such glowing financial talk about an impending deal in which Capone—if mum were the word—could make a quick killing, so to speak, that Capone was persuaded to loan the Kid two thousand dollars until later.

Later never came.

Capone sent two men to locate Lemon Drop and bring him back to Capone's home.

"Why did you pick on me?" asked the incredulous Capone.

"I didn't pick on you," replied Lemon Drop. "You picked on yourself."

Capone was supposedly so charmed that he turned and called to his wife, "Mae—set another plate for dinner, we've got a guest."

Another time, Swifty tried to sell a gold wrist watch to a certain famous gentleman he noticed in a restaurant. Swifty slipped uninvited into a seat beside the famous man, who did not know Swifty. "J. Edgar," said Swifty to Mr. Hoover of the FBI, "why don't you dump that rotten watch you're wearing and buy yourself a good one, which I happen to have right here."

Hoover looked over Swifty's watch and offered a hundred bucks. "Damn," said Swifty, "look at that watch. The insurance reward alone is worth more than that!"

His sense of the outrageous was his most compelling trait, even when he was dying at age ninety-two in a hospital. A friend entered his room for a visit and Swifty pointed to the fire extinguisher on the wall. "Open that bottle of Scotch and take a drink," said Swifty, barely audible, "and pour one for the nurse, too."

The King learned from Swifty some of these techniques, though he, of course, never quite carried them off with the velvety aplomb of his mentor. But he has given it a noble try, attesting to the gladiator he once was.

When people ask him today how it was to be in the same ring with Joe Louis, the King's craggy voice lowers as though he is about to share a deep confidence. "Rough," he says.

His memory, however, is not so terrific. He says he was knocked out in the second round, stretching the event to twice its factual length.

He was asked how business is. He shook his head. "Quiet," he related. "Nixon fucked it all up."

# BARNEY BALABAN

—Who is Barney Balaban? He was the president of Paramount Pictures. There was a Balaban "success mystique" within the industry. Paramount was, financially, the most solid of all the major film companies. Paramount stock was almost blue chip. . . . A fine, upright man, they said. A financial wizard; a magician at analyzing box office figures. There was a Paramount board of directors. Oh yes. But Paramount was Balaban, and Balaban was Paramount. [He was] money-wise, [but he was also] art-foolish.

> *Frank Capra*
> *THE NAME ABOVE THE TITLE:*
> *AN AUTOBIOGRAPHY*
> *1972*

———————◆———————

BYRAM, Connecticut. Barney Balaban . . . died today after a short illness at his home, 251 Byram Shore Road. He was 82 years old. . . . A member of the Balaban family that built the Chicago movie theater chain of Balaban & Katz. . . . He was called to straighten out Paramount's [sinking] finances in 1936. . . . Mr. Balaban was born on Chicago's West Side, a son of Israel

Balaban, a grocer, and his wife, Gussie
Mendebursky. They had both emigrated from
Russia. . . .

NEW YORK *TIMES*
*March 7, 1971*

---

Of Barney Balaban's six brothers and one sister, only Elmer
(born in 1903) and Harry (1909) are still alive. They share a
large office in the State-Lake Building in downtown Chicago, in
that building that housed one of the 125 theaters the Balaban and
Katz company (Sam Katz was a brother-in-law) once owned in
Chicago and other Midwestern cities. The surviving brothers own
three small theaters today, but their primary business interest is in
cable television.

Barney Balaban's son, Leonard, called "Red," is owner of
"Eddie Condon's," a highly regarded jazz nightclub in Manhattan.
He is also the bass player and leader of the house band. The band
is called, nostalgically, "Balaban and Cats."

---

To say that there was a tradition of show business in the family
may be stretching a point only a little. Barney Balaban's maternal
grandfather was, in fact, the fiddler at all Jewish weddings in their
shtetl near Odessa, Russia. His in-laws, or *machetunim,* scorned
him as a "loafer" and expressed their grief that he preferred
fiddling to his farming. His son, Barney Balaban's Uncle Luzor,
also was in the entertainment field, so to speak. He played fiddle,
like his father before him, but he added drums to his repertoire.
When he came to America, he played fiddle and drums in the
Jewish theater, on Jefferson Street, and earned what was considered good wages.

His wages were particularly good in comparison to Barney's father and mother, Israel and Gussie Balaban, who were always in
debt, a few times being forced to declare bankruptcy, and strug-
gling to feed their ever-increasing tribe.

They lived in the back three rooms of their grocery store, in a wood-shingle, two-story, pitched-roof building at 1137 South Jefferson Street, a block south of DeKoven Street, the site of Mrs. O'Leary's charred barn, and about two blocks north of Maxwell Street. On June 8, 1887, Gussie gave birth to Barney. He was the firstborn; nine more children followed in rather rapid succession.

Abe, later known as A.J., was born two years later; Ida came a year and a half later, then Max, John, Dave, Harry, and Elmer. There were two others. Anna died at age six months. Another boy died at birth, in tragic circumstances. A certain policeman, as family lore has it, came with a couple of henchmen to collect an overdue bill. As Gussie Balaban, swollen with child, tried to check the goods being taken away as quid pro quo for the bill, she was knocked down in the excitement by a heavy box of canned goods. It was believed that this accident caused the premature birth and death of the child.

Times were hard for Israel, or Izzy, Balaban. He owed money to among other his suppliers at the South Water Market, where he went with his creaky horse and old wagon to buy. Sometimes he took along his sons, who, in the cold, gray dawn, might fall asleep among the sacks of onions and crates of fruit. He owed because he in turn was owed.

The more he owed, the more he had to pay by cash. No credit. He fell into this sorry predicament like this: Many people coming over from Russia had no place to go and no money to buy food, so they opened accounts with the Balabans. The Balabans could not force them to pay. After all, they had been in just such a situation not too long before. Israel Balaban had been drafted into the czar's army, but escaped by swimming across a river, then whisked up his new wife, and together they stole across the borders, boarded a ship at a Baltic port in Germany, and sailed with a deep sigh of relief to the New World, and to Chicago, where home folk were.

So money was perilously tight. There was no end to the flow of children. Relatives and friends continuously came and lived with them off and on until they found their own place. It was the custom. Nobody was turned away.

The home was noisy, and it was smelly. The smell of the food from the store—the pickles and herrings and salamis—wafted into the back rooms. In summer, the front door of the store was left open at night to allow in the breeze to the stifling and over-crowded rooms.

Israel Balaban was short-tempered at times, bawling out customers, arguing with salesmen, whacking one of his meddlesome kids on the side of the head with the back of his hand. "Izzy," his wife exclaimed, cuddling one of the whimpering kids, "how can you be so mean?" But it was Pa who undressed the kids when they fell asleep at the table, and it was Pa who carried them off to bed. And it was Pa who understood quietly when his wife took one of the children in the buggy to the park ten blocks away to get fresh air.

The Balabans moved from Jefferson Street to a couple of places on Roosevelt Road to nearby Edgewood and Trumbull and Spaulding and Ogden avenues. Seeking, like their fellows in the area, just a little bit better way of life.

By the time Barney Balaban was twelve, he had quit school in the fifth grade to earn money to help the family. He first was a Western Union messenger boy, later stacked fruit in a wholesale market, and then became a clerk in a cold-storage company.

A.J., however, felt the music that unquestionably flowed in the veins of some of his ancestors. He enjoyed the Jewish theater, and he and Barney delighted in going to the Bijou and Academy nickelodeons on Halsted Street. By 1907, A.J. at age eighteen had developed aspirations. He had cards printed which read, "A. J. Balaban, Singer of Character Songs." He began to sing at weddings, Bar Mitzvahs, and in shows at some theaters. He also got a job singing at a little storefront theater on Kedzie and Roosevelt, called the Kedzie Theater. Ida accompanied him on the piano between films. He played in the evenings only, since he had to hold down a job crating woolens at Gutwillig's mill.

One evening, Gussie Balaban decided to go to the Kedzie to see what the nickelodeon was all about. She went with Barney. They were standing out in front of the theater, watching the people come up and drop nickels into a box. This was amazing to her. She turned to her son and said, "Barney, this is the business for us. It's a cash business. People pay *before* they get the goods. Nobody can owe us money."

Barney was somewhat surprised at her reaction. Nickelodeons and the newfangled moving pictures were in disrepute generally. The films were short one-reelers with silly situations, often nothing more than cop-chasing comedies. There was none of the depth, none of the soul-wrenching, none of the many-layered humor of the Yiddish theater.

Also, this particular theater was at once shabby and garish. It was merely an old store converted into a movie house—typical of the "store shows" of the day. A ticket window was built out on the sidewalk between the "Entrance Door" on the right and the "Exit Door" on the left. Over the window extended a huge gramophone horn which blasted out cacophonic tunes to attract the neighbors for blocks away. There was also a "circus spieler" who marched up and down the sidewalk waving his arms, shouting the name of the picture and the price of the show: "Right this way, half a dime, step right up!"

Inside the theater was an ordinary white sheet for a screen, 103 weak-jointed camp folding chairs, and a noisy projection machine. There was no ventilation, and the smell was particularly loathsome because of the bums and drunks who regularly slept in the theater.

Nonetheless, Gussie Balaban was mightily impressed. "You never have to worry about the fruit and vegetables spoiling! And you get the money on the spot! It's a great business," she insisted. She wanted to buy the Kedzie.

There was a family meeting. Abe and Ida laughed about approaching their *boss* with an offer to buy him out. But that's exactly what they finally decided should be done.

The entire wealth of the family was counted up. It came to about $350, including savings from the grocery store, savings from Barney's job and A.J.'s job, and the receipts from Max's newspapers. They were able to borrow ten dollars here, twenty dollars there, from relatives and friends, and soon had a total capital of $750.

The boss had been losing money and agreed to rent.

The Balabans decided the place had to be run like a theater and not a freak show. Immediately, they removed the gramophone and the outside spieler. It was a welcome refinement. Abe said, "The whole place looks better when it's quieter."

They turned their attention to the smell. The bums were shoveled out. At a junkyard, Barney paid forty dollars for an electric fan and motor so they could clear the air in the theater. However, the fan made such a racket that it drowned out the piano and the violin—a violinist had been hired at a dollar a night to add "class" —and so the fan was run only between pictures and musical selections.

The floor was raised at a cost of sixty dollars to give the customers a better view.

They showed one-reeler films: Society dramas like *The Blacksmith's Daughter*, Westerns like *His Last Cartridge*, comedies like *Nervy Jim and the Cop* or *Scratch My Back*, and thrillers like *The Yellow Peril*. They had illustrated song slides like "I'm Tying the Leaves So They Won't Come Down So Nelly Won't Go Away."

A.J. was still working at Gutwillig's woolen mill, laboring for ten dollars a week, but "thinking show business" and booking films on his lunch hour, running to the theater right from work to learn his songs and sweep out if "Pa's janitor was too drunk to do it." Israel Balaban carried his son's supper to him on a plate before the doors opened at seven o'clock.

The violinist, who was an assistant shipping clerk at Gutwillig's, worked with A.J. and had claimed to be a fine musician.

But the first night, there was trouble. The violinist was absorbed in watching *The King's Messenger*, a Biograph thriller advertised as "A Story of Love, Intrigue and Heroism." The denouement occurs when the hero dismounts his horse to assist a damsel in distress and is stabbed in the back by the villain who had hidden in the brush.

The shipping clerk-violinist watched this scene with his whole soul, while playing madly, "If the Man in the Moon Were a Coon, Coon, Coon." A.J. had to drag him away from the music stand in the middle of the show. He was furious when removed because he wanted to see the finish of the picture. He was eventually convinced to play music that fit the mood of the film.

Leonard Balaban recalls his father, Barney, telling the story.

"Apparently the guy also got a very terrible sound out of the instrument. It was scratchy. And not knowing the instrument too well, A.J. said, 'You're pressing down too hard on the strings.' He says, 'What do you mean telling me about my business? I'm an expert violin player.' So the next night he played, and the same thing happened. He said, 'I'm *not* pressing too hard. Just to prove it, my mother, my father, my cousin, my sister—they're all out there. And they also say I am not pressing too hard!'"

A.J. found it necessary to devote full time to running the theater. The family agreed, as long as Barney kept his steady twenty-five-dollar-a-week job. Barney and Max took turns at the box office and the door, and Ida played the piano for the pictures and the songs.

The first month's business was terrible because of the traditional January blizzards and trouble with the electricity. The light often went out unexpectedly. It was heartbreaking to return the nickels to the audience of eight or ten, who seemed to rattle around among the camp chairs.

Receipts for the first week were $88.75. Soon, the receipts rose to around two hundred a week. This was relatively unbounded wealth. The Balabans were the envy of their competitors, who were openly looking for "locations" on their street. It worried A.J. "We must build a bigger place," he said. "Or somebody will come and take our business away."

Owners of butchershops and delicatessen stores were bragging about the "theater" offers they had or what they expected to get for their places. News of half-finished deals buzzed around, and every day a new rumor was spread about "a big show coming in." There was one empty lot a block away on Sawyer and Twelfth. The Balabans were able to borrow enough money to buy the property and to build the Circle Theater for $25,000. It was opened in September 1909, one year and nine months from the time the Balabans had purchased the Kedzie Theater. The Circle was considered the finest Chicago had ever seen in the way of motion-picture houses.

"We knew by then [beginning of 1909]," said Barney later, "that moving pictures were more than just a novelty." Even during their first few months at the Kedzie the Balabans could see a great improvement in pictures. One-reel films, lasting ten minutes, supplanted the two- or three-minute comedies. The first one-reeler they played was entitled *The Merry Widow*. It was the cue for what was to follow.

They thought that the Circle was the ultimate in movie houses. They installed a pipe organ, hired a four-piece orchestra, and before the theater was half-finished decided to add a balcony, increasing the seating capacity from seven hundred to one thousand. There was also a good duct-ventilation system.

The Circle opened to play vaudeville for ten cents and fifteen cents admission. The best and most expensive acts were sought, despite the pressing debts. Many times they were asked on Monday how much profit was expected by the next Sunday, and from that guess, Barney would lay out a scheme to pay this creditor five dollars, that one ten dollars, and thus everyone could be paid something.

A.J. struggled to get good acts from the Western Vaudeville office downtown. It was there he met, according to A.J., "the energetic, red-haired mother of the Four Marx Brothers, Minnie Palmer. She sympathized with my ambitions and struggles to 'put over' the Circle because of her similar efforts for her talented young sons. . . . Their famous act, 'Fun in High Skul' was a tremendous favorite with our Circle patrons."

| | |
|---|---|
| GROUCHO: | Why were you late? |
| HARPO: | My mother lost the lid off the stove, and I had to sit on it to keep the smoke in. |
| GROUCHO: | If you had ten apples and you wanted to divide them among six people, what would you do? |
| GUMMO: | Make applesauce. |
| GROUCHO: | What is the shape of the world? |
| HARPO: | I don't know. |
| GROUCHO: | Well, what shape are my cufflinks? |
| HARPO: | Square. |
| GROUCHO: | Not my weekday cufflinks, the ones I wear on Sundays. |
| HARPO: | Oh, round. |
| GROUCHO: | All right, what is the shape of the world? |

HARPO:       Square on weekdays, round on Sundays.
GROUCHO:     What are the principal parts of a cat?
GUMMO:       Eyes, ears, neck, tail, feet, etc.
GROUCHO:     You've forgotten the most important. What does a cat have that you don't have?
GUMMO:       Kittens.*

Sophie Tucker was already a recognized star, playing the American Music Hall for $150. A.J. pursued her for a year and finally persuaded her to play the ten- and fifteen-cent house for $250. She was a smash there. And she may never have known that her first appearance at the Circle rocked the social structure of the West Side. The young ladies in their teens, according to A.J., were breathless as they told about her performance. "Oh, my face was so red when Sophie Tucker sang 'All Alone' into a telephone handed to her on the stage from the wings! Don't you think it was *suggestive?*"†

Meanwhile, the Balaban brothers would watch the audience from a hole in the wall they had made. A.J. said, "I felt responsible for making these people happy and gay, to release them even for a moment from the depression of their drab homes and usually burdened lives.

"It was wonderful to make people live in a fairyland, to make them forget their troubles."

Not all of the audience was trouble-free at the theater. Young Harry Balaban remembers one day when he and friends carried on in the balcony and the manager, a family friend, came up and said, "Harry, out!"

The Balabans also provided unique innovations, such as a "Baby Carriage Service," to make mothers feel welcome during the day. Sleeping babies in buggies with duplicate tags were left on the sidewalk. If a baby cried during the show, a slide would be flashed on the screen: "Mother, number 47, your baby is crying."

Pictures continued to improve, along with such stars as Pearl White, Ruth Roland, Francis X. Bushman, and the cowboy star

---

* Joe Adamson, *Groucho, Harpo, Chico and Sometimes Zeppo: A Celebration of the Marx Brothers* (New York: Simon & Schuster, 1973), p. 49.
† Carrie Balaban, *Continuous Performance: The Story of A. J. Balaban* (New York: A. J. Balaban Foundation, 1964), p. 34.

G. M. Anderson, known as Broncho Billy, from the local studio, Essanay. The first five-reel picture was, as Barney remembered, Sarah Bernhardt in *Queen Elizabeth,* around 1912. Soon, there were full-length pictures with a running time of fifty minutes, and motion pictures were becoming dignified.

There remains a family portrait of the Balabans taken at Passover, 1913, and is indicative of their growing affluence. They were now living in a relatively comfortable apartment on Douglas Boulevard. The family of ten is gathered before dinner at one end of a table with place settings, candles and a squat decanter of wine. The white linen tablecloth has deep folds along with wrinkles which shows it is brand new. Five lights on chains hang from a tilty support above the middle of the table. Behind the family is a wood-and-windowed cabinet with dishware, and floral-patterned wallpaper. The father and the boys are dressed in suits with vests, except for the youngest, Elmer. He stands in shirt sleeves with arm drapped on his mother's shoulder, her hand on his knee. Three of the boys, including Barney, wear bow ties. Both Gussie and her daughter wear V-necked dresses but with material demurely covering the chest. All but two of the Balabans seem to be taking the moment with cheerful assimilation. Elmer, the four-year-old, is serenely curious. The father, mustachioed and (like Barney) with high forehead, oval face, small, close eyes, goodly nose, sits with rigid collar and rigid back, wary of this New World apparatus before him. He sits with his strongly veined right hand in his lap, in a fist.

The Balabans began to purchase other small theaters. In 1914, Barney gave up his job as chief clerk of the Western Cold Storage Company to devote full time to the theater business.

By now, too, the grocery store had been closed. Gussie Balaban was put in charge of purchasing for the family. She bought clothes and new beds and chairs to furnish bedrooms and the parlor in the new steam-heated apartment she had found for the family. She bought luxuries, including furs and jewelry. Israel Balaban carried films and did some odd jobs, but mostly now was "retired" to become a full-time member of the synagogue.

The city was growing westward, and the Balaban brothers understood the need to expand. They realized that the Circle, as stupendous as they thought it was, was not enough to meet current needs. In 1915, they began construction of the Central Park Theater, considered the first "deluxe" theater in America. It would cost about $275,000 to build. They raised the money with the help of such financiers as Julius Rosenwald and John Hertz.

The Central Park seated two thousand. There was a mezzanine and a "horseshoe balcony." It was intended to give the audience the feeling of being part of a stage set. Added to the usual center stage, there were side stages, decorated like tiny gardens with green and marble statuary. The colored stage lighting was extended to take in the whole house. The gently changing colors traveled from wall to ceiling melting from soft rose to blue to lavender and yellow, as they touched the velour seats, chandelier crystals, and the extravagantly painted murals.

It was used as a model in various parts of the country, including the Paramount Theater in New York.

The stage show was also a new development by A.J. It was a production not strictly vaudeville. It was a production of music and singing and dancing—the same type of production that would later be presented at Radio City.

Perhaps the most interesting aspect of the Central Park, and the most revolutionary in the theater business, was the air-cooling system.

The purpose of the first air-conditioning equipment was to try to keep from losing a lot of money in the summertime when it was too hot to go to theaters. The Balabans hoped that they could just break even at least in the summertime. As a matter of fact, the whole thing became reversed. People went there to cool off. So the summer business was as good or better than the winter business.

The idea came about because Barney was looking for a way to make it a year-round business. Working in cold storage, he was aware of when cooling could be accomplished. It was done with ice. They chilled the water with ice and they ran it through a great big duct and it cooled the air as it came through. That was probably the first air conditioning.

When the Central Park was a year old, the Balabans opened the Riviera Theater on the North Side. It outstripped even the Central Park. It held thirty-two hundred seats. The lobby was modeled after the lush architecture of the royal chapel of Versailles. Fountains, statues, carpets, oriental paintings, mirrors, chandeliers. One of the most spectacular innovations had to do with the ushers. A West Point graduate trained them. They wore white gloves, red uniforms, yellow epaulets. "And when a new shift came on," says Harry Balaban, "that group of ushers marched to their stations. They didn't just mosey up. They marched."

The opulent Tivoli was built on the South Side, seating four thousand. Mobs clamored to get in to see it. It was followed by the Chicago Theater in the Loop: five thousand seats. Twin organs were played in the lobby to entertain people while they waited to go into the theater.

Paramount Pictures Corporation, observing the huge success of Balaban and Katz, grew interested in purchasing the burgeoning empire of theaters, which had grown to over a hundred. B and K eventually sold two thirds of the stock to Paramount for $13 million. The Balabans believed that they would gain financial freedom for the rest of their lives. They continued on, however, in executive capacities with Paramount. A.J. found little satisfaction, though, in his job, providing shows for the chain of fifteen hundred theaters Paramount owned. Working in an office with booking sheets, production managers, and public relations men was deadly for him. He wanted the touch of the audience, the involvement with ushers, musicians and stagehands.

Care of family finances was gradually left almost entirely to Barney. All profit could no longer go into brick and mortar, into larger theaters and larger stages. They began to invest in real estate.

The general idea of business is that somebody builds up a surplus of earnings. There wasn't any surplus for many years because a large family had to live out of one little business, and as this family grew up and expanded, their needs and demands grew in proportion. A few years after B and K came into existence, they hunted up all of Pa's old creditors and paid off the bankruptcy debts. Some of the old wholesale grocers had retired or gone broke in the meantime, and the money was doubly welcome.

In 1931, A.J. and his family moved to Geneva, Switzerland, to escape the bogey of "Money, Money, Money." What under the sun was money? he asked. It wasn't security, it wasn't contentment, it wasn't satisfaction. He said, "In Geneva, I could see, mentally, my pattern in comparison to the thrifty, contented Swiss family life, so peaceful and beautiful, unburdened by artificiality and extravagance. I used to say to my wife, 'This simple living reminds me of my childhood when our lives were so genuine and uncomplicated.' "

In 1931, A.J. sold all his stock in Paramount, at a time when it was a quarter of its former value. He said he had enough to live on for the rest of his life. He retired but later unretired and returned to manage the Roxy Theater in New York.

By 1936, B and K was the only Paramount subsidiary that did not wobble financially. Big companies were having a bad time of it, especially the big theaters that charged more for tickets (usually seventy-five cents) than the smaller neighborhood shows (charging ten or fifteen cents). But B and K was, apparently, the best run of all of Paramount theaters. Barney Balaban was president of B and K.

In New York, Adoph Zukor was stepping down at Paramount, now on the verge of bankruptcy. A turnover at the top was demanded.

This is the story according to how Leonard Balaban recalls his father telling it to him:

"Zukor and my father had become very close friends. Zukor now wanted my father to become president of the company in New York. Zukor would remain as chairman of the board in Hollywood.

"Meanwhile, Joseph P. Kennedy, the father of JFK, who had been in the motion-picture business, had a desire to own the company. He got himself hired as a financial consultant. Kennedy's idea was to show up at this membership meeting at which Zukor was stepping down, bring his report in, in person, read it in person, recommend that all directors step down, and the following directors who were friends of Kennedy's be appointed in their place. Hence, he would take over the company.

"Well, Zukor got wind of this. So when Kennedy came to the meeting, they met him at the door, paid him for his report, said thank you, and sent him home. And my father eventually got the gig.

"I can remember, too, this was in '36, I was in Chicago and Dinah Stein, a Jewish woman with a strong Russian accent, came rushing into our home yelling, 'Barney is president, Barney is president.' I thought my father was President of the United States for a while there until I found out it was Paramount Pictures. At the age of six, it really didn't matter that much."

ELMER BALABAN: "Just before Barney came to New York, Paramount was doing everything it could to stay afloat. It sold some of its big, white elephant theaters across the country. And at the time, Paramount owned about half of CBS, which wasn't what it is now. You know, they had good radio stations, and it was a radio network. But Paramount sold it in order to keep the operation going. The company was losing a million dollars a week, or something like that. They sold their part of CBS for $5 million to keep going a few minutes longer. It was probably one of the great financial boo-boos of all time."

As president of Paramount, Barney consolidated various overlapping departments and cut down home-office expenses by some $800,000 a year. His company was the first of the major film studios to wipe out its B-picture department.

Barney, earlier on, had the reputation for financial wizardry. It was he who worked out the operating system of the first Kedzie theater, cutting down the overhead, building up the entertainment, and pressing the younger brothers into service.

At that time, the receipts soared from ten dollars a night to twenty-five dollars a night. All his life he kept the first ledgers: Rent twenty-five dollars a week, light bill eight dollars. He paid the light bill, so he made sure the lights were turned off. The reputation for turning off lights followed him all his life.

He would laugh that the main theater of the Paramount chain, Paramount Theater in New York, was in 1940 paying ten thousand dollars a week for one feature. He remembered paying twenty-four dollars a week for films at the Kedzie.

And while once he handled the books for a movie business that grossed a couple thousand dollars a year, he now headed a company that grossed over $100 million a year. "He was always a great one for cleaning out the house, throwing away, and not accumulating things," said his son, Red Balaban. "I think he ran

Paramount Pictures pretty much that way—tight. He paid strict attention to detail around the house. If my mother bought something—furniture, artwork, whatever—he'd say, 'What is this bill? We're paying too much for this.' I don't think he had an artistic bent. All he wanted was the figures."

And his marshaling of the figures turned Paramount into a highly successful company again. Balaban soon saw fit to "explode his shocker," as Frank Capra termed it, "one of the slightly more than extraordinary edicts in theatrical history." To wit:

"Based on the industry axiom that a film breaks even when its take reaches twice its cost, Balaban declared that his 'figures'— which never lied—predicted that NO FUTURE BOX OFFICE HIT, NO MATTER HOW GREAT OR HOW COSTLY, COULD EVER AGAIN TAKE IN MORE THAN THREE MILLION DOLLARS! Therefore, THE PRODUCTION COST OF OUR TOP FILMS MUST NOT EXCEED ONE AND A HALF MILLION IF WE ARE TO SURVIVE!"

Capra, the esteemed director of such hits as *It's a Wonderful Life, State of the Union,* and *It Happened One Night,* said that the other company presidents shouted "Amen" and were grateful that Balaban could blame company deficits on "shrinking markets rather than on shrinking visions."

"I am not blaming Balaban for starting Hollywood's grand downward glide," said Capra, "for he was a real-estate man hostage to real-estate logic." Capra said that he *could* blame himself for not taking independent action and breaking away when he worked for Balaban at Paramount.

The top Paramount men in Hollywood could make financial decisions *only* if it dealt with sums of three thousand dollars or less. Capra recalled: "If an actor, truck, or an office remodeling cost one dollar *more* than three thousand dollars, New York—that is, Balaban—had to approve the expenditure in writing. From three thousand miles away, Barney dictated all policy decisions: stories, budgets, schedules; and all personnel decisions: writers, actors, directors, cameramen, film editors, musicians, etc. Thus a 'figure' man, who spent most of his time receiving, digesting, and analyzing the daily box office returns from every theater in the world, based and made Paramount's creative decisions on 'what the box-office figures tell me.'

"And so, because I could not agree to make them for Balaban's limit of one and a half million dollars, Paramount turned thumbs down on *Roman Holiday, Friendly Persuasion, Woman of Distinction* and *Westward the Women,* among others."‡ Eventually, though, Balaban's Law had to be amended, and costs for making movies escalated. By the mid-'60s, Balaban was reluctantly investing $17 million to $20 million for *Paint Your Wagon, Catch-22,* and *On a Clear Day You Can See Forever.*

Balaban also had firm opinions on what types of movies ought to be made. Eugene Zukor, son of Adolph Zukor, and himself a Paramount executive in Hollywood, remembers an instance at a meeting when Balaban vetoed a picture. The movie was *The Lost Weekend,* dealing with the problems of an alcoholic.

Balaban said he did not like the subject. "He felt that movies were entertainment, and he didn't think that movie was entertainment," said Zukor. "Others said, 'But, Barney, you have to go with the times and with the wishes of the public. The public wants to know things. They can't always be entertained. They want to be informed.' 'Well,' Barney said, 'I only vetoed it out of not being familiar with how pictures are made or what the content should be. Under those circumstances, go ahead with it. But if it was up to me, I would burn the negatives.'"

The movie was a great hit, and Barney admitted his mistake. In later years, Balaban would be most enthusiastic about two films in particular.

"He was very big on *Gulliver's Travels,* Paramount's answer to *Snow White,*" said Leonard Balaban. "But it never made it the way *Snow White* did. My father was also very big on *The Ten Commandments,* naturally, since he was so religious. It was a Paramount picture, and one of the few movies I ever walked out on. It was just too long. But he loved it."

Barney remained closely aligned to the Jewish community. "I guess he was closer to my parents than any of us, being the oldest son," said Harry Balaban. "Barney more or less took charge of the family. At a very early age. He didn't want to bother my mother and father with any problems. They had worked terribly hard, going to the South Water Market in hot weather and in bitter, bitter cold weather. Rainy weather. On a rickety old wagon

‡ Frank Capra, *The Name Above the Title: An Autobiography* (New York: Bantam Books, 1972), pp. 442–47.

pulled by a horse. Trying to make a living for everybody. My father was very religious his whole life and became president of the synagogue and kept the position for twenty years. He was very proud of that."

"My father was very involved with the temple, with Judaism," said Leonard Balaban. "He made major charitable contributions, and especially to the Westchester Jewish Center.

"He was very corney, looking back on it, in raising a kid. He had no idea. He didn't get married until he was forty-two years old. I guess he was too busy with business to settle down. Well, I think you share your philosophies by example more than by lecture, although he did lecture me quite sternly as a kid, I forget on what—on being good, mostly. Corny stuff.

"I can remember one Yom Kippur, we were walking in to the temple and I said, 'I wonder what's going to happen in the Notre Dame-Georgia Tech game today.' He said, 'Don't you dare think of anything like that on a High Holy Day like today.'

"But he could be ecumenical, too. One time my brother was making fun of Spiro Skouras, a Greek and the president of 20th Century Fox. My brother called him the High Priest, and the Grand Mufti. My father tore into my brother, verbally, that you don't make fun of other people's beliefs.

"I went through the motions of being religious as long as he was alive because it meant a lot to him. We had our kids Bar Mitzvahed and everything, but once he died, that was it."

In numerous ways, Barney Balaban kept close to his roots. For several years after taking the presidency of Paramount in New York, he retained a home in Chicago, in case he planned to move back. He held tight to his religion and to the necessity for frugality he learned as an impoverished youth.

"My parents were not wasteful people," said Harry Balaban. "They were always aware of money. They didn't throw it around. My father—I used to have to go buy him a hat for Pesach! You know, everybody used to wear new clothes on the Passover holidays. He said, 'Oh, I'll wear my old hat.' Fine. Then I would take him down and I'd buy him a hat and a suit of clothes. If the suit was fifty-five dollars, I'd tell the salesman to tell him it was thirty dollars.

"If you put something on his plate, he finished everything on it. But the one thing he wouldn't eat, and it was never served in our home, was bananas. When my parents came over on the boat from Europe, all that they had to eat for a few weeks were bananas. From then on, they hated the sight of bananas.

"My mother liked nice clothes, some jewelry. Rings and earrings. My parents and my brothers, Elmer and Dave, and I moved into a luxury apartment on Roscoe and Lake Shore Drive. A lot of wealthy Chicagoans like the Armours lived there. It was a tenroom apartment. The living room had paneled walls. There was a crystal chandelier, expensive furnishings, a walk-in refrigerator. And we had a Japanese butler. A world apart from our four rooms for ten people behind the old grocery store.

"But my mother still went to the West Side to shop for groceries and so forth in the Kosher markets. She went out in a chauffeurdriven car, and she wouldn't let the chauffeur park the car in front of the grocery store. She didn't want to make the people feel bad who were selling the groceries."

Barney did not forget where he came from either. He once said, "Once when my daughter brought some friends home from college —we had about eighteen rooms—she came to me and said, 'Daddy, we ought to move. There just aren't enough bedrooms here.'" And he smiled, he said, and recalled to her the crowded back rooms of the grocery store where he grew up.

Barney Balaban collected many of the original American documents, like a copy of the Bill of Rights, and gave them to the Library of Congress. He gave Lincoln's handwritten draft of his first proposal to abolish slavery to a church in Washington that Lincoln used to attend. Balaban presented the gift in the presence of President and Mrs. Dwight Eisenhower.

"I want people to see them and to understand how this country was formed, what sacrifices it took, and how everyone had a part in it," Barney once said. Balaban was also a prime mover in launching the tour of the famed Freedom Train in 1946 and a leader in the American Heritage Foundation.

"I can remember as a kid that I rarely saw my brothers, A.J. and Barney," said Elmer Balaban. "They were always working. They'd get up before me, and they'd get home after I was in bed.

My father could never understand them. He never participated in the growth of the theaters. He really resented the whole thing. What did they need it for, you know? They had enough, he thought. And yet they kept driving as Americans often do and, you know, he just really didn't appreciate it at all.

"But Barney. He knew nothing but work all his life. He never took a vacation hardly. There's a story that he was going on a cruise on a yacht but had a phone installed at dockside and never left it for three weeks. That was his vacation.

"And I know his wife lived for several months of the year in Paris. She didn't see him that much, I don't think. He was a good man, but always busy. He watched films seven days a week, every week of the year, and was always pouring over the books."

The dividends for this determination and energy were, certainly, enormous, both in money and in prestige.

Barney Balaban visited Pope Pius in 1945, as part of a motion-picture delegation seeking ways to help with films in solving the problems of the postwar world. Barney Balaban was several times a guest at the White House. He knew all the Presidents from Roosevelt to Nixon, but was closest to Eisenhower and Johnson. When President Eisenhower in 1957 made an appeal to American Jewish leaders to try to win Israeli withdrawal from disputed Mideast areas, he called in Barney Balaban and five others to discuss it with Secretary of State John Foster Dulles.

"Politically, he was a big FDR man," said Leonard Balaban. "He voted for Truman in '48 and Eisenhower in '52, and then he became a Nixon fan. I don't think he would have stayed that way if he had lived long enough to know about Watergate. But I understand his feeling toward Nixon, in a sense. It went back to Joe McCarthy. He was friendly with McCarthy, though he never liked McCarthy. But he gave McCarthy money. Now, don't forget, this was not too long after Hitler. It was evident to him that these things could again happen anywhere. Let's face it, anti-Semitism was pretty strong in this country, too. But when I heard he was helping to support McCarthy, I said, 'Dad, how can you give money to that son-of-a-bitch?' And he says, 'Things could get very bad.' This is the same reasoning for being with Nixon—he wanted both Nixon and McCarthy to have a Jewish friend. In other words, he was afraid of what might happen to the Jews in this country if Nixon or McCarthy got out of hand. Being a contributor to them and a supporter of theirs, he figured he might have their ear and would be able to stem any problem of anti-Semitism.

"And he said to me once when I was ranting and raving against McCarthy during the '54 Army-McCarthy hearings, he said, 'You'd better keep quiet. You're a Jew, remember.'

"I guess he picked up this mentality from his folks. You know, you don't oppose the czar, you try to stay on his good side. His mother once said to him, 'To meet the ruler of your land is a blessing, no matter what you think of him.'"

# THE STREET, 1938

## MAXWELL STREET MUST GO, DECLARE JEWISH LEADERS

— . . . Plans for a campaign by Chicago Jewry to stamp out the picturesque old mart were drawn Saturday night by a group of Jewish business and professional men meeting at the South Side Hebrew Institute. . . .

"These centers are like a cancerous growth gnawing at the vitals of American Jewry," declared A. Lincoln Wisler, chairman of the institute board. "They should cease to be sectional or racial phenomena. Seeds of anti-Jewish feeling come from such districts. They must be eradicated, not only in Chicago but in every other American city where they flourish.

"Rather than fight anti-Semitism," Wisler declared, "our committee shall endeavor to seek out its causes and in a candid way attempt to eradicate them."

The move follows unnumbered efforts to eradicate the Maxwell Street market. . . .

CHICAGO *DAILY NEWS*
*June 27, 1938*

# RAY NOVICK

Ray Novick was a clothing-store "puller" and salesman on Maxwell Street in the 1920s, as a youngster, until he went to the Army in 1943. He now owns a large drapery and linen store on the Northwest Side of Chicago. He is a neatly groomed, candid-seeming, pleasant man. The following conversation took place while he sat in a black leather chair in the den of his suburban home.

"Oh, you fought hard to make a sale in those days," he said. "When you had a customer, you worked with that customer because you knew the moment he left your door, you'd never see him come back because the next guy would work him. That's why we used every trick in the book to sell him.

"Usually, you had a ladies' clothing store, then a men's clothing store, then a shoe store, then a general merchandise store. Then it would start over again, ladies' store, men's store, shoe store, general merchandise store.

"So you had to sell your customer or he'd vanish into the store down the street. So, sure, we were physical sometimes. Take when we were outside, pullers. We'd ask a person to come in nice. 'We've got what you want,' and so forth. And we'd give you a little push.

"'Get out of my way.' You'd block him. We grabbed their hands, pulled their coats, this, that. Like I was small, but I wasn't afraid. I knew the moment he started a fight with me, I had four other guys to rush over and take my part in it, and we never showed fear. There was no such thing as fear. I don't care how big he was and how small I was. Like we had kids, like the Medlevines, or the Schumans. All they wanted was to walk down the street where there was a fight going on so they could come in and finish it. That's right! And half the pullers—they had as many fights in a day. . . . Remember King Levinsky? He used to stay with his sister Lena at the fish stand. If anybody needed help, bang!, he was there. For no reason at all, bang!, you found somebody twice your size helping you out. That's the way it went. But there were a lot of physical fights in those days. It was a way of life. You expected it.

"We tried our best not to let the customer by. And if they squirmed away, fine. After you talked to them, say, two, three minutes, and you knew definitely they did not want to buy your product, you left them alone because somebody else would come along.

"You know who didn't want to buy. Take the word 'puller.' It sounds like he was just an ignoramus standing outside. That isn't true. He had to know a lot about people—who he could bring into the store, who he couldn't bring in. You could tell their interest just the way they glanced at the merchandise. If a guy came up, and you asked him to buy a pair of shoes and he says, 'No, I want a suit,' you say okay. You'd holler—say Maxie was the puller over there—'Maxie, he wants a suit of clothes.' And you'd let him go to Maxie.

"If the boss was watching the puller, he'd talk to everybody who walked by. If not, the puller would pick and choose a little more. If somebody'd touch a suit hanging outside, you'd approach. If he asked you how much, you'd give him a low figure. 'You can get a suit inside for five dollars, two dollars, one dollar.' Just to get him inside so the salesman can work him over.

"Now, you have to learn to put words in people's mouths. Because when somebody is looking to buy, you are dealing with the mind, you're not dealing with the body.

"And you are not necessarily dealing to give him what he wants. But you still want him on your side. You don't want to antagonize him. Say he wants a jacket. And he wants to spend five dollars. I remember in the early '40s that the trend was for black horsehide-leather jackets. That's what they really wanted. So we'd start them off with suede jackets. At the time, suede jackets we'd sell for anywhere between five dollars and seven dollars apiece. A horsehide sold between seven dollars and ten dollars, which was quite a jump. Today it's nothing, but then it was quite a jump.

They'd come in for a black horsehide jacket and we'd say, 'Well, let's try on for size just exactly what you need.' And we'd try on a suede jacket first.

"The man would say, 'I don't want it. I want leather.'

" 'Okay, but let's see what size you wear.' That way we'd more or less get him to stand still.

"Invariably we'd pull out a real large size first and he'd put it on and say, 'Oh, that's too big on me. I can't use that.' You tell him the reason for this big size is that a horsehide jacket runs bigger than a suede jacket. We don't give him the right size for a couple of reasons.

"If we gave him the right size, he'd be making a decision on the coat immediately. That would allow him to think he still has his own mind. We want to change his mind. We know he only wants a garment that cost us five dollars; we could sell it for six or seven, but not for five. If we gave him the right size, then the next thing we have to go is to a leather jacket. Then we'd have to go to ten dollars—to ask him for ten—in order to bargain with him to come down to six to be a sale. And at this time, he's adamant about spending five dollars, so you'd be wasting time.

"Now, a jacket too small would automatically make him feel that you're trying to push him into something because it doesn't fit him. He feels all snugged up in it. Feels tight in it. A big jacket, he's comfortable. Like we're lulling him into a false sense of security. He should be able to swing his hands and so forth.

" 'Okay, now we'll try a smaller size.'

"As I'm taking the suede coat off of him, I'm telling him what this coat costs even though he doesn't want it. I want to plant a price in his mind. I tell him the suede jacket costs seven dollars. I'm only thinking of how much money I can get for the leather jacket out of him.

" 'Well, this is a nice jacket at seven dollars, if you want to change your mind and you don't want something as heavy as leather.'

"And he says, 'Oh, no. I want a leather jacket.'

" 'Fine. You're the boss.' Inflate him a little bit and lull him.

"And now when I do fit him right, and with what he wants, it's perfect. Okay, suede is out. But I'm hoping he remembers I told him the suede was seven dollars. Next thing I do, I bring out a cheap leather coat, not horsehide, a calfskin jacket or something like that. And I'll try that on. Now, this is his right size, and this I tell him is ten dollars. He says, 'Haven't you got a black horsehide jacket like I want? Don't waste my time.' I say, 'Of course I have. All I want to do is make sure I give you the right size. I don't want to pull them all down because I've got to go way up there to bring them down. They're heavy!'

"Then I bring him down the regular leather coat, the one he wants. I tell him it costs fifteen. He looks at it, he studies it, he feels it all around, and he says, 'This is a beautiful jacket.'

"And then he says, 'But all I want to spend is five dollars.'

"'Man, you're crazy! The suede jacket is seven dollars. Where do you come with five for a black horsehide-leather jacket like this one? Even if you want to buy this calfskin jacket, it's ten dollars. I'll tell you what I'll do. Forget the suede jacket. I know you don't like the suede jacket. Here, you can have the calfskin jacket for seven.'

"He says, 'I want that black horsehide.'

"I says, 'But, fella, all you want to spend is seven dollars. You can't buy a fifteen dollar jacket for seven dollars. I'm trying like hell to erase the five dollars from his mind.'

"He may come right back to me and say, 'This ain't worth no seven or ten dollars; the guy next door wanted to give me a jacket like this for five.'

"I says, 'No, you must have been talking about the suede. The suede is seven dollars.'

"Then he's got two friends with him. I pull him over to the side, I'll say, 'Look, if you can get your friends to buy coats, because I think they need them also, I'll let you have these calfskin jackets for seven dollars, providing you buy three of them, you and your two friends.'

"And he'll come back. 'My friends don't want to buy. But maybe I can talk them into it. What will you give me?'

"I says, 'I'll tell you what, instead of fifteen, you can have it for ten.'

"He says, 'Will you give it to me for seven dollars?' I says, 'Man, the calfskin is ten, and you want the horsehide for seven?'

He says, 'If you give it to me for seven, I'll try to get my friends to buy.'

" 'Okay, you've got it! But don't tell your friends you got it for seven. You see this seven dollars?' And I stick it in my pocket. I says, 'I don't want my boss to know I sold it to you for seven. Put the coat on and just walk out. He won't know whether you walked into the store with it or bought it. Then come back with your two friends and demand two fifteen-dollar jackets for ten apiece and I'll fight for you.' More often than not, he says, 'Yeah.'

"Now, my boss is often in the background. And he would sometimes come over to me and he would talk price with me in Hebrew—never Yiddish, never German, because the average person there, the Polish, the Russian, the Lithuanian, they could understand Yiddish and German, but Hebrew? Who in the hell heard of Hebrew?

"The next thing we did, we turned the customers back and forth between me and my boss, just to confuse them. And if my boss said I wasn't going anywhere with a customer—I couldn't implant a price into his head—he would come over and say, 'Look, you can't sell this. It's already sold.' And I'd say, 'Nobody told me it was sold already. This man wants to buy it. He wants to pay seven dollars.' Then my boss would say, 'I don't care if he wants to pay twenty. I promised it to a man for ten. He gave me a deposit. It's that man's. You can't sell it to this man. You can't replace it.' And I'd say, 'Look, you want to talk to him? I promised it to him. Now you go to talk to him,' and I'd walk away.

"He'd come in again, and he'd say to him, 'If you want it for ten, you can have it for ten, and I'll get another one almost like it and he won't know the difference.' And the customer says, 'Well, he told me I could have it for seven. What kind of place is this? He works for you, doesn't he?' Now the five-dollar price he came in with has been entirely forgotten. So now you've put words in the customer's mouth. He came in saying five, and he goes out saying seven."

Ray Novick recalls that the pressures on the salesmen and the pullers were great, particularly during the Depression, because there was always somebody waiting to take your job. "Let me put it this way," he said. "You feared your boss very much. You were never sure of your job, or when you'd be working. You might expect him to say on Sunday night when you got paid, 'You don't have to come in Monday. Maybe come in Wednesday if it's a nice day.'

"Every puller's dream in those days was to work inside and not outside, even though the work inside was much harder. But it was cold and damp in winter outside and miserably hot in summer.

"For most, there was another point of insecurity. Most salesmen were immigrants there. And the immigrant was afraid to, say, go downtown to a department store to work or to a neighborhood store. He figured he wouldn't be able to be hired because he had an accent. And after he saved a certain amount of money, then he'd leave the street and go into any neighborhood, but he'd open his own place. Invariably, he'd do well. If you learned on Maxwell Street, you learned.

"One of the lessons that we learned at a very early age, part of our experience, was that all people are alike. Meaning, you shouldn't have any trouble talking to a president of a company or talking to a stockboy. You talk to both the same way. They're both human. You don't have to be afraid of anybody.

"The tone, the respect, you don't put anybody down. If you want something out of a stockboy, you give him the same respect as if you were talking to the president of the company. On the same basis, you don't take a step back from the president any more than you'd take a step back from the stockboy.

"The biggest principle of any merchandising is to have merchandise in order to make money. The store has to be stocked. During the early war years, you just couldn't get merchandise. It was rationed—so much went to Marshall Field's, so much went to Sears. You were nobody. Who were you I should give merchandise? But there was plenty available for the right people. Even though you weren't the right people, you shouldn't have any trouble just talking to the person that was in charge of this merchandise, going up and saying that you'd like a part of it.

"We'd go to the mills, directly to the mills, in Tennessee or North Carolina or what. The mills were all booked up, sold out. But we knew there was a certain amount of merchandise that the regular accounts would not accept unless it was pushed on them.

You knew you couldn't get the first-quality merchandise right off, so you came up to them and said in a nice way you'd like the seconds, the irregulars. If we came in and asked for regulars and said we'd also take some of your irregulars, it would be a hassle. They wouldn't like it. So we said we'd pay the same price for the irregulars that they were getting for your regular merchandise. They'd listen because you weren't asking for their prime stuff.

"Now, going back to what we learned on the street. I've got to put words in your mouth. You're no different than the shnook I work over in the store. All people are human. So I've got to work the same tactics on you that I did the average guy off the street. We use the same principles, only it had to be on a higher level. You work in reverse—meaning, what you want to sell, I don't want to buy. You're thinking I'd want to buy your regular hosiery, for example. No. I want your scrappings. And I want to pay you the same price as your regulars.

"Right. And you look at me, 'Jeez, I've really got myself a dummy here. I'll give him the shit.' I don't care what I pay. I buy some scrappings. The first time. Next time, I ask for a lot of scrappings. He says, 'Well, maybe I've got ten dozen, fifty dozen.' I say, 'Jeez, I had in mind a hundred dozen, a hundred thousand dozen. Is there anything you can do for me? Look, maybe you can create some of this other merchandise.' Your price on your regular merchandise is ten dollars for stockings. For irregulars it's two dollars. I'm willing to give you ten dollars across the board.' He does it. Now I'm in. And the deal gets better every time I see him.

"What happened to the scrappings? Well, some people on Maxwell Street would sell them as irregulars and get the low price. And in those days, everything went. But some people on the street, they'd get the seconds and re-mark them as firsts and sell them at firsts price.

"Finally, there was the black market. Lot of people got rich in it. There were price ceilings in those days, but they often didn't mean anything because if you had merchandise that was hard to get, people would pay as much as they could if they needed it.

"We might go into a big department store, buy all they had of, say, towels. Say fifty dozen. They sold fifty cents each. We'd then sell them for seventy-five cents each. And people could only come to us. Only we had it. How did we get it from the department stores, when the department stores were only supposed to sell a limited amount to each customer? We'd pull the salesperson to the side, or his manager. We were generous with spreading the wealth. And also we talked to the mills people, the managers there. We diverted stock: instead of sending a hundred dozen to the department store, they sent fifty dozen to them, fifty dozen to us, and told the department store they'd owe it. Soon they began taking from Peter to give to Paul. But remember, this wasn't just Maxwell Street. This is the way it went up and down the line. This was the way business went all over the country, up to the biggest department stores. The only way you could make money in those days was to have merchandise in your store, and you had to be smart enough to know how to get it. Everyone had the same problem; it was just a matter of proportion. The only people who got caught were the pigs. There is a favorite saying in the stock market: Bulls make money, bears make money, but pigs never make money. The pigs flaunted everything openly. They got out of control. Like some jobbers—they had tie-in sales that were soon outlawed: if you wanted to buy a dozen curtains, say, you'd have to buy two dozen place mats. Who in the hell wanted place mats?

"Prior to those days, the average income of a Maxwell Street merchant was, tops, maybe twenty to twenty-five thousand dollars a year. His income not only doubled but quadruled in this era.

"These people had paid their dues and learned their lessons in earlier years. And now they put everything they knew into practice.

"Now, a lot of people who started on Maxwell Street, they'd deny it today. They might say they began on Halsted Street or Roosevelt Road. But he never mentioned Maxwell Street because there was just a funny tinge to that particular name.

"On the other hand, there was another element that came off the street. I think I was a part of it. I wasn't ashamed. When I'd be asked, 'Where did I work? What experience do I have?' 'Experience? Shall I put it to you this way? From '25 to '43 I had my training on Maxwell Street. Show me a better place.'

"And everybody I met, all the way in the world, no matter where I went—I don't care whether it was all the way down South or all the way up in the East or where—I tell 'em the same thing. I mean the top boys in my industry. Burlington Mills. Seneca Textiles. When I was starting out in the business, I was able to make inroads with them because of my background and not because of my business. They heard Maxwell Street, and they respected. And, you know, this was what we always strived for. The average boy on the street—it wasn't his dream to open a store one day on Maxwell Street. Our biggest dream was to get away from the street and open a store on State Street, say. To be a rich merchant, a respected merchant. Maxwell Street helped us become that more than a lot of us would admit."

# THE STREET, 1939

## OLD WORLD BAZAAR FACES
## MODERNISM'S THREAT

—Maxwell Street, Chicago's famous old-world bazaar, is to be modernized.

This sad, earnest bit of news comes from the Maxwell Street Merchants' Association. They plan to streamline the 4½-block market, to make pushcarts and street stalls a uniform size and to pull storefronts back in off the sidewalks.

They plan to encourage a friendliness instead of rivalry, to ban the puller-in who shoves the shopper into the shop, and to introduce a new word, ethics, into the Maxwellian vocabulary.

Gone will be the Maxwell Street that teems with humanity . . . where the streets are filled with stalls and no stall is like any other and the cries of hawkers blend into shrill, strange music.

Pushcarts of the present prevailing type, battered, unsightly and with creaking wheels will be replaced by streamlined pushmobiles, brightly painted, clean and with sanitary covering, according to Ira W. Wolfe, industrial engineer, who has just been made director of the rehabilitation work.

Sidewalk booths will be uniformly ornate

and sanitary and the buildings refurbished. A lighting system and improved police protection will extend night business. Elimination of fire hazards will reduce insurance rates and an advertising campaign will draw thousands to the district. . . . There will be a central bureau for handling complaints and adjustments. . . .

Maxwell Street must be modern. . . . A fishwife reposing in layers of fat beside her piles of fresh shrimp, shrugged her shoulders, chased a fly from her whitefish. "So?" she said, indifferently. "So how can they?"

CHICAGO *TRIBUNE*
*May 25, 1939*

# BENNY GOODMAN

### BENNY GOODMAN MARRIES
### INTO THE '400'

—Benny Goodman, who shook the dust of
Maxwell Street off his feet a few decades ago
and began shaking the foundations of theaters and clubs with that romping, stomping
thing "swing," today had become an heir of
the Vanderbilts, a connection of British peers
and a candidate for the social register.

Benny, the king of swing (royalty in his
own right), stormed the social ramparts by
marrying in Las Vegas, Nev., Lady Alice
Hammond Duckworth, great-great-grand-
daughter of the original Commodore Vander-
bilt and former wife of Lord Duckworth. . . .

CHICAGO *HERALD-EXAMINER*
*March 21, 1942*

---

David Goodman and Dora Rezinsky, Russian immigrants, met
and married in Baltimore in late 1894. The first three of their
eleven children were born in Baltimore. David Goodman, a tailor,
heard that there might be opportunities for him and his family in
Chicago. They moved in 1902. They came to the Maxwell Street
area. They lived at, among other places (according to the annual

Chicago City directory), what is now 1227 South Sangamon, in 1902; 1242 West Fourteenth Street, in 1905; and 1342 Washburne, about a block west of Maxwell Street, in 1909. At that Washburne address, on May 30, 1909, the seventh child of David Goodman and his wife was born. They named him Benjamin David.

"Pop was a tailor who, even in a good week, rarely made more than twenty dollars. He didn't have his own place but worked in a factory, when there was work," Benny Goodman would write in his autobiography, *The Kingdom of Swing*.* "My memory of those early days is hazier than that of most kids because we moved around quite a bit. But I can remember a time when we lived in a basement without heat during the winter, and a couple of times when there wasn't anything to eat. I don't mean *much* to eat. I mean *anything*. That isn't an experience you forget in a hurry. I haven't ever forgotten it. . . .

"Mom was always too busy with the youngest of the family to bother very much about the others. Because of this, Pop would get up before any of us, about six o'clock, make the fire and fix breakfast for us. This usually consisted of a huge pot of coffee and a dozen rolls. We started to drink coffee as soon as we were weaned, because milk for so many kids cost more than he could afford.

"Pop would be off to work before we were dressed, so we often didn't see him again until evening. Then he would come home with the food for the next day's meals, because he generally did the marketing. In fact, one of my earliest recollections is the picture of him staggering into our flat with a big bag or basket of apples which he had bought at a pushcart on the way home from work. . . ."

Goodman remembers moving farther west with his family, to Francisco Avenue. "It was one of those old three-story brick houses they have all over the West Side, with dark stairways, small rooms, not much light. This was a pretty hopeless neighborhood. . . .

"One game we played pretty nearly all the time was cops and robbers. A funny thing about this was that the cops always got the

* Benny Goodman and Irving Kolodin, *The Kingdom of Swing* (New York: Frederick Ungar Publishing Co., 1961), pp. 15–25.

worst of it, because in that kind of neighborhood the cops represented something that never did much for the poor people.

"Nobody had to remind us kids that someday we'd have to go out on our own and earn a living. That idea was with us from almost the time we were old enough to talk. I grew up with pretty much of a resentment against the way folks like my father and mother had to work, trying to take care of a big family, making a go of things with most of the breaks against them. Even in the hottest part of the summer they never could get anything like a rest or a vacation. The best we could do would be to go to one of the parks."

Benny Goodman heard the first music he can remember at Douglas Park, several blocks from his home at 1125 South Francisco. It was a typical Sunday afternoon band concert and many of the neighborhood people were there. It was free.

Dora Goodman had started working at age eight, in Russia, and imagined that all her children would be working by twelve or thirteen. David Goodman had some other dreams. He envied people with culture or "book learning" and emphasized this to his kids. "Whatever any of us may have amounted to may be traced pretty much to him," said Benny Goodman. "He was constantly scheming things that would make life go a little easier for us."

Neighbors moved in next door, and the man of the house happened also to be a tailor who worked in the same factory where David Goodman worked. The man had sons who went to high school and played musical instruments. Sometimes they earned money playing at various affairs.

Goodman was impressed that money could be earned in such an easy, enjoyable way, no long hours, no laborious sweat in a tailoring factory. He thought of his children.

"A few days later, on a Sunday, Pop went out for a walk. We didn't know anything about it at the time, but he came back a little later in great excitement," says Benny Goodman. "He had walked farther than usual and while out he heard some music from a distance. He found that it came from the Kehelath Jacob Synagogue, about a mile and a half from our place. Small boys were playing in the band, and when he asked he found out that the instruments were lent to them, and they paid maybe a quarter for a lesson. This really appealed to him and on the day of the next rehearsal he took the three of us—Harry, Freddy, and me—down to the synagogue.

"The idea was that the synagogue lent the instruments to the kids. They had a couple of rehearsals a week, and before the rehearsals the band leader gave lessons in rudiments.

"I remember going down to the place for the first time with my two brothers—Harry, who was about 12, and Freddy, who was a year older than me. This was 1919, when I was ten. Harry was the biggest and he got a tuba. Since Freddy was bigger than me, he was given a trumpet. The only thing left for me, the smallest, was the clarinet. There have been stories that I went for the clarinet in a big way because it had shiny keys and looked pretty. There might be something in that, but I know that if I had been twenty pounds heavier and two inches taller, I would probably be blowing a horn now instead of a clarinet."

The boys began taking lessons and playing in the synagogue band. When the synagogue ran out of money for the band, David Goodman took his boys to Hull House, a settlement house on Halsted Street, a few blocks north of Maxwell. He had heard about a boys' band they had there.

He had become quite proud of his boys' musical abilities. "He used to show us off to his friends over on a Sunday afternoon. He'd invite them up. I remember he'd stick us in a corner of the living room, and tell us to begin. He'd sit back, but his chest would be stuck out this far."

By twelve, Benny was doing well in the Hull House band, which played Sousa march music and wore snappy red uniforms. At home, his brother Charlie got hold of a phonograph with a horn. Charlie brought home records. One record he brought was by Ted Lewis, "who we figured was a pretty hot clarinet player." Goodman listened to it so much that he was soon able to imitate Lewis remarkably well. Charlie had heard about a "Jazz Night," at the Balaban and Katz Central Park Theater, every Thursday. It was comparable to an amateur night. One night Charlie persuaded the manager to allow his brother Benny, in Buster Brown collar with bow tie, to play clarinet. Benny did so well that a couple of weeks later, when one of the acts didn't show up, the manager in desperation sent for Goodman to fill in. "I was on the street playing 'shinny,' but I grabbed the clarinet and hustled around to the theater," Benny recalled.

He did an impersonation of Ted Lewis, with battered old top hat. He was paid five dollars. It was his first professional engagement.

He began to take classical lessons with a renowned teacher, Franz Schoepp, who once taught at the Chicago Musical College. Benny began playing for money. Still a kid in knee pants, he caught on in the famous Bix Beiderbecke river-boat band that made excursions to and from Chicago and Michigan City, Indiana, on Lake Michigan.

He had joined the American Musicians' Union and began playing more and more jobs. He was learning a new style playing with bands such as Beiderbecke's. Besides that, he found it necessary to buy a tuxedo to be properly dressed for nightclub dates. It was the first formal suit ever owned by anyone in the Goodman family. By the time Benny had begun attending Harrison High School, he had become the family's principal breadwinner. His father had died.

At sixteen, Benny had earned a great enough reputation that Ben Pollack, leader of a rising band of the day, sent Benny a wire from California to come out and join him. He signed Benny to a salary of one hundred dollars a week. Eighty dollars a week more than the highest salary his father ever earned. Benny, while still a teen-ager, would also play with the famous Red Nichols band. He returned to Chicago, eventually, and played in some of the top nightclubs and dance halls. Recordings and radio dates followed. By 1934 he had decided to form his own band, one that would play primarily dance music "in a free style"—in a way most musicians wanted to play and weren't allowed to on the ordinary job. He had his pick, virtually, of numerous good musicians.

"The point was that no white band had yet gotten together a good rhythm section that would kick out, or jump, or rock, or swing (all these expressions being ways musicians describe the vitality that comes from music played at just the right tempo with a lot of rhythmic snap), using arrangements that fit in with this idea, which would give the men a chance to play solos and express the music in their own individual way," said Goodman.

Goodman believed that if the musicians really enjoyed what they were playing, then the public would, too.

The Goodman band opened in the Grill Room at the Roosevelt Hotel in New York City. It was in May of 1935. Though there were few people in the audience, they applauded with enthusiasm. However, the manager was not impressed. He felt the "newfangled swing" was monstrous and, on opening night, gave the band its two weeks' notice.

Goodman, not daunted, kept knocking around with his band. In Denver, Colorado, he underwent what he termed, "the most humiliating experience of my life." On opening night at Elitch's Garden, people began asking for their money back after listening to the first few swing numbers. The manager hurried over and ordered Goodman to begin playing waltzes.

Shortly after, however, the mood suddenly began to change. The band played a one-night stand in Oakland and scored its first triumph. People waited outside in line to hear the new group, and responded with great cheers to each swinging number. "From there the band went to the most famous of the West Coast ballrooms, Hollywood's Palomar," wrote George T. Simon in *The Big Bands*.

" 'Apparently, Benny still wasn't too sure how the band would be received because on the first night,' drummer Gene Krupa recalls, 'we played the first couple of sets under wraps. We weren't getting much reaction, so Benny, I guess, decided to hell with playing it safe and we started playing numbers like "King Porter Stomp." Well, from then on we were in.'

"The engagement was a smash. Kids gathered around the bandstand and screamed for more. Their cheers and the band's swinging sounds swept coast to coast via a series of broadcasts from the Palomar.

The Goodman orchestra was now playing to record houses everywhere it went. "Riding on the crest of fame in 1937," said a United Press Dispatch, "the Goodman orchestra opened at New York's vast Paramount Theater. When the sun came up, on a cold morning in January, several thousand youngsters, most of them truants from school, were waiting in line for tickets.

"A riot call for police went out when the crowd burst over into the streets. Inside the theater, when the band began to play, the audience sat spellbound, then began to clap its hands in beat with the music, to stomp its feet. The less restrained leaped into the aisles or onto the stage to dance, and bedlam broke loose.

"Goodman had become a national phenomenon. He was the king of swing, threatened by few and challenged by none."

On January 16, 1938, the Benny Goodman orchestra played the august Carnegie Hall in New York City. It was the first swing-jazz performance in Carnegie Hall and is widely considered to be a landmark in the history of popular music.

It brought together many of the jazz stars of the age, such as Goodman on clarinet, Gene Krupa on drums, Lionel Hampton on vibraphone, Teddy Wilson, Jess Stacy and Count Basie on piano, Harry James, Cootie Williams, Ziggy Elman, and Bobby Hackett on trumpet, John Hodges and Lester Young on saxophone, Walter Page on bass, and Freddie Green on guitar.

Songs were by Gershwin, and Berlin, and Rodgers and Hart, and Duke Ellington, among others. "One O'Clock Jump," "I Got Rhythm," "Stompin' At the Savoy," "Blue Skies," "Loch Lommond," "Honeysuckle Rose," "Swingtime in the Rockies," and, finally, what turned out to be a pulsating, improvisational twenty-minute crescendo, "Sing Sing Sing."

Goodman would say in later years that he was not awed by Carnegie Hall. "We were a pretty cocky bunch," he said. But an on-the-spot observer, writing in the music magazine *Metronome,* said, "Goodman, in tails and with clarinet in hand, entered to a huge applause and, quite nervous, beat off 'Don't Be That Way' a bit too slow. And for one chorus it was obvious that his men were not relaxed.

"Suddenly, though, Gene Krupa emitted a tremendous break of drums. The crowd cheered. Gene's hair fell into his eyes. The band fell into a groove, and when it had finished . . . the concert was in a groove, too."

Some two hours later, the finale of the program: "Krupa began the tom-tom-tomming that started 'Sing Sing Sing.' After many choruses, the band began to build to a climax. . . . Then, Benny and Gene alone hit the musical highlight of the concert. . . .

"Came the full band, and then suddenly, softly, church music by Jess Stacy at piano. It was wonderful contrast. Benny started to laugh. And the audience started to applaud as the band went into the number's final outburst."[†]

Nearly four decades later, the album of that performance remains the best-selling jazz album of all time. The evening marked a turning point in the acceptance of jazz in American culture. Although conservatives like Ollin Downes, music critic of the New York *Times,* felt that the symphonic home of Beethoven, Bach, Mozart and the like had been defiled, the concert was overall a tremendous hit.

Also, there grew from it an acceptance of jazz musicians, who had been considered unsavory upstarts by "polite society." The "society" that, four years after Carnegie Hall, Goodman would marry into.

Goodman has saved the letter that Sol Hurok, the impressario who produced the concert, sent to him shortly before the concert engagement. The letter read in part, "Be sure to tell the boys to be on their best behavior."

Almost every man who played in that concert went on to lead his own group. Reportedly, bitter feuds dealing with personalities and musical style eventually broke up Goodman's quartet. Goodman (known now by musicians for his stern stare called "the ray" which expressed displeasure at a wrong note or toot) lost Krupa a week after Carnegie Hall. Hampton and Wilson followed.

Goodman was considered by colleagues a genius and a perfectionist, but with personality quirks that could amuse, intimidate, and/or irk.

Goodman seemed as insensitive with people, at times, as he was sensitive to his music. His "ray" was one thing. Another was his penchant for the verbal knife. Once, when a new musician had come on to play with him and missed a couple of notes in rehearsal, Goodman took him aside and said, "What's wrong, kid? The Big Leagues too much for you?"

[†] George T. Simon, *The Big Bands* (New York: Collier Books, 1974), p. 215.

Some musicians who played with him called him a "sadist."

Money was important to Goodman. Some of his musicians quit because they thought him "cheap to the point of being a chiseler." "If we had a gig and Benny would make ten thousand, he'd pay the band members maybe two hundred dollars apiece and then bill them for their hotel room," recalled one trumpet player.

But Walter Iooss, Sr., a bassist for the Goodman Orchestra in the early 1940s, saw a different side. Iooss had left the band to get married; Goodman learned where the Ioosses were honeymooning and sent severance pay, much to Iooss's surprise and appreciation.

The eccentric side of Goodman is legendary. Iooss recalled an incident in a Jewish delicatessen in Cedar Point, Ohio, near Sandusky. "A bunch of the band was sitting at a table and there were a lot of fingers going in a big discussion about something," said Iooss. "Benny was arguing as much as anyone else. Now, this is 1941 and there was an Artie Shaw record out called 'Concerto for a Clarinet.' Shaw really wasn't in the same league with Benny as far as being a musician. But Benny was very competitive. And, well, the record came on the jukebox. But nobody, it seemed, was really listening. We were arguing. Then, near the end of the record, Goodman says, 'Shhhh, I want to hear this. I want to see if he can hit the high note.' Benny must have heard that record dozens of times. Shaw *always* hit the high note. It was always the same record. It was things like that that made people wonder about Benny."

He is absent-minded to the core. Once, he got into a cab, sat down, and then asked the taxi driver, "How much do I owe you?" It was said that he sometimes called his two daughters and three grandchildren "Pops" because he didn't remember their names too well.

Despite a querulousness, Goodman has also demonstrated heart. He was deeply disappointed when Harry James quit his band to form one of his own, but Goodman understood and even helped James out financially. At the height of his popularity, Goodman would return to Hull House. He played a jam session there in September, 1938, to stimulate charitable contributions to the old settlement house. And in 1945, he gave five thousand dol-

lars to the settlement's music school. He played a charity concert
there as late as 1976.

Goodman is also credited with being the first to integrate
"Negro" musicians into a white band, in 1937. "The thought of a
white and colored group playing in a hotel room was pretty revolutionary at that time, but we worked it out so that Teddy played
intermission piano [while the band was off the stand], but soon
the trio was made a part of the floor show," said Goodman. "After
a few days' trial it was apparent that the thing was a natural from
every standpoint."

Soon after Teddy Wilson came another black to the group,
Lionel Hampton. Hampton later said, "What Benny did in 1937
made it possible for Negroes to have their chance in baseball and
other fields. He was a real pioneer and he didn't grandstand about
it."

Goodman, recalling this some forty years later, said, "I wanted
them because nobody played piano or vibes just the way they did.
They had something unique, and I wanted the best playing with
me.

"If we felt that there was going to be resistance to a black with
us, we just wouldn't go there. That's all. We could pick our spots
in those days."

Do you think it was courageous on your part in any way? he
was asked.

"Then?"

Yes.

"I didn't think so. I think there was more good to it than harm.
And, you know, it was never on my mind. Never. It couldn't be
on your mind because how could you perform? Couldn't think
about it. Had other things to do."

The Swing era began to wane after the war. But from 1935 to
1945, more than $80 million was paid to see and hear the Good-
man band. Goodman still played top dates, but he was no longer
in the kind of demand he had been. The era of "the Boppers" was
crowding him out. By now he lived on a huge estate in Connecticut and said, "I guess I've passed the stage where I want to knock
myself out." In 1950, a full-length Hollywood motion picture star-

ring Steve Allen was released and titled, *The Benny Goodman Story*. Goodman was critical. "It wasn't dramatic enough," said Goodman. "I hadn't died yet."

In the summer of 1962, he took a group of American jazz stars for a six-week, U. S. Government-sponsored goodwill tour of the Soviet Union. It was the first American jazz band to tour Russia.

Goodman had wanted to make the trip for some time. It was a return, of course, to the homeland of his parents. The United States had been reluctant to send Goodman and his group because it was worried about the treatment he would receive from the Russians; and the Russians were worried about the Russian audience's reaction because they had heard about rock 'n' roll bands causing riots.

There were no riots but there was a huge acceptance. A dispatch from Reuters on June 24, 1962, described the Goodman orchestra's last concert of the tour in Leningrad: "When stewards switched out the indoor arena's lighting, the 5,000 fans went frantic with delight. . . . The American 'Ambassador of Jazz' was forced to call on the band to play encores lasting an hour as the young Leningraders crowded up to the stage clapping and cheering.

"Each member of the 19-man band got a bouquet of flowers."

Goodman remembers that he wanted to visit his mother's birthplace but never was able to cut through the red tape to get there. She was born in the Republic of Georgia. "Funny thing about it," recalls Goodman, "is that my mother's maiden name was Rezinsky. That's the Russian word for 'Georgia.' Everyone was talking about Rezinsky. I said, 'Well, that's my mother's Russian maiden name.' They said, 'Comrade!' "

Something that would have been unimaginable for the Goodmans and the Rezinskys, who were born and raised in the Jewish ghettoes of Russia, took place on July 4, 1962.

The son of the tailor David Goodman met and spoke cordially and equably with the leader of the Russian nation. Nikita Khrushchev and Benny Goodman met on the lawn of the American Embassy in Moscow. Goodman shook hands with the premier under a spreading tree.

"Ah, a new jazz fan," said Goodman.

"No," said Khruschev, smiling, "I don't like Goodman music; I like good music." He laughed at his pun.

Khrushchev indicated what he thought of jazz by saying it started out "boo boo booo boo" and he did a little jig step.

"I don't understand it," Khrushchev continued. "I don't mean just American jazz. I don't understand our own Russian jazz, either."

The talk shifted to modern art. Khrushchev said: "When I talked to President Eisenhower, he said he was an amateur painter. When he talked about modern trends in painting, he said, 'It makes me sick to my stomach.'

"I said, 'It's the same with me.'"

Goodman defended modern painting, saying that painters had to experiment. He cited Gauguin, Matisse, and others and said that in their time they were not universally popular.

"I am not too well versed in the arts," said Khrushchev. "I think good art is always recognized."

Khrushchev told a story about a visit to the American exposition in 1959 at which he saw a painting of a woman "that was something to scare kids."

Khrushchev said he liked paintings in the formal Russian museums—"There you can go and really relax."

"Artists must do strange things to get somewhere, to create," said Goodman.

"But if a man lies on his back and swings his legs in the air, is that creation?" asked Khrushchev. "What would people think if you started doing it? If I did it, they would think I was out of my mind and they would be right."

Goodman remarked that he had found Yehudi Menuhin doing yoga exercises and didn't think it was crazy in the great violinist.

But Khrushchev simply said that was "just physical culture, not art." He said he had been told Prime Minister Nehru stood on his head as part of his exercise, then added: "If a man stands on his head in the street, then that is another matter."

When Goodman returned to America, President Kennedy called him to the White House to discuss the trip. The President recalled to Goodman that back in 1937 and 1938 he used to go up to the Ritz Hotel roof in Boston to hear the Goodman band. He said that he had sent a note to the premier thanking him for his graciousness to Benny Goodman and that when the Bolshoi Ballet came to Washington the following month he looked forward to attending.

Goodman today still is a vigorous concert performer. He still draws good crowds. He lives the comfortable life of a squire. He has his estate in Connecticut and a large office-apartment in the penthouse of a Sixty-sixth Street high-rise in Manhattan.

He is no longer the lean kid from Hull House. His face is roundish and looks raccoony with his horned-rim glasses. He has somewhat of a paunch. Original Monet and Picasso paintings are on the wall. He still plays classical clarinet, and on a music stand near his couch he had a Mozart piece for clarinet.

It is at times disconcerting to be with Goodman. While a visitor is talking to him, Goodman may begin to whistle. One is not certain whether he is working on a score or seeking relief from temporary boredom. He then may shuffle papers and say, "Go ahead, I'm listening." He may also get up without saying one word and leave and go into the next room for a few minutes. He returns.

But when he is right with you, he can charm. When he laughs, his eyes squinch up with the joy of a boy.

"You know," he said, "I don't talk much about my childhood. Many times I've been asked to talk in depth about it. But I've resisted. I don't know why. I guess there are things that I simply want to block out.

"Probably because I never found it all that enjoyable. Growing up poor. Living in certain parts of Chicago. I'm not a great one for remembering.

"I didn't cross the railroad tracks because of the Irish on the other side. I remember we used to walk down Halsted Street and somebody might get beat up. You give somebody the bird, you set up a challenge, and that's all. I really didn't have much to do with gangsters, though. I mean, they knew who they were after.

"One thing I've kept is my first clarinet-lesson book. It was on parchment paper. And I've had it redone in antique style.

"Playing music, well maybe it was a great escape for me from the poverty. I don't know. I wanted to do something with myself. And music was a great form with me. I was absolutely fascinated by it. So I set out at an early age to do what I could do—and devote my efforts to it, and enjoy it."

Did he think, then, that growing up as he did in poverty was a blessing in disguise?

"Well, I've thought about it. I've considered the possibility that if I had been born with a silver spoon in my mouth I might not have had the drive. My conclusion is, I could have come from Seattle, come from anyplace, and done the same thing. No doubt about it in my mind. I loved music. Some people are like that."

# SY BARTLETT

LONDON. Major Sidney Bartlett of the United States Army Air Force, a former newspaperman and scenario writer in Hollywood, claimed today the distinction of being the first American officer actually to bomb Berlin. . . . Of the 900 tons of bombs dropped (last night), Major Bartlett made the sighting and pressed the electric control button that released a two-ton, high-explosive "cookie," as he called it, to hit "right smack in the center of the target." "The whole of Berlin seemed to vomit dust and smoke and steel," he said. He said he saw the flames reflecting a glow in the sky when his plane was 120 miles away en route back to England from Hitler's capital.

NEW YORK *TIMES*
*March 28, 1945*

"I came to America from England when I was ten and a half years old, and I didn't even know how to make a fist. When my family came to live in the Maxwell Street area, I learned how to make a fist pretty damn quick," Sy Bartlett recalled in 1975 at age seventy-two. "And when I learned to fight, I didn't take anybody's shit. I'd knock 'em down first. I learned the American way. Hit 'em first, knock 'em down, and make 'em know who's boss.

"Jack Keeshin taught me my first lesson in all this. You see, I had a slight English accent. So he always called me 'Greenie.' He was a needling son-of-a-bitch. He was built like a butcher. Well, I brooded about this abuse until I challenged him to a fight. The fight was right in the alley off of Maxwell and, oh Christ— everybody was around. By this time, my friend Sam Siegel had shown me how to make a fist. I had never seen a fistfight before coming to America. Or violence. Suddenly, Jack is facing me and he's kind of giggling. He puts his head down like a bull, rushes at me, and I find myself tripped by one of his pals and my face and my hands—well, I fell right into a pile of horse shit. Jack leaned down and he punched me right in the eye. Gave me a black eye. I found him amusing as time went on and rather liked him, you know? But it took a while.

"But my first real encounter with violence was with a guy named McGovern who still bears the marks of his acquaintance-ship with me. Every time he'd see me he'd knock me down. For no reason. I'd be playing handball and he'd catch the ball and fling it over the rooftops. He'd trip me; he'd knock me down. I used to kill him in my sleep every night. I became psychotic about it. I used to dream of tearing his gullet out. I found a piece of cable and I lay outside his door on a winter's day, and as he stepped out I slashed him three times across the face. The marks of which he still bears. And when I can last remember, twenty people were trying to pull me off his chest. I was frothing, literally frothing at the mouth. They took me and put me to bed and sedated me. That's when I started going to the gym and boxing and learned how to fight. And my hatred of violence took over after a while and I never sought a quarrel because I knew I had developed a horrible temper. I couldn't remember for days after a fight what had happened. I've had to fight this ungovernable temper all these years. Eventually, guys like Jack, they began to accept me. I wasn't so alienated anymore, so out of things, because of my ac-cent."

In his townhouse now on North King Street in Los Angeles, Bartlett had been working on a script for a movie called, it hap-pens, *Days of Rage*. Pages of the manuscript lay about him on the floor. He is lean, blue-eyed, wears a silky, patterned shirt which is unbuttoned enough to see the white hairs on his chest. He wears white pants and white shoes. He lives alone, having been divorced for some time from the former Hollywood actress Ellen Drew. He was born Sasha Baranov in Kazakastan, Russia. The family name was changed to Bartlett because an uncle who had preceded them to London and to Chicago called himself Bartlett. "Nobody could pronounce Baranov," said Sy Bartlett.

"We landed in Boston. It's vague to me, but the excitement was overwhelming, and the tension was almost impossible. I was a stranger in a new world.

"My father started in business in a clothing store on Roosevelt Road and Union Street. My mother was kind of an intellectual. She was the daughter of the Tea King of the World. She went to school in Switzerland. My father was part Cossack, came from a harsh, rigid background. He was very much disliked by his father-in-law, who thought his daughter had married below her station.

"My parents were not religious, but they were highly moral. If you didn't keep your word, you were no good with him. He was a good man. A man's man. A hard-drinking man. And of course I never saw my father drunk. To him, it was crime to be seen drunk by your fellow man.

"My father and mother got the four of us—the four kids, that is —the typical rags-to-riches books to read. They thought this way we'd learn about America. I fantasized a lot as a kid, dreaming up stories. And it happened that I began hanging around with press guys, and I got a job with the Chicago *Examiner* as a copy boy. In those days, they had a rewrite battery team of Charlie MacArthur —who wrote *The Front Page* with Ben Hecht—and Joe Swirling and Jim Whittaker. I was drinking a lot and running around. Well, I got run-down, and I got TB. I was sent to a guest ranch in Arizona. I got completely healed in about four months. While there I wrote a story called *The Big Brain*. I had never been to California and I went there and I sold that story to the movies. I sold three more stories to the movies, then wrote four more that were rejected. Soon I was writing movie scripts."

Bartlett's best work was done *after* the war. He has written and produced since then such films as *Twelve O'Clock High, The Big Country, The Beloved Infidel, The Gathering of Eagles,* and *13 Rue Madeleine.*

"I've written nothing but dramatic stories for years," said Bartlett, "but I used to write comedy. Nobody believes that I was one of the writers of *The Road to Zanzibar*. It's still playing. It's the craziest goddamn comedy. It shocks people today when they see my name on the screen credits. I can't believe my mind worked that way, either. But my favorite line that I wrote in that movie—nobody ever heard it because there was such a big laugh before it. Bob Hope walks into this jungle hut and there's nothing but skeletons sitting around. As he passes one of 'em he briefly shakes his hand and says, 'Don't bother to get up.' It broke Bob up.

"That was before the war. The last thing I wrote when I was called up was *The Princess and the Pirate,* another Hope movie.

"I was called up before we were in the war. The first assignment they gave me was a special job. There was a German spy ring in Los Angeles and a guy named Werner Plack was in it. We wanted to embarrass him and get him out of the country. I was assigned to create a nuisance. One night I see him in a restaurant in Los Angeles. He's posing as a wine salesman. I shouted out loud from the next table, 'How dare you 'Heil Hitler' you Nazi son-of-a-bitch and I hit him right in the face with a bottle. And I proceeded to beat the shit out of him. I broke his nose and his jaw. And then I started breakin' up the joint. He's bleeding and he's shouting, 'You vill answer to the Third Reich for this, Herr Bartlett.' Well, they had to get him outta the country. And I began getting postcards from him as the Nazis marched through Poland and Czechoslovakia. He sent the postcards to Chasin's Restaurant. He knew I habitually went there. Postcards that read like, 'I am drinking a steindel of beer from town so-and-so. We will see each other soon, I hope.' He kept threatening me.

"Years later, a newspaper friend of mine named Ed Beatty is captured along with Jock Whitney, who owned the New York *Herald-Tribune*. The Germans find out who they are and they are brought to Goebbel's office at the Press Ministry. They are introduced to this Plack; he is now General Plack. And Beatty says—and later he told me he didn't know what the hell got into him—he says, 'General Plack, I talked to an old friend of yours recently.' He said, 'Yah? How's dat?' Beatty says, 'Sy Bartlett.'

"And Plack broke out in a big grin. He says, 'Ahhh, good ol' Sy.' He says, 'Ahhh, dem vas da wonderful days ven he was hitting me in da head with bottles instead of every day his fuckin' bombing.'

"Now, this is not the end. I'm in the Pacific when Plack is caught in the net. And the son-of-a-bitch—I get a communication from the Prisoner of War Commission asking me about Plack. He had given me as a reference! Can you believe this? I said, 'Hang the son-of-a-bitch with the speed of light.'

"The next thing I know, somebody shows me a Walter Winchell column. 'If Sy Bartlett knew that General S. S. Werner Plack was enjoying the premieres, the first nights on Broadway, blood would run. Plack is here as a witness for the State Department against Werner Best, the Boston newspaperman who had been charged with treason.' I sent the State Department the hottest goddamn wire and a copy of Winchell's remark. I confirmed that I would shoot Plack on sight. Because I'd read my dossier from the Nazi files. My boss had brought a photostatic copy of it. The Nazis were going to kill me on sight. When I flew over Germany, I always flew with a pistol. I had no intention of bailing out. I knew I had to kill myself."

Before the United States had entered the war, Bartlett went to England where he was schooled by the British in intelligence operations. He became head of the tactical section of the Eighth Bomber Command.

"While the British were training me, I would go on bombing missions with them as an observer, to write the manuals later for the American pilots in their bombing missions.

"Then I got an assignment on a seven-man team. I was the communicator. We were dropped behind enemy lines in Nazi-occupied Belgium and Holland. We were not supposed to engage the enemy. Our mission was to cut every road by laying mines and blow up all bridges to delay Nazi reinforcement of their troops. We were to avoid the enemy as much as possible. But we had this Lieutenant Colonel. He was a Harrow boy, and he was a wild bastard. He couldn't pass a Gestapo post without throwing a couple of grenades in it, and then we were on the run. We blew up over a hundred bridges.

"I was on this assignment for fourteen and a half months. Naturally we moved only at night and holed up in the daytime. You had to think like a Gestapo patrol—you know, where would they look for us.

"We were supposed to attend a meeting of all the resistance leaders. It was to be in this farmhouse, a beautiful farmhouse, in Belgium. Oh hell, we'd been on the move for seven solid nights in order to make this rendezvous. I walked into that house and, God, that groaning board! The hams and the meats and the drinks were just—you never saw. It was a page out of *Good Housekeeping*. Well, living the way we were, naturally I was too goddamn tired to eat.

"So I was shown to a small room in the back of the house, and I took my communication pack off and fell down to the bed. With my boots and all my clothes on. And, Jesus, I fought against falling asleep. Something just kept at me. It took a hell of a pull to pull myself out of the bed and get my pack I went out the window and I didn't follow the trail. Usually there's a small trail through the woods. But I went off the trail about a half mile in and about, oh, maybe another half mile away from the farmhouse. And I holed up in a potato patch, covered myself to make sure none of the metal of the communications glistened, laid my sleeping bag down, and went right to sleep. At three-thirty in the morning I hear this rat-ta-ta-ta and five of 'em died right there. This Welsh boy's the only one that survived besides me. The Nazis had been informed of the meeting. They executed everybody in the house.

"Now, I'm ordered to cross Normandy and come back home. I'd been away for ten months. I survived on potatoes and beets. It took me four and a half months to get back. Eventually I contacted this man in Normandy, and he buried me under a load of beets and penetrated the Nazi patrol that patrolled the Isle of Jersey. I was hidden on a boat that took me to the Isle of Wight. From there I was flown to the Oxford Hospital. And debriefed— after I had slept forty-eight hours. I didn't need any urging. I weighed 103 pounds. I started the mission weighing 148 pounds.

"Well, I later flew with the RAF. First I flew nineteen missions. Night missions. Then I flew seventeen more with the B-17s. The first bombing of Berlin was particularly dangerous because soon after takeoff, one of the Lancaster's four motors went dead. But the pilot decided to keep going. So the bomber never gained the altitude or speed it should have had over Berlin. And on the way back, a second motor went dead. We thought we'd have to make a crash landing, but we didn't.

"You know, I was ashamed of being a Hollywood writer all this time. I was self-conscious about it. Some of the Hollywood guys buddied up to Germans in the consuls in California. And some Hollywood guys used influence to avoid the military. So I tried harder and I did more than I should have, and that's what triggered me into becoming a very straight-line officer. And like in *Twelve O'Clock High,* the scene where I have a West Pointer brought in under house arrest. It was a natural occurrence from my own experience.

"This West Pointer, everytime he was set to go overseas, he would dog it. He'd make an excuse not to go. I called him in and I told him I understood his racket. Well, he continued to give me some trouble. So one day I had him stay in a brace position. Stand stiff. I had him standing there weaving with the sweat running down his clothes. And he'd ask permission to sit down, and I'd say, 'No! You may not sit down. You take a brace.' I kept that bastard standing for four hours. Oh my God. I never thought I could do that, never thought I could be so cruel. When it was over I went outside and puked. He went overseas and was a hell of an officer. And before I left, right after the war, he came into my tent and he took my hand and thanked me for saving his life. He's a Two-Star General now.

"But when it happened, it was just a horrible thing for me. Toward the end of the war, in Japan, I flew a mission with a freshman crew, as they say. We came back and were waiting for debriefing. See, I'm also Chief of Intelligence of all four groups and the wing. And this pilot said to me, 'Colonel, you're a West Pointer, aren't you?' Jesus, I wanted to reach over and kiss him. I thought, 'Here's a guy in the Air Force that doesn't know I'm Sy Bartlett, the Hollywood writer. I made it. I made it on my own.' I mean, I was always dealing with West Pointers who showed all the hostility that they had in them. And I just kept my nose clean. I never got caught with a boob. I had to be that good. To stay in that job.

"And that's the way it was. And when I got back, I had great bitterness against guys like Ronald Reagan. I could have knocked him outta the box when he ran for governor if I just picked up one magazine and read the contents of this magazine. Yeah, he went to war. There's a picture of him—I remember early in the war, there was one magazine that was so fingered and greasy—we had just lost five airplanes and just come back. It was bitter cold sitting in the tent, and every guy's eye is on me because the only magazine was a *Modern Screen* and it was automatically opened to a story, 'Ronald Reagan Goes to War.' There's his wife, Janie Wyman, holding one child. He's wearing a Cavalry Officer's hat from World War I. His boots are right out of Wardrobe. His britches, Warner Brothers. And as you read this tearful story, you learn that he's driving five miles up Ventura Boulevard where his job is to supervise the issue of underwear and socks and uniforms to GIs. This is the war Ronald Reagan fought. And what angered me more than ever was when I was on terminal leave. I'd been away from Hollywood six years, most of it in combat. And I see him at a Screen Actors' Guild dinner and he's shouting his face off. Which he was noted for. And he's saying, 'We ought to go to war with Russia now.' As I walked up to the table I looked at him and I said, 'When you say, "We," does that mean you, too, you son-of-a-bitch?' I turned around and walked outta the place and left my wife there and everybody. That's how sick I was. Alienated from my best friends. I couldn't stand to be around people. And the only people I was comfortable with were Air Force guys. And five of my officers moved out here and my sergeant, and it was—it was two years of a horrible struggle.

"I thought I could never write again and that I was fallow. I was, too, when I first came back to America after the war. This was the second time in my life that I had to start new in America, and each time it was one hell of a struggle."

# COLONEL JACOB MEYER ARVEY

One of the most stunning upsets in American political history was Harry Truman's victory over Thomas Dewey for the presidency in 1948. It was so close, so dramatic, so unexpected, in fact, that the Chicago *Tribune,* in a rush toward deadline, anticipated the outcome with its now-famous headline, "DEWEY WINS."

In *Inside the Democratic Party,* John M. Redding has described the days leading up to the election, and Jacob Arvey's involvement. Illinois was a pivotal state. Arvey was the powerful chairman of the strong Cook County Democratic committee.

REDDING: "One of the greatest demonstrations of the campaign was in Chicago only a week before the election. Plans had started modestly for a rally in Chicago Stadium which could accommodate about twenty-nine thousand. But Jack Arvey, all out for Truman since the (Democratic National) convention, sensed victory in the state. To get that victory he needed a tremendous vote in Cook County. So the plans were expanded and the effort intensified.

"We went to the Stadium on the West Side by bus, following behind the President's car. . . . Five thousand large pictures of Truman and the same number for [Vice Presidential candidate] Barkley. Every storefront along the route had at least one such picture and most had the glass solidly lined. The crowds were stupendous, massed fifty deep, for the twenty-four blocks from downtown to the stadium. . . . The massive crowds did come out for Truman, but they were triggered by Arvey's efforts. . . .

"At the Stadium, it was a noisy, enthusiastic crowd that cheered anything that moved. When the President was introduced, there was bedlam. The introduction was made by Mayor Kennelly. Oddly enough, Kennelly had been reluctant to introduce the President, for he was convinced Truman would be defeated. It was only when Arvey put on the screws that Kennelly agreed to do the job. . . .

"[On the night of the election in Truman's campaign head-quarters] Dorothy Vredenburgh, the party secretary, turned from her phone. 'I've got Arvey.' Howard McGrath [the campaign director] picked up the receiver. 'How are you Jack? . . . Tired? . . . How does it look?'

"Arvey was talking. '. . . Close, Howard, very close. By twenty-five thousand either way. I think it'll go our way. . . . If the edge is that close, the margin can come from the city wards here in Cook County.'

"McGrath nodded. 'Good man.'

"Howard was on the telephone talking for the twentieth time to Arvey. His face brightened and for the first time he showed real emotion. He looked at his wrist watch. . . . The time was 5:40 A.M. Then he looked at me and said, 'You can take it easy on those Illinois returns. We've got Illinois. Close, but we've got it for Truman and it's a landslide for [Senator Paul] Douglas and [Governor Adlai] Stevenson.'*

Not long afterward Harry Truman, before a mass of micro-phones at his headquarters, told a national radio audience, "If we've got Illinois, we've got the election."

---

Jacob M. Arvey was born in 1895 in Chicago on La Salle Street between Polk and Harrison. As a youngster he also lived on Taylor Street, between Clinton and Jefferson, just north of Max-well Street. His parents, Mr. and Mrs. Israel Arvey, were immi-grants from Russia.

Arvey and his wife today spend half the year in Miami Beach and the other half in Chicago. Arvey is still a senior partner in the huge and successful law firm of Arvey, Hodes, Costello and Bur-man on LaSalle Street, about a half mile from where he was born. Arvey is a sturdy-looking, vigorous man, an ardent golfer. He

---

* John M. Redding, *Inside the Democratic Party* (New York: Bobbs-Mer-rill, 1958), pp. 14–21.

stands five four and is unself-conscious about it. (Once, when Arvey was Illinois Democratic National Chairman, President Johnson invited him to the White House. "When I came into the room, the President hugged me," said Arvey. "Johnson was six four. It was the most comical scene you could imagine.") Arvey is bald except for a rim of white hair around the back of his head. He wears gleaming gold-rim glasses. His neck skin is surprisingly taut for a man over eighty. But his eyes and chin are the most remarkable features. There is both a steeliness and compassion in his eyes. His jaw juts and looks if not in fact fierce, then determined.

We talked in his Miami Beach apartment, with elegant furnishings amid a soft-blue motif. He wore sport shirt, dark slacks, and black shoes with laces. He speaks with the slightest trace of a lisp, but speaks distinctly, choosing his words carefully and cordially.

"My father came to Chicago because my mother's sister was married to a man who had a grocery store and was affluent. That is, affluent compared to my father who had no money at all. My father borrowed money from my uncle, his brother-in-law, to buy a dairy and bakery route. Bought a horse and wagon and peddled through the streets best he could. He'd get up at five in the morning to get the milk at the railroad siding and then he'd go to the bakery at six and get the hot rolls and the bread. In those days, the milk was in cans. And they had a dipper. He kept it on ice. No refrigeration, of course. And he was a very strong man. He could toss a can onto the wagon with his hands—not slide it on. Then he'd get on the wagon. I'd go with him once in a while. This was at the turn of the century.

"Well, when I was thirteen, something happened.

"One morning, as he was loading milk cans on his wagon, a train went by and the horse moved. The wagon went forward and my father fell on the railroad platform and a can of milk crashed down on him. He went into shock, what they call paralysis of the bowels. In those days, the medical technique for a bypass was not perfected. He lost an enormous amount of blood. Five days after the accident he died.

"Now, my father's wish was that he have a son who graduated from the university. I had three older brothers. One lived in California, one lived in New York, one was going to the University of

Chicago. He wanted us to be cultured. He had me take violin lessons. He used to sit there and listen to me practice for an hour. I musta been the worst violin player in the world. And I was soon in an orchestra, a children's orchestra. But the day he died, I put my violin away and never played it again. I suppose Freud could explain it, I can't. Maybe I somehow associated the violin with my dad—that was sixty-six years ago. And he's still with me. He made such an impression on me.

"I was the first child born in the United States. I wasn't my father's favorite, but I represented America to him. The new order. That for which he came. And as a child born in an atmosphere of liberty and opportunity, well—you know, where they came from in Russia and were poor not only in money, but poor in liberty and opportunity and in freedom and dignity. And they had no part in their government. They could not participate in the choice of who would govern them. And they were always in fear of the raids and assaults of hooligans and Cossacks, with or without government acquiescence. It's no wonder my father kept dreaming of America. He taught me always to be grateful to this country, even though we were very poor here, too. We lived in the rear of a store. No bathtubs, no inside plumbing, no money. But it was a better life than he had."

After his father's death, Arvey went to live with his aunt on Taylor Street. His involvement in politics began at the nearby Chicago Hebrew Institute—later named the Jewish People's Institute—where he helped organize a "Curventic Club," a combined form of "Current Events." His family moved farther west when his mother bought a candy store on Kedzie Avenue and Arvey went to John Marshall law school at nights while working. One job he had was covering basketball and softball games in the parks and settlement houses for the Jewish *Sentinel*, a weekly magazine. He campaigned for a professor who ran for judge. He made such a good showing that the regular Democratic organization leaders—the opposition—asked him to come into the fold. He joined the organization, headed by Mike Rosenberg, the ward committeeman, who had also moved west from his former home on Maxwell Street.

"I had become a good precinct captain," Arvey continued. "I

used to carry my precinct. And when Mike Rosenberg ran for Sanitary District Trustee in 1922, he asked me to manage his campaign. And he won. Now it came time to run a new alderman. He ran me. And I won.

"In 1931 I was the floor leader for the Democratic administration in the city council. And something happened then, a remarkable coincidence that had a great meaning to my life. Mayor Cermak called me into his office for a meeting of the representatives of all the medical schools in Chicago. The anticruelty society had protested the right of the city to deliver dogs to hospitals for the purpose of vivisection. The problem was this: Up to that time, dogs—unclaimed dogs, stray dogs—would be delivered to these hospitals for research. And they would be put to death after three days if no one claimed them. Blinded and put to death in gas chambers the same way minority people were put to death by Hitler.

"Well, the anticruelty society had appealed to the mayor. And so I proposed a kind of compromise ordinance. A dog must be held for five days, his loss advertised, and permit anybody to come and see him and claim him, owner or nonowner. And if at the end, after the dog was turned over to a hospital which the State had recommended, this dog would be given an added dose of anesthetic which was sufficient to put him to sleep. Without pain, without suffering, without torture.

"The head of the anticruelty society, a socialite woman, said she was going to sue us in court to prevent this from being done. She said we had no right to kill these dogs. There commenced at that time a campaign of vilification. I was very young, new, in '31, thirty-six years old. And the ordinance bore my name, the Arvey Ordinance. I got postal cards like 'Well, we can understand it. Your ancestors killed Christ. Why shouldn't we expect you to kill fine dogs?'

"Regardless, the ordinance passed.

"Now, let's jump to January 1946. I was operated on right after the war for bleeding ulcers, after I had come back from serving in the Philippines. Strangely enough, it was the same thing that my father died from, paralysis of the bowel. But by this time, the technique was perfected whereby they could operate by bypassing the colon with a catheter. While recuperating, I got a call from the dean of the Medical School at the University of Illinois. He said, 'I want you to know that the operation that saved your life, the technique which was employed in the saving of your life, was provided by experimentation with dogs. . . .' "

In 1934, Moe Rosenberg, the Twenty-fourth Ward committeeman, died. (He had taken over from his brother, Mike, who had died in 1928.) Arvey was now chosen as ward committeeman.

"For years the Jews were stanch Republicans, and they turned in big Republican majorities in the Maxwell Street area, the 'Bloody Twentieth' they called it. But Roosevelt made Democrats out of the Jews. Not only Roosevelt the man, but what he advocated. He was against restrictive immigration laws. He advocated collective bargaining by unions—now it turns out later, and this is an aside, that Roosevelt considered himself an emperor. He thought he had the ability to appease anybody. I don't doubt that in his heart he was for Jews. But I don't deny at all that he tried to appease the Arabs.

"Roosevelt told Jewish leaders, 'Why don't you go and buy up their land? You've got the money. They understand the value of a dollar. They'll do anything for money.' He said, 'You can outwit them. You've got everything on your side.' And this is what led to the founding of the nation of Israel. If it weren't for the buying of the land by the Jewish National Fund, we wouldn't have an Israel there today.

"I realized when I became ward committeeman that to get anything, you had to have power and let people know you have power. The history of the Jewish people is that they had to pay for things that they were entitled to under the law. They were denied things. They had to grease the palms of the authorities. Pay tribute in the shtetls. And the story of Maxwell Street is like the story of the Jews all over the world for centuries. They are raised amid violence, muscle, corruption, distortion. And I think it has been a mark of distinction that they've been able to survive it Endure it and then survive it and rise above it. Well, I was understanding that things could be better for the Jew The opportunity was there. We needed the power.

"And this is what we did in the Jewish community in Chicago. They did it in New York. This whole political evolution on that part of ethnic groups is the result of power. Political power.

"And I've been preaching that to my black friends for twenty years. Elect your own representatives. Have people in public office. Instead of coming on hands and knees to the supervisors and to the aldermen and committeemen and being obliged to grease palms in order to get what you deserve. When I'd address mass meetings I'd say, 'This is a political entity. Ninety-five per cent of this ward is Jewish. When we support the Democratic party in substantial fashion, they respect that power and you give your representatives a powerful voice in government.'

"In 1936, our ward gave Roosevelt 29,000 and some odd votes. Landon, seven hundred votes. When President Roosevelt was shown the returns, he said, 'This is the greatest Democratic ward in the country.'

"When I went before the county committee and wanted a man for judge, whether he's in our ward or elsewhere, if I wanted a Jewish man, they respected me. Some people say they feared me. They didn't fear me. But they respect that vote, and everyone wanted to gain my favor.

"We had a very strong organization. We worked with all the civic groups. A man could not be a precinct captain of mine unless he was a member of B'nai B'rith, a synagogue, a church, Elks, Mason, what have you. Any organization that had its roots, that had a power base or branch in the Twenty-fourth Ward. I served as alderman during a period when to fix a parking ticket and to run a handbook was the pattern. I admit that quite freely. I didn't bother them because they flourished all over the city. They never gave me any money. But it did widen my scope of influence. I felt you had to give something to the ward healers and those they felt responsible for in order to elect the good men you wanted.

"Before this, there were very few Jewish judges in the city, for example. Then the vote started to come in with tremendous majorities, 26,000, 27,000, 28,000 majorities. And we got more people on the tickets, a fire commissioner, Abe Marovitz in the state senate, and numerous judges. It came to such a pass that someone in the city council complained that too many Jews were judges.

"It was what is called a machine. Machine politics. *I am not ashamed of it*. There is only one meaning to machine: A disciplined organization. Strong enough to discipline its members.

"In 1939 I joined the National Guard. I had been working with the local commander, General Keehn, building armories, passing legislation. He got me to join by appealing to my Jewish instincts. I had told him I didn't want to join because I was not a soldier. Finally, he showed me—and this is when the Hitler thing was going on—he showed me on paper the number of Jews in the National Guard compared to their population. Woefully low. I was ashamed of it. He said, 'If you join, it will serve as an example to other Jewish boys to join.'

"One night in 1940 I was called in and told our division was going to be inducted into the regular army. Under the law, I had a right to resign my commission in the National Guard. If I stayed on, I'd have to resign my political and governmental offices. That was a hard decision for me to make.

"I was not poor, but I certainly wasn't wealthy. I had a fair legal practice and I had some real estate investments. So I said to my wife, 'This is one way I can serve in the Army and do my bit, which I couldn't do in World War I.' In the First World War, I had been a young married man with a small family and no one but me to support them. I now took the Army physical. I passed it only after faking the eye examination—I memorized the chart. I asked my law partner for a leave of absence, and he agreed. I resigned as alderman, resigned as ward committeeman, and went into the Army, the 33rd Infantry Division. I thought we'd be away a year or two. I was gone for four and a half years.

"When I returned, I found that some of the elements in our party were feuding. But they all accepted me. I had the fresh plume. You know, no scars. Just back from a long absence. Now some political writers said I got religion in the Army. Well, the war had influenced me to a great extent. It gave me a greater feeling for humanity. I felt politics could be more noble than it was. I hoped to be above petty party politics.

"I was named chairman of the Cook County Democratic Committee, and later Illinois member of the Democratic National Committee. In 1947 I was the one assigned to ask Mayor Kelly to step down. It was not my sole decision, but that's what happened. Immediately, then, I started thinking about elections of 1948. I wanted Martin Kennelly for mayor because he seemed a man of integrity, a businessman who was not sullied by the infighting of politics.

"And I made up my mind that I was going to sponsor Paul Douglas for senator. Why? Because he was so fine and genuine and the incumbent, a Republican, wasn't. Douglas was a distinguished college professor and had also been in the city council. Every one of the incumbent's speeches was punctuated with the same clichés:

"'And when the shrapnel which I got at Chateau Thierry starts acting up, when my back aches, I think of the sacrifice thousands of soldiers made for this country. . . .' Now, in 1946, I had organized a big political meeting at the Chicago Coliseum and Paul Douglas' wife was there as a candidate for congresswoman-at-large. Paul had just gotten out of the Marines. He had enlisted at age fifty, and his left hand had been shattered by a grenade. I had accompanied his wife, who spoke. I saw him at the back of the audience. I invited him up to the rostrum to speak. He said, 'No.' But he waved to the audience with that hand. And they went wild. That mere gesture indicated to them what he had done. Past the age of fifty, resigned from the city council, enlisted as a buck private in the Marines—he didn't have to make any speech about shrapnel or service or loyalty or patriotism.

"Now Truman was very unpopular at the time, and I believed that the only way we could win offices in the state was by getting fresh faces. Douglas was one. I also sought new blood for governor. I had been sounding out a number of people, business people and so forth, about who they'd recommend. One day on a train to Washington a friend named Dutch Smith mentioned Adlai Stevenson. I went to Washington for the purpose of picking a candidate for U. S. Attorney. I had been asked to make a recommendation. Scott Lucas, the Democratic senator from Illinois at the time, made a little luncheon for me in a caucus room. While there, I

spoke with James Byrnes, then Secretary of State, about my looking for a candidate for governor. He said, 'Why, you've got a gold
nugget in your backyard. I came across a man named Adlai
Stevenson in the Navy. He was an assistant to the U. S. Secretary
of the Navy. He's brilliant. His knowledge of world affairs
surpasses anything I've ever heard.' The name stayed in my mind.
I came back home, made inquiry about Stevenson. I got a speech
he had recently made to the United Nations. Then I called Dutch
Smith, who helped arranged a luncheon between me and Stevenson.

"This was in the fall of 1947. Over lunch that first time, I said
to Stevenson, 'I'm going to be very candid with you. I can't promise you that it will be done. I can't promise you that I would want
to do it. But how would you like to run for governor of the State
of Illinois?' He said, 'You must be kidding.'

" 'No, I'm not kidding.'

"I was already impressed with him, his speeches, his recom-
mendations, and his presence. He was modest to a fault. He kept
downgrading himself all the time: he had no experience at this, no
experience at that. None this, this, and that. Everybody else was
asking to be made a candidate. And this man, 'Oh, no. No, I
wouldn't run for governor under any circumstances.' He said, 'If I
have any experience at all, it's in the field of foreign relations. I
have no administrative experience.'

"Well, then, I started working on him. And the more he said he
didn't want it, the more anxious I was to have him. Finally we
went out to Libertyville, Illinois, with Dutch Smith. We met with
Adlai and his wife at their home. First of all, he asked me who I
had in mind to run for senator. I said, 'Douglas.' He said, 'He's a
very fine man. A good man.' He said, 'Well, what do you want me
for?' I said, 'I'll tell you why, because you're the very opposite of
the Republican incumbent, who is a tool of the Chicago *Tribune*.
There's a lot of scandal in the administration. You're fresh. We
can sell you to the public. With the help of Dutch Smith and his
wife, who agreed with me, he was finally convinced. And he gave
me his word that he would run if he received the party endorse-
ment.

"I took him before the Cook County Committee. Made my presentation. Told them that I was very happy to be his sponsor. And I made a motion that they endorse him for the office of governor. Subject to the primary, of course. And they did.

"I had the chairman of the state committee call a meeting of the state committee in Springfield. And Adlai Stevenson and I went to Springfield for the purpose of having him endorsed by the state committee. We went by train. Had a drawing room. And with me was our press secretary, Spike Hennessey. Now, this will show you how naïve Stevenson was in politics. He turned to me on the train and said, 'Jack'—by this time, we're on a first-name basis—he said, 'Jack, will I be required to say anything?' I said, 'Certainly.' He said, 'I've never made a political speech in my life. What do I say?' I said, 'Suppose you were honored by the Lion's Club or Masonic Order or Chicago Civic League. If they expressed confidence in you and advanced it by giving you an honor, wouldn't you respond? Wouldn't you thank them? That's all you have to do.'

"He said, 'Well, why can't you have Mr. Hennessey write something for me?' I said, 'No. You write it. And then we'll look it over.' Well, he went into the other room and on the back of a Western Union telegram wrote for what seemed only four or five minutes. He came back and he read it. I looked at Spike, and he looked at me. The papers have given me credit, but Spike Hennessey said, 'Stevenson, you don't need any speech writers. This is a new style in American politics, and don't let anybody change it.' It was just beautiful. He talked about—as I remember—for a man to enter public life was not an honor, it was an obligation. It was a duty. Just like a man being called to serve in the Army.

"But he still felt he didn't have the attributes to be governor. You know, a lot of people said he had an inferiority complex. Like when we tried to draft him to run for President. He couldn't imagine himself following in the shoes of Washington, Lincoln, Roosevelt, Truman. He was very unpretentious. A real Yankee. He never threw away any clothes. Like the famous hole in his shoe. I went to meet him once. I was in Washington and he was coming in. He called me, and I told him I'd pick him up at the airport. I met him and got his bag. He had a suitcase that was so worn out that it fell apart. We had to tie it with string. This is as

God is my witness. That Christmas I bought him a set of luggage. He wrote me and thanked me for being so observant. It was funny.

"By 1952, people are talking about Stevenson for President. Paul Fitzpatrick was the National Committeeman for the state of New York. And in order to raise funds for the upcoming campaign, he arranged a big banquet at the Waldorf Astoria Hotel. Invited Barkley, Kefauver, Harriman, Stevenson. . . . All possible presidential candidates. This is in about March or April. And then in between, about a week before the event, Stevenson announced that under no circumstances would he be a candidate for the nomination. He wanted to run for governor again. Well, this was a bombshell. And Fitzpatrick called me in Florida. I had a home down here then. And I hadn't been well. He said, 'Jack, you've got to get Stevenson to come. He's my headliner. We've advertised him.' So I called Stevenson, and said, 'Governor, I think you owe it to the party to go there.'

" 'But I'm not a candidate.'

" 'What difference does it make? You're the governor of Illinois. There are a great many people who want you to be their candidate. And in any event, you said you'd go and you ought to go.'

" 'Okay. If you say so, I'll go.'

"I called Fitzpatrick. He was jubilant. So the night before the event, I'm down here fishing, playing golf, whatever. I get a call from Bill Blair, Governor Stevenson's trusted assistant and buddy.

" 'The governor wants to know where you're staying in New York.'

" 'I'm not going to New York.'

" 'What do you mean you're not going?'

" 'I'm not invited. They don't want me. They want the governor.'

"The governor called me five minutes later. He said, 'What do you mean you're not going? I'm going there on account of you. Frankly, Jack, I'd want to speak to you about Harriman. I'd like to have you meet Governor Harriman.' He was interested in Harriman, the governor of New York, running for President on the Democratic ticket. And then he said, 'But if you won't go, I won't go.' So I went. I didn't know I was going to sit at the speaker's table. I'm seated in the center, right behind the microphone. And I'm in almost every picture that was taken of the speakers. I'm the only one in the crowd of four thousand who is not in a dinner jacket or dinner dress.

"Well, it was at that dinner that Harriman, who's a marvelous man, laid an egg in the streets. And Stevenson, with his wit and appropriate remarks, stole the crowd. For instance, some newspaper columnist said that there was a big romance between Eleanor Roosevelt and Adlai Stevenson. Adlai had been divorced from his wife, you know. He got up to speak at the Waldorf and he took note of that statement. He said, 'There is a romance between us, but it's on my part. I admire her. I respect her. I revere her. If she would even think of me as worthy of her, I would feel . . .' He went on like that. He had this knack. During the campaign for governor, his opponent said, in criticism of Stevenson's background, 'Are we going to have a striped-pants' governor?' Stevenson replied to him the next night, 'Well, I think I'd much rather want the striped pants of a diplomat than the striped pants of a man who's committed a crime.'

"After that banquet, I'll never forget it, Congressman Emanuel Celler of New York came over to me and said, 'Jack, you've got to make him run. He's our salvation. He captivated this crowd. He'll captivate the country. This is a new style.' Now when I met Stevenson, I said, 'Governor, don't ask me to go to Harriman. I respect him. I have great affection for him. But I cannot promise to be for him for President. Whether you run or not.'

"You know, Stevenson did not lose in '52 or '56, the two times he ran for President. Eisenhower won. Every once in a while, you have a wave of adulation, reverence, hero worship. Now, we had that with Kennelly, the mayor. Nobody could touch him at the time. Yet he was impotent as a mayor. He didn't know what was going on. But that's the way it was for Eisenhower. I'm an Army man, and I was for Eisenhower in 1947. I wanted him to be the candidate for President. I recognized his appeal to the people. I thought Eisenhower would make a great president. He's the leader of the Armed Forces. He spoke well. It was later that I discovered that it was General Bradley and a few more who were the heroes of World War II. That Eisenhower was a representative of them.

But when Eisenhower refused to defend General Marshall from attacks by Joe McCarthy because he didn't want to offend Joe McCarthy, he lost me. And he lost Truman, and lost many others.

"But Eisenhower had the capacity to pull the people together, and this is why I was for him in '47. And he did pull the people together. Now, from '52 to '60, people grumbled and complained, but never against him. He presented a united front, throughout the country, to the world. Looking back on it, those were some of the best years we've had as a country.

"But he could have done much more. See, always judge a man by what he could have done with the power. Eisenhower could have gotten away with almost anything; he had just that much respect and admiration. He could have done a lot with Russia. He could have gone to China. He could have straightened that out. But he didn't want to do it. He did only that which he had to do. He was more interested in his golf and social amenities. He's a typical Army man. I served in the Army, and I'm proud of that service and I respect Army service and the men in it. But there are some bad eggs there. In the main, they are loyal and dedicated men. But, unfortunately, sometimes when they get high up in power, they become lazy and indolent. I think Eisenhower, as President, was a lazy man. He was superficial. He let his staff work things out.

"But I didn't know any of this in '47. So I sought Eisenhower."

At this point Arvey referred me to a passage from Redding's book, *Inside the Democratic Party:* "The Palestine question and the civil rights problem combined to scare a number of Democratic leaders, particularly in the big cities. They were ignoring all of the political facts of life in a frantic search for a candidate with whom they might win. Jack Arvey of Chicago was one of these. . . . He wanted Eisenhower and was willing to ignore Ike's withdrawal as a Republican candidate. Apparently Jack rationalized Ike's refusal on the Republican side indicated the general was a Democrat and would be available to replace President Truman at the head of the Democratic ticket. No one knew whether Ike was a Democrat or a Republican because he had never voted. . . .

"I pointed out (to President Truman) that Arvey, O'Dwyer (of

New York City), and other defections resulted from Jewish political pressure in their areas. . . ."†

"Truman knew that the attempt to draft Eisenhower was in a way a ploy. And I knew he knew it," Arvey continued.

"I called in every Jewish leader in Chicago. All of us wanted the state of Israel recognized by the United States. Israel was the dream of all of our fathers—so Jews could have a place to go and live in dignity as first-class citizens. United States recognition would lead to recognition by the United Nations. I said to the leaders I had called in, 'I'm going to do something that may hurt many of you. Maybe all of you. But I've got to do it. I won't be able to sleep nights if I don't make this effort. I hope it works.' And then I said, 'I don't except any of you, out of loyalty to me, to embrace my position.'

"That's when I felt Eisenhower out about being the Democratic candidate. And he turned it down. Which was marvelous as it turned out. Why? Because I wanted Truman. I wanted to *be* for Truman, but I didn't think Truman could win. But I still was trying to force his hand."

Ralph Berkowitz, the first assistant state's attorney for Cook County, says today, "Jack Arvey told President Truman that if he does not recognize the state of Israel, then he couldn't guarantee that he could carry the Twenty-fourth Ward, let alone the county and the state." Truman knew he needed the Jewish vote to carry the state to win. Arvey intimates that that is what occurred.

On March 16, 1948, Truman recognized the state of Israel. "A week before the convention in '48, I took a train to New York City, and at Gracie Mansion issued a statement: 'I am for Harry S Truman as the Democratic nominee, and I will support him.'

"I got back to Chicago, and Truman called me. All I can tell you is this: He said, 'Jack, I know why you acted the way you did. But never have any qualms or doubt me.' I thanked him. I worked harder for him in '48 than I've ever worked for a candidate in my life.

"At the convention we met several times. We worked hand in hand. I was chairman of the party in Illinois at the time. The civil-rights plank was a major issue. It was still touch-and-go about

† Op. cit., pp. 147–49.

what should be done. We all went to see President Truman behind the stage. This was holding up the whole shebang. He said he'd support the civil rights plank. And we pointed out to him, 'Mr. President, you know the South will walk out.' He says, 'Well, if it's the right thing to do, let 'em walk out. If it's the wrong thing to do, they oughta walk out.' And someone said, 'You're doing it too soon.' And Hubert Humphrey, then the mayor of Minneapolis, said, 'We're 172 years too *late*.' That's why I've always liked Humphrey. He said, 'The Declaration of Independence was adopted, and the Bill of Rights provides that every man is equal—bing, bing, bing.'

"I was very active in the convention and I think that's what formed the close bond between the President and myself.

"We—the Illinois delegation—went back and we organized the whole state. And I was worried about some maneuvering. I asked the U. S. Attorney's Office to appoint men from the County Clerk's Office to make sure there would be no voting skulduggery downstate. And Truman knew about all these activities of mine.

"And then on election night when he found out we had carried Illinois for him, Howard McGrath, Truman's campaign director, got on the air and said, 'I've just had a telephone call from Jack Arvey in Illinois. That we will win Illinois. If that is so, we have won the election.' That's when he claimed it.

"He called me the next day and thanked me personally. And when he vacationed in Key West, and I was in Miami, he never failed to visit me at my home. He talked to me not as a President, or politician, but as friend to friend. We used to sit in a room with a couple of drinks and talk. And his wife, Bess, she was even warmer, if possible, more down-to-earth than he was.

"She never had been in our home that she didn't send Mrs. Arvey a little note thanking her, and with a couple handkerchiefs or flowers or something for our hospitality. There are some people who are warm, they're witty, they're obliging, they're kind. But they're patronizing. They feel they're doing you a favor by being with you. The Trumans were not like that. I'm rather proud that he personally invited me to his funeral. The arrangements were made well in advance. I was the only Chicagoan invited.

"I remember the night he started telling me about his anguish over the firing of MacArthur. He had great admiration for MacArthur as a general. And respected the pride MacArthur took in his military record.

"Well, Truman told me that MacArthur, if he had let MacArthur go, let him refuse to obey an order from the Commander-in-Chief to halt the invasion of North Korea, it would pave the way for a military dictatorship in this country. He said we must always subordinate the military to civilian authority. 'It was tough for me to do. I felt MacArthur was a hero, like everyone else. But I was doing it for the future of America.' Now this is over a Bourbon. He wasn't before an audience.

"And we also talked about the dropping of the A-Bomb on Japan.

"He told me he had relied on the advice of the Pentagon. That if we made a frontal attack upon Japan we would lose 750,000 to a million men. We had made warnings to Japan. To no avail. After the surrender, someone palmed a Japanese war plan. They knew about our invasion of Japan. Somehow they cracked our code. And we'd have lost a terrible high number of men. By the way, our division—the division I was in, the 33rd Infantry—was supposed to be one of the divisions attacking Japan."

Arvey was Illinois Democratic Committee chairman from 1950 through 1972, and as late as the '70s is credited with being a strong man-behind-the-scenes in national affairs. In Lawrence O'Brien's book, *No Final Victories*,‡ he mentions that it was in part Arvey's strong influence that persuaded him to assume the chairmanship of the Democratic National Committee.

Arvey's influence in Chicago and Cook County politics had waned much before that. In 1950, he made what he admits is a "blunder" for his choice for a sheriff on the county ticket. His blood pressure was up to 220. He said he was exhausted. And he resigned as county party chairman. "Governor Stevenson pleaded with me to withdraw the resignation, but I would not," said Arvey. Not long afterward he was elected State National Committeeman, a less trying job than that of county head.

He was also involved in a scandal of sorts in the late '40s. He and his law partner had purchased property along Congress Ave-

‡ Lawrence O'Brien, *No Final Victories* (New York: Doubleday & Co., Inc., 1974).

nue. It was there that a large expressway had been planned to be built. The newspapers hit the story hard. But a committee of the Chicago Bar Association looked into it and absolved Arvey of any wrongdoing. "If that's the only thing I've done wrong in my life," said Arvey, "I need have no worry."

Len O'Connor has written: "Arvey, who had a brilliant mind . . . gained such a reputation [for his skill in the law as well as in politics] that all the younger men, including Richard Daley, were openly in awe of the tough little man who was called Jake. . . . [In the 1930s] Daley watched Jake at all times, ingratiating himself with the budding city council leader at every opportunity. . . . Arvey was at pains to encourage the young man to keep at his books and get his law degree, promising Daley that great public offices were certain to be his reward. Like a Plato listening to Socrates, Daley was enthralled. . . ."*

I asked Arvey if he saw his influence in anyway in the Daley administration?

"No," said Arvey. "I helped him attain in a small way his leadership. I certainly did not stand in his way. I assisted in every way I could. But I've had nothing to do with his administration. He hasn't asked me. I served as the Park Commissioner for some time under him, but I was there when he got to be Mayor."

"I can't claim any credit for what Daley has done," said Arvey. "Of course, I can't be blamed or should not be blamed for any defects in his administration.

"If I accomplished anything during my years as Chairman, it was that I brought in young, new men to the party. I'm not proud of all of them. Don't misunderstand me. Kennelly was a bust as a mayor. But I had no means of knowing that. Douglas was a good senator. Sidney Yates is a good congressman. Bill Rifkin would become ambassador to Luxembourg. Abe Marovitz became a federal court judge. Otto Kerner was a good governor. Mike Howlett, the Illinois Secretary of State. Stevenson was a great national figure.

"President Kennedy flattered me one day. It was at a banquet in 1962. He said, 'We're having trouble in New York, Jack. If our

* Len O'Connor, *Clout: Mayor Daley and His City* (Chicago: Henry Regnery, 1975), p. 43.

people in New York had your sagacity and foresight and courage in picking a Douglas, picking a Stevenson, we'd have been in good shape there.' And Kennedy said very often it was in the 1952 Stevenson campaign that he got his urge to be President. He became a Stevenson follower. He was a great Stevenson follower.

"I made mistakes. I made a lot of them. But they're mistakes of judgment and not of the heart. I can live with them."

# MANNY STEIN

—Manuel D. (Manny) Stein, 42, lone Republican candidate for representative of the West Side 7th Congressional District in next month's primary, admitted yesterday that he had been found guilty of misdemeanors twice and had served 10 months in the Bridewell House of Correction for receiving stolen properties in one of the cases [when he was 15 years old].

Stein's case came to light after he had filed his nomination papers in the district long represented by A. J. Sabath, Democrat, 86, who has been a Congressman since 1906. Sabath is now seeking his 24th term, the longest continuous service record in American Congressional history, but is in failing health.

It was disclosed that Governor Stevenson had granted Stein a pardon last February 21 from the Bridewell sentence. . . . The Pardoning Board said it had received letters attesting to Stein's uprightness in recent years from Judge Abraham L. Marovitz and other prominent citizens.

Stein was an obscure West Sider until a few days ago when it was disclosed he had a police record.

"I have tried to live down my past," said Stein. "I have stayed out of trouble, and I

thought that this pardon meant my debt to
society was discharged."

Stein eventually withdrew from the race.

CHICAGO *DAILY NEWS*
*March 1, 1952*

———◆———

Manny Stein today owns a general merchandise store on the
North Side of Chicago. He also owns real estate. He has been embittered by the building inspectors who come in, he says, and say
to him, "Look, you got ten violations here that I can report if I
want to; I could make fifty violations out of it." And so he says he
must pay the tribute. "I could make $10,000 in repairs and it still
wouldn't be fixed as far as they're concerned." He calls Chicago
"Scum City." He is a thin, sallow-faced man with a heavy beard.
He wears glasses and has black hair. He grew up on Maxwell
Street. He is now out of politics.

He was asked how he first got into politics.

"By stealing a ballot box, in front of a policeman," he said.
"The policeman turned his back and let me steal the ballot box
and bring in another one that was full of ballots for the party that
paid me. That's it. I was sixteen at that time. I got five dollars for
changing ballot boxes.

"The elections in those days were like this. They had a policeman in the polling place. One particular place that I remember
was a barbershop called John Scarlotta's barbershop, near the
corner of Roosevelt and Blue Island. There was a backyard, and
a screen door to the barbershop. I parked my small Model-T
truck in the alley. I walked into the polling place through the
back door. The cop seen me come in. The election judges and
the cop all walked to the front window to look out as though
something happened there, and I put my box down, picked up
the other one, and carried it out.

"I got paid by the party organization of the ward. Both parties
did things like that. Although at the time it was for the Republicans that I did it. They'd be glad to give you five or ten bucks to
change ballot boxes. If I'd got caught, I'd of got ten years.

"Everybody in the place got paid off, too. There were such rotten things done over there, and I'm sorry to say that I was part of it. But I didn't know any better. I knew in a way it was wrong, yes. But I didn't realize to what degree it was wrong.

"I mean, who knew what politics was? To me and guys like me who were fourteen, fifteen, sixteen years old, politics was a game of who's the boss in the ward. But looking at it now, it means we survive on electing the right politicians. That's the only incident in which I ever did anything like that. If I could slap the shit out of myself for doing it, I would. I'd knock the shit out of myself

"But Watergate was a mud-pie game compared to some of the shit that went on *before* Watergate.

"But all of us, we were all trying to make a few bucks in those days. We were all poor. We were just hungry kids. In order to survive, in most cases, we would steal. A quart of milk, a few bagels, a can of sardines off the shelf, fruit off a fruit stand. We didn't go in for holding people up or breaking into homes or causing people pain. In our neighborhood we also developed some of the finest men in the country. You take for example the Honorable Abraham Lincoln Marovitz. We used to call him Abie years ago. One of the greatest men in the country. And Judge Ben Schwartz. We called him Shorty. See, our parents were hard-working people. Some of our fathers wouldn't make fifteen dollars a week to take care of a family of six. Some made as little as nine dollars a week.

"And when I got my five dollars from the politicians, I remember I went and got the dollar bills changed into coins. I went to the pool hall and stood around rattling the change in my pocket to let people hear that I got a lot of money. Then I went to a restaurant and I ate like pig eyes, you know?

"But by 1952, when I ran for Congress, politics was the same dirty game as when I was a kid, except it was being done on a bigger scale. That's all.

"I pulled out of the race because I saw that a lot of monkey business was being pulled. To the point where Congressman Sabath died about seven days before the election—but nobody knew it outside of the hospital. They kept him on ice in the hospital under orders of the mayor. Mayor Kennelly. That's how strong the mayor was. They didn't let anybody know Sabath died so that his name would still appear on the ballot as a legitimate candidate.

So he won the election. Had they immediately let the news out, my name was on the ballot, on the presidential ballot with Eisenhower, I could still have won the election and gone to Congress.

"I ran as a Republican on the same ticket with Eisenhower and with William Stratton for governor. And it was a landslide. I automatically would have been declared the winner because anybody else who would step in immediately to take Sabath's place would have had to be a write-in candidate. No write-in candidate could have beat me as a printed candidate on the ballot. I would have been elected congressman of the Seventh District.

"Sabath was supposedly in the hospital as a sick man. About three or four days after the election they announced he had died. The truth never came out that he was dead during the election because automatically Congress would have put me in.

"I withdrew because of pressure. I knew that I'm bucking the Democratic machine, and I wasn't getting much Republican support, and I knew that they're going to pull something and they're eventually going to win. And why throw any more money into the thing? I already had $40,000 of my money in it. President Eisenhower's secretary called me from Washington and asked me to get off the ticket about a month before, that I might hurt the Republican Party. The *Daily News* had come out with 'Ex-Convict!' headlines. A kid I was then. I want you to know how rotten the newspapers are. I want you to know how rotten the world is. I had bigger headlines than Eisenhower's victory. But I got letters and I got contributions from oilmen and from people all over the country, telling me to stay in it, not to pull out.

"So Eisenhower's secretary calls and says, 'Get off the ticket. The general wishes you to get off.' So I said, 'You tell him to kiss my ass and you, too.' Stratton was running for governor and he called me and he says, 'I'll give you a good job. I'll give you a $16,000-a-year job. Get off the ticket.' He says, 'We'll put somebody else in that's got a clean record.' I said, 'You, too, like I told the President-to-be, you can kiss my ass. I ain't gettin' off. . . .' Directly on the phone I talked to him. And I told him to go fuck himself. When I pulled out I pulled out on my own, not with pressure or not with anybody telling me what to do. I saw there was no way of winning. No way. No way. I got in to the race hoping that the son-of-a-bitch would die. I had it figured out that he wasn't going to last.

"But they covered it up. Nobody knew, but I had a hunch. And then my hunch came out about ten days after the election. And I got it. I got it direct from a doctor's assistant in the hospital who I knew very well—very well. And I was told in all confidence, 'I want you to know he was officially pronounced dead four days before the election.'

"There were people in politics at that time who would steal the eyeballs right out of your sockets. I knew many of them personally. Like I knew what the Twenty-fourth Ward was. It was the chosen ward of Chicago. No one there could do wrong, no matter how bad it was. Every precinct captain would have fifty or a hundred ballots already marked and in the boxes, and nobody ever dared question the count in the Twenty-fourth Ward. I mean, the Twenty-fourth Ward, you might say, was like the Mafia of the wards in Chicago. But what I knew about the Twenty-fourth Ward was after Alderman Arvey. Arvey, as far as I know, was a gentleman. A big man, but I don't think anybody could point a finger at him for being illegitimate.

"The Twenty-fourth, when I knew it, was run so tight and so crooked and so crummy. It was like the old Twentieth Ward used to be—the Maxwell Street district. The old 'Bloody Twentieth' Ward. Years ago that was the Mafia of all the wards. You could buy the police off with a buck and a quarter.

"It goes back to the days of Morris Eller, alderman of the Twentieth. The Twenty-fourth was an outgrowth of it. Eller was a two-bit whore in his heart. He tried to buy everything and everybody. He had a favorite saying—he spoke with a bad accent—'A vote for me is a vote for you.' He acted as a helper of people, but he made people pay through the nose to him to help. He bled 'em dry. But that was life in that time. Nobody dared say anything. If anybody did, he might wind up in an ash can. You'd see shooting on the streets. And nobody would say a word. I recall a certain fellow whose name I won't mention was killed under a pushcart. A fruit peddler's pushcart. He was shot about twenty times by a certain fellow, who in fact was his friend. They would go out stealing together. And because of a certain division of their ill-gotten gains, one tried to screw the other, and this one fellow shot the hell out of the other kid. When they buried him, his head looked like an apple. A hundred people saw it, and this guy was never apprehended. The following day he walked the streets. Walked right past the place where he killed this other fellow. People were afraid of their own skulls, so they never talked."

# MEYER LEVIN

Meyer Levin has been called by Norman Mailer one of the finest writers in America. However, numerous critics do not share Mailer's view and Levin, author of at least twenty published books and two famous plays, has felt he has been the target of a cabal of the "literary Mafia."

In one instance, beginning in 1953, Levin wrote, "In the middle of my life I fell into a trouble that was to grip, occupy, haunt and all but devour me." It dealt with the writing of the play, *The Diary of Anne Frank*—the diary which Levin first brought to public attention.

He is the author of *Compulsion,* the best-selling novel and play about the infamous Loeb-Leopold murder case; his novel, *The Old Bunch,* delineates life on the West Side of Chicago in the 1930s.

Levin was born on October 7, 1905, on Sangamon Street, just off of Maxwell. His father, an immigrant from Lithuania who went into tailoring, soon moved the family to nearby Racine and Taylor streets.

He was fifteen years old and in high school when his first story was published. The periodical, long defunct, was called *Ten Story Book* and was "a lurid little magazine," according to Levin.

"The story I sent them was a sort of Fannie Hurst ghetto tale about a Jewish boy who was ashamed to have his gentile sweetheart encounter his Maxwell Street family," Levin wrote in his autobiography, *In Search.* "One day his girl insisted that they go slumming along the pushcart ghetto street, and when she stopped to bargain at his father's stand, he pretended not to know his own father. I received ten dollars for this unconscious bit of autobiography, and a warm note from the editor. . . .

"Like so many of us, I seem to have begun with an unconscious resentment and rejection of my Jewish 'prison' which showed itself in my first story. Again and again through life, as I experienced difficulties and some forms of suppression in the publication of my work, I experienced the castration fears so evident in my early stories. . . .

"I began to struggle with the Jewish element first by trying quite unconsciously to 'pass,' as in [the novels] *Reporter* and *Frankie and Johnny,* where I eliminated the Jewishness of my characters. I then had a healthier perception of my difficulty and tried to absorb and understand my Jewish material, all through the years in which I wrote *Yehuda, The Golden Mountain* and *The Old Bunch.* But the extent of my self-understanding was so limited as to leave me with a typical sense of overrighteousness. . . . It was only in [covering as a reporter and writer] the Second World War was I able to recover my feeling of free and full identification as a Jew. For through my war experiences I came to recognize the universality of the guilt feeling, finding it even in the survivors, and I came to recognize the indestructability of the Jewish quality, in seeing its persistent life in the deepest spiritual ruins of Europe. . . ."*

Levin now lives with his second wife in a duplex apartment in the West Nineties in Manhattan. There is a winding steel staircase between the first floor and the ground-level floor. It is a neatly kept apartment, with a comfortable number of books in shelves, and a colorful collection of paintings on the walls in the otherwise darkish apartment. Levin writes in a room that seems hardly bigger than a pantry. The window overlooks a small yard. He had recently been at work on the late morning that I visited him. His sparse gray hair was rumpled. His voice is low and hoarse. He seems intense, brooding, preoccupied, and decent.

"All three kids—my two sisters and I—were born on Sangamon. I don't know if they considered them slums. See, today, when we go back and look at those streets, we consider them slums. Sure, there were the pushcarts on Maxwell Street. But on

---

* Meyer Levin, *In Search* (New York: Pocket Books, 1973), pp. 541–42.

Halsted Street were stores that were considered, well, fancy. Jewelry stores, fancy dry goods. I remember my mother once bought a *shventa,* a bronze little statue—a female figure—on a pedestal about this high, with sort of entwined tendrils of leaves. And that was inspiring to have art in the house.

"When we moved to Racine, I'd still go back to Maxwell Street because my grandmother lived there. My father had brought her and his whole family over from Europe—a sister, a brother, and his mother. And they worked for cigar makers. When we moved to Racine, the family considered itself on the way up. And at one time, just about when the Depression broke, my father was in those times fairly well-to-do, to the point where he closed his shop. He owned real estate, a few buildings. Then the Depression cleaned him out. So he opened another tailoring- and cleaning-and-pressing shop.

"I lived on a street in which on one side was all Jewish and the other side all Italian. And there was quite a lot of nastiness and threatening to beat us up. I don't remember any real beatings up, but threatening, you know. But I was always afraid of it. There were scrappier kids than I, I suppose, who did get into scraps. But since I was timid and a scaredy-cat, I—one time I did. A guy taunted me with sheenie. I knocked the guy down out of sheer fury and was surprised that I did. My dominant childhood memory is of fear and shame at being a Jew. Going to school each day was like running the gauntlet. At each house the Italian kids might be laying for us with knives. 'I'll cut your nuts off, you lousy little sheenie.'

"It was also a Mafia neighborhood. Just before Prohibition, I remember, two rival gangs fought it out for supremacy. There were shootings between them, and once from our front window we saw them shooting it out in the streets. And everybody was running to their houses. I stayed hunched down by the window.

"My first book was bought for me by my mother for my fifth birthday. She asked what I wanted. I said, 'Buy me a book.' In our house we had only religious books and religious stories. So my mother went to a store and the saleswoman figured that at my age I'd like a Horatio Alger book. That's what I got.

"We lived near the Jewish People's Institute on Taylor Street.

They had a library there. I went there as a kid and that's when I first started gobbling books—out of that library."

Levin began to write stories in grade school. He decided at that time that he wanted to be a writer.

"My mother and father were aware that the fundamental goal of Jewish family life was for the son to become either a lawyer or a doctor," Levin wrote. "However, they said, they would not try to influence me or hold me back from any path I chose. They would try to help me. But, my mother worried, could one make a living as a writer?

"I appealed to my father, as being in contact with the outside American world. Writers made fortunes, I pointed out. Especially since the invention of movies. . . . Although I sensed that my parents still hoped I would study medicine or law as a safety career, my nine-year-old self understood that they were too timid to advise me because they felt that even an American child knew better than a pair of immigrants about the way of the world. All through childhood I sensed, and resented, this terrible shame and inferiority in my elders; they considered themselves as nothing, greenhorns, Jews."

Levin said that some of the shame he felt about his father's foreign background may have emanated from his father himself.

"He didn't talk much about the life in Europe," said Levin, "except that America was a totally different civilization, and I never questioned him about it. I probably would just as soon have swept it under a rug at the time. So we just picked up what we learned as small children in the family get-togethers. My parents took the self-effacing attitude that 'Oh, that life was not worthy, really, of America.' Something like that. It wasn't an attitude that was spelled out; it was just in the air.

"I was reminded of that feeling a few years ago when I traveled to Russia. I visited Moscow. It was the only place in Russia that we saw Jews. We visited the Ukrainian villages, where the shtetls were, and there are no Jews left. But in Moscow, I found a curious parallel to us in America. The Jews there were assimilated to the Russian culture. Our guide was a Jewish girl, it turned out, and her mother was some kind of designer. Her father was an electrical engineer. They corresponded to our middle class. They

*Above left:* Muni Weisenfreund (later Paul Muni), vaudevillian, on stage of Yiddish theater in Maxwell Street area. Photo taken about 1911. He would then have been sixteen(?) years old. (Albert Fenn Collection)

*Above right:* Irving Jacobson, playing Sancho Panza in Broadway hit, *Man of La Mancha.* (Courtesy of Irving Jacobson)

Jake "Greasy Thumb" Guzik. At Senate Crime Investigation hearings in Washington, February 28, 1951. (UPI)

Jackie Fields, welterweight champion of the world, prior to defense of his title against Young Jack Thompson. December 26, 1929. (Wide World)

*Below left:* Fields, right, and Vince Dundee weigh in for title fight that night, January 24, 1930, in Chicago. (Chicago *Tribune* Photo) *Below right:* Fields, January 29, 1932, day after regaining welterweight title from Lou Brouillard. (Chicago *Tribune* Photo)

John L. Keeshin. In Washington, D.C., for transportation hearings, 1955. (UPI)

*Below:* Early Keeshin transportation service vehicle. (Courtesy John L. Keeshin) *Bottom:* Latter-day Keeshin trucks. (Photo by Pics, Chicago; courtesy of John L. Keeshin)

*Left:* Beatrice E. Tucker, age eighteen, at Bradley University, 1916. (Courtesy of Dr. B. E. Tucker) *Right:* Dr. Tucker shortly after delivering baby at a home, in 1975, at age seventy-seven. (Photo by Michael Mauney)

*Left:* Building in background is the Chicago Maternity Center, Maxwell Street Dispensary, on corner of Maxwell and Newberry streets, 1938. (Courtesy of Chicago Maternity Center) *Right:* Dr. Joseph Bolivar De Lee. (Courtesy of Dr. B. E. Tucker)

Gypsy family on Maxwell Street. Left to right, Prince Peter Bimbo (son), unidentified woman standing, King Tene Bimbo (father), Mary (mother) seated. Inset: Rose Bimbo (daughter), 1925. (Chicago *Daily News* Photo)

*Below left:* King Levinsky with his sister - manager "Leapin'" Lena Levy. At training camp, 1931. (UPI) *Below right:* Levinsky fish market, Maxwell Street, February 25, 1937. Sara Krakow, left, mother of King Levinsky, and Annie Minsky, daughter of Sarah and sister of King. (Chicago *Tribune* Photo)

*Left:* Birthplace of Barney Balaban in 1887. Address is 1137 South Jefferson Street, Chicago. The Balabans lived in the first-floor rear and entered their flat through the side door. The Balabans soon replaced "Frank A. Kapsa, tinner," in the storefront, with a grocery store. Barney Balaban, showing this picture to a reporter in 1940, said, "Behind those lace curtains above the store lived our 'rich' neighbors." Barney Balaban, when president of Paramount Pictures, lived in a twenty-two room house on an estate in Rye, New York. (Courtesy, Leonard Balaban) *Right:* Balaban family, Passover, 1912. Standing, left to right: Barney, Abe, Max, and John. Seated, left to right: father Israel, Elmer, mother Gussie, Harry, Ida, and Dave. (Courtesy of Leonard Balaban)

First two Balaban theaters. (Courtesy of the Chicago *Herald Examiner*)

*Left:* Chicago Theater, Balaban and Katz, 1922. (Theater Historical Society, Chicago) *Right:* Interior of Uptown Theater, Balaban and Katz. (Theater Historical Society, Chicago)

At ceremony on February 8, 1953, Barney Balaban unveils script of Abraham Lincoln's first proposal leading to the Emancipation Proclamation. President Dwight D. Eisenhower looks on, along with his wife, Mamie, and Mrs. Balaban. Balaban owned the document and presented it to the New York Avenue Presbyterian Church in Washington. Lincoln worshiped at that church. (UPI)

*Left:* Young Benny Goodman, 1939. (UPI) *Right:* Soviet Premier Nikita Khrushchev waves his finger at Goodman during conversation, July 4, 1962, at a reception in the U.S. Embassy in Moscow. (UPI)

Playing clarinet, Goodman leads a group at Carnegie Hall, New York, June 29, 1973. Slam Stewart is on bass, Gene Krupa is on drums, and Lionel Hampton plays the vibraphone. (UPI)

worried about getting luxuries and about whether their children could get into the university. And she would tell these little snide anti-Semitic stories that were pretty much like our own stories in the '30s. It was all quite familiar to me.

"What else was familiar was that the children were so far assimilated from their religious practices and beliefs that they corresponded to our own generation of breaking away from the old religious ways. So that one day our guide came to me and said, almost secretly or naïvely, 'Well, my mother told me that in Jewish houses there is some kind of a thing they put on your doorway. Could this be true?'

"I said it was a *mezuzah,* a kind of talisman. It is a sign and reminder of the faith. She considered this as if it were an anthropological curiosity but at the same time she felt very strongly that a bond existed between us. She was with us for two or three weeks. The bond grew stronger. But she never invited my wife and me to her house. And she would always find ways to reassert her Russianness. But it was perfectly clear that she was very, very confused about her background and that it was almost, you know, like a mulatto thing."

Levin was a prodigy. He was writing stories and plays even in high school. When he entered the University of Chicago at age sixteen, he quickly became part of the artists' circle of the university. And he got a job writing part time for the Chicago *Daily News.* A coup for a young man then. The *News,* at the time, was the center of the Chicago literary set.

"I was just one scant half-generation too young for that famous literary circle which was the last time Chicago had an importance in this area," said Levin. "That was *the* period when Chicago was the literary capital of America. Edgar Lee Masters, Dreiser, Sherwood Anderson, Carl Sandburg, Vachel Lindsay, Ben Hecht, Maxwell Bodenheim, and some lesser-known people all centered around the Chicago *Daily News.* And the major figure of this little circle was a very strange man named Henry Judson Smith. A kind of removed, sallow guy who was the epitome of the man who wants to write and has spent most of his time in a journalistic job —but who writes a few touching sketches, and encourages other writers through his job. He gave jobs to all these people that became this Chicago literary circle, like Sandburg. When I was on the paper, Sandburg was writing movie reviews perhaps once a week and doing a perfunctory job. All he'd do, he'd recite the plot of the movie.

"All these quite well-known and already famous men had a place, a restaurant named Shlogl's, near the paper, where they would foregather for lunch a couple of times a week. I was eight, ten years younger than they, and I would never dare come there as one of the group. I would occasionally be taken along in a patronizing way by one of the higher-level reporters who was almost a literati. No, for the most part, I lunched instead across the street from Shlogl's, at a little delicatessen counter where one could get a real, West Side corned beef sandwich.

"But that group of wits and great people eventually broke up when several of them moved to New York.

"I had become friendly with John Gunther, who was a year ahead of me at the university. I published in the literary magazine that he and a few others had started at school, called *The Circle*. When he graduated and became a correspondent with the *News,* I called him and he helped get me on the paper. When I graduated, I planned to go to Europe on a cattle boat. That was the traditional postcollege thing you had to do in those days. John Gunther had already gone.

"Well, I was on the paper writing feature stories and the Loeb-Leopold case broke. I had one foot out toward Europe. But then I thought I'd get assignments on that case. I covered the arraignment, but decided the case wouldn't come to court until I got back from Europe. I was in Paris when the trial came on and I read all about it. I missed covering it. The whole thing.

"When I returned I sat at the next desk to Alvin Goldstein, who covered the case, and uncovered the important typewriter evidence.

"So there is a confusion in which people think I was involved with the case in a way I was not. The use of a reporter as a storytelling device in *Compulsion* made people identify it with me."

For a number of years, Levin was a bright and promising writer, and then a highly praised, best-selling author. In the late '50s, when *Compulsion* was published, Levin said, "The book was an instant success. All at once I was a celebrity, an authority.

Every radio and TV program wanted me to discuss the psychology of crime, and whether Nathan Leopold should be on parole. I found myself virtually crusading for him.

"For the first time in my life I had real money. Just turning fifty, I could at last give up the time-consuming scramble for a living while writing. . . . Yet as to the obsession, the success changed nothing. All that happened on *Compulsion* would immediately be evaluated in my mind in relation to the struggle over the *Diary*."

Levin, through a mutual friend in London, had come across *The Diary of Anne Frank,* which had been rejected by numerous publishing houses. Levin helped Otto Frank, Anne's father, secure publication for *Diary* in English, Levin also precipitated the stage production of *Diary*. It had been agreed to by Otto Frank that Levin would write the Broadway stage play. Levin did. Frank came to New York to see to the authenticity of the staging. "But at that point," said Levin, "the prominent playwright, Lillian Hellman, and her producer, Kermit Bloomgarden, had persuaded him, he told me, that as a novelist I was no dramatist, that my work was unstageworthy, that it had to be discarded and someone else should write it.

A new drama was written. Levin fought it in the courts, in the press, on his analyst's couch.

"From the start," he said, "I had strongly suspected that some doctrinaire formulation rather than pure dramatic judgment had caused Miss Hellman's attack on my play. And after the substitute work written under her tutelage was produced, I became convinced that I had been barred because I and my work were in her political view 'too Jewish.' The whole affair increasingly appeared to me as rampant McCarthyism, a classic instance of declaring an author incompetent, in order to cover up what was really an act of censorship.

"The whole point centers around one speech of Anne's—a speech of her Jewish affirmation. Anne says: 'Who has made us Jews different from all other people? Who has allowed us to suffer so terribly up till now? It is God who has made us as we are, but it will be God, too, who will raise us up again. If we bear all this suffering and if there are still Jews left, when it is over, then Jews, instead of being doomed, will be held up as an example. Who knows, it might even be our religion from which the world and all the peoples learn good, and for that reason and that reason only do we have to suffer now. We can never become just Nether-landers, or just English, or just . . . representatives of any other country for that matter, we will always remain Jews, but we want to, too.'

"In its place, Anne Frank is made to say, 'We're not the only people that have to suffer. There have always been people that have had to. . . . Sometimes one race . . . sometimes another.'"

Levin said, "Now, the actual psychological effect of omitting such a passionate Jewish speech from the stage . . . who can imagine it? The attitude is that the Jew would assimilate and disappear. To take out 'Jewish suffering' and put in 'all people suffer' is to equalize the Holocaust with any kind of disaster. If you do this, you unhook the search for meaning, you unhook the wrong to the Jews. Then you go on over the years with statements like 'There weren't six million. There were four million. There were two million. There were a lot of Russians and Poles who were killed in those camps. So the Jews are just exaggerating. And you end up with what they're using now. The bottom line reads: 'The Jews did worse to the Arabs in Palestine than the Nazis ever did to the Jews.' It's been stated that way by any number of leaders in the United Nations.

"My version of the play was suppressed, though great chunks of what I originally had were used in the Broadway version. And for all that, I got destroyed for fighting it. That's the Anne Frank issue in a nutshell."

Fifteen years after it began, Levin was awarded fifty thousand dollars by a jury for his part in the stage version of *The Diary of Anne Frank*. But the attempt to get his version staged continues. He says that the desire to perform his play grows. He gets more and more requests for it.

"They got their version, now, this literary Mafia, and they made millions of dollars on it, and eventually smeared or destroyed my career so that all I have left, in certain areas, is a moral victory."

Even his greatest literary triumph, *Compulsion,* became a kind of tragedy for Levin. Nathan Leopold sued him for invasion of pri-vacy, though Levin never used Leopold's name in the thinly disguised portrayal of the crime and the men involved. Leopold lost in court.

"In the *Diary* affair I was being represented as a troublemaker, a man who had harassed poor Otto Frank, and in a similarly inverted way the claim of Nathan Leopold again made me out to be a devil," wrote Levin. "In those strange depths where public sentiment is determined, Leopold was now a victim, a man who had suffered 30 years of imprisonment as if in a death camp; he was a kind of culture hero—my book had helped make him so. . . . Whereas Meyer Levin was an exploitive writer who had first of all tried to make a fortune from Anne Frank, and then had battened on the miseries of Nathan Leopold, out of which he had become a millionaire!

"And for me, just as the Frank troubles had been truly an issue of literary suppression, so the Leopold case involved a whole area of artistic freedom, the freedom to use personages and events from living history. Dostoevski had done so in *Crime and Punishment,* Dreiser in *An American Tragedy;* an entire area of literature was occupied by such works, and this lawsuit threatened to close off the use of living material."

Levin adds now: "Well, I managed to get by. But I think I might have become a better writer if I hadn't had to devote such an awful lot of energy to this Anne Frank thing, which has become a consuming fight for some 20 years. Also, the tangential effects on my career as a whole has not allowed the point of interchange of ideas and feelings with contemporaries in that time. I've been more or less shut off from them because of the Anne Frank thing and there's been a kind of Mafia-like, underground literary attack on me so that by now, when a book of mine is published, the chances are it will not be reviewed very widely, or well.

"Outside of the New York influence, the reviews are good. But in the magazines and on radio and television, where exposure really counts, I get the silent treatment. I feel a kind of blacklisting. Shows that I once got on won't have me anymore. I feel angry, but there is also this curious aspect to rejection: no matter what the reason for it, it brings a sense of shame.

"It's so similar to those fearful, unforgettable experiences I had as a child, as a Jew, growing up in a Chicago gangland neighborhood."

# THE STREET, 1957

## MAXWELL STREET MARKET TO FADE WITH $5-MILLION SLUM PLAN

—The eastern end of noisy, colorful Maxwell St. Market may be displaced in a proposed new $5,000,000 land-clearance project. One of the city's most notorious slums also will be cleared.

Since another portion of the Maxwell Street Market will be used for the South Expressway, the market where some 70,000 people haggle on Sundays probably will be shifted to the west side of Halsted. . . .

Industry already has moved heavily into the proposed Clinton-Roosevelt area. Long before it came, however, the old houses, in which one wave of newcomers after another had lived, had deteriorated badly.

More than 90 per cent of the residential structures, according to Phil A. Doyle, executive director of the Land Clearance Commission, are dilapidated or lack air and sanitary facilities for the 1,650 people living in the area. . . .

CHICAGO *SUN-TIMES*
*April 16, 1957*

# MORRIE MAGES

Morrie Mages recalls: "When I was a little boy we used to get up at four-thirty or five on a Sunday morning to open our sporting goods store on Maxwell Street. . . . I had three brothers and as we got older we joined my parents in the business. I'll never forget when I was eleven or twelve—that would be 1928 or 1929—I stood on a pushcart on a Sunday. My father had bought a special deal on jackets similar to team jackets for semipro football teams, and I was up there on the stand yelling my little heart out to sell the jackets for . . . I don't know, maybe five or eight dollars. I was on top of the thing for maybe eight, ten hours yelling, 'Jackets, jackets, jackets.' We sold out every one to the last jacket. We must have had five hundred of 'em."

The Mages family's business grew tremendously. The Mages Company eventually owned fourteen stores in Chicago. The family had left Maxwell Street by 1960 when, because of family clashes, the fourteen stores were sold. Each member of the family was relatively wealthy. Morrie Mages, the youngest brother, had assets totaling about one million dollars. But in about five or six years he had, he says, "forty cents left in my pocket." He returned to Maxwell Street with merchandise and with an agony that was beyond embarrassment, he says.

Mages today owns a sporting goods store again, in Chicago, on North La Salle Street. It is five stories high and a big sign in the front proclaims it, "The World's Largest Sporting Goods Department Store."

Mages is a stout man with a quick step. He remains a mass of energy and enthusiasm. His hair is dark and so are his eyebrows. He makes good eye contact. He is a kindly hustler. He was particularly well-known in Chicago in the 1950s because he would be seen on television advertising the "Mages Moment of Madness," dealing with special sales for his sporting goods stores.

"Our business life and the struggle to make a living was a twenty-four-hour-a-day business," said Morrie Mages. "All conversations, whatever went on in our house in most instances, were about business. How can we improve? How can we give our kids better education? My mother was working right alongside my father. We were all in the business. My brother Ben, he was with my father all through the years. And my brother Sam who became an attorney. And my brother Irving who was an accountant. Irving opened his own store. Ben stayed on Maxwell for a good while. I was in college, class of '38, but I only made it to '37. My mother knew that when I came back from the University of Illinois that I'd have to make a living. So she was planning. She said to my father, 'Maybe we can open up another little store*kala* for Moishe.' So I went into a new store.

"We became the largest sporting goods stores in the world. We had a store where we sold nothing but boats. We had a store where we sold nothing but foreign cars, sports cars. We built two big bowling alleys. And we became a public company. In 1960, we sold out our interest. All the brothers decided that they weren't getting along with each other too well, and there were jealousies or whatever have you.

"My dad died in 1945; my mother died in 1958. Both died before we sold the business. But I think we would have sold out whether they were on the scene or not. The brothers squabbled. I guess this is par for the course. Take the Goldblatt brothers or the State Street Mandel brothers. Their families split apart, broke up, and the business was divided.

"And there were jealousies. For example, people knew me from being on television. I don't know; I was just the one to do it. And like I know when my brother Irving would go on the street, they'd call him 'Morrie.' I guess he didn't like that very well.

"So we decided to split and we found a customer and we sold out the stock in the Mages Sporting Goods Company to someone else. Everybody came out smelling like a rose. I stayed with the new owners for about a year, and then I left them and decided to go into other businesses, away from sporting goods. And as a result, inside of from 1960 to 1968, I lost practically everything I had, and I had to go back to work.

"I bought a department store that I didn't belong in. It's a different ball game. I had no business selling ladies' slips, dresses, coffee pots. . . . And other investments—whatever I touched—turned sour. That's when there were tears.

"I looked around and I looked in my bankroll and you don't have nothin' left. I went from the department store to selling whiskey. And I had big debts to pay off. And I began drinking too much, maybe. Well, I mean, I was selling whiskey so I had to sample it. That's a joke, but I wasn't joking then.

"The whole pallor of my face was serious, that the whole world around you is. . . . How can you do such a thing to yourself? It was so stupid. You gotta be smarter when you got money than when you haven't got it.

"When you get a success under your belt and you've made money and you've got substantial assets and everything is going well, you have a tendency of looking at things and saying that everything is good. That's when you gotta get tougher with a buck. You gotta look at things and you gotta say, 'This might be good, it might be bad.' And instead of where you think to yourself that you know everything and you're the greatest and, you know, if a guy could know everything about one thing, that doesn't mean he knows everything about everything else. When you have money, like they say in *Fiddler on the Roof,* 'When you got money, everybody thinks you know.'

"So I began to avoid people that I knew, that knew me. Out of embarrassment. I put myself in a shell.

"What about my friends? Didn't have any. Lost them all. I had had lots of friends. But everybody likes a winner and if you're a loser, or if you can't pay your own way and travel in style like your friends can afford to do, you lose your friends, of course. Not that it's their fault. It's just the way the ball bounces. I'm talking about social friends. Real down-to-earth love and affection and help comes within your family.

"My wife, she kinda broke away from me a little bit, too, because I was unlivable, let's say. You know, I was wrapped up in my own shell. I came and went. There was no conversation, hardly. She took a job and she was working. And we would meet at home and that was it. She worked. My father-in-law is Meyer Gold, who used to own that great restaurant on Roosevelt Road. And he was always supportive. You know, he's eighty-three years old and he works in my store now and he's terrific. He doesn't have to work, but he does.

"Well, I was working then for the Union Liquor Company and as a result of losses taken on my income tax forms, there was a tax audit. Which was a normal thing. My taxes were generally audited every two years by the Internal Revenue Service. But now they claim that I owe them an additional three thousand dollars. I didn't have the money. I tried to make an arrangement where I would pay them so much every week or every month, and because of my name being so well known, they couldn't believe that I went through this kind of money. . . . They said, 'No, we want it all at one time.' So they put a lien on my bank account, my salary, my wife's salary—she was a manager in a very exclusive dress shop. So I'm walking around with about forty cents in my pocket and I got nowhere to get money. And the only way I can drag anything up and get my salary is to pay off three thousand dollars. So I went to my brother Irving, who at the time had an office at 4 North La Salle. He was involved in an oil company and was reputed to be very, very wealthy at that time. Now this goes back to '65, '66. I asked him for this money. Well, after five conversations, he finally found a note long enough for me to sign.

"Oh, he wanted a big, long note. He gave me the three thousand. I paid it to Uncle Sam, and they released the lien.

"I didn't like working for someone else. I wanted to get back in business for myself. Not that I'm a big shot or anything, but when you're laying in the gutter that's when you have to have the strength to do something. And tears ain't going to give you no strength. You just have to say, 'I'm going to get it done.'

"I went back to what I know, with what little money I had. I began picking up various close-outs from friends of mine in the sporting goods business. That's when I went back to Maxwell Street and tried to sell this merchandise. So on Sundays, at about four in the morning, I would load up a little vehicle I had and then head off for Maxwell Street. I wound up back there in 1968 and '69. For two full years every Sunday I was there. Rain or shine. Snow or sleet. I was there. It was on Newberry right off of Maxwell. Right around the corner from where my father, a Russian immigrant, started his business in about 1918, when he'd pick up odd bits of crockery to sell on a pushcart, then bought a couple baseball gloves, sold them, bought more, soon opened up a basement with sporting goods, then a store, two stores on the street. I was back starting from scratch here like he did.

"But I didn't feel good about it. When you're going backwards, you don't feel too good. And I had lost my embarrassment. When you're out of money, you have to lose your embarrassment if you want to come back. I had a fellow, Joe Austin, that worked for me. The two of us stood there together. It was a wooden stand about ten, twelve feet long. You rent a piece of wood and a couple of horses from people in the marketplace.

"I began to take in two, three hundred dollars on a Sunday. Four hundred dollars. If I'd get lucky, it was over five hundred dollars.

"Now, with this money, I opened a little store on Chicago Avenue. I was back in the sporting goods business, the so-called wholesale sporting goods business. While I'm on Chicago Avenue, a friend of mine named Dave Perling calls me and says, 'Morrie, I got some skis. I got some boots.' I said, 'Eh, what do I know about skis and boots? Lemme alone. You got shirts? You got jackets? You got athletic equipment for teams? . . .' Well, he didn't give up. He called me again maybe two weeks later. Then he called me again two weeks after that. I figured, well, maybe I better go out and take a look at this stuff. I went over to his place and I knew nothing about skis and boots or anything else. But I saw a roomful of stuff over there, and I figured maybe I should take a crack at it. So I bought the whole thing for five hundred dollars. And I'll tell you the truth, I didn't know what I had there. But it was a lot of everything. I had to make three or four trips with my little truck. I brought it into the store. I put a classified ad in the Chicago *Tribune* to run on Sunday morning that I'm running a ski sale. I didn't even know that at the time, '68, skiing was going like this—straight up!

"That morning when I came down to the store, at nine Sunday morning, there was a line of people in front of that store. Oh maybe thirty, forty people waiting. I was all by myself with Joe Austin. And these people start coming in and they'd ask me how much this is. Well, I'd kinda guess. For the first sale, I told the guy it was ten bucks. He bought it so fast that the next guy that asked how much this thing was, already it was fifteen. He bought it, too.

"That was a whale of a thing. I kept advertising in the classified section. Here, after having spent close to half a million dollars a year on television, I am back spending fifty bucks for an ad.

"I'm taking a wild guess, but I would say that being in the right place at the right time, latching onto that stuff, following it through the way I did, I probably received for that five-hundred-dollar investment, without exaggeration, probably took in five thousand.

"I had had a relatively small room. I moved around the corner to a bigger place. I did well, moved out of there and into an even bigger place in a year. I eventually get enough capital to go into a full line of sporting goods.

"So now I got a little success behind me. People are talking. But just when I began a little something, in '67, my brother Irving is looking for his three thousand. Well, I was still in no position to give him anything. I was still diverting my profits into more merchandise, building the business.

"I had made an arrangement to pay him so much a week or so much a month. I made two payments or so and I'm unable to make the other payment. Well, he turned this note over to a bank and they start dunning me for the money. I had no obligation to them. I had an obligation to him. With my brother Irving, everything is done on a very formal, businesslike basis, whether it be your brothers or sisters or anybody else. 'Talk to my lawyer.' To give you a phone call and say, 'Morrie, how're you doing? Can you send me something?' He's not that kind of guy. I couldn't pay him, although I wanted to. I knew I owed him the money.

"Finally, because he was doing everything so formal, without any heart, without any brother concept, without any phone call, I decided I don't owe him nothing. I don't know what I want, but I'm not going to send this guy nothing. So he got a lawyer after me. Brother. Anyway, we finally negotiated a settlement with his lawyer. I think I paid him fifteen hundred dollars and tore up the note. That's in 1968. In 1972 I never heard from my brother Irving a hello or good-by. Just from what I hear other people saying, he's gone on an African safari; he's involved in the Livingston Oil Company; he just sold his interest in the oil company for perhaps a lot of money. Maybe half a million or thereabouts. So now I'm in a store on Wells Street, a pretty good-sized store, and in walks Irving. He's down in the dumps. I'd heard something about marriage problems with his new wife. We say hello. Then he calls me aside and he says he's had such a bad time, lost a bundle—a bundle of money in the market and other things. He's got to get into something; he has no income. What can he do? I took my brother Irving around the shoulder, and I brought him into my office in the back there, my little office, and I said, 'Irv, how much was the settlement that we made on that note?' He had the figure right in his head. I made him out the check for fifteen hundred dollars and I said, 'Thanks very much. You really helped me when I needed it.' And I didn't say it derogatorily, either. So I said, 'Now, how are we going to help you?' I said, 'Irving you're gonna need income. Why don't you go back in the sporting goods business?' He says, 'I'm sixty-five. I'm too old.' I says, 'You gotta work.' Now, he still owns a house in Palm Springs, California, and he's trying to sell a co-op apartment here in Chicago, which he eventually did. He finally rents a little store in Palm Springs and he lives there now all year round. He reminded me—walking around the way he was walking around—he reminded me of me five years previous, six years previous. I figured to myself I went through it. So I know what he needs. He needs encouragement. I can't help him with money. I can't help him do the job. But he needs a push. He went out to Palm Springs and got himself a little place. He called me about two or three months later. I flew out there and I sat down with pencil and paper and I mapped out what he should have in the store and I built him the same kind of a store that I put together for myself. Good lighting, cool, nice carpet. And I gave him the catalogue of practically every source. He'd been out of the sporting goods business for so many years, he couldn't remember. So he had to refresh himself. He opened a nice little store and his name is Mages and he's doing business. And he's probably happy. But I still don't hear from him. That's the way he wants it, I guess.

"But I have to worry about myself. I stand at this counter in my store twelve hours a day. I hear people talk. In most instances, they will say, 'This place is incredible.' From a selection standpoint, from a merchandising standpoint, from a housekeeping standpoint. It's not a glamorous setup with fixtures or anything like that. It's just a place that oozes with merchandise and personality. There's four floors here. And we're going to go up because there's four more floors that we can rent. I'm proud of it, a five-floor dynasty. Especially after going down and coming up like an escalator. And I did it.

"And I learned it all on Maxwell Street. It's the greatest university in the world, to teach a guy life and values and struggle and accomplishment and success and disappointment. Fantastic. It was a challenge every day to go there and make yourself better. Pull yourself up by the bootstraps every day. I am the world's greatest sporting goods merchant and I learned it all on Maxwell Street. But I don't advertise it now. What's there to advertise? Do I have to advertise where I put myself in the gutter? I think the first time I've ever even talked about it to anyone at any length is right now. As a matter of fact, by coincidence, yesterday, a young fellow came in to buy something, and he walked over to the counter where I stood and he says, 'You know, Morrie, you don't remember me, do you?' Well, a nice, young fellow, looked to be in his late twenties. He said, 'I was the fellow who used to sell pillows right next to you on Newberry Street on the stand. On Maxwell, in '68 and '69.' And he's reminding me of Maxwell Street. . . .

"When I was down there, some people came by and said, 'Aren't you Morrie Mages?' Something like that. I would pass it off like it didn't even occur. I'd say to them, 'That's my father, you mean,' or 'That's my brother,' or 'That's my uncle.' But no more. Morrie Mages is Morrie Mages again."

# ADMIRAL
# HYMAN GEORGE RICKOVER

—Hyman Rickover is in the headlines as a national hero and pioneer of the age of the atomic submarine. . . . [But] in the small Chicago apartment of his elderly parents the memories are of a boy who wept when he left home to journey to a place called Annapolis. . . .

The future history-making admiral spent his boyhood and got his early education on Chicago's West Side in modest surroundings.

The Rickover family saga in the melting pot land of America is in the classic tradition of immigration. The father, Abraham, traveled to New York alone from his native Poland in 1899, worked as a tailor and by 1906 had saved enough to send for his family, his wife, Ruchal (Rose), his daughter, Fannie, and his son, Hyman, who had been born in Makow, Russian Poland in 1900. . . .

Capt. Rickover attended the June 14, 1952, ceremonies laying the keel of the *Nautilus*. President Harry S. Truman said that the vessel provided the first tangible proof that the atom could be harnessed to serve man's peaceful pursuits, and that Capt. Rickover more than any other single individual is responsible for its construction.

The following month Sec. of the Navy Dan

Kimball presented Rickover with a gold star
and citation. Of the one-time Western Union
messenger boy from the West Side, Kimball
said: "He has accomplished the most important piece of development work in the history
of the Navy."

The citation took note of the captain's long
struggle with these words: "He has held
tenaciously to a single important goal
through discouraging frustration and opposition. . . ."

But the day after these glowing words were
broadcast the Navy's Selection Board by-
passed him in making promotions to rear admiral.

This meant that Rickover, reaching the
age of 53, would be forced to retire in
1953. A storm of protests developed in Congress. . . .

CHICAGO *SUN-TIMES*
*September 3, 1958.*

———————◄◆►———————

Admiral Rickover himself had nothing directly to do with Maxwell Street. He says that he recalls only that "it was a street with
pushcarts." The Rickover family lived on the West Side in the
Lawndale district, the budding Jewish community that was developing a few miles west of Maxwell Street. The Rickovers had
come to Chicago in 1907, after Abraham Rickover had lost his
nest egg in an apartment building in Brooklyn. Abraham decided
that Chicago offered greater opportunities than New York. Some
of Abraham Rickover's relatives had already moved from the
Maxwell Street area to the West Side, and so that's where he settled. His first apartment was located at 3243 Grenshaw, virtually
around the corner from the Kedzie Theater that the Balabans
would buy in 1909.

Families like the Rickovers, though not living in the immediate Maxwell Street area, still were dependent on it in numerous respects. As Rabbi Leonard Miskin said, "The West Side for the Jews was truly the Greater Maxwell Street Area."*

For one thing, many men like Abraham Rickover were compelled to work around Maxwell Street where the factories and shops were massed. In 1910, of the total number of tailors in Chicago, 68.6 per cent were Jews. And the great percentage of tailoring establishments were in that Maxwell Street area (where they worked twelve to thirteen hours a day for as little as six and seven dollars a week).

The Maxwell Street area, even for those Jews living farther west, remained a great shopping and cultural center. Many of the best kosher meat and poultry markets were located there, as were the most appealing clothing stores. The most popular department stores were L. Klein's at Fourteenth Street and Halsted, and the 12th Street Store, at Roosevelt and Halsted. It wasn't until World War II that immigrant Jews began to shop regularly in the Loop. The finest delicatessens were on Maxwell Street. Gold's was the plushest Jewish restaurant. The Yiddish-language newspapers were published and sold around Maxwell Street. The Yiddish theaters were there. It was still an Old Country meeting place. And, of course, it was where the bargains were.

To a recently emigrated, poor, orthodox Jewish family like the Rickovers, Maxwell Street would surely seem integral to their lives.

The first time Hyman Rickover saw a ship was when he took one to America. With the money sent by his father, the three remaining Rickovers in Russia traveled across Germany, sleeping in what they had described as "bleak dormitories" provided by German Jews. They were to board for America at Antwerp. His sister, Fannie, who at eight was two years older than Hyman, recalled that the future admiral burst into tears. "The boats were so big," she said, "they frightened him."

At seven, Hyman was already a tinkerer and builder. He constructed a small table which his parents used for the next fifty

---

* R. L. Mishkin, author and historian, was, when interviewed in 1975, a rabbi at a North Side Chicago synagogue.

years. "He was always clever with his hands," his mother once recalled. She also remembered that as a boy selling newspapers or delivering messages after school, he would often return home with some kind of present: a pot to boil potatoes, spoons, dishtowels. All practical things. "We had to watch our pennies," said Ruchal Rickover, his mother. "We taught the children to spend wisely."

Work quickly took on deep significance for Hyman Rickover. At eight, he was delivering papers before school, had a job in a grocery store after school, while attending Lawson grade school. While at John Marshall High School, he worked a four-to-midnight shift as a Western Union messenger.

"Brought up under strictest parental supervision, the Rickover children learned the meaning of frugality early in life," wrote Clay Blair, Jr., in *The Atomic Submarine and Admiral Rickover*. "In the Spartan household, waste was met with severest punishment.

"By the time [Hyman] Rickover had reached high school age, he had worked at a variety of jobs. Slight of build, he was a stubborn child. Once his father had to chip away at his front teeth in order to force medicine down his throat. He was proud of his self-sufficiency and asked for nothing."*

His grinding work schedule allowed him no time for parties, for football games, or much association with friends. He was very much a loner. He also studied hard, though he did not receive the best grades. He once failed two subjects because he was too sleepy from outside work to digest the schoolwork. He did well enough at Marshall High School, however, to have a friend intercede for him with the U.S. congressman of his district, Adolph J. Sabath, and seek appointment to a military academy. Since his father could not afford to send him to college, Hyman knew that a tuition-free military school was his only chance for higher education. Rickover was offered an appointment at Annapolis.

In order to cram for the tough Naval Academy entrance examinations, Rickover decided to enroll in a prep school in Maryland. He paid three hundred dollars, his life's savings. But after two weeks he realized that he could be better prepared for the upcoming tests if he studied on his own. So he quit the school, passed the exams, and entered the Academy in 1918.

---

* Clay Blair, Jr., *The Atomic Submarine and Admiral Rickover* (New York: Henry Holt, 1954), p. 35.

He was a diligent student, and no social butterfly. He did not "drag" like the others on weekends in Baltimore or Washington because he could not afford it. His parents sent him two dollars a month. Rickover also frowned upon the traditional hazing and harassing by upperclassmen. He shunned athletics. He tried and failed at swimming and fencing. He received poor marks on the drill field. "Scornful of the juvenile rituals at the Academy," wrote Blair, "Rickover finally withdrew to the privacy of his room. Dedicated to a life of hard work and scholarly pursuit, he read almost constantly, storing up odd bits of knowledge." He graduated in the upper quarter of his class.

"In Rickover's time (class of '22), life for a Jewish midshipman at Annapolis was marked by unpleasantness," wrote *Time* magazine,† without going into detail. But Clay Blair said in an interview in 1975, "This class was extremely anti-Semitic. There was a Jew named Kaplan who stood number one in the class, and in the school yearbook they had the page of this guy perforated so that everybody could tear it out more easily.

"The Navy was notoriously anti-Semitic. No Jew could ever hope to make Admiral. There may have been one other Jew in all of American Naval history who made Admiral.

"And whichever Jews stayed in the Navy, they almost never received command of ships. Rickover in the '30s was given command of a target towing ship. Some little repair tug. It was ridiculous. You could hardly call it a ship."

Whatever Naval pursuits he undertook after graduation from the Academy, Rickover applied himself with an almost obsessional diligence.

"Rickover's severely practical approach, his tireless energy, and his refusal to compromise on technical excellence paid off handsomely during the war," wrote Richard G. Hewlett and Francis Duncan in *Nuclear Navy 1946–1962*. "His own inspections of the fleet revealed electrical equipment of poor reliability and obsolete design; circuit breakers that would pop open when the ship's guns were fired; cables that would leak. . . . In addition to correcting scores of such deficiencies, the electrical section under Rickover developed fundamental engineering data on such subjects as

† *Time* magazine, "The Man in Tempo 3," January 11, 1954.

shock-resistance and took the lead in designing new and improved equipment. . . . By 1945 . . . Rickover had built the most creative, productive, and technically competent section in the Bureau of Ships. . . . [But] Rickover had anything but an ingratiating personality. He remorselessly pointed out flaws in Navy equipment even when they were outside his responsibility. He could speak with devastating frankness, never put his personal feelings above his mission, and did not try to conceal his contempt for such military traditions as captain's inspections of full-dress parades. These predilections had sometimes antagonized Rickover's fellow officers. . . ."‡

Regardless, by the end of the war he had won the rank of captain.

Rickover, who had obtained a masters degree in electrical engineering from Columbia University in 1929, was in line now to head a new nuclear technology project at Oak Ridge, Tennessee. Despite his proven abilities and his engineering background, many higher-ranking officers feared that Rickover would be too single-minded, too bullish, too unmanipulative for their purposes. In the end, Rickover's tremendous capabilities proved the last word.

"Rickover," wrote *Time* magazine, "had a vision. At Oak Ridge, he and his little command of four eager young officers painfully fought their way through mathematical entanglements to the strongholds where dwelt the atom. They came to the conclusion that the Navy, to remain a vital fighting force, must have nuclear propulsion, and that the logical place to apply it first was in submarines."* Submarines, because they were battery-run, were too slow, too vulnerable—always needing to surface for more "air"—to be useful against the modernized sonar systems. Much of military concern in those days was the stockpiling of atomic bombs. The atomic submarine seemed to many a waste of time and energy. But Rickover finally convinced Admiral Chester Nimitz, then Chief of Naval Operations, of the importance of the project.

When he got the money, Rickover and his crew went feverishly

‡ Richard G. Hewlett and Francis Duncan, *Nuclear Navy 1946–1962* (Chicago: University of Chicago Press, 1975), pp. 33–34.
* *Time* magazine, op. cit.

to work. He would phone "my gang," as he called them, even in the middle of the night, if need be, with instructions or questions. He had little tolerance for mediocrity and none for stupidity.

Rickover is five five, weighs one hundred and twenty pounds. He now has snow-white hair with a soft wave in front and a little cowlick in back. His nose is hawklike. He walks rapidly and straight. He has been described as "elfinlike" and "wispy" and "a slight, spare human tornado." There is still apparent in his voice a coarse, flat Chicago West Side inflection.

He was demanding of his workers. Scientist Alan Laser, working on the building of the ship the *Nautilus,* in the huge black-walled building in Arco, Idaho, and whose father, Meyer, was born and raised and ran the family feather-bedding business on Maxwell Street, recalls that Rickover would come in like a whirlwind, checking, asking, poking, prodding. "We all had the greatest respect for him because he certainly had a genius and knew how to get things done," said Laser. "But still, you could not deny my feeling that he had a personality like a prune."

Laser, however, adds that Rickover indeed was a colorful character and that many stories and legends were circulated about him. "One I remember," said Laser, "gives an example of his sense of humor. They tell a story about when he had his first heart attack—he subsequently had a second, by the way—anyway, he was at Bethesda Naval Hospital. His wife had gone out and bought a very expensive cemetery plot. When he found out about that he raked her up one side and down the other. He said, 'How could you spend money so foolishly. You know I'm going to be in the ground for only three days.' "

Rickover was a driving aesthetic. "For most of his life, if not all of it, he has denied himself the usual pleasures of food, drink, flesh and so forth," said Clay Blair. "I don't know. I think it probably grew out of his childhood. I believe his parents were probably that way, by necessity. And it was a condition that he found not unappealing and continued it as a matter of routine.

"I remember having lunch with him a few times, in his office, which was very uncluttered. The floor was bare. He was allergic to wool. He had his secretary bring him this lunch on a tray. It would consist of a cup of chicken broth, a hard-boiled egg, and an apple. Honest to God, that was what he was served. For the two of us, we would each have that. Plus a couple of Saltine crackers. And we'd sit and talk. Then I'd leave. And go have lunch."

In 1949 a young ensign fresh out of Annapolis entered Rickover's office seeking a job in the nuclear submarine program. The recruit was James Carter of Plains, Georgia.

Carter, in his 1976 presidential campaign autobiography, *Why Not the Best?*, wrote: "Admiral Rickover had a profound effect on my life—perhaps more than anyone except my own parents." The title of the book is taken from a remark in their initial interview.

The two sat alone in a large room and talked for two hours. Rickover allowed Carter to pick the subjects he felt he knew best. Whatever it was, from gunnery to music.

"Rickover soon proved that I knew relatively little about the subject I had chosen," wrote Carter. "He always looked right into my eyes and he never smiled. I was saturated with sweat.

"Finally, he asked me a question (in which) I thought I could redeem myself. He said, 'How did you stand in your class at the Naval Academy?'

". . . I had done very well, and I swelled my chest with pride and answered, 'Sir, I stood ninth in a class of 820.' I sat back to wait for the congratulations—which never came.

"Instead the question: 'Did you do your best?' I started to say, 'Yes, sir,' but I remembered who this was, and recalled the several times I could have learned more about allies, our enemies, weapons, strategy, and so forth. I was just human. I finally gulped and said, 'No, sir, I didn't always do my best.'

"He looked at me for a long time, and then turned his chair around to end the interview. He asked one final question, which I have never been able to forget—or to answer. He said, 'Why not?' I sat there for a while, shaken, and then slowly left the room."†

Carter got the job in the nuclear submarine program.

In the course of five years, from 1947 through 1952, the nuclear submarine was constructed. It was completed in at least half the time that anyone had expected. And done over the obstacles of

† Jimmy Carter, *Why Not the Best?* (New York: Bantam Books, 1975), pp. 63–64.

bureaucrats and officers who tried to keep rein on Rickover. The remarkable submarine used uranium for fuel; its engine needed no air; it could cruise around the earth without coming once to the surface. It could make an attack across the Pacific without poking more than a periscope into the atmosphere. It could sail under the arctic ice. It could also launch missiles. Rickover also saw how these nuclear reactors could save much money as conventional sources of power.

Despite all his accomplishments and encomiums, Rickover was passed over for admiral by the Naval Selection Board, a group of the highest-ranking Navy officers who secretly decided on promotions. Theoretically, they can be overruled but they hardly ever are. And if they "pass over" a candidate, there is usually no appeal.

*Time* and *Life* magazines leaped in with querulous stories on this "injustice." The Secretary of the Navy, the head of the Atomic Energy Commission, Rickover's superior at Oak Ridge—all were vocal in his support. Rickover, disappointed, continued working, still being rigid and, as some would think, antisocial. He would not even deign to be photographed by *Life* magazine, until his superior at Oak Ridge ordered him to do it.

Rickover was not interested in publicity. Even at the laying of the keel, he stood in the background in a gray civilian suit. He would rather have been back at his office, doing "the more important things."

One year after the first "passing over" and one day after receiving the legion of merit medal from Secretary of the Navy Kimball, Rickover was again passed over by the selection board. This seemed to mean that, at age fifty-two, Rickover, at the height of his powers, would be forced to retire.

Why was he passed over? His personality clashes was one reason, of course. He was not over-awed by the tradition that was so great a part of the standard Naval officer's world. Rickover seemed too narrow and, unstated, too uncompromising in pointing out waste and inefficiency in the Navy.

"Unquestionably some of the opposition in the Navy to Rickover's promotion was based on personal animosities, spite and even religious prejudice," said Hewlett and Duncan. "Although none of the naval officers, including Rickover, interviewed by the authors would acknowledge that religious prejudice was an influence in the Navy during these years, the authors concluded on the basis of all the oral evidence that Rickover's Jewish origins did in some instances fuel the antagonisms between Rickover and his fellow officers. Religious prejudice was in our opinion a reinforcing but not a controlling factor in Rickover's unpopularity in the Navy."‡

Blair said, "The factor of Jewishness was studiously avoided in the battle to keep Rickover in the Navy. It didn't seem tactically wise to raise it."

Rickover's case was strongly defended in Congress by U. S. Representative Sidney Yates, from the district where his family resided on the North Side of Chicago, and from U. S. Senator Henry Jackson of Washington.

Said Representative Yates on the floor of the House of Representatives: "Mr. Speaker, we are moving into an atomic age. We are engaging in a desperate race with a deadly enemy for the discovery of the secrets of nuclear power, the control of which may well determine our fate and the fate of other free nations. At such a time it is unthinkable that service politics . . . should be permitted to throw into the discard knowledge which is essential to our well-being. . . . It is in the best interests of the nation that he be given the promotion in order that his talents may continue to be used for national defense. . . ."

President Eisenhower, moved by these appeals, called in his highest Naval commanders. In 1953, in an unprecedented set of circumstances the Naval Selection Board after passing over Rickover twice made him admiral on a third try.

Today, he continues to work in nuclear projects for the Navy, with an office and secretary in Washington, and as a retired but still active and volatile vice-admiral.

He continues to be a thorn in the side of many Naval bigwigs. He continues to rip the "red tape" of the service, and the incompetence. For example, in 1975 he suggested, among other things, a reduction of twenty thousand in the number of Navy officers and the overhaul or closing of the service academies.

‡ Hewlett and Duncan, op. cit., p. 245.

He believes much of higher education in America is a waste, and has been for years a gadfly in this area. "It comes out," he has said, "that we have many more children in high school and universities than Europeans have in secondary schools and universities, and this makes us proud. But all these comparisons are meaningless because the European secondary school graduate has learned more than most of our college graduates. As to the high school diploma, the less said about it the better."

His feelings about America, his adopted country, may be summed up by a characterization he wrote of George Bancroft, who had written a monumental history of the United States. Rickover included Bancroft along with men like Edison, Washington, Lincoln, Will Rogers, George Washington Carver, and John Marshall in his book *Eminent Americans*. About Bancroft: "He did not observe and report the doings of his historical figures with the detachment of a scientist describing the movement of atoms and neutrons. . . . He was a fervent patriot, deeply committed to democracy."*

Rickover, needless to say, was himself a passionate American. But the "Old Country" ways of his family caused him some discomfort, according to *Time* magazine: "The Rickover family in Chicago had never been outwardly affectionate. Violent conflicts and bitter resentments were an integral part of its life, but it was close-knit and loyal. Captain Rickover had drifted out of this clannish environment. He did not follow Jewish customs; he did not go to a synagogue; he had married a gentile. At last he wrote a letter to his parents, telling them that he no longer considered himself exclusively Jewish in religion. A later generation might not have taken this too hard; he is still earnestly religious in a nonsectarian sense. But Rickover's parents did not forgive him for many years."

Rickover's father had retired as a tailor when he was seventy-five years old, but then resumed work "to get some financial security for old age," he said. He was still working on West Adams Street in the Garfield Custom Tailor shop until his death at eighty-four in 1959.

* Willard Edwards, "Eminent Americans," by Rickover, the Chicago *Tribune*, December 19, 1972.

His problems with his son had been somewhat resolved. "I'm proud of Hyman but I'm not surprised by his success," said Abraham Rickover. "When you work as hard as he has, you can't fail."

Then he recalled the time his son left home for Annapolis.

"I knew from a few things he said that he loved the water and wanted to travel on ships," said Abraham Rickover. "He tried to explain what Annapolis was. I told him that if that was what he wanted it was all right with us. I never let him know I was disappointed. He was such a fine scholar. I had hoped that he would be a rabbi."

# ARTHUR GOLDBERG

Arthur Joseph Goldberg took his seat on the bench of the U. S. Supreme Court for the first time on October 1, 1962. He was fifty-four years old, of medium height and weight, with steel-gray curly hair, small, close-set eyes, wore thick-lensed glasses with black rims, was rather pouchy in the cheek. He had been named to the Court by President Kennedy upon Justice Felix Frankfurter's resignation. Before coming to the Supreme Court, Justice Goldberg had been in Kennedy's cabinet as Secretary of Labor, was before then a renowned labor lawyer and negotiator, had practiced law in Chicago, had been first in his class at Northwestern University Law School, had during all his school years worked in construction, run errands for a shoe factory, delivered groceries, sold coffee at Cubs Park, stacked books in a library, packed suits in a clothing store, wrapped fish in a market, and, as a small child, would rise before dawn from the cot in the kitchen of his family's apartment—a half block from Maxwell Street—and then go with his father, a Russian-immigrant potato peddler, to the shack-stable behind the house, hitch up their wagon and horse, a blind horse, the only horse his father could afford, and, with the snap of the reins and a light cry of urging by his father, all three would begin the day's rounds, young Arthur holding tight to the bench of the jouncy wooden wagon as the horse clopped down the cobblestones in the gray morning.

---

Arthur Goldberg was born in Chicago on August 8, 1908, in a house on the 1300 block of Washburne, just off of Maxwell Street. The family soon moved a few blocks east to the corner of

Halsted and O'Brien. When Arthur Goldberg was eight years old, his father died, leaving his wife, Rebecca, and nine children, of which Arthur was the youngest.

Joseph Goldberg was born and raised in a small town named Zinkov, near Kiev, in Russia. His wife was from a town nine miles away. In 1892 Joseph Goldberg left his job as a sort of town clerk and with the blessings of his wife went to America. He traveled by way of Siberia and Manchuria, landed in San Francisco, and peddled notions for two years in the Southwest before going to Chicago, where, he said, his *landsmen* lived. He earned enough then to send for his family.

The first home Arthur remembers was on Halsted and O'Brien, in which the family crowded into a few rooms. The lone toilet was shared by other families in the hallway that connected the apartments.

He recalls that he would sometimes sleep in the bedroom, but sometimes he would be moved out. One of the reasons the Jews lived in the Maxwell Street area, Goldberg believes, is that it was so close to the railroads. He remembers going with his parents and carting a few wagons to meet relatives and friends from the Old Country coming off the trains. They would all return to the Goldberg residence. The newcomers would stay until they found places of their own. Meanwhile, as guests, *they* slept in the bedroom. Arthur moved to the kitchen. That was in summer. In winter, everyone slept as close as possible to the old wood stove in the kitchen, the only heat in the home.

Arthur Goldberg says that he taught himself to read at age three. He says he doesn't know how he did it. The only books in the home were religious books in Hebrew. There were, however, the Yiddish papers and at times one of his older brothers or sisters would bring home the popular English-language Hearst paper. It was popular with the Jews because the Hearst papers were against the restricting of immigration quotas.

Goldberg's education at home, he says, "was sacred, not secular." He would accompany his grandfather, who was a rabbi, and his father to synagogue. He remembers following with fascination as, after services, the men of the temple sat around and argued in Yiddish points of the Bible and Talmud. He has pleasant memories of a taffy pull at the temple during holidays.

As he grew older, he of course spent more time on the streets. He recalls the continuous street fights between Jews and the neighboring Irish. ("I used to fetch bricks for my brothers to throw," he has said.)

The marketplace intrigued him. On mornings he would go with his father to pick assorted fruits and vegetables—particularly potatoes—from the marketplace. His father sold them to hotels downtown. Goldberg says he has retained an affection for markets and wherever he goes in the world he likes to wander through the market areas.

Working as a delivery boy, he got his first lesson in collective bargaining. He and a companion, who toiled after school and on Saturdays, were asked to work on Thursday nights for supper money. They refused and were fired. "I found out," said Goldberg in later years, "that if there is strength in unity, there's got to be more than two."

He remembers another early "labor influence." He was working as a page in a library near Halsted Street. A bunch of "rowdies" began throwing books on the floor and causing a general disturbance. Goldberg was able to intervene and reason with them and helped squelch the outburst. That was the first group negotiation he remembers participating in.

After his father died, his mother held the family together by sending all of the older children out to work as soon as they completed grade school. At the time, Goldberg recalls, "we were poor as church mice."

As his brothers and sisters brought in money, it became clear that perhaps Arthur could continue further in school than the others. Realizing the sacrifices they were making for him, he worked hard in school.

He finished Harrison High School in three and a half years, at age fifteen. While still in high school he attended the headlined Loeb-Leopold case. Clarence Darrow's dynamic and profound conduct of the defense helped Arthur make up his mind to become a lawyer. He went to Crane Junior College and then Northwestern University Law School, moonlighting as a clerk in a law office all the while, to pay his way through school. He was editor of the school's law review.

One of his moonlighting jobs was with the firm of Kamfner and Halligan, at twenty dollars a week. Within a few months he was writing virtually all of the firm's briefs. One of the partners, Edwin Halligan, recalls that Goldberg had an uncanny talent for integrating and memorizing a welter of detail and could dictate a brief at high speed, without referring to notes. "When it came to the law," said Halligan, "Arthur's mind started where most of ours finished. For him, reading law was like reading a novel for someone else."

One of his first full-time law jobs after law-school graduation was with the firm of Pritzker and Pritzker. The Depression was now in full stride and the majority of Goldberg's duties had to do with foreclosing mortgages and reorganizations. There was much money to be made but not the way Goldberg wanted to make it —by divesting people of their homes and businesses. In 1933 he opened up his own law office on La Salle Street. He did a variety of legal work. Times were mean. Goldberg and his wife, Dorothy Kurgans, whom he married in 1931, struggled.

He became involved with labor unions, he says, out of no particular conviction but out of circumstance—that is, the Depression and the presidency of Franklin D. Roosevelt.

"In my youth," Goldberg had said, "there were plenty of radicals around, but I was never even a socialist, nor was anyone in my family. Roosevelt was the first man who had any strong political appeal for me. In that, of course, I was fairly representative of many young Americans at the time. Roosevelt was not only a political leader; in a very real sense, he was the great labor leader of his time. I am sure that if you had gone to any American worker of that period and asked him who best represented the aspirations of the labor movement, his reply . . . would have been Franklin D. Roosevelt."

Goldberg began doing some legal work for unions, particularly the Amalgamated Clothing Workers. He saw that the unions were relatively weak. He was first asked to represent the American Newspaper Guild in strike negotiations in Chicago between reporters and the Hearst paper in town, the *Herald-Examiner*. Goldberg quickly assented. "The Guild situation in Chicago was a particularly nasty, bitter one," said Goldberg, "in which a new union was battling an employer in economic difficulties who had not accepted the concept that newspaper reporters as well as clerical help had a right to organize. The atmosphere was one of terrible confusion and controversy." Goldberg was in court nearly every day for eight months, fighting a passel of lawyers to get pickets released from jail and, in the end, wrestling to just win the issue of simply allowing unions the right to exist. "It was a far cry from the fancy arguments over wages and so-called fringe benefits that go on today," said Goldberg.

As he got deeper into labor, he found that communists were often imbedded. He fought them, believing that you could be a militant labor man and not have to be a communist, too.

He represented the steelworkers union in Chicago and the Chicago and Illinois branches of the Congress of Industrial Organization. He served as a major during World War II on the staff of Brigadier General William J. "Wild Bill" Donovan, director of the Offices of Strategic Services (Goldberg was credited with organizing European railroad, river barge, and other workers into a spy network whose reports were of great value to the Allies), and then became general counsel for both the CIO and the United Steelworkers.

Goldberg played a lead part in negotiations over the years in contract negotiations for better pay and more fringe benefits. The first and perhaps the most important strike was in 1949. The steelworkers' union obtained a court ruling that pensions paid for by management were a legitimate bargaining concern and, that summer, the union demanded a pension plan. Management refused to hear of it. The workers struck for forty-two days. Goldberg was unwavering. Management gave in. "Today Goldberg maintains that a hundred million Americans are protected by social-insurance schemes of some sort because the labor movement led the way—a circumstance that he likes to cite in answer to critics who are so busy deploring the movement's current apathy that they forget its long-term contributions to social progress," noted an article in *The New Yorker* magazine in 1962.*

Goldberg was sometimes surprised at his effectiveness in negotiation, particularly since he had had no experience or training in it.

* Robert Shaplen, "Peacemaker—1," *The New Yorker,* April 7, 1962.

"I hold very strongly," he said, "that this art, or science, or whatever you may call it, of collective bargaining is something that probably cannot be taught. It must be largely intuitive, and in this sense I suppose it's like any creative process. You either have the qualifications or you don't.

"The main thing you must have is the ability to realize there are two sides to the story, and so to be generally calm and courteous in the handling of people in inflamed situations, but at the same time not to relinquish a position of leadership, which on occasion will require the calmness and courtesy to be submerged in a show of vigor and strength and even anger."

He was in the forefront of the merger between the American Federation of Labor and the CIO. He co-operated with the McClellan Permanent Investigations which began looking into labor corruption in 1956 and with the Select Committee on Improper Activities in Labor-Management Relations which took over the job in January 1957. This is where he came to know the Kennedys. Robert Kennedy, then chief counsel for both committees, said "Goldberg was our best friend in the movement. We had great confidence in his judgment."

In 1958 Goldberg backed a labor reform bill introduced by the then Senator John Kennedy.

Goldberg was instrumental in persuading labor to support John Kennedy's candidacy for President, that Kennedy truly had labor's best interests at heart. Goldberg had earlier been an Adlai Stevenson supporter (having worked with Stevenson in Chicago as far back as the early '40s). Goldberg now believed that Stevenson could not win and that Kennedy could. He also was influential in having labor look benignly upon Lyndon Johnson for Vice-President. Neither Kennedy nor Johnson ever forgot Goldberg's pivotal contributions to their elevation.

When Kennedy became President, he chose Goldberg as his Secretary of Labor. On the very first day in office, Goldberg hurried to New York to help settle a harbor tugboat strike. This was in accordance with his theory that federal government should take a new role in labor-management relationships. This was supported by the President. Goldberg called for a policy in which there was government guidance to parties in labor disputes that would take into consideration what the Administration believed was the over-all public interest. He explained that, in the past, federal media-tion had been concerned primarily with the immediate issues of a labor-management dispute. Now, he said, federal mediators would reflect government concern with the national interest. He added that this did not imply government dictation of terms of the settle-ment.

Goldberg was later involved in mediation of steel industry strikes and, oddly, was even called upon by President Kennedy to help settle the strike of musicians at the Metropolitan Opera. Goldberg successfully arbitrated. Kennedy excused the use of so high-powered an arbitrator for so seemingly small an issue by saying, "The Metropolitan Opera is important to the nation. I'm glad we found a way for it to continue."

Although Secretary Goldberg was now circulating in the highest circles of the government and culture, Arthur Goldberg the man might still be seen as the boy from the ghetto.

He retained a concern for money. When he made a visit to Scandinavia as Secretary of Labor, he was entitled by law to first-class plane accommodations. But he and his wife went tourist. He was paying for his wife's way and didn't think he could afford first-class for her. They sat far back on the plane; the Swedish del-egation in Stockholm there to greet him waited for so many peo-ple to deplane that they wondered if he had missed the flight.

The couple later stopped in Amsterdam and visited the home of Anne Frank, where Goldberg lay a wreath.

He would invite non-Jewish congressmen and senators and Su-preme Court justices to his home at Passover to partake in the *Seder,* celebrating the exodus of the Jews from Egypt. A rabbi friend noted that Goldberg reads from the *Haggadah,* or "telling" of the story, and then ties it in with the present-day evils of colo-nialism and bad housing so that "he makes the whole thing the story of all the oppressed and outcast of the world, as if he were presenting a brief before the Supreme Court of history that will forever put Pharaoh in outer darkness."

*The New Yorker* quoted a labor leader as saying that Goldberg was a "first-class operator." "Operator," *The New Yorker* said, "is a word that is frequently applied to Goldberg, sometimes favorably and sometimes not." "Operator" is also a commonly used word on the streets of Chicago, including of course Maxwell Street, and, equally, sometimes the word is used favorably and sometimes not.†

Another point associated with Goldberg, and one that may be related to his youthful experiences, is "toughness." It was often applied by the Kennedys, who equated "toughness" with loyalty. Bobby Kennedy often said that Goldberg had "the guts" and the integrity to stand up for his convictions.

Goldberg has said that "toughness" may not be the word he would choose to point up the influences of his youth. "I would prefer," he has told me, "the word 'self-reliance.' "

Upon Justice Frankfurter's resignation, President Kennedy, aware that the Supreme Court was an ambition of Goldberg's, decided to name his labor secretary for this "Jewish seat" on the Court, following the Jewish Justices Frankfurter, Louis D. Brandeis, and Benjamin N. Cardozo.

Goldberg wondered aloud to Kennedy how he felt the various factions in American public life would accept his nomination. Kennedy foresaw no problems whatsoever.

Goldberg happened to ask: "What about the American Bar Association." The President said: "Fuck the Bar Association! How can they oppose your appointment?" Then he reeled off Goldberg's credentials, as if to fortify his own convictions.

Perhaps, Goldberg had asked about the ABA, knowing its hidebound history, and perhaps he had been thinking of Henry Drinker, onetime chairman of the ABA Ethic's Committee, who had said in 1927 (when Arthur Goldberg was in law school) that he deplored the ethics of "many Russian Jew boys who came up out of the gutter [and] were merely following the methods their fathers had been using in selling shoestrings and other merchandise."‡

Robert Kennedy, the Attorney General of the United States, soon cleared Goldberg's appointment with the appropriate committee of the Bar Association. And the President announced his decision. Goldberg was easily confirmed by the Senate.

† Robert Shaplen, "Peacemaker—2," *The New Yorker,* April 14, 1962.
‡ Alan Dershowitz, "Counselor, Counsel Thyself," *New York Times Book Review* (reviewing *Unequal Justice* by Jerold S. Auerbach), January 25, 1976.

Goldberg's appearance on the bench changed the temper of the court. Frankfurter had been the leader of a five-justice majority that counseled caution, deference to the political branches of government, and respect for states' rights. Goldberg became a member of the school that was willing to exercise judicial power in this area. At the end of the 1962–63 session a 5–4 liberal, or activist, majority had emerged. A year later the conservative wing appeared to be breaking up and there were 8–1, 7–2, and 6–3 decisions.

The Associated Press had noted that "Goldberg had a talent for discovering the 'sleeper' issue in a case—the aspect that could turn a routine decision into an important precedent for future decisions.

"In one of his most famous decisions he held that the Connecticut antibirth-control law was an unconstitutional infringement of the fundamental right of privacy of married couples regardless of the fact that no specific provision of the Constitution guarantees such a right.

"He argued that this was one of the rights 'retained by the People' by the Ninth Amendment and therefore was protected from state infringement by the due-process clause of the Fourteenth Amendment.

"Another famous decision of his came in the case of *Escobedo* v. *Illinois*." Coincidentally enough, Danny Escobedo, the defendant in the case, was living on Twenty-ninth Street and Princeton, in Chicago, about a mile and a half from Maxwell Street. Goldberg wrote an opinion striking down a conviction based on a confession taken after police had denied the defendant the right to see his lawyer. But his language cast doubts on the constitutionality of all confessions taken before a suspect is informed of his right to counsel and to remain silent. This triggered a wave of cases invalidating noncoerced confessions and caused a fresh national examination of methods of law enforcement and crime detection.

Justice Goldberg said: "No system worth preserving should have to *fear* that, if the accused is permitted to consult with a lawyer, he will become aware of, and exercise [his] rights. If the exercise of constitutional rights will thwart the effectiveness of a system of law enforcement, then there is something very wrong with that system." Justice Goldberg's familial history and personal experiences made him deeply conscious of repressive tactics, from the czarist Russia of his parents to the Stalinist communists in the labor movement.

To Goldberg, "the major accomplishments of the Court during . . . the years . . . in which Earl Warren was Chief Justice [including the years Goldberg served on the bench] . . . were a translation of our society's proclaimed belief in racial equality into some measure of legal reality, the beginning of a profound change in the mechanics of our political democracy and the revolution in criminal justice, both state and federal."

As for racial equality, Justice Goldberg wrote his opinion in the *Bell* v. *Maryland* case in which blacks were refused service in a public restaurant: "It is, and should be, more true today than it was over a century ago that 'the great advantage of the Americans is that . . . they [are] born equal' and that in the eyes of the law they 'are all of the same estate.' The first Chief Justice of the United States, John Jay, spoke of the 'free air' of American life. The great purpose of the Fourteenth Amendment is to keep it free and equal. Under the Constitution no American can, or should, be denied rights fundamental to freedom and citizenship."

In her book *A Private View of a Public Life,* Dorothy Goldberg summed up her husband's views of the disparity between the rich and the poor throughout the area of criminal law:

"The rich man may be summoned to the police station; the poor man is more often arrested. The rich inebriant may be escorted home by the policeman; the poor drunk is almost always tossed into jail. The rich accused is released on bail; the poor defendant cannot raise the bail and remains in prison. The rich defendant can afford the best legal advice; he can summon psychiatrists and other expert witnesses; he can afford a thorough investigation of the facts of a case and can raise every possible defense. The poor defendant, until the *Gideon* decision, often had to defend himself, and even today in many jurisdictions he is denied many other important tools of advocacy. After conviction, when a fine is imposed, the rich man pays it and goes free, the poor man, who cannot afford to pay the fine, must go to jail. The rich man, who can be guaranteed a job, may qualify for probation or parole; the poor man, lacking a job, more often goes to or remains in prison."*

On Tuesday afternoon, July 14, 1965, Adlai Stevenson, then the United States Ambassador to the United Nations, fell dead of a heart attack in Grovesnor Square in London. Two days later Justice Goldberg received a phone call from President Lyndon Johnson. The President said that because of a current debate in the UN that threatened to destroy the international body [the Soviet Union, its satellites and France had been unwilling to pay their dues], a "great American" was needed to fill Stevenson's job immediately. "You're the best negotiator in the world, and the country needs you," President Johnson told Justice Goldberg.

It was a most difficult decision for Goldberg, who loved his work on the Court. Dorothy Goldberg wrote, however, that "Art felt he owed a great deal to the country that had honored him publicly and had afforded him great opportunities, and he was convinced—as was really the case—that the country was in great trouble over the Vietnam War as well as over the UN crisis."† Goldberg sought assurances from Johnson that he would be no figurehead and would truly participate as a foremost negotiator in trying to end the Vietnam War. Johnson gave his assurance.

Ambassador Goldberg formally accepted the UN post at the White House on July 20, 1965. He said: "With the death of Adlai Stevenson, a great voice of America in the world has been stilled, but the message of Adlai Stevenson to the world must go on. The message is man's ancient supplication: Grant us peace, Thy most precious gift.

"What has been prayer throughout the ages is a necessity today.

"Adlai Stevenson was the voice of a great and powerful nation, at once dedicated to peace and implacable in its commitment to freedom. The eloquence of his words no more than reflected the richness of his spirit and the righteousness of his cause. We, and the world, are different because he lived. Of Adlai Stevenson's de-

* Dorothy Goldberg, *A Private View of a Public Life* (New York: Charterhouse, 1975), p. 181.
† Goldberg, op. cit., p. 193.

parture and my appointment I can only borrow words uttered on a similar occasion by Thomas Jefferson: I succeed him. No one can replace him.

"I shall not, Mr. President, conceal the pain with which I leave the Court after three years of service. It has been the richest and most satisfying period of my career. Throughout my life I have been deeply committed to the rule of law. The law gives form and substance to the spirit of liberty and to mankind's sacred stir for justice.

"It now comes that the President has asked me to join the greatest adventure in man's history—the effort to bring the rule of law to govern the relations between sovereign states.

"It is that or doom—and we all know it.

"I have accepted, as one simply must."

He later added, "I have no illusions that peace can be achieved rapidly. But I have every confidence that it is going to be possible to inch forward to it, inch by agonizing inch."

Goldberg used his negotiating powers in helping keep the India-Pakistan war in 1965 from spreading, trying to keep an international cool in the *Pueblo* crisis in Korea, and seeking solutions to the Middle East confrontations. The journalist, Jimmy Breslin, observed Goldberg during an emergency meeting of the Security Council to discuss the Middle East crisis on May 24, 1967: "10:30 A.M. Out in the streets, people read of ships that moved toward the Gulf of Aqaba. But in the Security Council, the delegates stood around in groups and smoked and talked and were in a hurry to do nothing.

"Ambassador Goldberg moved through the crowd. His black horn-rim glasses stood out against his gray-white hair.

"He kept talking, his finger pointing at people, jabbing at their chests, then the whole hand coming out to touch the shoulder of somebody he wanted to speak to."

Goldberg's deepest disappointment was his inability to be persuasive with President Johnson on the Vietnam war. Goldberg moved to negotiate and de-escalate. Johnson opposed both of those. Goldberg had thought about quitting the UN post early on but decided to try to get the President's ear. Sometimes he did.

"At one of the briefings of the Wise Men (of Johnson's senior advisors) it was Arthur Goldberg, much mocked by some of the others, who almost single-handedly destroyed the military demand for 205,000 more troops. The briefing began with the military officer saying that the other side had suffered 45,000 deaths during the Tet offensive.

"Goldberg then asked what our own killed-to-wounded ratios were.

" 'Seven to one,' the officer answered, 'because we save a lot of men with helicopters.'

" 'What,' asked Goldberg, 'was the enemy strength as of February first when Tet started?'

" 'Between 160,000 and 175,000,' the briefer answered.

" 'What is their killed-to-wounded ratio?' Goldberg asked.

" 'We use a figure of three and a half to one,' the officer said.

" 'Well, if that's true, then they have no effective forces left in the field,' Goldberg said. What followed was a long and very devastating silence."‡

However, Goldberg in private to friends said he felt he had accomplished precious little in regards to peace in Vietnam. He felt he was helpless to reverse the course of the war. Hawks like Secretary of State Rusk and the Joint Chiefs of Staff were the main influences on Johnson.

"The most successful negotiator of the 1960s obviously sees no future in his work and so is bowing out, silently, like the Secretary of Defense, but nonetheless speaking volumes about the mood within the Johnson administration," wrote columnist Mary McGrory in the Washington *Star*.

By April of 1968, Ambassador Goldberg had returned to private life.

Goldberg did not complain in public over what turned out to be Johnson's double-dealing. But a sense of his deep bitterness was exemplified in the book by his wife, Dorothy.

One night Ambassador and Mrs. Goldberg had had President Johnson over for dinner. In the course of the evening, the President expressed admiration for Dorothy Goldberg's art work and asked to have a painting. A few days later she sent him one, one that happened to have been hanging in her husband's office.

‡ David Halberstam, *The Best and the Brightest* (New York: Random House, 1973), pp. 653–54.

All this was forgotten until a few years later when Johnson's memoirs were published. In that volume, the former President wrote that Goldberg had left the Supreme Court for the UN because, among other reasons, he was bored with judicial work.

". . . When Arthur read Johnson's distorted version . . . he was so outraged he phoned the President, insisting that I get on the extension," wrote Dorothy Goldberg. "He told him that I was there and said, 'I want her to hear me tell you what I think.' Then he said, 'And another thing, I want that painting of hers she sent to you. It's mine and you don't deserve it.' "*

Goldberg is a lawyer again, in Washington. He has worked quietly, except for a few celebrated clients, such as Reverend William Sloan Coffin, Jr., the controversial Yale chaplain, and Curt Flood, the black baseball player who challenged the Major League reserve clause.

Goldberg has an office well in the back of the large, plush offices of Caplin and Drysdale law firm on Seventeenth Street. There is an American flag hanging in the corner of the darkly wooded room. There are pictures of Goldberg and Presidents. There are a number of framed honorary degrees.

We sat and talked on a couch there. A secretary brought in coffee, in paper cups in plastic holders. Goldberg's voice is gravelly; he has a characteristic in which he speaks slightly out of the right side of his mouth. He is genial and pleased to recall his background, of how he slept in the kitchen, worked with his father, met Old World family and friends coming by train into Chicago, how his father once tried to go into a grain business but failed, and that, yes, his background was an influence on him as a judge. "You try to be dispassionate," he said, "but you have predilections. You can't help that. You can't escape your past. You think along the path you've come."

How did you become a liberal?

"Damned if I know. There was no liberal tradition in our family. I imagine the first time I really found out about labor was when I worked summers as a rodman in a construction company. It was in Elgin, Illinois. I was the first Jew worker in that construction company. I remember eating and talking with the other workers in a commissary. I was a curiosity because Jews were

* Dorothy Goldberg, op. cit., p. 223.

supposed to be too smart to work hard—or by the sweat of their brow. But I knew that construction paid more than other jobs I could get. So that's why I did it. I think I helped liberate myself there from any kind of shtetl mentality, but without ever diminishing my strong attachment to Jewish traditions. I came to understand what other people were like, understood where they were from, but saw where I was from and who I was in relation to them. And I was proud of my heritage. So I was not afraid to go out and meet the world."

He recalled that once at a dinner party he had an opportunity to speak with Bruno Kreiske, chancellor of Austria, a Jew, and a survivor of the Nazi concentration camps. He was a socialist and a nonbeliever. "I reproached him that Austria had a very poor record in war reparations to Jews," said Goldberg. "At the time, Kreiske said that his Parliament had been reluctant to do more in regard to reparations for Jews.

"Then he told me a story about when he was in a concentration camp, and he was down to about ninety pounds, and he was walking with an old rabbi. He said to the rabbi, 'Since we're both going to starve or end up in the gas chambers, tell me, Rabbi, how do you still believe in God?' And the rabbi said, 'It's not God's fault that we're here. It's your fault.' Kreiske said, 'Me? I didn't bring it about.' And the Rabbi said, 'You never practiced your faith, your Jewish life. And this is a visitation that God has put upon you— put upon us.' I know that this discussion made an impact on Kreiske, but perhaps he had submerged it for a while. Anyway, soon after our talk he made some friendly statements about Israel."

In 1969, a year after the Ambassador had left the United Nations, he and his wife made a trip to Russia. He had tried to get permission to visit his parents' hometown, Zinkov, but was rebuffed by Russian bureaucrats. They contended that it was an out-of-the-way small town and that new roads were being built in the area and, because of recent rains, were muddy and impassable.

One evening the Goldbergs were invited by Deputy Foreign Minister Vasily Kuznetzov to join him for lunch at the Kremlin. Goldberg and Kuznetzov had met when the two were representing their countries at the UN. A mutual respect and affection grew.

Goldberg, in passing, told his host about the problems he confronted in attempting to visit his parents' hometown. "I told him how disappointed I was," said Goldberg. "Well, he was a bigwig and he said, 'You'll make the visit.' And I did.

"There was one big road going there. It was indeed off-limits to tourists. The one main road was used for military transports. The town had a population of about fifteen thousand. The mayor took me around like I was a long-lost hometown boy who had made good. We had lunch. The town was like something out of *Fiddler on the Roof*. It was a kind of service town, in which farmers and peasants brought in their produce and wares to sell there. No industry. The mayor gave me a gift, an urn with dirt in it. He said that this was the land of Zinkov, the land of my father. But it was hard to place my father here. Because as I went around the town I realized that there were no Jews left. At one time over half the town was Jewish. It was incredible to think that an entire community had vanished. They all had gone to either America or Auschwitz."

# JACK RUBY

—Why did Lee Harvey Oswald shoot President Kennedy? Because of Jack Ruby, no one is ever to know. Was Oswald acting alone? Because of Ruby, that is unlikely to be proved to a certainty.

Was it to keep these questions unanswered, then, that Jack Ruby lunged between careless policemen to kill Lee Oswald? There are only Ruby's maundering words, and a lack of contrary evidence, to show that it was not. . . .

For [these reasons], Jack Ruby, the [Dallas] strip-tease proprietor who could throw hecklers down the stairs of his club but who anguished over the fate of the Jews and at the end longed to go home to the Chicago that shaped him, will linger grotesquely in history.

*Tom Wicker*
NEW YORK *TIMES*

———————◆———————

"The strangest part is that I made an illegal turn behind a bus at the parking lot. Had I gone the way I was supposed to go—straight down Main Street—I would never—I would never have met this fate because the difference of meeting this fate was thirty seconds one way or the other."—Jack Ruby (speaking to his brother Earl) shortly before his death on January 2, 1967.

Jack Ruby was born Jacob Rubenstein in 1911 in his parents' residence near Fourteenth and Newberry, just south of Maxwell Street. There is some confusion about his exact birth date. School records report it as June 23, April 25, March 13, and March 3, 1911. Other early official records list his date of birth as April 21 and April 26, 1911. During his adult life the date Ruby used most frequently was March 25. The police arrest report for November 24 gave his birth date as March 19, 1911. Since the recording of births was not required in Chicago prior to 1915, Ruby's birth may never have been officially recorded. No substantial conflict exists, however, about whether Jack Ruby was born in 1911.

Jack Ruby was the fifth of eight children (at least one more, and possibly two, died at childbirth) born to Joseph and Fannie Turek Rutkowski Rubenstein. Jacob (Jack) Rubenstein, like Jacob (Jack) Arvey, was the first male born to his family in America.

Jack Ruby's father was born in 1871 in Sokolov, a small town near Warsaw, Poland, then under the rule of czarist Russia. He entered the Russian artillery in 1893. There he learned the carpentry trade, which had been practiced by his father and at least one brother. In the Army, he picked up the habit of excessive drinking that would plague him the rest of his life.

While in the Army he also married Jack's mother. The marriage was arranged, as was the custom—just as my grandparents' wedding was arranged—by a professional matchmaker, or schatchen. Joseph Rubenstein served in China, Korea, and Siberia, detesting these places and Army life. Eventually, in 1898, he simply walked away from it and about four years later he went to England and Canada, entering the United States in 1903.

He settled in Chicago, joined the carpenters' union in 1904 and remained a member until his death in 1958.

Jack Ruby's mother was probably born in 1875, also in a town near Warsaw, though not the same town as her husband. When I think of Jack Ruby's parents, I think of my grandparents, since Joseph Rubenstein and my grandfather, Max Halperin, lived in nearby houses off of Maxwell Street for several years and spent much time together elbow to elbow in local saloons. And I think of the agony this debauchery caused my grandmother, Mollie, and the agony, according to the Warren Commission report, that it caused Ruby's mother, Fannie.

When the Rubensteins courted in Poland, though, I imagine it was also similar to the courting of my grandfather and grandmother, for they, too, lived in neighboring shtetls in Russia.

Jack Ruby's mother, with his oldest brother Hyman and oldest sister Ann, followed her husband to America in 1904 or 1905. She was an illiterate woman who went to night school in 1920 to learn how to sign her name. The Warren Report assumes she failed in this endeavor, however, "for an alien registration form, filed after 35 years in the United States, was signed 'X.'" Although her speech was predominately Yiddish, the primary language of the Rubenstein household, she did learn some English.

The Rubensteins and the Halperins moved from Fourteenth Street to Morgan Street in 1916. The Rubensteins moving to 1232 Morgan, the Halperins to 1302 Morgan. In the second-floor apartment at the latter address, my mother was born on May 15, 1916. I have a brown-and-white pebbled photograph of my mother and two older brothers taken five or six years later. When my mother was suddenly called to pose for the picture, she had been playing in the alley with her brothers and some of the other neighborhood kids, possibly some of the Rubensteins—Jack would have been only nine or ten, the age of my uncles. In the picture, my uncles Al and Jerry flank my mother. They are standing in front of the stoop and stairs of the three-story, pitched-roof apartment building where they lived. It was the same sort of building the Rubensteins lived in. The clothes they wore were similar to the kind generally worn by the kids in the neighborhood. The boys wore skullcap, knickers, ankle-high sneakers, sweaters, and wary, alley-wise grins. My mother, then aged five or six, wore a quiet smile and a dirt-blotched, uneven-hemmed garment that, she said, it took her mother about twenty minutes to create. The kindest comment one could make about the style of the dress is that, like a snowflake, there could never have been another exactly like it.

The apartments themselves were crowded with kids and much discomfort. ("Write about the bedbugs, Ira," my mother told me. "Don't forget them. And how we'd flush the bugs out of the coils with a candle, and then kill them with a hammer.") "We had a potbellied stove," my Uncle Jerry recalled to me, "and in winter for entertainment we'd spit on it and watch it sizzle. And we'd stay close to it in winter and keep turning around in front of it. When you'd stand facing it, you'd be warm in front but your ass would be freezing, so you'd have to turn around again to get your back warm. But sometimes we wouldn't have any stove because my father in a drunken fury would kick it and break it. Oh, the number of times he kicked in the celluloid-covered door of the stove!

"My mother—your *bubbie*—would throw him out of the house and he'd go live someplace else. Just like what Ruby's mother did with her husband, Joe. We called him Papala Joe. I remember one place he lived. It was on Sangamon, a block away from where we lived.

"So he lived upstairs in some kind of flat there. I think it must have been a one-bedroom apartment or something like that in the back. And I remember the copper wires he had put up and they traced to the bathroom where he had a homemade still and made what they call bathroom gin. His sons Jack and Earl would come and we'd all put in cherries to give the gin some color and we'd help Papala Joe make the gin.

"He was a great storyteller and we could sit and listen to him for hours. Sometimes he'd say things that would have shocked our mothers. His favorite saying was 'Six-and-seven-eighths measurement.'"

Why would he say that?

"He was a carpenter."

Yes, but why would—

"You figure it out. He would laugh and say, 'It's six and seven-eighths.'"

"One other thing I remember about where he lived. On his kitchen table he had newspapers flattened out and piled real high. When he'd finish eating, instead of cleaning off the table, he'd wrap up the top paper and throw it way in the garbage. No crumbs. The table was clean and ready for the next meal."

The Warren Report says that "The Rubenstein home was marked by constant strife and the parents were reported to have occasionally struck each other. Between 1915 and 1921, Joseph Rubenstein was frequently arrested because of disorderly conduct and assault and battery charges, some filed by his wife. In the spring of 1921, his, Jack Ruby's, parents separated. The predominant causes of the separation were apparently Joseph Rubenstein's excessive drinking and Fannie Rubenstein's uncontrollable temper. She resented her numerous pregnancies, believed her husband to be unfaithful, and nagged him because he failed to make enough money.

"Young Jack soon showed the effects of parental discord. On June 6, 1922, at age of eleven, he was referred to the Institute for Juvenile Research by the Jewish Social Service Bureau. The reason for the referral was 'truancy and incorrigible at home.' On July 10, 1922, the Institute recommended to the bureau that Jack be placed in a new environment and where he might be afforded the supervision and recreation that would end his interest in street gangs."

It is purely of personal interest to me—though it may add to an understanding of growing up in that neighborhood—but just before Ruby's earliest known problem, my Uncle Julius, the eldest child of my grandparents, Max and Mollie Halperin, got his name in the newspapers. This is a story dated November 12, 1921, that I located in the morgue of the Chicago *Tribune:*

## ROBS IN SHADOW OF "HOOSEGOW"; CAUGHT ON ROOF

### BOY BANDIT DODGES COPS FOR FOUR BLOCKS.

After robbing Charles Mroz, 2609 North Talman Avenue, at the point of a gun, within four doors of the Maxwell Street police station, a 16-year-old youth named Julius Halperin, was captured after a merry chase and a running gun fight on the roof of a four-story building.

Sergt. John F. Mangin saw the lad thrust the revolver at Mroz and take his belongings.

The policeman fired two shots at the robber, who took to his heels.

The shots attracted the attention of Policemen Andrew Atcher and Daniel O'Reilly, in the station. They joined the chase. The fleeing boy led his pursuers through icy areaways and alleys and tried to shake them off by scaling a wall by means of a fire escape. Other policemen joined the chase, emptying their guns as they ran.

The spoils of his stickup he threw away, as access baggage hindering his flight. Finally, poised on the roof of a four-story building at 1305 S. Sangamon Street, prepared to leap across a chasm to the building beyond, he was captured.

Taken before Capt. Patrick Kelleher at the Maxwell Street station, Halperin refused to tell where he had thrown the money or where he had obtained his weapon.

With familial discord, the temper of the streets and the times, and given, crucially, a certain nature, it is conceivable how an individual might erupt in violence.

A psychiatric report on eleven-year-old Jack Ruby revealed he was "quick-tempered" and "disobedient." He had little respect for his mother or her rules because she beat him and lied to him, he said.

"He could give no other good reason for running away from school except that he went to amusement parks. He has some sex knowledge and is greatly interested in sex matters. He stated that the boys in the street tell him about these things. He also claims that he can lick everyone and anybody in anything he wants to do. . . .

"He is egocentric and expects much attention, but is unable to get it as there are many children at home. His behavior is further colored by his early sex experiences, his great interest in sex and the gang situation in the street. From a superficial examination of his mother who was here with him, it is apparent that she has no insight into his problem, and she is thoroughly inadequate in the further training of this boy."*

A foster home was recommended. Jack spent four or five years in foster homes as determined by the courts. Subsequently the three brothers lived together in a foster home.

Jack Ruby's father remained apart from the children at least until 1936. When the children returned to live with their mother, there remained chaos in the house. Mrs. Rubenstein was, by most accounts, a careless housekeeper, selfish and a disagreeable woman who, said Marion Rubenstein, her daughter, "Never took much interest in the children's welfare."

In 1913, when Jack was two, Mrs. Rubenstein developed a delusion that a sticking sensation in her throat was caused by a lodged fishbone. She went regularly to the doctor for several years because of it. Nothing was ever found. An operation was performed. She continued, however, to complain of the fishbone.

In about 1940 the parents were reconciled. Mrs. Rubenstein died of a heart ailment in 1944. The Warren Report says: "Because she favored the education of her children and they recognized her difficulties in rearing them during a turbulent marriage, they all remembered Mrs. Rubenstein with warmth and affection. The evidence also indicates that Jack, notwithstanding his earlier attitudes, became especially fond of his mother."

Joseph Rubenstein died at age eighty-seven in 1968.

How violent Jack was in his youth may be disputable. The former boxing champion Barney Ross, for example, said that Jack was "well-behaved," never was a troublemaker, never got involved with law-enforcement agencies.

However, he did have a good reputation as a street brawler, and though he claimed never to have started fights, would be lusty once in one.

Ruby in young manhood sold pennants at the ball parks and scalped tickets, sold tip sheets at the race track, was a door-to-door salesman.

He was inducted into the Army Air Forces on May 21, 1943. He

* *The Warren Report: Report on the President's Commission on the Assassination of President John F. Kennedy* (published by the Associated Press, 1964), p. 350.

spent his military days in air bases in the South. He earned marksmanship and sharpshooter ratings for the firing of weapons. His character and efficiency ratings, when determined, were excellent. After attaining the rank of private first class and receiving the good conduct medal, Ruby was honorably discharged on February 21, 1946.

Warren Report: ". . . Ruby while in the Army Air Forces . . . was extremely sensitive to insulting remarks about Jews. When, during an argument, a sergeant called Ruby a 'Jew bastard,' Ruby reportedly attacked him and beat him with his fists. . . .

"Ruby frequently expressed to some fellow soldiers his high regard for Franklin Delano Roosevelt. Two independent sources reported that he cried openly when informed of Roosevelt's death in April 1945. This did not indicate any sudden political interest, however, since none of his known military associates reported such an interest, and Ruby's admiration for President Roosevelt anteceded his military days."

After the Army, Ruby went into business with his brothers. Earl was the sole investor, though each brother received an equal ownership interest upon his return from the service. The company manufactured and sold small cedar chests and distributed punchboards.

Eva Rubenstein opened a nightclub in Dallas in 1947. Jack had sent her a thousand dollars to help finance it, and then he decided, after some bickering with Earl, to leave the Chicago business and go to Dallas.

At about this time, in 1947, the Ruby brothers changed their name from Rubenstein. The shortening or amending of a name that is easily identifiable with the group was a common thing among Jews. "I changed my name for business reasons," was an oft-heard refrain. It was assumed that one would do better "in business" if he were not Jewish than if he were. Many Jews felt that giving up their full ancestral name was not necessarily giving up their soul. Small, assimilative concessions have been a part of Jewish tradition for two thousand years. So: Rasofsky into Ross, Issur Danielovich into Kirk Douglass, Irving Wallachensky into Irving Wallace, Bronstein into Trotsky, a Goldenberger into Gold, Schmulovitz into Small, a Berkovitz into Berkow or Berko or Berke or Berk, a Rubenstein into Ruby.

Between 1949 and November 24, 1963, Ruby was arrested eight times by the Dallas Police Department. The arrests included: suspected of carrying a concealed weapon, disturbing the peace, allegedly violating state liquor laws by selling liquor after hours, allegedly permitting dancing after hours, simple assault, ignoring traffic summonses. He was never convicted of any charge.

His place, "The Carousel," was a strip joint, but he wanted it to be "class" and sought respectability.

"Decorum meant a great deal to Jack Ruby," wrote Ovid Demaris and Gary Wills, in an *Esquire* magazine article. "He did not smoke or drink (his father was a drunkard); he rarely talked Yiddish (the language of his childhood); he was intent on perfecting his Bottom-the-Weaver English (his mother could not write her own name). . . . His ardor for decorum manifested itself primarily in a readiness to flatten any patron who put his feet on the table. His determination to run a 'clean club' made many strippers wonder how they could find protection from his protection. One girl told Jack she was given a black eye by her husband, and she was leaving him. The next time the poor fellow appeared at the club, Ruby pitched him down the stairs, though the couple had been reconciled and the girl was pleading, 'Jack, I don't *want* you to hit him.' He never married. He dated a blond gentile divorcée in Dallas for eleven years, but said he had promised his mother that he would never marry a woman who wasn't Jewish."†

Ruby stood five nine, weighed 175 pounds, with weight-lifter's arms, brawny and thick, and heavy shoulders. He often wore a hat to cover his thinning hair and strove to be a natty dresser. He had a few chins despite sweating and exercising at the Y. He had been described as having the eyes of one ready for a challenge. "You learn in the ghetto," Ruby had said, "to be a jungle walker."

Ruby, wrote the Dallas writer Gary Cartwright, "had the carriage of a bantam cock and the energy of a steam engine as he churned through the streets of downtown Dallas, glad-handing, passing out cards, speaking rapidly, compulsively, about his new

‡ "You All Know Me! I'm Jack Ruby," by Ovid Demaris and Gary Wills in *Smiling Through the Apocalypse: Esquire's History of the Sixties* edited by Harold Hayes (New York: The McCall Publishing Co., 1969), pp. 62–99.

line of pizza ovens, about the twistboards he was promoting, about the important people he knew, cornering friends and grabbing strangers, relating amazing details of his private life and how any day now he would make it big."

Bill Willis, a drummer at Ruby's Carousel, remembers how impressed Ruby was when he learned that Jackie Kennedy had cultural interests, such as the ballet. "And her being as famous as a star. . . ." said Ruby.

Willis said, "The night before Kennedy's assassination, [Jack] was up on the stage to demonstrate a twistboard he was promoting. 'Even President Kennedy tells us to get more exercise,' he said. A heckler shouted, 'That bum!' 'Don't ever talk that way about the President,' Jack shot back. The next day, when he called me all broken up by the assassination, he said, 'Remember that man making fun of President Kennedy in the club last night?'

"Well, he was crying and carrying on: 'What do you think of a character like that killing the President?' I was trying to calm him down. I said, 'Jack, he's not normal; no normal man kills the President on his lunch hour and takes the bus home.' But he just kept saying, 'He killed the President.'"

Ruby had ingratiated himself with local police authorities. He thought it was good business, as well as something to satisfy his urge for respectability. He did the same with the newspapermen and with various businessmen. He always seemed self-conscious about his looks, his lisp, his background, his business, always seemed to be trying to prove something, always seemed to be trying to be bigger than life. Lenny Bruce has called him "the Jewish cowboy."

On the morning of November 24, 1964, Ruby was up about ten-thirty in his Dallas apartment. He showered, applied Ban deodorant, combed his hair carefully, achieving a slightly off-center part. He shaved his heavy beard. His hands were hairy. He had a stump for a finger on his left hand, having been chewed off in a fight. He wore a three-diamond sapphire ring on his left pinkie. He dressed in a gray suit. He soon left, got into his car—a two-door Oldsmobile, 1960 model. His dachshund, Sheba, took the back seat. He told the man he was living with (someone he had befriended) that he was "taking her (Sheba) down to the club." He had been mumbling around the house about the President and the assassination. He now flicked on the transistor radio in his car.

Those who do not subscribe to a conspiracy association believe that Ruby drove by City Hall just to see what was going on. He had to be in on everything, his friends said.

"He drives 'on up Main,'" wrote Demaris and Wills. "There are four or five people talking to a policeman as Ruby drives past the rabbit hole in City Hall that lets police cars underground to park. On the other side of the building, an armored car has just jockeyed with difficulty backward into the small mouth of the exit. Ruby hugs the curb to see what is going on. There is still something down there—TV crews, perhaps packing up their equipment. Now he must get back to the left lane; he wants to pull into a parking lot across the street. But a moving bus blocks the other eastbound lane beside him; he cannot race ahead of the bus or ease in behind it in time to make the turn. He slows till he is even with the lot, waits for the tailgate of the bus to clear, then swings hard left into the lot from the far-right lane. Ruby—who is almost superstitious about the law, reverencing it and tempted to break it and feeling remorse afterward—has just committed his penultimate infraction of the law.

"The lot is on the corner of Main and Pearl. . . . He opens the trunk. He has a file cabinet there. He rummages through, puts his hand into the money bag where he keeps his weapons. (Take the gun now. God! How I'd like to use it on that character!) He puts the snub-nosed Colt revolver in his right-hand pocket. . . . Slams trunk. . . .

"Oswald is pulling on a sweater in Captain Fritz's office. Ruby adjusts his glasses—bifocals, he wears them as little as possible . . . and fills out the parking-lot receipt. It is stamped: 1963 Nov 24 Am 11 16. Ruby puts his glasses away. . . .

"Something strange *is* going on. A car is nosing out of the ramp, and this is an entrance door only! Ruby quickens his stride.

"History has always broken her date with Jack Ruby before now, despite his careful efforts to arrange a meeting. In fifty-three seconds, she will keep it. . . .

"The entrance to the ramp is narrow. . . . A car drives up and out, and Ruby glances down, turns smoothly left and down. As he is about to reach the line of men at the bottom, he hears a cry: 'Here he comes!' The brightest TV lights blink on, turns the glow in City Hall's belly to a flare. 'He's coming out!' He? The character? Ruby's shoulders tighten instinctively, a jungle walker's reaction when the enemy is near.

"Just as he reaches the line of people, Capt. Fritz's Stetson bobs into view, brilliant in the camera glare. At that moment, Ruby is looking straight ahead, on camera, though he does not know it. He stands in the penumbra of those lights. . . .

"Detective Leavelle, a movie Texan, moves the human chain of handcuffed men toward the car. He wears a white Stetson and white suit—the good guy. ('Hell, man, Dallas is still a shootout town.') He dwarfs the young man beside him, tense in his dark sweater—the bad guy, face logy with fatigue and bruises, jaws faintly dusted with morning growth.

"The orange stab of light in this dark place turns Oswald's face to the side, for a moment—toward the dim figure just arrived. Some will later claim he looked at Ruby, looked *for* him—but he could not see in those first seconds of the dazzle. The glare makes him tighten his lips further, in a slight grimace. . . . Ruby pushes through the line. No one has a chance of stopping him now, but one policeman raises his arm. As usual, his first act is decisive— dead on target. ('Jack was a first-puncher.') He mates in one move. ('You have to take the play away.') The job is done. . . .

"When policemen swarm toward him, Ruby the scuffler does not try to take this play. They are friends. They'll understand. But why are they so rough? Why turn on him? They must know I did it for Jackie, for Caroline. They must see that: 'YOU ALL KNOW ME! I'M JACK RUBY!'"

In jail, the prisoner was guarded twenty-four hours a day. He spent much of his time playing gin rummy with the guards. He cheated, the guards said, in keeping score.

He read newspapers, a Hebrew Bible, novels with erotic themes, and dictionaries. He prided himself on being a faultless speller. He told those policemen he became close to that he had acted "to show the world Jews had guts."

Dr. Roy Schafer, a psychologist, tested him after the arrest: He put Ruby's IQ score at 109, or in the 73rd percentile of the general population.

"The total set of tests results," the psychologist's report said, "indicates that Mr. Ruby's thought processes and speech fluctuate between two positions: One position is clear, alert, perceptive, socially appropriate and well-organized; the other position is confused, disoriented, arbitrary, inappropriate and loosely organized."

Ruby would tell the Warren Commission about that historic Sunday morning:

"I saw a letter that morning to Caroline. . . . Someone had written a letter to Caroline Kennedy. The most heartbreaking letter. I don't remember the contents. . . . alongside that letter on the same sheet of paper was a small comment in the newspaper that, I don't know how it was stated, that Mrs. Kennedy may have to come back for the trial of Lee Harvey Oswald. . . .

"I don't know what bug got ahold of me. I don't know what it is. . . .

"I am taking a pill called Preludin. It's a harmless pill, and it is very easy to get in the drugstore. It isn't a highly prescribed pill. I use it for dieting.

"I don't partake of that much food. I think that was a stimulus to give me an emotional feeling that suddenly I felt, which was so stupid, that I wanted to show my love for our faith, being of the Jewish faith, and I never used the term and I don't want to go into that—suddenly the feeling, the emotional feeling came within me that someone owed this debt to our beloved President to save her the ordeal of coming back. I don't know why that came through my mind."

Ruby worried that attempts to link him with a conspiracy would result in harm to his family, to Jews generally. He insisted on a lie detector test, or the use of truth serum to prove conclusively that he acted alone. Ruby testified before the Warren Commission in Dallas County Jail on June 7, 1964, in the presence of Chief Justice Earl Warren. At one point Ruby said, "Now, Mr. Warren, I can't tell you just how much confidence I have in it (the lie detector test), and so on."

CHIEF JUSTICE WARREN: "I can't tell you just how much confidence I have in it, because it depends so much on who is taking it, and so forth.

"But I will say this to you, that if you and your counsel want any kind of test, I will arrange it for you. I would be glad to do that if you want it. I wouldn't suggest a lie detector test to testify the truth.

"We will treat you just the same as we do any other witness, but if you want such a test I will arrange for it."

RUBY: "I do want it."

A polygraph or lie detector examination is considered to have some validity only if the subject is "normal." One psychiatrist for the court believed that Ruby was a "psychotic depressive." FBI director J. Edgar Hoover said that in view of that diagnosis of Ruby's mental condition, the test "cannot be relied upon."

However, FBI agent Herndon, who administered the testing, said that if Ruby had been in control of his faculties while taking the test, then the tests, he believed, proved that Ruby had in fact acted alone in the murder of Lee Harvey Oswald and had never known the victim.

By 1966, Ruby had developed cancer. He was apparently also a tormented man mentally. His lawyer, Elmer Gertz, said, "He was fifty-five and he looked like a man of eighty."

Gertz said, "At various times, apparently depending on the subject, Ruby appeared sane or insane during his final illness. He thought the Dallas jail was a Buchenwald."

Jack Ruby died on January 2, 1967, at 9:30 A.M., in Parkland Hospital in Dallas, the same hospital in which President Kennedy had died. His body was returned to Chicago for burial.

John Justin Smith covered it for the Chicago *Daily News*. He wrote for the January 6 editions:

"Under a moody gray sky and in frozen snowy ground, Jack Ruby was buried here Friday.

"The man who killed Lee Harvey Oswald was home forever. . . .

"Three squad cars led the procession [of some 20 autos] to the Westlawn Cemetery. . . . Jack Ruby would have liked that. He was given to hanging around policemen and police stations. . . .

"About 50 persons gathered at the grave for the burial service, and some 35 of the uninvited looked on from the other side of a wire fence about 50 feet away from the Ruby burial plot. . . .

"'Shall we condemn Jack Ruby?' asked Rabbi David Graubart in the eulogy before the burial. 'Because he loved the martyred President as we all did, he made it his personal duty to avenge his death.'

"'This act we cannot condone. Neither do we dare to sit in judgment. Let us understand and be sympathetic.'

"The rabbi also told mourners: 'Do not harshly condemn a person who succumbed to temptation until you are faced by a similar temptation and you overcome it. Judaism long ago taught that no man sins unless a spirit of folly overtake him.'

"'Jack Ruby thought he would acquire his world in one moment. But Jack Ruby unfortunately destroyed his world in one moment.'

"Ruby was buried in the same plot as were his father and his mother. His brothers—Earl, Sam and Hyman—were called upon to say Kaddish, the traditional memorial prayer in Aramaic. The centuries-old prayer of glorification of God contains the soaring phrases: 'May His great name be blessed forever and for all time.' The mourners also included Ruby's four sisters.

"At the end, the American flag, draped across the coffin because Ruby was a World War II veteran, was folded and handed to a sister, Mrs. Eva L. Grant of Dallas. She wept bitterly as the coffin was lowered into the frozen earth."

# EARL RUBY

Earl Ruby, the second youngest of nine children of Joseph and Fannie Rubenstein, is the executor of his brother Jack's will, was with Jack when he died, and was perhaps the one person closest to his brother. Earl was born in 1916, and was five years younger than Jack. Earl Ruby lives in Detroit where he owns one of Michigan's largest dry-cleaning establishments. He owns the block on which the store and plant is located and has ten trucks picking up cleaning.

There is a hub of activity in the establishment. In the back, there is a labyrinth of clean clothes hanging on hangers. There are hisses and slams from the pressing machines and eddies of smoke. Tumbrels of dirty clothes rumble in front of workers pushing them.

Earl Ruby's office is in the rear, beside his bookkeeper's office. It is a small office. On the wall is an official White House color photograph of President Kennedy; Ruby put the picture up in 1961, when he took over the business. The first dollar he took in in the dry-cleaning business is taped below the picture.

Earl Ruby wears glasses, has graying sideburns, bears a slight resemblance to his brother but is not as jowly as the pictures of his brother. He sits on a couch, pulls out a drawer of his desk and props his leg on it. He suffers pain from an old high school football injury to his right knee, which has been operated on. He limps because of it. He had picked me up when I came in to Detroit by plane and graciously invited me to his home for dinner. He was not reluctant to talk about his brother.

"On that Sunday morning, November 24, 1963, I'm sitting in this office talking to a friend of mine in Chicago. He was in the hospital. So I called him. Listen to this coincidence. We're talk-

ing and he says, 'I gotta hang up. Somebody just shot Oswald.'
Now, he knows my brother very well, but they didn't know instantly who did it. I didn't think anything of it. I was with a friend
named Jim Stewart. I told him, 'Somebody shot Oswald.' Well I
was finished with my business for the day and I said, 'Jim, let's go.
I'll drive you home.'

"We get in the car. We drive off. I turn on the radio and about
a block away we hear, 'A man named Jack Ruby has been
identified as the one who shot Lee Harvey Oswald. . . .' You
know, I stopped the car, pulled over to the side. 'I can't believe it,'
I said. My friend said I turned white as a ghost. And so I was all
shook up, of course. Jim said, 'You better not drive for a while.'
But I dropped him off and went home. By the time I got home,
you know, the word was out, and the news people were calling us.
And from then on, really, the tumult started. That night I went to
Chicago, to the home on Loyola Avenue, where my brother and
two sisters lived.

"A couple guys came to the door and said they're the FBI.
Well, there'd been so many reporters at the door, we wouldn't let
'em in. So they went up to the corner drugstore and called and
told us to call a number which would verify that they were the
FBI. They interviewed each of us separately and talked to us
about the story at length and made notes and all.

"It's a funny thing, but when I first heard of the President's assassination and then the capture of Oswald, my first reaction was
—I told friends—'If I could get hold of him, I'd kill him with my
bare hands.' Yeah, really, I made that statement. And I wasn't
alone. Oh, my goodness. My brother, while he was in jail,
received hundreds of Bibles from Catholics, Protestants. I don't
know if they knew he was Jewish or not—I saw a Bible must have
cost a hundred dollars. It was this big, brand-new. Inlayed gold
and silver. He asked me what to do with them. I said, 'Well, you
have no use for them. Give 'em all away.'

"My business didn't suffer in any way because most of my customers were very happy with what my brother did, believe it or
not. I had so many comments favorable. I don't remember any
unfavorable. For example, I was a Big Brother for a while. That's
an organization where adults help orphan kids. The head of Big

Brother locally was a reverend or some type of religious person. When I first went for the interview, he said, 'I know who you are.' He says, 'I want you to know one thing. Don't be ashamed of what your brother did because if I had the chance, I think I would have done it myself.' So it made me feel good.

"The only negative thing I can remember dealt with my youngest daughter, Joyce. She was nine years old at the time, and she had a little problem in school. They called her 'Killer' Ruby. But the principal, from what I understand, summoned all the students into the assembly and told them that this has got to stop. And it stopped right there. Yeah, I was disturbed by what happened. But those kids didn't realize. . . . They thought it was a joke, to call her 'Killer' Ruby."

His daughter, at the time this interview took place, was a senior at Michigan State, majoring in criminal psychology.

"Why does she major in criminal psychology? I never asked her, never did. Maybe because Jack Ruby is her uncle. She is concerned because she does bring it up. She says, 'My friends that I—they say that Jack, that your brother Jack was in the CIA, and they even think you're in the CIA now.' I say, 'Joyce, I would tell you, Joyce, if I was in the CIA. And you know I'm here all the time. CIA people gotta be away like a traveling salesman or something. And you know I'm at the plant for so many hours. I couldn't be in the CIA.' She says, 'Yeah, but they—but different people come and lecture at the school and they say that Earl Ruby and Jack Ruby were CIA.' And I tell her, 'You tell those people, honey, that your uncle was not in the CIA, he was not in the FBI, he was not involved in any way. And neither is your father.'

"Jack always used to brag to his friends about me, that I was a successful and respectable businessman. I loaned him money for the club. One time I sent him six thousand dollars. Altogether I loaned him about fifteen thousand. In fact, believe it or not, when I was in Washington to testify before the Warren Commission, they said, 'We know you loaned your brother money on several occasions for the nightclub. Why did you continue loaning him money if he never paid you back?' I said, 'He was my brother, that's why. I wanted to help him get on his feet. And I thought one of these days he's gonna hit it. And do well.' So that's the way we were. We were brothers. And we were very close.

"I don't know if you would say I'm 'proud' of what he did. But I'm not ashamed of him, that he did it. I'm really not ashamed. But I, like a lot of others—you have to understand, the people of our generation had a very deep feeling, a very deep love for President Kennedy. He was a man our age. He was our generation. Our President. Everybody loved him, you know. That's why I put this picture up on my wall in '61. He was also kindly toward the Jews, toward Israel. He put a Jew, Arthur Goldberg, into his cabinet. Come to think of it, Sirhan Sirhan killed Bobby Kennedy because of his friendly views toward Israel and Jews.

"I think Jack was a very good Jew and a very good American. He believed in America. He really did. He liked the Presidents. Roosevelt. Eisenhower. Truman. But especially Kennedy, and his whole family. He loved 'em all. That's the way he was.

"My brother was a very good fighter. Strong and fast. Good hands. Barney Ross actually told me, he said, 'Your brother, Jack, if he'd of been in the ring, he coulda been a champeen.'

"But I think Jack had more fights than the average professional. I'm sure of it. On the street, any insult to a friend, he'd immediately fight.

"Jack had a fiery temper, but he was also very softhearted. He'd be giving money away to all those people in Dallas, down-and-out people, and in the meantime he was borrowing money to do it. He would take people off the streets and help 'em. The irony of it, one fella he took into his apartment. Can't remember his name. But he didn't have any place to eat, any place to sleep or eat. My brother took him in, found him a job, everything. And then after the Oswald thing, the guy helped burglarize my brother's apartment. Stole some of his suits and then sold 'em. . . .

"You know, there is only one reason I wouldn't have wanted Jack to do what he did. I would have liked Oswald to have been alive long enough to tell the world that Jack had nothing to do with it.

"From what I read and the knowledge I have about Oswald, I'm positive he did it alone. I don't care what all these conspiracy theories say. . . . Guys like Mark Lane have made a million dollars fabricating events. . . . Oswald was a loner. His brother believed he did it alone; his wife believed he did it alone. And he tried to shoot other people. He tried to shoot General Walker, he told his wife he was gonna kill Nixon when he was Vice-President. If he had lived a little longer, it would have been proven that he operated alone. It would have looked a lot better for my brother. The only unfavorable thing everyone says is, 'Why didn't he wait until we got all the information from Oswald?' But there really was no information.

"No. Jack showed no remorse that he had killed Oswald. His greatest worry was that he caused a lot of problems for the family. But he didn't, really. We never had any problems. Nobody ever threatened us or anything like that. In fact, we got all kinds of favorable mail. And thousands and thousands of telegrams. I'd need a big truck to take 'em. And they sent us money for his defense. Walter Winchell sent me a hundred dollars.

"Sometimes, sometimes he'd say, 'Earl, I'm sorry I caused you embarrassment.' And he felt sorry that we spent money in his behalf. He felt he caused us hardships, which he didn't. The money, yes, but not real hardships.

"Something funny. We spoke in Yiddish when we wanted to discuss something confidential, like family matters. And that's when some reporters thought we were really talking about secret things.

"For me, growing up around Maxwell Street was, well, let me give you an example. We had some neighbors living upstairs, Polish people. On Morgan Street and Maxwell. And one of the sons became a hood—a holdup man. And he was killed. He was only eighteen or nineteen years old. And, you know, this registered with me. To stay clean. I used to see him and visit with him and then one day I read in the paper he was killed in a holdup of some kind.

"That helped me stay straight because a lot of 'em, a lot of people I went to school with, they became real bad people. And some were killed.

"It wasn't necessary. I managed to get along. I don't see why they shouldn't. I always worked, always had a job—for as long as I can remember. I had a bakery route when I was like ten years old. I had a newspaper route. I worked on a milk wagon. I would run up the stairs for the milkman, drop off bottles, pick up empties. I worked in a grocery store. I'm thankful I had such an upbringing. I always remember those days. And I must admit, for that reason, I probably never squandered money. I never became a gambler. I know how hard it was to make money.

"Our greatest problem then was surviving. I had one pair of pants when I went to high school. I never had a suit. We wore sweatshirts. I would wear the same sweatshirt, but I would wash it every night and hang it up to dry. And I would wash and iron my own pants. Many days I didn't even have carfare. I would hitch a ride or sneak on the streetcar.

"Luckily my father had steady jobs, so we didn't starve. He was a carpenter. And I remember he never left the house with his tool kit without at least a pint of whiskey. When he came home it was all gone. All the carpenters and all construction people drank. First of all, because of the cold winters. They didn't have the heating facilities for keeping workers warm as they do today. And then it was also a part of the European tradition. My father, I remember, would make his own whiskey. I would help him cut up apples to put in the alcohol. But I never drank—I've always hated the taste. To this day.

"So I grew up working, knowing the value of working, knowing the value of money. And I enjoy working. I really enjoy working. I appreciate the things I have now, and it all came from hard work.

"I mean, this business I'm in. I put in a lot of hours here, but I'm compensated for it. It's mine. It was rough here at first. In the second year, in '62, my half partner and I had a bad year. In '63, we were in the black.

"I worked hard. Some people can't believe that I work seven days a week. From seven in the morning to seven at night. On Sunday I work four, five hours.

"Once my daughter came home and said somebody at school had told her, 'Your father's got to be a member of the FBI or CIA. How else could he have such a big cleaning plant without the help of the government maybe buying it for him?'

"How else? I said to my daughter, 'Joyce, honey, have any of those people ever heard of something called sweat and tears?' "

# BARNEY ROSS

—CHICAGO. Barney Ross, the former lightweight and welterweight champion of the world, died today at age 58 in his Lake Shore Drive apartment. The funeral will be held on Friday, at the Original Weinstein and Sons Chapel.

A student of the Talmud who turned to prize fighting, Barney Ross was regarded as one of the toughest champions.

Outside of the ring, moreover, his heroism on Guadalcanal and his victory over a narcotics habit brought him further recognition as a man who had never been knocked out and had never quit.

NEW YORK *TIMES*
*January 18, 1967*

Barney Ross was born Barnet David Rasofsky on December 23, 1909. His parents, Isidore and Sarah, always called him by his Yiddish name, Beryl or Beryle. His mother was a woman of five two, but his father was almost six feet tall, stood erect as a soldier, and wore a pointed, reddish-brown beard with sideburns, which he clipped and combed but never shaved, in accordance with Orthodox Jewish law.

Ross's parents decided to leave Brest Litovsk, Russia, after a howling mob during a pogrom broke into the synagogue in which he was praying, smashed the mahogany doors of the Holy Ark, spat at and tore up the holy scrolls while Isidore Rasofsky begged them in vain to stop.

Isidore Rasofsky came to America in 1903 without his wife and firstborn son. He began teaching in a Hebrew school on the Lower East Side of New York. It was not lucrative. He gave it up to begin selling vegetables and groceries from a pushcart. He worked one hundred hours a week and in two years was able to send for his family, who came over on a dirty cattle boat.

Two years after Barney was born, Sarah Rasofsky's uncle in Chicago wrote that there was a small grocery store for sale in Chicago's Maxwell Street ghetto. "At least in a store we won't be out in the street in the wind and snow," reasoned Isidore Rasofsky. In March, 1911, they moved to Chicago.

"Rasofsky's Dairy" would be recalled by Ross in later years as "a hole in the wall, that when we had more than four customers they'd be jammed up against the shelves and the pickle barrels." The family, which now included five sons and a daughter, lived in a tiny, dingy apartment across the street. There was one bedroom and another small room, little more than a glorified hallway. There was just one window. Ross would remember that the air was always stale.

Pneumonia and TB were rampant and the free clinic on Maxwell Street was usually packed and had a monumental waiting list. "Fire," recalled Ross, in his autobiography,* "was another terror. I can't remember a week when we didn't have at least three big fires in the neighborhood. The old wooden buildings used to burn like tissue paper. . . . The fire barn was on Maxwell and Jefferson and every time we kids heard the fire bell, we'd run like crazy to the barn and watch the firemen harness the horses to their engines with their hoses. . . . Every time a fireman burned to death trying to carry women and children out of a blazing tenement, we used to take off from school and form a kids' brigade at the funeral."

Discipline was strict in the Rasofsky residence. Any misbehavior and Pa Rasofsky brought out his cat-o'-nine-tails. "Unless you are punished," he told his children, "how will you be able to follow the right path, to know that you must not break God's laws, and to earn God's blessings?" The children cried, but they

---

* Barney Ross and Martin Abramson, *No Man Stands Alone: The True Story of Barney Ross* (Philadelphia: J. B. Lippincott Co., 1957), p. 28.

also felt loved and saw that their parents put away what little money they earned for their education. Pa Rasofsky used to say in Yiddish, "We'll get our happiness from enjoying the good fortune that will come to our children."

Barney's parents felt shamed when he came home from the numerous street fights that he had. "Pa would collar me and let fly with that cat-o'-nine-tails whip," said Ross. "It was no use trying to tell him I hadn't picked a fight, that I fought only in self-defense. Pa's mind was made up that I had disgraced my heritage by descending to the same level as the other 'bums' and 'tramps.'

"As far as Pa was concerned, anybody who lifted a hand in anger or violence against a stranger was committing a shameful sin. Pa believed that physical force was something you used only to discipline your children or punish them for breaking the holy law. . . . Once when somebody told him about the great Jewish boxing champ, Benny Leonard, Pa's face turned blood red, 'What shame this Leonard has brought on his father and mother!' "

Barney's father added, "The religious man, Beryl, prizes learning above everything else. Let the atheists be the fighters, the *trubeniks,* the murderers—*we* are the scholars."

At seven-thirty on the morning of Thursday, December 13, 1924, Isidore Rasofsky was murdered in his grocery store on Jefferson Street just south of Maxwell.

"That morning," recalled Ross, "Pa was in the store early getting the milk, butter and cheese perishables ready for the breakfast trade. In the Jewish ghetto, and in the poor Italian and Polish slum districts just north and west of the ghetto, few families could keep food overnight in their ratty little wooden iceboxes. So as soon as they got up, they'd run to the local grocery to buy what they needed. Ma would go into the store a little later, after she'd given us breakfast.

" 'Did you *daven* yet, Beryl?' Ma wanted to know when I sat down to eat. 'Did you say your prayers?'

" 'Holy smoke, Ma, I forgot,' I answered.

" 'Less than a year after your Bar Mitzvah and you're forgetting already! From you I don't expect such things, Beryl. *Daven!* ' "

He recited his morning prayers from memory.

When he finished breakfast, Barney went to his father to get carfare to high school (Medill) and to get a cheese sandwich for lunch. His mother called, "Tell Pa to watch out for the *gonovim*." She was concerned about people who came into the store early, when her husband was busy with his morning chores, and tried to steal foodstuffs. Barney yelled back okay.

"I went bounding down the steps two at a time and nearly collided with one of my chums, little Jackie Broad," said Ross. " 'I was just coming for you, Barney,' he said. 'Hurry-up. Something's happened at the store.' His face was chalk-white. An unreasoning fear suddenly clutched me.

"A crowd was gathered in front of the store. I ran across the street, screamed, 'Let me in, let me in.' Pa was lying on the floor his face twisted in agony. Blood was pouring down the front of his white apron. Frantically, I tore open the apron. His shirt, money belt and *tzitzith*—a small praying shawl which Pa wore day and night—were torn and soaked with blood. 'Pa, Pa,' I cried. His eyes, which had been staring into space, suddenly focused on me and recognized me. 'It's all right, Beryl,' he mumbled. 'Don't tell Mama . . . the shock . . .' His eyes closed and his words trailed off.

"Two men rushed forward to hold my father's head up off the floor till the ambulance came. One of them accidentally kicked something hard across the room. It was a revolver. I stared at it open-mouthed. Suddenly, there was movement behind me and I heard a hysterical cry. It was Ma. She tried to grab Pa, but some neighbors held her back. Now the noise of the people outside the store sounded like a mass roar and there was a squeal of automobile brakes. Ambulance attendants hurried in with their stretcher and lifted Pa up tenderly. The blood was still dripping from his body."

His mother continued to shriek. Neighbors called a taxi and tried to pack the family into it. Barney refused to go. "I've got to find 'em," he said. "I wanna kill 'em with my bare hands."

There was one witness, a Mrs. Farbstein, and the police were questioning her. She said two young men who knew Isidore Rasofsky carried a few dollars in his money belt tried to stick him up. They had come in under the guise of buying lox and bagels. They asked if they could warm their hands at his potty stove.

"Sure, go ahead," he said.

Mrs. Farbstein said she didn't like the looks of the boys and told Isidore Rasofsky that, but he motioned her off with a smile. "By you, every stranger is a trubenik," he said.

She had gotten only a few feet outside the door when she heard a shot. In their fright, the perpetrators ran out without taking any money at all and dropped the revolver as they fled.

No one was sure what they looked like. But the cops fanned out in the teeming neighborhood, and people came streaming from the tenements to see if they could help. Barney and several of his friends grabbed up sticks and lead pipes and began a hunt.

"On one corner, a peddler whose pushcart had been knocked over by the fleeing punks pointed in the direction of Roosevelt and Halsted," wrote Ross. "Like madmen, we ran to the intersection and got more contradictory gestures and directions. A block away, there was a culvert which lay rusty and unused and led to a wooden area. A kid shouted at us, 'They went into the opening. . . . I saw 'em!'

"We ran to the culvert and I squirmed inside. It was so dark I couldn't see a thing. 'Come outta there,' I yelled, and began to curse. Jackie pulled me out. 'They're not gonna listen to you, Barney. We'll stand guard on all sides of this thing and grab 'em when they come out. They can't stay there forever.' "

The watch eventually ended there when sign of the two culprits never materialized. Isidore Rasofsky remained unconscious in Jewish Hospital for thirty-two hours. He awakened once, put a hand on his rheumatic shoulder—grown weak from the dampness of the Maxwell Street flat—which had bothered him for years, and whispered, "It doesn't hurt any more." He rubbed his beard and muttered, *"Shema Yisrael* [Hear, O Israel]." A few minutes later he died.

"I couldn't cry," wrote Ross. "The tears wouldn't come. My cousin Rose came up to console me, then looked at me in surprise because I wasn't showing grief. She started to say something and stopped when she realized that I was in a blind fog. She put her arms around me and mumbled soothingly, 'For a while, it'll be terrible without your pa, but you'll get over it, and your life will be just the same.'

"But it was never to be the same. Everything that happened to the Barnet Rasofsky who became Barney Ross happened only because of that senseless, stupid murder on Jefferson Street."†

Most of the money the family made by selling the dairy was used for Isidore Rasofsky's funeral. Ma Rasofsky was then sent off to stay with her husband's blind mother in Connecticut. The youngest children went into an orphanage; the older boys took an apartment.

The death of his father embittered Barney. He lost faith in religion. The anger welled up in him and he took it out often in the streets. Once, he tried to avoid brawls—no more. And he found that although he was four inches shorter than the average fourteen-year-old and weighed less than a hundred pounds, he was so fast and agile on his feet, so quick with his hands, that he was a superior street battler.

He quit school. During the week he hauled heavy ashes in the ghetto. On Sundays he worked as a "puller" and barker for a dry-goods store on Maxwell Street. "I used to scream 'Get your bargains! Get your bargains!' And I'd try to outshout the other barkers as well as the peddlers on the street selling the same thing. If one of my rivals started yelling, 'Best woolen sweaters, $1.39,' I'd immediately howl, 'Best cashmere sweaters in the whole world, $1.29,' wrote Ross.

Barney by his own admission was developing into a real troublemaker. He said he was "spitting fire." When the neighborhood was quiet, he'd goad his friends into going into rival racial neighborhoods and getting into gang fights, of which he was now a loving and vicious participant.

He remembered that one of his neighbors had been Samuel "Nails" Morton, a natty racketeer, who had been kicked to death accidentally by a horse in a riding incident in the same year "Pa" was killed. On impulse one day, Ross went to Morton's friends "Two Gun" Altarie and Frankie Yale, sometimes spectators at gang fights, and asked them for work. They discouraged him because he was "a rabbi's son." He insisted. They told him to "Go down to see Capone at his club." He did. Al Capone said, "You got no business getting mixed up in the rackets. You couldn't be a hood if you wanted to."

† Ibid., pp. 11–19.

But Capone capitulated to Ross's pleadings. He gave him odd jobs to do, such as buying his cigars and sending him for new packs of playing cards because he couldn't stand cards that were even a little worn or thumbed.

"My career as a messenger-boy there ended abruptly one morning when Capone told me it was time for me to stop hanging around his place and time to 'get off the streets.'

" 'Here's a twenty,' he told me. 'Buy your family something and go back to school or get a job.' When I started to protest he gave me a hard look and said, 'Look, I told you something. Now beat it before I get mad.' "‡

Ross says he accepted this and acknowledged that he was not meant "to be bad." "Too much of what Pa and Ma had taught me through the years was still inside me," he said.

One of the fellows from the neighborhood, Jackie Fields, had become a professional boxer and his career was watched closely by his old friends. Soon, more and more of them began going to gyms. Barney was one. His talents were quickly recognized. He soon became the top amateur for his weight in Chicago. He had changed his name to "Ross" because his name was now appearing in the papers at times and he didn't want his mother to find out. He chose Ross, being so close to Rasofsky.

One day Capone and his pals came to see Barney train. "I been hearin' about you," said Capone to Barney. "Who ever thought a skinny runt like you could do all right for himself in the ring? I wanna see a neighborhood kid make good and get ahead. If you're fighting at Howard's gym Saturday night, I'll buy out the whole place. Tell your pals they can come as my guest."*

After that, said Ross, Capone and his lieutenants were always in attendance at Barney's fights.

Ross's mother, back living in Chicago, was distraught at her son the fighter. But he eventually convinced her that it was a worthy occupation. As a symbol of her acquiescence, she sewed a Jewish Star of David on the inside of his boxing trunks.

"I took it to Rabbi Stein and he made a blessing over it," she said to him. "Now I want you to wear it every time you fight so

‡ Ibid., pp. 66–67.
* Ibid., p. 84.

you'll have protection from God." He wore it in the ring from then on.

Ross became a Golden Gloves champ, turned pro, won fight after fight. He grew cocky, neglected training, lost, got a lecture from Capone one night ("Take it from me, you're a goddamn dunce"), straightened out, won enough money to get the youngest of the Rasofsky kids out of the orphanage, brought the family back together under one roof.

"Beryl," his mother said to him, "Pa is looking down on you and he's very proud of you."

A few weeks later, on June 21, 1932, Barney Ross beat Tony Canzoneri, "with thirteen thousand fans screaming for the kid from the ghetto," to become the world's lightweight champion and also the junior welterweight champion.

Ross also rediscovered religion and would read the Talmud and other religious books even in training camp. He got married.

He was fighting championship fights and winning. He went on to win the welterweight title and gave up his other two titles. He was earning more than he ever imagined, "and I played with it as if it were a box of new toys." He became a sucker for loans to "friends" and a target for race-track touts. The money drained. Fortunately, the big fight nights eased that pain. But the "gambling curse" had taken about half a million dollars from him.

On May 31, 1938, he lost his welterweight title to Henry Armstrong in one of the bloodiest, bruisingest champion fights on record. It went the full fifteen-round distance. And Ross got the worst of it. He could hardly raise his arms for the last several rounds and the punishment he took was merciless. "My mouth was torn and ripped to a pulp. . . . It was agony to breathe." Ross begged the referee not to stop the fight, and the referee did not. "I wanted to go out a fighting champ, and on my feet," Ross said.

Ross left the ring, stumbling up the aisle, hanging onto his trainers. "Funny, I thought," he wrote, "I don't hear any shouting. I don't even hear talking. How come they're not raising the roof for the hero of the night, the new champ? I saw faces, faces, faces, and they were all looking at me, not up at the ring, and in the whole arena, 35,000 people were sitting in silence. And then I suddenly realized that this unbelievable, fantastic silence was the most wonderful tribute I had ever received. It spoke louder, a thousand times louder than all the cheers I had heard since the day I put on a pair of boxing gloves and won my first fight. . . ."†

Ross retired. He opened a cocktail lounge in Chicago that was a money-sapper. He got divorced, met a showgirl, fell in love. Just when they planned to get married, the war broke out. Ross joined the Marines.

He eventually landed on Guadalcanal. "Jap machine-gun and rifle bullets were raining all around us [in the foxholes]," wrote Ross. At least twenty bullets ricocheted off a log he had found, and those bullets hit his tin helmet. By night, he had fired 350 rounds of ammunition. His hand was burning from it. Out of bullets, he began to throw grenades.

"The bugs and malarial mosquitoes were around now too, and crawling in my hair and taking nips." He was thirsty, hungry, fatigued; it started to rain. "The dampness and the mud underneath cramped my feet and a chill went through my body. I felt terrible pain. . . ." He began to dream of his girl friend, Cathy, his family, his "ghetto pals," wondering if they'd ever see him again. Suddenly he was snapped out of his reverie. The Japs were back and firing again, this time just thirty yards away. "The firing went on all night." All he had left were twenty-one grenades, and he threw all of them just before dawn, after he had been in the hole about thirteen hours. He began saying the Shema Yisrael prayer over and over. Not long after, the firing miraculously stopped, he said. He was found later by a medical soldier and taken to an aid station. He was burning with fever. And he discovered that overnight his hair had turned gray "just as Pa's hair had once turned white in a Russian pogrom."

He had malaria. He was taken to the Ifati field hospital.

He had sharp pains throughout his body. His ears rang. He had migraine headaches. He kept vomiting. He had dysentery. Since his night in the shell hole, he had lost thirty pounds. "To help fight the pain, the corpsmen gave me half-grain Syrettes of morphine. The morphine lifted me out of the snake pit and let me climb high in the clouds.

"I was supposed to get the morphine only in case of emergency, but the corpsmen were well-meaning fellows and, when they saw me in agony, they gave me extra shots. . . . I came to depend

† Ibid., pp. 166–67.

Sidney "Sy" Bartlett and film actress Alice White, soon to be married. Los Angeles, November 7, 1933. (Acme)

*Below*
*left:* Governor Henry Horner, of Illinois, and Chicago Councilman Jacob Arvey, 1936. (Chicago *Sun-Times*) *Bottom left:* Arvey, right, and President Harry Truman ride in open car, following the President's arrival in Chicago, October 29, 1952, to make speech on behalf of Stevenson for President. (UPI) *Right:* Governor Adlai Stevenson, of Illinois, and Colonel Arvey, March 30, 1952. (Wide World)

Meyer Levin, 1932. (Wide World)

Meyer Levin, 1972. (Wide World)

Arthur Goldberg, at age eleven.
(Courtesy of Arthur Goldberg)

*Left:* Goldberg, Secretary of Labor, reporting to President John F. Kennedy in the Oval Room of the White House, September 2, 1961. (UPI) *Right:* Goldberg poses in his robes prior to being sworn in as an associate justice of the United States Supreme Court, November 1, 1962. (UPI)

Goldberg, United States Ambassador, addresses the opening session of the United Nations General Assembly, September 22, 1965. (UPI)

*Left:* Western Union messenger, lower left, is Hyman G. Rickover, standing ready at Republican National Convention in Chicago on June 7, 1916. Rickover was then a high school student in Chicago. (Chicago *Tribune*) *Right:* Admiral Rickover, bottom, rides in tickertape parade down Broadway in New York City. The parade was in honor of the crew of the *Nautilus,* the first atomic submarine. Rickover is credited with being the father of that submarine. Waving is *Nautilus* skipper Commander William Anderson, August 27, 1958. (UPI)

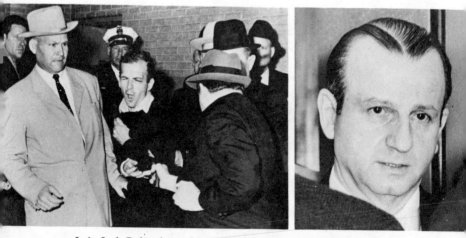

*Left:* Jack Ruby shoots Lee Harvey Oswald in Dallas, November 24, 1963. (UPI) *Right:* Ruby during his trial in Dallas for shooting of Oswald, February 22, 1964. (UPI)

*Left:* Barney Ross proclaimed winner of bout over Tony Canzoneri, which gave Ross the lightweight boxing championship of the world, June 24, 1933, at Chicago Stadium. At left is Ross's comanager and trainer, Art Winch. (Wide World) *Right:* Ross's mother, Mrs. Sarah Rasofsky, December 4, 1942. (Chicago *Tribune*)

*Left:* Ross receives cheers from fight fans as he returns to New York's Madison Square Garden a Marine war hero, March 13, 1943. (UPI) *Right:* Ross, seated, and former middleweight champion Tony Zale inspect tickets for "Salute to Barney Ross," in 1966. Ross was suffering from throat cancer. (Wide World)

*Left:* William Paley, 1966. (Wide World) *Right:* Mrs. William Paley (the former Barbara Cushing Mortimer), 1948. (UPI)

*Facing page*
*top:* La Palina cigar wrapper. Woman pictured is claimed by some to be the mother of William Paley. La Palina was the name of the cigar brand owned by the Paley family. (Courtesy of CBS) *Bottom left:* Mr. Samuel Paley, father of William Paley. (CBS) *Bottom right:* Mrs. Goldie Drell Paley, mother of William Paley. (CBS)

Joseph "Yellow Kid" Weil, at age fifty-one, 1926. (Chicago *Tribune*)

One of Weil's bogus business cards. (Courtesy of John Vidovic)

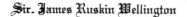

Sir. James Ruskin Wellington

LONDON, ENGLAND

Weil, at age one hundred, 1975. (Chicago *Tribune*)

on those shots the way a drowning man depends on a life pre-
server. When I couldn't get them I felt like jumping out of the
window."

He returned to the States, and he found that, still, the pain
subsided only when he was drugged.

"I became so wild for dope I was ready to tear up the town to
get it." He began injecting himself with dope, using a syringe
and an eye dropper. He lied to friends that he was using his
money for investments. But it all went for dope. "The pushers
were bleeding me for every penny I had. I was spending up to
$500 a week on it. I ran up debts of tens of thousands of
dollars."‡

In Hollywood one night, he almost collapsed. He was taken to a
doctor. He told the doctor he needed an injection—some morphine.

The doctor said he'd seen too many cases like his not to know a
dope addict. He advised him go to the U. S. Public Health Service
addiction hospital in Lexington, Kentucky.

Ross began to think about it, particularly since he was losing
the woman he loved—his new wife, Cathy. He checked out of the
hospital and decided he would have to do it. He was assigned to a
"withdrawal" ward.

"The withdrawal gave me the miseries, because the limited
amount of morphine [they kept cutting his dosage daily] wasn't
enough to kill the cramps and the sweats. I soon learned where
the expression 'kick the habit' came from. When the drug quota
was progressively cut down, I got spasms in the muscles of my
arms and my legs actually kicked."* He had nightmares of wild
animals, of fighting the Japs in the mud at night, of his father's
murder.

Three months later, on January 12, 1947, he was released from
Lexington. He was reunited with Cathy. He was joyous. One sour
note, however, was that he learned that John Garfield had decided to quit his plans to film *The Barney Ross Story* because of
Ross's drug addiction. Garfield had decided instead to make a
"fictitious picture" of a boxer and to call it *Body and Soul*. Ross,
however, realized sixty thousand dollars from that in a legal suit

‡ Ibid., 222.
* Ibid., p. 235.

because of the amount of material used in the movie from Ross's life.

Ross became a kind of crusader against drug addiction. He testified about his experiences before a Senate committee in Washington, talked with kids around the country. He also worked as an entertainment promoter and helped arrange the personal appearances schedule in the late '50s of an up-and-coming singer named Eddie Fisher.

The *Times* obituary on Ross added, "In recent years, Ross was frequently present at major fights hired to do promotional work. A small round man with gray hair, chain-smoking cigarettes and softly talking of the years when boxing was more important and its heroes were hungrier."

He was elected to the Boxing Hall of Fame and earned a rating in the top ten welterweights of all time.

However, many of the friends that had flocked around him when he was champ, had deserted him. One who did not was Ira Colitz, a boyhood friend of Ross's from the Maxwell Street area. It was Colitz, an insurance executive and onetime state senator in Illinois, who befriended Ross both with financial and emotional support. In his last days, Ross moved from New York back to Chicago, lived in a fine Lake Shore apartment due to Colitz's benevolence.

Colitz recalls that the two of them were walking to a hospital in which Ross was scheduled for a checkup, and Ross said, "It's almost over, Ira. I've got the Big C."

"Naw," said Colitz, "you don't have it."

"I know I do, Ira. No use fooling anybody. And I'm past the age when I should be trying to fool myself.

"Ira, do me a favor. Don't forget. When I check out, make sure you give my business to Hershey."

Hershey was one of the Weinstein brothers who owned a funeral parlor in Chicago and was a long-time friend of Ross's.

Ross died on January 18, 1967. On January 20, the body of Barnet David Rasofsky, known to the world as Barney Ross, lay in an open coffin among the throngs of flowers and mourners in the funeral parlor of his friend, Hershey Weinstein.

Barney had gotten his favor.

# THE STREET, 1957

## MORE TROUBLES FOR
## MAXWELL ST. MART

—Maxwell Street is having troubles. Business is said to be off ever since Cardinal Stritch banned unnecessary Sabbath work. Including shopping. And Sunday is the big day on Maxwell Street. That's when the narrow old throughfare blossoms into the new world's only rival to the flea market of Paris. . . . One merchant says he has dropped from $400 Sunday gross to $40.

CHICAGO *SUN-TIMES*
*May 2, 1957*

# JOSEPH RENÉ
# "YELLOW KID" WEIL

## CENTURY OLD LEGEND LIVES ON

### CON MAN NOW CHEATING FATHER TIME

Joseph [Yellow Kid] Weil, one of the slickest confidence men who ever parted a fool and his money, celebrates his 100th birthday Monday.

The wily Kid is holed up in a nursing home these days, where he needs help getting dressed. Having gone graciously through more than $8 million in his day, he's now on public assistance. . . .

The Kid was credited with being the first con man to fleece his victims by telephone; the first to use the sort of theatrics memorialized in the movie, *The Sting.* . . . [That is] setting up fake handbooks [and] promising some sucker a quick killing on a fixed horse race. The Kid would work his larceny with actors, props, delayed race results and plenty of success. . . .

He made himself an expert on high finance and unloaded hundreds of thousands of dollars of worthless stock. He "salted" gold mines as a come-on to investors.

All this led to many arrests. . . . He wound up in federal prison four times. . . .

He passed himself off at one time or another under various disguises. . . . The Kid was ever a dapper dresser, and one yellowed newspaper clipping describes him with neatly combed reddish Van Dyke in frock coat, gates-a-jar collar, mauve cravat, dove gray spats, silk checkerboard socks, white silk shirt, cream silk waistcoat embroidered in lavender forget-me-nots and a golden tweed topcoat. His underwear is not mentioned.

*Donald Zochert*
CHICAGO *DAILY NEWS*
*June 20, 1975*

————◆▸◀◆————

The Yellow Kid's underwear was peppermint-striped boxershorts, when I visited him at the Lake Front Convalescent Home shortly before his one hundredth birthday. I was accompanied by John Vidovic, half The Kid's age, but a long-time friend of The Kid's and his conservator.

The Kid had been sitting on a chair beside his bed and looking out the window. He had been reading the New Testament and also had a copy of *The Autobiography of Charlie Chaplin* on a night table. A cane rested against the white wall. The Yellow Kid's brown-flecked custom-made suit with vest was tailored in London many years ago, but still looked swell, if baggy, since the white-haired, wizened, small man was down to ninety pounds from his standard hundred and thirty. His thin tie was askew on his waffled neck. The zipper on his pants was at three-quarters' mast and a swatch of his dapper shorts showed.

All of his family, including his wife and daughter and two brothers, and most of his friends are long dead. Sometimes his mind did not now stick tenaciously to a subject the way it once did, but his innocent blue eyes behind steel-rim glasses remained deceptively bright.

Before coming to visit, I had read The Yellow Kid's autobiography, *Yellow Kid Weil—Con Man*. He was born on June 23,

1875, on the west side of Clark Street between Harrison and Polk, several blocks northeast of Maxwell Street. He was the son of Mr. and Mrs. Otto Weil, Alsatian-Jewish immigrants, "who were reputable hard-working people." They ran a grocery store. Later, his mother stayed with the store while his father opened a saloon. He recalls that he was "a bright pupil. Proficient in all my studies, I was particularly good at mathematics. After classes I helped in the store. . . ." He was quick-witted enough to understand human nature even at eight years old. He noticed how eggs came straight from the farm and were sold with the dirt still on them; so he decided to clean the eggs off and sell them for twice the price. And he sold twice as many.

He quit school after the eighth grade and worked as a bill collector. He found that his fellow collectors were not turning in all they collected. "If there was a scrupulous one in the lot, I don't recall him," wrote Weil. "By various means, they managed to cover up their peculations. . . . When I quietly made it known to my fellow employees that I was aware of their peccadillos . . . they contributed small sums so that I would keep their secrets. These sums amounted to considerably more than I was ever paid in salary."

During this time he had met a beautiful girl and became engaged to be married. He brought the girl home. His mother took young Joe aside and said, "She is a beautiful girl. But she is a girl for a rich man. She could not be a poor man's wife."

" 'And I'm not going to be a poor man!' I replied. . . ."

Weil wrote, "Having seen my parents struggle for their existence—my mother got up at five in the morning to open the store—I knew that such a life was not for me. Further, I had seen how much more money was being made by skulduggery than by honest toil."*

He began to frequent race tracks and saloons. One of his hangouts was the saloon of the notorious alderman "Bathhouse" John Coughlin, who in 1903 gave Weil the name "Yellow Kid." It was in respectful reference to a popular and cunning comic-strip character of the day.

* Joseph Weil as told to W. T. Brannon, *"Yellow Kid" Weil—Con Man: A Master Swindler's Own Story* (New York: Pyramid Books, 1957), pp. 7–8.

It was also at a saloon that he met Doc Meriwether, who would influence him profoundly. He went to work for Meriwether as a shill in the Doc's medicine show. Meriwether wore a Van Dyke beard and black frock coat and flowing cravat and sold "Meriwether's Elixir," said to be especially good for tapeworm, a fad disease of the day. "I don't remember the exact recipe," said Weil. "But the chief ingredient was rainwater . . . plus cascara [a laxative] and alcohol. . . . I cannot truthfully say whether anyone who took the Elixir ever got rid of tapeworm. But many thought they did, for the cascara worked on everybody. . . ."

Weil was also discovering the power of words. He went to church services once and was moved by the power of the preacher. "I said to myself, 'Joe, you are not capable of hard physical labor. You are too frail. Whatever you accomplish in life must be done through words. You have that ability. You can make words beautiful and scenic. What marble is to sculpture, what canvas is to painting, words can be to you. You can use them to influence others. You can make them earn your living for you.'"

He began to read "voraciously"—the Bible, encyclopedias, the dictionary, the lives of Moses, Buddha, Mohammed, Jesus. "There were so many inconsistencies that I became an iconoclast. I arrived at these conclusions: Man has all the bestiality of the animal, but he is cloaked with a thin veneer of civilization; he is inherently dishonest and selfish; the honest man is a rare specimen."

He said now, in his sterile room in the convalescent home, that he served his con-man's apprenticeship in the marketplace around Jefferson and Maxwell streets.

"The Jews located around through there because they were starving and had no place else to go," he said. "The city was highly anti-Jewish, and they had an awful tough go of it. They couldn't get anything to do. Nobody would hire them. They had to do something to make a living, so the market got started over in there. And it came to be Jewish headquarters.

"I would go there and peddle around. Peddle anything I could get. The first time I can remember going down to the marketplace there was when I was nine years old. Something like that."

In the following years he developed a con game with bum watches.

"I'd bring in a good gold watch and pawn it," he said. "Then I'd take it out. I'd pawn it a second time. And take it out. The third time, I'd bring in a phony that looked like the real gold watch. Then I'd sell the pawn ticket. The guy thought he was getting the McCoy when he was paying for the paste. You could make five hundred dollars on a ten-dollar watch. And then we'd sell these watches also on the street. Absolutely perfectly duplicated. There was something about it that you could tell it was a phony—by a click or something. I've forgotten so much. But I remember that they went flyin'.

"There were pushcarts on the street, I remember. It was loaded with Hebrews. And then they began to open little stores around Maxwell Street. I worked for one, a garment store. I can't think of the name of it now. I was mostly a salesman.

"Then I met Doc Meriwether, an Englishman, well versed in the language. I joined up and then I finally elevated myself out of what I was doing and went for the big money.

"I found that it was easy to get a big man with big money because they were accustomed to those real deals, you know. When a phony one come up, they couldn't set 'em aside.

"The bigger they were the more gullible they were. They believed that nobody had the gall to come to them with something that was nothing."

A most famous ploy was his stock-selling technique, involving false fronts and offices peopled with lesser con men in his employ. It was impressive enough to dispel the doubts of his intended victims. The day after the investor had paid Weil a huge amount, he would return to the huge office that had had rows and rows of secretaries and find nothing but bare walls.

"Each of my victims had larceny in his heart," said Weil. "I never fleeced anyone who could not afford to pay my price. . . . A truly honest man would never have gone for my schemes." Professional ethics precluded dealings with widows and orphans, he said.

He took a banker from Indiana for $200,000, a banker from Omaha for $250,000, and a banker from New York for $350,000.

"A chump who wants to get something for nothing usually winds up getting nothing for something," he said. "But I wasn't doing anything much different from the way bankers and merchants go about their normal work. Clarence Darrow was my lawyer in several cases and he once told me that mostly all wealthy people obtain their money by theft or misrepresentation. 'So don't be a bit concerned about what you do. Do it.' He was a nice person, Darrow was. And he was a splendid lawyer."

Weil said that not all big businessmen were thieves. He recalls when he approached Philip Wrigley, Sr., of the famous gum company, and wanted to have him invest a hundred dollars in a scheme.

"I'll tell you what," said Wrigley. "I know you. I know you're a con guy. Here's a hundred dollars. It's yours. It's a gift. But don't ever bother me anymore."

Weil expanded his operations to include a money-making machine, in which he had a cigar box with a crank on the side. You put a dollar bill in and you crank out a ten-dollar bill. The ten-dollar bill had already been placed in there before you had come to watch this magic. Of course, the build-up to this money may have taken a few months until you were begging to see this machine and, by then, were prepared to believe anything.

Weil also latched on to an accomplice, Fred Buckminster. "Buckminster," said Weil, "was a detective in the detective bureau. He was a big man there. He arrested me three or four times. And then he said, 'Fuck this, I'm going with you.'

"He was so good because he had been an English teacher at a university. And language was so much a part of being a good actor in our profession.

"For myself, my father would speak French to us and my mother would speak German. So we had the two languages. My older brother, he was a dumb ox, and my younger brother Louie —now, I'm not pattin' myself on the shoulder—they never adopted the livelihood or the manner of getting money that I did. But they had the languages also if they wanted them. And then I went on to make it my business to learn the words of high caliber. We knew words were money-getters. We'd get money by the gift of education that you were presumed to have, that you were college bred."

What words would you use?

"Every one that you could think of. It's hard to remember now."

Can you think of one?

"Well, like 'insofar.'"

(Vidovic, his conservator, added "charismatic" and "chauvinistic"; "He used them well before they came into general popularity," said Vidovic.)†

Weil went on to another subject. He said, "You know, nearly every con man is a sucker for a pretty face and a neat figure. And I was certainly no exception." When Vidovic mentioned the lady jockey Joe had employed when he owned race horses, and asked if Joe had in fact taken her to bed, Joe nodded in confirmation.

"But, Joe," said Vidovic, "weren't you a married man at the time?"

"Yes," The Kid replied, slowly, somewhat distantly, "but who's going to resist a beautiful girl?"

He had elaborate calling cards made up, with names on them like "Dr. Wellington Wallford," or "Dr. Marmaduke Wilson," or "Dr. Walter Weed."

Vidovic said that during all the years he was on the lam he would stay in tourist homes along roadsides in Indiana and Wisconsin and Iowa. He'd meet a woman and pass himself off as a doctor. He took advantage of the fact, says Vidovic, that all women always have an ailment and love to talk to a doctor.

"I always carried a little medical case with me," interjected Weil, "and I had those embossed cards."

Vidovic continued: "So invariably these women would invite 'Dr. Wilson' in for a cup of tea, and invariably they'd have some kind of itch, and in no time at all the doctor's examining her on the bed and he is saying, 'You know, I've never done this before

---

† In a letter of con-artistic persuasion when hustling donations for a church group, in 1965, he wrote (in part): "Man is not made to understand life, but to live it. The wise person does not expect consistency or harmony in the pattern of life or any other man's life, for they see that man is a mosaic of characteristics and qualities that only rarely achieves intrinsic harmony. Man is an accidental juxtaposition of discordance. . . . May the omnipotent and omniscient architect of the universe bestow upon you, and yours, His beatific benedictions. Yours in felicitations, Joseph R. Weil."

in my life, and the Hippocratic oath shouldn't be violated, but you've done something to me,' and pretty soon he's bouncing up and down on her.

"In a city, Joe might meet a gorgeous girl, and get a hotel suite—never a room. He was never, never forward. Very gentle. And he'd take her out to dinner. Wine her and dine her. You see, Joe could never go into a whorehouse and get laid. He had to put up a stage, you know. And he'd say, 'Now tomorrow, we'll go and pick out a fur coat.' They go to the fur store. He tells her to pick out anything she wants. Every coat is ten thousand dollars and more—this is sixty years ago, too! She picks one out. Joe calls the salesman over. They decide the fit, the styling—a big haggle. Everything is decided. The coat is perfect. Now, Joe says, for the lining. She wants red, so then Joe wants green. Some type of argument. And finally it gets kind of hot, and the salesman is completely taken in, too. And eventually Joe calls the salesman over to the side and says, 'This is just a recent bride and you know how funny girls are. I just want this particular lining. I'm paying for the goddamn coat. Please hold it. Put it off to the side. I'll stop in tomorrow personally and tell you what we've decided. Let us sleep on this thing.' And the salesman's tickled to death. He's sold a coat, see?

"So then Joe comes back to the gal, and says, 'All right, you won—I want the green but I'll give you the red. I slipped the guy a few bucks. Instead of waiting two weeks to get this fur coat you'll have it—today's Monday—you'll have it by Thursday. We can pick it up.' In the meantime, he has three days where she would do anything in the world he wanted. And then, of course, Friday morning, he was gone."

Once, on an ocean liner traveling from New York to London, Weil and Fred Buckminster, his accomplice, met two beautiful and sophisticated women. Weil introduced himself as Dr. Henry Reuel and even showed her a medical book he had purportedly written and with his own picture bound as frontispiece to make it appear he was the author. They became fast friends. And they met again in London. Eventually she confided to him that she was traveling incognito. That in fact she was the Comtesse de Paris, and her brother was the Duc d'Orléans, the last of the Bourbons and the rightful heir to the French throne. The brother, she said, had been arrested, and she had been to America to try to get finances to support his cause and get him out of jail.

Weil began seeing her regularly. One night at dinner, her pearl necklace broke, the pearls scattering on the floor. She was so upset. She asked Weil for a favor. Would he get them restrung? He said of course. Out of professional curiosity Weil asked the jeweler what the necklace was worth. He said, eight thousand pounds, or about forty thousand dollars.

About a week later this comtesse comes to Weil and Buckminster and says she is in desperate financial straits. She needs two thousand dollars to help her brother immediately. All she has is her necklace. Both Buckminster and Weil leaped up and insisted on helping her. She thanked them profusely and then she insisted on giving them her necklace as collateral. They demurred, but accepted. (Under normal circumstances, they would have disappeared with the necklace. But Joe had allowed Cupid to interfere with business.)

The comtesse said she would have the money for them the next day. They were to meet at a restaurant. The two con men waited and waited. She never showed up.

Buckminster got up and said to Weil, "I'll be back shortly." He returned and tossed the necklace in Weil's lap. "Paste," he said. "We've had a con game worked on us. We've been taken."

Weil asked how he knew.

"I walked over to Old Bond Street," said Buckminster. "I showed the necklace to the jeweler. He said it was a very clever imitation, worth about twenty-five dollars."

Weil wrote in his book: "It was particularly ironical for one reason: I had worked the switch on dozens of gullible people. I had used virtually the same tactics in the buildup. It had been one of my rainy day schemes. I had fallen back on it at various times through the years when I was in need of ready money. And at last I had become victim of the same scheme!"

For the most part, though, he apparently had extraordinary success in his pursuit of women, even into old age.

Vidovic recalled a time when there was some discussion about a movie of Weil's life, starring Adolphe Menjou as the dapper flimflam man. Weil would meet a terrific-looking woman and convince her she'd get a starring role in the film. Her first big Hollywood break! Said Vidovic:

"One night—I'll never forget it—I was walking down Clark Street at about four in the morning on my way to pick up my car. And I happen to look in the window of the Clover Bar. The place is empty, except for a couple in the center of the dance floor. Here's Joe dancing with Miss Riley—I still remember her name—who was an inspiring actress. She was nineteen, Joe was seventy-two or seventy-three. She was about twelve inches taller than him. Joe was lookin' up, dancing gracefully, he was a fantastic dancer, and he's singing, 'I wish this night could last forever.'"

Weil went into retirement in 1942 after serving twenty-seven months in a federal prison on a mail-fraud charge involving phony oil leases.

He lived off some real-estate holdings and supplemented this income with now and then a small little foray into the past, such as soliciting money for a church group and going under the name of Father Ferdinand.

But more and more he began to find how "satisfying peace of mind is." That is, living the legal life.

He remained a high liver. I asked him what happened to his money.

"Went, like everything else," he said. "Expensive way of livin', buyin' jewels. Squandered it away. Yep."

Are you sorry you didn't save more of it?

"I didn't save *any* of it. Well, of course, I'm sorry. But in those days we were broke today and wealthy tomorrow."

Are you happy now?

"No, I can't say I'm happy. I'm satisfied with the condition that exists under the circumstances . . . don't permit myself to get depressed. You see, I know so many wealthy men that went broke. And I used that as a ladder to climb out of my depression. See. And I, then I say this, 'Well, I'm an old man now and young girls don't mean nothin' to me, champagne is on the shelf. I have no earthly use for it.' We used to drink a lot of champagne in those days. We had big sumptuous food. We lived to enjoyment."

Did you ever worry about getting caught?

"No, that didn't bother me. I just didn't permit fear to become a part of my operations. I always knew that if you had sufficient money you had sufficient liberty. All you had to do was get acquainted with a top-ranking lawyer.

"My mother was the one who worried. She once threatened to commit suicide when I got arrested for the first time. My father told her, 'Forget it. Everyone else is doing what Joe is doing.'"

Do you have any regrets?

"No, I had a lot of money. I didn't earn it. I took it by theft. And by confidence game. Consequently I had no regard for money. I wasn't like a man that earned his money."

Are you fearful of dying, Joe?

"No. I never was. The church has made it wonderful; you wonder why the priests want to live. . . . No. I'm not afraid to die. I always said, 'Death will teach me something or nothing.'"

---

CHICAGO, Feb. 26, 1975—(UPI)—Joseph R. Weil, the confidence man known as the Yellow Kid, died today at the Lake Front Convalescent Center here. He was 100 years old.

He was buried in a pauper's grave.

# WILLIAM S. PALEY

Opulence is synonymous with Palm Beach, Florida. Some of the nation's most powerful and wealthy families have winter homes here, great, sprawling homes of twenty and thirty rooms set in splendiferous green acreage and within lapping sound of the Atlantic Ocean. The homes themselves may be only partially glimpsed from the adjoining tree-shaded thoroughfares because of the walls and woods that buttress them. One of the homes was owned by Mrs. Goldie Drell Paley, widow of Samuel Paley, who once owned the largest cigar-manufacturing business in the United States, and the mother of William S. Paley, chairman of the board of the Columbia Broadcasting System, America's greatest entertainment factory and most powerful communications empire.

Mrs. Paley, at age ninety-three in 1975, lived in a home overlooking the bay of Palm Beach. Closed in is her own swimming pool. One morning she sat on her canopied veranda heavy with fresh flowers and drank tea and ate toast. She was a wispy, gray-haired woman, quite lively, and wore a bright green robe.

She was born in Kiev, Russia, as was her late husband, though they did not meet there. Both her family and her husband's left Russia, with the thousands and thousands of other Jews there, when the pogroms began in dead earnest after the death of Czar Alexander II. Her husband, who was born in 1875, came to America in 1883. The families settled in Chicago and in the common West Side neighborhood of the other immigrant Russian Jews there. Samuel Paley, like many young immigrants, became a cigar maker, one of the few American industries open to unskilled foreigners.

The Paleys were married in 1896. The Chicago City Directory, a kind of telephone book before there were telephones, lists a

"Samuel Paley, cigarmaker, 283 W. 14th Street,"* which (after the renumbering of streets in the early 1900s) would have been 812 West Fourteenth Street, about a block from the corner of Maxwell and Halsted streets.

A following listing for a Samuel Paley is in the 1902 directory: "Samuel Paley, cigars, home 258 Ogden Avenue (new address: 1767 Ogden)." Samuel Paley had moved up a bit in the world. He had left forever the world of being an employee, wrapping cigars under Yiddish signs in the window of a storefront factory. He now had his own place, a mile or so west of Maxwell and Halsted. It was here on Ogden Avenue that he and his wife endeavored to make and sell their own cigars. And it was in their living quarters in the back of that store that on September 27, 1901, their only son was born. (Several years later their only other child, a daughter, Blanche, was born.)

From the city directory one may see the continued progress of the Paleys.

1905: "Samuel Paley, cigar manufacturer, home, 395 Marshfield." They were now living on Marshfield near well-appointed Jackson Boulevard. An address to be reckoned with: it meant moving dramatically up in the world and farther away from the congestion of the ghetto.

1910: "Samuel Paley, cigar manufacturer, 235 Van Buren." He had moved his factory to a large building on Van Buren.

1915: "Samuel Paley, president Congress Cigar Company, 404 South Racine." A bigger factory. And he was moving farther north: "2934 Logan Boulevard." Like so many immigrants, he kept seeking improved residences, higher-toned neighborhoods— palpable examples of success.

1917: "Samuel Paley, home, 1456 Fargo Avenue." He had moved his family to the northernmost section of Chicago, and one of the most sparsely populated.

The next year the family moved to Philadelphia. Because of labor problems, most of the many cigar-manufacturing businesses moved out of Chicago. Samuel Paley and his brother, Jacob, a

* Only one "Samuel Paley" is listed in the Chicago City Directory in any year that William Paley's father lived in Chicago.

partner, built the Congress Cigar Company—with its famous "La Palina" brand cigar—from one small storefront factory to eventually twelve humming factories in Pennsylvania, New Jersey, and Delaware. In 1931, at the height of the Depression, Samuel Paley sold his prodigious business for $30 million.

His son, meanwhile, had left the cigar business in 1928 to become the owner of a small radio network and by 1931 was building it into an immense corporation. In his own right, young William Paley was a wealthy man by this time.

Mrs. Paley, during my visit to her home, told me in a surprisingly unquavery voice for a woman of ninety-three, "The gods have been good to me. I don't deserve any more than a poor person, but I was fortunate to get it. My family when I was young was never wealthy—otherwise we wouldn't have left Russia. But I often say, 'Who am I to have all this luxurious surrounding? Who am I to have what I have now?'"

She sipped her tea slowly and looked out at her small pool. Along the sides are small sculptures such as, one imagines, adorned the sides of pools of Roman consuls and their wives. Curiously enough, floating in the quiet pool was a large indifferent inflated rubber toy goose. The obvious but insistent symbolism kept bobbing up about the fabled goose who laid the golden egg.

---

Meyer Patur is the last of a breed who continues to hand-roll cigars for his livelihood in Chicago. A crusty, sturdy eighty-two-year-old, he maintains a small store on West Chicago Avenue. Meyer Patur began making cigars after he had come over from Russia in 1909 at age sixteen. He went to work for the Congress Cigar Company on Van Buren Street.

Even in midday, now, old Meyer Patur must unlock several locks on the front door of the store to allow in a visitor. Times are dangerous. He has never been robbed, but police tell him to take those precautions. The store is redolent with tobacco. Patur sits on a tall stool and leans on a table wrapping tobacco and leaf into long rolls. He then takes a blade to snip off the top; then sticks the rolls in slots like vises. There are thousands of big brown-green cigars in the store, one of which is lit and smoking and clenched between Meyer Patur's teeth.

"Sam Paley had a big shop, maybe fifty, sixty people working there. Sam, he was nice. He was a cigar maker and he started up like the other guys. He happened to be a success. The reason he was a success is he took a chance with a particular salesman, and he paid him at that time about seventy-five hundred dollars a year," said Meyer Patur, wrapping another cigar. "That was a lot of money to pay a salesman, or anybody else.

"The story I was told is that this salesman made connections with big jobbers and distributors. They made good distribution, and that's how he got to be famous, Sam Paley. He also used to use Java wrappers—wrappers from Java. And it was the best wrapper you could get. You know, he thought he was going to make a success with cigarettes, too. He started to manufacture them, but he couldn't make it in cigarettes.

"Now, the cigar makers got paid for piecework. I made fifteen dollars a thousand. The most I would make is three hundred a day. And you worked five days and a half day on Saturday.

"The conditions were not good. It was hot and crowded and noisy. But we had freedom there. We used to argue. There wasn't a subject that the cigar makers didn't cover. Politics, labor, everything. We wrapped and we argued. All day.

"There was a lot of unionizing, and the demand for union labels on cigar boxes was big, especially in the saloons where the workingmen congregated.

"So one day there was a big strike. We wanted 50 per cent increase in wages. So the manufacturer's association made up, 'We'll fix them. We'll move out of here.' And all the factories moved out, and they all went broke except La Palina, which was Sam Paley's famous brand. That's the only one that really was a success. They all went broke, El Cenalto, Ben Bay, Pan Palmer, Ball and Concert, Lanfield's. They moved different places outside of Chicago. Sam Paley moved to Philadelphia."

What kind of man was Sam Paley?

"He was a man. What was he like? He was a cigar maker who worked up, that's all. It's history. It's gone. Nobody knows La Palina any more."

Did he ever walk through the factory?

"Yeah, sure he'd walk. What do you mean? He had to go in a wheelchair? Sure he walked."

Did you ever talk to him?

"Sure, I said hello to him. So what? What is he to me?—like you or any human being. I didn't look up on him more than any-body else."

Did you know his son?

"No. I just knew he had a son."

Do you know what happened to his son?

"No. Something happen to him?"

---

William S. Paley recalled to me in an interview that his father's father, Isaac Paley, "had been a well-to-do man in Russia, with a special position assigned to him by the czar. He had special privi-leges." Paley said he wasn't certain what his grandfather did, but it had something to do with being an emissary of sorts and he traveled a great deal. He said his grandfather came to America on a visit and decided to stay and subsequently sent for his family.

"He had money, but invested badly and lost it," William Paley told me.

When William Paley's father, Samuel, began to make money himself, he sent his son to what he considered the best schools. William attended Western Military Academy at Alton, Illinois, and then went to the University of Chicago for one year. When his family moved to Philadelphia, he transferred to the Wharton School of Finance in Philadelphia.

After graduation in 1922, Bill Paley joined his father's cigar company.

Bill Paley, according to Robert Metz in *CBS: Reflections in a Bloodshot Eye,* even then "possessed a shrewdness and a talent for managing money. As Wharton crew manager, he turned in record-low expense accounts, a suggestion that his father's money hadn't affected his common sense.

"Few believed, however, that this playful ladies' man and heir to millions would find a direction of his own; likely he would remain in the comfortable niche his father had prepared for him in the cigar business. Indeed, when he entered the family business, he lived at home, drove expensive cars, enjoyed the girls and learned the business—from a high perch. He was probably well prepared to begin as production chief; his father, a business genius of sorts, had been schooling Bill in the cigar trade for years (even sending him to tobacco farms in Havana during summers). Still, there was something slightly indecent about his quick promotion to advertising manager as well as vice-president and secretary of the company in 1925. His salary: $30,000 a year. Not bad for a boy three years out of college."*

Bill Paley developed an interest in radio while doing advertising for the cigar company. One summer, his father and his uncle Jacob went on a trip to Europe for the summer. Bill Paley took it upon himself to invest fifty dollars a week to put Miss La Palina and a ten-piece orchestra on a local station. When his father and uncle returned, they were furious at what they considered wasted expenditure. His uncle Jacob said it was "the dumbest thing" he'd ever heard of. They made Bill cancel it. But requests by listeners to the station began to come in asking about the show. And the senior Paleys realized that they might have an advertising bonanza. They put the show back on the air. Sales of cigars jumped. Bill Paley grew more and more interested in radio. In 1928, Jerome Louchheim, a friend of the family, was ailing and wanted to sell his interests in a small network of radio stations he owned. Speculation of what Paley paid for it ranges from $275,000 to $400,000 to a million dollars.

The cigar business was just too tame for Bill Paley, for his creativity and for his adventuresomeness. And three days before his twenty-seventh birthday, on September 26, 1928, Bill Paley became president of the Columbia Broadcasting System and moved to the headquarters in the Paramount Pictures building on Times Square in New York.

CBS was well behind the National Broadcasting Company in network affiliates. Paley began to make his move to catch up by offering affiliates his unsponsored shows for free. Paley wisely

* Robert Metz, *CBS: Reflections in a Bloodshot Eye* (Chicago: Playboy Press, 1975), pp. 12–13.

figured that the more affiliates he got, the more people would listen to his programs, and this in turn would impress more advertisers, who soon would be sponsoring those shows. The affiliates were delighted as well, since they were getting free entertainment —and this during depression days. Such a bargain! The number of affiliates jumped from an original 16 to 114 within a decade. Gross earnings went from $1.4 million in 1928 to $4.7 million in 1929 and $28.7 million by 1937.

It wasn't just money matters that Paley excelled at. He had taste in programming as well. He was on a ship once, heard the voice of a young man on the air, and told his assistants to hire him for CBS. The young man was Bing Crosby. He was told that Crosby had the reputation for being unreliable. Paley retorted, "We're not buying his reliability; we're buying his talent. Sign him."

Paley would also discover Kate Smith and hire away Jack Benny from NBC, and he took the lead in such programming as "School of the Air," a remarkable series of educational broadcasts; "Lux Radio Theater," and, much later, such a dramatic television innovation as "All in The Family."

He was also battling newspapers to bring news to radio on a regular basis. Newspapers wanted news coverage to be exclusively theirs, and some newspapers even began eliminating radio listings.

Another aspect of Paley's success was his desire to have good people around him. David Sarnoff, head of NBC, once noted that, unlike himself, Paley likes to have geniuses around him. It was similar to Sam Paley's desire to hire the best salesman possible for his cigar company and pay him the best salary.

"A revolution was taking place in communication and advertising, and young Bill Paley was at the center of it," wrote David Halberstam. "He seemed perfectly designed for his new role—tall, handsome, always seen with good-looking women on his arm. He was something of a ladies' man and a man to savor, to enjoy life. A man of the world. All things would soon be possible for Bill Paley despite his Russian-Jewish origins. (This was and is a point of some sensitivity. When . . . Robert Metz [in his book] described Paley as a Russian Jew, Paley's public relations man, Kidder Meade, sent out a letter to book reviewers purporting to correct factual inaccuracies in the book and noting, among other things, that Paley was not a Russian Jew—which, in the pecking order of the American Jewish Community, was not as good as being a German Jew—he was an American Jew.)"†

Metz describes how Bill Paley "not only was discriminated against by gentiles" at Wharton, but also by German Jews who refused him entrance into their fraternities because of his Russian ancestry. "He settled for a Jewish fraternity described by a former dean as 'Class B.' "‡

When he came to New York, it was obvious, then, that he was not a part of the Jewish aristocracy there. "The smell of cigars was still on his money, a problem of which he was acutely aware," writes Halberstam. Years later, a story goes that his aides had gotten an option on the play, *Fiddler on the Roof*. All were sure it would be a big hit. "They were surprised when Paley, after reading the script and listening to the music, turned it down," according to Halberstam. "To one assistant he said that it seemed good, but wasn't it too *Jewish?* He told another friend, 'I couldn't do it —it's the story of my own family.' "

Paley, however, seemed to move swiftly into the highest levels of American society.

He married Dorothy Hart Hearst, recently divorced from John Randolph Hearst, son of William Randolph Hearst. So now Paley married one of the three so-called fabled Cushing girls of Boston, Barbara "Babe" Cushing Mortimore, who would be named to the Best-Dressed Hall of Fame in America. A blueblood of the first order. Marriage to her gained, for Paley, Jock Whitney as a brother-in-law and Mrs. Vincent Astor as a sister-in-law. Besides this, he was courted by his country. In 1943 Paley took a leave from CBS and went to London to serve as a head of Eisenhower's psychological warfare staff.

In some circles, none of these enormous successes were good enough.

† David Halberstam, "CBS: The Power and the Profits," *The Atlantic Monthly*, January 1976.
‡ The public relations office of CBS disclaimed this: "At the Wharton School, Mr. Paley was not 'discriminated against by prideful German Jews for his Russian ancestry.' He was tapped by the premier Jewish fraternity, Zeta Beta Tau, hardly a 'Class B' fraternity. He was head of the fraternity before he graduated and looks back on his ZBT days as among the happiest in his life. . . ."

"In the late 1950s," wrote Halberstam, "Philip Graham, publisher of the Washington *Post,* suggested to Paley that he join the F Street Club; the perfect club for him in Washington, said Graham, the right combination of good men, powerful, attractive, effective. He would be at home there. Paley, knowing the byzantine ways of clubs and of restricted apartment houses, was nervous. He did not really like the idea of clubs, he told Graham; his experience was that he was better off without them. But Graham, a man of infectious enthusiasms, said not to worry about *that,* these were modern, serious, humane men of the world and he, Phil Graham, would personally lobby it through. Paley, encouraged by the idea of Phil Graham as floor manager, reluctantly agreed to let his name be put up. Phil Graham was very nearly as good as his word. He lobbied with great vigor and intelligence. A few weeks later he met a friend on a Washington-New York flight and seemed almost desperate for companionship. Graham's customary enthusiasm was gone and he seemed sober. The friend asked what was wrong. 'Oh, God,' said Graham, 'this is one of the worst days of my life—this is the day I've got to go to New York and tell Bill Paley he was blackballed at the F Street Club.' "

Paley's predilection for prestigious circles is evidenced by this story by Halberstam: "In 1962, after CBS had done a documentary on school integration called 'Storm Over the Supreme Court,' Arthur Goldberg wanted it screened at a reception honoring his appointment to the Court, an occasion when all the justices would be present. Would someone please represent CBS at the reception? Fred Friendly, who had produced the show, mentioned the invitation to Frank Stanton (president of CBS after Paley moved up to Chairman of the Board), and Stanton seemed cool to the occasion. He saw no great merit in it for himself or the Chairman. So Friendly went for CBS. Friendly later made the mistake of mentioning the reception to the Chairman, who exploded. Clearly this was a rare *good* occasion in Washington. (It was generally known that Paley disliked the aura of the capital.) What right did Fred Friendly have to represent the company? This was an occasion when the Chairman and Mrs. Paley should have been there."*

* Halberstam, loc. cit.

Paley is also known to have that requisite for successful businessmen—a ruthless streak. A story is told, for example, of how he traveled from New York to Hollywood to have dinner with the comedian Danny Kaye. Kaye, a noted preparer of Chinese food, served a splendid meal to his guest and boss. Shortly after, Paley informed Kaye that the ratings for his television show were low and it would have to be dropped. Robert Metz reports that when Frank Stanton, Paley's long-time friend and right-hand man at CBS, reached retirement age, 65, and a decision had to be made whether to retain Stanton, "Paley acted as he had a hundred times before. He just did what pleased Bill Paley: Frank, you're sixty-five—good-by."

Yet Paley continued on—by 1976, at age seventy-five, he was still on top of the entire, mammoth CBS operation, running it with that personal concern that marked, it seems, the way his father before him had run the cigar business, starting from the small storefront cigar store on Ogden Avenue.

In mid-April of 1976, Robert Wood, the successful president of the CBS television network, surprisingly resigned. The New York *Times* carried this report by its television news analyst, Les Brown:

"Mr. Wood [said] without being specific: 'There are internal pressures.'

"Close associates of Mr. Wood believe the 'internal' stresses—those that came from within the company—were the most punishing of all and the ones that finally wore him down.

"The source of those unrelenting pressures, they said, was 'CBS pride'—the code phrase for the fierce determination of William S. Paley to keep the network he founded perpetually the leader in general popularity and advertising sales, and to maintain its prestige.

"Although Mr. Paley is responsible for the entire multifaceted business organization that CBS Inc. has become, he continues to watch over the progress of the television network, even to the point of participating in the selection of programs."

By 1975, CBS had over two hundred affiliates, with more than $100 million in profits. Its power to persuade and influence the nation's millions upon millions of viewers was incalculable. The network's commentators, from Edward R. Murrow to Walter Cronkite, helped destroy the reckless Senator Joseph McCarthy (televising the Army-McCarthy hearings) and helped to topple a President (the unrelenting reportage on Richard Nixon and the Watergate affair).

Of course, the network must also carry the burdens of contributing to "the vast Wasteland" of insipid programming, including numerous soap operas and situation comedies of the most saccharine and insulting varieties.

Besides radio and television, CBS Inc. branched out and bought two publishing companies, Fawcett Paperback and Holt, Rinehart and Company; a toy company; a record company, Columbia, and, from the mid '60s to the mid '70s, a baseball team, the New York Yankees.

Despite his desires to become attached to social worlds and his impelling business involvement, William Paley retained a closeness to his family. He retained his father as a member of the board of CBS until his death on March 30, 1963. Paley's sister and her husband, Leon Levy, are two of the biggest stockholders next to Paley himself (who owned 1,683,337 CBS shares as of 1975).

In 1967 he built for $1 million a small lovely park with a waterfall on Fifty-third Street in Manhattan and named the park for his father.

Severals years later he organized an ecumenical charity in Jerusalem and named it for his mother.

He also keeps an interest in his parents' charities, such as the Paley Clinic at the Einstein Medical Center in Philadelphia, the Samuel Paley Lectureship on American Culture and Civilization in Jerusalem, the Allied Jewish Appeal, and the Federation of Jewish Charities.

Although Paley has been thought to downplay his Jewish heritage, a long-time associate, John Minary, says that Paley on the contrary is proud of his background; both of the children that Paley had with "Babe" were brought up Jewish with, Paley liked to say, "the very best Jewish teachers." He cherished the links with Jewish culture, said Minary, including the tradition of kissing his father whenever they met, even if it happened to be before the austere board meeting of CBS, with all the button-down Gentile members looking on.

---

"My son is very much like me," said Goldie Paley. "Neither one of us is spoiled. My parents weren't rich and I went through good times and bad times. You know, we all have good times and bad times. I don't care if you're rich, you have problems. . . . Well, I call myself a tramp. I can scrub a floor. I can drive a machine. I'm never afraid of anything. I have a personal maid, a gardener, a cook, and a chauffeur. But I could do most things by myself if I need to—even today. I certainly would. There's nothing wrong. I haven't allowed my system to get sluggish. I get up at six or seven in the morning. I'm just one of those tough guys. I used to play golf. I was a horsewoman most of the time. I'll never forget, my husband said, 'Goldie you shouldn't ride.' I said, 'Why?' He said, 'The horse is too high-spirited.' But if the horse knows that you got control of him, he won't do it. Just as soon as you give in, you'd be surprised that the animal feels it.

"Well, my husband respected me, respected my independence. You see, you had to work together if you're serious. I took part in the store in the early years. I was the saleslady. It was a retail store. My husband would open up a certain time, and I'd open up the place a certain time. We changed off. We figured things out together. And we were congenial with each other. I used to help him strip tobacco. I wasn't ashamed of it.

"I stopped working when we sold the store. My husband, he sold the La Palina cigar and it got on the market very big. He opened up a big factory. So he felt that he can give up the store—living in the back of the store—and have a nice home."

Cigars had always a part of much of Goldie Paley's life. Her father owned a cigar store. Sam Paley sold his cigars to Goldie Drell's father. "One day," she said, "my father didn't pay his bill right. He said to Sam, 'Come to my house and I'll pay you there.' So he came, and he met me. So after, he said, 'You tricked me into the marriage.' We had a lot of fun." They were married in 1896 when Goldie was eighteen and Sam twenty-one.

I asked her about Maxwell Street.

"Not Maxwell," she said, "Jefferson Street. That was the market where the poor people, where the Jewish people shopped." And it was there, presumably, where she too shopped for her family.

She now spoke about her son. "He never brought me any shame," she said. "He was always a credit. As long as I can remember, he was independent. And he made things good on his own. Parents can't make a child act—to be somebody—unless it's in him. My son believes in poor people. He became famous because he believes in people.

"He's like me in that we think Gentiles and Jews are the same. Years ago a Jew and a Gentile were just like at war with each other. We mix an awful lot more now. My son does and I think it's good. He's a nice chap. He's not a show-off. He has a fine reputation, Bill Paley. I am very proud of my son."

# THE STREET, 1962

## MAXWELL ST. KEEPS PACE
## —RELUCTANTLY

—Maxwell Street is changing. . . . For one thing Maxwell is bisected by the South Expressway, which slices across the street midway between Halsted and Jefferson.

East of the expressway the street has been torn up to make way for a warehouse.

The excavation began only a few weeks ago, but the vendors still stubbornly return to set up their stands on the dusty road and worry out loud about their future.

"Twenty-five years I've been selling here," said one merchant from behind his cardtable stand stacked high with socks and T-shirts. "Twenty-five years—and now? I don't know. They say we'll have to move west of the expressway but I ask, 'Where?' There just isn't any room."

When asked for his name, he smiled.

"Twenty-five years," he repeated. "I didn't last here twenty-five years by telling everyone my name."

CHICAGO *SUN-TIMES*
*July 9, 1962*

# SHELDON PINSKER

"I hated Maxwell Street because the street was a barrier between my father and me, and like I would see fathers and sons playing baseball, going to baseball games, going to football games, going to basketball games—I think he took me to one basketball game, no two. He never took me to a football game. He never took me to a baseball game. My father was always working on Maxwell Street."

Sheldon Pinsker is in his mid-twenties. He was born and raised on the North Side of Chicago. His father is Bernard "Barrel" Pinsker. In the early 1970s, father and son had clothing stores side by side on Maxwell Street. Barrel's store was a dingy, typical Maxwell Street store from the 1930s, with a dark and haphazard-seeming display of drab-colored clothes, primarily work clothes. There was no name on the window of the store. Sheldon's store was "modern"—bright, with the front painted yellow and red. A big sign read, "Mother's Threads." It had as hip a selection of clothes as there was on the street, denim and leather jackets, bell-bottom trousers, floral-patterned shirts.

Sheldon is lean but sinewy, stands about six feet tall. He wears glasses, has a mustache, and sometimes in the store wears weights around his ankles to build up the strength in his legs. He is interested in martial arts. His father is a thickset man. He has a broad leathery face and nose and, below it, often a stump of a cigar clenched between his teeth.

"Maxwell Street had always seemed to me a dirty street with a lot of people, a lot of confusion—My feelings were confused regarding Maxwell Street up to maybe my early teens," Sheldon Pinsker said.

"Somehow Maxwell Street was always a source of frustration

for me, and I never really could express why. But today I can. I know why. It always has been an almost insurmountable barrier between my knowing my father and my father knowing me.

"Initially, I think I came to work down here to do my father a favor, to help out when I was a teen-ager. As for this store, I originally came into it with the idea of my father moving out of his store and into this one and then my going into graduate studies in clinical psychology. But the clinical psych programs were closed for the time being, and I was tired of studying—I had just gotten my bachelor's degree in psychology from Roosevelt University— and I was content to just read and study on my own and pursue my interests on my own. But eventually I found my commitment to the store took on a longer-term aspect. So I was working seven days, and then I cut it back to six.

"I found myself doing it, not liking it, and seeing my father in me, and not liking *that* because I didn't want to be my father. I wanted to be myself and I was having a difficult time.

"I want fulfillment by myself for myself creatively in my work. I don't want my enjoyment centered around my nonwork activities only. I want to derive satisfaction from my work, and I can't derive satisfaction from making money and only money.

"Now, my father, he had business aspirations, which probably came about because this was the way to survive, as he saw it, as far back as when he was a boy in Russia. He had so many experiences in trading with people, and he enjoyed trading with people so that business was not unpleasurable for him. He always enjoyed talking to people on a business level, and I have never enjoyed speaking to people on a business level.

"I think that most people on the street, because they're on the street, especially those who have been on the street for a long time, have difficulty in expressing their emotions—and this has been a problem in the relationship between my father and me. The people down on the street can't allow their emotions to be expressed here because that would leave them too open, too susceptible, too vulnerable to customer tricks, to all sorts of ploys that are employed on the street by people who are familiar with the system. And they can't allow that. So they have to shut off their emotions to a large extent. And occasionally their anger flares up or their frustrations come out in the form of, maybe, violence.

"My father has been a violent person all his life. I've seen him take people and knock them down. I've never seen him back off from anybody. That's one very strong image I have of my father, a strong person physically, a strong person emotionally in that, regardless of what crisis would arise, he wouldn't find himself helpless, and he would have some way of dealing with it, whether appropriate or inappropriate. He wouldn't just break down and be so inundated and unable to approach the problem.

"I think this street serves as—not a lathe—but it hones the senses because you have to be able to sense what's going on, on the street, especially now because there are so many people, con artists, on the street trying to put something over on the merchants. And since the street has become more and more black, what I call the ghetto mentality has made its impact here, and that kind of serves too as an emotion deadener because emotions are expressed, are channeled into violence a lot of times among customers, and you can't allow that to happen if you're a merchant. You've got to repress those feelings.

"I remember not long ago some blacks came in and were sharp-tongued to my mother. She was amazed by it. She said, 'Why, what have I done to you to deserve that kind of language?' Well, she was white and she was Jewish. I think there's a great deal of hostility that's rooted in preconceived notions of Jews. And this is Jewtown. That's what non-Jews call it. That's an expression that I resent and have always resented.

"Because, number one, the merchants are not all Jewish—but that's the least important of my objections. Secondly, I've always had the feeling that it's been used in a derogatory manner, and I think it is. I think underlying it is a great deal of anti-Semitism, a great deal of violence and potential violence. That's evident in the way we react to each other here. . . .

"Part of the reason I'm here on the street now, though, and I guess I've finally admitted it to myself, is because of my love for my father. I wouldn't be here, in this store, if I didn't have more than somewhat of a fondness for him. Growing up, I hardly saw him. I'd catch a glimpse of him when I was waking up and he was going to work or when I was about to go to sleep and he'd come home. But the times that he saw me he was able to express enough love and care for me that I could reciprocate those feelings and like in later years, to the limits of his ability, he showered me with attention and affection.

"He would try to talk about what I was doing. He really wasn't too successful. He didn't know what questions to ask. I think most of what I know about him was as a result of having been at the store with him. I think I'm closer to him. But it's hard to get to know him. He doesn't speak easily about his feelings, about his values. He can't make statements about what he wants in life. Like he won't talk about, 'When I was ten I had dreams of being a rabbi or dreams of being a doctor or a teacher.' And I wonder about what his dreams were like.

"I had been awed by my father. He had been the strongest man in his village of five thousand in Russia, and he was a powerhouse. My grandmother told me a story of how he bet a man that he could lift a wagon and four men on his back and pick it up off the ground, and things of that nature that impressed me as a boy, especially when other people confirmed it. I remember as late as ten years ago, when I weighed 150 pounds or so, he'd lift me straight up and down like I was just a sack of potatoes. And me, I don't think I was ever genetically predisposed toward great strength.

"And then, growing up, I realized my father also possessed a strange knowledge. My father knew what customers were thinking and knew whether they were there to steal. It was almost like a mystical thing. He would know. He'd also know who would pay a better price and who was cheap. He knew people. He does know people. Without questions, without words, he knows pretty much how a person is going to act.

"And I, on the other hand, used to feel very klutzy, very awkward, very inept. I didn't know what I was doing and I was insecure. I was in a place where—hey, like all this stuff is going on, these people kind of looking at me? Am I doing something wrong? They were street educated and I had no street education.

"And now, I've got a little more of a street education, but I kind of don't want to relate to them on that basis. I'm stand-offish. If I try to relate to the seventeen-year-old black street gang member who walks in or the seventeen-year-old Mexican kid who has been in the ghetto all his life—'Hey, man, what's happening! Hey, dig that,' and go through all that hip stuff—I can relate on that basis and succeed doing that. But I've got to be true to myself and my origins."

Sheldon Pinsker added that he found the Maxwell Street tradition of haggling inimical to his instincts and interests.

"I'm not comfortable at it," he said. "I mean, when I go into a store to shop, I don't want to start a tug of war over price. But people come to Maxwell Street with those expectations.

"Now, I have a puller who works for me sometimes, named Jake the Fake. He's an old-timer. He used to hustle watches on the street years ago. He'd grab people and tell them we've got $89.95 coats for $40. I told him this *hurts* sales—it doesn't help sales—because this jeopardizes our credibility. You have to have the belief and trust of the customers. You want them to believe that they're getting a good price, but a price within reason. Okay, tell them $55 coats for $40, but not $89.95 for $40. Also, he tells people we have all kinds of goods that we really don't have. They come in looking for it, and when we don't have it, they get mad. So I get mad too. I go outside and curse Jake the Fake out and tell him to stop it. But Jake the Fake says, 'But, Sheldon, outside who can buy?'"

In the winter of 1975, Sheldon Pinsker gave up "Mother's Threads" for a job in psychology in a Chicago school program. The day after Sheldon left the street, Barrel Pinsker came down with a terrible cold. It was the first time that Barrel Pinsker had been too sick to come to work in over a decade.

# ISRAEL GREEN

On a wintry day in Chicago, with "the Hawk" in full fury, Israel Green stands in front of "Mother's Threads" clothing store on Maxwell Street. He is bundled to the core. A great red scarf is wrapped around his nose and mouth. A cap with bill and ear flaps is tied under his chin. He wears a huge fur-lined brown coat that seems so heavy it ought to make his knees buckle. He wears big gloves and big galoshes. He is a small-built man of sixty-eight, and his job is "puller." A couple walks by him. He says with a distinct accent, "Folks here we got some nice ladder coats."

They understand him only when he points to a leather jacket hanging from the store door. "Check 'em out," he says. It is a valiant but shaky attempt at American colloquialism.

Israel Green, who had spent much of the war years in a Nazi concentration camp, came to America from Belgium in 1951. He now lives with his wife in a modest second-floor four-room apartment on the North Side of Chicago. We sat at his kitchen table and spoke one afternoon.

"We left Antwerp, Belgium, because my wife she was afraid for the Korea war should break out in Europe," he said. "The Russians, they are in Germany, and in Belgium a lot of Jewish people left. They were afraid it's going to break out another war. But this time, it's not happen, thank God. So that's why I came to United States. I didn't come to United States to make money. I had it good over there.

"I came first to New York. So then my daughter got married in Chicago. She got in love in New York with a Chicago boy. Maybe you know this boy? Weiner his name is.

"In 1945 I came home from the concentration camp. In 1948 I met my wife and we were married because they killed her husband

and my wife. She had a small child from the first husband. A girl. And this is the daughter. I got a son, too. He lives in Boston. He graduate from college, University of Illinois, a CPA.

"In my first family, I had two boys, eleven and eight. The Nazis came into Antwerp in 1940. For two years we was free. They didn't bother us, nothing. Except we had to wear Jewish stars. But the day came, June 1942. I don't remember the exact date. They took me from my work. I was a diamond cutter. They took the young men from the Jew streets to France. The town of Camien. They promise us our families will be secure. Safe from harm. We did labor for the Nazis. I hear about my family. My friends later tell me the whole story what's happened. The Nazis come in in midnight. They close up our streets and they took the people out from their beds. On a Friday night. Shabbes. In a nice night, they took the people out from their beds and there was screaming and everything. But I didn't see it. I never saw—I never saw my wife with the children again. They told me they went to Auschwitz.

"I later was taken to Auschwitz, too. They put us on a train. A lot of people. So crowded. You know what I mean? We couldn't stand, we couldn't sit. It was like sardines. It took three days the journey. No water. No food. Did people die? Oh, and how! Screaming and—I don't like to talk about this. . . .

"It was in the train car that people went to the toilet. It was very dir—it was very—it was no good.

"We did not know we were going to a concentration camp. You know what they say? They say that we going to see the wives and children over there. They're going to unite us with the wife and children. And that means I am so happy I cannot tell you. But who figured this?

"When we got to the concentration camp there was the sign, *Arbeit Macht Frei*. Work Makes Free. And there was another sign that there was happiness here. Sure, it wasn't true. The whole thing what they did wasn't true.

"So we come off the train now, herded off the train. *'Raus! 'Raus!* So they separate the people. Young mens, old mens separated. For me they took me to work. I carry cement on my back. Fifty kilo. One hundred fifty pounds. And breaking rocks with picks, with shovels.

"So I have friends which I saw them in Auschwitz. And they knew my family and me. So sometimes I had a chance to talk with a woman, a friend from us. I ask her, 'Where is my wife? Did you see my wife?' And she asked me the opposite: 'Did you see my husband?' That was all we talked because we was afraid to talk. Well, sure, SS women and SS men watched. We couldn't be in connection with other people.

"Later I find out from friends they took my family to the crematorium.

"Four in the morning we wake up in the concentration camp. Work all day until eight. In the night. They give for breakfast, for four people, a small bread. They cut the bread so that one had a bigger portion than the other. So they didn't care for you. For lunch and dinnertime a cold soup. Soup? Water! With a little potatoes. But you didn't have enough. Believe me. You could live, with this, four weeks. After four weeks, you have to be in the cemetery. I organized food. I didn't survive on their food, what they gave me.

"So first of all, I had a lot of gold teeth in my mouth. I just fixed up my mouth in Belgium before they took me. There was gold in sixteen teeth. I took each one out myself. And I sold them to a German guard. He gave me money and I sold him teeth, because gold was expensive and valuable. I shake every night a tooth a little bit. Every night little bit because the gums are weak. Very weak. And not the first night, not the second night, little by little I took them out. I break them out. I have no teeth of my own left.

"I only was looking to see what can I do to have food. That's all. The others were like me. Sometimes I would be beaten up, hit, kicked. But not just by the SS. From Polacks. From Gentiles. They were foremen. One prisoner to the other. They wants to show the Nazis they are good. To get advantages. And then I had a neighbor, a Jewish fellow, who used to live in Antwerp in the next house to me. His name was Louie Littleman. He was my foreman over there, and he hit me. Oh, he hit me so much. He give me this. Oh, you see my ear? Take a look this ear. See the black? I never had it in my life before. He makes me a botch. He never stop hitting it. So when I came from the barracks, if I'm hurrying in the snow in the morning, a botch from Louie. They didn't let you sleep because they made patrols. And the beds? Five in a small bed. Two on this side and two the other side. One gives the feet in the mouth the other. It was so smelly, I'll tell you.

"And it was cold. We didn't have nothing to put on. We had only thin pajama.

"At night we must stay outside. They count the people. If somebody run away, we must stand there all night. No food all night. The Germans say, 'One for all and all for one.' So that's why we have to suffer all night if somebody run away.

"Some people escape. But many people they bring them back in the concentration camp to show us what's going to happen if we decide to run away. They took off their clothes from them and everybody must see this. Then they hang them. In the big yard. We must stay and see how they hang the people. And how they leave the people twenty-four hours. Saw sometimes twenty people, twenty-five people hang at a time. At dinnertime.

"Why I was able to live? I had feeling in mine heart that I am going to survive. I keep hope in God. I had friends, they lost hope. They get sick, and I say, please, don't go hospital. From there you go right to the gas chamber. But they went to hospital and next thing, I see them naked on a truck. They go to be burned up.

"I want to fight. I don't like to go suicide. There was nothing to live for, but I didn't want to be a murder over my own life. If I die, let somebody else kill me.

"I do a lot of things to sabotage. And if they catch me, they kill me. But I didn't care? I steal bread from the kitchen. That's sabotage. I sneak potato to a friend. He sneaks one to me. That's sabotage. So many times I wish they catch me. I prayed to die. I was jealous because I see others die, just lie down and die. I couldn't die. I called myself a devil. But all the time I believe God will help us. Maybe a miracle will come to help us.

"Then I was evacuated to Nordhausen concentration camp in January 1945, because the Russians was over there. I escaped just before the Americans came to liberate the camp. There was a very big bomb exploded by the Americans. And everything was on fire. And a lot of people got burnt. I told my friends to do the same thing what I planned to do. And they didn't want to listen to me.

They was afraid the SS was going to kill them. So I told them, 'They're going to kill us anyway. The last minute they're going to kill us.' And they got killed over there.

"When I run away—this is a very nice story—when I run away, three German soldiers captured me on the way. They saw me in my pajama. And they saw that I am a prisoner. So they start to scream at me. 'Halt! Halt!' So I didn't listen to them, and I was running faster. But then they start to tell me, I'll kill you. I shoot you away if you not stopping. This I was afraid. So I stopped. They came over to me and they asked me what I am. 'I'm a Jew. A Yehuda.' 'So what you doing here? So you were running away?' I say I am running away because I told them all the SS, they disappear, all camps, they are bombed. And the people, they are burning. So I told them, 'What do you want? What want you can do with me? I don't want to run away. I don't know where I have to go.'

"They told me, 'You know what I'm going to tell you?' 'No.' 'Take a look over there. It's not far from here. It's very big bushes. Go over there and hide yourself. In two, three days, you're going to be free. Americans are coming.' So one soldier gave me three packages of matches. One soldier gave me half a bread—his portion. He told me, 'Be careful. Don't give them a chance to catch you. They will kill you away. They're bandits, the SS.' I listened to them, and I went over there in the bushes.

"I had water over there. And I got mussels that was in the water. And I found potatoes in the fields. And I had this. It was delicious. Was good, was so delicious. All day I was cooking potatoes.

"And at night I hide myself up in a grave. Not a grave. Like the soldiers make for themselves?

"Foxhole, yeah. I was waiting. Two days. Three days. No Americans. A week maybe is passed. All of a sudden one day I hear a noise. I am collecting potatoes. It is not far from a house. A farmer sees me. So he comes running at me with a big butcher knife. And what I should do with him?

"He told me, 'You there—you there'—And I had a chance to, when he was running, I took my feet and I put underneath, and he fell. I took the knife and I killed him.

"I am in the bushes for two weeks. Till all of a sudden in a nice day I hear something. Tanks. They come through the bushes. I thought that this was the Germans back. So I hide myself again. American soldiers I never saw in my life. But English soldiers I saw them in Belgium. I recognized English soldiers. Then I went out and I gave myself to them.

"I went next three months in a hospital in France. I was skinny. I was sick. I was yellow. All my face, mine eyes was all completely yellow. I lose maybe a hundred pounds. I weigh at that time maybe sixty, seventy pounds. I was weak. I could hardly walk. My feets was swollen. I finally got stronger and I went home to Belgium.

"I saw Louie Littleman's father, my neighbor. His father asked me about him. So I gave him a nice regard from what he did. I showed him my ear. So when Louie Littleman come home, his father told him that Green is home, too. He said, 'You can't be here. Green gonna kill you. You hit him.' I would kill him. Yeah. I had a knife. I would kill him right away. I would kill him.

"I meet a new wife. She was hiding in Switzerland during the war. Then we come to America. When I grew up in Poland, I always hear of America. And many, many people went to America. Jewish people. But my family did not go. Not everybody was willing to go. My father was a Hebrew teacher. And he didn't have money for tickets for six children and a wife, who was sick. But my father used to say that, in America, the stones you walked on are *trayfeneh*. You know what trayfeneh means? They're not kosher. So the real religious people, they didn't like to go. Later I went to live in Belgium to make for myself a better life.

"Well, I came to America and to East Flatbush. I work in a factory. But there are so many people. In Belgium I worked in mine house. So then we come to Chicago to be near the daughter. I got a job in a little factory. But I need more money. Somebody told me there is a market, so take this and this bus, change here this and this, and go over there. I had a friend. He gave me plastics to sell. I went to Maxwell Street, work on Sundays, on Saturdays, on holidays. I make a few dollars. I was happy.

"I make enough from there that when my boy grow up, I send him to college. From this money that I make on Maxwell Street. I gave it for my son. He made me a big joy when he graduate from college.

"Right near where I stand on Maxwell, I met my boss, Pinsker. He had told me, 'Why you should stay with this? You can work for me. I hire you.' So I went because I'm ready to retire. So I pick up some extra money.

"It's a very nervous place, Maxwell Street now. A man comes in and he buys a suit and overalls and clothes and then the store owner totals it up and the man says, 'Too much money. I don't want to buy that. It's too much money.' And he walks out. And all the store owners carry guns. What kind of life is that?

"But Maxwell Street is safer than most places in the city, even in America. America still a nice country because whenever you want to work, you can make a few dollars—not like Belgium and other places. But it is a shame for America to have this trouble, this danger.

"I want to tell you. If you talk about freedom, I had more freedom in Belgium. You know why? Because I'm not afraid to walk over there the whole night. Nobody going to hurt me. That means freedom. If you have to be afraid for me, and I have to be afraid for you, is that freedom? If you are afraid to go out in the night whenever you want to go, is that freedom? Doesn't mean freedom to me.

"My wife visited a friend one night. When she walks back, two guys beat her up. They want to take her purse. She didn't want to give it. She was taken to the hospital, and she was very, very sick. She, thank God, is home. Was last year.

"When I lived in East Flatbush they kill away three butchers not far from me, three which they come from Europe. Young men.

"That means, believe me, if I have to go to bed and sleep in the night, I have to look all over my doors. Oop, I didn't—forgot to lock something, to lock good. That means I live in fear."

Does this bring back memories of the concentration camp?

"No, no. Concentration camp is different. A lot of times I got dreams, bad dreams from concentration camp. I want to scream from the sleep, but I can't. You know what I mean? When you sleep, your voice . . . doesn't go. You know?

"Because old memories from SS. Very bad dreams. Crematoriums and . . . beating. Smoke from the crematorium. I used to work in that part of the camp. I used to see smoke and hear screams from children. Papa. Mama. They come from the trains. The people got out. 'Raus! 'Raus! And the children, they was screaming. All the luggage. They separate the people.

"I dream of eating like animals. We never had a spoon to eat. We never had a fork. The whole three years we never had a knife. Four people and one plate and the guard gave a piece of meat to me and one *shlep* to the other one. The one pulled it away and that one pulled it away and the other one pulled it away. I want to tell you. I prayed to God when I was over there that if I survive, I only want to have bread, as much as I need, and potatoes. And water. Nothing else.

"So now I appreciate. I never throw away a piece of bread. When I go on the street, when I see bread, I pick them up and I put the bread somewhere, by a window—not to walk on bread.

"Sure, sometime I complain. I don't like this food my wife make and I don't like that. That's the way it is. But I am happy with my life. I'm not looking to be rich. I say, 'I got enough.' My parents didn't have this, either. Why shouldn't I be happy? I got food. Or if I'm going to sit with people and talk like a human being. Is very nice. In the concentration camp, you talk this and this, they hang me up. Sabotage. Everything was sabotage. And I look at grass and trees now. So beautiful. I didn't see a tree for three years.

"But with the dreams I have, and with this on my arm—it is hard to forget."

He rolls up his sleeve. Engraved in black in his skin just above the left wrist is the number 66242.

"This is what I was known by. They never call you by name in the concentration camp. I see this now every morning when I wash.

"But you can't live all the time with this memory. It would be very serious thing if you would dream every night about this. If you would talk every night about this. You don't have to forget completely, but you have to forget little by little.

"But I still have the fear of walking in America, of waiting at a train platform. I would like to go back to Belgium. But my wife told me we can't leave the children. So, for my part, believe me, I would leave the children. Because children, they don't care too much about their parents.

"My son, I start to tell him about the concentration camp, but he used to say, 'Daddy, I'm American. Please don't tell me any of your stories from the old country.'

"As soon as he graduated college he told me he going to move to Boston. So I ask him, 'Why you have to move to Boston? The same money you can make here.'

"He said, 'Daddy, I got my own life. I like living over there and I think I can make more money.' I feel very bad. Very, very bad. So he left. I don't care so much now. But my wife, she feels lonely. We have no relative, only the two children. But I tell her, 'He got a right to live any way he want. It's his life.' I did the same thing. When I left home from Poland to go to Belgium, my father asked me the same question, 'So why you leave me?' And I didn't listen to him either."

# III

# THE SMOKESTACK EXPRESS

"The Smokestack" was the name the southern blacks gave to the Illinois Central Railroad train, whose distant whistle in the night called to so many in drab shacks, and carried them up to Chicago. Migration began after the Civil War, increased steadily, and turned into a kind of stampede after both the First and Second World Wars when jobs loomed juiciest in the big northern industrial cities.

"The Smokestack" began its trek north from New Orleans and then quickly hit Mississippi and ran right up the middle of that State, making stops in McComb and Brookhaven and Jackson and Asylum and Yazoo City and Tchula and Durant and Greenwood and Grenada and Water Valley and, finally, Holly Springs. The IC traveled through the far western niches of Tennessee and Kentucky and then swung up through the belly of Illinois.

The blacks carried with them, in their metal suitcases bound with belts and packed with simple clothes, the same kind of dreams for their future and their children's future that the Jews sailed with from Europe, that the Mexicans swam with across the Rio Grande.

The black population of Chicago in 1900 was 30,150, which accounted for 1.8 per cent of the total population of the city. By 1920, there were 109,458, and 4.1 per cent of the city population. In 1950 there were 492,265 blacks, 13.6 per cent, and by 1970 the black population was estimated at over one million and better than one-third of the city population.

There were blacks living around Maxwell Street in the 1920s, and as the Jews left and no new Eastern European landsmen replaced them because of new U.S. immigration quotas, the blacks moved more and more into the Maxwell Street ghetto. In

1943, one of the last Jewish families to reside in the neighborhood, the Hessings, (who still own the hot-dog stand, "Buck's" on the corner of Union and Maxwell), moved west to the Lawndale district.

Even when blacks were not living on Maxwell Street, some worked there. Morrie Burres, in his early seventies in 1975, worked on the street for much of his life, having come up to Chicago from Memphis when he was a boy. Burres works today for Kelly's Sporting Goods Store. He is a careful dresser who wears a hat indoors in the style of the orthodox Jews, whom he spent years working for.

"In the early days, the only place where a black could get a job as a salesperson in a store was Maxwell Street—the Jews were the only ones who'd hire you," said Burres. "Nowadays, of course, you find plenty of blacks as salespersons downtown. But in them days? Oh, forget it! It was lucky if you got a job even. You couldn't get a job even cleaning the floor downtown, let alone as a salesperson."

Would the Jews pay you fairly?

"Well, you know, considering—after all, if a guy can't get a job anywhere, he can't be too fussy about what he gets. So you'd be making—this is in the '20s—maybe twenty dollars a week. Not bad."

Burres worked for years for an orthodox Jewish couple named Horowitz who sold sporting goods. Burres learned to speak a *gashmacht* Yiddish. That is, a Yiddish so rich that one, just listening to him from another room, might have thought he had recently come over on the boat from Kishinev.

One day in the 1930s he remembers walking into a store on Maxwell Street a few blocks from where he worked. The shopkeepers did not know him. "I walked in," said Burres, "and I says to the owner, 'Will you kindly show me something very nice in a nightgown for my wife?' The owner turns to a salesman and says in Yiddish, 'Show the *shvartzer* some cheap stuff.' So upon returning with the merchandise, why, I looked at it, asked the price. The price was not bad, but it wasn't good, either. So I told him, 'Well, this doesn't look like it's worth that much money.' He said, 'Well, of course it is. This is very good merchandise.' I says, 'In that case, I don't think you did what your boss told you to do.' He said, 'What do you mean?' I said, 'Well, he didn't tell you to bring me this good merchandise. He told you to bring me cheap merchandise. And now you tell me this is good merchandise.' He looked at me strange. I said, 'Your boss said to you—' I repeated the instructions in Yiddish. He looked shocked, and then he went back and brought me better merchandise, and the price was the same as the first merchandise he had brought. I bought the nightgown, and I told him where I worked. We got along fine after that."

Leeman Reynolds was twenty-one in 1923 when he took the train up to Chicago from Mississippi. He had family, he says, living around Maxwell—560 West Twelfth Place. He now owns one of the most remarkable places of business around Maxwell Street. He is the hubcap man. On a high rickety wooden fence on Union just north of Maxwell, he has placed a terrific jamble of hubcaps that glitter in the sun and, at certain parts of the day, are nearly blinding. He has hubcaps on the sidewalk and spilling into the street. He also sells old toilets and rusty tools and a used mop and cracked crutches, among other items. He wears a heavy black sweater under a printer's apron. He wears thick glasses, a blue railroad engineer's cap, and a serious mien.

He was asked if there is a market for used toilets?

"Is there a market for used toilets?" he replied. "There's a market for everything!"

A man came by and asked for hubcaps for a 1960 Chrysler. Reynolds went right to them. It seemed amazing.

How do you know where to go to find your merchandise?

"I know where I put them," he said.

His first job in Chicago was in the Union Stockyards. At first he worked in the refrigerator section, where he had to wear an overcoat for ten hours a day. He made enough money so that in about eight months he went back home with three hundred dollars. He bought a suit of clothes and a derby hat. He had seven brothers who were working on this poor farm. They saw Leeman and, he said, "They got crazy for the prosperity and all came up to Chicago."

He returned to the stockyards but this time got an even better job, or a higher-paying job, working in a slaughtering room where the blood was ankle-deep to his hip boots. In 1936 he left the stockyards to open a grocery store near Maxwell Street. When that finally busted out, he began his hubcap and toilet-bowl business.

"I'm makin' a living," he said. "I don't have any treasures stored up for my olden days. These are times now where you don't even try to save. You just try to break even. Everything is fucked up, and they don't know how to unfuck it."

Don Miller, a sixty-year-old black, grew up near Maxwell Street and early worked as meat cutter for Leavitt's Delicatessen on the corner of Halsted and Maxwell.

Miller is now the proprietor of the tavern on the corner of Halsted and Maxwell, directly across the street from where the now-defunct Leavitt's once was.

"My father butchered meat in the stockyards and my mother worked maid service," said Miller, who stands behind the counter and wears a hat with feathers tucked in the brim and a turtleneck sweater. "My parents had four kids, when they came up from Mississippi. But they were never on relief. They raised us to be independent and so forth. But now you find most of your black people, families, nine out of ten are on relief rolls around these neighborhoods, in these ghettos. And the kids are brought up on relief. Relief becomes more important than a job. I've had people workin' for me that tell me, 'I can't come to work because my caseworker's comin' to see me, and I can't lose my relief.'

"Relief has been here all this time. But I remember back in the years when they had WPA. And then I remember when they used to bring baskets of food to people. Well, that was their relief. I mean, they had welfare. And when the basket ran out, you were out of food until it came again, another month. So you'd better find yourself some work."

The blacks have been playing music on Maxwell Street to entertain—and some "to sanctify" souls—from the time they arrived in Chicago. One, Papa Charlie Jackson, who lived at 624 Maxwell recorded "Maxwell Street Blues" in 1926. Some lines were:

> I was walking down the market back on Maxwell Street
> I was walking down the market back on Maxwell Street
> Lord, I'm talking about your wagons, talking
>     about your pushcarts, too.
> Because Maxwell Street's so crowded on a Sunday
>     you can hardly pass through.
> Hey, hey—hey, hey, hey, hey. . . .
> If you ain't got no money, the women got nothing
>     for you. . . .
> The Maxwell Street women gonna carry me to my
>     grave. . . .
> I got the Maxwell Street blues. . . .

Maxwell Street would become the most important area in the most important city for modern blues in America.

Edward "Porkchop" Hines is one of the last of the old breed.

Porkchop is a short man of seventy-three who wears cap, glasses, vest, snappy pointy shoes, and is kind of crotchety. When he smiles, his teeth clamp tight on his cigar. He is a drummer and a vibrant one. He has played with Gene Krupa and Louie Armstrong, among others. Like many of the blues musicians around Maxwell Street, he is invited to play in college towns, where students relish this exotic taste of the big-city ghetto streets.

Porkchop's wife had recently died in a fire in their apartment on Newberry just off of Maxwell. The wife before that suffered blood problems due to overdrinking, and a leg was amputated. But gangrene had gone too far. So now Porkchop is wifeless. He says he needs a woman. He has to have a woman look after his affairs when he is on the road. He knows that if he leaves his apartment unattended, he will be stolen blind. He also needs a woman to walk his dogs when he is gone.

He did find one woman who he thought filled his bill. But she wanted him to give up his music because, she said, she was "a churchgoin' woman and music was like sinnin'." Porkchop proved her wrong when her deacon found out about him and asked Porkchop to play his drums before the flock.

Porkchop still dances, too. "That old man," said Don Miller, "is as active as he can be. I mean, he can do buck dancin' just like he was a kid."

Who knows why Porkchop never made it bigger than Maxwell Street? Was there a character defect? Too much booze? Never received that blessed opportunity? Not quite enough talent? Whatever, he lives his life in a small apartment where hookers sometimes are heard in the hallways with their johns. And thievery and dope are rampant.

"Nowadays," said Porkchop, "you got to sleep with one eye open at all times."

"Maxwell Street" Jimmy Davis, going on sixty years old, rheumy-eyed, a hard knife-scar on his cheek, plays guitar and came up north from Greenville, Mississippi, when he was a boy. He had his first show business experience as a minstrel in the tap dancing Rabbit Foot Show.

"I used to dance in them big carnivals, dance on broken glass barefoot," said "Maxwell Street" Jimmy Davis, sitting on a chair in an empty lot on the street with his guitar. He wore a nice suit and a red carnation in his lapel.

"Yes, barefoot," he continued. "I was nothin' but a boy then. 'Bout twelve years old. There was a trick to it. Take glass bits and stack 'em up in a sack so the sharp edges are smoothed. Then you put 'em in a large cardboard box, and you keep the sharp pieces near the edges, and you try to dance in the middle of the box.

"It was a real popular side show. Onliest thing I didn't like so much was that I had to wear a grass skirt. I like to make people happy and make 'em clap.

"Like on Maxwell. You get the feelin' out there. Yeah, you get feelin' 'cause a whole lots of people crazy about ol' Jimmie Davis. Maxwell Street Jimmy Davis. I knowed it. I play 'em blues and everybody gets happy. We gets 'em to dancin' in the street.

"I had one album done. I was goin' to get others, but it never worked out good. A man promised me some things. He from the big record company in New York. But he die. I see some of 'em make it good—Howlin' Wolf and Muddy Waters and Hound Dog Taylor and Little Walter and B. B. King and them, and I'm feelin' good. I want to see the boys go big. See, 'cause we been in that field a long time, a long time together. Forty-some odd years in the blues line. I say to myself what my mother used to say to me, 'A bad dog always got one day, and a good dog is got two days.' She says, 'Set and wait, Jimmie, your time will come.' Meanwhile, I got to take what jobs I can. I just finished a dishwashing gig in a restaurant. But I'm one dog who's gonna have one more day. I feels it."

Bernard Abrams, who owned a record and appliance store at 823 Maxwell, opened opportunities for those musicians on the street who did achieve success. Abrams recalls:

"Little Walter and Johnny Young were the first to cut records here. These fellas that were down here, they used to come in to my store. I used to have a little disc recorder, and I'd have a mike and they'd sit on a box or something and sing. Well, one day I thought this might sell. I took it to a pressing plant and had records made. A thousand or so. Little Walter played his harmonica. The songs were 'Just Keep Lovin' Her,' on one side, and 'Ora Nelle Blues,' in honor of his girl friend Ora Nelle, on the other. From there, they got in with Lenny Chess of Chess Records and it got national distribution. I still get requests for this record from all over the world—from Japan and Austria and Germany."

Muddy Waters recalls playing down on Maxwell Street, but not liking it. "A lot of peoples was down there trying to make a quarter," he said, "but I didn't like to have to play outside in all the weathers and I didn't like to pass the hat around and all that bullshit.

"But, man, when you get a dude like Little Walter blowin' harp, he can set a fire behind you. That's when me, Walter, and Jimmy Rogers, who used to play down there all the time, got our trio together. And Bernard Abrams sold my first records there. It was a good place, but I'm glad I don't ever have to go back."

Muddy Waters is an internationally acclaimed blues artist, unlike Maxwell Street Jimmie Davis.

Jimmy says: "A man named Pete Welton named me Maxwell

Street Jimmie Davis. And now everybody knows me by that name. I likes the Davis and the Jimmie pretty good. But I don't like Maxwell Street too good.

"I don't know, man, maybe I believe it give you a bad name. I'd rather be Jimmie Davis. See, Maxwell Street is where you started at. It's where you wanna get known. You can get known on Maxwell Street. But after you done be known, you oughta dust your broom from there."

Jimmie, wearing a suit, sat on a chair on the sidewalk on Maxwell. A cord from his guitar slithered up through a first-floor window where it was nestled in a socket. Maxwell Street Jimmie began a song, rocking slowly back and forth in his folding chair, a rose in his lapel sometimes brushing his cheek. He sang:

> My baby don't wear no drawers, my babe.
> My baby don't wear no drawers,
> She wash her clothes in alcohol
> And hang 'em up on a hook in the hall.

Except for a few blues musicians, no black from Maxwell Street ever gained national recognition and none, at least from a so-called legitimate standpoint, ever experienced the rags-to-riches rise that their Jewish predecessors from Maxwell Street enjoyed.

Ben Lewis is the lone black from the neighborhood to rise even in city-wide circles, according to long-time Maxwell Street residents and businessmen.

Lewis became one of the few black aldermen in Chicago. In 1958 he became the head of the Twenty-fourth Ward, the ward that Jack Arvey had led years before.

Lewis had shined shoes on Maxwell Street and cut corned beef behind the counter at Leavitt's Delicatessen. He was a clever man and played party politics wisely. He had a dignified mien and was considered a mainstream member of the Democratic machine of Mayor Daley.

On the morning of February 26, 1963, Lewis was discovered sitting in his private office in ward headquarters on Roosevelt Road. He had been bound and shot through the head with three .38-caliber bullets. The motive is still unknown and the murder remains unsolved.

# NATE DUNCAN

It was nearly six o'clock Sunday evening, June 30, 1973, when Ben Lyon, who had been checking out the cash registers in the rear storage room, walked into the front of his basement Jewish delicatessen at 807 Maxwell. This was Ben Lyon's last day as owner of Lyon's Delicatessen, which had been on this site for forty-nine years and had been the family business, starting on Jefferson Street, for sixty years. His parents began the business when Benny was five, and he grew up cutting corned beef on the slicing machine while wearing knickers and standing on an orange crate.

At the slicing machine now, washing it with a soapy rag, was tall, black, brawny, gentle-eyed Nate Duncan, hired by Lyon twenty-five years ago at seventeen to be porter and factotum. By dint of his warmth and capability, Nate became a nearly indispensable employee. Not only did he learn the basics of business, wait on customers, deal with wholesalers, but, from Ben's Russian-born mother, learned to make kosher dill pickles and gefilte fish and schmaltz herring and chopped liver so well that he became the envy even of those elderly Jewish women who still worked on the street.

Sitting at one of the three small tables in the delicatessen were Nate's mother and sister, Patsy, who is a few years younger than Nate. They often stopped to chat with Nate and with Ben and with Ben's wife, Cele, who, though not here now, regularly worked in the store. Nate's mother and sister had made a special point of being here this night, for tonight was Ben's last as owner of the delicatessen, and Nate's first. Ben had decided to sell the business because, he said, he owed himself a long rest and also his wife's failing health demanded more of his time.

Over the years, there had been many opportunities for him to sell the business, in which people came from all over the city for Lyon's corned beef, and on a Sunday afternoon there might be forty or fifty people packed into this madly active small store. The orders, the jokes, the questions, the expletives, the gallons of cups of coffee and the strong smell of salami sandwiches filled the place. In recent years, though, as the neighborhood turned more and more black, prospective buyers for the store grew fewer. And when Lyon decided to get out, the best person he thought he could sell to was Nate.

He also knew Nate had little in the way of liquid cash.

But that didn't bother Lyon. If Nate accepted the responsibility, Lyon knew he would meet whatever the regular payment arrangement would be. The agreement began with no money down, and then weekly checks to follow. Now, Lyon walked in and greeted Mrs. Duncan and Patsy Duncan. Nate finished on the machine, dried it, and wiped his hands. It was his last official act as an employee. Nate came out from behind the counter. And Ben took his set of store keys and handed them to Nate, and then the two of them, the thin elderly Jew and the younger, stocky black man, had tears in their eyes as they embraced in their grease-stained aprons. And the two women in turn hugged and kissed Ben.

---

It is two years later. It is midmorning. The store remains much the same as when Ben Lyon left it. There are still salamis of various sizes and lengths hanging from the ceiling behind the counter. Eggs are still fried in the far corner. The gold-chrome banister on the three stairs leading from the door into the store is still wound with white tape at the big knob. One difference, though, is that the plate glass window with the neon sign that once read "Lyon's Delicatessen," now reads "Nate's Delicatessen." Also, the window is patched with long strips of tape. The day before, a merchant and a man he caught stealing had had a fistfight for a block that ended with the thief being punched through Nate's window. The people in the place were, even for Maxwell Street, stunned to find two men crashing in through the window. The thief lay unconscious at the foot of Nate's meat cutter. The merchant, who now lay on top of the thief, said to Nate, "What's that window cost?"

"A hundred dollars," said Nate.

The man got up, dug into his pocket, ripped one hundred dollars off his roll. "Here," he said to Nate. "It was worth it."

Don, from the liquor store at the corner, happened to be eating a corned beef sandwich in the delicatessen. He said, "Nate, you got some luck. When somebody comes through my window, he's always broke."

Another difference in the store from when it was Lyon's is that Nate tiled the ceiling and the floor and seems to have a penchant for keeping it neat in a way that eluded Ben. Ben periodically drops into the store and always makes note how much nicer it looks today.

"I found out Ben wanted to sell the store when one day he took me in the back and said, 'Nate, I've had enough. I'm getting tired.' He asked me if I wanted the store," said Nate.

"At first I didn't say yes or no; here's a guy throwing money at me, man. I didn't know what the situation was. And he told me, 'Don't worry about the money.' He told me what the deal was and it sounded beautiful. I didn't give him my okay right away because I had to talk to my family—my sister and brother and mother. Because if I take over a store and got no good help, I'm in trouble.

"You see, Ben was leaving and so was Al Ariew, who had worked with us all these years. Al is Ben's old friend. All that was left was Kenny, who was the other black fellow behind the counter, and me.

"My family had no experience in the store. My mother used to make her own ice cream and sell it outside on the street, and my brother and sister had other jobs. But they said, okay.

"It was very tough for all of us. Here's a black family in a Jewish delicatessen. Of course we had a lot of Ben's white customers. But some of them were very mean. For example, a lot of them at first didn't want nobody to wait on them but me. Very impatient. The customers used to bring it to me. So and so didn't give me this or they forgot this. Knowing that they're new but not giving a damn, not giving us a break.

"I remember once someone got a cup of coffee and sent it back, said it was full of salt. That was just to aggravate us. Others complained that my sister didn't put enough cream cheese on the bagel or enough butter on the onion roll. Someone else complained that they'd put too much cream cheese or butter on. All of my family at one time or another got so angry or so hurt, we wanted to fight or cry. We had talks. We decided to keep trying.

"Now, we also had black trade, of course. And one day one of the white merchants said to me, 'You wait on all the blacks now first? You don't wait on the Jews no more? What's the matter, you gotta be black to be waited on?'

"I think a couple of 'em resented Benny lettin' me have it in the first place. I don't know, maybe they felt a threat that the store would change, and they had been comfortable with the way it was. But we didn't lose too many customers.

"But they'd come in . . . like these two brothers. They always have a bitch, these two yo-yos. And then they'd go up the street sayin', 'The coffee's no good at Benny's no more.' Stuff like that. I was real tight with them when I was working there. But after I got the business it was different. Now, I'm getting a little hot at them. They're the type of people that don't want to see nobody get ahead, no matter the color. One day I'm behind the counter and I hear the one guy tellin' his brother, 'Take the coffee back, go ahead. Don't drink it.' They don't know I'm listening. And I'm burning up. I come out. I'm through with it then. I took enough. I said, 'Look, don't come in here no more. Leave me alone. Let me run my business. Don't come in here. Do me a favor and never come back.' They haven't been back, though I know that they send in every day for coffee.

"I didn't need them in here no way. They'd go in the back nine times a day and use up my toilet paper, my paper cups, water, everything. I was losing money on them.

"Some just have strange habits that you have to learn. One guy never would take dirty bills for change. There'd be a million people in the store and you've got to riffle through the cash register for clean bills for him.

"Another guy eats a piece of pie in his hands. You can't give him a plate and fork. But when you give him a pickle, it's got to be with a fork.

"A lot of them down here have a trick that when they buy coffee, they pay twenty-five cents. They know coffee is twenty-six cents. They got the penny in their hand, but you got to ask them for it. If you don't ask them for it, they'll walk out with the penny in their hand. This is what it's all about on the street. They always look for the edge. Always. At all times.

"The one thing I had to teach my family was that with the religious Jews you can't use the same knife to cut the meat and the cheese. At one time, the religious people would wait a long time for me because they thought that I was the only one who could do it right. Well, this and some of the other things could have been explained, instead of trying to make my family feel like dummies. So it was rough, and I'd talk to my family. What was my argument? I just said, *Nem the Gelt*. In Yiddish, that means, 'Get the money.' Wait on the customer, ring up the register, and forget it. I told 'em that it happened to me, too, when I began.

"Meanwhile, a lot of beautiful things were happening, too, believe me. Small things, but nice. Like Willie and Ann who run the panties stand on the corner of Halsted and Maxwell. He'd say to my sister or mother or brother, 'Look, this is new to you. Take your time. You're gonna make some mistakes.' He never complained. And Louie Steinberg, he's the one who started my sister on cooking eggs. She had never considered herself an egg cooker. She hesitated. He said, 'Go ahead.' So she made him eggs and he said, 'Now that's good.'

"And we've got a small bunch that meets in the mornings here around six or six-thirty. Called 'The Pumpernickel Gang.' It's with Gerard the ice man, and Stuart Hessing the hot-dog guy from Union Street, and Julie who works in Oscar's wholesale store, and a few others—beautiful people. We celebrate birthdays with cakes and have a sweet time in the mornings. So things like that, people like that, made it good.

"And of course there's always Benny Lyon. I called Benny quite a few times about situations that happened. Not so much as far as customers, but as far as commercial things. You see, I knew the front of the store well. I mean, how to cook the corned beef, how to slice the tongue, that sort of thing. But the back of the store, the prices and the ordering, I wasn't as certain about. Like, I called Benny when the lox was going up, going crazy. I called

Benny often. Whenever my meats go up, I call him. About how far can I let them raise me before I raise it. And he tells me.

"The big question when I took over was whether I'd lose the white trade. Benny explained to me that I might have to switch over our business, as far as having hamburgers and all that bullshit. But I said to myself, 'No way.' He actually felt I couldn't hold up the Jewish trade. But I knew this business as good as he did on this side of the fence. In regard to the Jewish products. I don't know anything about hamburgers and soul food and so on. What's funny is, a lot of black customers are getting away from pork and foods they used to eat. And you'd be surprised, we get a lot of black Jews in. Like for Passover, it's amazing. They have their own synagogues all over the city."

What did they say to you when you took over the business?

"They said, '*Mazel tov.*'"

Lyon's concern that Nate might not be able to hold the Jewish trade was, as it turns out, unfounded. Although Nate's homemade kosher dill pickles, gefilte fish, and chopped liver get high marks by the regular customers, it is the schmaltz herring that has raised his reputation to the highest levels of Jewish cuisine.

"Benny's mother taught me," said Nate. "I used to spend hours and hours with her, watching her make it, asking questions. She was a beautiful person. We were very close. I used to go to her house and watch television with her. My mother and sister were close with her, too. Well, our two families were tight, period.

"She taught me the tricks of making schmaltz herring. How to mix the spices, the right amount of time to soak the fish in salt water. The old Jewish ladies come to me and ask how I make it. I won't tell them. Of course not. A lot of them boil vinegar, or add water to the vinegar. They do a lot of silly things. I tell them 'You're doing it wrong.' That burns 'em up because I won't tell 'em how to do it right.

"And like one time, one of the ladies was sitting here and trying to get the recipe out of me. At the next table a guy is eating my schmaltz herring. He finishes it and says to me, 'I haven't had herring like this since I left the old country.' The lady I was sitting with got up and walked out.

"I've been teaching my mother how to make it. She messed it

up bad the first time. Man, she really messed it up. But she's starting to catch on now. In fact, she made the last batch. Not too bad, either. My mother's a very good cook, but Jewish cooking has not been her specialty."

Nate's mother, Roberta Duncan, is called "Bu" by her children. It was the only way Nate, the oldest child, could say "Ma" as an infant. She is a husky, bosomy matron; her intelligence and good nature are amply reflected in her children. She came to Chicago from West Virginia. Her husband had worked in a coal mine there, where he lost his arm in an accident in the pits. She did not want her children working in the mines and had relatives in Chicago. She moved to Chicago and to the Maxwell Street area because her husband's family lived there and, also, because she liked the community feeling of the area.

"It was 1937," she said, "and there were Blacks and Jews living here. It was like one big happy family then. Everybody knew everybody. In the morning everybody was on the street. In the evening everybody would get out and just sit around and laugh and talk. It was beautiful. I could have moved many times to the South Side. But I chose to stay around Maxwell Street. It was just so homeylike."

Nate's father worked as an elevator operator in a building on Chicago Avenue. Nate remembers that his father liked to gamble and could shuffle and deal cards with his one hand with extraordinary dexterity. He died in 1958.

Nate says that growing up on Maxwell Street holds no regrets for him. "It was different," he said. "There were all the chicken markets then and the meat markets. It had a liveliness it doesn't have any more. There was a park, Stanford Park, a beautiful park, and I'd play baseball and basketball day and night. Used to play with Ben Lewis, in fact, when we were kids.

"None of the kids in our family ever got into trouble. Never. Now I see guys on the corner here today, some who I was raised with and know very well, who have always been in trouble. Winos, thieves, drug addicts. I could have been one of those guys. I coulda been the same thing. I coulda made the wrong turn around the corner."

Why them and not you?

"Could be the difference in upbringing, I guess. I've seen guys take their first shot of dope when I was a kid in the alley. But I was afraid. I had to be home at a certain time. And if I wasn't home at a certain time, my mother'd come out and look for me. Where other parents, they would never do that. They could have been drunks, or just didn't care. My mother knew where I was at all times when I was growing up. At all times.

"At the time I might not have realized that that was a good thing. But in later years I did. I feel I was very lucky. It coulda happened to me very easy. I coulda been one of those guys noddin' on the corner."

# SHIRLEY WALKER

Shirley Walker arrived for an appointment at the medical clinic wearing trench coat, brown boots, luxuriant black wig, and her right arm and hand wrapped in bandages. She had developed an infection from having been pricked with an unclean needle. Her eyes are large and her fake eyelashes are thick. Her skin is of a smooth, milk-chocolatey shade. She is of medium height, carries herself with a nice poise, and speaks articulately and softly. One of the neighborhood cops once described her as "the princess whore of Maxwell Street."

She was born at 656 Maxwell Street in 1948, and grew up on the street. She now lives a few blocks away but still comes back often to work and to talk to old friends.

We met at the clinic and then took a drive and chatted. Her boyfriend is the head of a West Side drug and rehabilitation clinic, and we will call him Tom. He has tried to persuade her to "clean up her act" and get a different profession. She has thought about it, since she does enjoy being treated by him "as a true lady." The high point in such treatment came in 1971 when Tom put Shirley's name on a list of guests to attend in Washington a huge dinner party at the Washington Hilton honoring the new head of the federally funded department that Tom is connected with. Shirley, the "princess whore of Maxwell Street," received a signed invitation by President Nixon. At the dinner, she also was photographed with the President of the United States.

Shirley and I began to drive around the Maxwell Street area, and she pointed out the several houses she lived in and reminisced. At one point, though, she slunk down in the seat. "That looks like my boyfriend," she said. "He wouldn't understand me and you together." She peeked up, watched a Cadillac turn the corner. "No," she said, "that's a white dude. That's not him."

"Did you ever see the movie *Irma la Douce?*" she asked. "Do you remember the marketplace in it, and when Irma was prostitutin'? That's what Jewtown was like. Fruits and stuff on the stands and clothes and things hanging. And it was just fine, just walkin' up and down the street or beggin' people for nickels, dimes, quarters. And sometimes if we wanted to be bad, we would sneak by a stand and snatch somethin'. They might chase us—me and my sister Mabel or my cousin Lavon. But we were faster, and once we got into the crowds and then hit those alleys, it was over.

"Prostitution came natural to me. When I was small and I went on the corners of Maxwell and Halsted, Maxwell and Union, Maxwell and Newberry, I used to see the girls all workin' and makin' money and this fascinated and excited me.

"There would be nine or ten women on the corner, twenty-four hours a day. And I used to go to the store for 'em. They would tell me how big and pretty my eyes were and I was going to grow up to be a real pretty girl. There was one, I told her I wanted to be just like her when I grew up. Her name was Boots. She was so pretty.

"Even at six or seven or eight I knew what they was doin'. I had a girl friend, Beverly, that lived about four doors from me. And my mother was working during the day, so I'd go to Beverly's house. Her mother was dead. But her father lived there. He would be home in the afternoon. So, like when we would get home, he'd say, 'It's time for us to take a nap.' And he would put us in separate bedrooms and, believe it or not, I was hot and frustrated at six years old. So I would play at being asleep and this man, he'd come in there and play with me. It was nice.

"But one day he made straight advances toward me. He grabbed me and tried to kiss me. And he was a man. It was okay as long as I was playing asleep. But he frightened me and I ran out. I never went back.

"Another thing was, I was close with the Gypsies who lived next door to us. They would look out for me and my sisters.

"There was one particular Gypsy woman named Rachel who I still come by to see. She was like a second mother to me. When I was a kid, I'd peep out our second-floor window and see the Gypsy ladies and how they'd get the men in the back—take 'em through the back door of their home, through the gangway which led to the back stairs, and into the alley. Now, some of these Gypsy ladies was beautiful, and they'd fix up so they looked whorish type, to draw customers. Sometimes two or three women were around one man. One would be holdin' one hand, and one would be holdin' the other hand. And one would be tellin' his fortune and pressin' her body up against his. And one would be in his pocket, just pickin' pockets. But the women never went too far sexually. And if the man got out of hand, the Gypsy men would come flooding out."

Shirley remembered the first time she ever fornicated for money.

"Every now and then on a Sunday, a man they called 'the Hundred-dollar Man' came around. He wanted girls like ten or eleven years old. He'd give 'em a hundred dollars. When I was sixteen I looked thirteen, because I was flat-chested. I hadn't matured yet. A dude named Sykes who had a whore on Maxwell named Lorrece came to me and said, 'You can pass for twelve or thirteen, why don't you go buy you some socks, put on a little girl's dress and I got a hundred-dollar date for you. But you gotta give me twenty-five dollars.' I borrowed a dress with a bow in the back from this little girl. And the man saw me. Oh, he really wanted me. You know, I didn't have no titties or nothin'. And I was kinda scared.

"He said, 'How old are you?' I said, 'Twelve.' He say, 'You look older than twelve, but you'll do.' And he felt my chest. I said, 'Give me the money,' because this Sykes had told me to get the money first. And Sykes was right there at the door. I wasn't going to do it unless he was there because I was scared.

"After I took my dress off he saw my little knobs. And he just knew I was a virgin."

But you weren't really a virgin, were you?

"Are you kidding? My boyfriend was nineteen. And, shit. I had been fuckin' since I was twelve. Okay. So he pulled his thing out and he had a little-bitty dick. But you could see the class and richness of this man. He wore silk mohair suits, tailor made. Drove a

Lincoln Continental. Had white hair, was in his sixties. One time he got stuck up and he chased the cat for four blocks.

"So now the dude he got on top of me and put it in. I tried to fake it off like it was hurtin'. Hey, the man didn't even come and got up. He said, 'You're not twelve or thirteen years old!' Just as simple as that. He got up and walked out, told Sykes I was no virgin.

"I learned somethin' from that. But I had to have it explained to me. I learned it when I was seventeen or eighteen, from another white trick. He said, 'Honey, if you're gonna be in this business, here's the first thing you got to learn about people with class. Be straight with 'em—and do not ask for no money first. You'll get more money by not askin' for no money.'

"But I had seen how easy it was to make money doin' this. When my mother found out I was screwin', she told me I should get somethin' for it. She say, 'Don't ask me to buy you no cigarettes or nothin'.' I was about thirteen then.

"I also found it could be fun turnin' tricks. A girl is lyin' if she says she never been out with a trick and has never come with one. It's supposed to be just a job, and they're supposed to be there just for the money. But it doesn't work like that all the time.

"I'll never forget this one white dude from the South. He had the biggest Johnson I've ever seen."

How big was he?

"It was from—I would say as big as my arm."

Your *arm?*

"I would say as big as my arm. I was in a motel at the time. He gave me fifty dollars and he said, 'Take a douche and come back and get into bed.' When he took off his clothes, I told him he was going to have to give me fifty *more* dollars if he wanted to put *that* in me.

"And he said, 'Oh, no, honey. I'm only gonna French you, that's all.' And honest to God, this man made me feel like I've never felt before in my life. He knew exactly what he was doing. And he didn't stick his dick in me. And I came about ten times, I believe it was.

"He told me that he couldn't take a chance on catchin' somethin' because he was married. And this man, while Frenchin' me, oh, I was so involved and high and so frustrated until I had no idea that I was gonna start comin'. And I'll admit it, he made me jump outta the bed. Jumped out from under him because it was so good. He looked at me and laughed. He said, 'You oughta give me my money back.'

"Now, I wanted to fuck him. Bad! And then after I seen his dick, I really wanted to fuck him because I do like big dicks.'

That big?

"I believe I coulda took it. I wanted it. I asked him to fuck me. He said, 'Don't you like that?' Told him, 'Yeah, I liked it. But I couldn't stand it, though.' He never did fuck me. I was weak when he left.

"He deserved that fifty dollars back, but of course I didn't give it to him. I mean, I got me a habit I got to support. And you know that cost cash. Some of the girls will stick you up. And one of my friends can make a lot of money pickpocketin'. She is gifted. A dude couldn't crawl on her with his pants on without her takin' his wallet.

"Sometimes we'd work together, like we did in the house we worked in on Newberry just off of Maxwell. We'd be creepin' and tippin'."

What's "creepin' "?

"Well, if a dude take his pants completely off and lay 'em over in a chair and walk over to the bed, somebody creep on in the room and get it."

And "tippin' "?

"Tip-toe in there."

There were two whorehouses down the block from each other on Newberry and Maxwell. The one Shirley Walker worked in was called the Maxwell Street house because the girls there were all local product. The other was known as the South Side house because all the girls were imported from the South Side of Chicago. One day the two houses engaged in a terrific fight.

"The South Side girls, there was Sugar and Pearl and LaVerne and Candy and Gert and Barbara and Toni and a couple others. Of the Maxwell Street girls there was Charlene, who owned the house, and Emma, Mable, Ida, Pam, Betty, Little Barbara, Bow-legged Barbara, Leola, Sandra, Bernadine. . . .

"Now, one of the girls in the other house, name of Barbara, she told Baby Joe to kiss her ass. And so he went upstairs and kicked the whorehouse down. He was a young dude, a young punkish-type dude. Supposed to be tough. Baby Joe from Jewtown. He goes up there and he whips that girl, he stomps that girl every which way. Stomps her, beats her, kicks her, and tells her, 'Bitch, you tell *your* man to kiss your ass. You don't tell *me* to kiss your ass.' When her man comes down and see how she look, Baby Joe got her lookin' like Frankenstein.

"Baby Joe musta felt he really beat her too bad for just that, when he coulda told her man what she did. He goes back down there and apologizes. And the dude won't accept it! They say he pulled a gun. But anyway, Baby Joe got killed. Now, Baby Joe was one of us, Jewtown. And when he got killed we decided that them South Side whores gotta go, because Baby Joe would be alive if it wasn't for them broads down there. We had a meetin'. And we sent them a kite that it was time for them to leave. The message was that they had to leave Jewtown, otherwise we were going to burn their building down.

"So here comes Gert, with a knife in her hand. This is in broad daylight. She say, 'Don't nobody tell me where I can't work.' So here comes Sandra and Bernadine. . . . I mean, the worst girls that we got, there they go. With knives and iron pipes and things. Gert sees all these wild young girls comin', she race back up in that house. So Sugar, the one that I would say everybody liked— real cute, real pretty girl, real skinny, dressed sharp and all, made most money—she tried to talk to us outta the window. Charlene— she owned our house and she was jealous of Sugar because Sugar had a steady flow of business—Charlene wanted her action. She said, 'You oughta drag that skinny bitch out, too.' Sugar said, 'No, y'all don't have to drag me out. Y'all can have this house 'cause I been down here five years and I made enough money.'

"So now Gert, she gonna be Miss Tough, she comes back out with the knife in one hand and an iron pipe in the other. The other girls from her place follow her. And our girls come streamin' out. We all still had on short dresses and wigs and eyelashes and high heels. Bernadine says to Gert, 'Bitch, what you step out for?' Gert say, 'Well, I ain't scared of none of you. I'll fight you all, one by one.' Bernadine says, 'All right; fight me first.' Bernadine is the huskiest and the biggest. Bernadine was boxin' like a man. She whips Gert's ass. When Bernadine let her go, Sandra grabbed her. And Gert said, 'Oh, you're all jumpin' on me at once!' Sandra said, 'Oh, no, you smelly fish, it's one at a time like you said.' A policeman came by and tried to stop the fight. He had just started rookin' down there, and he was new. He couldn't get close to the fight because the girls had made a circle around it. We turned him around and we even took this dude's gun!

"Later on Sergeant Murph came down and said that he wanted that gun or else every girl was gonna go to jail, no if, ands, or buts about it. I don't know why, but he pointed to me and said, 'Shirley, I'm gonna give you fifteen minutes to bring me the gun down.' I got it to him.

"But meanwhile, there was another girl named Toni that got her head busted. Toni was messin' with Ida's old man. And this is when Ida said, 'While I'm at it, let me bust this bitch's head for fuckin' my man.' And she took a pop bottle and she busted Toni upside the head.

"Now, Barbara's girls backed off from us. And we went upstairs to their place, kicked the door down, drove Barbara out, drove her sister out, and just started throwin' clothes out the window. That was the last we saw of them for a while. Until a few months later. Sugar had a lot of policemen that were dates of hers. Some local, some from Tactical. And they also liked a few of the other girls. So we eventually gave the house back to them under the persuasion of the police. And things between us two houses was peaceable."

Unlike most of the working girls, Shirley Walker has no pimp. "I used to," she said, "but I came to never respect a man that depends on a woman for his money. I had one once for a year. Van was his name. We bought an El Dorado, mink-trim suits, leather suits, oh, we were flyin'. I was makin' a hundred fifty dollars a day, minimum. Sometimes $300 a day. But he started sneakin' 'round with Bernice. We had a showdown and I split from him.

"And it was from him I started snortin'. Then when I woke up in the morning I didn't feel right unless I snorted some cocaine. And then I met Tom and I thought I'd give Jewtown the air. But not for very long. I couldn't stay away from Jewtown. Are you kidding? Jewtown is addictive, too. Ask Meathead. Ask Mike. Ask any of the police. They can transfer him today and he'll still come back to Jewtown.

"Tom didn't want me comin' to Jewtown. He thought it was a bad influence. He said he'd rather see me dead than down there. But I had friends I wanted to see. Like Ida. She got strung out and OD'ed not long ago. She had stayed with me about a week before she died. She was twenty-three years old, and she was very attractive. Big, pretty legs. Nice shape. Red natural. Sexy. She told me she wanted to die 'cause she didn't think her man loved her. Skeets. She say, 'Sometimes I just wanna die.' She had no business shootin' no dope because she could shoot only a three-dollar bag and nod to the floor. Others might spend forty or fifty dollars on a bag and not nod off. One night I came home and the house was dark, and I went to turn on a light and I tripped over somethin'. I screamed. I turned on the light. There was Ida, on the floor, starin' up at me, dead.

"It's things like that that made Tom want me to stay away from Jewtown. But it gets in your blood. Tom told me, 'I'm gonna have to get handcuffs to keep you from there.' But it's fun. Just bein' out there. Hey, it's something when you can be out on the streets and you're able to survive. Because there's a street life just like any other life. And if you can survive out here, you can make it anywhere in the world. It can be prostitution; it can be sellin' buttons. It gives you an independent feeling. But there's a helluva lot of people died that couldn't survive down here. Did things to people whereas they couldn't smooth it off, whereas street life, you can't do things bogush. You don't do things to rip somethin' off and leave yourself wide open for the penitentiary or for whoever you did it to come back and kill you. You do it with finesse. Whatever you do to anybody, you do it whereas that they'll like it.

"Take my tricks. I leave 'em with a satisfied feeling. I would say I stood out among all the other girls because, for one, I was different. I didn't have a man. I had more regular tricks than any other girl down there. My tricks would come and wait for me.

Some other girls would hit on 'em, but they'd still wait. They couldn't figure it out. But they don't know that in order for a man to enjoy himself, do not rush him. Do not rush him. And anybody with any class, do not ask him for money first.

"In bed, I found that all men like to have his balls massaged. Played with, rubbed. I mean, even while I'm fuckin' or just lyin' down. All men like that. It's relaxing.

"And if you want a dude to come in a hurry, you can put your arms around his neck and say a few sounds, even if it's not good for you. You tell him how good it is. And, hey, he's gonna come. But the best prostitutes, just to be blunt about it, like to fuck. They enjoy their work. I enjoy sex very, very much. I enjoy the buildup most of all. And I enjoy Frenchin' a guy. And some guys need it before his dicky get hard. Some people think that if a broad suck a dick, 'Oh she's a worm or something.' Whereas I think oral sex is cleaner than body contact. But, hey, I dig body contact, too.

"You got to be delicate with a man's feelings, too. Like I've done it on steps, I've done it standing up, I've done it layin' down on the floor in a hallway. When all the rooms were busy, and I'd say to the date, 'Well, baby, all the rooms are filled. If you want to go out, you don't mind goin' in the hallway, do you?' And they'd be ready, they'd be stickin' out and it didn't take 'em but two, three minutes to come. Soon as they put it in, they come. Yep, I did it every place."

When Shirley Walker went to Washington at the President's invitation, she had visions of a whole new world opening up for her.

"My thoughts were these: If I could knock me off a Senator and get a picture of him and me in the bed in a motel, boy, boy, boy. I could live comfortably."

How about the President of the United States?

"That didn't strike my mind 'cause I never thought that I would get that close to him. Never. Had no idea. None whatsoever. I was about as close to him as this, we shook hands, but the Secret Service say, 'Hurry up.' And we took a picture. I wanted to be like a Fanne Foxe. I sure would like to be. I've been savin' her articles. What she did with Wilbur Mills got so wide open that I know she did it purposely. I believe he was set up for it. Are you kidding?

From seven hundred a week to thirty-five hundred a week. That's how much her income jumped.

"Oh, yeah. I would love to have a Wilbur Mills of my own.

"But Tom was not into this for me. Like afterward we went to a party at a doctor's house. And the doctor cornered me off in a corner. He gave me his card, told me he was gonna wire me money to come back to Washington. I told Tom and he said, 'But we don't play that.'

"That's where I met Sammy Davis, Jr., and his wife Altovese. I told Tom I had never seen a movie star in person. He said, 'Wait a minute and I'll introduce you to him.' I was dyin' to meet him and I was so excited. He said, 'Sammy, this is my woman, Shirley, Shirley this is Sammy. . . .' He was real nice. 'Oh, hi, Shirley.' And he shook Tom's hand, 'Say, man.' And then Sammy kissed me on the jaw. I told Tom I wasn't gonna wash my face till I got back to Chicago.

"That night I had on a gown and my nice wig and a couple pairs of eyelashes, and, matter of fact, some people looked at me twice because they thought I resembled Diana Ross. Lot of people tell me that. And once Diana Ross herself came to Jewtown. She was filming a movie. I think it was *Mahogany,* and I went up to the film truck. I said, 'I would like to see Diana Ross.' The guard said, 'Well, she eating now.' So like she peeked around, and she waved. Well, she had to turn and look at my face twice. One of the guards looked at me twice, too, and said I could be her double, that I have eyes like her, but I'm a little too fat for her. Well, she look like a skeleton. I could see the bones in her neck.

"When I came back to Chicago from Washington, it was an adjustment. I had been up that far and now it's like I went backwards. Tom gave me the opportunity to actually meet some people and do somethin' for myself.

"And nowadays I look in the mirror and I see I'm gettin' different, gettin' older. I'm not as pretty as I used to be. But I think if I can stop drugs now and take care of myself, I won't age as fast. I've still got somewhat good looks, and I think with a little medical attention I'll get myself back in order. I know I've wasted myself. I think of some of the women from Maxwell. Remember Boots, the pretty whore who I admired when I was a kid? Well, she lives in Rockville, Illinois, now, and she's had TB and a number of other things. Her health isn't too swell. And Juanita. It was her house I first went to work in. She was a prima donna, a real elegant lady. She was mixed blood and high cheekbones and thin and beautiful. And her house had wood paneled walls and leather couches and soft lamps. And a piano, too. Have you seen her recently? She sits around Don's Liquor Store in galoshes and raggedy coat. She drinks all day. Ain't got no teeth, losin' her hair, and she's half outta her mind. Goes back and forth from an institution. Poor thing's a hag now, just waitin' to die.

"So I look at this, and at how Ida died, and I want to do something constructive with my life. The one thing I'd like to work toward is get prostitution legalized. If I don't, my whole life would have been for nothin'. If prostitution was legalized, we'd stop venereal disease. There'd be less crime, less dudes gettin' pockets picked, beat up, killed. And less rapes.

"So this is why I want to go in a hospital and get the cure. So then I can come back and be ready for this project. I can type and with practice I can build my speed up. So I said I would go back to school to take typin' over again. Because I've already made myself the assistant secretary of the organization to legalize prostitution. I'm not qualified to be a secretary, but I'm qualified to be the assistant secretary. And I'd go out and hustle up backers to donate money. You'd be surprised who would donate toward it. . . .

"I guess I'd have to work in an office downtown. I'd miss workin' in Jewtown. But, you know, Jewtown ain't quite the same since they started tearin' it up. They tore down all those buildings so fast, it was unbelievable. Make way for the highway. And then the university. The first thing they tore down was our park. Stanford Park, and hey, it was beautiful for the neighborhood. It was some place for the kids to go. We loved it. I even took tap dancing lessons there as a child. And swimming lessons. This could have caused a lot of kids to wander because they didn't have anything to do after the park was bulldozed. And I remember I'd walk through the alleys and streets, like when I was five years old, and I'd pick up cigarette butts along the curb and smoke. My

# BENNIE MAURICE,
## or MAURICE BENNIE

The most startling aspect of Bennie Maurice's dark brown face are his blue eyes. And not simply because he is, uncommonly, a black man who possesses blue eyes. The eyes are as much curious as they are curiosities. They are also warm and penetrating and intelligent, as well as watery.

Another striking detail about the fifty-seven-year-old Maurice is his thinness. His face is gaunt, cheekbones prominent, arms bony, clothes baggy. This had to do with at least two facts: one, he drinks more than he eats; second, a recent injury has set him back.

Maurice—known to the people on the street as "Cuz," as in "cousin," because he calls everyone "Cuz" and so everyone calls him "Cuz"—broke his hip in a fall. On a recent Christmas Eve, he had finished a holiday glass of wine at Don's as guest of Mike the Cop. Snow had begun to fall and the streets were slippery. When Cuz got up to leave, Mike thought perhaps he ought to help the old man across Halsted Street, then decided not to, that Cuz's pride might be injured. As Cuz neared the far curb in the white night, he slipped and fell. Mike, seeing it all through Don's window, rushed out and hurriedly drove Cuz to a hospital, cursing himself for not following his original instinct.

Cuz now is a sometime handyman for an eye doctor in a medical clinic on Halsted just north of Maxwell Street. In the tavern he will also hustle cheap watches and various other pieces of jewelry. Once, he came to Mike with an idea.

"Hey, Cuz," said Cuz to Mike, "let's you and me open a newspaper stand on the corner here."

Mike brightened at Cuz's thought because there were no newspaper stands for miles around, for one thing, and, for another, it was a nice, legitimate enterprise.

"That sounds great, Cuz," said Mike. "The only trouble is, you know that nobody around here reads."

"Hey, no problem, it'll just be a front for a bookie and numbers thing," said Cuz. The idea never materialized.

That would be tame stuff, though, for Cuz, who has been a pimp, a thief, a drug peddler, a drug addict, and who had "a couple jolts in prison," the longest stretch being for the stick-up of another drug pusher.

"The first time I got hooked up with anything like that was accidentally, in December of 1924, when Barney Ross's daddy was killed," said Cuz. "I was only about six or seven years old. I was living on Maxwell Street then, and there was a little brother to one of the suspects who I was friends with. I come by his house. And there was a bust. When the police made the bust, they raked in everybody. Little kids, too. Yeah, they raked up everybody. Then they started weeding us out. They turned me loose on this because there was no part I could play because them was much bigger boys than me that done it. But, boy, they worked me up before they turned me loose."

Cuz was a boy of the streets. He was that way in New Orleans before he moved to Chicago, where he was the son of Annie Mae.

"When I was just little stuff, many guys would come and give me a dollar to go tell Mama to come to such and such a place," he recalls. "They knew I was Annie Mae's boy. So they catch me, say, 'Where's Mama?' I'd say, 'She at home.' Say, 'Go tell her I be over at Miss Mary's'—or any broad that was running a house.

"I began to get up in age. It didn't take me too long to wake up to the fact what was really going on. And then I know how she come by this bread. Like I needed money for clothes for school. I always had a dollar or so to take to school.

"See, she worked in the French Quarter. And she was a beautiful woman. She was what they call mulatto. You dig? She was part Indian, and they say that's where I get my high cheekbones. She couldn't read or write, but she wanted me to go to school. That was her one ambition. In summertime she even hired a teacher for me at home. So she was hookin' up with all the farmers and planters and workingmen. I remember she had a sayin', that a man could pat her ass if she could pat his pocket.

"She was sweet. She was Ma. But she had her own thing. She made out. I remember when I was shinin' shoes and it was Mother's Day. I knew that on Mother's Day you're supposed to bring your mama something. Well, I saw a lady, a Gypsy lady it musta been, and she was sellin' flowers. But they was fake flowers. I bought one for a nickel. I am so excited and so happy and I run all the way home. I go poundin' up the stairs. My heart is beating like it's gonna jump out. I run in and give the flower to Ma. She took it and looked at it and threw it to the ground. And she stepped on it. She say, 'I don't want nothin' artificial. I am a real mother. I'm no artificial mother. Always remember that, boy.'

"So when she told me that, I started playin' my hand behind reality. Everything I've tried to do in life, I've tried to let it be real. No phony nothin'.

"She had hooked up with a man, but they had a rumble and she wind up coming to Chicago and getting a regular job. She cut all that other life loose, gave it up completely, when we come to Chicago.

"Funny thing, I began makin' extra money in Chicago by runnin' errands for the prostitutes and whatnot. All the girls around Maxwell Street area that works in these houses, they always would send me because I was a little boy and I wouldn't run off with their money. I was a pretty decent kid. So that gave me a nice hustle when I was ten and eleven years old. I made maybe three or four dollars a day from the girls. I'd run and see they connect and get their package. Their dope connect. This had been going on better than a year before I knew what was in them packages. I happened to be in a house when the lady, this particular girl, started takin' off. She injected in her arm. It begun to dawn on me there was somethin' wrong here.

"But I was amazed when I found out how much money you can make in narco. Okay. Time marches on. I start operatin'. I thought in order to get anywhere in life, I better start dealin' instead of deliverin'. And I'm a teen-ager and I'm into this thing right up to my neck. I got cousins buyin' fifty, sixty, seventy dollars worth of stuff in a day. But I'm spendin' thousands of dollars on bonds to keep me outta jail. The onliest thing I can look back at here and be proud of is I come up with a good chunk to help Mama buy a home.

"But I'm in and outta jail regardless. But when I'm out one night, I'm with this girl who was usin' it and one morning she say, 'You want a little taste?' I said, 'Yeah. Just a little.' So I took a little taste. I began to taste more. About two, three weeks later I find out I'm hooked. I stayed hooked four, five months. I didn't like it. There was no drug programs then. So I quit mine by walkin' the street. I sweated it out. I put on a sweatshirt because sweatin' so much you could very easily catch pneumonia. I walked around for three days. On the third day I got into a crap game. I had thirty-five dollars in nickels and dimes. I didn't wanna win no thousand dollars. I just wanted to kill time, to forget about my pain. I stood up there gamblin' all night. The people there knew. I was shiverin' and wringin' wet. 'He sick, he a narco.' They let me alone. I went home the next day, took a bath, and ate a whole chicken. That's the best thing, to be hungry. When you broken the habit, your best thing is to start eatin' because before you can't. Everything comes back up."

Cuz went to prison for ten years for sticking up another dope dealer named Cotton.

"The judge knew this was a smutty case, but like he tell me, 'It make no difference what another guy done. That don't mean you can stick him up.'" Cuz spent the next ten years in Statesville Penitentiary.

"Now, the first times I was in, like in reform school and my first short bit in prison, I was in and out so fast, by the time I got through runnin' off at the mouth, the time was up. Oh, you're talkin' to the guys 'bout the girls you gonna get and how fast you live out there and all the clothes you got and how much money you made. That's fast talk. When you got a year. But when you get ten, that talk run out.

"That's when it dawned on me what a damn fool I was, and I tried to pick up all the knowledge I could that didn't go with committing crimes.

"Lookee here, man. In Statesville, I was up on the fourth gallery, and I can lay in my bed and look right out on the highway. I can see my whole entire life that I have already lived from a kid up come through that window. I thought about what I could have done. And what I didn't do. And what I can do. And what I hope to do. But I know one thing. I got to change my life. Because I don't want no more of this.

"So when I come out I tries to take a different road. I copped me a good girl who had a nice job. That give me a chance to get around and try to maneuver myself. And I did. Start runnin' crap games at a nice club—wasn't doin' no bad things.

"You see, in this town, what's crooked someplace else is straight here. This is a gangster town. It's always been a gangster town. The town consists of everything that is hooked up with the underworld. They first tried to make it a religious town. It ain't no religious town. Gangsters. Thieves. Thugs. Prostitutes. Anything that go with the underworld is Chicago. And it's a town where everybody has got their hand in a pie of some kind. And Jewtown is right in the middle of it. And Jewtown, it be around since Jesus Christ's day. That's where Jesus met a whole lot of people, in the market. He was a Jew. And this is tradition for them, for the Jews. But it also bring in everybody else. Crowds bring crowds. And this bein' Chicago, it naturally bring in the underworld. And I'm part of it 'cause I'm raised up in it.

"And so I was always with a nice little hustle here and there to keep me sweet. But I stayed outta hard trouble. And now I'll sit in the tavern and I'll see the young kids comin' up in the game and I talks to 'em. They calls me 'The Godfather.' I'm not puttin' no roses on me. I just been a guy. And I kept my mouth shut through the years. But guys come to me for their knowledge. I'm their daddy.

"They come to me with the pimpin' problem. They want to pimp. I say, 'Well, how many kids you got?' 'I got three.' 'Well, why don't you get a job? You gonna pimp with three kids?' I talks to 'em. Later I've had guys come to me, say, 'Cuz, I got a job like you tole me. And I'm not kiddin' you, I can go home, go to bed, get up and go to work, and not worry. I feels much better.'

"Now, others say, 'Cuz, I'm gonna have to try thievin'.' I say, 'If you be a thief, be a good one. Be somebody. Take off somethin' without hurtin' anybody.'

"Mostly I tell 'em to stay clear the dope. It's the worst thing in the world. That go for all white kids, all black kids, all kids. This narcotics gonna ruin this country without a bullet being shot from another country. Mothers and fathers, sisters and brothers, every mother-fucker better get on this case.

"I been so close to it. I seen kids six years old, five years old, know how to get Mama's towel or needle and dunk the stuff in the cooker. When the kid get to be eight or ten years old, nine times out of ten he gonna try it hisself. 'Cause he watchin' Mama.

"Now, a lot of mamas and pops don't know about it, like in the suburbs. Daughter sittin' up and say, 'I got a bad cold,' and eyes runnin' water, don't want nothin' to eat, she sick, man. Doin' it right under their nose. I see it happenin' all over. I'm tellin' you, this is an eyeball thing. But people don't know what they seein' until it hits 'em right in the face. You go to court and find out your daughter, your son has got a habit. Maxwell Street is still a center for a lot of dope dealin'. But, you know, one of the things I respect Don for is that he won't allow no connectin' in his tavern. He'll throw you out before you can do that."

Don's tavern, though, is the scene of a lot of other things. There are periodic murders, like one not long before Cuz broke his hip, in which one fellow accused another of not paying money owed and shot him cold as the other stood leaning on the jukebox. Cuz sat stiff, watching. ("There was no place for me to go," he said.) "But generally," says Cuz, "it's an all right place. It's not one of them places you're a dead bird no quicker than you hit the door." Since it is in the heart of the market, a lot of people stop by Don's for a drink and to see what's being talked about and what's being sold. Cuz is in the middle of this action.

In recent years he also worked as a clerk for a Japanese import firm and as a sorter in the Post Office, and has had a couple of desk jobs from political patronage. But it is the street where he remains most comfortable.

"I had thoughts of bein' a boxer once, and of bein' a dancer. When I was a boy I went to Jack Johnson's gym on Thirty-first Street. Jack Johnson, the great heavyweight champ. First black world champ. I remember he say, 'If a guy ever knock you down when you in the ring, if the referee start countin', try to raise up and spit on the referee.' Said, 'Referee lose the count. He'll get mad 'cause you spit on him. And it might mean that one second for you to get up.' I thought Jack was nice. In every respect, he was so kind and nice. When I first went there he asked my name. I said, 'Bennie.' 'Bennie, that Benjamin?' I said, 'No, it's Bennie.' 'How you know it ain't Ben?' He said, 'What they call you?' Say, 'Bennie.' He said, 'I'm going to call you Ben.' He was talking to me like that. I got thrilled.

"I seen him spar. He was a big man, over six feet tall. He'd shadowbox, jump a little rope, beat the big bag, and then he'd play with the little bag. Oh, everybody watchin'. We'd be crowded around. Just to see him with the boxin' gloves on, that was enough. Yeah. That's Jack. He'd work that bag. He could play a song on that little bag. 'Nearer My God to Thee.' That's right. That's a Christian song. And that's what he played on that little bag. So you know he was whuppin' it nice.

"Well, I liked boxin'. But I never followed it up. The other thing, I was a professional dancer. I danced in shows. But when I got into these jams, I quit. I had two opportunities in life, to be a nice fighter or to be a nice dancer. I could have made it in either one. But something like this must be in the makings from the gods of fate: 'I educated you for this and thus you do.' Something keeps telling me this. I've asked myself a thousand times, 'Where shall I go from here?' So I have but one alternative and that's this. It's to go which way the gods of fate lead me. I can make no destination for myself."

Don't you have anything to do with your destination?

"To tell the truth, I am bewildered by this. What happened to me was something I cannot understand. What drove me into this thing of going to jail? But I wanted to make dough. I wanted to get over, and I thought that narco was the quickest way. I liked it instead of breakin' in somebody's house or stickin' up somebody. But once I got my records, it done made things so tough for me when I wanted to keep honest.

"I learn when I grow old that what ain't for you, ain't for you. You could move a mountain to try to make it so, but it won't. So it wasn't for me to be a fighter or a dancer. And I still wonder, 'There musta been somethin' else for me. What could the "else" be?'

"But number one, you know what I'd like to know? I'd like to know who is operatin' this action? That's what give me a little concentration. Who is operatin' this action?

"But I'm gonna get over. I ain't worried about gettin' over. I'll make it. There's no doubt about me makin' it."

In Cuz's apartment, one may sense this feeling of optimism. In the morning, the place is dark and old. He sits at the kitchen table, a naked light bulb dangling from the ceiling. There is a bottle of vodka, emptied, on the table, and some leftover scrawny chicken wings in a plate. But there is also some old Christmas tinsel on the walls. And between the old stove and refrigerator are a number of photographs ripped out from newspapers and magazines and taped to the peeling wallpaper. One photo is of Jacqueline Kennedy, who Cuz describes as "a royal lady." Another is of Jackie Robinson. The photograph shows Robinson, the first black baseball player in the Major Leagues, looking drawn, in a business suit. He is heavy in this picture and white-haired at age fifty-three, a few months before his death. In the photograph, Robinson is smiling.

Cuz said, "Every morning when I comes into the kitchen, I says to the photograph of Jackie Robinson, 'Good mornin', Jackie, you made a million of us clap.'

"At the end, he was so blind from diabetes that he couldn't even see the baseball to put his autograph on it. It was so sad. He lived a real life. It's a block-and-tackle world, and Jackie fought the most terriblest fight. They tells the story of one day in St. Louis Jackie come up to bat and they had thrown a black cat on home plate to hurt him. Well, he looks at the cat. Then he goes back to the milkman in the dugout and now he got a bowl of milk and puts it down at home plate. When the cat was finished sappin' it up, Jackie dusted off home plate and hit the mother-fuckin' ball over the mother-fuckin' fence. And that made the rest of that bullshit dead."

# HOUND DOG TAYLOR

—Last Christmas, stately Philharmonic Hall
in New York City surrendered to [the] rocking graces of Hound Dog Taylor and his
House Rockers trio. "Yeah, we had a ball,"
said the Dog. "Look here, you know, out in
the audience, about eight hundred peoples
on the first floor. Second balcony, you got
the same thing. And the third . . . you know
they got *seven?* Philharmonic Hall, man, and
when I quit, let me tell you, [them floors] was
comin' down. And I'm thinkin', maybe these
people didn't like it, you know, maybe they
raisin' hell on account of they hate this shit. I
went back out there, played half a number,
and [they] started jumpin' again. Boy, we laid
them sons of bitches in the aisles."

*ROLLING STONE*
*September 12, 1974*

———————◆———————

Hound Dog Taylor began playing his bottleneck blues guitar
(with its "Mississippi wompa-domp domp choking sound") on
Maxwell Street when he first arrived in Chicago from Natchez,
Mississippi, in 1940, at age twenty-three.

"You used to get out on Maxwell on a Sunday morning and
pick you out a good spot, babe. Dammit, we'd make more money
than I ever looked at. Sometimes a hundred dollars, a hundred

twenty dollars. Put you out a tub, you know, and put a pasteboard in there, like a newspaper? . . . When somebody throw a quarter or a nickel in there, can't nobody hear it. Otherwise, somebody come by, take the tub and cut out. . . .

"We were all down there. Muddy Waters was down there. . . . Howlin' Wolf was down there. . . . Little Walter was down there. . . . I'm over there. . . . And Jimmy Rogers, too. We were all in Jewtown. I'm tellin' you, Jewtown was jumpin' like a champ, jumpin' like mad on Sunday morning. And I had the biggest crowd there was in Jewtown. All them cats would beat me playin', but I, you know, put on a pretty good show.

"I had a mike, amp, everything like they do in a hall or nightclub. And I went to actin' the fool, movin' around, jumpin' up. When you stand up straight and just play, don't do nothin' but just stand there and with a frown on your face, well, maybe they go for the music all right, but it ain't like a cat always grinnin' and actin' fool. I played with another guitar player—can't remember his name, now. They done threw him out a window and killed him. Well, I'd sit on his lap, he'd sit on my lap, or he'd hoist up and sit on my shoulders. It was crowded on the street and people could see him for long way 'round. It was like a sign.

"We'd get there at about eight in the morning, set up, and then play through till like four in the afternoon. Never eat nothin' 'cept some chicken in the bottle. Was rainin' or cold so many times. But we was always there, man."

I visited Hound Dog Taylor in the third-floor Chicago South Side apartment he shared with his common-law wife, Freddie, and their three sons. Their stone building stands next to a burned-out apartment building. The window of the entrance at 5828 South Calumet, Hound Dog's building, is broken.

The apartment has six rooms, and their hallway is covered with photographs of Hound Dog playing at various nightclubs, and his two album covers, *Hound Dog Taylor and the House Rockers,* and *Natural Boogie.* The latter cover is particularly striking in that it depicts Hound Dog, seated on a simple chair, rearing back with one leg up, guitar shaft pointed up and out like a rifle, and a huge toothy grin caught in eternal mirth.

It was now 11 A.M., and he had not been up very long. He sat in rumpled white T-shirt and pants, an amber amulet hanging from his neck. He sipped from a glass that held some of the contents of the Seagram's V.O. bottle on the table before him. His voice is rather guttural, and he reminds one of a thin Louie Armstrong. His legs are quite bony and his pointy black laced shoes are size 13A. Rhythm and blues plays on the stereo to his right. He sits on a sunken greenish couch. Behind him, there is a jagged hole in the red and white wallpaper. On the wall is a sign, "Peace Be In Our House." There are pictures of Lincoln and John Kennedy.

He was born in Natchez and raised in a shack ("You could see through the roof") in Greenwood, Mississippi. His father left home before he was born. He remembers he was an undisciplined boy and refused to go to school. He began working at age nine in the fields picking cotton beside his grandmother, who had been a slave, and remembers the music that was sung by the laborers.

"Cats just be hollerin' and singin'," said Taylor. "Some of 'em hollerin' the blues, some of 'em hollerin' church songs. And they be workin'. And I just stand there and look at 'em, damn fools I thought. They be out in the sun from dawn to dark, choppin', bendin', haulin'. Only rest you get is when the bell ring at noon, then you take your sack off your shoulder or put down your saw or ax, get your little bucket you done brought from home, and sit and eat your salt pork or molasses, then go back at one. All for seventy-five cents for the whole entire day. And while we workin', I look over there and see the bossman sittin' up on that horse, you know. Up under the shade tree, sittin' up on that horse, legs crossed, smokin'. And I said, 'You son of a bitch, you. You got it now, but goddamn it. . . .' I said, 'one of these days when I get grown, he ain't gonna be sittin' up over me. One of these days I'm gonna get outta this town.'

"And if a cat just standin' 'round, talkin' a little too long, 'Hey, Nigger!' "

Hound Dog said that on the weekends, he'd go into town and cut up. "Man, I'd cuss and play my guitar up and down the street."

He had purchased a guitar at a Sears store after being taken there by a local blues singer, Blind Jesse. He took to the instrument immediately, he said. It was pleasant escape from a harsh life. He says he remembers hiding on the wood floor of his shack when Ku Klux Klansmen tramped past on the gravel road in front. He remembers peeking out the window and looking at the shoes of the white-sheeted, white-hooded men. "You pay attention to their shoes, then you see the shoes in town or wherever, and you know who it was," said Taylor. He remembers one day after such a harrowing night when, hunting rabbit in the nearby woods, he came across a black man he knew dangling by rope from a tree. "I thought, 'Lord have mercy. . . . I wish I was big enough to—Well, that gonna happen to me one day. But one thing about it, I won't be the only one dead. . . .'" At about the same time he purchased his guitar, in 1935, he also got hold of a .45 pistol. "I was a young man," he said, "and I was crazy." One day in 1940 the bossman's "old lady" made an overture to him. He said he sneaked around and "laid up with her" and then he was found out. The bossman came looking for him with a rifle. "I figured I'd better get the hell outta there," said Hound Dog. He had twenty-four dollars and took the bus to Chicago, where he had a sister.

"I'd heard about Jewtown and went to see it for the shoppin'. You meet all your friends there from the South. You go over there when it's warm and just stand around on the corner. And you'll see 'em walkin' by. I used to say, 'Hey, how you doin', man? I know you from so and so place.' 'Yeah, yeah, yeah, man.' You know, have a conversation. And then me and him be standin' there talkin' and here come somebody else he know, and I know 'em, too. 'Man, lookee there so and so.' Yeah. Ain't nobody down South I know now. All them cats is split. Goin' to New York or Boston or Detroit or Chicago."

But from the time he came to Chicago in 1940 until 1957, Taylor did not play on Maxwell Street. He just "jammed around," at home and with friends. He had been assembling wooden cabinets for television sets, when he was laid off. "Well, jobs was scarce. And I had no education. Hell, they started a thing, you had to have education to be on a garbage truck. The only thing I know how to do is go get me a guitar and give it some licks. A friend named Willie say, 'Let's go to Jewtown.' He tell me, 'Man, you make more money in Jewtown than you can make on your job.'

"So Maxwell Street was the start for me. And people come over to me and listen and say, 'Why don't you come over to my club and blah blah.' Okay. I went first to a little spot at South Water Street Market, near Maxwell.

"First one, I get eight dollars for the night. Then we'd sneak around and be in a place where we hear they pay more money. 'Hey, man, can we play a piece.' Then we get that job 'cause people say, 'Hey, can you play another one?'

"Then I started goin' on the road with my trio, with Brewer Phillips and Ted Harvey—the House Rockers. We started playin' across the country in colleges. The kids, they don't want no more of that old stuff, 'The Yellow Rose of Texas' and all. Everybody wantin' hard rock or bop or blues or rock 'n' roll or boogie woogie. They go for it like hot cakes. It's real nice. You see the people all out there and appreciatin' you, and you appreciatin' them. But man, when you get through, all the whistlin' and clappin' and stompin'. Make you feel good.

"When we was in Philharmonic Hall, I remember Ted was scared. I said, 'Man, play your drums and don't worry about it. You ain't playin' with no wildcats. You playin' with human beings. Don't be scared. You ain't gonna get ate up, man.'

"The only time I got scared was overseas. It was in Holland someplace. After we play we get in a bus and split. But they lined up out there, the peoples. They got their autograph books in their hands. Paper. Matchbook, anything. Ooooo, man. And when you come outta there and get on that bus and the cats try to fasten that door and there be hands with books comin' through, you can't close the door. And they be hollerin', man, and bangin' on the window and kickin' on that bus till we get away."

Hound Dog said he got the nickname because of his deep interest in women. "Went after 'em like a hound," he said. And indeed much of his music relates to the fickleness of women. But the sounds of his music are what is called "good times blues."

Except for the few nationally renowned blues singers, like B. B. King and Muddy Waters, it is necessary for those a notch below in fame to work other jobs. Hound Dog continued to pick up extra cash to help support his family by doing woodworking during the day and playing nights. "It sure takes a lot out of you, but if you want to play the blues, don't mess around," he said. "It don't matter if you got one finger on each hand, you can manage."

He was managing well enough that he owned four cars, a sports car, a station wagon, a Pontiac. He also has a white Cadillac. ("That's my bad motor scooter.") "You don't get no good deal on trade-ins no more," he said. "So when you buy a new car you might as well keep the other cars you got."

In an interview in 1970 in the magazine, *Living Blues*, Hound Dog said, "I'm gettin' better jobs now and more of 'em, but I don't know if I can make it from here. I'm gettin' to be an old man, 55 now, and from here I just don't know, man. If I'd had someone to handle me right and made me a few more records, I could have got somewhere. But from here, man . . . I just don't know."

He was asked if he meant he was quitting.

"No sir! I'll be jammin' till the day I die!"

On Thursday, December 17, 1975, the New York *Times* reported that the blues singer and musician Theodore Roosevelt "Hound Dog" Taylor, "whose 'bottleneck' style influenced many rock musicians," had died the day before in Chicago. He died from cancer of the lungs.

# ARVELLA GRAY

Arvella Gray, sixty-nine, is a black sidewalk troubadour who favors bright suspenders. His black shoes are glossy and his sport jacket is shiny, though not threadbare. In winter he thrums his all-weather metal guitar wearing gloves. He had cut one album, called *The Singing Drifter: Blind Arvella Gray.* He was blinded when shot in the face as a young man.

He sings and plays on Maxwell Street and on Halsted Street every Sunday and often during the week as well. He has been there for forty-five years. The song he plays more than any other is "John Henry." His voice is a reflection of his being, husky but mellow; a lilt may be heard even in his most low-down blues. He wears no glasses, and his eyes have a white, faraway mystic quality. His cane is tucked in his belt. His cup is pinned to his jacket so nobody can run off with it. He turned seventy in 1976. He also plays in coffee shops around the city and performs at colleges, including Purdue and Illinois and Bowling Green.

We sat in the living room of his three-room apartment on the South Side of Chicago. A sophisticated stereo is set up. He had his several guitars nearby. When he crossed his legs, his white woolen socks seemed as white as his eyes.

"I was not blind when I first came to Maxwell Street," he said. "It was 1923 in July. It was excitin' to be around there. You'd get the whole of what you call middle class and upper class on holidays and Sundays. And of course the poor peoples was there. All a-crowdin' in. People everywhere. You never seen so many people. The stores was decorated very nice. There was up the street the musicians with guitars and tubs and Jew's harps and harmonicas. There was sideshows. More like a carnival place. Like a dream. Very colorful. I'd get up on a building and look around, look all four ways. I'm glad I could see then to see the sight. I had never seen nothin' like it.

"Maxwell Street stayed open all night. They had a different group of people there in them days. They hadn't learned to snatch, steal, and all that. If a bum or hobo did come by, he'd take maybe a shirt or a suit, just what he could use himself. He didn't go out and peddle it. I don't know if they was stupid in them days or not, but that's that way they operated."

Arvella Gray was born in Temple, Texas, on January 28, 1906. He began working at age four, and remembers working in darkness.

"I was a real small kid, and we didn't have no electric light and stuff in them days. My peoples said, 'Come in and go to bed. If you don't, the devil gonna get you.' Now, sometimes be stars shinin' and sometimes be clouds, but it be dark. And we'd go in and go to bed and, the next morning at four it's still dark. They tell you, 'Get up and go get the cattles and drive 'em up so they can be fed and be milked.' And what puzzled me, if the devil was out there the first part of the night, was it he got tired of waitin' on me and went to sleep or somethin' or other? It was kinda confusin'. And then when you had to go through them places, when the dew was on them vines and cool like that, and then the vines strike you across the face, and you're feelin' your way through there, and I'd be glad to get them cows or horses so I could get 'em by the tail and tell 'em, 'Git up and git on back to the barn.' 'Cause I'd hold 'em good by the tail and some kind of way they'd find their way back and I'd be stumbling along there, holdin' on to the tail in the dark.

"Sometimes you'd step on a cold snake or like that. And sometimes a rabbit would get scared and jump up and that would scare you. I didn't know whether the devil comin' after me or whether he's tryin' to run from me. But I know it would send shivers all over me. I can just feel it now.

"I remember I had to gather eggs, too. I mostly had to follow the chickens around, especially in the springtime after it got warm enough for the snakes to come out because the snakes would swallow chicks and suck the eggs. Well, I'd have to try to beat the snake to the egg. And then I had to drive the chickens to the proper roostin' place for the night. So that means I had a job all day.

"We had rattlesnakes—copperheads, mostly—and we just had a gang of snakes. When you're growing up with them things, you know how to handle 'em. I just had to stay out of the way from them strikin' at me when they coiled up. But I knowed how to do that, even at that age.

"They'd be coilin' up and havin' their head right in the middle of the coil, and you know he's fixin' to spring at you. And then you got to think about how far you can jump. We used to pick 'em up by the tail and we'd put a fork over the head to hold 'em and then take and pop it like you would a whip and pop the head and it would come right of.

"One time I got in a hassle with what they call a black snake or coachwhip. It was the spring of the year. And I'm comin' along this road and I'm drivin' oxen then. I was haulin' logs, and I was 'bout seven or eight. I see these snakes all coiled up together. Of course, I didn't know what they was doin'. I know now 'cause I figured it out later after I got older. But they was matin' in the springtime. I gets down there and I takes and throws some rocks at them to break 'em up. And they run up a little sapling tree. So then instead of me going on about my business, I got to still throw rocks at 'em and knock 'em down. When the rocks hit the tree, they just turned around and come down and come after me. And they was comin' like mad after me! And so then by me catchin' up with this wagon, the back end of it, the oxen was steady goin', I jumped up and into the seat. These snakes, they wrapped around a wagon wheel, still determined to get me, and the wagon wheel went over and kinda crushed 'em. But I didn't fool with no more snakes that spring. You better believe it."

Another indelible memory from his childhood was the lynchings.

"Now, you seen some of them people who are not no violent type, but they just stare at you—just a little bit mentally deformed. This fellow in Temple, Texas, went around there for years, but he'd look like he just starin' at you and things like that. And the white men one day say he lookin' at the white woman. Which I guess he was, but not in any lust way. They was just wantin' to hang somebody anyway. So at that time they say, 'Niggers, come to the square, we're goin' to hang this guy cause he lookin' at the woman.'

"They had us all to come there. Now, all the colored peoples standing there, about a hundred of us, and they hung him to this oak tree. Put him up there and hanged him till he's dead. But now in the meantime all the young kids like me, we're holdin' on to our parents. And our parents was cryin' and moanin'. They had some of the queerest moanin' you ever wanted to hear. Somethin' like that just send shivers over you, the moanin'.

"And so anyway they said, 'I'm gonna show you niggers what happens to you if you look at white women.' And the comical part of it—it wasn't comical to the people and it wasn't comical to the one who was hung either—but at the time they cut the rope and let the body fall to the ground. Now this banker, the president of the bank or whatever, he gets his knife outta his hip pocket and bends over the body and take the guy by the ear and says, 'Way you tell a nigger's dead, you cut his ears off and if he don't bleed, he dead. But if it bleed, he still alive.'

"And he bends over, and he was a show-off. And he lookin' all around. And he go to cut the guy's ear off. You know, they take the ears and joints of the fingers and they put it in alcohol for souvenirs. And put it on the mantle piece over the fireplace and show the colored people who work there, and say, 'This comes from that nigger that got uppity.' So when the banker bends over, lookin' all around, takes the ear—he falls dead over the body. At the time, the people didn't say he had a heart attack. That's the comical part. They said, 'God done struck that man dead.' The black folks said that. The white people heard the colored people with all this kind of strange moanin' and they got superstitious. Then they made the black men take the two bodies and bury 'em because they said, 'If we take 'em, we're going to have bad luck.' Yackkedy-yak like that. So then the white people got so they didn't want to lynch the black people in that town no more. They didn't mind shootin' 'em. But they was through hangin' 'em.

"Sure, I saw the shootings and the beatings. When they used to tie you 'cross the barrel. The hands and the feet, just your naked backside up there, and they'd beat you until the blood come outta you with them rawhides and whip ropes and things. And then they'd take and put the salt and stuff on you which burned like hell. Oh, and the screamin' you'd hear.

"I never had that happen to me. My people taught me to do what the white person say and don't look after white women. Which I wasn't old enough. I wasn't payin' no attention to no girls and things like that.

"But one of the reasons I didn't pay no attention, I didn't go to school to learn anything. White people say no reason for nigger boy to get schoolin'. So I was workin' in the fields. When I wasn't with the animals and chickens, I was pickin' cotton, and that's where I first heard singin'. They'd sing like . . . 'We're gonna pick more cotton/Than a gin can gin.'

"When I was thirteen or fourteen, my mother died. I went to live with my father in Hugo, Oklahoma. I was haulin' these logs that weighed about one hundred pounds each, and my shoulders would get raw from that. Now, my father been gone so long from Texas, he like a stranger to me. And I looked him up 'cause I was tryin' to look for somebody to just give me a kind word. You know, to take the place of Mother. He got a second wife now and two daughters and so I was just like a outsider. So that's what made me desperate to leave.

"One day the circus come to town, Ringling Brothers Circus. I wanted to go with the circus when it left. But me bein' skinny and young, the foreman didn't want me to go 'cause if I run off with the circus, he believes my people'll be comin' after me and probably want to give him some trouble. So he said he didn't want me.

"But when they takin' the tent down and after they load 'em up on the train to travel to the next town, I hitch on. I figured the only place the trainmaster wouldn't find me was I'd get up under the wagon where they had the canvas pulled down over the lion's cage. And I got up under that. The lions was in there, in the cage. And I'm up under there between them two back wheels because I could ride on that coupling up under there. But all night, the lion, he just kept pawin' at me. And the trainmaster come along there and hit his stick upside the bars and say, 'Keep quiet in there' to the lion. . . . So when I got to the next town, I was out helpin' put up the big top and the foreman come along and he said, 'I thought I told you not to come.' So I just ignored him and kept working. So then he seen I was determined to go with the circus and so then he let me slide. I worked hard and I did what the mens did. I worked like nobody's business.

"I traveled from town to town. After I put up the tent then I would walk all over the town, observin' different things, and I didn't know I was gettin' conditioned for to be blind 'cause I didn't have that on my mind. But after I lost my sight, I found out any place I been, I can go back and get around in.

"The circus eventually put up out in South Chicago. And I'm walkin' around the area. I met this white man—Greek or Italian. He was a tall fellow and by me bein' little and skinny he looked huge to me. But he didn't smile or nothin'. He say, 'Hey, boy.' I say, 'Yes, sir.' He say, 'You want a job?' I say, 'Yes, sir.' He say, 'Come with me.'

"At this time, the circus isn't payin' me. Just give me food. So I'm going to get money. This would change things for me. I started washin' dishes. I work twelve hours a day for eight dollars. So I kept that job as long as I could. But then a problem was created. I was from the South. And livin' like I was down there, you know, white people superior over black peoples, and I seen the lynchin' and everything, and I had no schoolin, no learnin', and I couldn't talk plain, talked like we done in the South—so while I was workin' in the restaurant, they had three waitresses. I think they turned out to be Polish. I was peelin' potatoes in the kitchen and moppin' the floors and things. But these waitresses when they wasn't busy, they'd come in the kitchen where I was. And they'd put me in the corner. And they'd come up there to me and then they started talkin'. And they'd be gigglin', but they'd be havin' fun. So when they started talkin' to me, these white women, and started gettin' close to me, I started breakin' out in big drops of sweat. Because this big Greek fellow, he looked mean in the first place.

"So now these girls are gettin' me up there and so I'd have to stop peelin' potatoes because I'm tryin' to figure out how to get outta the way of 'em, but when they come on both sides of you, you ain't got too much room. They put their arms around me and kiss me on my cheeks and then I'd have all kind of expression and

I'd break out sweatin'. It'd start rainin'. I'd be so frightened. It wasn't exciting to me at all, because I didn't want to get hung. See, once you ever seen one of them hangings, like I did, well, you know there was no fun in it at all. So I quit workin' there.

"I met another fellow who was a hobo, who had friends living around Maxwell Street. It was on Miller Street, just behind the Maxwell Street police station. And I eventually got a job helpin' the produce people. That's when Maxwell Street went all the way down to Jefferson Street. So you could always pick up a quarter or fifteen cents helpin' them unload or load. And then you could get hot dogs for a nickel apiece. And when you got to be common like I was around there, then you got a lot of hot dogs for nothin'. So now Maxwell Street put me in the mind of like the carnival and circus I had been with, especially in the evening times when the lights come on, and there used to be two or three picture shows along there and they was ten cents, more or less, and you could stay all night and we hobos, we bums, we didn't sleep on boxcars, we slept in them shows because they had washrooms in there, water and everything.

"But I still itched for travel. And I got all around. I was workin' as a gandy dancer on a railroad in Peoria in 1930. I was puttin' down double tracks and buildin' shoulders and things. And meantime, I'm livin' with a woman. Now a friend come to me one day and says, 'Listen, that LaMar fellow, you know, the night watchman out on them steam shovels, he layin' up there in the house with your woman in the daytime.' So I went to him and told him, 'LaMar, stay away from the house when I'm not there and don't be layin' up in there with my woman.'

He said, 'You ain't married to her, and I got as much right as you have.'

"I say, 'LaMar, if you want the woman, you get her and get another place for her and take her.'

"LaMar say, 'I don't want the responsibility. I just wanna lay up with the woman.'

"I say, 'You can't do that.' I told him I'd give him a whuppin' if he don't stop. And I had already whupped some peoples on the job. One of 'em happened to be the foreman; he was like you call a slave driver. He just hollered and cussed, 'Hurry up! Hurry up!'

And I was in the sun, and it burned down. I stopped and went over and told him to stop. And we got into it.

"So then LaMar told me, 'I will shoot you, but I won't fight you.' It was payday, on September thirteenth. I had been downtown gamblin'. I got off the train and it was about midnight. It was about a four- or five-minute walk to my house. I stepped up on the porch. And I tried the door. But it had a bolt. I knocked and I said, 'Open the door.' And this Lisa, she said, 'Just a minute.'

"Well, I thought she was gettin' up to open the door. And I ain't thinkin'. I had taken a cigarette in my mouth and struck a match and a shotgun blast came through the glass window of the door. I didn't see him at all because the green shade was pulled down. Now at first I didn't feel no pain. It was about two or three seconds before blood started runnin'. And so I said, 'What the hell is going on?' And LaMar says, 'Get away from that door.' And about that time I discovered my finger was gone. And then it commenced to bleeding. And I said, 'What the hell? You done shot half my hand off.' Then I got myself together and walked a block and a half to the police station. And I'm mad because I didn't even get a chance to defend myself.

"I done bled until I was unconscious. And then the next thing I know, I was in a hospital. They told me LaMar still in the house at eight the next morning because he scared he missed me and that I was waitin' on the outside with my .38.

"So I lost the index finger and middle finger of my right hand. And the shots knocked my eyes out. I still got a bunch of lead pellets in the bridge of my nose and things like that. They didn't penetrate my skull but they did penetrate my nose. I'd wake up and some of 'em would be droppin' outta my nose, and some of 'em worked out my face and went through my jaw.

"After the trial, when LaMar got sent to jail, I got sent to a hospital in Kankakee. It was a combination old folks' home and insane asylum. See, I don't have no people. My sisters scattered all over and I don't know where. So they said, 'This is your home until you die.' Now, I'm twenty-four years old, and I got a problem. I sure enough had a problem. So now I got to think of somethin'. I thought of one aunt who lived in Miami. They told me, 'If you could get in touch with any relative, we could sign you out. And that's the onliest way you be able to leave here. Otherwise, you're here.' I had them write my aunt in Miami. And I love my aunt today. 'Course she dead now, but I really loved her 'cause she wrote back.

"In her letter—and they read it to me—well, my bones and everything turned to jelly and they had to sit me down 'cause it was a shock to me. The letter said, 'Due to the fact I got five kids of my own and my nephew, he's blind, keep the boy in there 'cause I ain't going to be leadin' him 'round to the bathroom and feedin' him and a-waitin' on him hand and foot 'cause I got my own five kids.' And that's when I was shocked. Now I know I'm in a world of trouble. I can't get away."

And you say you love your aunt to this day?

"I loved her 'cause what she did—'cause perhaps if she hadda signed me out, I probably been a helpless person right today. I'd got in a condition like that. She didn't sign me out and that's what makes it much better. That made me have spunk enough to get up on my own. 'Cause a lot of blind people right now, and they don't do nothin' unless somebody's leadin' 'em and everything. And I do everything myself. Even domestic work around here. My cookin'. I take movies, home movies. I take 'em even if I do cut the heads off. I got a whole lot of film."

But if you can't see what you're taking, how can you shoot movies?

"Because if you sit down and get bored and don't be active, I imagine you could get stiff and die and then get to reminiscing and such. You just go outta your cotton-pickin' mind. So I take movies in the house, I take 'em swimmin', I take 'em out on Maxwell Street.

"But so now my aunt turned me down. So one day I'm eavesdroppin' on the supervisor, and I hear he and his girl friend are goin' to town. I got tight with the supervisor. He tells me, well, if I get hurt on the outside, the state could be sued. But I plead. Okay. Well, in town, they left me for a while. Now, I got this hoe, like a walkin' stick. And I trained myself in the institution to get around. And I takes off. I hops a train, goes to Peoria. Gets in a big gamblin' game, right near where I was shot. So I said, 'Here I am.' And I put my hat in the middle of the table and start to gamble. And I was pretendin' I was happy. But I wasn't happy. I was just about to go out of my mind from bein' blind and the doctors done told me I'm going to be blind the rest of my life. But in the gamblin' game, I get lucky. I been lucky all my life. And I win $125.

"Now, I'm scared there's an alarm for me from the institution. So I hop the next train and eventually I make it back to Chicago. I look up some friends of old friends of mine on Forty-eighth Street. I get in a rooming house. The next day I go on the street. And I'm sittin' flat down, Indian style, on the sidewalk, and this other blind fellow bumped into me and tripped over me.

"And he asked me what I was doin' sittin' there. I told him I'm blind. What the heck. We started talkin'. He took me to a moonshine joint and we loaded up. I stayed with him a few days and then he carried me out and showed me how to hustle. I had just a cup 'cause I wasn't even able to buy any pencils. I think I made thirty-five cents the first day. Now, he was a pro hustler. And he come back and said he made three dollars. Now this is during the Depression. There's not a whole lot of money around, you know.

"So then I thought about Maxwell Street and then I went to goin' back to Maxwell Street. But I was kind of timid. I didn't want to bump into stands and have people bawlin' me out. So I'd mostly get over on one place on Maxwell Street, until later on in life I started movin' around. I was talkin' to some of the hot-dog stands and askin' didn't they remember me? I told 'em I was one of the old-time.

"I had another problem. That was learnin' how to play the guitar. I didn't want to just stand on the street corner with a cup and pencils. 'Cause it was slow hustlin', and then I was young and I was embarrassed. I just felt uncomfortable. But I always liked music and so I got a guitar at a pawnshop, even though I never had played one before. And a blind fellow I met taught me how to play, even with my couple fingers missin'. And I learned and been playin' around Maxwell Street ever since.

"Generally they don't allow street singers in certain places in Chicago. But they leave me on Maxwell Street. See, I'm one of the old-time. The police is very nice to me 'cause a lot of these policemen used to be children what used to come around me.

"But years ago it was bad. In 1939 I remember I was locked up thirteen times for singing on the street. I was locked up when I tried to sing in the Loop. They say the reason they didn't want me down there is because then these institutions would bring people out there in wheelchairs and clutter up the street with all kind of handicap.

"I even got locked up once on Maxwell Street. But now the police protect me, help keep people from rippin' me off so much. I had people attempt to steal, that go in my pocket. Like one time, they come along and hit my cup under the bottom and knocked my money out. Then they scooped it up and went. But now I pretty well keep the cups clean. But by forty-five years bein' blind and out there scufflin', well, you know, I done been held up. One time they got fifteen cents and the other time they took ninety-five cents.

"I knows who the second stick-up people was. That was Tommy and Sanford. They was needle pushers. And I run into them in a restaurant and I told 'em. 'Hey, you bums, you. If you ever try that again, I'm gonna cut your ears off.'

"I would have, too. I don't feel handicapped in no way. I feel like this, we all can't be the same. But even if we can see or not see, we all gonna have our share of problems. It's just a matter of whether you can handle it or not. If you have a problem and I have a problem and we wrote 'em out on a piece of paper and put it on the table and you read mine and I read yours, I'd say, 'I'm gonna take mine back because you know how to handle your problem. And I know how to cope with mine.'

"I get money from the State to live on, and I'm a licensed musician with the Musician's Union. And I play all around, and I know I can always pick up a good enough buck playin' on Maxwell Street.

"And I built me up quite a prestige. I can get credit from anybody. I got my first credit at Lyon and Healy music store in 1939. I bought my steel guitar from them. So my life has been very nice to me.

"I been happy all my life because I never was geared to be

Maxwell Street at the end of its heyday. . . .
(Photos courtesy of Chicago Historical Society, City of Chicago,
Department of Urban Renewal, and Chicago *Daily News*)

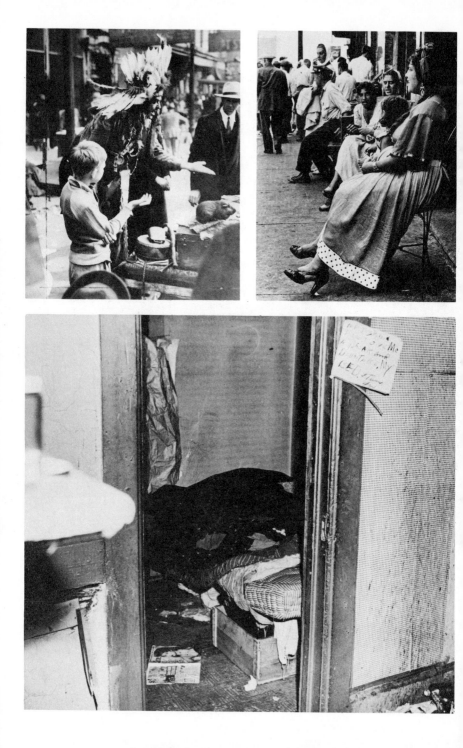

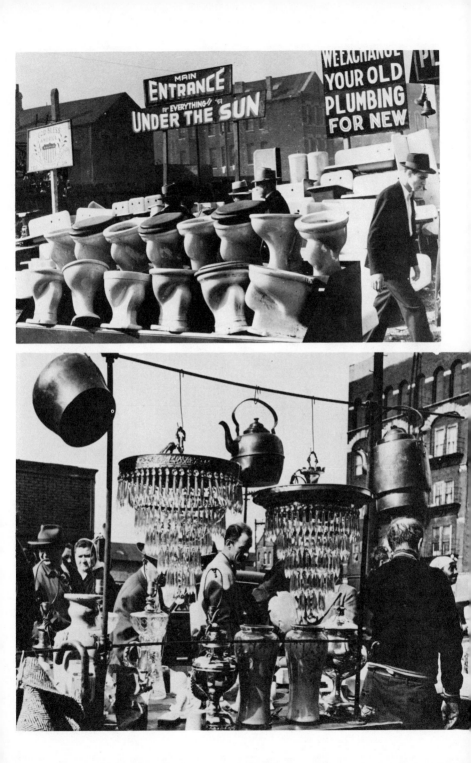

Bennie "Cuz" Maurice in his flat at 707 Maxwell. (Walter Iooss, Jr.)

Sheldon and Barrel Pinsker. (Walter Iooss, Jr.)

Theodore Roosevelt "Hound Dog" Taylor. (Photo by Peter Amft; courtesy of Bruce Iglauer)

*Below:* "Blind" Arvella Gray. (Photo by Jim O'Neal)

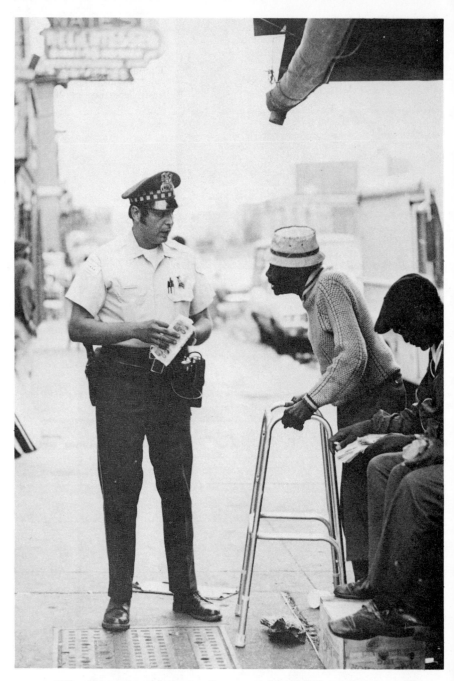

Mike Chiappetta, night-beat policeman on Maxwell Street, known as "the shamus of Maxwell Street," speaking to Bennie "Cuz" Maurice. (Courtesy of Mike Chiappetta)

Rich Mrozek, left, and John Corcoran. Maxwell Street policeman in plain-clothes on a Sunday. (Walter Iooss, Jr.)

Maxwell Street police station house.

*Left:* Mrs. Channa Friedman Carl, about 1926, at age twenty. (Courtesy of Morris Carl) *Right:* Morris Carl, in about 1930, at age twenty-six. Then a Maxwell Street store owner. (Courtesy of Morris Carl)

Howard Carl, lower left, All-American guard on nationally ranked De Paul University basketball team, 1960. Carl poses with coach Ray Meyer and rest of starting team. (*Sports Illustrated*)

Morris Miller selling baseball gloves in Kelly's Sporting Goods at 729 Maxwell, 1976. (Walter Iooss, Jr.)

Nate Duncan, owner of Nate's Kosher Delicatessen, 807 Maxwell, 1976.

*Below:* View of Nate's from outside the window. Maxwell Street buildings are reflected in the window, 1976. (Walter Iooss, Jr.)

Irv Gordon, Maxwell Street's last market master, in his "office" at a table in Nate's Delicatessen. (Walter Iooss, Jr.)

Jimmy Stefanovic seated beside bushels of onions in backroom of his hot-dog stand at Maxwell and Halsted. (Walter Iooss, Jr.)

Getting into his chauffeur-driven limousine is Jimmy Stefanovic, owner of the nearby hot-dog stand on Maxwell and Halsted. Eddie Thomas, a security guard in the area, opens car door for the frankfurter baron, 1976. (Walter Iooss, Jr.)

Andy Jones and dog, on Maxwell Street. (Courtesy of Mike Chiappetta)

Maxwell Street, end of day. Sunday, 1976. (Walter Iooss, Jr.)

# THE STREET, 1926

## DOOM HANGS OVER
## MAXWELL STREET

—Progress is again threatening the Maxwell Street Market. This time, it's a land clearance proposal to reduce further the size of Chicago's Old World Bazaar.

Indeed, there are some who are predicting that the market may fade into oblivion before many more seasons pass. Mere mention of this possibility is enough to bring a tear to the eye of a sensitive Chicagoan.

"Why, they might as well tear down the Water Tower, or dry up Buckingham Fountain and turn it into a hot dog stand." That's the sort of lament you hear. We know one man who ranks the market only slightly below the Art Institute and the Chicago Symphony on the scale of civic assets. . . .

CHICAGO *DAILY NEWS*
*December 28, 1962*

# THE STREET, 1965

## IT'S HARD TO FIND A TEAR
## TO SHED FOR MAXWELL STREET

—There has been a constant trickle of tears in some circles because the Maxwell Street Market is slowly slipping towards extinction. . . .

Ah, but the pungent odor in the air, say the stories [of nostalgia]. The outdoor sandwich stands. The fruit mellowing in the sun. The teeming bodies of shoppers in July. What an atmosphere.

Less romantic persons, plodding along on a regular shopping trip, might paraphrase it and say, "It stinks. . . ."

If the Mourners of Maxwell Street really want something to cry about, they can join me in shedding a tear for the countless small neighborhood businessmen—grocers, bakers, gas station operators, druggists, clothing shops, butchers, tailors.

They smiled pretty, didn't twist any arms, put the prices on the merchandise, gave a little friendly credit, knew your name and made a living.

When progress and the Big Operator come after them, each becomes a committee of one to save himself. And they are sinking fast.

CHICAGO *DAILY NEWS*
*January 13, 1965*

# IV

# POTPOURRI

This section deals with people other than Jews and blacks who had to devise some of the most creative and fantastic ways to survive in the great bazaar.

Maxwell Street draws people from the spectrum of humanity. Three current Maxwell Street cops are examples: the Irishman, John Murdock; the Pole, Rich Mrozek; and the Italian, Mike Chiappetta.

Mike worked on Maxwell Street starting at age eleven. He had a movable "snowball" stand on a street corner there. (A snowball is ice with syrup served in a paper cone.) One day a policeman ordered a cherry snowball, took it, and asked the price. Mike said, "Five cents." The cop paid the nickel then ordered the boy to move his stand because it was illegally blocking the sidewalk.

The boy went home to nearby Taylor Street in tears. His father, an Italian immigrant, listened to the story, then berated his son for being so stupid. The following day, the boy returned to Maxwell Street. The cop came by again, asked the price of a cherry snowball. The boy said, "My father told me never to charge a policeman." The cop winked and went on. The stand stayed.

Mike's father had learned from his father the hard lessons of the ruling class and the serfs.

Mike's grandfather was from a small town near Palermo, Sicily, and his hero was a man named Mussolini. Not Benito, but Giuseppe Mussolini, who stole from the rich and gave to the poor —and there was a plethora of poor in Sicily. Mike's grandfather had told Mike how the family was starving in Italy and decided to come to America, "the golden land." The family came to Louisiana, worked in strawberry fields, earned enough to return to Italy, and hoped for a better life there among the olive trees. But little

had improved. So the family decided to return to America and
Chicago, where there were promises by relatives of better jobs.

Mike recalls that until he died, his grandfather was wary of the
ruling class. He used to say, "Mike, never trust a man who wears
a suit." And when someone would ring his doorbell, he'd say, "If
he wants me and he's wearing a suit, I'm not home."

John Murdock's* grandfather came from County Cork in Ire-
land. There was a large family living in a virtual shack. Rarely was
there enough food for the family. They, too, made the trek to
America seeking fuller stomachs.

John's grandfather came to Chicago and, through relatives, got
a job as a policeman. The biggest break of his life, John recalls, is
that he got the "walking post" on the beat outside the Metropole
Hotel—Al Capone's hotel—on Twenty-second and Clark streets.
John's grandfather had the plum job of opening Capone's car
door whenever the gangster came or went. He received twenty
dollars a day from Capone. He was making ninety-six dollars a
month from the police force. John's grandfather passed the walking post on to his son, John's father. The job lost its financial
luster when Capone went to jail for income tax evasion.

Rich Mrozek grew up on Seventeenth and Paulina, in the Polish
neighborhood adjoining Maxwell Street to the southwest. He
remembers coming early to the street with his mother, right after
Mass on Sundays, to get "first-sale" bargains. Get there first, went
the legend, and you get the best price because the merchants are
hungry to "break the ice." When Rich got his first paycheck from
his first job as a kid, he hurried that first Sunday to Maxwell
Street. Early. He bought a leather coat, after the customary haggle. He was very proud of the price he had finagled and very
proud of the coat. He returned home immediately to show the
coat off. He put it on for his family and turned around to model
it. He happened to be standing next to the steamy radiator. The
coat made a crackling sound, and another. The coat slowly began
to melt before their eyes. The leather coat was actually plastic.

Mrozek's grandparents were born in the hill country of Poland,
in a town translated to mean, "Black City." Mrozek says he un-

* John Murdock is a pseudonym by request.

derstands that area is as "primitive" today as when his grand-parents left it.

"They still have dirt floors in their shacks," he said. "Yet my father used to tell me how much he loved Poland, the countryside, the farming areas—and especially the horse he owned. My father, John, was born in America, but moved back to Poland as a child with his mother when she began to yearn for it. She stayed there until she died. But his father remained in America.

"When my father was sixteen, he decided to come back and live with his father in Chicago. My father never got much schooling here, but he kept working different jobs to try to improve himself —stevedore, stockyards worker, punch pressman—in order to send his four kids to Catholic school. He was proud of the fact that he accomplished it.

"My dad always spoke of returning to Poland. But he never did. He used to wear the Highlanders' uniform in parades—it's a woolen shepherd's outfit with a hat that has horses' teeth in it and a single eagle feather sticking out.

"He appreciated America for the opportunities it provided his children, that it would be an easier life for us. But it was never God's country for him. To tell you the truth, I don't think my dad's heart was ever really in America at all."

# JEWTOWN BROWN

Bernard Brown wears a hat, a black hat. It is narrow-brimmed. He calls it "stingy-brimmed." In the days from 1946 to 1960 when he was a plainclothes foot cop around Maxwell Street, he wore a wide-brimmed black hat. But Brown tries to stay with the times, tries not to look too conspicuous. Bad for business. He still wears black suits, black shoes, dark tie, white shirt, dark lines on a lean and pallid face. He could pass for a mortician as easily as he could a policeman, and indeed has probably seen as many stiffs in his line as any undertaker. He was called "Jewtown" Brown because Maxwell Street, where he became a fixture known city-wide, was and is called "Jewtown." Jewtown Brown was also called "Rooftop" Brown because the junkies and dope pushers he pursued would often congregate on rooftops around Maxwell Street and Rooftop Brown would invariably show up there.

Jewtown, or Rooftop, Brown was also known as "Garbage Can" Brown. The dope guys would sometimes hide their junk in and around garbage cans. Brown admits to having hidden behind garbage cans to nab an offender. The drug participants said they never knew when he'd pop out of a garbage can. But he insists he never hid *inside* a garbage can. Jewtown Brown or Rooftop Brown or Garbage Can Brown was also known as "Water Faucet" Brown. He was given that name from a fellow on the street named Woo Woo. He was called Woo Woo because he had big bulging eyes and looked as if he was amazed all the time at what he was seeing, and his eyes, to the person who named him, said, "Woo, woo." Brown was always catching Woo Woo at trying to break into cars. That was the only thing he ever did, said Brown. Brown would arrest Woo Woo three times or more a week for breaking into cars. After one such pinch, Woo Woo made a confession to

Brown as they headed for the station house. Brown recalls: "Woo Woo said to me that time, 'Mr. Brown'—very respectful when he said it, and he looked at me with those big eyes—'Mr. Brown, I'm afraid to turn on the water faucet for fear you'll come out of it.' "

———————

Jewtown Brown, etc., and I met in the rear of a restaurant across from the courthouse on Twenty-sixth and California. He is broad-shouldered but walks a little hunched, like a cat. He is six feet one, weighs about a hundred eighty. The skin of his left eyelid is a little baggy and gives the impression he is squinting. He came in wearing his usual funeral garb.

"In 1946, I was twenty-six and I came out of the service and joined the police force and was assigned to the Maxwell Street Station," he said, in his sober but off-hand manner.

"For a rookie cop, God, the place was colorful! But it was also considered one of the heaviest districts involved with crime and narcotic drug peddling and narcotic drug use. Not so much maybe with the people that inhabited the area, but people came from all sections of the city and many sections of the suburban towns.

"In them days Maxwell Street was mainly a Jewish business district. Blacks lived there, some Mexicans lived there, and you had the Gypsies lived there. All different bands of Gypsies lived there.

"But Fourteenth and Halsted was for a number of years considered the hub of all the narcotic activity in the city. You had an Italian syndicate there, too, and they were like behind the drug thing. I remember at one time there was a tavern there called the New Harlem Tavern, a place for all nationalities, and I helped get an undercover federal agent to make purchases of dope there. Buys, they're called. They bought $150,000 worth in one crack. That was in the year 1954. And they busted out maybe thirty or forty of these syndicate guys and a lot of 'em were eventually machine-gunned to death on the street because the big guys were fearful that they might talk to these federal agencies. And a lot of 'em that were out on bond went in and surrendered voluntarily. They wanted their bonds revoked; they wanted to go into jail for safekeeping.

"Maxwell Street was the center of this activity since it was such an easy place to congregate and to hide because it was so busy, so many people there. It was a booming street in them days. It was an area that they felt safe in to conduct their business.

"A lot of times they felt so safe they'd transact right out in the open. My partner Morgan Gardner and I used to hide behind the stands on Maxwell Street and the dope dealers would be on the other side. As soon as the one handed the dope to the other, we'd jump out and grab 'em.

"Sometimes I'd be alone, hiding behind a stand. Then I'd jump out. Well, one guy would run away but I'd have the other guy cornered. He might get a stand behind you and him, and they'd go one way and you'd be goin' the other way, and you play tag going around the stand. You know, guys figure eventually they'll wear you down. You might be four or five minutes running in between the stands until you either head him off or your partner shows up.

"I was a fast runner. I never lost too many people when I started after 'em. Even today, somebody downtown or someplace will come up to me and say, 'Boy, I'll never forget how fast you could run.'

"I remember one time I chased a fellow for about three blocks. He was much younger than I was and he had a pretty good start, but anyway I finally did catch him. He was heading for the Meadowmoor Dairy. I caught him right in front on Maxwell and Sangamon. A lot of them in those days were great for the switchblade knife. It would flash open and boom! He pulled out a switchblade and he made a slash at me and he cut my topcoat from here, you know, down the sleeve. And then he broke away from me and he ran into the dairy. Evidently he worked there part time. He was a colored fellow. And when he ran into the dairy, he called to a bunch of these guys, 'Help me. This guy's tryin' to rob me.' Well, the next thing I know, I had about nine of them dairy employees on top of me. You know, they were really beltin' me. So finally I broke away from 'em and I pulled a gun out and I backed 'em into the wall. I was so mad I was going to arrest the whole bunch of 'em for interfering with an arrest.

"My partner Morgan was a fast runner, too. He was much older than I was, twelve years older. He was about six feet four and he was real skinny. But he could go like a deer. We went through yards, over fences, across roofs, down streets, up alleys—I'm talkin' about the whole Maxwell Street area. We knew just about every back yard and fence and building and passageway. When I was chasin' somebody, I knew what route I could take to cut him off.

"I remember the time Morgan and I climbed over this big cyclone fence at the house at 1407 South Peoria. It was quite a house for dope. We walked in the yard to the back door and sneaked down and hid behind a big mound of dirt that was next to a garage. Now, this was in the early '50s. There were still a lot of horses on Maxwell Street at that time. A lot of these peddlers had their own horse and wagons and everything. A lot of your colored fellows at that time sold coal over there with the horse and wagon. The garage we hid beside was a stable for those horses. And the rats over there were tremendous. In fact, I don't know if they have a regular mating season, but there musta been three, four hundred rats in there and they were jumpin' on each other's backs and squealin' and hollerin' like it was that time of year. Oh, you could hear the squealin' and hollerin' and my partner Gardner says, 'Let's get the hell outta here. These son-of-a-bitches will eat us up.' I don't remember if we made an arrest or not. I only remember the rats.

"We used to chase people a lot across roofs. Three stories high. We'd surprise them and they'd go out the window and across roofs. And, well, you might just jump a gangway or something like that, over from one roof to another. It was kind of dangerous now that I think about it. If you slipped it would not be so wonderful. But being younger and that, you never, ever think of them things.

"The only time anything serious ever happened to me, I kicked in a door. I was chasing a guy and he ran into this house and he slammed the door behind him. I kicked the door. I thought it was a wooden door. It was painted. But it was a glass door. I kicked the glass out and I cut an artery in my leg and the blood was squirting. We got the guy, but the blood was squirting all across the room.

"I was chasing another fellow down Halsted Street and he ran in this hallway and slammed the door. And I was coming so fast behind him and it was a big plate-glass door there from the top to the bottom and he slammed the door and it just caught in the latch there and I went right through the glass. I chased him up to the third floor and got him. I bled all over this place, too."

Did you ever have anybody try to swallow the stuff?

"Oh, yeah."

Did you choke them to get it out of them?

"Well, I have tried to get it out. But the courts frown upon choking, you know. But see, that's all it is, is swallow today. Because everything today is packaged in balloons. Most of your dope now comes in a rubber balloon. Depending on the size of the balloon, that's how much you'll pay for the dope. A marble-sized balloon might cost twenty-five dollars. Now, they carry the balloon in the side of their mouth. If I was to run up to a guy, he'd probably swallow that balloon. I might search him, but I won't find anything. I can't lock him up. He's got the balloon down in his stomach. After I let him go, he might walk a block away from me and go in an alley and pick up a stick and jam it down his throat and try to force himself to throw up. That balloon will probably come back up and there's nothing wrong with it.

"Or, if what we call it's past the point of no return by mouth, then he might—if he's anxious to get it in a hurry—he might go in the drugstore and get a bottle of Milk of Magnesia and drink that and when he goes to the bathroom, it'll come out there. And then he just has to sift through that dirt to get it. There's nothing wrong with it because—you and I, that sounds like a terrible thing—but you know we're talking about a drug that's the whole life of the people that's either using it or selling it.

"Yeah, you can see their cheek is out and that's when I'll go over to them. Sometimes they might have twenty-five or thirty different-size balloons. And when them balloons get wet, they just glide down your throat. You figure you wouldn't be able to swallow so many at once, but you can.

"A lot of times, these guys will make like a string of pearls out of the balloons. And they'll line it around their gums and down through their mouth. And they'll leave the end out a little bit. Now, if a guy comes up and says, 'I want two balloons,' the seller will just pull that string of pearls and bite off between two balloons. And he'll keep the rest in his mouth.

"Now, I very seldom ever recall choking a guy. Because I'll tell you, once they have it in their mouth, we have tried to open their teeth with our fingers, but you stand the possibility of getting bitten, and once you get bitten you got to go for that tetanus shot or they order you home to put your hand in boiling hot water. I've been bitten many times. You know, the human bite is the worst thing in the world. It's the dirtiest thing in the world. Worse than a dog bite. A dog has a cleaner mouth. Humans have the dirtiest mouths in the world. And some of the people chomp fast. So I endeavor to keep my fingers as far from their teeth as I can."

Jewtown Brown's work would sometimes take him into the area of prostitution.

"They had an old fellow over there at Fourteenth and Newberry who they called Old Man Yancey," said Brown. "Yancey used to run a house, and a lot of them girls used to work for him. Yancey was about ninety years old when he died, and I think that Yancey did about thirty years one time for murder and then he got out, and then I guess he became a pimp.

"Okay, so now one day a policeman on Maxwell arrests a colored girl for prostitution. They brought her into narcotics court because she's a junkie. The girl said, 'Well, your honor, I was brought from the South Side by Old Man Yancey. And every trick I got I had to give him so much of the money.'

"I'm standing off to the side, so the judge says, 'Officer Brown, do you know this Old Man Yancey?' I said, 'He's been pinched a million times,' which he had. The judge said he would issue a warrant for his arrest and wanted him in the courtroom tomorrow morning. I pinched him and we locked him up with a real high bond so he couldn't get out. Took him into court the next morning. And they had this girl brought back at the same time, so she's testifying against him. Now, Yancey denied the charges that he drove this girl from the South Side to the West Side for the act of prostitution purposes. He said, 'No, Judge, I didn't do that. I didn't drive her over.'

"The judge says to him, 'Do you have a car?'

" 'Yes, I have a car, but it don't run,' says Old Man Yancey.

"The judge says, 'What do you mean it don't run?'

"Yancey says, 'Well, it won't go in first.'

" 'Well, will it go in third?'

" 'No.'

" 'Will it go in reverse?'

" 'No, your honor, it won't go in no mother-fuckin' speed. It won't go.'

"The judge gave Yancey eighteen months in jail.

"Okay, but then the judge said, 'Mr. Yancey, just a minute. I'll tell you what I'll do. If you're willing to take a lie detector test and you pass the test, I will drop the charges against you in court.'

" 'Well, Judge,' says Yancey, 'I'll take the lie detector test. But I don't know where to go.'

"The judge says, 'We'll make the arrangements for you. It's at Harrison and Michigan.' And Yancey says, 'I wouldn't know how to get there. I never leave Maxwell Street district. I'm Maxwell Street. I'm gonna die on Maxwell Street.'

"Well, the judge made the arrangements. And myself and my partner picked Old Man Yancey up and took him to take the test. You see, he really couldn't drive.

"Old Man Yancey passed the lie detector test with flying colors.

"It was also true that some of the people there never left the Maxwell Street area. Like Woo Woo. There was once a rape on Sixty-ninth Street and he was picked out in a photograph as the rapist.

"I went to see him. I said there's been a rape out South. He said, 'Where's South?' I said, 'Sixty-ninth Street.' He said, 'Mr. Brown, you know I never been south of Fourteenth Street. I wouldn't know how to get out to Sixty-ninth Street.' Which was true.

"You see, some of them people were strictly Maxwell Street. Now, we had a lot of other people come *into* Maxwell Street. But the ones from Maxwell Street never, never left the district. They had their little show on the corner there and if they were junkies, they had their dope peddlers, they had their cars to break into, but they never ever left Maxwell Street. They needed the security of the neighborhood. And I suppose they maybe felt, why leave? Why go outside? They had everything there. And you go into a strange neighborhood you might get hurt. And I think that a lot of 'em felt that even if they committed a crime, they knew we knew 'em and that they wouldn't get beat up. They'd be arrested and might be sent to jail, but they'd never get beat up. Even though they were thieves and burglars and this and that, they felt a sense of security about the neighborhood. It was home sweet home.

"And some of 'em got to make the Maxwell Street station house like a second home. And you should have seen that place. It's an old building, one of the oldest in Chicago. They closed up the basement lockup in 1952. In the lockup in Maxwell Street you had the cells in the basement, although with the exception of the rats it was a very clean place. The janitor there, Joe Molina, hosed the thing down with hot water every day. There were no bugs there. We had the kitchen down there where we fed the prisoners. We had maybe I would say thirty cells down there. Two benches on each side of the cell. But the sewer rats down there were tremendous. They were big enough to eat you. You see, there were no toilets down there. The prisoners would urinate and defecate in the trough that ran alongside the cells, and the water continually ran through there and carried it out. And even your rats would come right outta them troughs, soakin' wet with the water and the piss and the shit. We had all these hot-water pipes connected to the ceiling of the basement that went up into the building. And the rats used to get up there on them warm pipes, and they'd lay there. And maybe their tails would be hangin' down this far. It was kind of a scary thing in a way, you know, because you could throw a tin cup up at one of them rats there and it wouldn't move. It wouldn't scare 'em. Because they probably had been through everything. But with the exception of that, I had to say that the Maxwell Street lockup was a very clean place.

"But it was declared unsanitary in 1952. They outlawed all basement lockups then. From then on, when we made a pinch we'd take the person downtown."

During the conversation, Jewtown Brown and Rooftop Brown and Garbage Can Brown and Water Faucet Brown recalled that he had another nickname. It was "Blue-eyed Mother Fucker."

"The Gypsies nicknamed me that," said Brown. "This is how it came about. The Gypsies were great for pickin' pockets. When Maxwell Street was in its heyday, you had tourists coming from all over the world. The Gypsy women would be standing and sitting in their windows. They had the big plate-glass storefront windows. They'd call a guy in, and naturally the guy'd go in and they'd want to tell their fortune for a dollar. But, you see, while in the act of tellin' their fortune, they'd back 'em up into a curtain that separated two rooms, and while the Gypsy would be tellin' the guy's fortune and maybe massaging his balls, why somebody from behind the curtain would be pickin' his pocket. Now, they made some tremendous scores. Oh, they might get a conventioneer for a thousand, fifteen hundred dollars.

"And the minute the guy would miss his wallet, why they'd get this woman out of town who had told his fortune. Or they'd get her to another Gypsy place out of the area so she couldn't be identified. So we put a lot of heat on the Gypsies. Every time we'd catch 'em tellin' a fortune, we'd lock 'em up. Always locked 'em up. Tellin' fortunes at the time was against the law in Chicago. We charged 'em with disorderly conduct or something like that. But they continued to do it. So we used to hide behind the stands on Maxwell Street, trying to catch 'em at tellin' fortunes. And they'd send their little kids up and down the street to see if we were around. I remember one time this little girl who was about six came down the street. We didn't know what she was there for. You know, looking around behind the stands and everything. And finally she spotted me. So she went running down the street to this storefront, and she is hollering, 'Blue eyes, Blue eyes, Blue-eyes Mother Fucker.'

"The Gypsies were probably the best pickpockets in the world. There's a lot of techniques to picking pockets. The Gypsies mainly used the two-finger approach. Like a prong. They would be trying to get a guy excited. And of course they wore the low-cut dresses. They had a way of getting the wallet no matter where it was. Or if they suspected a policeman, they'd feel him up for the gun. They knew the ins and outs of all that stuff.

"Gypsy girls are always sold by the Gypsy family. The marriages were all arranged. If you had five thousand dollars and you'd give it to the father, then he'd give you the girl. But you'd pay according to how adept she was at picking pockets. Could she go in with the two fingers and come out with money?

"In 1960, I was moved to Downtown and away from Maxwell Street. The guy who was in charge of narcotics at that time asked me to come down and help him. I said okay. Well, the first day on the new job, I was lost. I ended up back on Maxwell Street. And I met one of my informers—policemen live by informers—and he took me to a place on the South Side where I broke a case.

"You know, I enjoyed every day of it there on Maxwell Street. I looked forward every day to it. I loved every day of it. I loved the people, and I knew hundreds and hundreds. Even the thieves. I think I loved 'em. I loved the merchants. I got close with a number of them. I even liked those that were rough, that would sell a guy a pair of pants with holes in 'em and when the guy brought 'em back the pants man wouldn't give the money back. I'd have to go in and try to pacify the store owner.

"There was never a dull moment down there. Always something to watch, always a case to be made. There's a certain amount of excitement that gets in your blood. God, I broke up hundreds of robberies there, and there was just always something to be done.

"And I made a kind of name for myself. In fact, I remember one time I was in court and a case was going on, and this defendant said to the judge along the way, 'I know Jewtown Brown.' The judge took offense at this, thought it was a racial slur. He says, 'I'll have none of that in my courtroom.' But, see, the fellow actually didn't mean anything by that. This was just the way of associating me with Maxwell Street.

"I've slowed down in recent years. I had a heart attack about three years ago. But knock on wood, I bounced back and I'm active again. But I'm trying to hold down the running. I'll walk up five flights of stairs to make an arrest, but I mean I won't walk 'em real fast. I'm no Maxwell Street spring chicken anymore."

# "TONY RAGUSA"*

Tony Ragusa is a junkie, a thief, a swindler, a liar, a stool pigeon, a brawler and, best of all, as far as the Chicago Police Department is concerned, an informer.

For a number of years he has been a close associate of John Murdock, a Maxwell Street area cop whose main line is the drug traffic in the general area.

I asked Murdock how he first met Ragusa.

"One night he threw an outfit underneath my unmarked car," said Murdock. "An outfit is a hypodermic needle and a syringe. I recovered it and I was going to arrest him. And he said, 'No, no, don't arrest me. I'll help you with cases. I'll do anything you want me to do, but don't arrest me. I'm a good guy.'

"Unfortunately, that's the way the Chicago Police Department has to get their information, from people who make cases on other people. So it's like a vicious circle. You just make a case on this guy, and he makes three more for you and you let him go. Every police force in the country works relatively under the same principles as far as I know.

"Of course, Rags knows how the police force works. Not only has he had firsthand experience at dealing with it, but his uncle is a police sergeant. He also claimed that Fifi Buccieri was an uncle of his, but Fifi wasn't. Fifi, you may know, was the Godfather of Chicago. There's a book I have that's called *Bloodletters and Badmen* by Jay Robert Nash and it calls Fifi 'the lord high executioner.' Fifi owned a gas station around here, and Rags's mother used to date him. So sometimes Rags would be seen with the two of them, and then he'd hang around the gas station. That was enough for everyone to assume that Rags was in tight with the

---

* "Tony Ragusa" is an alias.

Syndicate. He wasn't. They didn't trust him. But he had a lot of people believing he was part and parcel.

"He took advantage of it. For example, Rags had a car, a '67 Mustang, and I remember him selling it at least six times."

What do you mean, sold it six times?

"He would give a guy the keys to his car and tell him, 'Here's my car. Take the car. Give me two hundred dollars down. I'll come over to your house tonight when you've got the other hundred,' or whatever he sold the car for. 'Give me the two hundred you've got now. And I'll come over to your house tonight with the title. Where do you live?' The guy would tell him. In the morning Rags would come over and get in the car and boogie. He always had two sets of keys. One for the customer and one for himself.

"So when the guy found Rags, he'd say, 'Where's my car?'

"'What car? It's my car. I got the title to this car.'

"Now, Rags, who is about forty and wears a beard, is five nine, weighs about two hundred pounds and he's a fighter! One of the baddest dudes around! After he screwed you, he'd stand up to you and say, 'I've got you. What are you going to do about it?' And if you made a good threat, he'd always use Fifi Buccieri's name. 'If you touch me, anything happens to me, I already told my uncle where you live. Remember that. Did you ever get a hot poker in your kid's eyeball.' He was that ruthless.

"He made every waitress in the area. He and his partner, Ray. He would make you in a minute. You would think when you met him he was the greatest guy in the world. He would joke around with you, everything else. You'd say, 'Hey, this is the first guy that never tried to make me. All he's doing is joking around, and he's a great guy.' He'd come and if he had money he'd buy you a cup of coffee, get to be your friend. Then finally him and Ray would set up a little gig. Ray would call a waitress at the restaurant, 'Hey, honey, Rags got busted.' And you'd say, 'Oh, he's such a nice guy.' Ray'd say, 'Yeah, well, listen, do you have any spare change for a bond? He'll pay you back tomorrow.'

"She'd say, 'How much is bond?' They would say that bond was whatever amount of money she had saved. And they knew how much she had saved. They found out by talking to her in the past.

Rags would say, 'You know, you should be saving your money.' And she'd say right away, 'I do save money.'

" 'Really? That's nice. How much do you put away?' And they'd have an estimate of how much dough she had, and that's what bond would be. Then Rags would call her and say, 'You know my uncle, Fifi Buccieri? He's a top Syndicate hood. I'll have the money for you tomorrow, honey. Five hundred dollars,' or whatever she had saved.

"Now, if she said, 'Well, I don't know,' Ray would say he just wants to take her for a drive. Then they go to police headquarters at Eleventh and State, brazen as hell, and there would be Rags. And he'd wait for Ray's car to pull up, and he'd walk up and there's got to be a hundred uniformed policemen there and ten of 'em are trying to get on the elevator every time the elevator comes down. Rags would walk over to one and say, 'Hey, how about it? You got a match?' And she's outside, and Ray would say, 'Look, look, they've got him! Look at the police. They're taking him upstairs now! Give me the money. I'll go and bond him out.' And Rags would go up to the coffee shop at police headquarters and sit down and have a cup of coffee. In a few minutes Ray's got the money, goes up, has a cup of coffee with Rags, and then the two would finally come down. Rags says, 'Wow, honey, thanks a lot. I really appreciate it. I'll pay you back tomorrow. Listen, could you loan me ten dollars? I ain't got nothin'. I haven't eaten, they didn't give me nothin' to eat.' Tomorrow would come and no money for the waitress. He would keep giving her excuses for two, three weeks. And then he'd fade away. So what can she do about it, go to the police and say she lent somebody money and you want to get it back? It's impossible.

"He was screwing people left and right. He's always paying you back tomorrow. I've heard that a thousand times if I've heard it once. 'John, I'll pay you back tomorrow.' He must have beat me for four hundred dollars."

He beat *you* for four hundred?

"Oh, definitely. The loan got so big and he would come with such stories that you couldn't say no to him."

Like what?

"Oh, the kids are sick. They need some milk. Oh, I got to get this. Lend me ten dollars. I'll make a case tomorrow. And it all came out of my pocket. The Chicago Police Department doesn't give anything back.

"But he had already set me up. You see, he was instrumental in my first big dope buy. Now, when I was going to pinch him that time with his outfit, he said he'd rip someone off for me.

"He got me and him together with a Mexican guy. And the guy trusted Rags, just as everybody did who didn't really know him— or even if they knew him! But the guy wouldn't trust me. He didn't like the way I looked, as if I was scared or something. It was my first buy. Rags told him, 'Listen, go get the stuff.' And the guy said, 'Well, give me the money. What do you think I am— crazy? I don't give anything C.O.D.' Rags said, 'The only way I pay for anything is C.O.D. Nothing goes up front. Go get the stuff.'

"So the Mexican guy went and got the stuff, came back, sat in the car. I gave him the money. He wanted to give the dope to Rags but Rags knew the procedures. The dope had to go into my hand. Otherwise it would have been a delivery to Rags. So Rags turned around and started talkin' to the guy and he said, 'Can't you see I'm drivin', you asshole? You got the stuff? Give *him* the stuff. Give *him* the stuff. Don't give *me* the stuff.' Fifty-miles-an-hour double talk. 'Who gave you the money, you asshole? Give him the stuff. If I gave you the money, wouldn't you give me the stuff? Give it to him! He gave you the money, you fucking creep!'

"The guy turned around. He's all confused. And I'm scared, it's my first, and I'm scared. So the guy, his head is spinning, and he hands the stuff over to me. And I put the cuffs on him and tell him, 'You're under arrest, you asshole. Where'd you get the stuff?'

"Well, now he doesn't want to go to jail, either. 'If you can say something for me when I go before the judge, I'd appreciate it.' Okay, fine, what'll I say? He tells me he'll take me someplace where he gets the stuff. I run out, get a warrant for the place, and hit it. Rags is with us all the time, stays with us till the end. So we go in the place and kick the door in. There's this Polish guy that owned the building, and he says, 'Hey, what's going on?' There's a bunch of guys there. The place was going crazy. 'Who are you? What's this?' So Rags was the spokesman at the time. He could al-

ways play the police role like he was the Man. He'd slap you
around. He said, 'Listen, pal, we're police. You rent your apartments to dope dealers and we're raiding the place and if you don't
want to go to jail, you'd better get out of here.' He said, 'I'm
sorry. I'm sorry. I'm sorry.' Everything went down fine. I don't
know what else Rags said to the Polish guy. I just saw him leave.
The next day I stopped by Rags' apartment and I walked in and I
looked around and I said, 'Oh, God!' I said hello to his wife,
'How are you doing?' And I said, 'Rags, where did all this shit
come from? It looks familiar to me.'

"'Well don't worry about it.'

"I said, 'What happened?' He said, 'Well, you know that place
we raided? It's a shame to see all that furniture and everything go
to waste. So I went back there and I told the Polack that it was all
confiscated, and I brought my brother's truck and I made the
Polack load it onto the truck.'

"I said, 'Well, that's a nice thing to do, very nice. You can get a
guy in trouble that way.'

"Rags would screw his best friend. And he did. He screwed Ray,
oh, a thousand times. Ray was a chump. He was Rags' patsy.
Once they made a score on a Timex machine. They went into a
drugstore and there was a machine with about a hundred Timex
watches. They ripped it off. Ray walked right out with it, while
Rags was making a phone call. When the druggist saw his machine disappearing out the door, he began running over. But Rags
walked out of the phone booth and fell in front of the guy. The
guy was apologizing and Rags said, 'You go call the police and I'll
get the license number.' Rags disappeared.

"Okay, Rags sold the watches to a fence for five hundred dollars. So Rags went out and copped four hundred dollars worth
of dope for the three of them who were involved, including a
driver, and kept a hundred dollars for himself. He told them he
copped five hundred dollars. He gave each one of them five dollars
besides the dope. Rags said, 'Listen, I've got to stop and give my
old lady my five dollars. I'll stop up and be right down. Then
we'll split the dope.' He was talking a mile a minute. He went
upstairs, came down in a few minutes. He said, 'My old lady is
hot on my ass. I've got to get back upstairs. Here's your share of

the dope.' He went upstairs, took the phone off the hook, and shot himself up. Ray and the other guy went back home, and they took the bags that Rags gave them and put them in a cooker. They began to perk! Rags had switched coffee for the dope.

"The next day he came out high as hell and he told his pals, 'Yeah, that son-of-a-bitch burned us yesterday. I got hot chocolate. What did you guys get in yours?'

"Once Rags used Ray as a front man with his wife. Rags' old lady had this rabbit coat, her prize possession. That's about the only thing she ever had and that was from her ex-husband. So Rags snatched the rabbit coat and he sold it for dope while she wasn't looking. The same night he takes her out to the corner taco joint for dinner—which is all of about three bucks. And he made Ray babysit so he'd have a cover story, somebody to throw the heat on when she saw the coat was missing. He threw the weight on Ray right away.

" 'It must have been Ray. Remember when we went out to dinner? You know I wouldn't do anything like that. May my mother go blind if I would steal anything from you, honey.' So she of course stopped talking to Ray. Rags can put people in a trance.

"Even though Ray was his fall guy, he'd always take care of Ray, but never as good as he took care of himself. Once they went into a liquor store boosting. Rags was wearing his boosting clothes —usually a pair of pants that's about eight inches bigger in the waist than he needs. And he's got pockets sewn into them to fit whatever he's boosting, like he had his wife make patches for his pants which would fit a bottle of whiskey. So he could load up with four bottles of whiskey in a matter of seconds, put them in pockets around him, and he always had an oversized coat and he could walk out and he would look like Santa Claus, ho, ho, ho, and stop at the door and talk to the owner. 'How you doin'?'

"One time, he's in with Ray and a bottle fell down Ray's leg. Clunk. It hit the floor. Ray froze in the aisle, he was so scared. The bottle is lying on the floor. Rags hollered, 'Hey, help me, the guy collapsed. He zonked out. This guy's crazy. I don't know what's wrong with him. Open the door.' The guy opens the door and Rags picks Ray up and carries him out of the store.

"He'd screw anybody. Anything to get his dope. He had more

policemen waiting for a Puerto Rican with red pants and a pencil mustache, and there's five thousand of 'em on Halsted Street.

"Maybe he's driving down the street and he and a pal have made a score. The pal has recently been busted, and he's trying to figure who busted him. Rags says, 'See that guy on the sidewalk there, that's the guy who got you.' And his pal would get infuriated. 'I saw him downtown. He's a narc. He's the stoolie.' The guy jumps out of the car and begins to beat up an honest citizen. The guy being beaten up could have been you or me. Rags probably never saw him before in his life. Rags pulls away and drives off with the whole score. Any way he could figure to make some bread, he'd stop at nothing.

"Once, he tried to pull somethin' slick on a narc agent. And the guy tripped him up and was going to send Rags up for five years. Rags pleaded to let him finger as many guys as they needed. Well, Rags went out and made about seventeen or eighteen black guys on Roosevelt Road in a period of weeks, just to get his five years' probation. And after those few weeks, he and the federal agent go to a bar to celebrate. The bartender knows that the guy with Rags is an agent and, of course, trusts him. The agent is dancing and having a good time. Rags is double-talking the bartender like crazy and winds up selling him five hundred dollars worth of invisible booze."

# MEATHEAD O'CONNOR

The second floor of the Maxwell Street station house is the quarters for the detectives. The several offices are, however, separated by wire mesh and makes them look like either prison cells or chicken coops. The room is large, very uncluttered, peely, and contains that indefinable but unmistakable drab aura of "the Heat." In the middle of the room is a row of moss-green lockers. "Meathead" O'Connor, whose mother calls him Michael, has a locker here. He is a detective who has been assigned to the Maxwell Street district since 1961, when he was twenty-seven. In the locker is a bound leather photo album. It contains pictures, primarily head shots, of men and women with faces generally dreary, drawn, grimacing, melancholy, glazed, skulking, madcap, or humbugging. They populate Meathead O'Connor's small but strange world. They are the flower and fauna of the Maxwell Sreet criminal culture.

Meathead started the album when he was a rookie cop on the street. The collection is for the purpose of easier identification of suspects by victims. Early on, Meathead decided it would not be a bad idea if the transgressing community of Maxwell knew such an anthology existed. Maybe they'd be fearful of him, stay out of his territory because he knew who they were, had something extra going for him. "Try to psych 'em out," was his phrase. First chance he got, he took the pictures to court when he had a Maxwell Street case. At this time, he was known only as O'Connor or Officer or, of course, Heat. A first name did not really exist in the community at large, as it were. So he's sitting in the courtroom and beside him is a gentleman named Billy, a Maxwell Street pimp. Billy said, "Can I look and see your pictures?" Meathead handed them over. Billy browsed through them. Handed them back. O'Connor was secretly pleased as could be. Soon, Billy left. When he did, a lady sitting behind O'Connor tapped him on the shoulder. "Officer," she said, "that man stole some of your pictures." And that's when people on the street began to call O'Connor "Meathead," meaning stupid.

O'Connor is a burly man, with a sense of humor but who also possesses a controlled fury. When he hits you, it must hurt. He would hit people, he said, who called him "Meathead." He soon realized, however, that the name had spread and that all he could do was live with it because it was not going to go away.

"And now," he said, "I like it." He was sitting in a room in the corner of the police station. It was barren except for a simple wooden table, two wooden chairs, and venetian blinds that could be drawn so nobody can see what's going on inside and can't make out shadows, either, the way they could with standard shades. He was seated in a chair, feet propped up on the table, a holster with gun at his beefy side.

"The name's like a calling card," he said. "People know me, know the name. Once you get a name here, it makes you somehow closer to the people. You know, I get in doors—like in the project buildings—that I couldn't get in otherwise. I mean, people open 'em for me, 'Hi, Meathead.' "

Sometimes it is not necessarily an advantage. Meathead recalled that once he bought a curly blond wig in a dime store. Cost him twenty-five cents. And he'd drive around with it in an unmarked car. It was such a good disguise that when he walked into his own station house the cop at the desk threw him out, and he heard one cop say to another, "Geez, we got to keep these degenerate hippies out of the police stations." So O'Connor started walking down the street in his wig, laughing at how successful he was when Gwen, a local hooker, called to him from across the street, "Hey, Meat, what're you doin' with that wig on?"

Meathead was wearing the wig and pink glasses and dressed in old Levi jeans and driving a cab, with a walkie-talkie hidden under the cap on his seat. It was a clunker of a Yellow Cab. This was a ploy to try to ferret out a guy who was robbing cabdrivers. They could never catch him, but they knew who it was: Tumor Top Tompkins, who always had a wrinkled forehead and who lived in, and operated around, the Green projects just west of Maxwell and in sight of the second-story offices of the Maxwell station house. They told Tumor Top to stop, but he didn't. Tumor Top got so bold as to tell the Heat he'd never stop robbing cabbies.

Now, a beat-up inconspicuous-looking Volkswagen with two plainsclothesmen would follow Meathead, according to a plan. They drove around and then Meathead radios that he's going into the projects. This was unusual. "Few cabs ever go into a project without being ripped off," said Meathead. In fact, everybody is always being robbed in the projects. If you go for two dollars worth of groceries, for example, you'd better bring two dollars. "If you bring two and a quarter," said Meathead, "they'll think you're 'flashing' and rip you off." So Meathead pulls into the project. He honks the horn, and hears a shout, "She'll be right down."

Meathead sat back, suppressing a grin, because of course no one had called for a cab. And he waited.

Suddenly, Marvin Ramsey appears. Now, Marvin is not Tumor Top. But Marvin is another cab rip-off and stick-up artist. Marvin came up so fast that Meathead was unprepared. "Marvin was on me before I knew it," said Meathead. He had opened the door and stuck a gun in Meathead's side, and said, 'Where's your money?" Meathead pointed to his left shirt pocket. As he did, he also began to reach for his walkie-talkie. "Marvin saw this, saw the walkie-talkie, and began to run like hell," said Meathead.

Meathead threw the car into park. Unfortunately, it was a clunker of a car and it went into reverse instead and smashed into the car behind him. Meathead feverishly threw the car into drive because there was no neutral or emergency brake and jumped out and began to scream, "Stop! Stop, Marvin!" Marvin did not stop.

Suddenly Meathead realized the Volkswagen wasn't there! And he wasn't being backed up at all! It hit him that the backup squad must have gone to a different project. "I was really shaking and really pissed off," he said. "I was beside myself." The car started rolling again. Meathead grabbed a brick and put it under a tire to stop the car. He took the walkie-talkie and yelled for his men to come over. Then he ran up to Apartment 802. That's where he knew Marvin lived.

Meathead began banging on the door and Marvin's mother looked through the peephole and she said, "What do you want?" And he said "I'm a cop." She said, "You ain't no cop." He said, "Aw, c'mon I *am* a cop." She was looking at his pink sunglasses and his yellow wig with a headband. "Open up or I'll kick the door in," he said. He finally busted in and she tried to body him back out and they started arguing and all of a sudden the other cops came running in and they ran into the bedroom. Marvin was behind the door, against the wall. They grabbed him and they pulled him out. And he was arguing, "I didn't do nothin'. Let me alone." Then Meathead walks over, pulls off his wig, and very docilely Marvin put his hands behind his back.

Meathead has a partner named Skinhead, who is bald to the core. Sometimes their signals get crossed, as they did in the taxicab caper. Another time, Meathead chased a pair of bandits through Maxwell Street alleys. Skinhead caught the action and, unbeknownst to his partner, began running to help. Meathead began firing at the bandits. Skinhead began firing at the bandits. But Skinhead did not seem to realize that Meathead and not the bandits was the beneficiary of his bullets. Meathead dived over a fence and cowered behind it, wondering who in the hell was shooting at him, until he saw Skinhead fly by.

Once there was a fellow named Fishsticks. He was called Fishsticks because he was so skinny he looked like the bare bones of a fish. Fishsticks was a con man and a stick-up man. His milieu was the South Water Market area, a couple blocks south of Maxwell Street. He would go to a truck driver there and tell him that he can get him a terrific deal on a hot color-television set. He'd say he might be able to get a seven-hundred-dollar set for a hundred fifty dollars. He takes the truck driver to a shopping center and the driver points out which TV set he wants. Then Fishsticks calls up an accomplice. He tells the driver that he's got to call up this woman because she can get the TV for him. So she says on the phone that, well, the only person she trusts to come up to her place and get it is Fishsticks, because this is a Mafia deal and they're afraid the Mafia is going to try to cut in on it or something. So she'll say, 'Give Fishsticks seventy-five dollars down payment.' The truck driver can hardly resist. He gives Fishsticks the money and never sees him again.

One particular time, a truck driver made a complaint. The truck driver said he had been stuck up by some skeletal creature. Meathead needed no other descriptive details. It happened that Meathead had been talking on the radio to Skinhead, who said he had just seen Fishsticks go into a drugstore that he frequented. Meathead shot over to the drugstore. But Fishsticks was gone from sight. He was hiding.

Meathead wasn't sure where he went. But he did not want to cause a commotion in the store. So he quickly composed a plan. It's called "Playin' on him." Meathead makes believe that he gets into the squad car with his partner and the automobile pulls away. But Meathead has flattened himself against the wall. When Fishsticks figured the heat had simmered, he strolled out of the drugstore. A hand from behind clapped on his shoulder. "Got you now," announced Meathead.

This kind of hurt Fishsticks' pride, according to Meathead, because he had been played on, and that's *his* game. So they went to the police station. To try to convince Fishsticks to come clean, Meathead chains him to a thick hook on the wall. The hook is secured by a big bolt. It's impossible to escape from, Meathead knows. Fishsticks told Meathead that the cuffs were a little tight on him. Meathead, a gentle compromiser, loosened them a little. Fishsticks said, "Thanks, Meat, and now I'm going to help you out. I'm going to tell you where the Big D is. He's at the Medical Center right now." Big D was a top dope pusher. Meathead said, "That's enough for me," and he bit and raced off with his partner, leaving Fishsticks chained to the wall.

The cops crashed into the Medical Center, but there was no Big D there. Meathead remembers getting a very sick feeling. He raced back to the station house, flew upstairs and all he saw on the wall was a pair of handcuffs hanging. They were still locked.

He remembers running back down the stairs like a crazy man. And then he began combing the neighborhood for Fishsticks. They spotted Fishsticks' father. Meathead said to Skinhead as they pulled closer, "I'm going to kill that Fishsticks son-of-a-bitch." And Skinhead said, "You can't say you're going to kill somebody. That would be premeditated murder."

They stop the car and get out. Meathead says to the father,

"Well, where is Tyrone?" Tyrone was Fishsticks' real name. "You know we're looking for him."

And Skinhead blurts out, "If you don't tell us where that son-of-a-bitch is, we'll kill him!" Meathead winced.

Skinhead was really cooking now. He added, "You won't ever be looking up at him no more, you'll be looking *down* on him." The old man got so scared he ran and produced his son.

Meathead chained him back up to the gates on the window, after pulling the venetian blinds. Fishsticks was spread-eagled. "The guy was very vulnerable," recalled Meathead. Then Meathead got a cup of coffee, put his feet up on the table and said, "Right now I'm too mad to beat the shit out of you. So I'm going to drink my coffee, and then I'll beat the shit out of you methodically." And Meathead began to sip slowly. Meathead stared at him, "mind-fucking him," he calls it. After several minutes, Fishsticks says, "Okay, what do you want to know? I'll tell you."

He told how he had escaped. His wrists are so thin that he slipped out of the cuffs, and then walked into the next room to an officer and asked casually, "What time is it, Officer?" And then walked out, whistling.

He also admitted duping the plaintive truck driver, and Fishsticks departed the street for several months. When he returned, he went back into the television business.

Meathead said that the tactics of policemen today have changed. There is much less brutality, he says. He remembers when suspects were beaten up regularly. Not so much slugging, he said, but slapping. He also felt that there was some rationalization for it. "A slap opens a guy's mouth, while a punch—for some reason—closes it," he said. He also contends that the pride of the suspect is hurt if you talk to him without belting him. One of the most ambivalent police devices was to wash the blood from a suspect's face in the toilet bowl, and if the guy was partly drowning at the same time, well, that's the chance you take in being a Good Samaritan.

Sometimes there is utter defiance on the street. Meathead remembers one Saturday night when he went to help a guy who had fallen drunk in front of a tavern. Someone hollered that a fight was breaking out inside between two women with knives.

Down the street, someone was hollering, "Robber! Robber!" And as Meathead was getting up from the drunk to see which way he was going next, some other guy comes by and blows a green cloud of smoke in his face from a reefer. To apprehend a reefer smoker was the least of Meathead's problems. The defiant smoker luxuriated in the moment.

Dope, said Meathead, was the biggest problem on the street. He said three-quarters of the crime centered around dope. To deal with dope, you've got to first deal with the language of it. "You can't ask a guy if he's taking dope," said Meathead. "That marks you as square. You got to say, 'You messin' 'round,' And you listen to how a guy says 'drugs.' The people who love it, need it, live by it, they'll draw the word out as if they're tasting it, 'Dru-u-u-u-u-ugs.' They kill each other for it." Meathead recalls that one of the junkies had written to a girl friend from jail, asking her to reform. He wrote, "Powder your nose if you want, but don't stick holes in your arms, honey." "Powder your nose" means you can use cocaine but don't shoot up heroin. A cocaine user "snorts" the narcotic from a plastic card.

There was a guy in the neighborhood named Good Hittin' Bob, who had a peg leg. Sometimes they called him Doc Bob. He carried a stethoscope around with him. He liked to pretend he was a doctor, but what he had been was an embalmer. In that line, he learned all the veins of the body. This helped him eventually earn the name, Good Hittin' Bob. Women junkies would come to him to be shot up. Women have smaller veins than men, and the more you shoot them up, the blacker they become and, for black-skinned women, kind of disappear under the skin. They can't find the veins to shoot up by themselves. So they have to go to the jugular. And somebody else has to administer the shot. That's where Good Hittin' Bob came in. Bob had the reputation for never missing, since he was a veins expert, being an ex-embalmer. He'd charge three bucks a hit. Once, during an operation of this nature, a patient was dying. He took out his stethoscope, took the pulse beat, and called a cab. By the time the patient arrived at the hospital, she was dead. Bob himself passed on not long after. He was getting on in years, and it seems that one evening he missed on himself—his final miss.

Most of the prostitutes on the street are junkies. And most of their pimps are junkies. This causes the cops many difficulties. Robberies were once rampant. Some whores would take their tricks, or johns, to the old Newberry Hotel, a musty, dingy joint that has since been torn down. The charge was ten dollars for the trick and two dollars for the room. Some stick-up men were charging the whores three dollars to let the johns out of the building without robbing them. Sometimes the whore herself would rob the john, or he'd be robbed by a stick-up man in the hallway, or when he got out onto the street or a little bit down the block. And there was competition to see who could get to him first, like hungry wolves with a piece of carrion.

Sometimes a couple of pimps would jump a john. There followed fights among the pimps about who got there first. The pimps robbed each other, and their apartments. A would-be john would sometimes be shooed away by Meathead, but they'd go around the block and come back looking for action. When Meathead first got to the street, he and his partner Skinhead and about ten other cops decided that the way to curb crime there was to hang around the corner as much as possible, in full uniform and with pistols showing. Now, the cops generally looked a little sideways at prostitution, it being one of their lesser concerns compared to murder and burglary and robbery. Also, the whores made good informants. The cops didn't want to be so nasty to the whores, but crime was on the upsurge. Soon, the whores grew lean due to the Heat. One Sunday afternoon, a delegation of about six of the women, with their hands on their hips, and dressed in all their high-heeled, short-skirted finery, confronted the cops at the corner of Maxwell and Newberry. "You're killing us," they complained. "So we have decided we definitely want to co-operate with the friendly local police." The cops soon relented and got their own kind of *quid pro quo,* such as with the whore Irma.

Irma came to the station house on crutches one day and said, "Meathead, Butch stuck up my apartment last night. Butch thought I was holding out money on him. He said, 'Bitch, that's how people end up in cemeteries.' And he beat the shit out of me with a table leg." When Meathead caught Butch, he locked him up. And there followed a line-up in which Irma refused to identify

Butch. She said she was leaving and went to the top of the stairs, and then turned and hobbled back. "Fuck it," she said, "if I'm goin' to die, I might as well die for a good cause." And she signed a complaint against Butch. Butch got two years for, in fact, beating up a junkie whore. "Meanwhile," said Meathead, "Irma went back to the street, trickin' on crutches."

# JACK SHAW

When Jack Shaw moved to Maxwell Street from the South Side of Chicago in 1961, he was eleven years old, and became the only white boy growing up in the neighborhood.

As a man he still lives around Maxwell Street where he spends his days hustling various goods and persons, visiting friends, just enjoying the aspect of being on friendly turf.

He cuts an eye-catching figure. He is about five ten and chunky, walks with thick-heeled, clunky leather shoes, yet there is an aura of the nimble cat about him. His dark blond hair is sleek and so is his mustache and beard. He wears a black leather car coat, magenta pants, and heliotrope shirt. His eyes are bright and alert. One imagines he misses little, including the amusing.

He talks the way ghetto blacks talk. He walks with "a scoot" the way ghetto blacks walk. He says that it's all "natural" to him, growing up as he did. He seems a black man except for his ruddy, pink skin.

"The way it went down, my mother busted up with my father and then went and married a colored dude," said Jack Shaw. "This was when the Jewtown Cobras and all was down here. It was really bad then. So when I gets down here, by being the only white dude, they tried this harassment, this racial stuff and all. They would cuss me and my sister out, throw bricks in the window, shit like this. My old man had a shotgun. So I said to my sister, next time they run me home from school, they're going to run up in the hallway and wait for me to come out. I'm going to come around the back way. Okay. That's what happens. They jump on me and run me home. About nine or ten dudes.

"I got it all set up. I runs in the house, I grabbed the shotgun, and my sister and Ma look at me, and I run out the back door.

Now these guys are hollering and cussing in the hallway. I come around the front, kick the door, and I just start shooting. I seen everybody in the hallway. I hit every one of 'em.

"One guy I crippled for life. Another one was shot up pretty good. This is not the first trouble I been into. My first father and me would rip off stores, pop trucks, and things like that, when I lived on the South Side. Okay, so they send me to reform school at St. Charles, Illinois. I come back and now they're going to put me in the Jewtown Cobras because I proved myself and now I got some rank in the neighborhood.

"And then I come up here with some guys and we snatch purses and we slit guys' pockets, like at the hot-dog stand on the corner of Maxwell and Halsted. We'd just grab a guy and rip off his pocket and he'd walk around here in his drawers. We had the wallet and we was gone.

"And then I started stealin' cars. I had maybe six or seven on one block or in a vacant lot. We'd steal for the joy ride. One day my friend says, 'Hey, let's go to Florida.' So we steals a car and head south. We end up in a cemetery not far from Chicago, running over graves. We get stuck and we go to sleep and the police catch us. We go to court on a Friday afternoon, and there's a teacher there from our school, a black dude name of Mr. Johnson. And he's badmouthin' us to the judge. We couldn't say anything in court. The judge turns us over to the custody of our parents. That afternoon we go to school and beat him up. We was going to throw him off the balcony, but the other kids stopped us.

"See, no stool pigeons at that time was in the neighborhood. I spend six months in St. Charles again. I get out. Two days later I snatch a purse and I get caught. Right back in St. Charles I go.

"I hadn't got tired of jail yet because I would rather be in there than out here on the streets. Because my mother and them weren't doing nothing. Everything I did, I had to do on my own. All the money I got I had to get on my own. And by eight, I had to steal the food to get it just about. My parents are alcoholics. So they drank up all the money they had. They would get drunk and I wouldn't go to school; I was going to Garfield School. It didn't make no difference what I did. I just did it. I was on my own. So that's why it was no loss. I felt in St. Charles that I was doin' all

right being there. I get out, but go into Vandalia on an armed robbery charge. I'm sixteen going on seventeen. On my release day, I
stop off in Springfield, and I think I'm the baddest guy to hit the
streets. I know I'm good at boxing now 'cause I been boxing in
prison. So I'm layin' in this tavern and drinkin' a beer even
though I'm not old enough to be there. And these three guys from
over there, I guess they didn't like the way I was dressed. They
start mellin'. And I get into it. 'Hey, dig this dude.' See, at the
time, everybody was wearing blue jeans and plaid shirt and stuff.
Well, I had a green suit on, with lizard shoes and all this shit. And
the hat. It was a felt hat with the fur around it and feathers on it
and I got it cocked ace, deuce, trey, you know, the way we block
it in the place, and it's layin' in on the side. The whole bit. All
right. So, these guys they start up mellin'. We get into it and they
charge me with aggravated battery and I go back for six more
months.

"This time I get out, I played it cool. I'm sayin', 'I can't outdo
these walls.' But then I start stealin' tires and car seats again. This
is the way I'm makin' my money. I'm tough. So I get caught. Into
the House of Correction. Another six months. I break out, me and
a few other guys. One night we sneak past the towers and we
throw a blanket over the barbed wire and just crawl over it. We
run. Then we stop in a restaurant about a mile away. One of the
other guys breaks into a laundrymat coin machine to get enough
money to eat. We're sittin' and eatin' and in comes a couple of
House of Correction guards in plain clothes.

"They recognized us. And that was it, see. Took us back. Another year.

"Now, I really start gettin' an education in a lot of ways. I get a
high school diploma. I learn about electronics. I was interested in
that subject to learn about burglar alarm systems. And you learn
how to steal a car better, how to bypass the ignition by jumping
from the battery to the coil, and this and that. You learn how they
wire a house, and you learn how to disconnect the wire with a
magnet to keep the current going where you can get in and out
without disconnecting something. So that's why everybody up
there is in school now. The average guy that goes to the penitentiary, he will go to school.

"And you learn a mess of things from different guys. Forgery. Air games—sellin' something that don't exist for something that does.

"Prison is supposed to be a place for rehabilitation—impossible. It never happens. You learn more in jail than you do out here on the streets. The people in there *are* criminals. The peoples you sleep with and associate with in there are criminals. It's like a criminal university. You listen to a guy and say, 'Wow, man, I could have did this,' like steal a car. So when the guy get out, he's going to try it.

"The way I used to only know how to steal a car was with a screwdriver. I wouldn't mess with no cars but a Chevy and a Buick. I didn't think you could do any other. After I get in the joint, man said, 'Any kind of car's easy to steal.' I said, 'Man, you crazy.' He said, 'Show you the wires.' He did. I say, 'Oh, man!

"Something else I learned. I learned I don't like the joint. After I got out I started thinking, 'Man, I'm gettin' busted here and there, and in and out.' So I got enough sense to put other guys up to doing my dirty work after I done got out. Dudes come to me, 'Hey, man, heard you rippin' off. Can I go with you? I wanna learn.' Instead of me stealing a car, I'd teach guys what I learned. How to burglarize. That's cool. The money was coming in. But then things started getting real hard. All my guys started getting busted, and then I'm out here by myself now. 'Oh, man, this ain't workin'.'

"Now, I started getting friendly with Mike Chiappetta, the night cop on Maxwell. And I thought I might try to change. He was also on my case pretty heavy. He began to figure that whenever I was with him, weren't no crime on the street. When I was out of sight, there was burglaries.

"He'd be coming around to get me before he went on duty. And sometimes he'd handcuff me to his car.

"Mike would give me five dollars a night. I'd get to drive his car, a Thunderbird. Okay. Now I got no car. He's got a car, and it just got good to me because a car was my weakness. And we'd sit in there and watch his portable TV all night. He'd buy me a hot dog, anything I wanted. And then he started taking me to his house. And I started doing work around there and getting extra money. His wife cooked me dinners. And we got real tight, Mike and me.

"At first, I kinda liked it until I found out I was being used. I said, 'Now he using me 'cause he's frontin' me off. Everybody think I'm stool pigeon because I'm with the police. Because they start bringin' it to me. They say, 'Hey, man, we heard you talking to the police. You stool pigeon.' I say, 'Man, get on off. . . . I don't want to hear this. Don't come to me with that because I know I'm not doin' it.' Then I started wondering, 'Well, maybe he telling people this.' And I found out he was. So I started thinking. I said, 'I'll tell y'all what. I'm going to show you how to get this place and I'm going to be with Mike.'

"Okay, so I'm sitting now with Mike and we're drinking coffee and watching TV. All of a sudden, it's a burglary. Oh, man. This starts happening and happening. One night. The next night. Mike knows what's in the air.

"Mike had also got me a regular job. I started work in an auto-body shop. It was cool for a while. Then comes a recession and they cut the hours and I got to get more money because now I'm livin' with a little girl, you know, and I got to go back on the street. I can't survive on workin' two days a week at the shop. When hard times come, the crime rate shoots right up. If a guy's a thief and he ain't got no regular job, he's got to go back on the street. And if you go to jail, you don't care because you got a place to stay and you got something to eat. And he don't think about getting killed or nothing.

"It is exciting and it is a challenge, but when you realize that crime don't pay, it ain't. See, if you work all week long for a hundred dollars, you make that in a half hour on the street. Okay. But if every time you hear a knock on the door and you gotta jump and run or something, it ain't worth it.

"So I go back to stealing cars and being a fence, as well. But I don't like fencin'. I'm better on the street. I'm white and the average guy around there was black or on dope and they'd be the ones breaking in. Now, the university was built around 1966, and you get a lot of white college dudes. So I dress like 'em. Get a brief case. I'd just walk up to a car, get in, and that's it.

"The police think I belong. They looking for the guy who looks like a dope fiend, dirty and looking like he could kill the world—and when he goes to a car, he looking up and down the street. I'd slip in like the car's mine.

"The cops, they don't know what's happening. I steal a hundred cars. No kidding. I even got one commander transferred. Sometimes at roll call, at 4 P.M., I'd stroll into the police station, supposedly for a drink of water. But I'd be there checking the faces, see if they got any new recruits to watch out for. And nobody got no idea what I'm doing, just drinking water.

"Finally, there was a setup. On the Fourth of July, 1966, I walks past the church and I look in a car. And there's a trailer across the street. I see a tuxedo in the car and I see a television set. I walk past, look in the window, there's a piece of paper, like it's a new car. Out of town name and address. The door is unlocked. I look around. I don't know. I walk around the block. Okay, it looks good. So I gets my little brother and a friend named Eli. See, you never, ever work alone. You got to have a back.

"When we return I get a warm feeling. I said, 'Man, something ain't right. Let's go y'all.' Eli said, 'No, man, let's undress her and get the TV.' I said, 'Don't feel right.' He said, 'I'm goin' in.' He went in, picked up the TV, and I looked and I just started running. He picked up the TV, but it was too light—it was just a cabinet, a frame. Nothing inside. And then I seen all the officers, about twelve of 'em, come piling out of the trailer. I hit the alley. Boy, we running. I'm two hundred pounds now and I got the high heels on, but I'm flyin'. But I'm tiring. I see this fence, and when I see it, it's too late. I done hit it. Bam! I go right through. . . . They scraped me up and I got sent away for a year.

"That's the last time I been behind them walls."

Shaw says he has since become more aware than ever of the style and habits of plainclothes policemen.

"You can spot 'em the way they dress, the way they walk, by the way their hair is made or anything. No matter how hard they try, they don't have the true sense of being down here. They never really can blend in, can't adjust because they got the suburban life or something.

"Like the walk, this is maybe a hump or a scootin' your feet or something. It's like you got rhythm, you know, it's 'Hey, what's happenin'?' Cops walk too straight. And when the cops talk, they always hit one word real plain. I mean, they can hold a whole conversation, but then they hit one word plain and bam!, you know. Like a dude say, 'Well, it ain't this.' And they'll say, 'It isn't this.' It catches you.

"We used to look for bulges, for a pistol, because you know ain't no cop gonna be without protection—especially down in Jewtown. But they got hip to bulges and now strap a pistol to their ankle.

"But the slickest they got was with them bicycles. They'd walk around with a bicycle. Walkin' it, not ridin' it. Lookin' like a hippie. And they woulda got me, but happen they bust a trick and I was watching 'em. Now I got my mind I'll go around with the trick and snatch his wallet. So I'm sitting there with a couple more guys and these two guys come up. One's Mexican and one's Indian. They look like normal people. Now, these guys actually coulda fooled us. They're walkin' with their bicycles and all of a sudden I see one guy reach down there and get his pistol. I said 'Man, lookit, they're going to rip this guy off.' I said, 'God darn, they done beat us to it.' So they grabbed the guy and they got him against the wall, search him, and they got the whore, too. All of a sudden this guy with the bicycle opens the box behind his seat and pulls an antenna up. I said, 'Oh, man, this can't be!' Yeah. And he's a policeman. A wagon pulls up and I look. Oh, man, I coulda died when I seen that. I said, 'They're gettin' slick now, and we really gotta get on the case now.'

Would you ever sell the merchandise you stole from stores and cars to the merchants or vendors on Maxwell Street?

"You see, any place you go, any neighborhood, there's a fence. Somebody's always buying something. I don't care where you go. All right. Jewtown, anybody's the fence. Anything you got, there's somebody know you can double his money; he's gonna buy it from you.

"Most merchants won't go through with it because they got a store business, and it's too hard to handle that merchandise. But any stand around here, 90 per cent of the stuff is stolen. Ninety per cent. I know for a fact, 'cause I even had all the stands going at one time. And the way had it going, like an old guy would be on the streets like ten, fifteen years, go out and say to him, 'I got some tires. You sell 'em, I give you so much commission.' Well, I might put twenty tires next to his stand. If somebody come around, they figure these are his. They don't figure that he stole 'em. Okay. And if they were, they couldn't prove it. And here's a brand-new tire that'll sell for sixty dollars. He say, 'Gimme thirty dollars.' Well, the average guy ain't gonna say no. He gonna buy. So this is what keeps it going on.

"And you gotta figure, how many places get burglarized? All right, all that stuff is going on the streets. Most of it. Between burglaries and stick-ups and stuff like that, it's all hot stuff what goes on the street.

"You see a watch. They probably done stole it in another town. But it's still here, and if a guy got a five-hundred-dollar watch and he's askin' a hundred, you know it can't be legit. There's no way. But as easily as you can get a five-hundred-dollar watch down here for a hundred you can get a two-dollar watch for a hundred.

"You gotta be careful. I'm more careful now. Like I won't have a hot TV in my house. I put it in a store because you got to account for it. So I say why pay fifty dollars for a hot TV when you can pay a hundred for a legit one and you know if something go wrong, you even got a guarantee plus the backing up if the cops come by.

"And now I try to avoid doing my own breaking in, I'm careful like that way, too. I got about nine or ten guys I'm teaching the ropes to. Each one of them is pretty pro now. They could come down here and do something and get away with it.

"What they learn from me is the beginning. . . . Then they can go and get past certain burglar alarms or get in through windows or soft spots in the wall or roof.

"Now, I always think about me getting caught. I didn't too much before. I think ahead now. Try to stay clear of the mess."

At twenty-five, now, and with so much experience and thought, do you ever look back and resent your upbringing down here?

"Definitely. Because I figure I shoulda come up another way. I didn't pick my neighborhood. I didn't pick my parents to be alcoholics. I didn't pick nothin'. But this is what it was. And like I say, by me spending most of my young life in jail, this is where I learned everything. So, I had to try it because that was the only way I could survive out here.

"Since the older I got and the way things started getting hard, I figured, you know, 'Wow! Why I had to be like this?' One time, Mike the Cop had got me really getting myself together. Reading, cutting all my slang out, quit messing around and all. Doing nothin' but enjoying myself and trying to get with a different crowd. So I started hanging with a lot of white guys and white broads. First time in my life. I said, man, you know, I just couldn't get into it and they couldn't accept me. Because I always got this slang or this walk or the way I dress, and I couldn't change because I can't see myself puttin' blue jeans on with a checkered shirt. It ain't me. And then someone'll say, he got a colored old lady, or his stepfather's colored. Some kind of way it come out.

"But one day I meet this white broad, a waitress in a restaurant on Wabash Avenue. Another woman there told me that this broad is a virgin, twenty-seven years old, she's a nice girl and everything. I took her out. I never approached her in no kinda way. I just felt good because I could take her at places I wanted to go, where I couldn't with a colored chick. So when I got with her and started going in these places, I felt good.

"Like, we would go in Cicero to the bowling alley. Well, this something I hadn't done, but I enjoyed it. So we would go bowling, we'd go swimming, like up in Crystal Lake. Not with no bunch of colored and 'Hey, mother fucker this and that.' Peoples treat you like, 'Excuse me, I'm sorry this and that.' If you pull in to park and another guy pull in at the same time, they say, 'Go ahead.' I mean, hey man, it was different. I said, 'Man, this is my style.'

"I would sit on her porch and just look at the peoples. Quiet, grass, I mean nothing to worry about. Then when I'd leave there, I'd come back to Maxwell. No grass. No trees. Man, you know, it seemed funny, day and night.

"But then she met some other guy who she dug. So she shot off with him. And he took advantage of her and he took her virginity.

I never even kissed her. I never been like that with no chick before. She liked me, she enjoyed me, but she also knew I was still messing around with the colored.

"But it seemed like the average white broad I ever went out with always took somebody else, and I get along better with the colored broad. So I couldn't—I mean, I'd try to match it up with the white broad, but it wouldn't work out."

# THE STREET, 1964

### URBAN RENEWAL?
### NOT FOR PEDDLERS
### ON MAXWELL STREET

Urban renewal nearly caught up with Maxwell Street Sunday. But this weekend, open-air merchants, probably the most flexible in the world, staved off calamity, at least temporarily.

When the pushcarters and pitchmen went to set up their wares as usual early Sunday at Jefferson and Maxwell, they found their sidewalk marketplace destroyed by some construction work.

As one pushcart merchandiser put it:

"You can't be a sidewalk merchant without a sidewalk."

Like the pioneers before them, they began trundling goods westward all the way to Sangamon St., which may not exactly have been the promised land, but which at least had sidewalks.

They moved their goods by car, by wagon, by cart and truck and on their backs on a slow, three-block trek under the Dan Ryan Expressway.

And the customers, many of them regulars who shop Maxwell Street every Sunday, tagged along. Policemen in the district station at 943 W. Maxwell were a bit puzzled and bemused as they watched the merchants setting up their stands. . . .

CHICAGO *SUN-TIMES*
*March 23, 1964*

# TENE BIMBO

Gypsies have been a part of Maxwell Street for a very long time. What was probably the largest winter colony of Gypsies in the United States was located around Maxwell Street in the 1920s and 1930s. Some of the first newspaper accounts of the Gypsies there center around the self-proclaimed king of the Gypsies, Tene Bimbo, a blocky, mustachioed man. He had a reputation for carrying a gun and also cutting off the ears of enemies. He settled in Chicago with his family around 1920. The supposed leader of the Chicago Gypsies at the time was Eli Miguel. Within a year, Tene Bimbo swore out a warrant for Miguel's arrest because Miguel and two others had "assaulted a helpless Bimbo female" and ripped her off for twenty-five gold pieces that had adorned her neck. He went to police headquarters, demanded immediate justice, and then emerged and told a gathering of reporters, "Eli Miguel, he is not the king. He is the bunk! I am the king of the Gypsies," and then he patted himself on the chest in a manner "lordly, but restrained."

His problems with the law in various ways escalated. Once he was arraigned on a charge of "mayhem," and said he would be forced to buy a dictionary to find out what he was being arrested for.

Perhaps his most publicized problems dealt with his daughter Rosalie whom, he said, "even the *Gadje* [non-Gypsies] would turn in the street to stare at as she walked by, she was so beautiful." Indeed, a newspaper account of her in court in 1923, when she was fifteen years old, described her as "slim, but sinewy, five feet two, as erect as a West Point cadet and brown as a berry from outdoor living. Oval face, slender, shapely nose, firm red lips, luminous brown eyes. Glistening black hair hanging in two braids that reached to the waist. Gorgeous skirt of voluminous garment as colorful as Joseph's coat."

She was in court because she had been caught as a runaway. Rosalie said she left home "to turn civilized." She said to Judge Harry McEwen, "I run away. I want to grow up to be a good girl. I want to eat with a knife and a spoon instead of tearing meat to pieces around a camp fire. I'm tired of lying, stealing and telling fortunes. Who wants to be picking pockets from people who honestly earn their money? I want to sleep in a real bed instead of mattresses on the floor. I want clean white linen. And I want a school education. My father don't think Gypsy children should go to school." Then Rosalie, according to the newspaper account in the Chicago *Tribune* of September 12, "began winking and flirting with the judge" and asked the judge, "Isn't there somebody who will take care of a little girl like me?" The story said the judge grew suddenly nonplused.

Tene Bimbo was called up to the bench. He said, "I don't know what's wrong with Rosalie, Judge. She's getting like American girls. She wants to be the boss. I know American girls. Excuse me, Judge, but they are all powder and paint, and my Rosalie wants to be like that. Two years ago I couldn't buy my women any red shoes. Not for a hundred dollars. Now they come in carloads into the city. The American women are all turning Gypsies, and my Rosalie wants to turn American."

Rosalie had said that she was afraid to return home because she would be beaten up. She did return home. The next time we run across Rosalie and father in the newspapers is the following year when Tene Bimbo is hauled back into court by a complaint of Amelie "Queen Millie" Marks, one of the few Gypsy matriarchs, who headed a small but aggressive bunch of Gypsies. Queen Millie contended that she had paid Tene Bimbo $2,250 for Rosalie to marry one of her sons. But Rosalie vanished a few hours before the ceremony was supposed to take place. Tene swore out a complaint of his own, saying that the alleged bridegroom and a brother had, in fact, assaulted and raped Rosalie. It turned out that the strong-minded Rosalie wanted nothing to do with Queen Millie's suitor. There was a trial but amid the panoply of charges and countercharges, a second trial was ordered. It was eventually dropped when Tene Bimbo agreed to return the money to Queen Millie. But it is doubtful he did because he proceeded to run her entire band out of Chicago.

The Gypsies justify their double-dealing with a piece of folklore. They say that a Gypsy man wiped Christ's brow on the cross and loosened the nails to make him more comfortable. Because of that, the story goes, Christ gave permission for them to cheat and steal.

An example of how they worked was reported in the March 2, 1938, Chicago *Tribune*. The story is about Mary Bimbo, Tene Bimbo's wife, whose address was given as Fourteenth and Halsted. It seems that a Stanley Koshak and his wife were visiting Chicago from Kenosha, in 1937. Mr. Koshak had not been feeling well. As they walked past Bimbo's home, a Gypsy woman, Mary Bimbo, "promised miraculous cures." She told him to go home and bring back all the money he could and then go buy a rooster. A nice, lively rooster. When he returned, the Gypsy woman wrapped up his $615 in a handkerchief and directed him to hold the money over his heart. She held the rooster in front of him. She said that if the rooster died, he'd live, and vice versa."

There was a wild shriek from the rooster, and blood spurted up into Koshak's face. And the rooster fluttered and died. Mary had surreptitiously broken one of the rooster's veins. Then she told Koshak to go back home and not to untie the handkerchief for five days. When he did, he found only a lot of paper wrapped around an egg.

Mary Bimbo got one to ten years and was shipped off to Dwight Women's Reformatory.

# BOB MONTES

There are several Gypsy families still living around Maxwell Street. Bob Montes is the head of one of them. The Gypsy families living around Maxwell Street are some of the few non-black or non-Hispanic people living in the area now. Maxwell Street, said Montes, is still a lucrative place for Gypsy fortune-telling. He says the women make ten, fifteen, thirty dollars a day at it. "Lotta people come on the street to shop, not as much as the old days, but still it's a crowded tourist street," he said. "It's somethin' we're brought up to know. It's our tradition for survival, 'cause they didn't know no other trade. You try to live the best. You got kids, family. You need food, rent money. So every bit helps. You try to survive. Just like the American people do. You try to survive."

One evening in the fall of 1975, he had returned home to Maxwell Street from the funeral of his old Gypsy aunt; Gypsies from all over the country had descended to pay their customary last respects and to help send the dearly departed on her merry way.

The Gypsies had gathered at the funeral parlor where on the wall behind the open casket was the name of the woman, "Peggy Mitchell," in neon lights that flashed on and off. Bob Montes and the others then proceeded to the cemetery. After the burial, they danced and sang to violin music and ate and drank from a long table set up on the grass and which overflowed with whiskey and soft drinks, hot dogs and pork chops and turkey and ham. Nearby, whole pigs roasted on an open, steamy pit.

In death as in life, Gypsies remain Gypsies. However, there have been great changes made within this remarkable race of people, a race which has been among the most unalterable in the history of civilization. For one thing, Gypsies today—at least those in the United States—no longer travel in caravans of gaudy, gingerbread horse-drawn wagons with emblazoned eagles on the sides. Those who live within a five hundred-mile radius or so roll in by automobile. A majority of the automobiles at the funeral were either Rolls-Royces or Mercedes-Benzes or Cadillacs.

"Outside of five hundred miles," said Montes, "we usually take a plane. Gas is so expensive these days—especially for our big cars that drink up so much."

Montes was sitting now in the second-floor apartment and on a deep-sunk couch, styled so that one's knees are well-raised, allowing, supposedly, for loose change to trickle from an unsuspecting visitor's pockets into the deep cracks of the couch. Montes became head of his family upon the death of his father a year before and of his mother nine months later. He is a chunky, round-faced dark-complexioned twenty-five-year-old with thick, carefully combed black hair. He wears a conservative gray slipover sweater, black knit slacks, and fashionable black boots with large heels. He looks comfortably middle-class America.

A roofer and car-fender mender by trade, Montes even has had business cards made up. He drives a three-year-old Chevrolet station wagon. He is not as rich, he says, as some of his fellow Gypsies who populate the "hot sheets" in police files because of various con games. The most prominent con game is the water-meter trick. One Gypsy with false identification impersonates a water-meter reader. He takes a homeowner into the basement while other Gypsies silently ransack the upper parts of the house in a matter of minutes. Montes said he is simply too weak in the stomach for it, that once he went and while the scam was being enacted, sat in the car sweating abundantly.

His wife, Rosie, is a little more traditional. She tells fortunes. ("I can tell people what they are worrying about because it's usually what I'm worrying about. We all have the same troubles. You know, I say, 'There is sickness in your family' or 'You have money problems.'") But few of the women do the boojo anymore, according to Montes. The boojo is an ancient Gypsy trick in which a Gypsy woman tells some rube that she will ward off evil spirits if she will be given some of the person's money; the

money, you understand, may be "tainted." When some of the
money is brought in, it is discovered to be duly cursed, and only
by bringing in all the rest of the person's money can the devil be
fully exorcised. Jail sentences and the growing Americanization of
women has changed some of these machinations.

Once, it was the women who did all the work in Gypsy families
and would never even cross in front of a Gypsy man. No more.
The women often dress like American women and demand more
creature comforts. Once, Gypsies ate on the floor and used no
eating utensils. Now they have tables and tablecloths and knives
and forks. Once, they rarely went to school. Now, says Montes,
they do. "For years we could not read or write—all we could do
was money counting," he said. "But there are some Gypsies today
who are even lawyers."

Gypsies are also wandering much less than ever before. "It's too
expensive, for one thing," he said. "Also, we used to make money
by sprayin' and fixin' farmhouses along the road. There aren't that
many farmers no more. And then if we have to get someplace
like a funeral, you get there faster and easier by airplane, just like
anybody else."

Gypsies, in a most unusual switch in tradition, are becoming
homeowners. "We are learning that if we aren't going to be wandering so much then we have to pay rent. So why not own your
own home? It's cheaper. Sometimes people are afraid of us. So it's
hard to get property. Sometimes they think we're hippies."

The modernization of Gypsy life has its drawbacks. "Gypsies
are dying of diseases they never had before," said Montes. "Gypsies never had cancer or leukemia or strokes or brain tumors, now
they got 'em because they going modern. They're eating all the
sweets and bad meats that the others been eating."

Montes also laments the younger generation of Gypsies, who
are respecting their elders less and taking dope and getting
venereal disease.

"And Gypsies are breaking into the houses of other Gypsies,"
said Montes. "You can't even trust your own brother today—
same thing like in Americans."

When his parents died and when the family went to the funeral,
he hired Mike the Cop's moonlighting security agency to guard

the apartment on Maxwell Street from burglars—burglars presumably of another Gypsy tribe who knew the apartment would be vulnerable. In fact, as a security guard sat on the couch, a pair of Gypsy men did try to enter. They were surprised to find the guard, introduced themselves as cousins, and retreated down the stairs.

Montes was born and raised with his seven sisters and one brother in a storefront home on Maxwell Street. He went to Garfield School until the eighth grade, when at age thirteen a marriage was arranged with Rosie, who was eighteen. The marriage cost his father, Joe, twenty-five hundred dollars, the going rate for the hand of a pretty daughter. They now have five children, the oldest being a son ten.

They are intent on their children going to school. Rosie, slim with long, straight black hair and frilly and tastefully low-cut blouse and simple blue skirt, sitting across from her husband, smoking a cigarette and flicking the ashes at the potbellied stove near her, said, "I want my children to have what I didn't have. See, I don't know how to read or write. I didn't think it was important, and neither did my mother and father. But I feel shame when I go in a restaurant. I say, 'I don't read English. I read Rumanian. So tell me what's for dinner.'

"It was hard to go to school because we used to travel so much. Now we're at home and so the kids will go to school."

"But the way we used to live," said Bob, "we could survive on our know-how and our wits. They don't go out and take a gun and shoot somebody or stick up somebody. They'll con you, but they won't harm a person."

One of the few times they are known to fight, is among themselves. Mike the Cop has broken up internecine fights in empty lots in the area, in which Gypsy men and women are slugging it out with fists and rolled up newspapers and the women are using their shoes as clubs.

"But then," said Montes, "maybe a month later the grudge is all simmered, like nothing happened."

The most violent of the Gypsies was the notorious "King" Tene Bimbo, Bob Montes' grand-uncle.

"We have no kings," said Montes. "Only we have a President of the United States, and we have the head of a house, and there are a lot of houses. But this Tene, he was high-tempered. And every-body was fearing him. He was a powerful man. Moneywise, policewise, connectionwise. He had a lot of connections and every-thing in the city. There was nobody like him. He called himself King of the Gypsies and nobody was there to doubt him. He was the only Gypsy that would a gun. For instance, there was a Gypsy person dead in the Jackson Boulevard funeral home. He went there and threw a bomb. Blew up everybody in there. He wanted to do business with Al Capone. But Al Capone was even scared of him. Bimbo was violent, was crazy.

"Gypsies were all afraid of Tene Bimbo, just like a lot of people have been afraid of the Gypsies, and still are afraid. But for no good reason. You know why this is? Because years ago they used to say, 'Oh, Gypsies. Watch your childrens. They're gonna steal 'em.' Let me tell you: Gypsies never stoled any child."

Rosie interrupted, "They had too many of their own!"

"They had their own and they never, never in their life stoled a child," said Bob Montes.

"We were trained not to have a bad name. To have dignity within our customs. And we believe in the best. To make the best of yourself. Sure, we go about things different from the Gadje, or the non-Gypsy. But we have dignity within our customs. When they die, they go the best. When they live, they wanna live the best. That's the way it goes with 'em.

"Look at the big cars Gypsies drive. You put a big down-pay-ment down and you get credit. That's how we drive those cars. Anybody can get credit with a big down-payment. They work to get the down-payment, or they steal. A good water-meter trick can make you thirty, forty thousand dollars. It takes longer when you're black-toppin' a driveway for someone. But you eventually get it."

Gypsies have been known to prey on superstitious people. I asked Montes if he believes in curses.

"No, there's no such thing as a curse," he said.

Do you believe in fortunetelling?

"No."

Astrology?

"No."

Any of that stuff?

"No."

Why not?

"What's meant to happen is going to happen. It was meant for my mother to die. It was meant for my father to die. We tried to get them the best doctors in the city of Chicago. It was meant for them to die. They died.

"We made no special potions or anything. We just lit a candle and prayed. All the Gypsies are Catholics. We all believe in God. And the old ways now are dying with the old people.

"The Gypsies now are not really strict. The daughters marry now who they want to marry. The sons pick their wives. There's nobody who cares to keep the old strict ways. There ain't no more leaders. The older people, like they used to have hearings, meetings. If something go wrong or somebody make a disgrace, like use profoul language to a woman for no reason, there is no hearing no more. No respect for the old customs, the old people. You should have seen at the funeral, the old woman Zuza Hybota. She wore the old-style long dress with an apron, a big handkerchief on her head and a shawl. The young people laughed at her. It made me sad. We have a proud history. People tried to change us for centuries and thousands of years. And we stayed Gypsies. We kept our ways because we thought our ways were better than yours.

"We were wandering before even the Bible, coming from India and Egypt. My grandparents came over on boats from Yugoslavia, from Rumania. Why did they come to America? Why do people from all over the world come to America? Opportunity. Better chance to make a living. More economy. More everything. They came over, they stayed. They sent for their relatives. And most of the Gypsies that came from the old country came to Chicago, to New York, to the major cities. More people, more work. Like, they would never go into St. Paul or a little town like Kenosha or Des Plaines. They would come into a main big city. Most of the Gypsies that came to Chicago originated on Maxwell Street.

"Then in the wintertime we'd go south, to Florida or Texas or somewhere. And wherever we wandered, we tried to make a buck."

"And the women did all the work," said Rosie. "I remember when I was small and we went in horses and wagons. Caravans of fifty, seventy-five people. The women would walk for a mile from our camp to get water. Or we'd go to a dairy and carry back those big containers of milk. The men would be sitting around the fire, sleeping or eating or joking. They wouldn't even watch the kids while the women went. Then we'd clean the chickens while the men sat around and smoked. And then when we ate the women weren't allowed to sit around the table where the men ate. But all over the world that's changing."

"When she goes outside now," said Bob Montes, "she makes me babysit."

# JIMMY STEFANOVIC

Jimmy Stefanovic, owner of the thriving hot-dog stand on the northwest corner of Halsted and Maxwell, was born on July 11, 1901, in Gostivar, Macedonia, Yugoslavia. ("Was that time Turkish rule in our country.") He came to America in 1939, landing in New York harbor with seven dollars in his pocket. The customs official said, "Lucky seven." Jimmy, who spoke no English repeated respectfully, "Lucky seven. Lucky seven." Jimmy traveled first to an uncle in Detroit. He asked his uncle, "What means this, 'Lucky seven'?" The uncle explained. Jimmy took it as an omen.

Jimmy is husky, pouchy, pale, mild-tempered. He arrives at the stand each morning at about eleven and enters at the rear where he has an office and where the bags of onions are plopped, the Polish sausages and Vienna hot dogs and hamburgers and pork chops are stored, the barrels of pickles and peppers are kept, and the cases of soda pop are stacked. It is from here that he orchestrates his twenty-five employees at this twenty-four-hour-a-day stand which, at peak hours, may have forty or fifty customers jamming up to its steamy open windows.

At seven-thirty each evening, he slips off his white apron, tugs into his jacket or coat, pushes a fedora on to his baldish head and walks out to the corner where his chauffeur-driven Cadillac awaits.

"I grow up in Russia, in Kamenets Podolskiy, where my father have candy manufacturing business," said Jimmy, seated at a table in the back of the hot-dog stand. "And that's when first time I hear Chicago. One old man named Faranya work as a chauffeur for my father. He drive the buggy with the horses. I ride all the time with him. He like whiskey. I give him always a nickel to buy bottle. I am nine, ten years old. He drink one gulp, finish bottle. He was once in Chicago. He tell me, 'You young boy. You go over there to Chicago. Over there is future.' And I put it in my head and I never take it out, Chicago.

"There come the time the Revolution—1919. That time in Russia was very bad. The Russian Red Army was retreating through our town. Two blocks south already was Rumanian Army. When the Russians retreat, they rob the stores. Break the stores and everything. They come to our store. My brother Daniel is fifteen and he say to them, 'What kind liberty you give? You criminals. You steal. You not give liberty.'

"Then we left Russia in a hurry. Left everything behind. We want to travel to Rumanian border and get to Yugoslavia. It is twenty-five kilometers away, but we walk through forest for a hundred days. Why so long? We was sitting here three days, after one mile five days, after two miles five days. You cannot go through. They was fighting, fighting. War, fighting. Oh, guns! No stop. Night and day. My three sisters, two brothers and mother and father and my uncle and me. We get to the border and stay forty days in the forest. We meet a Frenchman, a Chinese, and one Italian, who is famous violinist. We hide together. We wait for moon to get dark. And we eat only green corn that we steal. They call it *carroosa*. And then we are able to get bread. Across in Rumania near the border is a town where there are men who did business with my father. So now, my uncle has a big dog, name Dooruff. My uncle shave him like a sheep except for around the neck, so he look like a lion. The dog was trained good. So smart this dog. He understand everything what you say to him. He used to go with the buggy from our town in Russia to Rumania. He knows the way. My father take Dooruff, put message around his neck and with some gold pieces, and tell him, 'Go to friends in Rumanian town across the river and get bread.'

"Before you know it, Dooruff swims back with basket of bread around his neck. We take the bread all wet and dry it in the sun. He do this twenty, twenty-five times. Our whole family eat, and the Frenchman and the Chinese and the Italian eat. Dooruff save our life.

"All the time dog was going, we hear shooting. One night

Dooruff comes back, he has blood all over. They shot the dog. He return to us and then he lay down. Everybody was cry. And my uncle, 'Oh, they killed the dog. Son-of-a-bitches,' and this and that. He died, dog. We make grave, everything. Everybody was in his funeral. Italian man play the violin. Everybody was sorry for dog."

The Stefanovic family eventually crossed the river in a canoe into Rumania. The other men did not leave the forest yet. The Frenchman asked Jimmy to take a letter with him and mail it when he got to Yugoslavia. Jimmy put it in his boot. When the Rumanians searched Jimmy, he tried to say his boots were so tight they wouldn't come off; he was afraid the letter just might get him in trouble. "But two soldiers try to get boot off," said Jimmy. "I pulled my foot. It hurt so much. Finally I lose my foot and the soldiers fall down over there and I fall down in the middle of the room. They see the letter. 'We gonna kill him,' they say. 'Shoot! He's a spy!' But they wait. They take me to jail. Prison full of people who are communists. The Rumanians kill the communists like fly over there. When I see this I say, 'What the hell. Good-by my friends and family.' They call me. I am ready to die. But I am taken to the commandant. He says he knows my father, asks about the letter. I tell him. He let go of me.

"In my mind is still Chicago. After I come home, I apply for passport at American consul. They tell me immigration is now strict. Yugoslav quota nine hundred people yearly. And he tell me we got sixteen thousand in line already. He say, 'When I put your name, you have to wait at least twenty years. Maybe fifteen years, if somebody die.' I figure, 'What the hell, it cost me nothing,' and I put my name down. They say, 'Okay, when time come, we gonna call you.' And I forget about it.

"I go to Bucharest, Rumania. There is a big marketplace, like Maxwell Street. Two thousand people come in a day. I open up a candy and ice cream store, like my father had. But they don't like foreign people. They say, 'Rumania for Rumanians.' So I go back to Belgrade. I work with my family.

"One day I get letter from American consul. It is 1939. I say, 'What do they want with me?' I forget altogether. Fifteen, sixteen years. My number come up and I can get visa. And it's one month time they give to decide. Now, I have one brother-in-law from my first wife, who had died. He come back from America. He say it is Depression times. 'What the hell, peoples in America not working.' He said, 'You got good job here. Stay.' I was making six dollars a day in Belgrade. He say in America the best people make only six dollars a week! Everybody was counter for me to go. I say, I kid with myself, 'After sixteen years, I cannot renounce.' But also I see the newspaper. 'Hitler take Czechoslovakia.' 'Hitler take Prague.' 'Hitler take Vienna.' Hitler. Hitler. I see Mussolini take Albania. I say to family, 'Now is time to go. Now is trouble. You see yourself. I gonna go over there. In case you get in trouble, I gonna help you.'

"I got to Chicago, where I have an aunt. At first I sell on street corners what they call—Affy Taples? Tappy Affles?"

Taffy Apples?

"Taffy Apples."

Jimmy saved $280 in three months. His aunt owned the hot-dog stand on Maxwell and Halsted. She was sickly, didn't care much for the stand. Jimmy saw a future in it much brighter than the taffy-apple business. He borrowed money from friends and relatives and bought the stand from his aunt.

I asked how he built it up, from a small business with five or six employees to a minor empire.

"I build like this: Take care of the stuff; give fresh stuff; no put too much; no fry too much; be nice to people. Somebody no like, I take back; I give money back, and I throw this away; I never sell it again. And like this. I never buy cheap stuff.

"I learn that in marketplace in Bucharest. I want best vanilla ice cream. Salesman come and say, 'Sell it to you for ten cents.' I say, 'I pay twelve cents and I don't want no water in it.' Competitors think I am crazy. But soon I work eight hours a day and make five thousand a week. They work twelve hours and make one thousand a week.

"My trade now come from all over. Only make one-fourth from around Maxwell Street. Maxwell Street hot dog is famous all over the world now. Example: Man stop and say, 'I heard about your sandwich in Vietnam.' When he was discharged he come from San

Francisco to New York and make special stop for pork chop and hot dog on Maxwell.

"People say, 'Oh, the smell of the hot dog on Maxwell is so special. How come it is?' Keep fresh water. Watch the fire is just right. When you take care, you gonna smell good ones. When you keep too long, you not gonna smell nothing but burnt."

Jimmy has three sons and a daughter in America, all in their twenties. The boys worked at the stand briefly, but he says, "I took them off."

"They too naïve," he said. "For example, I gonna tell you some story like this: A guy, he say, 'Listen, Joe, keep this package here. I gonna come back in an hour.' Now my son could make close friendship with this man. Maybe in the package is dope. Or he say, 'Joe, take this package for me for favor to Roosevelt Road and this and that.' They do it. You see, it is dangerous. They can make bad friends. From bad neighborhood, you see, you cannot find good friends here."

In recent years, Jimmy has suffered various internal ailments. He has spent a number of weeks in the hospital, and then recuperated in his spacious Oak Park home. He has also suffered some distress of the heart. Several years ago he helped bring over two nephews from Yugoslavia. He brought them into his business. Without consulting him, they took the newly learned know-how and opened first one hot-dog stand down the street, and then a second. And sometimes even when Jimmy was in earshot, they might mimic the old strong man growing sickly. Jimmy does not speak about this.

But his business, nonetheless, still thrives. And it is still open all day and all night.

"Ah, is too many reasons why we open all night," he said. "When you keep closed, they break inside, they steal everything. One time I closed, they steal a hundred twenty cases of pop from in the back. Nighttime here on the corner is dead when we be closed. When we open, traffic little bit is. Truckmen stop. Buy a hot dog. Or milkman coming, buying pork chop. Or policeman come and buying soda. Or somebody else come and want three can soda or something. You see, when I'm open, corner is life."

# MARIO DOVALINA

On a muggy night in 1947 a twenty-four-year-old Mexican named Mario Dovalina crossed the Rio Grande River into America. He crossed illegally and he landed penniless. He is the owner today of the Taqueria Restaurant on Halsted Street, a few doors south of Maxwell Street, and is also president of Pepe's, Inc., a Chicago-based chain of fourteen Mexican restaurants. In the March 1975 issue of the "Food Service Chain Executive," Dovalina was named "chain executive of the month." Profits may run to a half million dollars a year or more.

He has also begun to sell to the nation's supermarkets his frozen tacos, tostadoes, tortillas, and shrimp fritters.

At the time of his honor in the "food chain" monthly, Dovalino was fifty-one years old. He is broad-shouldered, tawny-skinned, gray-haired, and balding, with heavy gray sideburns, dark heavy eyebrows, grayish mustache and goatee, baggy Beagle eyes. He has an office in his factory on Randolph Street. It is rife with the pungency of Mexican spices. When we spoke, he puffed on a black pipe and wore a red ascot.

Why did you come to America?

"Why do people come to America?" he asked rhetorically. "I guess the great public relations that this country has with all the other parts of the world. They tell everyone that America is the greatest country in the world for opportunity for young people. And I believed.

"I had come from what in Mexico is considered a middle-class family, by that is meant we never went hungry. My father was a justice of the peace in Saragossa, which is about sixty miles from the Texas border. I wanted to be an aeronautical engineer and went to college in Mexico City. I stayed with relatives. But the saying in Mexico is that dead fish and guests stink after three days. I wasn't very happy. So I quit school, got a job as a radio announcer. And I wasn't making any money at all. I decided to come to America. When you are young, you have dreams. You want to do something, and you have that adventurous attitude in your mind. You're not happy with your status, and you're looking for something better. I tried to get a visa to come to America. The immigration quota was strict and I was turned down. No soap. I was determined, and with two friends we went.

"It was very exciting. We paid a man five or ten pesos, I don't remember which, to take us across. We went with a *patero*. A *pato* is duck in Spanish. And a patero owns a light canvas boat which is called a pato. It was just big enough for the four of us. It was hidden in the bushes by the river. We came across at night. One of the fellows I crossed with had done it before. And he was confident he could take us to a ranch where we could work and make money.

"We landed near Macalla, Texas. We quickly ran up on shore and slipped into the trees and the bushes. We headed for the ranch this fellow knew about. But after fifteen or twenty minutes, we realized we were lost. There were no signs except "No Trespassing!" and "Government Property." It began to drizzle. With the last money I had, I had bought a pair of new shoes, which was the biggest mistake I made because we had to walk and walk. Oh! You see my other shoes were a shame. I was really ashamed of them. I thought I should make a good impression when I came to the new country, the land of opportunity, and I should be dressed to take advantage of it. I also wore a suit, a gabardine suit. I didn't own very much in the way of clothes at the time.

"We walked and walked. It was so muggy. It was rainy. My feet in the new shoes were burning up. We came across a lot of orchards—orange groves. At one point we could see lights, automobile lights from a highway. 'Oh,' I said, 'let's go towards the highway. That would be the most logical. . . .' So we crossed fences and then suddenly we saw a pickup truck and with a guy on the running board. He had a spotlight and they were shooting from the truck. I thought, 'They're after us!' We dived behind bushes. They drove by, still shooting, and I now think they were hunting for animals, not for us. Anyway, it scared the hell out of us.

"We continued on in the dark and in the rain. We walked for hours. I had blisters all over the place. But we couldn't stop because if we did, we'd never get up.

"Soon, we hit the highway and we heard Mexican music. We found some people who gave directions to the farm we were heading for. It was about twenty miles away! We go back along the highway. And every time we see headlights, we figure it's the police, and we dive off the road. After a while, we stopped doing that. We were in such pain, we didn't care anymore. We figured, 'Well, heck, that's the best thing that can happen to us if they catch us, bring us back.'

"We arrived at the farm at seven in the morning. Soaking wet and tired. So tired. It was a packing company that packed oranges, citrus fruits, and they protected the wetbacks—which is what they called illegal Mexican immigrants, because they could pay 'em a lot less than the regular people in the town. As a matter of fact, they were paying forty-five cents an hour at the time to us, and their regular people from the area they were paying a dollar twenty-five, a dollar fifty an hour.

"So we come in, they let us go to the basement of the plant, and we laid down on the top of crates and bags and we were out in a minute. In about an hour the foreman came over to ask us if we wanted to work. That was the biggest decision. After walking with blisters and no money in your pocket and your bones ache so much—and then be offered a job! Two of us rose. The other kid said, 'I can't get up.' We unloaded a trailerful of crates. We must have been a sight because other people started to help us. You can just imagine! They felt sorry for us, the way we looked. I stayed for a few months and saved up twenty-eight dollars and decided to move on.

"I was disappointed in the discrimination as far as pay was concerned. But we couldn't say anything because we were here illegally, so you have to put up with it. You have no choice. You either take it or leave it. And then I heard that when things were bad, when the crops were over, then the company would call the immigration authorities. The company doesn't need the wetbacks anymore so they send 'em back. Hypocrites, you know.

"I didn't want to go back until I made maybe a few thousand dollars. It's every Mexican's dream—every foreigner's dream, I guess—to come to America and get a business, make your goal, and return to your country. That is until the person starts to grow roots in America. Then he stays.

"But this life on the fruit farm was not my idea of America. I had been practically brainwashed in Mexico by all the Hollywood movies. The standard of living portrayed was just fabulous. And in Mexico, jobs are very scarce. I had an uncle in Chicago, and so that's where I wanted to go to look for the America I had seen in the movies.

"I began to talk to the truck drivers and ask 'em for rides. 'Will you take me to Chicago?' 'No, we don't go to Chicago.' One day there was a fellow and I said, 'You going north?' He said, 'Sure, I'll take you.' I ran to my room. I picked up everything I had. Some clothes on the line drying, got my Mackinaw jacket, tied it into a bundle—like a regular bum—and I ran and he took me.

"Then I went with this truck driver. He drove me all over Texas. I was helping him load and unload. I'd say, 'When are we going north?' A week passed and I'm still in Texas. I was buying my own meals and sleeping in the truck. Finally, he's in Houston and he says, 'That's as far as I go.' He dropped me off! I had left only eleven dollars. I hadn't shaved. I was carrying my bundle. I went over to a Mexican coming out of a supermarket to ask him where a barbershop is where they speak my language, but the guy didn't give me a chance. He looked at me and figured, 'Well, this guy's a bum. He's going to ask for a dime.' The second guy that I approached, also Mexican, put me on a bus and told the bus driver where to let me off. It was a Mexican neighborhood.

"I asked around and found out that Texas City was nearby. I had an uncle there. So with the last money I had, I took a bus to Texas City. My uncle wasn't too happy with me coming in the way I was. You know, illegally. He was settled in the community and was respected, and he doesn't want to be bothered. Here it comes again, the dead fish and guests stink after three days. I told him I wanted to go to Chicago. Right away he says, 'How much do you need?' He lent me forty dollars and put me on a bus.

"It was November, one day after Thanksgiving Day when I arrived in Chicago. It was cold, and I mean cold. Oh, how the wind was blowing. I had never known such cold. I wore only an Army field jacket that my uncle had given me.

"I took a bus to my uncle's house on Roosevelt Road. This uncle was my father's brother. He was happy to see me. He helped get me a job washing windows at the Seneca Hotel. I learned there was better money in a factory where they made springs, and I went to work there. Now, I needed some identification to get around some places. So I signed up with the Selective Service to get a draft card, an ID card. And sure enough, I'm classified 1A and inducted into the Army. I've got a big mustache and I've got no English. Can you imagine! Yet I qualify for officer's school. They had given a test with multiple choice. I could read English because I had studied it in school, though I couldn't speak it.

"Well, I'm sent to Camp McCoy in Wisconsin and I remember one day talking to a sergeant, telling him my story, and he said, 'You mean you're in this country illegally? You know, they aren't supposed to draft you. Aliens aren't allowed to be drafted.' He talked with the captain. The captain talked to the commander. And pretty soon they called me into the office and they said, 'You're free to go. Just wait a couple of days until we process all these papers, but we have no right to have you here.' By then, I was up to here with the military life. I was an outstanding recruit, and I was happy. But let me tell you, when I found out that I could get out, heck, I was happier yet.

"They gave me an honorable discharge. But they reported me to immigration authorities. Immigration gave me three months to settle my affairs and return to Mexico. Now, before entering the Army, I had met a girl at the farewell party given me by my landlady. We corresponded while I was away and I'd come back every weekend to see her. We had made out that as soon as I got out of the Army, we'd marry. Which we did. A little sooner than we expected, though.

"Since she was an American citizen, I became an American citizen. I started selling vacuum cleaners. That's when I came to know that there were no decent Mexican restaurants in Chicago.

"There were a lot of greasy spoons that catered to Mexicans. I figured, 'Well, anybody that can come in here with a halfway decent place can clean up. Make a fortune. Which—well, then I opened my first place on Roosevelt Road near Ashland, where my uncle lived. It was strictly tacos at first. Then I brought my brother up from Mexico to help me. We opened a place on Halsted Street, about two blocks north of Maxwell Street. We were very, very successful there. Then we opened up another place around the corner on Roosevelt and Halsted—we bought Gold's Restaurant. It was a very famous Jewish restaurant. And we took over the second floor which they had as a banquet hall. [It was in this hall that Benny Goodman played when he was a young professional, and where Jake "Greasy Thumb" Guzik, the Capone mob brain, threw the fiftieth wedding anniversary party for his parents.] We converted the banquet hall into a nightclub called El Mirador. That was good, but we lost our pants in the restaurant downstairs. We expanded too fast. Also, we had kept it a Jewish restaurant. And we kept the same help, which was a mistake. They stole us blind. They gave the food away to customers, and the stuff they could serve themselves they wouldn't put on the ticket.

"From there, we moved to our location on Halsted by Maxwell in 1963, when the University of Illinois took over the area where our restaurants were.

"I figured we had a future on Maxwell Street because the market in itself was a landmark of the city. I had the idea it was going to remain the same. It didn't. And during the '60s the neighborhood changed so much. It became a jungle. It is so dangerous in that store. We have an armed guard there. That's how bad things are. I rarely go there anymore. I'm busy with other things, and I have good people working there for nearly fifteen years and they seem happy. They're making a living. And it's still profitable."

Dovalino became a voice in the community when he took over the Spanish-language paper, *Prenza Libre,* which means *Free Press.*

"We fought the city on some issues, particularly at the time when the site was chosen for the University of Illinois at Chicago.

"I don't know if I should tell it to you, this story, but you see, when you run a paper and you are an honest man, it's a big responsibility. And when you start mixing up politics and business and a newspaper, you get into trouble. You start—especially in Chicago—if you start writing editorials against the machine, especially against Mayor Daley, which I was doing at the time . . . I don't know if I should tell you these things. . . . I trust that you will be discreet about it. . . .

"I was against the university site because I was prejudiced, naturally. My restaurants would be torn down. Many of my people lived there. But it was also a great melting pot. Greeks, Jews, Italians, Scandinavians. Everybody lived happy. Well, I came to the conclusion I could not stay in the restaurant business and in the newspaper business at the same time . . . you know, inspectors and things like that.

"They would come and they would be more strict than . . . Like when I opened my place near Maxwell Street. I did everything according to the books. But I couldn't get license approval. The inspector was coming in, measuring the steps going down to the basement . . . he said, no good. The joints on the floor in the basement were supposed to be twelve inches apart instead of sixteen inches. . . . The beams weren't right. Every little thing was wrong. It was obvious that they weren't going to co-operate with me if I wasn't going to co-operate with them. The newspaper was more a hobby than a business. And so why have a paper if you cannot say what you want? I didn't stop saying what I want; I just gave up the paper."

After having been in America for twenty-seven years now, have your dreams as a youth in Mexico fit with your reality today?

"I'm very, very happy. I bought a home in Waukegan with my family. I have the most beautiful setting. It is on a hill overlooking a golf course—the golf course is my backyard. The home is not luxurious, but for me—and on the street we live—it's from a storybook.

"What's funny is that the success I made in the restaurant business is related directly to Mexico. And to my mother. She made us learn how to cook, made us self-reliant. She also wrote a cookbook. With all her recipes. She wrote it in fact for my sister. I use her recipes in the book to this day. They're all in Spanish. It is in pen-and-ink on notebook paper and it's thick. I carry it with me all the time. It is my Bible."

Do you know of many successful Mexicans in America?

"Some, but not too many, unfortunately. The big reason is the dollar. That's the reason everyone comes here. To make a fortune and return. But they are kept down by American society generally. There is such harassment of the poor people. It is inhuman. They will stop you on the street and, if you don't have any papers to prove you're a citizen, they just put you in a wagon and send you back to Mexico. They don't even ask if you've got a home or a family. . . .

"And the Mexicans are so naïve. So honest. They are asked, 'How did you come here.' The Mexican answers, 'Well, I crossed the border.' 'Where.' 'Oh, such and such.' And the police are typing. It's a full confession. The people don't know that they have rights. They by right can be given a visa. So they are sent back to Mexico and meanwhile their family is waiting for them to return to supper. Not only that, the authorities break into a home, with no search warrant, and ask all kinds of questions. It is inhuman.

"The people in authority are so blind. They think the poor Mexicans are a blight. They don't realize that if they were given immunity these people would become a thriving part of the economic life of this city, this country. What happens is the Mexican lives with the fear he will be kicked out tomorrow. So he doesn't buy a home, he doesn't establish himself. He is always with a suitcase, ready to go. And the money he makes, he sends back to Mexico.

"But if you come down to it and compare how it is here and how it is in Mexico or anyplace else, it is still the best country in the world.

"What made this country so great was that the land was open to people from all over the world.

"But we're losing that. We're sending people back that are contributing, or can contribute, to the culture.

"America has always liked the cheap labor, though. Mexicans built half the railroads in this country. And if you wanted to, you could go to the Hilton Hotel, or any big hotels, and send back all the cheap Mexican help and the big hotels would be out of business tomorrow. They rely on that help. A lot of industries do, too.

"But when the illegal immigrants begin to compete with U.S. citizens, they'll send the cheap help back. Otherwise they'll use them unfairly. Not just Mexicans. Look at the Greeks and the Italians who jump ship. I read where fifty Polish washerwomen recently were working in the John Hancock Building. Someone complained they weren't citizens and they are being deported. It's such a big country. We have room for them all.

"I think these newcomers are like I was. I came here with nothing in mind but a dream, and to look for a job. I was willing to work. I did not come to America to steal."

# THE STREET, 1967

## PLAN ELIMINATION OF
## MAXWELL STREET MARKET

—The department of urban renewal has announced plans for a large slum clearance program that will wipe out the famous Maxwell Street market.

However, merchants already have mapped plans for a new Maxwell Street market to be the first commercial condominium development in the nation. It will be known as the Maxwell International Shopping Center.

Also to be included in the urban renewal area, immediately south of the Chicago Circle campus of the University of Illinois, will be about 900 apartments and houses.

CHICAGO *AMERICAN*
*April 29, 1967*

# THE STREET, 1967

## MAXWELL STREET MARKET
## CLEARANCE OK'D

—The city has received approval for early purchase of properties in the Maxwell Street area for expansion of the University of Illinois Chicago Circle campus.

It is the first phase of the Roosevelt-Halsted urban renewal project that will eliminate the old Maxwell Street Market. . . .

The three blocks bounded by Roosevelt, Maxwell, Newberry and Morgan will be used for a new physical education building for the Circle campus.

CHICAGO *DAILY NEWS*
*October 2, 1967*

# V

# MARKET MASTERS

Early in 1976, a tradition on Maxwell Street that spanned nearly the whole of the century came to a shameful end. The post of market master was abolished, and the assignment of collecting the fees from the stands was turned over for regulation to the state Department of Revenue.

One Sunday morning in January of 1976 Irv Gordon, the market master of Maxwell Street since 1950, did not show up.

Irv Gordon was then fifty-nine years old and sickly. He had suffered two heart attacks and swallowed as many as twelve nitroglycerine tablets a day. He was once known as a physically powerful man, besides having the immense backing of city hall "clout," the Chicago term for political influence. He dressed in the latest *nouveau-riche* styles, in spring wearing even an all-white leisure suit with pink shirt and white shoes. Appropriate-looking perhaps for the lawns where he lived in suburban Skokie, but dramatically out of place among the grime and stench of Maxwell Street. His hair was white and sparse on top, where his reddish pate glistened in the sun as he made his rounds among the hundreds of stands. He had one or two policemen with him. He was supposed to collect seventeen cents per stand. When I had a small belt stand in the late 1950s, Gordon and his assistant, Sam "Suzi" Schuman, would collect from me two dollars every Sunday. It was said that better and bigger stands would pay as much as one or two hundred dollars a day. And who knows what a gold mine like Jimmy's hot-dog stand would shell out for the privilege of retaining the finest spot in the market?

Gordon's "office" was at the third table of three tables in Nate's delicatessen. He had owned a jewelry store on the street. But eventually, for reasons he would not discuss, he became the market master solely. He never made more than a ten-thousand-dollar-a-year salary from the city for his work as market master. But he lived and dressed in a manner quite unbecoming his modest salary.

Questions concerning Gordon, the market master, began as early as 1951, his second year on the job. In a confidential memo to his editor, a reporter for the Chicago *Sun-Times* wrote: "Gordon is a slick fellow, but I think we can catch him. . . . My informant at city hall said Gordon and the cop who works with him are probably getting a percentage of the take. . . . I dropped in on Gordon again. He's mad. He again protested his innocence in loud and strident terms. At which time, Carey, the cop, walked in. That jewelry store of Gordon's gets an awful lot of protection, it seems."

In 1965, Alderman John J. Hoellen charged in city council that "the market master is collecting extralegal fees."

In a Chicago *Sun-Times* article of November 30, 1965, Gordon denied the charges, declaring, "I'm sure he hasn't got anything to back them up."

Gordon remained on the job, and the matter dissolved, until the 1970s.

Investigations began to escalate around Maxwell Street. There were a couple of murders of men who owned stands, and it was learned that they had been dealing in stolen merchandise. There was a question of the role of the underworld on Maxwell Street. Governor of Illinois James Thompson, onetime U. S. Attorney and a man who was known as a fierce and unrelenting crime hunter, was an antique collector who would sometimes stroll around Maxwell Street on Sunday. He could not help but wonder about whether some of the goods there were ill-gotten.

As the heat increased, Gordon grew more nervous. He told a friend that he couldn't even go to bed anymore without hearing a G-man breathing a few feet away. When he noticed Willie the underwear-stand man speaking to someone he termed suspicious, he called Willie over and in a fit of paranoia berated him for being a stoolie.

One day in Nate's, Gordon and a policeman friend of his were

talking nervously. It was a bit loud in Nate's. Gordon said to the cop, "What?" The cop replied, "What?" Gordon: "What?" People nearby began to laugh.

Gordon had replaced Suzi Schuman as assistant market master when Schuman developed problems. He was eventually found to be a slumlord. When it came to light in the press, he quickly resigned his position as building inspector and as a precinct captain in the First Ward. Suzi was a legend of sorts on the street. He and his numerous brothers lived on Maxwell Street for many years. For a long time, Suzi was an assistant to several market masters. He was most conspicuous when he was assistant to the market master Harry Minsky who had a speech defect and could barely whisper. But he would relay a message to Suzi and Suzi would carry out the order. "Get your stand out of there," Suzi would say. "Get it the hell out!" Suzi was reputed to carry a gun.

Suzi remains friendly with John D'Arco, former head of the First Ward. The two see each other frequently in Miami Beach, where they both have winter residences.

Before Minsky, there was a market master named Marty Klass, who went blind. One former store owner, Morris Carl, remembers pleading with Klass to have a man move his stand from in front of his store since the man was selling the same items as Carl. Klass refused. Carl says that Klass went blind because people hated him so much.

Another previous market master was Harry Lapping. A story in the Chicago *Tribune,* dated May 19, 1926, said: "Acting on a report by Corporation Counsel Francis K. Busch that the Maxwell Street Market has become honeycombed with graft and political favoritism under the supervision of Harry Lapping, Mayor Dever today accepted the resignation of Lapping. . . . He recommended the appointment of Max Janowski as Lapping's successor." In approving Janowski to be market master, Mayor Dever expressed a desire to "clean up the Maxwell Street situation by abolishing the practice of granting favors to the peddlers and hucksters in return for political activities."

The man whom Lapping had replaced was Louis Krakow, who had himself been deposed by the city hall for "violations" unbecoming a city employee. However, the Krakow family, which included the soon-to-be-boxer King Levinsky, took this bitterly, particularly when Lapping, in March of 1923, attempted to shorten the Krakow family's nineteen-foot fish stand to the legal limit of nine feet. A riot ensued which included five Krakow women who began flinging fish in buckets and in singles at Lapping and his assistant. Then fists flew. A riot call to the Maxwell Street police station brought a squad of policemen who squelched the fish fight.

It didn't take long for the very first market master, A. I. Goldstein, in 1913, to run into troubles that in one way or another would plague nearly each of his predecessors. This pyramid headline in the Chicago *Tribune* of July 2, 1913, tells the story:

## SEEK TO ENJOIN
## MARKET MASTER

### MAXWELL STREET PEDDLERS
### TO HIRE LAWYER
### TO FIGHT OVERCHARGES

## ALLEGE DISCRIMINATION

Enemy of Manny Abrahams*
Forced to Pay 75 Cents Daily;
Legal Rate 10 Cents

* Manny Abrahams was then alderman of the ward.

# THE STREET, 1968

## ONCE BUSY MAXWELL ST. DYING

—Maxwell Street, they say at city hall, has but two or three more years to live. . . . Maxwell Street was born of immigrants of another century. The slums they left behind are gone now, flattened into rubble by urban renewal and usurped by the expanding University of Illinois campus to the south.

The Dan Ryan Expressway cut the street to less than four blocks and of these the market area now occupies less than two. . . .

Once, thousands pushed and shoved to get at what seemed to them like a king's ransom in beggars' treasures, a vast and motley display rivalling any castle keep on market day nine centuries ago.

The hysteria is gone now and only a handful wander about. . . .

CHICAGO *TRIBUNE*
*November 25, 1968*

# VI

# DEMOLITION

The destruction of the Maxwell Street area is plotted out neatly, precisely, coldly on a map on the wall of the Cleveland Wrecking Company on North Milwaukee Avenue in Chicago, some eight miles northwest of Maxwell Street. The map is a methodically detailed, blue-and-white representation of the "Roosevelt-Halsted and Roosevelt-Clinton slum and blighted area redevelopment project." Each block is numbered. Each house is numbered. It includes a total of nearly one hundred acres and hundreds of frame and brick buildings, some of which had been standing for a hundred years.

In the early 1950s city hall had decided that more roads were needed to transport the growing population of the metropolis. The thinking was the same in every city and, for that matter, virtually every village in America. The Age of the Auto was certainly upon us. For various reasons, many of them good, it was decided in Chicago to construct the Dan Ryan Expressway from downtown to the South Side. Part of that expressway would come through Maxwell Street. At first, the plan was to have it course down Halsted Street. But such a protest arose, a protest that had substance and clout, that the city then contrived to build the road two blocks east of Halsted, to Jefferson Street.

In the early 1960s, after a search of nine years, a site to build the new University of Illinois at Chicago Circle was decided upon. It would include a part of Maxwell Street west of Halsted. The bulk of the destruction, however, had to do with the area north of Roosevelt, in a neighborhood that was the melting pot of melting pots. Italians, Greeks, Swedes, Gypsies, Mexicans, Jews, and Blacks worked and lived side by side. The fight to save that area became a *cause célèbre,* led by Mrs. Florence Scala, a resident there. A two-year citizens' protest ensued, costing the community thirty-five thousand dollars. Street carnivals, raffles, and other fund-raising activities were held to pay for the battle.

Mrs. Scala was an outspoken leader, condemning Mayor Daley in particular and city hall in general for what she termed a devious, insensitive, probably graft-influenced decision to relocate some ten thousand residents. She sought help from politicians. Nothing. She tried the church: she visited Chicago's Cardinal Albert Meyer. He pointed a finger at her and said, "This is a secret conference. And remember, this meeting never happened." And nothing did happen. She sent two letters to the President of the United States, John Kennedy. No reply. She and her followers tried the judicial system. The case eventually reached the Supreme Court of the United States, in late May of 1963. The Supreme Court refused to hear the appeals of the community to preserve the neighborhood.

Meanwhile, her home was bombed, and her back porch and stairway demolished. The culprits were never caught. Her life was threatened by anonymous phone callers.

The city continued to buy land from residents, who feared repercussions if they did not sell.

In the area, also, was the famous Hull House, the old settlement house begun by Jane Addams, the only woman ever to win the Nobel Prize for Peace. It was at Hull House where Benny Goodman developed as a musician, where children from impoverished homes throughout the area would come for food, for recreation, for comfort.

Jane Addams' associate, Jessie Binford, was in her late eighties when the fight to save the neighborhood was in full fury. When the Supreme Court turned down the plea, and the fate of the area was assured, Mrs. Binford asked, "What has happened to justice in America?"

Only one small part of Maxwell Street was knocked down by the university project. At first, all of Maxwell was supposed to go, according to Florence Scala. "Then, when they began to tear down," recalled Mrs. Scala, "for some reason Maxwell Street was excluded. It drove us up the wall. When you looked at it, Maxwell Street was the area that should have gone because it was such a slum, but there was never a focus there. There never seemed much of a community rallying around it, either. The people were very poor and disorganized, and, besides, there wasn't very much for them to keep. And the merchants were usually the last ones to buck it because they depended on the city for all kinds of favors, and they depended on the city in order to exist, really, and they were all strong Daley people."

Bernard Abrams, the record-shop owner, said, "If they knocked down all of Maxwell Street, all that revenue, all that tax-free revenue for First Ward officials would be gone."

And top First Ward officials, such as John D'Arco and Buddy Jacobson, were acknowledged to have the ear of the highest elected officers in city hall, city hall being, like Maxwell Street, in the First Ward.

Hobby Sherman, owner of Sherman's Pants on Maxwell Street, believes Maxwell Street will stay alive because it provides a kind of buffer for downtown. "The Loop people know," said Sherman, "that if Maxwell Street died, all the people, all the dregs of humanity that come to Maxwell Street to shop, they'd go to the Loop. And the entire Loop would come tumbling down. It couldn't handle all the thievery. It would just be overrun by the worst element of society. We can handle the thieves better here. We know them and they know us. Our stores are smaller and we have a lot more help per square foot. I've heard that at Marshall Field television sets have walked right out the door. On Maxwell Street, we have about one helper for every customer. A customer comes in and immediately a salesman is with him. 'Can I help you?' 'No, just looking.' The salesman walks with him. The customer says again, 'Hey, I'm just looking.' The salesman says, 'Well, I'm just looking, too.' "

Many others, though, disagree with Sherman and believe it is simply a matter of time before Maxwell Street, what's left of it, is razed by the bulldozers unleashed from the Department of Urban Renewal. For all around the street itself, demolition has been occurring off and on for over twenty years.

Many of the residents, illiterate and unworldly except for the ability to survive on the streets, found it a trauma to be asked to move. And many in their own way fought it with whatever means at their disposal. One thinks of the Polish cavalry in 1939 trying vainly to hold back the Nazi's enormous, mechanized army: swords versus tanks.

Some Maxwell Streeters refused to be evicted from their shacks and lopsided wooden apartment buildings. One man sat in front of the door of his apartment, a rifle on his knees. An urban renewal officer dressed as a priest finally persuaded him to relent. A neighboring woman spoke from behind her door and said that if anyone tried to evict her, she'd kill them. It wasn't known how armed she in fact was. About ten squad cars were called to the scene. The police chief called from the hallway, "We're going to have to come in, lady, and if you take a gun, we're going to have to use our guns." She slowly opened the door. Cops were on either side of it, and cops were down the stairwell and cops were lining the sidewalk and cops were bunched in the street. Several cops burst into her flat. She was ready for them, and tried to fight them off with her weapon, a frying pan.

Another woman had an estimated thirty cats in her six-room apartment. The cats were not housebroken and the place reeked. She smelled so much like her cats that dogs chased her down the street. For months urban renewal people tried to convince her that relocation in a good apartment in a good neighborhood would be impossible with all those cats. "I'm not gonna move," she said. "I love my cats." She didn't move until the day she looked out the window and saw a wrecking ball poised just a few feet away.

An eighty-year-old hermit lived in the boiler room of a large basement. He lived without plumbing facilities, slept on a cot banked with rags and newspapers to provide a mattress. He admitted, when discovered, that he had not shaved or bathed in thirteen years. He received forty dollars a month Social Security, a small portion being paid to an upstairs tenant for one meal a day. He had a faithful cur and seventeen cats, for whom he bought food regularly. In a memorandum at the time, an urban renewal official wrote, "This tenant is not truly senile although his mind does wander. His conversation is full of recollections of his days on the high seas and work in laying railroad tracks across this country."

One old Italian man was found to be living in a little frame house with a horse. Manure and hay were all over the floor.

Though some fought to stay, Ed Lally, director of Urban Renewal for the area, said "others went meek and mild."

One family that went without problem was the one living in that Chicago landmark on DeKoven Street, the onetime home of Mrs. O'Leary whose cow supposedly kicked over the kerosene lamp that precipitated the Chicago Fire of 1871. An Italian family had been living in the old frame house and renting it from the city for fifteen dollars a month. It was assumed the family could not afford to pay more. But when they were told they had to move, they bought a forty-thousand-dollar home in a northwestern suburb.

When the Maxwell Street people moved out, the vultures moved in. There are people who follow the urban renewal department all over the city. These people steal radiators, chrome, knobs, light fixtures, anything they can rip out. Guards were hired around Maxwell Street to patrol the area.

The buildings and houses were some of the oldest in the city, and some of the worst tended. Some were so old they did not have inside plumbing. They did not have gas jets. No electricity. "It was amazing," said Ed Lally, "that in this day and age, in the city of Chicago, to find buildings so terrible. I've never run into any buildings like that any place else in the city of Chicago."

The first construction company to work on the demolition of the Maxwell Street area was chosen by low bid. It was a company from Michigan. Apparently, it was a new company, or a company used to toppling trees and not houses. The workers had few proper tools, shoddy equipment, and an incredible lack of knowledge. They first misread the map and began tearing down the wrong houses on the wrong street. When they eventually got the right place, they went wild, nearly maiming passersby and endangering themselves. "It was fantastic," recalls Ed Lally. "They'd be standing on the top of a building and using a sledge to hit under them."

The Michigan company was swiftly discharged, to ward off the taking of innocent lives. The Chicago company was brought in.

Alan Rose of the Cleveland Wrecking Company remembered the beginning of the end. "The houses there were so old and weak," he said. "They were pushovers. You just knock over one and go to the next."

Looming cranes with either claw-heavy clamps or wrecking

balls worked the buildings over, these buildings that housed the poor Jewish immigrants at the turn of the century. The big-toothed clamp was used more than the ball. The clamp chews the building up, slowly but certainly. There is a thud as the clamp batters into the wall, then a crunching as the house's inner whitish wood, like intestines, are bared, and then masticated by the chomping clamp. The wood is torn away and hangs from the clamp like stiffened spittle. Throughout, the machine groaned like a ravished animal noisily savoring the entrails of its captured prey.

It was sometimes seen fit to use more meticulous means to lay the last of a house low. Workers slid crowbars in between mortar joints, the way a street-wise guy could pierce a knife deftly under one's heart. The joints would loosen and loosen and finally the remainder of the building would come apart piecemeal. Then canary-yellow bulldozers would gaily churn up the rubble, as building after building collapsed amid swirling dust.

As the buildings began to come down, amazing things were discovered. Passageways, some very long, were found underground. These cryptic routes were used at the turn of the century for the "carriage trade" to the whorehouses. Pillars of the community would have their horses and carriages parked at the door of a respectable store, and then they'd enter, slipping through a door, and make their way along the passage to the brothel.

A cache of 30-caliber Thompson submachine guns from the Capone era was come upon. In another underground setup, dank and cobwebby bottles of wine and whiskey of every conceivable size and shape were found under arches beyond arches beyond arches. The arches seemed to stretch for miles. It obviously was hidden there during Prohibition days. But why it was not touched, and who used it, is a mystery. The only clue is from a little ledger found there. It listed all the people to whose funerals flowers had been sent. The names were mainly known gangsters.

One day a wrecking ball hit the building at 1313 Peoria— around the corner from Maxwell Street—and money began flying out from it. The money was in the large bills that were printed in America until the 1930s. The walls of this house were brick, and the man who lived in the apartment, and who had died and left it empty about a year before, had apparently saved his money in the wall. He had wrapped his money in a cloth and stuck it behind removable bricks. The cloth broke open and the bills flew up in the air like a great pigeon release. The man working the crane slammed on the brakes. He jumped out of the cab and scooped up all the money he could and ran off. People came running from all over, fighting to grab the bills that had floated down from the sky.

That night, hundreds of people continued to hover around the demolished building, digging at the spot. Garbage drums were rolled over to the now rubble-strewn area, and fires were burned for illumination for the hunt. People and their long shadows dug well into the night. Nothing more was found.

Money wasn't the only thing buried behind some walls. Also discovered were several skeletons.

One dark night, one of the neighborhood winos stole into a house that was soon to be demolished. He put his hand out to get hold of some piping and instead grabbed something soft and spongy. He lit a match. And saw a man, or what was left of him. He had been dead about a week. There was some skin left on his bones that the rats had not eaten. But the heart was still there, still soft and spongy. It was the heart the wino had grabbed in the dark. He screamed and ran out of the house.

Some people that were relocated could not stay away from Maxwell Street. They built little wooden shacks in the rubble where they had lived. They slept in abandoned cars, or sneaked back into buildings that had not yet been demolished.

They burned garbage in the empty lots and cooked their food there as well. But much of the neighborhood was collapsing, or had collapsed, around them.

Ed Lally recalls that at night he could see from a distance embers glowing in the night. It resembled ravaged and deserted battlefields, deserted but for the bodies and rubble left behind.

# VII

# DUSK

In a strident burst of optimism the Chicago *Tribune Magazine* ran an article on Sunday, August 25, 1974, headlined in big bold black type:

## MAXWELL STREET LIVES

> On a Sunday morning, it's still a crowded bazaar stocked with hubcaps, hot dogs, TV sets, tacos, lox and leg holsters. Herewith, an introduction to the people, wares and pulse of a marketplace some said was dead. . . .

The headline would have been defter had it read: "Maxwell Street Survives." For Maxwell Street as it had been known for over a hundred years was now a husk of itself.

Besides the gradual neglect of the neighborhood decade after decade—as one poor family moved in to replace one that moved up—and besides its demolition and the resurrection of an expressway and a university in its midst, another factor occurred to change the mood and look of the street: the assassination of Dr. Martin Luther King, Jr.

In the Memphis dusk on April 4, 1968, the Reverend King stood on the open second-floor level of a motel. A rifle peeked out from a corner of a hotel window across the street and narrowed Dr. King in its sights. A shot from that rifle exploded and touched off eruptions in 125 American cities. Chicago was one.

In the aftermath of Dr. King's assassination, large sections of the West Side went up in smoke. Those blacks who participated in the burning and looting of their own neighborhoods seemed to be articulating what they had long been unable to articulate to white society. It appeared to be an attempted release from their poverty and ignorance and "the accumulated debris of their existence." "At the first show of provocative white behavior," wrote Richard Kluger, in *Simple Justice,* "they put their run-down sections of the city to the torch and then stoned the agents of the power establishment who came to put the fires out."*

The rioting in Chicago resulted in 162 buildings being destroyed by fire, eleven deaths, $9 million in property losses, and a notorious order by Mayor Richard J. Daley to the police to "shoot to kill arsonists and shoot to maim looters."

The Maxwell Street station house called in nearly one thousand added police officers. They were armed with riot guns. The area around Maxwell Street was cordoned off. The blinds in the police station windows were rolled down in a puff of dust, the first time they had been down since perhaps they were put up, over one hundred years before, so that no potential sniper could peer inside.

Mike Chiappetta, the "shamus" of Maxwell Street, remembers standing on the corner of Roosevelt and Halsted with a phalanx of other policemen and watching the flames going up around the city and listening to the intermittent explosions. "It made your skin crawl," he said.

Maxwell Street was virtually barricaded and walled. It was again a ghetto in the strictest sense of the word. Morrie Burres, the elderly black salesman in Kelly's sporting goods store, recalls, "I was angry about it and embarrassed as well because people look at me and figure because I'm black, too, well, 'He's one of them.' I didn't feel it should have been done. There was no reason for that. Sure, we *should* have more access to better jobs—if we're qualified and capable—but this wasn't the way to go about it. I mean, we were destroying our own neighborhoods, our own shopping centers. Black mothers couldn't get food for their children."

Hymie Strom, who owned a grocery store on Maxwell Street then, said, "I can't blame them for what they did. I can only blame the individual black who comes in and shoots up a store

---

* Richard Kluger, *Simple Justice: The History of Brown v. Board of Education and Black America's Struggle for Equality* (New York: Alfred A. Knopf, 1976), p. 762.

and kills somebody. But I can understand the riots. Wouldn't you riot if you've been treated all your life like an animal?"

It is generally considered on the street that the riots of 1968 changed the face of Maxwell Street. Blacks—particularly young adult blacks—got bolder, more belligerent, according to shopkeepers, and this contributed to the leave-taking of some of the better-known shops on the street.

Jack Tuchten, who owned a fruit and vegetable stand on Maxwell for over twenty years, said that now black kids would walk by, "grab some apples right in front of you and defy you to do anything about it. 'Hey put that apple back!' They'd say, 'Fuck you.' "

Hymie Strom remembers a black man came into his grocery soon after the riots and got upset when Strom gave him change in a "scoop" at the cash register. "How come you don't put the change in my hand, man?" the customer asked. Strom said, "Hey, mister, you got a chip on your shoulder?" The man said, "It ain't no chip, it's a log."

In the Taqueria owned by Mario Dovalino, a black man ate his dinner, then got up and dropped his check at the cash register. He said to the woman behind the counter, "My name is Crime, and Crime don't pay." And walked out.

"It's changed here," said Sidney Goldstein, who owns a jewelry stand. "There's a tension down here now."

The white business people on the street no longer want to keep their stores open after dark. The street begins to close earlier than it ever had.

White people, who once came to Maxwell Street from other parts of the city looking for bargains and the challenge of the haggle, are more reluctant than ever to visit Maxwell Street. They will more likely shop in the burgeoning shopping centers in their suburbs, which in recent years are opening on Sundays. Once, Maxwell Street was one of the only places in the city where one could shop on Sunday.

Pilferage increased. Len Shavin, who owns Howard's Style Shop, one of the most prominent of the forty-five business stores in the two-and-a-half block Maxwell-Halsted street area, says pilferage is the number-one problem for the stores there.

When there is a robbery now, it seems scarier, like part of a monster out of control.

Some of the great and famous stores on the street begin to close.

Makevich's all-purpose store shuts down. Ira Makevich, in his late sixties now, closed it down. He had taken over from his father, who arrived in America with twenty-five cents, bought railroad salvage products—everything from a used stamp to a chair with three legs to a can of caviar—and built it into a business that even on some days in the Depression earned ten thousand dollars. Ira was sent to college, got a degree, and returned to Maxwell Street, working long hours almost every day of the week for years. "I was like a fire horse," he said. "When the gong rang, I was up and gone." Ira's sons were not interested in continuing the old family business, and he was frightened for them to do so.

Smokey Joe's, one of the most colorful stores on the street, moved to State Street downtown. Smokey Joe's invented the zoot suit that drove America batty for a short time. Smokey Joe was an innovator in pork pie hats and spangled suits as well. But Max Doblink, who ran Smokey Joe's, felt that when he had more help watching the customers than there were customers, it was time to leave.

Gabel's closed down. It was once the largest retail men's store in the Midwest. There were, in fact, two Gabel's. The biggest, Louis Gabel's, was advertised as "in the middle of the street." His brother, Sam, had a store on the southeast corner of Halsted and Maxwell. The two didn't speak to each other for the last fifteen years of their lives, even though they owned stores about a hundred feet apart. Sam had worked for Louis. There was a disagreement, and Sam moved out and opened his own place. Morris Gabel, son of Louis, remembers that it was agonizing for his father. "One remark of my father's that echoes in my mind," said Morris Gabel, "is that he told me, 'Whatever you do, see to it that you are always a friend of your brother's.'"

Louis Gabel had come to America from Russia. When he began to earn a sufficient amount of money, he sent for his family and then got a tutor to teach him better English. He even tried to read through the encyclopedia. He wanted his sons to go to college.

Morris had an aptitude for mathematics. Louis read about the Massachusetts Institute of Technology and when Morris graduated from high school, he went to MIT, where he graduated. He now owns a steel-fabricating business in Houston, Texas.

Morris Gabel said: "My son got his Ph.D. in math from Brandeis and today is an associate professor at Purdue. He knows very little about Maxwell Street. I think back about my father, who has been dead for fifteen years, and I think about his dreams. He was proud of me for having gone through college, and I know he would have been proud of his grandson. He worked so hard; it was so difficult for him to finally close up the store because he always thought there might be one more customer. He thought the country did great for him. I'm not so sure it did so great for him because he really sacrificed an awful lot to get what he got. He laid down his life for his work. Citizens of the country today don't do that. We're not accustomed to that kind of investment.

"Now, I see Maxwell Street dying a slow and painful death. I'm sorry to see it happen this way, but I don't think the street is necessary to preserve. I think it has served a need for both sides of the scale—the seller and the buyer—for a long period of time. That time appears over. Let the street die in peace."

Another remarkable store on the street has closed up. That was Ja-Mar jewelers, owned by Marv Cohen. It was an exclusive store known all over the country. Some of Marv Cohen's customers included Jimmy Hoffa and the Shah of Iran. Marv Cohen made excursions several times a year to Europe and to Asia in quest of spectacular gems. (He began on Maxwell Street with a cardboard table set in a dark, three-foot-wide gangway. He paid Abe Fogel, who owned the clothing store to the left of his stand, fifteen dollars a month to use one of Fogel's light bulbs.) There were several robbery attempts on the store. Marv Cohen began carrying two guns wherever he went. "I began to live with one eye always over my shoulder," he said. He had secret mirrors and elaborate security mechanisms and an electronic system with which he could listen to conversations quietly being carried on in the front of the store while he was in the back. He eventually moved to a onetime bank building with vaults in a northern Chicago suburb.

And Dunn's Hats shut down. And Turf's Shoes went out of

business. And Sidney Leibowitz, who owned as many as twenty stocking stands on the street (I worked some of them in the 1950s), was reduced to one stand.

One chilly afternoon, Israel Green, who had come to America in 1949 after Auschwitz, stood in front of "Mother's Threads" where he is a "puller." "Look at the street," he said. "It is like a cemetery."

But there is still life on the street. On a nice Sunday a concatenation of sounds, a blast of smells and, overhead, a silent hullaballoo of balloons.

There are the watch-selling con artists, the peanut salesman with quarters in his ears ("Just a come-on, so you'll buy some peanuts to ask why I have quarters in my ears"), the three-card monte man who invariably draws a crowd not experienced in *trompe l'oeil*.

There is still money to be made. Hy's lamp fixtures and rugs moved into Makevich's. Kelly's moved into Marv Cohen's place. Two men in their thirties, Harold Rappeport and Joel Kornick, moved into Smokey Joe's. The hot-dog stands are jammed. Nate's schmaltz herring still sells like hot cakes.

Some stores remain boarded up, after old-timers died or retired. But some young ones like Barry Spector, owner of a toy appliance store, and Cisco Rodriguez, owner of a shoe store, and Tony DeFalco, the porno store entrepreneur, give it a go, sensing a future there.

The future of Maxwell Street, though, is quizzical. Rumors are always rife—have been for nearly a century—that Maxwell Street is on its last legs. Many believe it is just a matter of time before the forces of urban renewal finally wipe it out.

"We got a reprieve a few years ago," said Len Shavin. "The bulldozers working on the university stopped at Roosevelt and Halsted. I think they just ran out of federal funds. It was dramatic. They came right up to the line and halted. We were saved for the time being."

Shortly after, there was a strong attempt to make Maxwell Street into a mall, called the Maxwell International Shopping Center. The organizer was Seymour Taxman, a lawyer and son of Sam Taxman, the old Maxwell Street clothier. Money was collected for research and for the drawing up of architectural plans. Some store owners contributed; some did not. The plan fell through. Some felt swindled; some did not.

There have been talks about putting Maxwell Street under the Dan Ryan Expressway, of moving it to a suburban field. A survey prepared by Loyola University for the Department of Urban Renewal recommended: "The 'relocation problem' presented by the Maxwell Street vendors is a unique one. If the city of Chicago should decide upon an urban renewal program for the Roosevelt-Halsted area which requires the displacement of the Market, it will be impossible to relocate the individual vendors separately; the entire Market, or a close facsimile of it, would have to be created in order to create a location where any individual vendor could operate satisfactorily. . . . There are reasons for discarding the idea of a permanent structure, which may be capsulized in the phrase, 'It simply wouldn't be Maxwell Street. . . .' The best possible relocation site for the Market would be one which, at least along one edge, actually touched Maxwell Street itself."

The street remains a source of nostalgia for many, a center from which their lifetime compasses point.

Sidney Mandel, a lawyer in Chicago, was raised on Halsted near Maxwell Street. "About a year ago I decided to drive south down Halsted Street. I was with my granddaughter, who was about six years old. She is a totally suburban girl. I wanted to show her where I had grown up when I was her age. I pointed up to the third floor of a building and said, 'Polly, that's where I slept as a child,' and with a plaintive expression on her face, looking around at these many, many people walking shoulder to shoulder on a Saturday afternoon, she said, 'Grandpa, you know I'd like to live there.' And I said, 'Polly, why?' She said, 'Because from up there I would sit at the window all day long and watch all these people.' I said, 'But, Polly, you live in such a beautiful neighborhood.' She said, 'Yes, but when I look out of my window, all I see are the Shapiros.'"

Mandel, the son of Russian immigrant parents, remembers sleeping three in a bed with his brothers. He remembers the smell of poverty—grease and unclean corridors. "It was my resentment of these things that gave me the impulse to come to the conclusion

I hate the ghetto and I hated it so damned much that I resolved I wanted to get out of this place.

"I remember visiting a friend of mine when I was a boy. He lived on the Northwest Side of Chicago, and I brought back a basket of earth from there. Then I went into a five-and-ten cent store and bought some seeds. And in that basket of earth that I carried from the Northwest Side, I put seeds in because this was a little bit of a never-never world. I put them in a wicker basket and put it in my window. And flowers grew. I was determined to live my adult life where there were flowers and trees. I'm happy to have escaped the ghetto, and proud of my accomplishments as a lawyer and proud of men like Federal Court Judge Abe Marovitz who came from that neighborhood and who recently recalled it to me, and I think living there and surviving there better equipped us for life. I worry that my grandchildren will be too isolated. But I'm also pleased that they don't have to suffer the life of poverty as we did. It was not glamorous."

Morris Weinger, now a stockbroker in the Sears Tower in Chicago, says he never wants to return to Maxwell Street. His family were the egg-and-butter-store entrepreneurs. He grew up there and says he feels so attached to that store and that house that to see empty lots of rubble there now would bring tears to his eyes.

Jack Tuchten, the former Maxwell Street produce man, remembers fondly growing up around Maxwell Street and the pranks of boyhood, when he and friends would dig a big hole and cover it with paper and ask another friend to come over for a moment, and when the unsuspecting fellow stepped over—Whoooop! Tuchten left shortly after the Dr. King riots. He says that he grew so disenchanted with the changes there that he tries diligently to drive around the area when he nears it. "It sickens me today," he said.

Life goes on: Andy the bum, drunk one night, burns to death in a shack while clawing to get out during a fire. Another wino freezes to death while drunk and asleep at the curb in subzero weather; he is found barefoot—his new pair of shoes having been stolen off his feet.

Kelly Miller, the sporting goods man, who is seventy-seven

years old, must go to the doctor every week to check his feet which still ache from peddling the lathes in a sweatshop on Maxwell Street when he was a boy.

Sidney Goldstein, in his small, eerie-looking jewelry stand, speaks in symbols about why he remains on the street. He is in his sixties, has been on Maxwell Street all his life. "When a worm crawls in a radish," he said, "and if he's never known anything else, then for all he knows he's in a peach."

The patrolman Al Muscalino walks his beat on a Sunday at noon. Some of the vendors begin to close up. "The thieves and pickpockets begin waking up and coming out on the street about now," he said. "The businessmen know it."

Mike Chiappetta is talking. He is in plain clothes this Sunday. He is a big broad man with at once piercing but smiling eyes. It is getting late in the afternoon. Mike has been on the street as the night cop for several years. He is only thirty, but he has had an amazing background. He was a boxer, a hairdresser, a dehaunter of houses, a fortuneteller, a baker. Recently he and another policeman, another Maxwell Street cop, started a security agency, which immediately began to flourish. Mike also wrote and published in 1976 a novel entitled, *The Policeman's Bible, or The Art of Taking a Bribe*. The teachings of Maxwell Street are evident in his introduction: ". . . You probably think this is going to be an unscrupulous book, written by an unscrupulous author primarily for unscrupulous readers. You're absolutely right. It should be of interest to millions.

"I believe that 99 per cent of the people in this country are hustlers. Personally, I think it's a beautiful system, and I like to think the silent majority shares my feelings. Why not? We're all in this together."†

Mike has taken a leave of absence from the police force. He does not know if he will ever return. He sees Shirley Walker, a tony lady of the streets, visiting now the old neighborhood. "Maxwell Street's in my blood," she explains to Mike. "I can't stay away."

Mike smiles and considers that.

† Nicholas Ross (pen name for Mike Chiappetta), *The Policeman's Bible, or The Art of Taking a Bribe* (Henry Regnery: Chicago, 1976), pp. ix–x.

Winter is coming on. The wind picks up. The sun is beginning to dip. Streaks of sun pierce the mauve clouds. The garbage and metal cans glint and sparkle in the sun. It is a poignant time of day. It is a beginning and an ending. It is a preparing for unseen eventualities—the night. The big neon sign, "Rush Liquors," lights up bright from the orange sun. The street takes on an orangey hue. At Jimmy's hot-dog stand, a worker in smudged apron is out brooming, as if to broom away the shadows. And the shadows are long. Eddie Thomas, a security guard, watches the broomer broom. Thomas wears aviator glasses. The sun reflects red in the glasses. The sun's rays beat off the cars. A few drunks, slumped in the saggy wooden stands, are now deep in shadows. The click and clang and shutter of locks and bolts are heard. Card-table stands are folded up. A vendor's last cry. The sun is falling behind the Maxwell Street police station. The telephone wires are slivers of silver. A solitary pitched-roof apartment house, a remnant from the turn of the century, is silhouetted in black. The sun suddenly becomes a deep, deep orange and seems for a moment to even expand, to flatten out on top of the roof of the project building to the west, before it descends behind the building and sinks without a trace.

## ABOUT THE AUTHOR

IRA BERKOW was born and raised in Chicago and now lives in New York City. He won a Front Page award when with the Minneapolis *Tribune*. He has been a syndicated feature columnist and sports columnist for Newspaper Enterprise Association. *Beyond the Dream,* his previous book, is a collection of his sports columns. He is also coauthor with Walt Frazier of *Rockin' Steady,* chosen by the American Booksellers Association as one of the best books published in 1974 and chosen by the American Library Association as one of the best books published for young adults in the last fifteen years.